THE PRINCIPLES OF LEARNING AND BEHAVIOR
ACTIVE LEARNING EDITION
FIFTH EDITION

MICHAEL DOMJAN
University of Texas

with contributions by
J. W. GRAU
Texas A&M University

with workbook by
Mark A. Krause
University of Portland

THOMSON
─────★─────
WADSWORTH

Australia • Brazil • Canada • Mexico • Singapore
Spain • United Kingdom • United States

THOMSON
™
WADSWORTH

The Principles of Learning and Behavior:
Active Learning Edition, Fifth Edition
Michael P. Domjan

Psychology Editor: *Marianne Taflinger*
Editorial Assistant: *Lucy Faridany*
Technology Project Manager: *Darin Derstine*
Marketing Manager: *Chris Caldeira*
Marketing Assistant: *Nicole Morinon*
Signing Representative: *Tamy Ryan*
Marketing Communications Manager: *Laurel Anderson*
Project Manager, Editorial Production: *Lori Johnson*
Creative Director: *Rob Hugel*

Art Director and Cover Designer: *Vernon T. Boes*
Print Buyer: *Doreen Suruki*
Permissions Editor: *Stephanie Lee*
Photo Researcher: *Terri Wright*
Compositor: *G&S Book Services*
Copy Editor: *Darlene Bledsoe*
Cover Image: *Tim Flach/Getty Images*
Cover Printer: *Phoenix Color Corp*
Printer: *R.R. Donnelley/Crawfordsville*

© 2006 Thomson Wadsworth, a part of The Thomson Corporation. Thomson, the Star Logo, and Wadsworth are trademarks used herein under license.

ALL RIGHTS RESERVED. No part of this work covered by the copyright hereon may be reproduced or used in any form or by any means—graphic, electronic, or mechanical, including photocopying, recording, taping, Web distribution, information storage and retrieval systems, or in any other manner—without the written permission of the publisher.

Printed in the United States of America
1 2 3 4 5 6 7 09 08 07 06 05

Library of Congress Control Number: 2005929532

ISBN 0-534-60590-7

Thomson Higher Education
10 Davis Drive
Belmont, CA 94002-3098
USA

For more information about our products, contact us at:
Thomson Learning Academic Resource Center
1-800-423-0563

For permission to use material from this text or product, submit a request online at
http://www.thomsonrights.com
Any additional questions about permissions can be submitted by e-mail to
thomsonrights@thomson.com.

Workbook Figure Credits
Figure 3.12 (p. 41): From Cole, R. P., Barnet, R. C., & Miller, R. R. (1997). An evaluation of conditioned inhibition as defined by Rescorla's two-test strategy in *Learning and Motivation,* Volume 28, 333, copyright 1997, Elsevier Science (USA), reproduced by permission of the publisher. **Figure 5.1, left** (p. 98): Chance, P. (1999). Thorndike's puzzle boxes and the origins of the experimental analysis of behavior. *Journal of the Experimental Analysis of Behavior,* 72, 433-440. Copyright 1999 by the Society for the Experimental Analysis of Behavior, Inc. Reprinted with permission. **Figure 10.7** (p. 136): From "Conditioned Suppression as a Monitor of Fear of the CS in the Course of Avoidance Training," by L. J. Kamin, C. J. Brimer, and A. H. Black, 1963, *Journal of Comparative and Physiological Psychology,* 56, pp. 497-501. **Figure 12.3** (p. 160): Based on Clayton & Dickinson, 1999a.

TO ALICE, KATHERINE, AND PAUL

ABOUT THE AUTHOR

Michael Domjan is Professor and Chair of the Psychology Department at the University of Texas at Austin, where he has been teaching undergraduate and graduate courses in learning since 1973. He has served as Editor of the *Journal of Experimental Psychology: Animal Behavior Processes* and Associate Editor of *Learning and Motivation.* He is noted for his research on food-aversion learning and learning mechanisms in sexual behavior. He is recipient of the G. Stanley Hall Award from the American Psychological Association, and his research on sexual conditioning was selected for a MERIT Award by the National Institute of Mental Health. He has served on the Governing Board of the Psychonomic Society and as President of the Division of Behavioral Neuroscience and Comparative Psychology of the American Psychological Association. In addition to *The Principles of Learning and Behavior,* 5th edition, he is author of *Essentials of Conditioning and Learning.*

BRIEF CONTENTS

CONTENTS

1 INTRODUCTION 1

4 CLASSICAL CONDITIONING: MECHANISMS 91

9 EXTINCTION OF CONDITIONED BEHAVIOR   251

10 AVERSIVE CONTROL: AVOIDANCE AND PUNISHMENT   279

11 ANIMAL COGNITION I: MEMORY MECHANISMS 315

12 ANIMAL COGNITION II: SPECIAL TOPICS 352

Human Examples

Human Examples

INDEX OF HUMAN EXAMPLES

Human Examples

Human Examples

WORKBOOK CONTENTS

PREFACE

The investigation of learning and behavior has been an integral part of the study of psychology since the late nineteenth century. Studies of learning provide important insights into ways in which long-lasting changes in behavior occur as a result of particular types of experience. Basic associative learning phenomena have contributed significantly to our understanding of the functions of the nervous system. They have provided useful models for various psychological disorders as well as conceptual tools for the construction of intelligent artificial systems and robots. They have also made possible studies of the evolution of cognition and intelligence in various animal species. The methods and analytical models developed to study conditioning and learning have been adopted in studies of infant cognition, behavioral neuroscience, psychopharmacology, behavioral medicine, behavioral toxicology, rehabilitation training, and special education. Thus, the study of learning is at the crossroads of many different aspects of the study of psychology and behavior.

A Bold New Revision

I'd like to give my thanks to Mark Krause, a psychologist and learning instructor at the University of Portland, who created the Workbook exercises and was kind enough to listen to my suggestions to change them in places.

In preparing the fifth edition of *The Principles of Learning and Behavior*, I reviewed all of the research that has appeared in the major journals devoted to this field since 1996, the year I prepared the fourth edition. In particular, I looked at all articles published since 1996 in the *Journal of the Experimental Analysis of Behavior, Animal Learning & Behavior*, the *Journal of Experimental Psychology: Animal Behavior Processes*, the *Quarterly Journal of Experimental Psychology*, and *Learning and Motivation*. I also consulted other sources as needed and reviewed the reprints that were sent to me by numerous investigators in the field. Although I thought I was reasonably well informed before undertaking this review, I was surprised by how much new work has been done in the last five years. I ended up including only about a third of the references that I reviewed, which nevertheless resulted in more than 550 new references being added to the text.

From the early twentieth century to the mid-1960s, the study of learning and behavior provided the foundations of the study of psychology in North America. Prominent investigators of learning, such as Hull, Spence, Mowrer, Tolman, N. E. Miller, and Skinner, were prominent in the field of psychology as a whole rather than major figures in a subspecialty. The thrust of the effort during this period was to develop a general theory of behavior based on extensive laboratory study of a few experimental situations. Much of the research employed laboratory rats and pigeons. Findings derived from this research were assumed to apply to a variety of species and circumstances. The concepts and findings were also used to construct models of abnormal behavior, personality, and the acquisition of special skills, such as language. Students training in psychology were taught the principles of learning and behavior, even if they planned to specialize in some other area.

The field of psychology has changed dramatically during the past 35 years, with the growth of specialties such as cognitive psychology, health psychology, social and developmental psychology, and behavioral neuroscience. The study of learning and behavior no longer has the dominant position in psychology that it once enjoyed, but it remains a vital area that addresses basic aspects of how behavior is governed by environmental events. A remarkably large number of new studies of learning, many with laboratory animals as subjects, continue to appear each year. This trend is evident in two prominent databases, PsycInfo and Medline. PsycInfo lists most of the published literature in psychology, and Medline lists much of the literature in the medical and biological sciences. There is, however, some overlap in the journals covered by the two databases.

Increased Emphasis on Animal Learning

Figure 1 shows the numbers of papers that are found in PsycInfo and Medline for successive 5-year periods since 1970, if one uses the search term "learning" and limits the search to "animal." Notice that Medline shows a steady increase in the numbers of

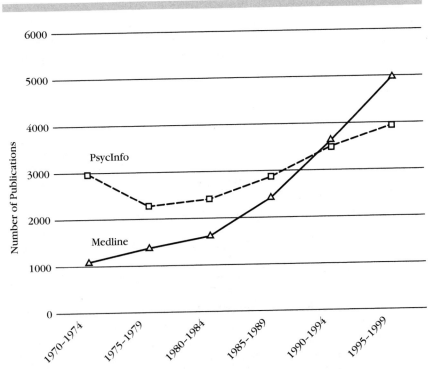

Figure 1 Numbers of papers in Medline and PsycInfo identified by using "learning" as a search term and limiting the search to "animal" in 5-year blocks between 1970 and 1999.

papers that were published on learning in animals from 1970 to 1999. A steady increase is also evident in PsycInfo from 1975 to 1999. The increase in the number of research reports dealing with learning and animals evident in the last quarter of the twentieth century resulted in part from an increase in the total number of published papers on learning in general. However, the proportion of all learning publications that involved animal subjects has remained steady since 1975 (see Figure 2). These data indicate that the investigation of learning with animal subjects remains a vital and growing area of scientific inquiry.

Because Medline covers the scientific literature in medicine and biology, the learning papers listed in Medline tend to cover the physiological or biological bases of learning. The dramatic increase in the number of papers on learning in animals during the last 30 years evident in Medline no doubt reflects increased research on the physiological or biological mechanisms of learning. Neuroscientists have focused on learning as one of the key phenomena they are trying to understand at the molecular level. Today, studies of the neural mechanisms of learning probably exceed studies that examine learning at the behavioral level. Notice that for 1995–1999, Medline lists about 5,000 publications dealing with learning in animals, whereas PsycInfo lists only about 4,000 publications. In addition, the numbers of papers dealing with learning in animals shows a much steeper increase from 1975 to 1999 in Medline than in PsycInfo.

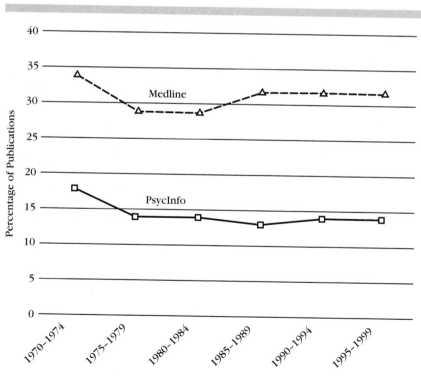

Figure 2 Proportion of papers on learning in Medline and PsycInfo that involves studies with nonhuman animal subjects in 5-year blocks between 1970 and 1999.

Reflects the Biological Bases of Learning

In keeping with increased interest in the biological bases of learning, the 5th edition of the *Principles of Learning and Behavior* includes, for the first time, summaries of some of this research. I am indebted to Professor James W. Grau of Texas A&M University for preparing these summaries, which appear in boxes in Chapters 2, 3, 5, 10, and 11. The emphasis of the book, however, remains on describing learning phenomena at the behavioral level. This emphasis is based on two considerations. First, as the new sections of this text show, scientists are far from having a full understanding of learning at the behavioral level. It therefore remains important to conduct behavioral studies. Second, investigations of the biological bases of learning require first understanding the behavioral characteristics of learning. We cannot study the physiological bases of something without first describing that effect at the behavioral level. Interpretations of the significance and function of various biological processes require relating those processes to well-characterized behavioral end points. The sharp increase in research on the biological bases of learning requires continued attention to the behavioral mechanisms of learning. Without relating the physiology to behavior, we cannot determine the function or significance of a physiological process.

Although the basic paradigms of classical and instrumental conditioning go back about 100 years, our understanding and conceptualization of these types of conditioning continue to evolve in significant ways. Those changes are reflected in numerous revisions I have made to the book. For example, Chapter 7 describes new research on the motivational mechanisms of instrumental behavior, and a new chapter on extinction has been added to the text (Chapter 9).

Balance: Contemporary Findings within a Historic Framework

The fifth edition, like earlier editions, introduces contemporary phenomena and theories about learning and behavior. The emphasis is on presenting recent findings and models, but within an historical framework. Rather than advocate a particular point of view, I strive to present a balanced perspective. I aim to point out the strengths and weaknesses of ideas in an evenhanded fashion. As before, I have tried to emphasize the development of contemporary ideas instead of just listing major findings. Although some contemporary ideas and phenomena cannot yet be fully integrated with earlier findings, I have tried to provide an integrated approach whenever possible.

As in earlier editions, I present information in order of increasing complexity, both within chapters and across chapters. The ideas presented in early chapters serve as a foundation for material presented later, with critical concepts repeated as needed. The order of chapters remains similar to earlier editions, but the material on Theories of Reinforcement and Classical-Instrumental Interactions now comprises a new chapter called Instrumental Conditioning: Motivational Mechanisms. In addition, a new chapter called Extinction of Conditioned Behavior has been added.

My goal has been to provide a captivating description of the field of conditioning and learning. To that end, I have selected interesting examples and added numerous new studies of conditioning and learning conducted with human participants.

More Instructor Support

The Instructor's Manual with Test Bank (0-534-56159-4) is an excellent resource for instructors. Each chapter contains Chapter Summaries, Key Terms and Concepts, In-class Exercises, Suggested Readings, Short Answer and Discussion Questions, Multiple Choice Questions, and material on using Sniffy the Virtual Rat in the classroom. The test items are also available: Examview (0-534-56166-7). The text can also be bundled with a copy of Sniffy, The Virtual Rat, Pro Version 2.0 (0-495-05476-3)— see endsheets in the front of the book for more information.

Acknowledgments

I am grateful to the friends and colleagues who provided me with material to consider and made useful suggestions for changes. I particularly appreciated Peter Killeen's wisdom and perspective, and Bertram Ploog's persistence. I am also grateful to Marianne Taflinger, who encouraged me to undertake the revision, Vicki Moran who guided me through the production process, and to all of the staff at Wadsworth who helped to make the new edition a reality. I also thank Kevin Holloway for preparing a marvelous instructor's manual and test bank for the book.

I am indebted to all of those who provided thoughtful reviews of an earlier draft of the fifth edition and made numerous helpful suggestions: Kim Dielmann, University of Central Arkansas; Judith Dygdon, Roosevelt University; David Falcone, La Salle University; Edmund Fantino, University of California, San Diego; J. Gregor Fetterman, Indiana University-Purdue University, Indianapolis; Adam Goodie, University of Georgia; Barbara Kucinski, University of Pittsburgh; Sheila Mehta, Auburn University, Montgomery; Thomas Minor, UCLA; Cora Lou Sherburne, Indiana University of Pennsylvania; Lynne Trench, Birmingham-Southern College.

Michael Domjan
Austin, Texas

INTRODUCTION

T he goal of Chapter 1 is to introduce the reader to the study of learning and behavior. I begin by describing the historical antecedents of key concepts in modern
learning theory. This is followed by a discussion of the origins of contemporary experimental research in studies of the evolution of intelligence, functional neurology, and animal models of human behavior, and the implications of contemporary research for the
construction of artificial intelligent systems and robots. I then describe the defining characteristics of learning and discuss different causal explanations of learning. Methodological
features of studies of learning are described in the next section. Because numerous experiments on learning have been performed with nonhuman animals, I conclude the chapter
by discussing the rationale for the use of nonhuman animals in research, with some comments about the public debate about animal research.

People have always been interested in understanding behavior, be it their own or that of others. This interest is more than idle curiosity. Our quality of life is dominated by our actions and the actions of others. Whether you receive a job offer depends on your prior education and record of employment and the decisions of your prospective employer. Whether you get along well with your roommates depends on how they react to the things you do and how you react to the things they do. Whether you get to school on time usually depends on whether you get up early enough and on how crowded the roads are.

Any systematic effort to understand behavior must include consideration of what we learn and how we learn it. Numerous aspects of the behavior of both human and nonhuman animals are the results of learning. We learn to read, to write, and to count. We learn how to walk down stairs without falling, how to open doors, how to ride a bicycle, and how to swim. We also learn when to relax and when to become anxious. We learn what foods we are likely to enjoy and what foods will make us sick. We learn how to tell when someone is unhappy and when that person feels fine. We learn when to carry an umbrella and when to take an extra scarf. Life is filled with activities and experiences that are shaped by what we have learned.

Learning is one of the biological processes that facilitate adaptation to one's environment. The integrity of life depends on successfully accomplishing a number of biological functions such as respiration, digestion, and fighting off disease. Physiological systems have evolved to accomplish these tasks. For many species, however, finely tuned physiological processes do not take care of all adaptive functions required to maintain life. Human and nonhuman animals are faced with climatic changes, changes in food resources, the comings and goings of predators, and other environmental disruptions. Adverse effects of environmental change are often met by behavioral adjustments.

Animals must learn to find new food sources as old ones become used up, they must learn to avoid predators as new ones enter their territory, and they must find new shelter when storms destroy their old one. Accomplishing these tasks obviously requires motor behavior, such as walking and manipulating objects. These tasks also require the ability to predict important events in the environment, such as when and where food will be available. All these things involve learning. Animals learn to go to a new water hole when the old one dries up and to anticipate new sources of danger. These learned adjustments to the environment are as important as physiological processes such as respiration and digestion.

We commonly think about learning as involving the acquisition of new behavior. Indeed, learning is required before we can read, ride a bicycle, or play a musical instrument, but learning can just as well consist of the decrease or loss of a previously common response. A child, for example, may learn not to cross the street when the traffic light is red, not to grab food from someone else's plate, and not to yell and scream when someone is trying to take a nap. Learning to withhold responses is just as important as learning to make responses, if not more so.

When considering learning, we are likely to think about forms of learning that require special training—forms of learning that take place in schools and colleges, for example. Solving problems in calculus or making a triple somersault when diving require special instruction. However, we also learn all kinds of things without an expert teacher or coach during the course of routine interactions with our social and physical environment. Children, for example, learn how to open doors and windows, what to do when the phone rings, when to avoid a hot stove, and when to duck so as not to get hit by a flying ball. College students learn how to find their way around campus, how to avoid heartburn from cafeteria food, and how to predict when a roommate will stay out late at night, all without special instruction.

In the coming chapters, I describe research on the basic principles of learning and behavior. This book deals with types of learning and behavior that are fundamental to life but, like breathing, are often ignored. I describe pervasive and basic forms of learning that are normal (and sometimes inevitable) even though they rarely command our attention. I describe the learning of simple relationships between events in the environment, the learning of simple motor movements, and the learning of emotional reactions to stimuli. These forms of learning are investigated in experiments that involve conditioning or "training" procedures of various sorts. However, these forms of learning occur in the lives of human and nonhuman animals without explicit or organized instruction or schooling.

Much of the research that I describe is in the behaviorist tradition of psychology that emphasizes analyzing behavior in terms of its antecedent stimuli and consequences. Conscious reflection and reasoning is deliberately left out of this analysis. I describe automatic procedural learning, which does not require awareness (for example, Lieberman, Sunnucks, & Kirk, 1998), rather than declarative learning, which is more accessible to conscious report. One might argue that this restriction leaves out many interesting aspects of human behavior. However, social psychologists who have been examining these issues empirically have concluded that many important aspects of human behavior occur without awareness. Gosling, John, Craik, and Robins (1998), for example, found that people are relatively inaccurate in reporting about their own behavior. Based on studies of the experience of conscious intent, Wegner and Wheatley (1999) concluded that "the real causal mechanisms underlying behavior are never present in consciousness" (p. 490). Bargh and Chartrand (1999) similarly concluded that "most of a person's everyday life is determined not by their conscious intentions and deliberate choices but by mental processes that are put into motion by features of the environment and that operate outside of conscious awareness and guidance" (p. 462).

HISTORICAL ANTECEDENTS

Theoretical approaches to the study of learning have their roots in the philosophy of René Descartes (see Figure 1.1). Before Descartes, most people thought of human behavior as entirely determined by conscious intent and free will. People's actions were not considered to be controlled by external stimuli or mechanistic natural laws. What a person did was presumed to be the result of his or her will or deliberate intent. Descartes took exception to this view of human nature because he recognized that many things people do are automatic reactions to external stimuli. On the other hand, he was not prepared to abandon entirely the idea of free will and conscious control. He therefore formulated a dualistic view of human behavior known as Cartesian **dualism.**

According to Cartesian dualism, there are two classes of human behavior: involuntary and voluntary. Descartes proposed that involuntary behavior consists of automatic reactions to external stimuli and is mediated by a special mechanism called a **reflex.** Voluntary behavior, by contrast, does not have to be triggered by external stimuli and occurs because of the person's conscious intent to act in that particular manner.

The details of Descartes' dualistic view of human behavior are diagrammed in Figure 1.2. Let us first consider the mechanisms of involuntary, or reflexive, behavior. Stimuli in the environment are detected by the person's sense organs. The sensory information is then relayed to the brain through nerves. From the brain, the impetus for action is sent through nerves to the muscles that create the involuntary response. Thus, sensory input is *reflected* in response output. Hence, Descartes called involuntary behavior *reflexive.*

Figure 1.1
René Decartes
(1596–1650)

Bettmann/CORBIS

Several aspects of this system are noteworthy. Stimuli in the external environment are assumed to be the cause of all involuntary behavior. These stimuli produce involuntary responses by way of a neural circuit that includes the brain. Descartes assumed, however, that only one set of nerves was involved, that the same nerves transmitted information from the sense organs to the brain and from the brain down to the muscles. This circuit, he believed, permitted rapid reactions to external stimuli—for example, quick withdrawal of one's finger from a hot stove.

Descartes assumed that the involuntary mechanism of behavior was the only one available to nonhuman animals. According to this view, all nonhuman animal behavior occurs as reflex responses to external stimuli. Thus, Descartes believed that nonhuman animals lacked free will and were incapable of voluntary, conscious action. He considered free will and voluntary behavior to be uniquely human attributes. This superiority of humans over other animals existed because only human beings were thought to have a mind, or soul.

The mind was assumed to be a nonphysical entity. Descartes believed that the mind was connected to the physical body by way of the pineal gland, near the brain. Because of this connection, the mind could be aware of and keep track of involuntary behavior. Through this mechanism, the mind could also initiate voluntary actions. Because voluntary behavior was initiated in the mind, it could occur independently of external stimulation.

The mind–body dualism introduced by Descartes stimulated two intellectual traditions. One, mentalism, was concerned with the contents and workings of the mind; the other, reflexology, with the mechanisms of reflexive behavior. These two intellectual traditions form the foundations of the modern study of learning.

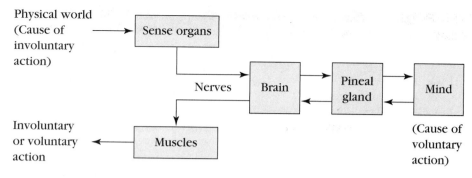

Figure 1.2 Diagram of Cartesian dualism. Events in the physical world are detected by sense organs. From here the information is transmitted to the brain. The brain is connected to the mind by way of the pineal gland. Involuntary action is produced by a reflex arc that involves messages sent first from the sense organs to the brain and then from the brain to the muscles. Voluntary action is initiated by the mind, with messages sent to the brain and then the muscles.

Historical Developments in the Study of the Mind

Philosophers concerned with the mind were interested in what was in the mind and how the mind works. These questions are similar to those that preoccupy present-day cognitive psychologists. Because Descartes thought the mind was connected to the brain by way of the pineal gland, he believed that some of the contents of the mind came from sense experiences. At the same time, he also believed that the mind contained ideas that were innate and existed in all human beings independent of personal experience. He believed, for example, that all humans were born with the concept of God, the concept of self, and certain fundamental axioms of geometry (such as the fact that the shortest distance between two points is a straight line). The philosophical approach that assumes we are born with innate ideas about certain things is called **nativism.**

Some philosophers after Descartes took issue with the nativist position. In particular, the British philosopher John Locke (1632-1704) believed that all the ideas people had were acquired directly or indirectly through experiences after birth. He believed that human beings were born without any preconceptions about the world. According to Locke, the mind started out as a clean slate (*tabula rasa,* in Latin), to be gradually filled with ideas and information as the person had various sense experiences. This philosophical approach to the contents of the mind is called **empiricism.** Empiricism was accepted by a group of British philosophers who lived from the seventeenth to the nineteenth century and who came to be known as the *British empiricists.*

The nativist and empiricist philosophers disagreed not only about what the mind was assumed to contain but also on how the mind was assumed to operate. Descartes believed that the mind did not function in a predictable and orderly manner, according to strict rules or laws that one could identify. One of the first to propose an alternative to this position was the British philosopher Thomas Hobbes (1588–1679). Hobbes accepted the distinction between voluntary and involuntary behavior stated by Descartes and also the notion that voluntary behavior was controlled by the mind. Unlike Descartes, however, Hobbes believed that the mind operated just as predictably and lawfully as a reflex. More specifically, he proposed that voluntary behavior was governed by the principle of **hedonism.** According to this principle, people do things in the pursuit of pleasure and the avoidance of pain. Hobbes was not concerned with whether the pursuit of pleasure and the avoidance of pain are laudable or desirable. For him, hedonism was simply a fact of life. The notion that behavior is controlled by positive and negative consequences has remained with us in one form or another to the present day.

According to the British empiricists, another important aspect of how the mind works involved the concept of **association.** Recall that empiricism assumes that all ideas originate from sense experiences. But how do our experiences of various colors, shapes, odors, and sounds allow us to arrive at more complex ideas? Consider, for example, the concept of a car. If someone says the word *car,* you have an idea of what the thing looks like, what it is used for, and how you might feel if you sat in it. Where do all these ideas come from given just the sound of the letters *c, a,* and *r*? The British empiricists proposed that simple sensations were combined into more complex ideas by associations. Because you have heard the word *car* when you saw a car, considered using one to get to work, or sat in one, connections or associations became established between the word *car* and these other attributes of cars. Once the associations are established, the word *car* will activate memories of the other aspects of cars that you have experienced. The British empiricists considered such associations to be the building blocks of mental activity. Therefore, they devoted considerable effort to detailing the rules of associations.

Rules of Associations. The British empiricists accepted two sets of rules for the establishment of associations, one primary and one secondary. The primary rules were originally set forth by the ancient Greek philosopher Aristotle. He proposed three principles for the establishment of associations: contiguity, similarity, and contrast. Of these, the contiguity principle has been the most prominent in studies of associations and continues to play an important role in contemporary work. It states that if two events repeatedly occur together in space or time, they will become associated. For example, if you encounter the smell of tomato sauce with spaghetti often enough, your memory of spaghetti will be activated by the smell of tomato sauce by itself. The similarity and contrast principles state that two things will become associated if they are similar in some respect (both are red, for example) or have some contrasting characteristics (one might be strikingly tall and the other strikingly short, for example). Similarity as a basis for the formation of associations has been confirmed by modern studies of learning (for example, Cusato & Domjan, 2001; Rescorla & Furrow, 1977). However, there is no contemporary evidence that making one stimulus strikingly different from another (contrast) facilitates the formation of an association between the two.

Various secondary laws of associations were set forth by several of the empiricist philosophers—among them, Thomas Brown (1778–1820). Brown proposed that a number of factors influence the formation of associations between two sensations, including the intensity of the sensations and how frequently or recently the sensations occurred together. In addition, the formation of an association between two events was considered to depend on the number of other associations in which each event was already involved, and the similarity of these past associations to the current one being formed.

The British empiricists discussed rules of association as a part of their philosophical discourse. They did not perform experiments to determine whether the rules were valid. Nor did they attempt to determine the circumstances in which one rule was more important than another. Empirical investigation of the mechanisms of associations did not begin until the pioneering work of the nineteenth-century German psychologist Hermann Ebbinghaus (1850–1909).

To study how associations are formed, Ebbinghaus invented **nonsense syllables**—three-letter combinations (*bap*, for example) devoid of any meaning that might influence how someone might react to them. Ebbinghaus used himself as the experimental subject. He studied lists of nonsense syllables and measured his ability to remember them under various experimental conditions. This general method enabled him to answer such questions as how the strength of an association improved with increased training, whether nonsense syllables that appeared close together in a list were associated more strongly with one another than syllables that were farther apart, and whether a syllable became more strongly associated with the next one on the list than with the preceding one. Many of the issues addressed by the British empiricists and Ebbinghaus have their counterparts in modern studies of learning and memory.

Historical Developments in the Study of Reflexes

Descartes made a very significant contribution to the understanding of behavior when he formulated the concept of the reflex. The basic idea that behavior can reflect a triggering stimulus remains an important building block of behavior theory. However, Descartes was mistaken in his beliefs about the details of reflex action. He believed that sensory messages going from sense organs to the brain and motor messages going from the brain to the muscles travel along the same nerves. He thought that nerves are hollow tubes and that neural transmission involves gases called *animal spirits*. The animal spirits, released by the pineal gland, were assumed to flow through the neural tubes and enter the muscles, causing them to swell and create movement. Finally, Descartes considered all reflexive movements to be innate and to be fixed by the anatomy of the nervous system. Over the course of several hundred years after Descartes passed away, all of these ideas about reflexes were proven incorrect.

Charles Bell (1774–1842) in England and François Magendie (1783–1855) in France showed that separate nerves are involved in the transmission of sensory information from sense organs to the central nervous system and of motor information from the central nervous system to muscles. If a sensory nerve is cut, the animal remains capable of muscle movements; if a motor nerve is cut, the animal remains capable of registering sensory information.

The idea that animal spirits are involved in neural transmission was also disproved. In 1669, John Swammerdam (1637–1680) showed that mechanical irritation of a nerve was sufficient to produce a muscle contraction. Thus, infusion of animal spirits from the pineal gland was not necessary. In other studies, Francis Glisson (1597–1677) demonstrated that muscle contractions were not produced by swelling due to the infusion of a gas, as Descartes had postulated.

Descartes and most philosophers after him assumed that reflexes were responsible only for simple reactions to stimuli. The energy in a stimulus was thought to be translated directly into the energy of the elicited response by the neural connections—that is, the more intense the stimulus, the more vigorous the resulting response. This simple view of reflexes is consistent with many casual observations. If you touch a stove, for example, the hotter the stove, the more quickly you withdraw your finger. Some reflexes, however, are much more complicated.

The physiological processes responsible for reflex behavior became better understood in the nineteenth century, and reflexes came to be used as an explanation for a greater range of behaviors. Two Russian physiologists, I. M. Sechenov (1829–1905) (see Figure 1.3) and Ivan Pavlov (1849–1936), were primarily responsible for these developments. Sechenov proposed that stimuli do not elicit reflex responses directly in all cases. Rather, in some

Sovfoto

Figure 1.3
I. M. Sechenov
(1829–1905)

cases, a stimulus can release a response from inhibition. Where a stimulus released a response from inhibition, the vigor of the response would not depend on the intensity of the stimulus. This simple idea opened up all sorts of new possibilities.

Since the vigor of an elicited response does not invariably depend on the intensity of its triggering stimulus, it is possible for a very faint stimulus to produce a large response. Small particles of dust in the nose, for example, can cause a vigorous sneeze. Sechenov took advantage of this type of mechanism to provide a reflex analysis of voluntary behavior. He suggested that complex forms of behavior (actions or thoughts) that occurred in the absence of an obvious eliciting stimulus were in fact reflexive responses. In these cases, the eliciting stimuli are so faint as to be unnoticeable. Thus, according to Sechenov, voluntary behavior and thoughts are actually elicited by inconspicuous, faint stimuli.

Sechenov's ideas about voluntary behavior greatly extended the use of reflex mechanisms to explain a variety of aspects of behavior. However, his ideas were philosophical extrapolations from the actual research results he obtained. In addition, Sechenov did not address the question of how reflex mechanisms can account for the fact that the behavior of organisms is not fixed and invariant throughout an organism's lifetime but can be altered by experience. From the time of Descartes, reflex responses were considered to be innate and fixed by the connections of the nervous system. Reflexes were thought to depend on a prewired neural circuit connecting the sense organs to the relevant muscles. According to this view, a given stimulus could be expected to elicit the same response throughout an organism's life. Although this is true in some cases, there are also many examples in which responses to stimuli change as a result of experience. Explanation of such cases by reflex processes had to await the experimental and theoretical work of Ivan Pavlov.

Pavlov showed experimentally that not all reflexes are innate. New reflexes to stimuli can be established through mechanisms of association. Thus, Pavlov's role in the history of the study of reflexes is comparable to the role of Ebbinghaus in the study of the mind. Both were concerned with establishing the laws of associations through empirical research. Pavlov, however, did this in the physiological tradition of reflexology rather than in the mentalistic tradition.

Much of modern behavior theory has been built on the reflex concept of stimulus-response, or S-R units, and the concept associations. S-R units and associations continue to play prominent roles in contemporary behavior theory, but these basic concepts have been elaborated and challenged over the years. As I describe in later chapters, in addition to S-R units or connections, modern studies of learning have also demonstrated the existence of stimulus-stimulus (S-S) connection and modulatory or hierarchical associative structures (Schmajuk & Holland, 1998). Quantitative descriptions of learned behavior that do not employ associations have gained favor in some quarters (for example, Gallistel & Gibbon, 2000, 2001) and have been emphasized by contemporary scientists working in the Skinnerian tradition of behavioral analysis (for example, Mazur, 2001). However, associative analyses continue to have a prominent role in both physiological and behavioral investigations (for example, Dickinson, 2001) even though some have supplemented associative mechanisms with other processes (for example, Denniston, Savastano, & Miller, 2001; Miller & Escobar, 2001).

THE DAWN OF THE MODERN ERA

Experimental studies of basic principles of learning often are conducted with nonhuman animals and in the tradition of reflexology. Research in animal learning came to be pursued with great vigor starting a little more than 100 years ago. Impetus for the research came from three primary sources (see Domjan, 1987). The first of these was interest in comparative cognition and the evolution of the mind. The second was interest in how the nervous system works (functional neurology), and the third was interest in developing animal models to study certain aspects of human behavior. As described in the ensuing chapters, comparative cognition, functional neurology, and animal models of human behavior continue to dominate contemporary research in learning.

Comparative Cognition and the Evolution of Intelligence

Interest in comparative cognition and the evolution of the mind was sparked by the writings of Charles Darwin (see Figure 1.4), who took Descartes' ideas about human nature one step further. Descartes had started chipping away at the age-old notion that human beings have a unique and privileged position in the animal kingdom by proposing that at least some aspects of human behavior (their reflexes) were animal-like. However, Descartes had preserved some privilege for human beings by assuming that humans (and only humans) have a mind.

Darwin attacked this last vestige of privilege. In his second major work, *The Descent of Man and Selection in Relation to Sex,* Darwin argued that "man is descended from some lower form, notwithstanding that connecting-links have not hitherto been discovered" (1897, p. 146). In claiming continuity from nonhuman to human animals, Darwin attempted to characterize not only the evolution of physical traits but also the evolution of psychological or mental abilities. He argued that the human mind is a product of evolution.

Figure 1.4
Charles Darwin
(1809–1882)

Bettmann/CORBIS

In making this claim, Darwin did not deny that human beings had such mental abilities as the capacity for wonder, curiosity, imitation, attention, memory, reasoning, and aesthetic sensibility. Rather, he suggested that nonhuman animals also had these abilities. For example, he maintained that nonhuman animals were capable even of belief in spiritual agencies (p. 95).

Darwin collected anecdotal evidence of various forms of intelligent behavior in animals in an effort to support his claims. Although the evidence was not compelling by modern standards, the research question was. Investigators ever since have been captivated by the possibility of tracing the evolution of intelligence by studying the abilities of various species of animals.

Before investigating the evolution of intelligence in a systematic fashion, a researcher must have a criterion for identifying intelligent behavior in animals. A highly influential proposal for a criterion was offered by George Romanes in his book *Animal Intelligence* (1882). Romanes suggested that intelligence be identified by determining whether an animal learns "to make new adjustments, or to modify old ones, in accordance with the results of its own individual experience" (p. 4). Thus, Romanes defined intelligence in terms of the ability to learn. This definition was widely accepted by comparative psychologists at the end of the nineteenth and the start of the twentieth century and served to make the study of animal learning the key to obtaining information about the evolution of intelligence.

As the upcoming chapters show, little research on mechanisms of animal learning has been concerned with trying to obtain evidence of the evolution of intelligence. Nevertheless, this issue remains of considerable contemporary interest (for example, Papini, 2002; Roitblat & Meyer, 1995; Shettleworth, 1998). I describe some of the fruits of contemporary research on animal cognition in Chapters 11 and 12.

Functional Neurology

The modern era in the study of learning processes was also greatly stimulated by efforts to use studies of learning in nonhuman animals to gain insights into how the nervous system works. This line of research was initiated by the Russian physiologist Ivan Pavlov, quite independently of the work of Darwin, Romanes, and others interested in comparative cognition.

While still a medical student, Pavlov became committed to the principle of **nervism.** According to nervism, all key physiological functions are governed by the nervous system. Armed with this principle, Pavlov devoted his life to documenting how the nervous system controlled various aspects of physiology. Much of his work was devoted to identifying the neural mechanisms of digestion.

For many years, Pavlov's research progressed according to plan. But, in 1902, two British investigators (Bayliss and Starling) published results showing that the pancreas, an important digestive organ, was partially under hormonal rather than neural control. Writing some time later, Pavlov's friend and biographer noted that these novel findings produced a crisis in the laboratory because they "shook the very foundation of the teachings of the exclusive nervous regulation of the secretory activity of the digestive glands" (Babkin, 1949, p. 228).

The evidence of hormonal control of the pancreas presented Pavlov with a dilemma. If he continued his investigations of digestion, he would have to abandon his interest in the nervous system. On the other hand, if he maintained his commitment to nervism, he would have to stop studying digestive physiology. Nervism won out. In an effort to continue studying the nervous system, Pavlov changed from studying digestive physiology to studying the conditioning of reflexes. Thus, Pavlov regarded his studies of conditioning (which is a form of learning) as a way to obtain information about the functions of the nervous system—how the nervous system works. Pavlov's claim that studies of learning reveal how the nervous system functions is well accepted by contemporary neuroscientists. Kandel, for example, has commented that "the central tenet of modern neural science is that all behavior is a reflection of brain function" (Kandel, Schwartz, & Jessell, 1991, p. 3).

The behavioral psychologist is like a driver who tries to find out about an experimental car by taking it out for a test drive instead of first looking under the hood. By driving the car, you can learn a great deal about how it functions. You can discover its acceleration, its top speed, the quality of its ride, its turning radius, and how quickly it comes to a stop. Driving the car will not tell you how these various functions are accomplished, but it will reveal the major functional characteristics of the internal machinery of the car.

Knowledge of the functional characteristics of a car can, in turn, provide clues about its internal machinery. For example, if the car accelerates sluggishly and never reaches high speeds, chances are it is not powered by a rocket engine. If the car only goes forward when facing downhill, it is probably propelled by gravity rather than by an engine. If the car cannot be made to come to a stop quickly, it may not have brakes.

In a similar manner, behavioral studies of learning can provide clues about the machinery of the nervous system. Such studies tell us about the kinds of plasticity the nervous system can exhibit, the conditions under which learning can take place, how long learned responses persist, and the circumstances under which learned information is accessible or inaccessible. By detailing the functions of the nervous system, behavioral studies of learning define the features or functions that have to be explained by neurophysiological investigations.

Animal Models of Human Behavior

The third major impetus for the modern era in the study of animal learning was the belief that research with nonhuman animals can provide information that may help us better understand human behavior. Animal models of human behavior are of more recent origin than comparative cognition or functional neurology. The approach was systematized by Dollard and Miller and their collaborators (Dollard, Miller, Doob, Mowrer, & Sears, 1939; Miller & Dollard, 1941) and developed further by B. F. Skinner (1953).

Drawing inferences about human behavior on the basis of research with other animal species can be hazardous and controversial. The inferences are hazardous if they are unwarranted; they are controversial if the rationale for the model system approach is poorly understood. Model systems have been developed based on research with a variety of species, including several species of primates, pigeons, rats, and mice.

In generalizing from research with rats and pigeons to human behavior, scientists do not make the assumption that rats and pigeons are like people. Animal models are like other types of models. Architects, pharmacologists, medical scientists, and designers of automobiles all rely on models, and the models are often strikingly different from the real thing. Architects, for example, make small-scale models and drawings of buildings they are designing. Obviously, such models and drawings are not the same as a real building. The models are much smaller, made of cardboard and small pieces of wood instead of bricks and mortar, and they support little weight.

As Overmier (1999) pointed out, "Models are basic and powerful tools in science" (p.17). Models are commonly used because they permit investigation of certain aspects of what they represent under conditions that are *simpler, more easily controlled,* and *less expensive.* For example, with the use of a model, an architect can study the design of the exterior of a planned building without the expense of actual construction. The model can be used to determine what the building will look like from various vantage points and how it will appear relative to other nearby buildings. Studying a model in a design studio is much simpler than studying an actual building on a busy street corner. Factors that may get in the way of getting a good view (other buildings, traffic, and power lines, for example) can be controlled and minimized in a model.

In a comparable fashion, a car designer can study the wind resistance of various design features of a new automobile with the use of a model in the form of a computer program. The program can be used to determine how the addition of spoilers or changes in the shape of the car will change its wind resistance. The computer model bears little resemblance to a real car. It has no tires or engine and cannot be driven. However, the model permits testing the wind resistance of a car design under conditions that are much simpler, better controlled, and less expensive than if the actual car were built and driven down the highway under various conditions to measure wind resistance.

Considering all the differences between a model and the real thing, what makes models valid for studying something? For a model to be valid, it must be comparable to the real thing in terms of the feature or function under study—the *relevant feature* or *relevant function.* If the model of a building is used to study the building's exterior appearance, then all the exterior dimensions of the model must be proportional to the corresponding dimensions of the planned building. Other features of the model, such as its structural elements, are irrelevant. In contrast, if the model is used to study how well the building would withstand an earthquake, then its structural elements (beams and how the beams are connected) would be critical.

In a similar manner, the only thing relevant in a computer model of car wind resistance is that the computer program provide calculations for wind resistance that match the results obtained with real cars driven through real air. No other feature is relevant; therefore, the fact that the computer program lacks an engine or rubber tires is of no consequence.

The rationale and strategies associated with using nonhuman animals as models for human behavior are similar to those pertaining to models in other areas of inquiry. Animal models permit investigating problems that are difficult, if not impossible, to study directly with people. A model permits the research to be carried out under circumstances that are simpler, better controlled, and less expensive. Furthermore, the validity of animal models is based on the same criterion as the validity of other types of models. The important thing is similarity between the animal model and human behavior in *relevant features* for the problem at hand. For example, similarities between rats and humans in the way they learn to avoid dangerous foods make a rat model valid for the investigation of human food aversion learning. The fact that rats have long tails and walk on four legs instead of two is entirely irrelevant to food selection.

The critical task in constructing a successful animal model is to identify the relevant similarity between the animal model and the human behavior of interest. The relevant similarity concerns the causal factors that are responsible for particular forms of behavior (Overmier, 1999). We can gain insights into human behavior based on the study of nonhuman animals if the causal relations in the two species are similar. Because animal models are often used to push back the frontiers of knowledge, the correspondence between the animal findings and human behavior always must be carefully verified by empirical data.

The rationale and strategy for the use of animal models of human behavior was stated succinctly by Dollard and Miller (1950):

> In using the results from [research with rats] we are working on the hypothesis that people have all the learning capacities of rats. . . . Even though the facts must be verified at the human level, it is often easier to notice the operation of principles after they have been studied and isolated in simpler situations so that one knows exactly what to look for. Furthermore, in those cases in which it is impossible to use as rigorous experimental controls at the human level, our faith in what evidence can be gathered at that level will be increased if it is in line with the results of more carefully controlled experiments on other mammals. (p. 63)

Dollard and Miller advocated an interplay in which laboratory studies with nonhuman animals are used to isolate and identify phenomena that can then be investigated in people more successfully. The nonhuman animal research is also used to increase confidence in human data obtained with weaker research methods. This interaction between animal and human research continues to make important contributions to our understanding of human behavior (for example, Branch & Hackenberg, 1998; Gosling, 2001) and has also informed our understanding of the behavior of nonhuman animals (for example, Escobar, Matute, & Miller, 2001; Miller & Matute, 1996).

Applications of learning principles got a special boost in the 1960s with the accelerated development of behavior therapy during that period. As O'Donohue commented, "the model of moving from the learning laboratory to the clinic proved to be a extraordinarily rich paradigm. In the 1960s, numerous learning principles were shown to be relevant to clinical practice. Learning research quickly proved to be a productive source of ideas for developing treatments or etiological accounts of many problems" (1998, p. 4). This fervor was tempered during subsequent developments of cognitive behavior therapy. However, recent advances in learning theory have encouraged a return to learning explanations of important human problems such as panic disorder (Bouton, Mineka, & Barlow, 2001).

In the upcoming chapters I describe animal models of love and attachment, drug tolerance and addiction, food aversion learning, learning of fears and phobias, and stress and coping, among others. Animal models have also led to the development of numerous procedures now commonly employed with people, such as biofeedback, programmed instruction, systematic desensitization, token economies, and other techniques of behavior modification. I provide examples of such applications at relevant points in the text. (For additional examples, see Carroll & Overmier, 2001; Haug & Whalen, 1999.)

Animal Models and Robotics

Animal models of learning and behavior are also of considerable relevance to robotics and intelligent artificial systems. Robots are machines that are able to perform specific functions or tasks. The goal in robotics is to make the machines as "smart" as possible. Just as Romanes defined "intelligence" in terms of the ability to learn, contemporary roboticists view the ability to remember and learn from experience an important feature of "smart" artificial systems. Information about the characteristics and mechanisms of such learning may be gleaned from studies of learning in nonhuman animals (for example, McFarland & Bösser, 1993; Meyer, Berthoz, Floreano, Roitblat, & Wilson, 2000; Roitblat & Meyer, 1995; Wilson, 1991). For example, associative mechanisms are frequently used in artificial intelligent systems to enable the response of those systems to be altered by experience.

THE DEFINITION OF LEARNING

Learning is such a common human experience that people rarely reflect on exactly what it means to say that something has been learned. A universally accepted definition of learning does not exist. However, many critical aspects of learning are captured in the following statement (see also Domjan, 2000):

Learning is an enduring change in the mechanisms of behavior involving specific stimuli and/or responses that results from prior experience with those or similar stimuli and responses.

This definition has important implications for the study of learning, as shown in the following sections.

The Learning-Performance Distinction

Whenever we see evidence of learning, we see the emergence of a change in behavior—the performance of a new response or the suppression of a response that occurred previously. A child becomes skilled in snapping the buckles of her sandals or becomes more patient in waiting to eat dinner until everyone has been seated at the table. Such changes in behavior are the only way to tell whether learning has occurred. However, notice that the preceding definition attributes learning to a change in the *mechanisms of behavior,* not to a change in behavior directly.

Why should we define learning in terms of a change in the mechanisms of behavior? The main reason is that behavior is determined by many factors other than learning. Consider, for example, eating. Whether you eat something depends on how hungry you are, how much effort is required to obtain the food, how much you like the food, and whether you know where to find food. Of all these factors, only the last one necessarily involves learning.

Performance refers to an organism's actions at a particular time. Whether you do something or not (your performance) depends on many things. Even the occurrence of a simple response such as jumping into a swimming pool is multiply determined. Whether you jump depends on the availability, depth, and temperature of the water, your physical ability to spring away from the side of the pool, and so forth. Performance is determined by opportunity, motivation, and sensory and motor capabilities, in addition to learning. Therefore, a change in performance cannot be automatically considered to reflect learning.

Learning is defined in terms of a change in the mechanisms of behavior to emphasize the distinction between learning and performance. The behavior of an organism (its performance) is used to provide evidence of learning. However, because performance is determined by many factors in addition to learning, an observer must be very careful in deciding whether a particular aspect of performance does or does not reflect learning. Sometimes evidence of learning cannot be obtained until special test procedures are introduced. Children, for example, learn a great deal about driving a car just by watching others drive, but this learning is not apparent until they are permitted behind the steering wheel. In other cases (next to be discussed), a change in behavior is readily observed but cannot be attributed to learning either because it does not last long enough or because it does not result from experience with specific environmental events.

Learning and Other Sources of Behavior Change

Several mechanisms produce changes in behavior that are too short-lasting to be considered instances of learning. One such process is **fatigue.** Physical exertion may result in a gradual reduction in the vigor of a response because the individual becomes tired or fatigued. This type of change is produced by experience. However, it is not considered an instance of learning, because the decline in responding disappears if the individual is allowed to rest for a while.

Behavior also may be temporarily altered by a *change in stimulus conditions.* If the house lights in a movie theater suddenly come on in the middle of the show, the behavior of the audience is likely to change dramatically. However, this is not an instance of learning, because the audience is likely to return to watching the movie when the house lights are turned off again.

Other short-term changes in behavior that are not considered learning involve *alterations in the physiological or motivational state* of the organism. Hunger and thirst induce responses that are not observed at other times. Changes in the level of sex hormones cause changes in responsiveness to sexual stimuli. Short-lasting behavioral effects may also accompany the administration of psychoactive drugs.

In some cases persistent changes in behavior occur, but without the type of experience with environmental events that satisfies the definition of learning. The most obvious example of this type is **maturation.** A child cannot get something from a high shelf until he grows tall enough. However, the change in behavior in this case is not an instance of learning because it occurs with the mere passage of time. The child does not have to be trained to reach high places as he becomes taller. Maturation can also result in the disappearance of certain responses. For example, shortly after birth, touching an infant's feet results in foot movements that resemble walking, and stroking the bottom of the foot causes the toes to fan out. Both of these reflex reactions disappear as the infant gets older.

Generally, the distinction between learning and maturation is based on the importance of special experiences in producing the behavior change of interest. However, the distinction is blurred in cases where environmental stimulation is necessary for maturational development. Experiments with cats, for example, have shown that the visual system will not develop sufficiently to permit perception of horizontal lines unless the subjects have been exposed to such stimuli early in life (for example, Blakemore & Cooper, 1970). The appearance of sexual behavior at puberty also depends on developmental experience. In particular, successful sexual behavior in primates requires interactions with playmates before puberty (for example, Harlow, 1969).

Different Types of Causal Mechanisms

So far I have referred to causal mechanisms but not defined them—and for good reason. Causes can be conceptualized in different terms or at different levels of explanation. In discussing causal mechanisms, it is important to keep in mind what kind of cause you are concerned with. Killeen (2001) has encouraged learning psychologists to think in terms of the four different forms of causality originally described by Aristotle. The first of these, *efficient cause,* is closest to the common definition of cause and refers to the necessary and sufficient conditions for producing a behavioral outcome. In the case of learning, the efficient cause is the training experience with specific stimuli and/or responses that produces the behavior change that is indicative of learning. In contemporary research on learning, efficient causes refer to the procedures that produce the learning. As the upcoming chapters show, there are many different kinds of learning procedures.

The efficient causes of learned behavior are mediated by changes in the nervous system. These neural changes are the *material causes* of learning. Material causes refer to the physical changes in the nervous system that mediate learning. These involve changes in synaptic mechanisms, among other things. Scientists who study the neural mechanisms of learning are studying what Aristotle termed material causes (for example, Greenough & Black, 2000).

Except for the boxes dealing with neural mechanisms prepared by Professor James Grau, this book does not deal with material causes. It deals with what are typically referred to as behavioral mechanisms, explanations of learning at the level of behavior. Behavioral mechanisms are what Aristotle referred to as *formal causes.* Formal causes are theories or models of learning. These theories or models may be expressed in mathematical or computational terms, or they may be stated in terms of theoretical constructs. Associative models of learning are examples of formal causes. This book focuses on such formal causes of learning.

As I noted at the outset of this chapter, learning is a pervasive feature of behavior across the animal kingdom because it is useful, because it enables animals to adjust to changes in their environment. Explanations of learning that emphasize its function or utility involve the fourth type of cause described by Aristotle, namely, *final cause.* In modern biology, the final cause of a behavior or biological process is how that process contributes to the reproductive fitness of the organism. Biological function or final cause is measured in terms of the number of offspring an individual leaves behind. Most scientists would agree that learning mechanisms probably evolved because they increase reproductive fitness. Exactly how the increase in reproductive fitness is achieved has not been identified in many cases, but a few examples of the contributions of learning to reproductive fitness are available (Domjan, Blesbois, & Williams, 1998; Hollis, Pharr, Dumas, Britton, & Field, 1997; see also Domjan & Hollis, 1988).

A common distinction among biologically oriented scientists is between the proximal or immediate causes of behavior and its ultimate causes. Proximate causes correspond to Aristotle's efficient and material causes. Ultimate causes correspond to Aristotle's final causes.

There are two prominent methodological features of investigations of learning processes. One of these is a direct consequence of the definition of learning and involves the exclusive use of experimental, as contrasted with observational, research methods. The phenomena of learning cannot be investigated without the use of an experimental methodology. The second methodological feature—reliance on a general-process approach—is more a matter of preference than necessity.

Learning as an Experimental Science

As I described earlier, studies of learning emphasize identifying the causal factors that are responsible for long-term changes in behavior that result from prior experience. Of the four types of causes, learning investigators have focused on efficient, material, and formal causes. Regardless of the type of cause, this emphasis dictates that experimental techniques be used in investigations of learning. Causes cannot be observed directly. They can only be inferred from the results of experimental manipulations.

Consider the following example. Mary opens the door to a dark room. She quickly turns on a switch near the door, and the lights in the room go on. Can you conclude that turning on the switch "caused" the lights to go on? Not from the information provided. Perhaps the lights were on an automatic timer and would have turned on without Mary's actions. Alternatively, the door may have had a built-in switch that turned on the lights after a slight delay. Or, there may have been a motion detector in the room that activated the lights.

How could you determine that manipulation of the wall switch caused the lights to go on? You would have to see what would happen under other circumstances. More specifically, you would have to instruct Mary to enter the room again, but ask her not to turn on the wall switch. If the lights did not go on under these circumstances, certain causal hypotheses could be rejected. You could conclude that the lights were not turned on by a motion detector or by a switch built into the door. To identify a cause, an experiment has to be conducted in which the presumed cause is removed. The results obtained with and without the presumed cause can then be compared. The conclusion that one event causes another requires such comparisons.

In the study of learning, the behavior of living organisms, not lights, is of interest. But observers have to proceed in a similar fashion to identify causes. They have to conduct experiments in which behavior is observed with and without the presumed cause. The most basic question is whether a training procedure produces a particular type of learning effect. To answer this question, the actions of individuals who previously received the training procedure in question have to be compared to the actions of individuals who did not have that training. The only way to prove that the training experience is causing the behavior change of interest is to experimentally vary the presence and absence of that experience. For this reason, *learning can be investigated only with experimental techniques.* Also for this reason, the study of learning is primarily a laboratory science.

The necessity of using experimental techniques to investigate learning is not adequately appreciated by allied scientists. Many aspects of behavior can be studied with observational procedures that do not involve experimental manipulations of the presumed causes of the behavior. For example, observational studies can provide a great deal of information about whether and how animals set up territories, the manner in which they defend those territories, the activities involved in the courtship and sexual behavior of a species, the ways in which animals raise their offspring, and the changes in the activities of the offspring as they mature. Many aspects of animal behavior are accessible to observational study, and much fascinating information has been obtained with observational techniques that involve minimal intrusion into the ongoing activities of the animals.

Unfortunately, learning cannot be observed directly in the same manner as activities such as grooming, aggression, or parental behavior. Researchers can form hypotheses about what animals may be learning by observing their behavior unobtrusively in nature. However, to be sure that the changes in behavior are not due to changes in motivation, sensory development, hormonal fluctuations, or other possible non-learning mechanisms, it is necessary to conduct experiments in which the presumed training experiences are systematically manipulated.

The General-Process Approach to the Study of Learning

The second prominent methodological feature of studies of learning is the use of a general-process approach. This is more a matter of preference than of necessity. However, in adopting a general-process approach, investigators of animal learning are following a long-standing tradition in science.

Elements of the General-Process Approach.   The most obvious feature of nature is its diversity. Consider, for example, the splendid variety of minerals that exist in the world. Some are soft, some are hard, some are brilliant in appearance, others are dull, and so on. Plants and animals also are in many different shapes and sizes. Dynamic properties of objects are also diverse. Some things float up, whereas others rapidly drop to the ground; some remain still, and others remain in motion.

In studying nature, one can either focus on differences or try to ignore the differences and search for commonalities. Scientists ranging from physicists to chemists to biologists to psychologists have all elected to search for commonalities. Rather than being overwhelmed by the tremendous diversity in nature, scientists have opted to look for uniformities. They have attempted to formulate *general laws* with which to organize and explain the diversity of events in the universe. Investigators of animal learning have followed this well-established tradition.

Whether or not general laws are discovered often depends on the level of analysis that is pursued. The diversity of the phenomena scientists try to understand and organize makes it difficult to formulate general laws at the level of the observed phenomena. It is difficult, for example, to discover the general laws that govern chemical reactions by simply documenting the nature of the chemicals involved in various reactions. Similarly, it is difficult to explain the diversity of species in the world by cataloging the features of various animals. Major progress in science comes from analyzing phenomena at a more elemental or molecular level. For example, by the nineteenth century, chemists knew many specific facts about what would happen when various chemicals were combined. However, a general account of chemical reactions had to await the development of the periodic table of the elements, which organizes chemical elements in terms of their constituent atomic components.

A fundamental assumption of the general-process approach is that the phenomena of interest are the products of more elemental processes. Furthermore, those elemental processes are assumed to operate in pretty much the same manner no matter where they are found. Thus, generality is assumed to exist at the level of basic or elemental processes.

Investigators of conditioning and learning have been committed to the general-process approach from the inception of this field of psychology. They have focused on the commonalities of various instances of learning and have assumed that learning phenomena are products of elemental processes that operate in much the same way in different learning situations.

The commitment to a general-process approach guided Pavlov's work on functional neurology and conditioning. Commitment to a general-process approach to the study of learning is also evident in the writings of early comparative psychologists. For example, Darwin (1897) emphasized commonalities among species in cognitive functions: "My object . . . is to show that there is no fundamental difference between man and the higher mammals in their mental faculties" (p. 66). Jacques Loeb (1900) pointed out that commonalities occur at the level of elemental processes: "Psychic phenomena . . . appear, invariably, as a function of an elemental process, namely the activity of associative memory" (p. 213). Another prominent comparative psychologist of the time, C. Lloyd Morgan, stated in 1903 that elementary laws of association "are, we believe, universal laws" (p. 219).

The assumption that "universal" elemental laws of association are responsible for learning phenomena does not deny the diversity of stimuli that different animals may learn about, the diversity of responses they may learn to perform, or species differences in rates of learning. The generality is assumed to exist in the rules or processes of learning—not in the content or speed of learning. This idea was clearly expressed nearly a century ago by Edward Thorndike, one of the first prominent American psychologists who studied learning:

> Formally, the crab, fish, turtle, dog, cat, monkey, and baby have very similar intellects and characters. All are systems of connections subject to change by the laws of exercise and effect. The differences are: first, in the concrete particular connections, in what stimulates the animal to response, what responses it makes, which stimulus connects with what response, and second, in the degree of ability to learn. (Thorndike, 1911, p. 280)

What an animal can learn about (the stimuli, responses, and stimulus-response connections it learns about) varies from one species to another. Animals also differ in how fast they learn ("in the degree of ability to learn"). Thorndike assumed that the rules of learning were universal. We no longer share his view that these universal rules of learning are the "laws of exercise and effect." Contemporary scientists do, however, continue to adhere to the idea that universal rules of learning exist. The job of the learning psychologist is to discover those universal laws. (More about the work of Thorndike is found in Chapter 5.)

Methodological Implications of the General-Process Approach. If we assume that universal rules of learning exist, then we should be able to discover those rules in any situation in which learning occurs. Thus, an important methodological implication of the general-process approach is that general rules of learning may be discovered by studying any species or response system that exhibits learning. This implication has encouraged scientists to study learning in a small number of experimental situations. Investigators have converged on a few "standard" or conventional experimental paradigms. Most studies of learning are conducted in one of these paradigms. Figure 1.5, for example, shows an example of a pigeon in a standard Skinner box. I describe other examples of standard experimental paradigms as I introduce various learning phenomena in later chapters.

Conventional experimental paradigms have been fine-tuned over the years to fit well with the behavioral predispositions of the research animals. Because of these improvements, conventional experimental preparations permit laboratory study of reasonably naturalistic responses (Timberlake, 1990).

Figure 1.5 A pigeon in a standard Skinner box. Three circular disks, arranged at eye level, are available for the bird to peck. Access to food is provided in the hopper below.

Robert W. Allan, Lafayette College

Proof of the Generality of Learning Phenomena. The general-process approach has dominated studies of animal learning throughout the twentieth century. As I show in the chapters that follow, the approach has provided an extensive and sophisticated body of knowledge. Given the successes of the general-process approach, it is tempting to conclude that learning processes are indeed universal. However, it is important to keep in mind that the generality of learning processes is not proven by adopting a general-process approach. Assuming the existence of common elemental learning processes is not the same as empirically demonstrating those commonalities.

Direct empirical verification of the existence of common learning processes in a variety of situations remains necessary in efforts to build a truly general account of how learning occurs. A general theory of learning cannot be empirically verified by investigating learning in just a few standard experimental paradigms. The generality of learning processes has to be proven by studying learning in many different species and situations.

The available evidence suggests that elementary principles of learning of the sort that are described in this text have considerable generality (Papini, 2002). Most research on animal learning has been performed with pigeons, rats, and (to a much lesser extent) rabbits. Similar forms of learning have been found with fish, hamsters, cats, dogs, human beings, dolphins, and sea lions. In addition, some of the principles of learning observed with these vertebrate species have been demonstrated in *newts* (Ellins, Cramer, & Martin, 1982); *fruit flies* (Cadieu, Ghadraoui, & Cadieu, 2000; Davis, 1996; Holliday & Hirsch, 1986); *honeybees* (Bitterman, 1988, 1996); *terrestrial mollusks* (Sahley, Rudy, & Gelperin, 1981; Ungless, 1998); *wasps* (Kaiser & De Jong, 1995), and various *marine mollusks* (Carew, Hawkins, & Kandel, 1983; Colwill, Goodrum, & Martin, 1997; Farley & Alkon, 1980; Rogers, Schiller, & Matzel, 1996; Susswein & Schwarz, 1983).

Examples of learning in diverse species provide support for the general-process approach. However, the evidence should be interpreted cautiously. With the exception of the extensive program of research on learning in honeybees conducted by Bitterman and his associates, the various invertebrate species in the studies I cited have been tested on a limited range of learning phenomena. Consequently, we do not know whether their learning was mediated by the same mechanisms that are responsible for analogous instances of learning in vertebrate species.

USE OF NONHUMAN ANIMALS IN RESEARCH ON LEARNING

Many of the experiments discussed in this book have been conducted with nonhuman animal participants. Many types of animals have been used, including rats, mice, rabbits, fish, pigeons, and monkeys. Nonhuman animals are used in the research for both theoretical and methodological reasons.

Rationale for the Use of Nonhuman Animals in Research on Learning

As I have argued, experimental methods are needed to investigate learning phenomena. Experimental methods make it possible to attribute the acquisition of new behaviors to particular previous experiences. Such experimental control of past experience cannot be achieved with the same degree of precision in studies with human participants as in studies with laboratory animals. With laboratory animals, scientists can study how strong emotional reactions are learned and how learning is involved in acquiring food, avoiding pain or distress, or finding potential sexual partners. With people, investigators are limited to trying to modify maladaptive emotional responses after such responses have already been acquired. However, even the development of successful therapeutic procedures for the treatment of maladaptive emotional responses has required knowledge of how such emotional responses are learned in the first place—knowledge that required studies with laboratory animals.

Knowledge of the evolution and biological bases of learning also cannot be obtained without the use of nonhuman animals in research. How cognition and intelligence evolved is one of the fundamental questions about human nature. The answer to this question will shape our view of human nature, just as knowledge of the solar system has shaped our view of the role of Earth in the universe. As I have discussed, investigation of the evolution of cognition and intelligence rests heavily on studies of learning in nonhuman animals.

Knowledge of the biological bases of learning may not change our views of human nature, but it is apt to yield important dividends in the treatment of learning and memory disorders. Such knowledge also rests heavily on research with laboratory animals. The kind of detailed investigations that are necessary to unravel how the nervous system learns and remembers simply cannot be conducted with people. As I pointed out in the Preface, a search for the biological bases of learning first requires documenting the nature of learning processes at the behavioral level. Therefore, behavioral studies of learning in animals are a necessary prerequisite to any animal research on the biological bases of learning. Neuroscience has to be grounded in behavioral science.

Laboratory animals also provide important conceptual advantages over people for studying learning processes. The processes of learning may be simpler in animals reared under controlled laboratory conditions than in people, whose backgrounds are more varied and often poorly documented. The behavior of nonhuman animals is not complicated by linguistic processes that have a prominent role in certain kinds of human behavior. Another important advantage is that demand characteristics are not involved in research with laboratory animals. In research with people, the investigator has to make sure that the actions of the participants are not governed by their efforts to please (or displease) the experimenter. Such factors are not likely to determine what rats and pigeons do in an experiment.

Laboratory Animals and Normal Behavior

Some have suggested that domesticated strains of laboratory animals may not provide useful information because such animals have degenerated as a result of many generations of inbreeding and long periods of captivity (for example, Lockard, 1968). However, this notion is probably mistaken. In an interesting test, Boice (1977) took 5 male and 5 female albino rats of a highly inbred laboratory stock and housed them in an outdoor pen in Missouri without artificial shelter. All 10 rats survived the first winter with temperatures as low as −22°F. The animals reproduced normally and reached a stable population of about 50 members. Only 3 of the rats died before showing signs of old age during the 2-year study period. Given the extreme climatic conditions, this level of survival is remarkable. Furthermore, the behavior of these domesticated rats in the outdoors was very similar to the behavior of wild rats observed in similar circumstances.

Domesticated rats act similarly to wild rats in other tests as well, and there is some indication that they perform better than wild rats in learning experiments (see, for example, Boice, 1973, 1981; Kaufman & Collier, 1983). Therefore, the results I describe in this text should not be discounted simply because many of the experiments were conducted with domesticated animals. In fact, laboratory animals may be preferable in research to their wild counterparts. Human beings in civilized society live in what are largely "artificial" environments. Therefore, research with animals may prove most relevant to human behavior if that research is carried out with domesticated animals that live in artificial laboratory situations. As Boice (1973) commented, "The domesticated rat may be a good model for domestic man" (p. 227).

Public Debate about Research with Nonhuman Animals

There has been much public debate about the pros and cons of research with nonhuman animals. Part of the debate has centered on the humane treatment of animals. Other aspects of the debate have centered on what constitutes ethical treatment of animals, whether human beings have the right to benefit at the expense of animals, and possible alternatives to research with nonhuman animals.

The Humane Treatment of Laboratory Animals. Concern for the welfare of laboratory animals has resulted in the adoption of strict federal standards for animal housing and for the supervision of animal research. Some argue that these rules are needed because without them scientists would disregard the welfare of the animals in their zeal to obtain research data. However, this argument ignores the fact that good science requires good animal care. Scientists, especially those studying behavior, must be concerned about the welfare of their research subjects. Information about normal learning and behavior cannot be obtained from diseased or abused animals. Investigators of animal learning must ensure the welfare of their subjects if they are to obtain useful scientific data.

Laboratory rats cower in a corner if they are sick and anxious. No useful information about their learning and behavior can be obtained under such circumstances. Investigators have to take great pains to make sure their animals are not upset by serving in an experiment.

The animals must be healthy and adapted to handling; the experimental chambers must be suitable for the species; and the animals must be comfortable being in the chamber.

Learning experiments sometimes involve discomfort. However, every effort is made to minimize the degree of discomfort. In studies of food reinforcement, for example, animals are food deprived before each experimental session to ensure their interest in food. However, the hunger imposed is no more severe than the hunger animals are likely to encounter in the wild, and often it is less severe (Poling, Nickel, & Alling, 1990).

The investigation of certain forms of learning and behavior require the administration of aversive stimulation. Important topics, such as punishment or the learning of fear and anxiety, cannot be studied without some discomfort to the participants. However, even in such cases, efforts are made to keep the discomfort to a minimum.

Electric shock is often used in studies of fear and avoidance learning. The term "shock" conjures up images of an electric chair or the pain a child suffers when she accidentally puts her finger in an electrical outlet. However, the shock used in learning experiments is much milder. Unlike other sources of aversive stimulation, electric shock can be precisely regulated, enabling an experimenter to administer shock at controlled low levels. The shock levels employed in studies of animal learning are far lower than the levels experienced from a wall outlet or an electric chair. In addition, in many procedures the animals are permitted to control their exposure by making escape or avoidance responses.

What Constitutes the Ethical Treatment of Animals? Although making sure that animals serving in experiments are comfortable is in the best interests of the animals as well as the research, formulating general ethical principles is difficult. Animal "rights" cannot be identified in the way we identify human rights (Lansdell, 1988), and animals seem to have different "rights" under different circumstances.

Currently, substantial efforts are made to house laboratory animals in conditions that promote their health and comfort. However, a laboratory mouse or rat loses the protection afforded by federal standards when it escapes from the laboratory and takes up residence in the walls of the building (Herzog, 1988). The trapping and extermination of rodents in buildings is a common practice that has not been the subject of either public debate or restrictive federal regulation. Mites, fleas, and ticks are also animals, but we do not tolerate them in our hair or on our pets. Which species have the right to life, and under what circumstances do they have that right? Such questions defy simple answers.

Assuming that a species deserves treatment that meets government-mandated standards, what should those standards be? Appropriate treatment of laboratory animals is sometimes described as being "humane treatment." However, we have to be careful not to take this term literally. "Humane treatment" means treating an individual as we would treat a human being. It is important to keep in mind that rats (and other laboratory animals) are not human beings. Rats prefer to live in dark burrows made of dirt that they never clean. People, in contrast, prefer to live in well-illuminated and frequently cleaned rooms. Well-kept laboratories typically have rats in well-lit rooms that are frequently cleaned. I cannot help but wonder whether the housing standards were dictated more by human considerations than by rat comfort.

Should Human Beings Benefit from the Use of Animals? Part of the public debate about animal rights has been fueled by the argument that people have no right to benefit at the expense of animals, no right to "exploit" animals. This argument goes far beyond issues concerning the use of animals in research. Therefore, I do not discuss the argument in detail here, except to point out that domesticated animals also gain substantial benefits from their relationship to people. In fact, many animals would not exist were it not for their relationship to people. Thus, the relationship is symbiotic rather than just one-sided and exploitative (Hefner, 1999). Furthermore, the use of laboratory animals in research represents but a small proportion of the other human uses of domesticated animals, such as for food.

The U.S. Department of Agriculture is charged with keeping records of the numbers of nonhuman animals (exclusive of rats and mice) that are used in all forms of research in the United States. Since 1973, when these data were first collected, the number of dogs, cats, hamsters, and rabbits used in research has decreased substantially (USDA, 2001). The number of nonhuman primates used in research has remained fairly steady, but only a small proportion of all research animals are nonhuman primates.

Table 1.1 provides estimates of the numbers of animals used in agriculture and all forms of research for 1997, the latest year for which complete data were available from the National Agricultural Statistics Service. More than 8.5 billion animals were used for food in the United States in 1997. Many fewer animals (less than 8.5 million) were used in various forms of research. In fact, all forms of research accounted for less than one tenth of a percent (0.099%) of the total number of animals used between agriculture and research. When the number of animals killed in hunting and in animal shelters is added, the percentage of animals used in research is even smaller. It is difficult to estimate the numbers of animals used in studies of learning, but it is certainly only a tiny proportion of the total number used in research in general.

In addition to the explicit human uses of animals for such things as food, clothing, and hunting, a comprehensive count of human "exploitation" of animals has to include disruptions of habitats that occur whenever we build roads, housing developments, and factories. We should also add the millions of animals that are killed by insecticides and other pest-control efforts in agriculture and elsewhere. In this context, the contributions of animal research to the total "exploitation" of animal life takes on even more trivial dimensions.

In a survey of animal rights advocates, 90% indicated that they would like to eliminate all animal research, and 38% said that this should be the top priority of the animal rights movement (Plous, 1998). Although this percentage is smaller than what had been obtained in an earlier survey (Plous, 1991), the focus of a sizeable proportion of animal rights advocates on curbing animal research efforts is puzzling given the far greater numbers of animals used in other ways. This anti-research focus is also puzzling when we consider that alternatives to the use of animals are much more readily available when it comes to food, clothing, and sports and entertainment.

Alternatives to Research with Animals. Increased awareness of ethical issues involved in the use of nonhuman animals in research has encouraged a search for alternative techniques. Russell and Burch (1959) formulated the "three Rs" for animal research: *replacement* of animals with other testing techniques, *reducing* the number of animals used with statistical techniques, and *refining* the experimental procedures to cause less suffering. Replacement strategies have been successful in the cosmetic industry and in the manufacture of certain vaccines and hormones (Murkerjee, 1997). However, as Gallup and Suarez (1985) pointed out, good research on learning processes cannot be conducted without experiments on live organisms, be they animal or human. Some proposed alternatives are the following:

1. *Observational techniques.* As I discussed earlier, learning processes cannot be investigated with unobtrusive observational techniques. Experimental manipulations of past experience are necessary in studies of learning. Field observations of undisturbed animals cannot yield information about the mechanisms of learning.

2. *Plants.* Learning cannot be investigated in plants because plants lack a nervous system, which is required for learning.

TABLE 1.1   NUMBERS OF ANIMALS USED IN AGRICULTURE AND RESEARCH IN THE UNITED STATES*

AGRICULTURE[1]

Chickens, Broilers	7,764,200,000
Chickens, Layers	303,604,000
Turkeys	301,251,000
Cattle & Calves	59,801,000
Hogs & Pigs	104,301,000
Sheep & Lambs	6,691,000
Total Agriculture	**8,539,848,000**

RESEARCH[2]

Dogs	75,429
Cats	26,091
Primates	56,381
Guinea Pigs	217,079
Rabbits	309,322
Farm Animals	159,742
Rats and Mice	7,452,186
Other	150,987
Total Research	**8,452,186**

Percentage of total used in research = 0.099%

*Data for 1997.

[1] Data for chickens (broilers) and turkeys from U.S. Department of Agriculture NASS Bulletin number 958. Data for chickens (layers) from U.S. Department of Agriculture NASS Bulletin number 944. Data for all other agriculture animals from U.S. Department of Agriculture NASS Bulletin number 959a.

[2] Includes all forms of research, not just psychological research. Data for animals, except rats and mice, U.S. Department of Agriculture Animal Welfare Report, Fiscal Year 2000, APHIS 41-35-071. Rats and mice estimated on the assumption suggested by the Institute of Laboratory Animal Research at the National Research Council that 85% of all research vertebrate animals are rats and mice.

3. *Tissue cultures.* Although tissue cultures may reveal the operation of cellular processes, how these cellular processes operate in an intact organism can be discovered only by studying the intact organism. Furthermore, as I pointed out earlier, a search for cellular mechanisms of learning first requires characterizing learning at the behavioral level.

4. *Computer simulations.* Writing a computer program to simulate a natural phenomenon requires a great deal of knowledge about the phenomenon. Before programmers could construct a computer simulation of learning, they would have to have precise and detailed information about the nature of learning phenomena and the mechanisms and factors that determine learning. The absence of such knowledge necessitates experimental research with live organisms. Thus, experimental research with live organisms is a prerequisite for effective computer simulations. For that reason, computer simulations cannot be used in place of experimental research.

Computer simulations can serve many useful functions in science. Simulations are effective in showing us the implications of the experimental observations that have already been obtained. Computer simulations are often used in studies of behavior to show the implications of various theoretical assumptions. They can be used to identify gaps in knowledge and to suggest important future lines of research. However, they cannot be used to generate new, previously unknown facts about behavior. That can be done only by studying live organisms.

Earlier in this chapter, I used the example of a computer simulation to measure the wind resistance of various automobile designs. Why is it possible to construct a computer program to study wind resistance but not possible to construct one to study learning processes? The critical difference is that we know a lot more about wind resistance than we know about learning. Wind resistance is determined by the laws of mechanics—laws that have been thoroughly explored since the days of Sir Isaac Newton. Application of those laws to wind resistance has received special attention in recent years, as the wind resistance of automobiles has become an important factor in increasing gas mileage.

Designing automobiles with low wind resistance is an engineering task. It involves the application of existing knowledge, rather than the discovery of new knowledge and new principles. Research on animal learning involves the discovery of new facts and new principles. It is science, not engineering. As Conn and Parker (1998) pointed out, "scientists depend on computers for processing data that we already possess, but can't use them to explore the unknown in the quest for new information" (p. 1417).

SAMPLE QUESTIONS

1. Describe how historical developments in the study of the mind contributed to the contemporary study of learning.

2. Describe Descartes' conception of the reflex and how the concept of the reflex has changed since his time.

3. Describe the definition of learning and the methodological implications of this definition.

4. Describe Artistotle's four causes and how they may be related to learning.

5. Describe several alternatives to the use of animals in research, and describe their advantages and disadvantages.

KEY TERMS

association A connection between the representations of two events (two stimuli or a stimulus and a response) such that the occurrence of one of the events activates the representation of the other.

dualism The view of behavior according to which actions can be separated into two categories: voluntary behavior controlled by the mind and involuntary behavior controlled by reflex mechanisms.

empiricism A philosophy according to which all ideas in the mind arise from experience.

fatigue A temporary decrease in behavior caused by repeated or excessive use of the muscles involved in the behavior.

hedonism The philosophy proposed by Hobbes according to which the actions of organisms are determined entirely by the pursuit of pleasure and the avoidance of pain.

learning An enduring change in the mechanisms of behavior involving specific stimuli and/or responses that results from prior experience with similar stimuli and responses.

maturation A change in behavior caused by physical or physiological development of the organism in the absence of experience with particular environmental events.

nativism A philosophy according to which human beings are born with innate ideas.

nervism The philosophical position adopted by Pavlov that all behavioral and physiological processes are regulated by the nervous system.

nonsense syllable A three-letter combination (two consonants separated by a vowel) that has no meaning.

performance An organism's activities at a particular time.

reflex A mechanism that enables a specific environmental event to elicit a specific response.

ELICITED BEHAVIOR, HABITUATION, AND SENSITIZATION

hapter 2 begins the discussion of contemporary principles of learning and behavior with a description of modern research on elicited behavior—behavior that occurs in reaction to specific environmental stimuli. Many of the things we do are elicited by discrete stimuli, and some of the most extensively investigated response systems involve elicited behavior. The chapter begins with a description of the simplest form of elicited behavior, reflexive behavior, and ends with a discussion of complex emotional responses and goal-directed behavior. During this discussion, I describe two of the fundamental and most common forms of behavioral change—habituation and sensitization—which occur in a wide variety of response systems and are potentially involved in all learning procedures.

All animals, whether single-celled paramecia or complex human beings, react to events in their environment. If something moves in the periphery of your vision, you will likely turn your head in that direction. A particle of food in the mouth elicits salivation. Exposure to a bright light causes the pupils of the eyes to constrict. Touching a hot surface elicits a quick withdrawal response. Irritation of the respiratory passages causes sneezing and coughing. These and numerous similar examples illustrate that much of behavior occurs in response to stimuli—that is, it is elicited.

Elicited behavior has been the subject of extensive investigation. Many chapters in this text deal in one way or another with responses to stimuli. I begin the discussion of elicited behavior by describing its simplest form, reflexive behavior.

The Concept of the Reflex

A light puff of air directed at the cornea makes the eye blink. A tap just below the knee causes the leg to kick. A loud noise triggers a startle reaction. These are all examples of reflexes. A reflex involves two closely related events, an *eliciting stimulus* and a *corresponding response,* which are linked. Presentation of the stimulus is followed by the response, and the response rarely occurs in the absence of the stimulus. For example, dust in the nasal passages elicits sneezing, which does not occur in the absence of nasal irritation.

The specificity of the relation between a stimulus and its accompanying reflex response is a consequence of the organization of the nervous system. In vertebrates (including humans), simple reflexes are typically mediated by three neurons, as illustrated in Figure 2.1. The environmental stimulus for a reflex activates a **sensory neuron** (also called **afferent neuron**) that transmits the sensory message to the spinal cord. There, the neural impulses are relayed to the **motor neuron** (also called **efferent neuron**), which activates the muscles involved in the reflex response. However, sensory and motor neurons rarely communicate directly. The impulses from one to the other are relayed through at least one **interneuron.**

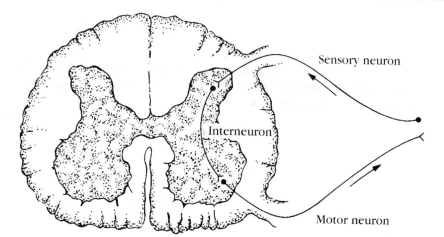

Cross-section of spinal cord

Figure 2.1 Neural organization of simple reflexes. The environmental stimulus for a reflex activates a sensory neuron, which transmits the sensory message to the spinal cord. Here, the neural impulses are relayed to an interneuron, which in turn relays the impulses to the motor neuron. The motor neuron activates muscles involved in movement.

Figure 2.2 Painful stimulation of one limb of a dog causes withdrawal (flexion) of that limb and extension of the opposite limb. (From "Reflexive Behavior," by B. L. Hart in G. Bermant [Ed.], 1973, *Perspectives in Animal Behavior.* Copyright © 1973 by Scott, Foresman. Reprinted by permission.)

The neural circuitry ensures that particular sensory neurons are connected to a corresponding set of motor neurons. Because of this restricted "wiring," a particular reflex response is elicited only by a restricted set of stimuli. The afferent neuron, interneuron, and efferent neuron together constitute the **reflex arc.**

The reflex arc in vertebrates represents the fewest neural connections necessary for reflex action, but additional neural structures may also be involved. For example, the sensory messages may be relayed to the brain, which in turn may modify the reflex reaction in various ways. I discuss such effects later in the chapter. For now, it is sufficient to keep in mind that the occurrence of even simple reflexes can be influenced by higher nervous system activity.

Most reflexes contribute to the well-being of the organism in obvious ways. In many animals, for example, painful stimulation of one limb causes withdrawal, or flexion, of that limb and extension of the opposite limb (Hart, 1973). If a dog stubs a toe while walking, it will automatically withdraw that leg and simultaneously extend the opposite leg (see Figure 2.2). This combination of responses removes the first leg from the source of pain and at the same time allows the animal to maintain balance.

Reflexes constitute much of the behavioral repertoire of newborn infants. If you touch an infant's cheek with your finger, the baby will reflexively turn her head in that direction, with the result that your finger will fall into the baby's mouth. This head-turning reflex probably evolved to facilitate finding the nipple. The sensation of an object in the mouth causes reflexive sucking. The more closely the object resembles a nipple, the more vigorously the baby will suck.

Another important reflex, the *respiratory occlusion reflex,* is stimulated by a reduction of airflow to the baby, which can be caused by a cloth covering the baby's face or by the accumulation of mucus in the nasal passages. In response to the reduced airflow, the baby's first reaction is to pull her head back. If this does not remove the eliciting stimulus, the baby will move her hands in a face-wiping motion. If this also fails to remove the eliciting stimulus, the baby will begin to cry. Crying involves vigorous expulsion of air, which may be sufficient to remove whatever was obstructing the air passages.

The respiratory occlusion reflex is obviously essential for survival. If the baby does not get enough air, she may suffocate. A problem arises, however, when the respiratory occlusion reflex is triggered during nursing. While nursing, the baby can get air only through the nose. If the mother presses the baby too close to the breast during feeding so that the baby's nostrils are covered by the breast, the respiratory occlusion reflex will be triggered. The baby will attempt to pull her head back from the nipple, may move her hands in a face-

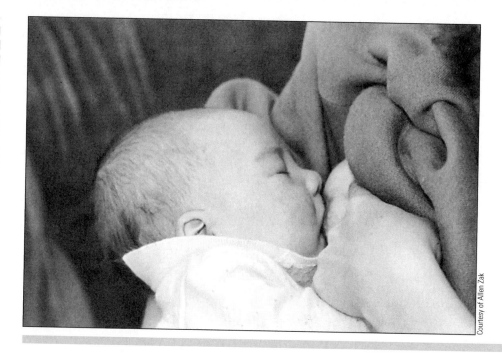

Courtesy of Allen Zak

Figure 2.3 Sucking is one of the most prominent reflexes in infants.

wiping motion that pushes away the nipple, and may begin to cry. Successful nursing requires a bit of experience. The mother and child have to adjust their positions so that nursing can progress without stimulation of the respiratory occlusion reflex (Gunther, 1961). (See Figure 2.3.)

Modal Action Patterns

Simple reflex responses, such as pupillary constriction to a bright light and startle reactions to a brief loud noise, are evident in many species. By contrast, other forms of elicited behavior occur in just one species or in a small group of related species. For example, sucking in response to objects placed in the mouth is a characteristic of mammalian infants. Herring-gull chicks are just as dependent on parental feeding as are human infants, but their feeding behavior is very different. When a parent gull returns to the nest from a foraging trip, the chicks peck at the tip of the parent's bill (see Figure 2.4), causing the parent to regurgitate. As the chicks continue to peck, they manage to get some of the parent's regurgitated food, and thus receive nourishment.

Response sequences, such as those involved in infant feeding, that are typical of a particular species are referred to as **modal action patterns** or **MAPs** (Baerends, 1988). Species-typical modal action patterns have been identified in many aspects of animal behavior, including sexual behavior, territorial defense, aggression, and prey capture. Ring doves, for example, begin their sexual behavior with a courtship interaction that culminates in the selection of a nest site and the cooperative construction of the nest by both male and female. By contrast, in the three-spined stickleback, a species of small fish, the male first establishes a territory and constructs a nest. Females that enter the territory after the nest has been built are courted and induced to lay their eggs in the nest. Once a female has deposited her eggs, the male chases her away, leaving him alone to care for and defend the eggs until the offspring hatch.

31

Figure 2.4 Feeding of herring-gull chicks. The chicks peck a red patch near the tip of the parent's bill, causing the parent to regurgitate food for them.

An important feature of modal action patterns is that the threshold for eliciting such activities varies as a function of circumstances (Camhi, 1984; Baerends, 1988). The same stimulus can have widely different effects, depending on the physiological state of the animal and its recent actions. A male stickleback, for example, will not court a female who is ready to lay eggs until he has completed building his nest. And after the female has deposited her eggs, the male will chase her away rather than court her as he did earlier. Furthermore, these sexual and territorial responses will occur only when environmental cues induce physiological changes that are characteristic of the breeding season in both males and females.

Modal action patterns were initially identified by ethologists, scientists who study the evolution of behavior. Early ethologists, such as Lorenz and Tinbergen, referred to species-specific action patterns as "fixed action patterns" to emphasize that the activities occurred in much the same way in all members of a species. Subsequent detailed observations, however, indicated that action patterns are not performed in exactly the same fashion each time, that they are not strictly "fixed." Because of this variability, we now use the term "modal action pattern" (Baerends, 1988).

Eliciting Stimuli for Modal Action Patterns

The eliciting stimulus is fairly easy to identify in the case of simple reflexes, such as the startle response to a brief loud noise. The stimulus responsible for a modal action pattern can be more difficult to isolate if the response occurs in the course of complex social interactions. For example, consider again the feeding of a herring-gull chick. To get fed, the chick has to peck the parent's beak to stimulate the parent to regurgitate. But what stimulates the chick's pecking response? There are a number of possibilities, but the answer cannot be determined on the basis of casual observation.

The adult herring gull has a long, yellow bill with a striking red patch near the tip. Pecking by the chicks may be elicited by the color, shape, or length of the parent's bill, the noises the parent makes, the head movements of the parent, or some other stimulus. To isolate which one of these stimuli elicits pecking, Tinbergen and Perdeck (1950) tested chicks with various artificial models instead of live adult gulls. Their research showed that a model had to have several characteristics to elicit strong pecking—a long, thin, moving object pointed downward and having a contrasting red patch near the tip. These experiments suggest that the yellow color of the adult's bill, the shape and coloration of its head, and the noises it makes are not required for eliciting pecking in the gull chicks. The specific features required to elicit the pecking behavior are called, collectively, the **sign stimulus** or **releasing stimulus** for this behavior.

A sign or releasing stimulus is sufficient for eliciting a modal action pattern. However, a given action pattern may be controlled by several stimulus features in an additive fashion. In addition, the most effective stimulus for eliciting a modal action pattern may not be one that is likely to occur under natural conditions. These principles are well illustrated by a study of the egg-retrieval behavior of herring gulls (Baerends & Drent, 1982). If a brooding herring gull finds an egg on the rim of its nest, it will pull the egg into the nest. To determine which features of the egg best stimulate this behavior, Baerends and Drent tested gulls with wooden eggs of various sizes, colors, and speckling.

The results indicated that the gulls preferred to retrieve green speckled eggs more than yellow ones, yellow eggs more than brown, and brown eggs more than blue. The preference for green and yellow eggs over brown eggs was remarkable because real gull eggs are brown rather than green or yellow. Increases in the number of speckles and their contrast with the background also increased egg-retrieval behavior, as did increases in the size of the wooden eggs (see Figure 2.5).

G. P. Baerends

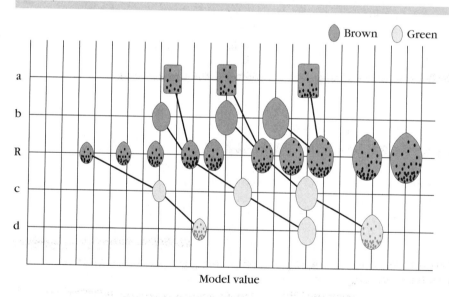

Model value

Figure 2.5   Relative effectiveness of various artificial eggs in stimulating egg retrieval behavior in gulls. From left to right, the models increase in effectiveness. Row "R" (for reference series) shows eggs of normal color and speckling. Row "a" shows block-shaped eggs; "b" shows plain brown eggs; "c" shows plain green eggs; and "d" shows speckled green eggs. The oblique lines connect models of the same size. Notice that eggs of a given type can be made more effective by an increase in size. (From "The Herring Gull and Its Egg. Part II: The Responsiveness to Egg Features," by G. P. Baerends and R. H. Drent [Eds.], 1982, *Behaviour, 82,* pp. 1–417. Reprinted by permission.)

BOX **2.1**

THE LEARNING OF "INSTINCT"

Because modal action patterns occur in a similar fashion among members of a given species, they include activities that are informally characterized as "instinctive." Instinctive behavior is considered primarily to reflect an individual's genetic history, leading to the impression that modal action patterns are not the product of learning and experi-ence. However, the fact that all members of a species exhibit similar forms of behavior does not necessarily mean that the behavior was not learned through experience. As Tinbergen (1951) recognized many years ago, similar behavior on the part of all members of a species may reflect similar learning experiences. In a more recent expression of this sentiment, Baerends (1988) wrote that "learning processes in many variations are tools, so to speak, that can be used in the building of some segments in the species-specific behavior organization" (p. 801). Thus, learning may be involved in what we commonly refer to as "instinctive" behaviors (Domjan, 1998; Hailman, 1967).

Color, speckling, and size appeared to control the egg-retrieval behavior in an additive fashion. Thus, the attractiveness of an egg could be increased by making it more green, more speckled, or larger. Optimizing all three of these stimulus dimensions resulted in a green, highly speckled, and abnormally large egg. Interestingly, such an egg was more effective in stimulating egg-retrieval behavior than was a real gull egg. Thus, once the stimulus features that controlled egg retrieval were identified, they could be combined to form an object that was more effective than a naturally occurring egg in eliciting the action pattern. Such an unusually effective stimulus is called a **supernormal stimulus.**

The Sequential Organization of Behavior

Responses do not occur in isolation of one another. Rather, individual actions are organized into functionally effective behavior sequences. To obtain food, for example, a squirrel first has to look around for potential food sources, such as a pecan tree with nuts. It then has to climb the tree and reach one of the nuts. After obtaining the nut, the squirrel has to crack the shell, extract the meat, and chew and swallow it. All motivated behavior, whether it is foraging for food, finding a potential mate, defending a territory, or feeding one's young, involves systematically organized sequences of actions. Ethologists called early components of a behavior sequence **appetitive behavior** and the end components **consummatory behavior** (Craig, 1918). The term "consummatory" was meant to convey the idea of *consummation* or *completion.* Thus, consummatory responses are actions that bring a species-typical response sequence to completion. In contrast, appetitive responses occur early in a behavior sequence and serve to bring the organism into contact with the stimuli that will release the consummatory behavior.

Chewing and swallowing are responses that complete activities involved in foraging for food. Hitting and biting are actions that consummate defensive behavior. Copulatory responses serve to complete the sexual behavior sequence. In general, consummatory responses are highly stereotyped, species-typical behaviors that have specific eliciting or releasing stimuli. In contrast, appetitive behaviors are less stereotyped and can take a variety of different forms, depending on the situation (Tinbergen, 1951). In getting to a pecan tree, for example, a squirrel can run up one side or the other or jump from a neighboring tree. These are all possible appetitive responses leading up to actually eating the pecan nut. Once the squirrel is ready to put the pecan meat in its mouth, however, the chewing and swallowing responses that it makes are fairly stereotyped. Consummatory responses tend to be species-typical modal action patterns. In contrast, appetitive behaviors are more variable depending on the environment. As is evident from the varieties of ethnic cuisine, people of different cultures have many different ways of preparing food (appetitive behavior), but they all chew and swallow in much the same way (consummatory behavior). Actions that are considered rude and threatening (appetitive defensive responses) also differ from one culture to another, but people hit and hurt one another (consummatory defensive behavior) in much the same way regardless of culture.

The sequential organization of naturally occurring behavior is very important to scientists interested in understanding how behavior is altered by learning, because learning effects often depend on which component of the behavior sequence is being modified. As I describe in later chapters, the outcomes of Pavlovian and instrumental conditioning depend on how these learning procedures modify the natural sequence of an organism's behavior. Learning theorists are becoming increasingly aware of the importance of considering natural behavior sequences and have expanded on the appetitive and consummatory distinction made by early ethologists (Domjan, 1997; Fanselow, 1997; Timberlake, 1994, 2001).

In considerations of how animals obtain food, for example, it is now common to characterize the foraging response sequence as starting with a **general search mode,** followed by a **focal search mode,** and ending with a **food handling mode.** Thus, in modern learning theory, the appetitive response category has been subdivided into general search and focal search categories (for example, Timberlake, 2001). General search responses occur when the subject does not yet know where to look for food. Before a squirrel has identified a pecan tree, it will move all about looking for potential sources of food. General search responses are not spatially localized. Once the squirrel has found a pecan tree, however, it will switch to the focal search mode and begin to search for pecans only on that tree. Thus, focal search behavior is characterized by considerable spatial specificity. Focal search behavior yields to food handling or consummatory behavior once a pecan nut has been obtained.

EFFECTS OF REPEATED STIMULATION

A common assumption is that an elicited response—in particular, a simple reflex response—will automatically occur the same way every time the eliciting stimulus is presented. This is exactly what Descartes thought. In his view, each occurrence of the eliciting stimulus would produce the same reflex reaction because the energy of the eliciting stimulus is transferred to the motor response through a direct physical connection. If this were true, a baby would suck with the same vigor every time it received a nipple, and you would react with the same pleasure each time you took a sip of your favorite drink. However, if elicited behavior occurred the same way every time, it would be of limited interest, especially for investigators of learning.

Contrary to Descartes' assumptions, elicited behavior is not invariant. One of the most impressive features of elicited behavior is its plasticity. Even simple elicited responses do not

Figure 2.6 Experimental setup for the study of visual attention in infants. The infant is seated in front of a screen that is used to present various visual stimuli. How long the infant looks at the display before diverting his gaze elsewhere is measured on each trial.

occur the same way each time. As the following examples illustrate, alterations in the nature of elicited behavior often occur simply as a result of repeated presentations of the eliciting stimulus.

Visual Attention in Human Infants

Human infants have a lot to learn about the world, and one way they obtain information is by looking at things in their environment. Visual cues elicit a looking response, which can be measured by how long the infant keeps his eyes on one object before shifting his gaze elsewhere (see Figure 2.6).

In one study of visual attention (Bashinski, Werner, & Rudy, 1985; see also Kaplan, Werner, & Rudy, 1990), 4-month-old infants were assigned to one of two groups, and each group was tested with a different visual stimulus. (The stimuli are shown in the right panel of Figure 2.7.) Both were checkerboard patterns: one had 4 squares on each side (the 4×4 stimulus) and the other had 12 (the 12×12 stimulus). Each stimulus presentation lasted 10 seconds, and the stimuli were presented eight times at 10-second intervals.

Both stimuli elicited visual attention initially, with the babies spending an average of about 5.5 seconds looking at the stimuli. With repeated presentations of the 4×4 stimulus, visual attention progressively decreased. By contrast, the babies increased their gaze at the 12×12 stimulus during the second trial as compared to the first. But, after that, visual attention to the 12×12 stimulus also decreased.

This relatively simple experiment reveals a great deal about visual attention. The results show that visual attention elicited by a novel stimulus changes as babies gain familiarity with the stimulus. The nature of the change is determined by the nature of the stimulus. With a relatively simple 4×4 pattern, visual attention progressively declines. With a more complex 12×12 pattern, attention initially increases and then declines. Thus, far from being invariant, the elicited behavior of looking at checkerboard patterns changes in different ways as a result of experience with the stimuli.

Infants cannot tell us in words how they view or think about things. Scientists are therefore forced to use behavioral techniques to study infant perception and cognition. The

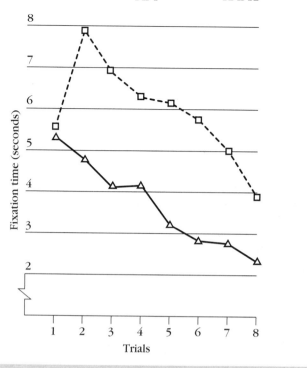

—— 4 x 4   - - - - 12 x 12

The 4 × 4 stimulus

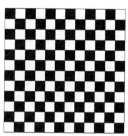

The 12 × 12 stimulus

Figure 2.7 Time infants spent looking at a visual stimulus during successive trials. For one group, the stimulus consisted of a 4 × 4 checkerboard pattern. For a second group, the stimulus consisted of a 12 × 12 checkerboard pattern. The stimuli are illustrated to the right of the results. (From "Determinants of Infant Visual Attention: Evidence for a Two-Process Theory," by H. Bashinski, J. Werner, and J. Rudy, *Journal of Experimental Child Psychology, 39,* pp. 580–598. Copyright © 1985 by Academic Press. Reprinted by permission.)

visual attention task can provide information about visual acuity. For example, from the data in Figure 2.7 we may conclude that these infants were able to distinguish the two different checkerboard patterns. The procedure has also been adapted to study a wide range of complicated questions about infant cognition (Fagen & Ohr, 2001).

Salivation and Hedonic Ratings of Taste in People

The taste of food elicits salivation as a reflex response. This can be observed as easily in people as in Pavlov's dogs. In one study, salivation was measured in eight women in response to the taste of either lemon juice or lime juice (Epstein, Rodefer, Wisniewski, & Caggiula, 1992). A tiny amount of one of the flavors (.03 ml) was placed on the subject's tongue on each of 10 trials. On each trial, the subject was asked to rate how much she liked the taste, and her salivation to each taste presentation was also measured. The results are summarized in Figure 2.8. Salivation in response to the taste increased slightly, but from Trial 1 to Trial 2, but response systematically decreased from Trial 2 to Trial 10. A similar decrease was observed in hedonic ratings of the taste. Thus, as the taste stimulus was repeated 10 times, it became less effective in eliciting both salivation and hedonic responses.

On Trial 11, the flavor of the taste was changed (to lime for subjects who had previously been exposed to lemon, and to lemon for subjects who had been exposed to lime). This produced a dramatic recovery in both the salivary reflex and the hedonic rating. Interestingly, this recovery persisted on Trial 12 when the original flavor was presented again.

People often eat because they like the taste of what they are eating. The results presented in Figure 2.8 indicate that people find the taste of a specific food less pleasant the

Figure 2.8 Salivation and ratings of pleasantness in response to a taste stimulus (lime or lemon) repeatedly presented to women on Trials 1–10. The alternate taste was presented on Trial 11, causing a substantial recovery in responding. (After Epstein, Rodefer, Wisniewski, & Caggiula, 1992.)

more often they encounter it. The taste of a different food is enough, however, to restore the hedonic rating of a familiar food. These findings suggest that overeating may be discouraged by not varying the foods that are available for consumption.

Startle Response in Rats

The kinds of effects presented in Figures 2.7 and 2.8 have also been extensively examined in laboratory animals. Many of these experiments have involved the startle response. The startle is a defensive response evident in many species, including humans. If someone unexpectedly blows a foghorn behind your back, you are likely to jump. This is the startle response. It consists of a sudden jump and a tensing of the muscles of the upper part of the body, usually involving raising of the shoulders. In rats, the startle reaction can be measured by placing the animal in a *stabilimeter chamber* (see Figure 2.9), which rests on pressure sensors. When startled, the animal jumps and thereby jiggles the chamber. These movements are precisely measured by the pressure sensors under the chamber and are used as indicators of the vigor of the startle reaction.

The startle reaction can be elicited in rats by a variety of stimuli, including brief tones and lights. In one experiment, Davis (1974) investigated the startle reaction of two groups of rats to presentations of a brief (90-millisecond) loud tone (110 decibels [dB], 4,000 cycles per second [cps]). Each group received 100 successive tone presentations separated by 30 seconds. In addition, a noise generator provided background noise that sounded somewhat like water running from a faucet. For one group, the background noise was relatively quiet (60 dB); for the other, it was rather loud (80 dB), but of lower intensity than the brief startle-eliciting tones.

Figure 2.9 Stabilimeter apparatus to measure the startle response of rats. A small chamber rests on pressure sensors. Sudden movements of the rat are detected by the pressure sensors and recorded on a computer. (Adapted from Hoffman and Fleshler, 1964.)

Pressure sensor

Cable to computer

The results of the experiment are shown in Figure 2.10. As in the other examples, repeated presentations of the eliciting stimulus (the 4,000 cps tone) did not always produce the same response. For rats tested in the presence of the soft background noise (60 dB), repetitions of the tone resulted in progressively weaker startle reactions. By contrast, when the background noise was loud (80 dB), repetitions of the tone elicited more vigorous startle reactions.

THE CONCEPTS OF HABITUATION AND SENSITIZATION

The studies described in the previous section show that both decreases and increases in responding can occur with repeated presentation of an eliciting stimulus. Decreases in responsiveness produced by repeated stimulation are technically referred to as **habituation effects.** Increases in responsiveness are called **sensitization effects.** Habituation and sensitization effects are two basic types of behavior change that result from prior experience. They are such fundamental features of how organisms adjust to their environment that they occur in nearly all species and response systems (for recent studies in nematodes and crabs, see Beck & Rankin, 1997). Habituation and sensitization effects can occur in any situation that involves repeated exposures to a stimulus. Therefore, an appreciation of these effects is critical for studies of learning. As I describe in Chapter 3, habituation and sensitization are of primary concern in the design of control procedures for Pavlovian conditioning. They also play a role in operant conditioning (McSweeney, Hinson, & Cannon, 1996; McSweeney & Roll, 1998; see also Bizo, Bogdanov, & Killeen, 1998).

Adaptiveness and Pervasiveness of Habituation and Sensitization

Organisms are constantly bombarded by a host of stimuli. Even a simple situation such as sitting at your desk involves a myriad of sensations. You are exposed to the color, texture, and brightness of the paint on the walls; the sounds of the air-conditioning system; noises

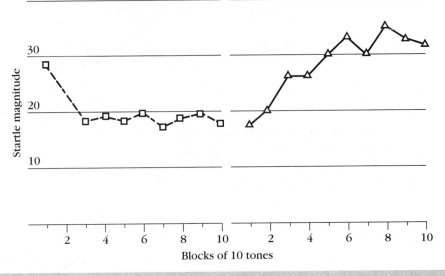

Figure 2.10 Magnitude of the startle response of rats to successive presentations of a tone with background noise of 60 and 80 dB. (From "Sensitization of the Rat Startle Response by Noise," by M. Davis, 1974, *Journal of Comparative and Physiological Psychology,* 87, pp. 571–581. Copyright © 1974 by the American Psychological Association. Reprinted by permission.)

from other rooms; odors in the air; the color and texture of the desk; the tactile sensations of the chair against your legs, seat, and back; and so on. If you were to respond to all of these stimuli, your behavior would be disorganized and chaotic. These effects help sort out what stimuli to ignore and what to respond to. Habituation and sensitization effects are the end products of processes that help organize and focus behavior in the buzzing and booming world of stimuli in which all organisms live.

There are numerous instances of habituation and sensitization in common human experience (Simons, 1996). Consider a grandfather clock, for example. Most people who own such a clock do not notice each time it chimes, because they have completely habituated to the clock's sounds. They are more likely to notice when the clock misses a scheduled chime. In a sense, this is unfortunate, because they may have purchased the clock because they liked its sound. Similarly, people who live on a busy street or near a railroad track may become entirely habituated to the noises that frequently intrude into their homes. Visitors who have not become familiarized with such sounds are much more likely to react and be bothered by them.

Driving a car involves exposure to a large array of complex visual and auditory stimuli. In becoming an experienced driver, a person habituates to the numerous stimuli that are irrelevant to driving, such as details of the color and texture of the road, the kind of telephone poles that line the sides of the highway, tactile sensations of the steering wheel, and routine noises from the engine. Habituation to irrelevant cues is particularly prominent during long driving trips. If you are driving continuously for several hours, you are likely to become oblivious to all kinds of stimuli that are irrelevant to keeping the car on the road. If you then come across an accident or arrive in a new town, you are likely to "wake up" and again pay attention to various things that you had been ignoring. Passing a bad accident or coming to a new town is arousing and sensitizes various orientation responses that were previously habituated.

If you visit a new place or meet a new person, you will likely pay attention to all sorts of stimuli that you ordinarily ignore. In a strange home, for example, you might take notice of the quality of the furniture, the drapes, and some of the knickknacks. You probably ignore such details in familiar places—so much so that you may not be able to either describe the color of the walls in a hallway you pass through every day or recall the type of knob attached to a door you use regularly.

Habituation versus Sensory Adaptation and Response Fatigue

The key characteristic of habituation effects is a decline in the response that was initially elicited by a stimulus. However, habituation is not the only effect that produces a decline in resonse. To understand alternative sources of response decrement, return to the concept of a reflex. A reflex consists of three components. First, a stimulus activates one of the sense organs, such as the eyes or ears. This generates sensory neural impulses that are relayed to the central nervous system (spinal cord and brain). The second component involves relay of the sensory messages through interneurons to motor nerves. Third, the neural impulses in motor nerves in turn activate the muscles that create the observed response.

Given the three components of a reflex, there are several reasons why an elicited response may fail to occur (see Figure 2.11). The response will not be observed if for some reason the sense organs become temporarily insensitive to stimulation. A person may, for example, be temporarily blinded by a bright light or suffer a temporary hearing loss because of repeated exposures to a loud noise. Such decreases in sensitivity are called **sensory adaptation** and are different from habituation. The response also will not occur if the muscles involved become incapacitated by **fatigue.** Sensory adaptation and response fatigue are impediments to responding that are produced outside the nervous system, in sense organs and muscles. Therefore, they are distinguished from habituation.

Habituation and sensitization are assumed to involve neurophysiological changes that hinder or facilitate the transmission of neural impulses from sensory to motor neurons. In habituation, the organism ceases to respond to a stimulus even though it remains fully capable of sensing the stimulus and of making the muscle movements required for the response. The response fails to occur because changes in the nervous system block the relay of sensory neural impulses to the motor neurons.

In studies of habituation, sensory adaptation is ruled out by evidence that *habituation is response-specific.* An organism may stop responding to a stimulus in one aspect of its behavior while continuing to respond to the stimulus in other ways. When a teacher makes an announcement while you are concentrating on taking a test, you may look up from your test at first, but only briefly. You will, however, continue to listen to the announcement until it is over. Thus, your orienting response habituates quickly, but other attentional responses to the stimulus persist.

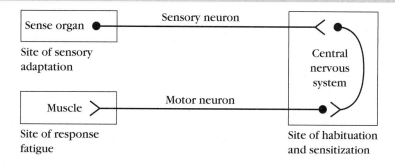

Figure 2.11 Sensory adaptation occurs in the sense organs, and response fatigue occurs in effector muscles. In contrast, habituation and sensitization occur in the nervous system.

Response fatigue as a cause of habituation is ruled out by evidence that *habituation is stimulus-specific.* An habituated response will quickly recover when a new stimulus is introduced. This was illustrated in the taste habituation study summarized in Figure 2.8. After the salivary and hedonic responses had habituated during the first 10 trials, presentation of the alternate taste on Trial 11 resulted in a recovery of both response measures. In an analogous fashion, after your orienting response to a teacher's announcement has habituated, you are likely to look up again if the teacher mentions your name. Thus, a new stimulus will elicit the previously habituated orienting response, indicating that failure of the response was not due to response fatigue.

The Dual-Process Theory of Habituation and Sensitization

Habituation and sensitization effects are changes in behavior or performance. These are outward behavioral manifestations or results of stimulus presentations. What factors are responsible for such changes? To answer this question, we must shift our level of analysis from behavior to presumed underlying process or theory. The dominant theory of habituation and sensitization remains the dual-process theory proposed by Groves and Thompson (1970).

The dual-process theory assumes that different types of underlying neural processes are responsible for increases and decreases in responsiveness to stimulation. One neural process, the **habituation process,** produces decreases in responsiveness. Another, the **sensitization process,** produces increases in responsiveness. These processes are not mutually exclusive. Both may be activated at the same time. The behavioral outcome of these underlying processes depends on which process is stronger. Thus habituation and sensitization processes compete for control of behavior, as illustrated in Figure 2.12.

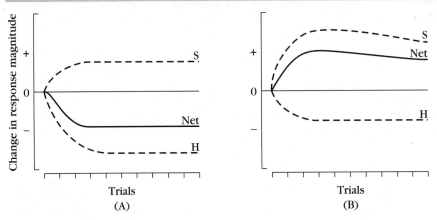

Figure 2.12   Hypothetical data illustrating the dual-process theory of habituation and sensitization. The strength of the habituation process (H) is indicated by the dashed lines that extend below the horizontal 0 line. The strength of the sensitization processes (S) is indicated by the dashed lines that extend above the horizontal 0 line. The solid lines indicate the net effects of the habituation and sensitization processes. In panel A, the habituation process becomes stronger than the sensitization process across trials, which leads to a progressive decrement in responding. In panel B, the sensitization process becomes stronger than the habituation process across trials, which leads to a progressive increase in responding.

The left side of Figure 2.12 illustrates a hypothetical situation in which repetitions of a stimulus intensify the habituation process more than the sensitization process. The net result and behavioral outcome of these changes is a decline in the elicited response across trials (an habituation effect). The right side of Figure 2.12 illustrates the opposite outcome. Here, repetitions of a stimulus strengthen the sensitization process more than the habituation process, and the net result is an increase in the magnitude of the elicited response across trials (a sensitization effect). The change in the elicited response that actually occurs always represents the net effect of the habituation and sensitization processes.

It is unfortunate that the underlying processes that suppress and facilitate responding are called habituation and sensitization. One may be tempted to think that decreased responding or an habituation effect is a direct reflection of the habituation process, and that increased responding or a sensitization effect is a direct reflection of the sensitization process. In fact, as illustrated in Figure 2.12, both habituation and sensitization effects are the sum or net result of both processes. Whether the net result is an increase or a decrease in behavior depends on which underlying process is stronger in a particular situation. The distinction between *effects* and *processes* in habituation and sensitization is analogous to the distinction between *performance* and *learning* discussed in Chapter 1. Effects refer to observable behavior, and processes refer to underlying mechanisms.

On the basis of neurophysiological research, Groves and Thompson (1970) suggested that habituation and sensitization processes occur in different parts of the nervous system (see also Thompson et al., 1973). Habituation processes are assumed to occur in the **S-R system,** which consists of the shortest neural path that connects the sense organs activated by the eliciting stimulus and the muscles involved in making the elicited response. The S-R system may be viewed as the reflex arc. Each presentation of an eliciting stimulus activates the S-R system and causes some buildup of habituation.

Sensitization processes are assumed to occur in the **state system.** This system consists of other parts of the nervous system that determine the organism's general level of responsiveness or readiness to respond. In contrast to the S-R system, which is activated every time an eliciting stimulus is presented, the state system is activated only by arousing events. It is relatively quiescent during sleep, for example. Drugs such as stimulants or depressants may alter the functioning of the state system and thereby change responsiveness. It is also altered by emotional experiences. For example, the heightened reactivity that accompanies fear is caused by activation of the state system.

In summary, the state system determines the organism's general readiness to respond, whereas the S-R system enables the animal to make the specific response that is elicited by the stimulus of interest. Changes in behavior that occur with repetitions of a stimulus reflect the combined actions of the S-R and state systems.

Applications of the Dual-Process Theory. The examples of habituation and sensitization illustrated in the experimental evidence I reviewed earlier can be easily interpreted in terms of the dual-process theory. Repeated exposure to the 4 × 4 checkerboard pattern produced a decrement in visual orientation in infants, presumably because the 4 × 4 stimulus did not create much arousal. In fact, the 4 × 4 stimulus activated primarily the S-R system, and hence activated primarily the habituation process. The more complex 12 × 12 checkerboard pattern produced a greater level of arousal. It presumably activated not only the S-R system but also the state system. Activation of the state system resulted in the increment in visual attention that occurred after the first presentation of the 12 × 12 pattern. However, the arousal or sensitization process was not strong enough to entirely counteract the effects of habituation. As a result, after a few trials, visual attention also declined in response to the 12 × 12 stimulus.

BOX 2.2

TALKING TO A FETUS OR A PRE-VERBAL INFANT

Habituation and sensitization do not require verbal competence. These forms of behavioral plasticity are therefore very useful in studies of the perceptual and cognitive abilities of fetuses and pre-verbal infants (Cohen, 1988; Fagen & Ohr, 2001; Hepper & Shahidullah, 1992; Leinbach & Fagot, 1993; Rose & Orlian, 2001; Smotherman & Robinson, 1992). For example, Kaplan, Goldstein, Huckeby, and Cooper (1995) investigated whether 4-month-old infants could tell the difference between a mother's speech directed toward the infant or toward other adults. To create the speech stimuli, Kaplan et al. recorded a mother saying, "Round and round she goes, and where she stops nobody knows." In one recording, the words were directed toward the mother's infant. In another, the mother was asked to say the words as if talking to another adult. The two kinds of speech were presented while infants were tested for habituation of visual attention to a 4 × 4 checkerboard pattern. Presentation of the infant-directed speech along with the visual stimulus slowed down habituation to the checkerboard pattern. Furthermore, less habituation occurred with infant-directed speech than with adult-directed speech. The babies evidently became more sensitized or aroused by infant-directed speech than by adult-directed speech. This result shows that the babies were able to tell the difference between the two types of speech and found infant-directed speech more stimulating.

A different type of application of the dual-process theory is required for the habituation and sensitization effects I noted in the startle reaction of rats (Figure 2.10). When the rats were tested with a relatively quiet background noise (60 dB), there was little to arouse them. We can therefore assume that the experimental procedures did not produce changes in the state system. Repeated presentations of the startle-eliciting tone merely activated the S-R system, which resulted in habituation of the startle response.

The opposite outcome occurred when the animals were tested in the presence of a loud background noise (80 dB). Stronger startle reactions occurred to successive presentations of the tone. Because the identical tone was used for both groups, the difference in the results cannot be attributed to the tone. One must assume that the loud background noise increased arousal or readiness to respond in the second group. This sensitization of the state system was presumably responsible for increasing the startle reaction to the tone in the second group.

Implications of the Dual-Process Theory. The preceding interpretations of changes in visual attention and startle responding illustrate several important features of the dual-process theory. As discussed earlier, the state and S-R systems are activated differently by repeated presentations of a stimulus. *The S-R system is activated every time a stimulus elicits a response,* because it is the neural circuit that conducts impulses from sensory input to response output. By contrast, *the state system becomes involved only in special circumstances.* Some extraneous event (such as an intense background noise) may increase the individual's alertness and sensitize the state system. Alternatively, the state system may be sensitized by the repeated presentations of the test stimulus itself if that stimulus is sufficiently intense or excitatory (a 12 × 12 checkerboard pattern, as compared with a 4 × 4 pattern). If the arousing stimulus is repeated soon enough so that the second presentation occurs while the organism remains sensitized from the preceding trial, an increase in responding will be observed.

The dual-process theory of habituation and sensitization has been very influential in the study of the plasticity of elicited behavior (for example, Pilz & Schnitzler, 1996), although it has not been successful in explaining all habituation and sensitization effects (for example, Bee, 2001). One of the important contributions of the theory has been the assumption that elicited behavior can be strongly influenced by neurophysiological events that take place outside the reflex arc that is directly involved in a particular elicited response. In the dual-process theory, the state system is assumed to modulate the activity of reflex arcs. The basic idea that certain parts of the nervous system serve to modulate S-R systems that are more directly involved in elicited behavior has also been developed in other recent studies of habituation and sensitization (for example, Borszcz, Cranney, & Leaton, 1989; Davis, Hitchcock, & Rosen, 1987; Falls & Davis, 1994; Frankland & Yeomans, 1995; Lipp, Sheridan, & Siddle, 1994). (For a detailed discussion of other theories of habituation, see Stephenson & Siddle, 1983.)

CHARACTERISTICS OF HABITUATION AND SENSITIZATION

Much research has been performed to determine how various factors influence habituation and sensitization processes. Although the characteristics of habituation and sensitization are not perfectly uniform across all species and response systems, there are many commonalties. In this section, I describe some of the most important ones.

Time Course

Most of the forms of behavior change I describe in later chapters are retained for long periods (weeks or months), a defining characteristic of learning phenomena (see Chapter 1). Instances of habituation and sensitization do not always have this characteristic, and therefore not all instances of habituation and sensitization are properly considered examples of enduring learning.

Time Course of Sensitization.   Sensitization processes generally have temporary effects. Although in some instances sensitization persists for more than a week (e.g., Heiligenberg, 1974), the increased responsiveness is generally short-lived. Davis (1974), for example, investigated the sensitizing effect of a 25-minute exposure to a loud noise (80 dB) in rats. As expected, the loud noise sensitized the startle response to a tone, but this increased reactivity lasted only 10–15 minutes after the loud noise was turned off. In other response systems, sensitization dissipates more rapidly. For example, sensitization of the spinal hindlimb-flexion reflex in cats persists for only about 3 seconds (Groves & Thompson, 1970).

In all response systems the duration of sensitization effects is determined by the intensity of the sensitizing stimulus. More intense stimuli produce greater increases in responsiveness, and with more intense stimuli the sensitization effects persist longer.

Time Course of Habituation.   Habituation also persists for varying amounts of time. With sensitization, differences in the time course of the effect usually reflect only quantitative differences in the same underlying mechanism. By contrast, there are two qualitatively different types of habituation effects: *Short-term habituation* is similar to most cases of sensitization in that it dissipates relatively quickly—within seconds or minutes. The other type, *long-term habituation* is much longer lasting and may persist for many days.

Figure 2.13 Startle response of rats to a tone presented once a day in Phase 1, every 3 seconds in Phase 2, and once a day in Phase 3. (From "Long-Term Retention of the Habituation of Lick Suppression and Startle Response Produced by a Single Auditory Stimulus," by R. N. Leaton, 1976, *Journal of Experimental Psychology: Animal Behavior Processes, 2,* pp. 248–259. Copyright © 1976 by the American Psychological Association. Reprinted by permission.)

Short-term and long-term habituation effects are clearly illustrated by Leaton (1976) in an experiment on the startle response of rats. The test stimulus was a high-pitched, loud tone presented for 2 seconds. The animals were first allowed to get used to the experimental chamber without any tone presentations. Each rat then received a single test trial with the tone stimulus once a day for 11 days. Because of the long (24-hour) interval between trials, any decrements in responding produced by the stimulus presentations were assumed to exemplify long-term habituation. The short-term habituation process was illustrated in the next phase of the experiment by giving the rats 300 closely spaced tone presentations (every 3 seconds). Finally, the animals were given a single tone presentation on each of the next 3 days to measure recovery from the short-term habituation effect.

Figure 2.13 shows the results. The most intense startle reaction was observed the first time the tone was presented. Progressively less intense reactions occurred over the next 10 days. Because the animals were tested only once every 24 hours in this phase, the progressive decrements in responding indicate that the habituating effects of the stimulus presentations persisted throughout the 11-day period. It is worth noting, though, that this long-term habituation did not result in complete loss of the startle reflex. Even on the 11th day, the animals reacted a little.

By contrast, startle reactions quickly ceased when the tone presentations occurred every 3 seconds in the second phase of the experiment, but this dramatic loss of responsiveness was only temporary. In the third phase of the experiment, when the animals were tested again just once a day, the startle response recovered to the level of the 11th day of the experiment. This recovery, known as **spontaneous recovery,** occurred simply because the tone had not been presented for a long time (24 hours). *Spontaneous recovery is the identifying characteristic of the short-term habituation effect.*

Repeated presentations of a stimulus do not always result in both long-term and short-term habituation effects. With the spinal leg-flexion reflex in cats, for example, only the

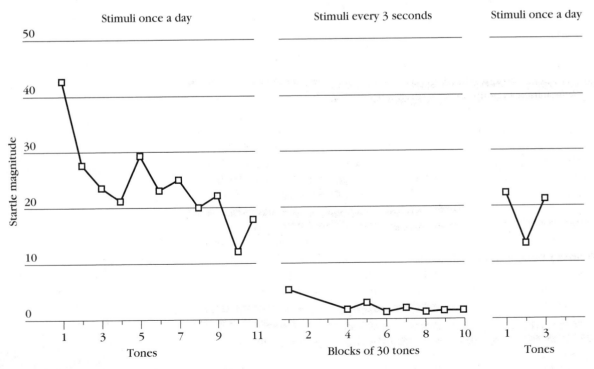

short-term habituation effect is observed (Thompson & Spencer, 1966). In such cases, spontaneous recovery completely restores the animal's reaction to the eliciting stimulus if a long enough period of rest is permitted after habituation. By contrast, spontaneous recovery is never complete in situations that also involve long-term habituation effects, as in Leaton's experiment. As Figure 2.13 indicates, the startle response was restored to some extent in the last phase of the experiment, but the animals did not react as vigorously to the tone as they had the first time it was presented.

Short-term habituation typically occurs when the eliciting stimulus is presented frequently, as in the second phase of Leaton's experiment. In contrast, long-term habituation is more likely with more widely spaced stimulus presentations (for example, Beck & Rankin, 1997; Pedreira et al., 1998; Staddon & Higa, 1996).

The dual-process theory of habituation and sensitization was formulated to explain only short-term effects and therefore cannot explain why habituation lasts considerably longer under certain conditions. The most successful explanation of long-term habituation is Wagner's priming theory (for example, Whitlow & Wagner, 1984). I do not discuss this theory here because it involves associative learning mechanisms that are not presented in detail until Chapters 3 and 4. (For recent studies of the associative mechanisms of long-term habituation, see Honey, Good, & Manser, 1998; Jordan, Strasser, & McHale, 2000; Tomsic, Pedreira, Romano, Hermitte, & Maldonado, 1998.)

Stimulus Specificity

Stimulus Specificity of Habituation. Habituation is specific to the stimulus that is repeatedly presented (Thompson & Spencer, 1966). A response that has been habituated to one stimulus can be evoked in full strength by altering a critical feature of the stimulus. This outcome was shown in the experiment on habituation of salivation and hedonic ratings in response to a taste (see Figure 2.8). After the salivary and emotional responses to one taste stimulus (for example, lime) had substantially habituated (Trials 1-10), the responses showed total recovery when a different taste (lemon) was presented (Trial 11). Similar effects occur in common experience. For example, after you have become habituated to the chimes of a grandfather clock, your attention to the clock is likely to be entirely restored if the clock malfunctions and makes a new sound. After complete habituation of the orienting response to one stimulus, the response will occur in its normal strength if a sufficiently novel stimulus is presented. Stimulus specificity has been considered one of the defining characteristics of habituation (Thompson & Spencer, 1966).

Although habituation effects are always stimulus-specific, some generalization of the effects may occur. If you have become habituated to a particular clock chime, you may also not respond to another clock chime that is similar to the original one. This phenomenon is called *stimulus generalization of habituation*. However, even in cases of stimulus generalization, as test stimuli are made increasingly different from the habituated stimulus, the organism will show progressively less habituation or suppression of responding to the test stimuli.

Stimulus Specificity of Sensitization. Unlike habituation, sensitization is not highly stimulus-specific. If an animal becomes aroused or sensitized for some reason, its reactivity will increase to a range of cues. For example, pain induced by footshock increases the reactivity of laboratory rats to both auditory and visual cues. Similarly, feelings of sickness or malaise increase the reactivity of rats to a wide range of novel tastes. However, shock-induced sensitization appears to be limited to exteroceptive cues, and illness-induced sensitization is limited to gustatory stimuli (Miller & Domjan, 1981). Cutaneous pain and internal malaise seem to activate separate sensitization systems.

Effects of a Strong Extraneous Stimulus

As I have noted, changing the nature of the eliciting stimulus can produce recovery of an habituated response. However, this is not the only way to quickly restore responding after habituation. The habituated response can also be restored by sensitizing the organism with exposure to an extraneous stimulus. This phenomenon is called **dishabituation.**

Figure 2.14 illustrates the results of a study involving dishabituation of the visual-attention response of human infants (Kaplan, Werner, & Rudy, 1990). The infants were shown a 4 × 4 checkerboard pattern during each of the first eight trials of the experiment and displayed a familiar habituation effect. During Trial 9, a 75 dB, 1,000 cps tone was sounded along with the visual stimulus for one group of infants, while the other group continued to receive the visual stimulus but without the tone. The presence of the tone greatly elevated responding. Furthermore, responding continued to be elevated in Trials 10, 11, and 12, during which the tone was again omitted and only the 4 × 4 visual stimulus was available.

It is important to keep in mind that dishabituation refers to recovery in the response to the previously habituated stimulus—the 4 × 4 pattern in the above example. Responding directly to the sensitizing or dishabituating tone was not of interest. In fact, the increased visual fixation that was observed when the tone was presented on Trial 9 could not be explained as a response to the tone because the tone was presented through a speaker located above and behind the infant. If the infant had oriented toward the source of the tone, he or she would have ended up looking away from the visual stimulus.

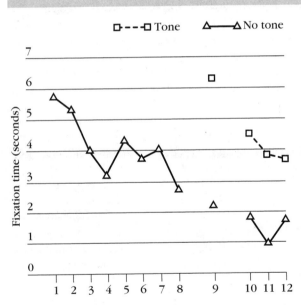

Figure 2.14 Fixation time of human infants plotted as a function of presentations of a 4 × 4 checkerboard pattern. On the 9th trial, some of the infants were exposed to a 10-second, 1,000 Hz, 75 dB tone. This caused an increase in responding to the checkerboard pattern. (From "Habituation, Sensitization, and Infant Visual Attention," by P. S. Kaplan, J. S. Werner, and J. W. Rudy, 1990, in *Advances in Infancy Research,* Vol. 6, pp. 61–109, C. Rovee-Collier and L. P. Lipsitt [Eds.]. Copyright © 1990 by Ablex Publishing Company. Reprinted by permission.)

BOX **2.3**

LEARNING IN AN INVERTEBRATE

How does the brain acquire, store, and retrieve information? To answer this question, we need to know how neurons operate and how neural circuits are modified by experience. Studying these issues requires that we delve into the neural machinery, to record and manipulate its operations. Naturally, people are not keen on volunteering for such experiments. Therefore, such research has to be conducted on other species.

Much can be learned from the vertebrates (rats, rabbits) that are typically used in behavioral studies of learning. Yet, at a neural level, even a rat poses technical challenge for a neurobiologist. Therefore, neurobiologists have focused on creatures with simpler nervous systems. Invertebrates are attractive because some of their neurons are very large (for example, the motor neuron that drives escape in a squid), and they have far simpler nervous systems. Using this approach, Eric Kandel and his colleagues have uncovered the mechanisms that mediate some basic learning processes in the marine snail *Aplysia*. Here I provide an overview of the mechanisms that underlie habituation and sensitization. For more information on this topic and others related to the neurobiology of learning, see Dudai (1989) and Kandel, Schwartz, and Jessell (2000).

The *Aplysia* has two winglike flaps (the parapodium) on its back or dorsal surface. These flaps cover the gill and other components of the respiratory apparatus (see Figure 2.15). The gill lies under a mantle shelf and a siphon helps to circulate water across the gill. In the relaxed state, the gill is extended (left side of Figure 2.15), maximizing chemical exchange across its surface. The gill is a fragile organ that must be protected, and thus nature has given *Aplysia* a protective gill withdrawal reflex. This reflex can be elicited by a light touch applied to the siphon or mantle. In the laboratory, the reflex is often elicited by a water jet produced from a Water Pik. While the mechanisms that underlie this reflex can be studied in the intact organism, it is often easier to study the underlying system after the essential components have been removed and placed in a nutrient bath that sustains the tissue.

With this simple preparation, it is an easy matter to demonstrate both habituation and sensitization (see Figure 2.15). Habituation can be produced by repeatedly applying the tactile stimulus to the siphon. With continued exposure, the magnitude of the gill withdrawal reflex becomes smaller (habituates). Interestingly, this experience has no effect on the magnitude of the gill withdrawal elicited by touching the mantle shelf. Conversely, if we repeatedly touch the mantle, the withdrawal response observed habituates without affecting the response elicited by touching the siphon. A modification in one stimulus-response (S-R) pathway has no effect on the response vigor in the other.

In vertebrates, a painful shock engages a mechanism that generally sensitizes behavior, augmenting a variety of response systems including those that generate a startle response (Davis, 1989). A similar effect can be demonstrated in *Aplysia*. If a shock stimulus is applied to the tail, it sensitizes the gill withdrawal response elicited by touching the mantle or siphon (Walters, 1994). Notice that this is a general effect that augments behavioral reactivity in both the mantle and the siphon circuits.

The essential neural components that underlie gill withdrawal in response to a siphon touch are illustrated in Figure 2.15. A similar diagram could be drawn for the neurons that underlie the gill withdrawal elicited by touching the mantle.

Touching the siphon skin engages a mechanical receptor that is coupled to a sensory neuron (SN). Just one receptor is illustrated here, but additional receptors and neurons innervate adjoining regions of the siphon skin. The degree to which a particular receptor is engaged will depend on its proximity to the locus of stimulation, being greatest at the center of stimulation and weakening as distance increases. This yields the neural equivalent to a generalization gradient, with the maximum activity being produced by the neuron that provides the primary innervation for the receptive field stimulated.

The mechanical receptors that detect a touch engage a response within the dendrites of the sensory neuron (SN).

(continued)

Box 2.3 (continued)

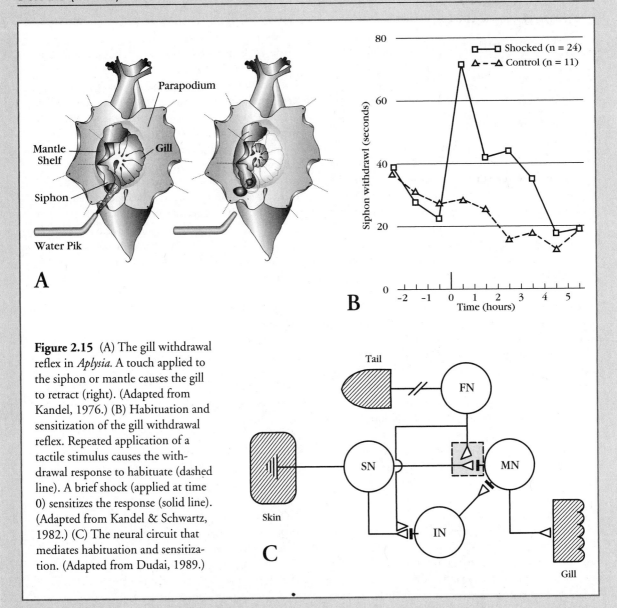

Figure 2.15 (A) The gill withdrawal reflex in *Aplysia*. A touch applied to the siphon or mantle causes the gill to retract (right). (Adapted from Kandel, 1976.) (B) Habituation and sensitization of the gill withdrawal reflex. Repeated application of a tactile stimulus causes the withdrawal response to habituate (dashed line). A brief shock (applied at time 0) sensitizes the response (solid line). (Adapted from Kandel & Schwartz, 1982.) (C) The neural circuit that mediates habituation and sensitization. (Adapted from Dudai, 1989.)

This neural response is conveyed to the cell body (soma) and down a neural projection, the axon, to the motor neuron (MN). The sensory neuron is the presynaptic cell. The motor neuron is the postsynaptic cell. The motor neuron is engaged by the release of a chemical (neurotransmitter) from the sensory neuron. The motor neuron, in turn, carries the signal to the muscles that produce the gill with-

drawal response. Here, the release of neurotransmitter activates muscle fibers that cause the gill to retract.

The sensory neuron also engages other cells, interneurons that contribute to the performance of the gill withdrawal response. However, because an understanding of the basic mechanisms that underlie learning does not hinge on their function, we will pay little attention to the interneurons engaged by the sensory neuron. We cannot, however, ignore another class of interneurons, those engaged by applying a shock to a tail. A tailshock engages neurons that activate an interneuron called the facilitory interneuron (FN). As shown in the figure, the facilitory interneuron impinges upon the end of the presynaptic, sensory, neuron. In more technical terms, the facilitory interneuron presynaptically innervates the sensory neuron. Because of this, the facilitory interneuron can alter the operation of the sensory neuron.

The magnitude of the gill withdrawal response depends on the amount of neurotransmitter released from the motor neurons. The more that is released, the stronger is the response. Similarly, the probability that a response will be engaged in the motor neuron, and the number of motor neurons that are engaged, depend on the amount of neurotransmitter released from the sensory neuron. Increasing the amount released will, on average, enhance the motor neuron response and gill withdrawal response.

Research has shown that repeated stimulations of the sensory neuron cause no change in the action potential generated within the sensory neuron, but result in less transmitter being released, thereby producing the behavioral phenomenon of habituation.

Sensitization, in contrast, engages the facilitory interneuron, which produces a change within the sensory neuron that causes it to release more neurotransmitter. Because more transmitter is released, the motor neurons are engaged to a greater extent, and the gill withdrawal response is more vigorous. Thus, behavioral sensitization occurs because tailshock augments the release of neurotransmitter from the sensory neuron.

—J. W. Grau

EXTENSIONS TO EMOTIONS AND MOTIVATED BEHAVIOR

My discussion of changes produced by repetitions of an eliciting stimulus has so far been limited to relatively simple responses. Stimuli may also evoke complex emotions, such as love, fear, euphoria, terror, or satisfaction. I have already described habituation of an emotional response to repeated presentations of a taste (Figure 2.8), but the concepts of habituation and sensitization also have been extended to changes in more complex emotions (Hoffman & Solomon, 1974; Solomon & Corbit, 1974) and various forms of motivated behavior such as feeding, drinking, exploration, aggression, courtship and sexual behavior (McSweeney & Swindell, 1999), and drug addiction (for example, Koob, Caine, Parsons, Markou, & Weiss, 1997; Solomon, 1977; Solomon & Corbit, 1973).

R. L. Solomon

Emotional Reactions and Their Aftereffects

In their review of examples of emotional responses to various stimuli, including drugs, Solomon and Corbit (1974) noticed a couple of striking features. First, intense emotional reactions are often biphasic. One emotion occurs during the eliciting stimulus, and the opposite emotion is observed when the stimulus is terminated. Consider, for example, the psychoactive effects of alcohol. A person who has a beer or a glass of wine becomes mellow and relaxed, feelings that are generally pleasant. These reactions reflect the primary sedative effects of alcohol. In contrast, something quite different occurs after a serious bout of drinking. Once the sedative effects of alcohol have dissipated, the person is likely to become irritable and may experience headaches and nausea. The pleasant sedative effects of alcohol give way to the unpleasant sensations of a hangover. Furthermore, both the primary reaction and the aftereffect depend on the drug dosage. The more you drink, the more se-dated or drunk you become and the more intense is the hangover afterward. Similar biphasic responses are observed with other drugs. Amphetamine, for example, creates feelings of euphoria, a sense of well-being, self-confidence, wakefulness, and a sense of control. After the drug has worn off, you are likely to feel tired, depressed, and drowsy.

Another common characteristic of emotional reactions is that they change with experience. The primary reaction becomes weaker, and the after-reaction becomes stronger. An habitual drinker is not as debilitated by a few beers as is someone drinking for the first time. However, an habitual drinker experiences more severe withdrawal symptoms after a bout of drinking.

Habituation of the primary drug reactions is called **drug tolerance,** which refers to a decline in the effectiveness of a drug with repeated exposures. Habitual users of alcohol, nicotine, heroin, caffeine, and other drugs are not as greatly affected by the presence of the drug as are first-time users. An amount of alcohol that would make a casual drinker a bit tipsy is not likely to have any effect on a frequent drinker. (I revisit the role of opponent processes in drug tolerance in Chapter 4.)

Because of the development of tolerance, habitual drug users sometimes do not enjoy taking the drug as much as naive users. People who smoke frequently, for example, do not always derive much enjoyment from doing so. Accompanying this decline in the primary drug reaction is a growth in the opponent after-reaction. Accordingly, habitual drug users experience much more severe "hangovers" on termination of the drug than do naive users. Most people who stop smoking cigarettes, for example, experience headaches, irritability, anxiety, tension, and general dissatisfaction. A heavy drinker who stops taking alcohol is likely to experience hallucinations, memory loss, psychomotor agitation, delirium tremens, and other physiological disturbances. For an habitual user of amphetamine, the fatigue and depression that characterize the opponent aftereffect may be severe enough to cause suicide.

Solomon and Corbit (1974) noted that similar patterns of emotional reaction occur with other emotion-arousing stimuli. Consider, for example, love and attachment. Newlyweds are usually very excited about each other and are very affectionate whenever they are together, but this primary emotional reaction habituates as the years go by. The couple gradually settles into a comfortable mode of interaction that lacks the excitement of the honeymoon. Furthermore, habituation of the primary emotional reaction is accompanied by a strengthening of the affective after-reaction. Couples who have been together for many years become more intensely unhappy if they are separated by death or disease than do most newlyweds. After partners have been together for several decades, the death of one partner may cause an intense grief reaction in the survivor. This strong affective after-reaction is remarkable, considering that by this stage in their relationship the couple may have entirely ceased to show any overt signs of affection.

The Opponent-Process Theory of Motivation

The above examples illustrate three common characteristics of emotional reactions: (1) Emotional reactions are biphasic; a primary reaction is followed by an opposite after-reaction. (2) The primary reaction becomes weaker with repeated stimulations. (3) The weakening of the primary reaction with experience is accompanied by a strengthening of the after-reaction. The *opponent-process theory of motivation* (Solomon & Corbit, 1973, 1974) was designed to explain these three prominent features of emotions.

The opponent-process theory assumes that neurophysiological mechanisms involved in emotional behavior serve to maintain emotional stability. Thus, the opponent-process theory is a *homeostatic* theory. It is built on the premise that an important function of mechanisms that control emotional behavior is to minimize deviations from emotional neutrality or stability. (The concept of homeostasis has been very important in the analysis of behavior. I discuss other types of homeostatic theories in later chapters.)

How might physiological mechanisms maintain emotional stability or neutrality? Maintaining any system in a neutral or stable state requires that a disturbance that moves the system in one direction be met by an opposing force that counteracts the disturbance. Consider, for example, trying to keep a seesaw level. If something pushes one end of the seesaw down, the other end will go up. To keep the seesaw level, a force pushing one end down has to be met by an opposing and equal force on the other side.

The concept of opponent forces or processes serving to maintain a stable state is central to the opponent-process theory of motivation. The theory assumes that an emotion-arousing stimulus pushes a person's emotional state away from neutrality. This shift away from emotional neutrality is assumed to trigger an opponent process that counteracts the shift. The patterns of emotional behavior observed both initially and after extensive experience with a stimulus are the net results of the opponent process and changes in the opponent process with experience.

The opponent-process theory assumes that the presentation of an emotion-arousing stimulus initially elicits what is called the **primary process,** or *a* **process,** which is responsible for the quality of the emotional state (happiness, for example) that occurs in the presence of the stimulus. The primary, or *a*, process is assumed to elicit, in turn, an **opponent process,** or *b* **process,** that generates the opposite emotional reaction (unhappiness, for example). The emotional changes observed when a stimulus is presented and then removed are assumed to reflect the net result of the primary and opponent processes. The strength of the opponent process subtracts from the strength of the primary process to provide the emotions that actually occur. Thus, the primary and opponent processes are internal mechanisms whose net effects are the emotional changes that are observed. (The idea is similar to the proposal, illustrated in Figure 2.12, that habituation and sensitization processes are internal mechanisms whose net effects are observed in the magnitude of the startle reflex.)

An additional assumption that is basic to the opponent-process theory is that the opponent process is a bit inefficient. It lags behind the primary emotional disturbance at first and therefore is not strong enough to entirely counteract the primary emotion initially. However, the opponent process becomes quicker and more powerful with practice or repeated experience with the emotion-arousing stimulus. In a sense, the opponent process becomes sensitized as a result of repeated activation. It eventually becomes strong enough to block most of the primary emotional reaction, at which point it also produces a very strong after-reaction when the emotion-arousing stimulus is terminated.

Opponent Mechanisms during Initial Stimulus Exposure. Figure 2.16 shows how the primary and opponent processes determine the initial responses of an organism to an emotion-arousing stimulus. The underlying primary and opponent processes are represented at the bottom of the figure. The net effects of these processes (the observed emotional reactions) are represented in the top panel. When the stimulus is first presented, the *a* process occurs unopposed by the *b* process. This permits the primary emotional reaction to reach its peak quickly. The *b* process then becomes activated and begins to oppose the *a* process. On the first presentation of the stimulus, however, the *b* process is not strong enough to entirely counteract the primary emotional response, which therefore persists during the eliciting stimulus. When the stimulus is withdrawn, the *a* process quickly stops, but the *b* process lingers for awhile. At this point, the *b* process has nothing to oppose, and emotional responses characteristic of the opponent process become evident for the first time. These emotions are typically opposite to those observed during the presence of the stimulus.

initial presentation

a – b

primary reaction

After-reaction

Figure 2.16 Opponent-process mechanism during the initial presentation of an emotion-arousing stimulus. The observed emotional reactions are represented in the top panel. The underlying opponent processes are represented in the bottom panel. Notice that the *b* process starts a bit after the onset of the *a* process. In addition, the *b* process ends much later than the *a* process. This last feature allows the opponent emotions to dominate after the end of the stimulus. (From "An Opponent-Process Theory of Motivation: I. The Temporal Dynamics of Affect," by R. L. Solomon and J. D. Corbit, 1974, *Psychological Review, 81,* pp. 119–145. Copyright © 1974 by the American Psychological Association. Reprinted by permission.)

Opponent Mechanisms after Extensive Stimulus Exposure. Figure 2.17 shows how the primary and opponent processes operate after extensive exposure to a stimulus. As I noted earlier, a highly familiar stimulus does not elicit strong emotional reactions, but the affective after-reaction tends to be much stronger when a highly familiar stimulus is terminated. The opponent-process theory explains this outcome by assuming that the *b* process becomes strengthened by repeated exposures to the stimulus. The strengthening of the *b* process is reflected in several of its characteristics: It becomes activated sooner after the onset of the stimulus, its maximum intensity becomes greater, and it becomes slower to decay when the stimulus ceases. In contrast, the *a* process is assumed to remain unchanged. Thus, after repeated presentations of a stimulus, the primary emotional responses are more effectively counteracted by the opponent process. This growth in the opponent process reduces the intensity of the observed primary emotional responses during presentation of the emotion-arousing stimulus. It also leads to the excessive affective after-reaction when the stimulus is withdrawn (see Figure 2.17).

Opponent Aftereffects and Motivation. If the primary pleasurable effects of a psychoactive drug are gone for habitual users, why do they continue taking the drug? Why are they addicted? The opponent-process theory suggests that drug addiction is mainly an attempt

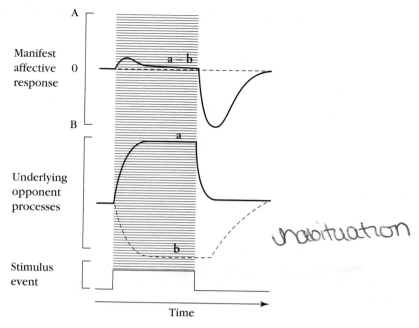

Figure 2.17 Opponent-process mechanism that produces the affective changes to an habituated stimulus. The observed emotional reactions are represented in the top panel. The underlying opponent processes are represented in the bottom panel. Notice that the *b* process starts promptly after the onset of the *a* process and is much stronger than in Figure 2.16. In addition, the *b* process ends much later than the *a* process. Because of these changes in the *b* process, the primary emotional response is nearly invisible during the stimulus, but the affective after-reaction is very strong. (From "An Opponent-Process Theory of Motivation: I. The Temporal Dynamics of Affect," by R. L. Solomon and J. D. Corbit, 1974, *Psychological Review, 81,* pp. 119–145. Copyright © 1974 by the American Psychological Association. Reprinted by permission.)

to reduce the aversiveness of the affective after-reaction to the drugs—the bad hangovers, the amphetamine "crashes," and the irritability that comes from not having the usual cigarette. There are two ways to reduce the aversive opponent after-reactions of drugs. One is simply to wait long enough for them to dissipate—an act known as "cold turkey." For heavy drug users, cold turkey may take a long time and may be very painful. The opponent after-reaction can be reduced much more quickly by taking the drug again. This will reactivate the primary process and stave off the agonies of withdrawal. According to the theory, addicts are "trapped" not by the direct pleasure they derive from their drug, but by their need to take the drug to reduce withdrawal pains.

Overall Assessment of the Opponent-Process Theory. The opponent-process theory was very attractive when it was first introduced because it encompassed a wide range of situations and provided a provocative account of drug tolerance, dependence, and drug addiction. The theory has been extended to research on social attachment in monkeys (Mineka, Suomi, & DeLizio, 1981; Suomi, Mineka, & Harlow, 1983) and ducklings (Hoffman & Solomon, 1974; Starr, 1978). It has also been supported by research on human breast-feeding (Myers & Siegel, 1985). Applications of the theory to other aspects of human experience, such as love and attachment, have been intriguing but have not led to much systematic research (Tzeng & Gomez, 1992). The most extensively pursued applications of the theory have been to the understanding of drug addiction (e.g., Koob et al., 1997). On balance, however, it is fair to say that the promises of the opponent-process theory of motivation remain to be fulfilled. It is not that the theory has been found wanting, but simply that its predictions in various situations have not been put to empirical test.

Although the theory has not stimulated as much research as predicted, it has made an important contribution in that it extended the concept of homeostatic regulation to the analysis of emotions and motivation. As I describe in Chapter 4, opponent-process concepts continue to have a prominent role in learning theory.

Variations in Goal-Directed Behavior

Responding to escape the discomfort of withdrawal is just one type of motivated or goal-directed behavior. I say a lot more about goal-directed behavior in Chapters 5, 6, and 7, focusing on situations in which individuals make a response in order to produce a desirable or rewarding stimulus. A rewarding goal object is technically called a **reinforcer.** Situations in which organisms repeatedly make a response to obtain a reinforcer show many of the common properties of habituation and sensitization (McSweeney & Swindell, 1999). Consider, for example, turning on a CD player to listen to a particular song. You become less likely to turn on the CD player if the outcome is the same song over and over again (habituation), but this loss of interest is specific to the repeated song (stimulus specificity). Furthermore, you will regain your interest in the original song if you don't hear it for a few days (spontaneous recovery). Your interest in the familiar song can also be restored by exposure to novel stimuli, such as the excitement of meeting a friend (sensitization).

Habituation and sensitization effects are common with sensory reinforcers such as pieces of music. Phenomena similar to habituation and sensitization also occur with consumable goal objects such as food and water. For example, repeated exposures to food will produce a decline in food-directed behavior. Decreases in food-directed behavior are often attributable to a reduction of hunger or satiation (Bizo, Bogdanov, & Killeen, 1998), but more general habituation mechanisms may also be involved (McSweeney & Roll, 1998).

CONCLUDING COMMENTS

The quality of life and survival itself depend on an intricate coordination of behavior with the complexities of the environment. Elicited behavior represents one of the fundamental ways in which the behavior of all animals—from single-celled organisms to people—is adjusted to environmental events.

Elicited behavior takes many forms, ranging from simple reflexes mediated by just three neurons to complex emotional reactions. Although elicited behavior occurs as a reaction to a stimulus, it is not rigid and invariant. In fact, one of its remarkable features is that elicited behavior is altered by experience. If an eliciting stimulus does not arouse the organism, repeated presentations of the stimulus will evoke progressively weaker responses (an habituation effect). If the eliciting stimulus is particularly intense or of significance to the individual, repeated presentations will lead to progressively stronger reactions (a sensitization effect).

Environmental events activate habituation and sensitization processes to varying degrees. The resultant level of responding reflects the net effect of the habituation and sensitization processes. Therefore, if one does not know the past experiences of the organism, it is impossible to predict how strong a reaction will be elicited by a particular stimulus presentation.

Repeated presentations of an eliciting stimulus produce changes in simple responses as well as in more complex emotional reactions. Organisms tend to minimize changes in emotional state caused by external stimuli. According to the opponent-process theory of motivation, emotional responses stimulated by an environmental event are counteracted by an opposing process in the organism. This compensatory, or opponent, process is assumed to become stronger each time it is activated, and this leads to a reduction of the primary emotional responses. The strengthened opponent emotional state is evident as an after-reaction when the stimulus is removed.

Habituation, sensitization, and changes in the strength of opponent processes are the simplest mechanisms whereby organisms adjust their reactions to environmental events on the basis of past experience.

SAMPLE QUESTIONS

1. Compare and contrast appetitive and consummatory behavior, and describe how these are related to general search, focal search, and food handling.
2. Describe the distinction between habituation, sensory adaptation, and fatigue.
3. Describe the difference between habituation and sensitization effects and habituation and sensitization processes.
4. Describe the two processes of the dual-process theory of habituation and sensitization and the differences between these processes.
5. Describe the opponent-process theory of motivation and how it explains habituation and sensitization effects.
6. Describe how habituation and sensitization are relevant to goal-directed behavior.

KEY TERMS

a process Same as *primary process* in the opponent process theory of motivation.

afferent neuron A neuron that transmits messages from sense organs to the central nervous system. Also called *sensory neuron*.

appetitive behavior Behavior that occurs early in a natural behavior sequence and serves to bring the organism into contact with a releasing stimulus. (See also *general search mode* and *focal search mode*.)

b process Same as *opponent process* in the opponent-process theory of motivation.

consummatory behavior Behavior that serves to bring a natural sequence of behavior to consummation or completion. Consummatory responses are usually species-typical modal action patterns. (See also *food handling mode*.)

dishabituation Recovery of an habituated response as a result of a strong extraneous stimulus.

drug tolerance Reduction in the effectiveness of a drug as a result of repeated use of the drug.

efferent neuron A neuron that transmits impulses to muscles. Also called a *motor neuron*.

fatigue A temporary decrease in behavior caused by repeated or excessive use of the muscles involved in the behavior.

focal search mode The second component of the feeding behavior sequence, following general search, in which the organism engages in behavior focused on a particular location or stimulus that is indicative of the presence of food. Focal search is a form of appetitive behavior that is more closely related to food than is general search.

food handling mode The last component of the feeding behavior sequence, in which the organism handles and consumes the food. This is similar to what ethologists referred to as consummatory behavior.

general search mode The earliest component of the feeding behavior sequence, in which the organism engages in nondirected locomotor behavior. General search is a form of appetitive behavior.

habituation effect A progressive decrease in the vigor of elicited behavior that may occur with repeated presentations of the eliciting stimulus.

habituation process A neural mechanism activated by repetitions of a stimulus that reduces the magnitude of responses elicited by that stimulus.

interneuron A neuron in the spinal cord between the afferent (or sensory) neuron and the efferent (or motor) neuron in the reflex arc.

MAP Abbreviation for *modal action pattern.*

modal action pattern A response pattern exhibited in much the same way by most, if not all, members of a species. Modal action patterns are used as basic units of behavior in ethological investigations of behavior. Abbreviated *MAP.*

motor neuron Same as *efferent neuron*

opponent process A compensatory mechanism that occurs in response to the primary process elicited by biologically significant events. The opponent process causes physiological and behavioral changes that are the opposite of those caused by the primary process. Sometimes referred to as the *b process.*

primary process The first process elicited by a biologically significant stimulus. Sometimes referred to as the *a process.*

reflex arc Neural structures, consisting of the efferent (sensory) neuron, interneuron, and afferent (motor) neuron, that enable a stimulus to elicit a reflex response.

reinforcer A stimulus whose delivery shortly following a response increases the future probability of that response.

releasing stimulus Same as *sign stimulus.*

sensitization effect An increase in the vigor of elicited behavior that may result from repeated presentations of the eliciting stimulus or from exposure to a strong extraneous stimulus.

sensitization process A neural mechanism that increases the magnitude of responses elicited by a stimulus.

sensory adaptation A temporary reduction in the sensitivity of sense organs caused by repeated or excessive stimulation.

sensory neuron Same as *afferent neuron.*

sign stimulus A specific feature of an object or animal that elicits a modal action pattern in another organism. Also called *releasing stimulus.*

spontaneous recovery Recovery of a response produced by a period of rest after habituation or extinction. (Extinction is discussed in Chapters 3 and 9.)

S-R system The shortest neural pathway that connects the sense organs stimulated by an eliciting stimulus and the muscles involved in making the elicited response.

state system Neural structures that determine the general level of responsiveness, or readiness to respond, of the organism.

supernormal stimulus An artificially enlarged or exaggerated sign stimulus that elicits an unusually vigorous response.

CLASSICAL CONDITIONING: FOUNDATIONS

 hapter 3 provides an introduction to another basic form of learning, classical conditioning. Investigations of classical conditioning began with the work of Pavlov, who studied how dogs learn to anticipate feeding episodes. Since then, the research has been extended to a variety of other organisms and response systems. Some classical conditioning procedures establish an excitatory association between two stimuli. Others serve to inhibit the operation of excitatory associations. I describe both excitatory and inhibitory conditioning procedures and discuss how these are involved in a variety of important life experiences.

Chapter 2 described how environmental events can elicit behavior and how such elicited behavior can be modified by sensitization and habituation. These relatively simple processes help to bring the behavior of organisms in tune with their environment. However, if human and nonhuman animals only had the behavioral mechanisms described in Chapter 2, they would remain rather limited in the kinds of things they could do. For one thing, habituation and sensitization involve changes only in responses that are already in the organism's repertoire. They do not involve the learning of new responses or responses to new stimuli. And for the most part, habituation and sensitization involve learning about just one stimulus. Events in the world, however, do not occur in isolation, independent of one another. They occur in predictable and consistent combinations.

Cause-and-effect relationships ensure that certain things occur in combination with others. A car's engine does not run unless the ignition has been turned on; you cannot walk through a doorway unless the door is first opened; it does not rain unless there are clouds in the sky. Social institutions and customs also ensure that events occur in a predictable order. Classes are scheduled at predictable times; people are better dressed at church than at a picnic; you can predict whether someone will talk to you by the way the person looks at you. Learning to predict events in the environment and learning what stimuli tend to occur together are important for bringing behavior in line with the environment. Imagine how much trouble you would have if you could not predict how long it takes to make coffee, when stores are likely to be open, or whether your key works to unlock your apartment.

Classical conditioning is the simplest mechanism whereby organisms learn about relations between stimuli and come to alter their behavior accordingly. It enables human and nonhuman animals to take advantage of the orderly sequence of events in their environment and learn which stimuli tend to go with which events. On the basis of this learning, organisms come to make new responses to stimuli. For example, classical conditioning is the process whereby we learn to predict when and what we might eat, when we are likely to face danger, and when we are likely to be safe. It is also integrally involved in the learning of new emotional reactions such as fear and pleasure to stimuli that initially do not elicit these emotions.

THE EARLY YEARS OF CLASSICAL CONDITIONING

Systematic studies of classical conditioning began with the work of the great Russian physiologist Ivan P. Pavlov (see Box 3.1). Classical conditioning was also independently discovered by Edwin B. Twitmyer. In a Ph.D. dissertation submitted to the University of Pennsylvania in 1902 (see Twitmyer, 1974), Twitmyer repeatedly tested the knee-jerk reflex of college students by sounding a bell 0.5 seconds before hitting the patellar tendon just below the kneecap. After several of these trials, the bell was sufficient to elicit the knee-jerk reflex in some of the students. But Twitmyer did not develop the implications of his discoveries, and his findings did not attract much attention.

Pavlov's studies of classical conditioning were an extension of his research on the processes of digestion. He made major advances in the study of digestion by developing surgical techniques that enabled dogs to survive for many years with artificial tubes or fistulae that permitted the collection of various digestive juices. With the use of a stomach fistula, for example, Pavlov was able to collect stomach secretions in dogs that otherwise lived normally. Technicians in the laboratory soon discovered that the dogs would secrete stomach juices in response to the sight of food, or even just upon seeing the person who usually fed

Figure 3.1 Diagram of the Pavlovian salivary conditioning preparation. A cannula attached to the animal's salivary duct conducts drops of saliva to a data-recording device. (From "The Method of Pavlov in Animal Psychology," by R. M. Yerkes and S. Morgulis, 1909, *Psychological Bulletin, 6,* pp. 257–273.)

them. The laboratory produced considerable quantities of stomach juice in this manner and sold the excess to the general public. The popularity of this juice as a remedy for various stomach ailments supplemented the income of the laboratory for several years.

Assistants in the laboratory referred to stomach secretions elicited by food-related stimuli as "psychic secretions" because they seemed to be a response to the expectation or thought of food. For many years, however, the phenomenon of psychic secretions generated little scientific interest.

The Discoveries of Vul'fson and Snarskii

The first systematic studies of classical conditioning were performed by S. G. Vul'fson and A. T. Snarskii in Pavlov's laboratory (Boakes, 1984; Todes, 1997). Both students focused on the salivary glands, which are the first digestive glands involved in the breakdown of food. Some of the salivary glands are rather large and have ducts that are accessible and can be easily externalized with a fistula (see Figure 3.1). Vul'fson studied salivary responses to various substances placed in the mouth, such as dry food, wet food, sour water, and sand. After the dogs had experienced these substances placed in the mouth, the mere sight of the substances was enough to make them salivate.

Whereas Vul'fson used naturally occurring substances in his studies, Snarskii extended these observations to artificial substances. In one experiment, for example, Snarskii first gave his dogs sour water (such as strong lemon juice) that was artificially colored black. After several encounters with the black sour water, the dogs also salivated to plain black water or to the sight of a bottle containing a black liquid.

The substances tested by Vul'fson and Snarskii could be identified at a distance by sight. The substances also produced distinctive texture and taste sensations in the mouth. Such sensations are called *orosensory stimuli.* The first time that sand was placed in a dog's mouth, only the feel of the sand in the mouth elicited salivation. After sand had been placed in the mouth several times, the sight of sand (its visual features) also came to elicit salivation. Presumably, the dog learned to associate the visual features of the sand with its

BOX **3.1**

IVAN P. PAVLOV: BIOGRAPHICAL SKETCH

Bettmann Archive

Born in 1849 into the family of a priest in Russia, Pavlov dedicated his life to scholarship and discovery. He received his early education in a local theological seminary and planned a career of religious service. His interests soon changed, and when he was 21, he entered the university in St. Petersburg, where his studies focused on chemistry and animal physiology. After obtaining the equivalent of a bachelor's degree, he went to the Imperial Medico-Surgical Academy in 1875 to further his education in physiology. Eight years later, he received a doctoral degree for his research on the efferent nerves of the heart. He then began investigating various aspects of digestive physiology. In 1888, Pavlov discovered the nerves that stimulate the digestive secretions of the pancreas—a finding that initiated a series of experiments for which he was awarded the Nobel Prize in Physiology in 1904.

Pavlov did a great deal of original research while a graduate student, as well as after obtaining his doctoral degree. Interestingly, he did not have a faculty position or his own laboratory until 1890, when he was appointed professor of pharmacology at the St. Petersburg Military Medical Academy. In 1895 he became professor of physiology at the same institution. Pavlov remained active in the laboratory until close to his death in 1936. Much of the research for which he is famous today was performed after he received the Nobel Prize.

orosensory features. Such learning is referred to as **object learning** because it involves associating different features of the same object.

To study the mechanisms of associative learning, the stimuli to be associated have to be manipulated independently of one another. This is difficult to do when the two stimuli are properties of the same object. Therefore, in later studies of conditioning, Pavlov used procedures in which the stimuli to be associated came from different sources. This led to the experimental methods that continue to dominate studies of classical conditioning to the present day.

The Classical Conditioning Paradigm

Pavlov's basic procedure for the study of conditioned salivation is now familiar to college students. The procedure involves two stimuli: (1) a tone or a light that does not elicit salivation at the outset of the experiment, and (2) food or the taste of a sour solution placed in the mouth. In contrast to the first stimulus, the second one elicits vigorous salivation the first time it is presented.

Pavlov referred to the tone or light as the **conditional stimulus** because the effectiveness of this stimulus in eliciting salivation depended on (or was conditional on) pairing it several times with the presentation of food. By contrast, the food or sour-taste stimulus was called the **unconditional stimulus** because its effectiveness in eliciting salivation was not dependent on any prior training. The salivation that was eventually elicited by the tone or light was called the **conditional response,** and the salivation that was always elicited by the food or sour taste was called the **unconditional response.** In other words, stimuli and responses whose properties did not depend on prior training were called "unconditional," and stimuli and responses whose properties emerged only after training were called "conditional."

In the first English translation of Pavlov's writings, the term unconditio*nal* was erroneously translated as unconditio*ned*, and the term conditio*nal* was translated as conditio*ned*. The *-ed* suffix was used exclusively in English writings for many years. However, the term conditio*ned* does not capture Pavlov's original meaning of "dependent on" as well as the term conditio*nal* (Gantt, 1966). The words conditional and unconditional are more common in modern writings on classical conditioning and are now used interchangeably with conditioned and unconditioned.

Because the terms "conditioned (unconditioned) stimulus" and "conditioned (unconditioned) response" are used frequently in discussions of classical conditioning, they are often abbreviated. Conditioned stimulus and conditioned response are abbreviated **CS** and **CR,** respectively. Unconditioned stimulus and unconditioned response are abbreviated **US** and **UR,** respectively.

EXPERIMENTAL SITUATIONS

Classical conditioning has been investigated in a variety of situations and species (Hollis, 1997; Turkkan, 1989). Pavlov did most of his experiments with dogs using the salivary-fistula technique. Most contemporary experiments on Pavlovian conditioning are carried out with domesticated rats, rabbits, and pigeons using procedures developed by North American scientists during the second half of the twentieth century.

Fear Conditioning

Following the early work of Watson and Rayner (1920), a major focus of investigators of Pavlovian conditioning has been the conditioning of emotional reactions. Watson and Rayner believed that infants are at first limited in their emotional reactivity. Given this belief, they assumed that "there must be some simple method by means of which the range of stimuli which can call out these emotions and their compounds is greatly increased" (p. 1). That simple method was Pavlovian conditioning. In a famous demonstration, Watson and Rayner conditioned a fear response in a 9-month-old infant, Albert, to the presence of a docile white laboratory rat.

There was hardly anything that Albert was afraid of. After testing a variety of stimuli, Watson and Rayner found that little Albert reacted with alarm when he heard the loud noise of a steel bar being hit by a hammer behind his head. Watson and Rayner then used this unconditioned alarm response to condition fear to a white rat. Each conditioning trial consisted of presenting the rat to Albert and then striking the steel bar. At first, Albert reached out to the rat when it was presented to him. But after just two conditioning trials, he became reluctant to touch the rat. After five additional conditioning trials, Albert showed strong fear responses to the rat. He whimpered or cried, leaned as far away from the rat as he could, and sometimes fell over and moved away on all fours. Significantly, these fear responses were not evident when Albert was presented with his toy blocks. However, the conditioned fear generalized to other furry things (a rabbit, a fur coat, cotton wool, a dog, and a Santa Claus mask).

Fear and anxiety are the source of considerable human discomfort, and if sufficiently severe they can lead to serious psychological and behavioral problems. There is considerable interest in how fear and anxiety are acquired, what the neural mechanisms of fear are, and how fear may be attenuated with pharmacological and behavioral treatments. Many of these kinds of questions are difficult to address experimentally using human subjects. Therefore, since Watson and Rayner's study with little Albert, investigators have examined fear conditioning using primarily laboratory rats. The aversive unconditioned stimulus in these studies is a brief electrical current delivered to the feet through a metal grid floor. Shock is used because it can be regulated with greater precision than striking a steel bar with a hammer. The shock US is of such low intensity and brief duration that no tissue damage occurs. The shock is aversive primarily because it is startling—unlike anything the animal has encountered before. The conditioned stimulus may be a tone or a light. Thus, the basic procedure involves presenting a tone or a light shortly before the presentation of a brief shock US. Unlike little Albert who showed fear by whimpering and crying, rats show their fear by freezing. Freezing is a species-typical defense response that occurs in a variety of animals in response to the anticipation of aversive stimulation (see Chapter 10).

Although the primary fear response of rats is to become motionless, investigators of fear conditioning often do not measure freezing directly. Instead, they measure conditioned fear indirectly by recording how the conditioned stimulus disrupts the animal's ongoing activity. A popular technique for the indirect measurement of conditioned fear is the **conditioned emotional response,** or **conditioned suppression,** procedure (abbreviated **CER**). The CER procedure was devised by Estes and Skinner (1941) and has since been used extensively in the study of Pavlovian conditioning (Kamin, 1965). Rats are first trained to press a response lever for food reward in a small experimental chamber (see Figure 3.2A). Food is provided for every few lever presses. After sufficient training, the rats press the lever at a steady rate. The classical conditioning phase of the experiment is then introduced. During each conditioning trial, the CS is presented for 1 or 2 minutes, followed immediately by brief exposure to the shock US. Trials are scheduled 15–30 minutes apart.

Rats cannot press the lever when they freeze because of fear. This makes the CER procedure useful for measuring response suppression induced by fear (Bouton & Bolles, 1980; Mast, Blanchard, & Blanchard, 1982; for additional factors involved in conditioned suppression, see Bevins & Ayres, 1994). The acquisition of fear to the CS results in disruption of the food-rewarded lever-press response. After several pairings of the CS with shock, the animals suppress their lever pressing when the CS appears. Within three to five conditioning trials, the conditioned suppression may be complete (Kamin & Brimer, 1963), with the rats not pressing the lever at all during the CS. However, the suppression is specific to the CS. Soon after the CS is turned off, the animals resume their food-rewarded behavior.

To measure the conditioned suppression quantitatively, a suppression ratio is calculated. The ratio compares the number of lever presses that occur during the CS with the number that occur during a comparable baseline period before the CS is presented (the pre-CS period). The specific formula is as follows:

$$\text{Suppression Ratio} = \text{CS responding} \div (\text{CS responding} + \text{pre-CS responding})$$

Notice that the *suppression ratio* has a value of 0 if the rat suppresses lever pressing completely during the CS, because in this case the numerator of the formula is 0. At the other extreme, if the rat does not alter its rate of lever pressing at all when the CS is presented, the ratio has a value of .5. For example, assume that the CS is presented for 2 minutes and that in a typical 2-minute period the rat makes 30 responses. If the CS does not disrupt lever pressing, the animal will make 30 responses during the CS, so that the numerator of the ratio will be 30. The denominator will be 30 (CS responses) + 30 (pre-CS responses), or 60. Therefore, the ratio will be 30 ÷ 60 or 0.5. Decreasing values of the ratio from 0.5 to 0 indicate greater degrees of response suppression, or conditioned fear. Thus, the scale is in-

Figure 3.2 (A) Representation of a rat in a Skinner box. The floor is made of metal rods. The response lever is located in the center of the wall above the food cup. (From *Sniffy, The Virtual Rat,* Wadsworth/ Thomson Learning.) (B) Sample results of a conditioned suppression experiment with rats (from Domjan, unpublished). Three conditioning trials were conducted on each of 3 days of training. The CS was an audiovisual stimulus and the US was a brief shock through the grid floor. A suppression ratio of .5 indicates that the participants did not suppress their lever pressing during the CS. A suppression ratio of 0 indicates complete suppression of responding during the CS.

verse. Greater disruptions of lever pressing are represented by lower values of the suppression ratio.

Figure 3.2B shows sample results of a conditioned suppression experiment with rats. Three conditioning trials were conducted on each of 3 days of training. Very little suppression occurred the first time the CS was presented, and not much acquisition of suppression was evident during the first day of training. A substantial increase in suppression occurred from the last trial on Day 1 (Trial 3) to the first trial on Day 2 (Trial 4). With continued training, responding gradually became more and more suppressed, until the animals hardly ever pressed the response lever when the CS was presented.

Interpreting conditioned suppression data can be confusing because the scale is inverse. Keep in mind that a suppression ratio of 0 indicates zero responding during the CS, which represents the greatest possible suppression of lever pressing. The smaller the suppression ratio, the more motionless is the animal, because the CS elicits more conditioned fear.

In the conditioned suppression procedure, the baseline level of responding is provided by lever pressing for food reinforcement. In a related procedure, thirsty rats are permitted to lick a waterspout. The presentation of a conditioned fear stimulus causes a suppression in this licking behavior. Hence, this is called the **conditioned lick suppression** procedure. Some investigators favor the lick suppression procedure because getting rats to lick a waterspout requires less training than getting them to press a response lever for food. In the lick suppression procedure, how long it takes subjects to complete a total of 5 seconds of drinking is recorded as a measure of response suppression. The more fearful the rats are, the longer they will take to accumulate the criterion 5 seconds of drinking (for example, Figures 3.12 and 3.13). (For an adaptation of the conditioned suppression in the form of a video game for testing human subjects, see Arcediano, Ortega, & Matute, 1996.)

Eyeblink Conditioning

The eyeblink reflex is a discrete reflex, much like the patellar knee-jerk response. It is an early component of the startle response and occurs in a variety of species. To get someone to blink, all you have to do is clap your hands near their eyes or blow a puff of air through a straw directed toward their eyes. If the air puff is preceded by a brief tone, the person is likely to learn to blink when the tone comes on, in anticipation of the puff.

Eyeblink conditioning was extensively investigated in studies with human participants early in the development of learning theory (see Hilgard & Marquis, 1940; Kimble, 1961) and is the topic of renewed interest in contemporary research (for example, Clark & Squire, 1999; Durkin, Prescott, Furchtgott, & Cantor,1993; Green, Ivry, & Woodruff-Pak, 1999; Tracy, Ghose, Stecher, McFall, & Steinmetz, 1999) because of advances in our understanding of the neurobiological substrates of this type of learning (see Box 3.2). Steinmetz (1999), for example, noted, "Eyeblink conditioning provides an excellent means for direct observation of simple behavior . . . [and] can be used to assess basic biological-psychological processes in humans, such as basic learning and memory, development, awareness, attention, arousal, and normal aging" (p. 24).

In a recent study of eyeblink conditioning, 2 groups of 5-month-old infants were compared (Ivkovich, Collins, Eckerman, Krasnegor, & Stanton, 1999). The CS was a 1,000 cps tone presented for 750 milliseconds, and the US was a gentle puff of air delivered to the right eye through a plastic tube. Each infant sat on a parent's lap facing a platform with brightly colored objects that maintained the infant's attention during the experimental sessions. Eyeblinks were recorded by video cameras. For Group 1, the CS always ended with the puff of air, and these conditioning trials occurred an average of 12 seconds apart. Group 2 received the same number and distribution of CS and US presentations, but for them the CSs and USs were spaced 4–8 seconds apart in an explicitly unpaired fashion. Thus, Group 2 served as a control. Each subject received 2 training sessions, 1 week apart.

The results of the experiment are presented in Figure 3.3 in terms of the percentage of trials on which the subjects blinked during the CS. The rate of eyeblinks for the 2 groups of subjects did not differ statistically during the first experimental session. However, the paired group responded to the CS at a significantly higher rate during Session 2 than the unpaired control group. Furthermore, additional research indicated that the high level of performance in the paired group during Session 2 was due in part to the CS-US association they started to learn during Session 1.

This experiment illustrates a number of important points about learning. First, it shows that classical conditioning requires the pairing of a CS and a US. Responding to the

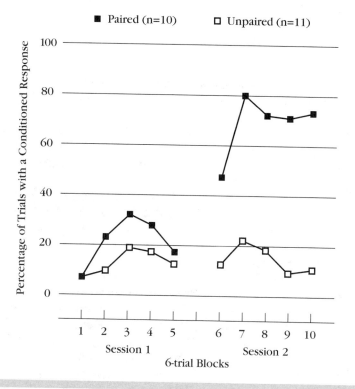

Paired (n=10)   □ Unpaired (n=11)

Figure 3.3 Eyeblink conditioning in 5-month-old infants. For the infants in the paired group, a tone CS ended in a gentle puff of air to the eye. For the infants in the unpaired group, the tone and air puff never occurred together. (After Ivkovich, Collins, Eckerman, Krasnegor, & Stanton, 1999.)

CS did not develop in the unpaired control group. Second, initial learning may not be directly observable. Although the infants in the paired group did not respond much in Session 1, they were starting to learn that the CS was related to the US. This learning was evident when the subjects were returned to the experimental situation for Session 2.

As I noted earlier, recent interest in eyeblink conditioning in humans stems from the fact that substantial progress has been made in understanding the neurobiological substrates of this type of learning. Neurobiological investigations of eyeblink conditioning have been conducted primarily in studies with domesticated rabbits. The rabbit eyeblink preparation was developed by Gormezano (see Gormezano, 1966; Gormezano, Kehoe, & Marshall, 1983). Domesticated rabbits are ideal for this type of research because they are readily available, they are sedentary and tolerate mild restraint well, and they rarely blink in the absence of an air puff or other irritation of the eye. In an eyeblink conditioning experiment, the rabbit is placed in a small enclosure and attached to equipment that enables measurement of the blink response. The unconditioned stimulus to elicit blinking is provided by a small puff of air or mild irritation of the skin below the eye with a brief (0.1-second) electrical current. The conditioned stimulus may be a light, a tone, or a mild vibration of the animal's abdomen.

In the typical conditioning experiment, the CS is presented for half a second and is followed immediately by delivery of the unconditioned stimulus. The US elicits a rapid and vigorous eyelid closure. As the CS is repeatedly paired with the US, the eyeblink response also comes to be made to the CS. Investigators record the percentage of trials in which a conditioned blink response is observed. Rabbit eyeblink conditioning is relatively slow, requiring several hundred trials for substantial levels of conditioned responding.

Courtesy of I. Gormezano

I. Gormezano

BOX **3.2**

EYEBLINK CONDITIONING AND THE SEARCH FOR THE ENGRAM

When an organism learns something, the results of this learning must be stored within the brain. Somehow, the network of neurons that makes up the central nervous system is able to encode the relationship between biologically significant events and use this information to guide the selection of ongoing behavior. This biological memory is known as an *engram*. The traditional view is that the engram for a discrete conditioned response is stored in localized regions of the brain. This raises a basic question in neurobiology: Where is the engram located?

This question has been pursued for nearly four decades by Richard Thompson and his collaborators (for recent reviews, see Steinmetz, Gluck, & Solomon, 2001). Thompson recognized that locating the engram would require a well-defined behavioral system in which both the conditions for learning and the motor output were precisely specified. These considerations led him to study the mechanisms that underlie eyeblink conditioning. In the eyeblink conditioning situation, a CS (for example, a tone) is repeatedly paired with an air puff to the eye (the US) and acquires the ability to elicit a defensive eyeblink response. To pursue his neurobiological investigations, Thompson studied eyeblink conditioning in rabbits.

The search for the engram began with the hippocampus. Studies of humans with damage to this region revealed that the ability to consciously remember a recent event requires that the hippocampus remain intact. In animal subjects, small electrodes were lowered into the hippocampus and neural activity was recorded during eyeblink conditioning. These studies revealed that cells in this region reflect the learning of a CS-US association. To the surprise of many investigators, however, removing the hippocampus did not eliminate the animal's ability to acquire and retain a conditioned eyeblink response. In fact, removing all of the brain structures above the midbrain (see Figure 3.4) had little effect on eyeblink conditioning with a delayed conditioning procedure. This suggests that the essential circuitry for eyeblink conditioning lies within the lower neural structures of the brainstem and cerebellum. Subsequent experiments clearly showed that the acquisition of a well-timed conditioned eyeblink response depends on a neural circuit that lies within the cerebellum (Steinmetz et al., 2001).

The unconditioned response elicited by an airpuff to the eye is mediated by neurons that project to a region of the brainstem known as the trigeminal nucleus (see Figure 3.4B). From there, neurons travel along two routes, either directly or through the reticular formation, to the cranial motor nucleus where the behavioral output is organized. Three basic techniques were used to define this pathway. The first involved electrophysiological recordings to verify that neurons in this neural circuit are engaged in response to the US. The second technique involved inactivating the neural circuit, either permanently (by killing the cells) or temporarily (by means of a drug or cooling), to show that the circuit plays an essential role in the unconditioned response. If the circuit is necessary, disrupting its function should eliminate the behavioral output. Finally, the circuit was artificially stimulated to show that activity in this circuit is sufficient to produce the behavioral response.

The same techniques (electrical recording, inactivation, and stimulation) have been used to define the neural pathway that mediates the acquisition and performance of the conditioned response. As illustrated in Figure 3.4B, the CS input travels to a region of the brainstem known as the pontine nucleus. From there, it is carried by mossy fibers that convey the signal to the cerebellum. The US signal is carried into the cerebellum through the climbing fibers. These two signals meet in the cerebellar cortex where coincident activity brings about a synaptic modification that alters the neural output from the cerebellum. In essence, the climbing fibers act as teachers, selecting a subset of connections to be modified. This change defines the stimulus properties (the characteristics of the CS) that engage a discrete motor output. This output is mediated by neurons that project from the interpositus nucleus to the red nucleus, and finally, to the cranial motor nucleus.

As a conditioned response is acquired, conditioned activity develops within the interpositus nucleus. Neurons from the interpositus nucleus project back to the US pathway and inhibit the US signal within the inferior olive.

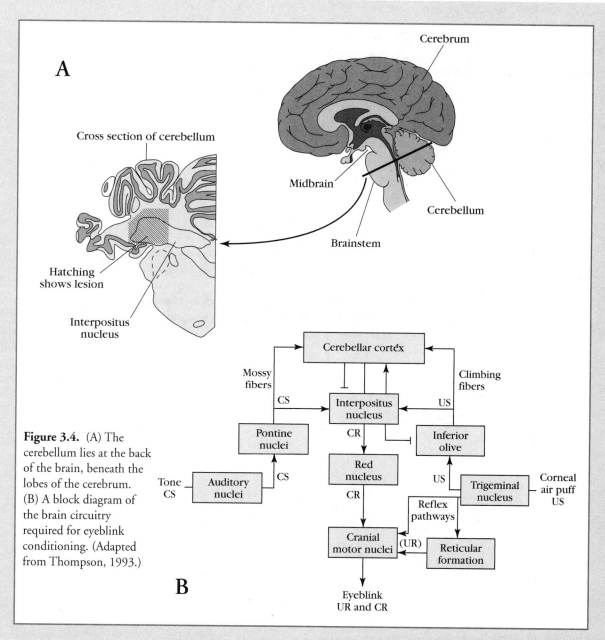

Figure 3.4. (A) The cerebellum lies at the back of the brain, beneath the lobes of the cerebrum. (B) A block diagram of the brain circuitry required for eyeblink conditioning. (Adapted from Thompson, 1993.)

This provides a form of negative feedback that decreases the effectiveness of the US. Many researchers believe that phenomena such as blocking and overshadowing occur because a predicted CS is less effective (see Chapter 4). Within an eyeblink paradigm, this might occur because the US input is inhibited within the inferior olive. Supporting this, Kim et al. (1998) showed that eliminating this source of inhibition eliminated the blocking effect.

(continued)

Box 3.2 (continued)

Earlier I noted that the hippocampus is not needed for simple delayed conditioning. It is, however, required for more complex forms of learning. An example is provided by trace conditioning, where a temporal delay is inserted between the end of the CS and the start of the US. A normal animal can readily acquire a conditioned eyeblink to a CS that ends 0.5 seconds before the US. However, it cannot span this gap if the hippocampus is removed. A similar pattern of results is observed in amnesic patients who have damage to the hippocampus (Clark & Squire, 1998). These patients cannot consciously remember the CS-US

relation. In the absence of this explicit memory, they fail to learn with a trace conditioning procedure. Learning in the delayed procedure is not affected, even though the patient cannot consciously remember the CS-US relation from one session to the next. Interestingly, disrupting conscious awareness in a normal subject undermines the appreciation of the CS-US relation with the trace procedure. Again, subjects who cannot explicitly report the relation, fail to learn.

—J. W. Grau

Sign Tracking

Pavlov's research concentrated on salivation and other highly reflexive responses and encouraged the belief that classical conditioning occurs only in reflex response systems. In recent years, however, such a restrictive view of Pavlovian conditioning has been abandoned (e.g., Hollis, 1997). One experimental paradigm that has contributed significantly to modern conceptions of Pavlovian conditioning is the **sign tracking** or **autoshaping** paradigm (Hearst, 1975; Hearst & Jenkins, 1974; Locurto, Terrace, & Gibbon, 1981).

Animals tend to approach and contact stimuli that signal the availability of food. In the natural environment, the availability of food can be predicted by some aspect of the food itself that is apparent at a distance (such as the visual appearance of the food). For a hawk, for example, the sight and movements of a mouse are cues indicating the possibility of a meal. By approaching and contacting these distant food cues, the hawk can end up with a meal.

Sign tracking is investigated in the laboratory by presenting a discrete, localized visual stimulus just before each delivery of a small amount of food. The first experiment of this sort was performed by Brown and Jenkins (1968) with pigeons. The animals were placed in an experimental chamber that had a small circular key that could be illuminated and that the pigeons could peck. Periodically, the birds were given access to food for a few seconds. The key light was illuminated for 8 seconds immediately before each food delivery.

The pigeons did not have to do anything for the food to be presented. The food was automatically delivered after each illumination of the response key no matter what the birds did. Since the birds were hungry, one might predict that when they saw the key light, they would go to the food dish and wait for the forthcoming food presentation. Interestingly, however, that is not what happened. Instead of using the key light to tell them when they should go to the food dish, the pigeons started pecking the key itself. This behavior was remarkable because it was not required to gain access to the food.

Since its discovery, many experiments have been done on sign tracking in a variety of species, including chicks, quail, goldfish, lizards, rats, rhesus monkeys, squirrel monkeys, and human adults and children (see Tomie, Brooks, & Zito, 1989.) These experiments have shown that sign tracking is a useful technique for the investigation of associative learning. In pigeon sign-tracking experiments, the *conditioned stimulus* is illumination of the response key and the *unconditioned stimulus* is presentation of food. Learning proceeds most rapidly

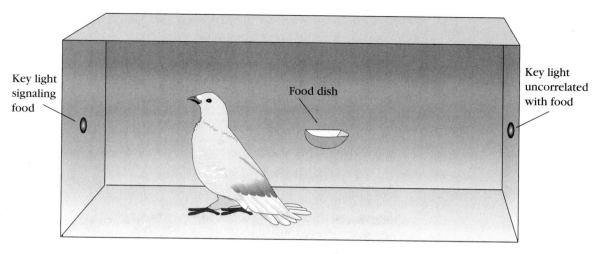

Key light signaling food

Food dish

Key light uncorrelated with food

Figure 3.5 The "long box" used in the sign-tracking experiment with pigeons by Jenkins. The conditioned stimulus was illumination of the key light at one end of the experimental chamber. Food was delivered in the middle of the chamber. (Based on Jenkins, personal communication, 1980.)

when the CS is presented just before the US. Pigeons do not approach and peck the CS if the CS and US are presented at random times in relation to each other (Gamzu & Williams, 1971, 1973).

The tracking of signals for food is dramatically illustrated by instances in which the signal is located far away from the food cup. In one such experiment (see Hearst & Jenkins, 1974), pigeons were placed in a 6-foot (182 cm) alley that had a food dish in the middle (see Figure 3.5). Each end of the alley had a circular disk or response key. Presentation of food was always preceded by illumination of the key at one end of the alley. The key light at the opposite end was uncorrelated with food. One other aspect of the experiment is important to point out: the food was available for only 4 seconds each time. Therefore, if the bird did not reach the food cup within 4 seconds, it did not get any food on that trial.

As conditioning progressed, the pigeons started behaving in a most remarkable manner. As soon as the key light came on, they ran to that end of the alley, pecked the key, and then ran to the center of the alley to get the food. Because the alley was very long, the pigeons did not always get to the food dish before the brief food presentation ended. The sign-tracking behavior was amazing because it was entirely unnecessary. The birds did not have to peck the key light to get the food US. They could have just stayed in the middle of the alley and waited by the food dish. The fact that they approached the key light is evidence of the compelling attraction of classically conditioned signals for food. The pigeons did not consistently approach the light at the other end of the chamber, which was uncorrelated with food presentations. (For similar experiments with domesticated quail, see Burns & Domjan, 2000.)

Sign tracking is possible only in situations where the conditioned stimulus is localized and therefore can be approached and "tracked." In one study, diffuse spatial and contextual cues of the chamber in which pigeons were given food periodically served as the conditioned stimulus. This time the learning of an association was evident in an increase in activity, rather than in a specific approach response (Rescorla, Durlach, & Grau, 1985). In another experiment (conducted with laboratory rats), a localized light and a sound were compared as conditioned stimuli for food (Cleland & Davey, 1983). Only the light stimulated conditioned approach or sign-tracking behavior. The auditory CS elicited approach to the food cup rather than approach to the sound source. These experiments illustrate that for sign tracking to occur, the conditioned stimulus has to be of the proper modality and configuration. Another important factor is how much time the subjects spend in the experimental

71

context relative to the duration of each CS presentation. Greater levels of sign tracking occur with longer exposures to the experimental context relative to the duration of the CS (Burns & Domjan, 2001). I say more about this variable in Chapter 4.

Taste-Aversion Learning

The normal course of eating provides numerous opportunities for the learning of associations. Rozin and Zellner (1985) concluded a review of the role of Pavlovian conditioning in the foods people will like or dislike with the note that "Pavlovian conditioning is alive and well, in the flavor-flavor associations of the billions of meals eaten each day, . . . in the associations of foods and offensive objects, and in the associations of foods with some of their consequences" (p. 199).

Taste aversions can be learned if ingestion of a novel flavor is followed by illness or other aversive consequences. In contrast, a taste preference may be learned if a flavor is paired with nutritional repletion or other positive consequences (for example, Capaldi, Hunter, & Lyn, 1997; Ramirez, 1997). Taste-aversion and taste-preference learning as examples of Pavlovian conditioning have been investigated extensively in various animal species (see Riley & Tuck, 1985; Pérez, Fanizza, & Sclafani, 1999; Sclafani, 1997). A growing body of evidence indicates that many human taste aversions are also the result of Pavlovian conditioning. Much of this evidence has been provided by questionnaire studies (Batsell & Brown, 1998; Garb & Stunkard, 1974; Logue, Ophir, & Strauss, 1981; Logue, 1985, 1988a). People report having acquired at least one food aversion during their lives. The typical aversion learning experience involves eating a distinctively flavored food and then getting sick. Such a flavor–illness pairing can produce a conditioned food aversion in just one trial, and the learning can occur even if the illness is delayed several hours after ingestion of the food. Another interesting finding is that in about 20% of the cases, the individuals were certain that their illness was not caused by the food they ate. Nevertheless, they learned an aversion to the food. This indicates that food aversion learning can be independent of rational thought processes and can go against a person's conclusions about the causes of the illness.

Questionnaire studies offer provocative data, but systematic experimental research is required to isolate the mechanism of learning. Experimental studies of taste aversion learning have been conducted with people in situations where they encounter illness during the course of medical treatment. Chemotherapy for cancer is one such situation. Chemotherapy often causes nausea as a side effect. Both child and adult cancer patients have been shown to acquire aversions to foods eaten before a chemotherapy session (Bernstein, 1978, 1991; Bernstein & Webster, 1980; Carrell, Cannon, Best, & Stone, 1986). Such conditioned aversions may contribute to the lack of appetite commonly found among chemotherapy patients. (For laboratory studies on the role of nausea in the conditioning of taste aversions, see Limebeer & Parker, 1999, 2000.)

Conditioned food aversions also may contribute to the suppression of food intake or anorexia observed in other clinical situations (see Bernstein & Borson, 1986, for a review.) The anorexia that accompanies the growth of some tumors may result from food aversion learning. Animal research indicates that the growth of tumors can result in the conditioning of aversions to food ingested during the disease. Food aversion learning may also contribute to anorexia nervosa, a disorder characterized by severe and chronic weight loss. Suggestive evidence indicates that people suffering from anorexia nervosa experience digestive disorders that may increase their likelihood of learning food aversions. Increased susceptibility to food aversion learning may also contribute to loss of appetite evident in people suffering from severe depression.

Many of our ideas about food aversion learning in people have their roots in research with laboratory animals. In the typical procedure, the subjects receive a distinctively flavored food or drink and are then made to feel sick by the injection of a drug or exposure to radiation. As a result of the taste-illness pairing, the animals acquire an aversion to the taste. Their ingestion of the taste solution is suppressed by the conditioning procedure (see Barker, Best, & Domjan, 1977; Braveman & Bronstein, 1985).

Taste aversion learning is a result of the pairing of a CS (in this case, a taste) and a US (drug injection or radiation exposure) in much the same manner as in other examples of classical conditioning and follows standard rules of learning in many respects (for example, Domjan, 1980, 1983). It also has some special features. First, laboratory studies have clearly demonstrated that strong taste aversions can be learned with just one pairing of the flavor and illness. Although one-trial learning also occurs in fear conditioning, such rapid learning is rarely, if ever, observed in eyeblink conditioning, salivary conditioning, or sign tracking.

The second unique feature of taste aversion learning is that it occurs even if the animals do not get sick until several hours after exposure to the novel taste (Garcia, Ervin, & Koelling, 1966; Revusky & Garcia, 1970). Dangerous substances in food often do not have their poisonous effects until the food has been digested, absorbed into the bloodstream, and distributed to various body tissues. This process takes time. *Long-delay learning* of taste aversions probably evolved to enable human and nonhuman animals to avoid poisonous foods that have delayed ill effects.

A dramatic example of long-delay taste aversion learning was provided by an experiment by Smith and Roll (1967). Laboratory rats were first adapted to a water deprivation schedule so that they would readily drink when a water bottle was placed on their cage. On the conditioning day, the rats were given a novel 0.1% saccharin solution to drink for 20 minutes. At various times after the saccharin presentation, ranging from 0 to 24 hours, different groups of rats were exposed to radiation from an X-ray machine. Control groups of rats were also taken to the X-ray machine but were not irradiated. They were called the sham irradiated groups. Starting a day after the radiation or sham treatment, each rat was given a choice of saccharin solution or plain water to drink for 2 days.

The preference of each group of animals for the saccharin solution is shown in Figure 3.6. Animals exposed to radiation within 6 hours after tasting the saccharin solution showed a profound aversion to the saccharin flavor in the postconditioning test. They drank less

J. Garcia

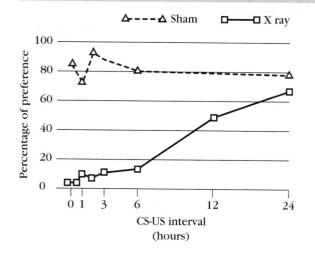

△ - - - - △ Sham   ▫——▫ X ray

Figure 3.6 Mean percent preference for the CS flavor during a test session conducted after the CS flavor was paired with X irradiation (the US) or sham exposure. Percent preference is the percentage of a participant's total fluid intake (saccharin solution plus water) that consisted of the saccharin solution. During conditioning, the interval between exposure to the CS and the US ranged from 0 to 24 hours for different groups of rats. (From "Trace Conditioning with X-rays as an Aversive Stimulus," by J. C. Smith and D. L. Roll, *Psychonomic Science,* 1967, *9,* pp. 11–12. Copyright © 1967 by Psychonomic Society. Reprinted by permission.)

than 20% of their total fluid intake from the saccharin drinking tube. Much less aversion was evident in animals irradiated 12 hours after the saccharin exposure, and hardly any aversion was observed in rats irradiated 24 hours after the taste exposure. In contrast to this gradient of saccharin avoidance observed in the irradiated rats, all the sham irradiated groups strongly preferred the saccharin solution. They drank more than 70% of their total fluid intake from the saccharin drinking tube.

EXCITATORY PAVLOVIAN CONDITIONING PROCEDURES

What I have been discussing so far are instances of excitatory Pavlovian conditioning. In excitatory conditioning, organisms learn an association between the conditioned and the unconditioned stimuli. As a result of this association, presentation of the CS activates behavioral and neural activity related to the US—in the absence of the actual presentation of the unconditioned stimulus. These US-related processes are responsible for the conditioned responses that are observed. Thus, dogs come to salivate in response to the sight of sand or black water, pigeons learn to approach and peck a key light that is followed by food, rats learn to freeze to a sound that precedes foot shock, rabbits learn to blink in response to a tone that precedes a puff of air, and rats learn to avoid drinking saccharin that is followed by illness. In all these cases, the conditioned stimulus comes to activate behavior related to the associated US.

Common Pavlovian Conditioning Procedures

One of the critical factors that determines the course of classical conditioning is the relative timing of the conditioned stimulus and the unconditioned stimulus. In most conditioning situations, seemingly small and trivial variations in how a CS is paired with a US can have profound effects on how vigorous the conditioned response becomes.

Five common classical conditioning procedures are illustrated in Figure 3.7. The horizontal distance in each diagram represents the passage of time; vertical displacements represent when a stimulus begins and ends. Each configuration of CS and US represents a single conditioning trial.

In a typical classical conditioning experiment, CS-US episodes are repeated a number of times during a *training session*. The time from the end of one conditioning trial to the start of the next trial is called the **intertrial interval.** By contrast, the time from the start of the CS to the start of the US within a conditioning trial is called the **interstimulus interval or CS-US interval.** For conditioned responding to develop, the interstimulus interval has to be much shorter than the intertrial interval. In many experiments the interstimulus interval is less than 1 minute, whereas the intertrial interval may be 5 minutes or more. (A more detailed discussion of these parameters is provided in Chapter 4.)

1. *Short-delayed conditioning.* The most frequently used procedure for Pavlovian conditioning involves delaying the start of the US slightly after the start of the CS on each trial. This procedure is called **short-delayed conditioning.** The critical feature of short-delayed conditioning is that the CS starts each trial and the US is presented after a brief (less than 1 minute) delay. The CS may continue during the US or end when the US begins.

2. *Trace conditioning.* The **trace conditioning** procedure is similar to the short-delayed procedure in that the CS is presented first and is followed by the US. In trace conditioning,

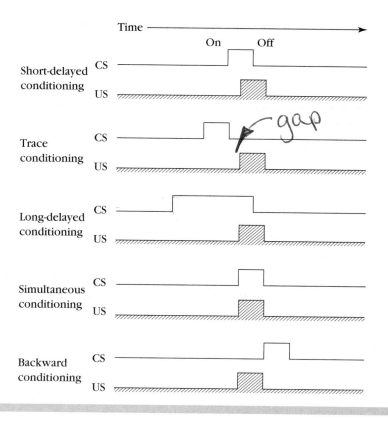

Figure 3.7 Five common classical conditioning procedures.

however, the US is not presented until some time after the CS has ended. This leaves a gap between the CS and the US. The gap is called the **trace interval.**

3. *Long-delayed conditioning.* The long-delayed conditioning procedure is also similar to the short-delayed conditioning in that the CS starts before the US. In this case, however, the US is delayed much longer (5–10 minutes) than in the short-delay procedure. Most important, the long-delayed procedure does not include a trace interval. The CS lasts until the US begins.

4. *Simultaneous conditioning.* Perhaps the most obvious way to expose subjects to a CS in conjunction with a US is to present the two stimuli at the same time. This procedure is called **simultaneous conditioning** because the conditioned and unconditioned stimuli are presented concurrently.

5. *Backward conditioning.* The last procedure depicted in Figure 3.7 differs from the others in that the US occurs shortly *before,* rather than after, the CS. This technique is called **backward conditioning** because the CS and US are presented in a "backward" order compared to the other procedures.

Measurement of Conditioned Responses

Pavlov and others after him have conducted systematic investigations of procedures like those depicted in Figure 3.7 to find out how the conditioning of a CS depends on the temporal relation between CS and US presentations. To make comparisons among the various procedures, the investigator must use a method for measuring conditioning that is equally applicable to all the procedures. This is typically done with the use of a **test trial.** A test trial

75

consists of presenting the conditioned stimulus by itself (without the US). Responses elicited by the CS can then be observed without contamination from responses elicited by the US. Such CS-alone test trials can be introduced periodically during the course of training to track the progress of learning.

Behavior during the CS can be quantified in several ways. One aspect of conditioned behavior is how much of it occurs. This is called the **magnitude** of the conditioned response. Pavlov, for example, measured the number of drops of saliva that were elicited by a CS. Other examples of the magnitude of conditioned responses are the amount of response suppression that occurs in the CER procedure (see Figure 3.2) and the degree of depressed flavor preference that is observed in taste aversion learning (see Figure 3.6).

The vigor of responding can also be measured by how often the CS elicits a conditioned response. For example, the percentage of trials on which a conditioned response is elicited by the CS can be measured. This measure is frequently used in studies of eyeblink conditioning (see Figure 3.3) and reflects the likelihood or **probability** of responding.

A third aspect of conditioned responding is how soon the conditioned response occurs after presentation of the CS. This measure of the vigor of conditioned behavior is called the **latency** of the conditioned response. Latency is the amount of time that elapses between the start of the CS and the occurrence of the conditioned response.

In the delayed and trace conditioning procedures, the CS occurs by itself at the start of each trial (see Figure 3.7). Any conditioned behavior that occurs during this initial CS-alone period is uncontaminated by behavior elicited by the US and therefore can be used as a measure of learning. In contrast, responding during the CS in simultaneous and backward conditioning trials is bound to reflect the presence of the US or its recent presentation. Therefore, test trials are critical for assessing learning in simultaneous and backward conditioning.

Control Procedures for Classical Conditioning

Devising an effective test trial is not enough to obtain conclusive evidence of classical conditioning. As I noted in Chapter 1, learning is an inference about the causes of behavior based on a comparison of at least two conditions. To be certain that a conditioning procedure is responsible for certain changes in behavior, those changes must be compared to the effects of a control procedure. What should the control procedure be? In studies of habituation and sensitization, only the effects of prior exposure to a stimulus were of interest. Therefore, the comparison or control procedure was rather simple: it consisted of no prior stimulus exposure. In studies of classical conditioning, our interest is in how conditioned and unconditioned stimuli become associated. Because this is a more complicated issue, it requires more complicated control procedures.

An association between a CS and a US implies that the two events have become connected in some way. After an association has been established, the CS is able to activate processes related to the US. An association requires more than just familiarity with the CS and US. It presumably depends on having the two stimuli experienced in connection with each other. Therefore, to conclude that an association has been established, one has to make sure that the observed change in behavior could not have been produced by prior separate presentations of the CS or the US.

As described in Chapter 2, increased responding could occur as a result of sensitization, which is not an associative process. Presentations of an arousing stimulus, such as food to a hungry animal, can increase the behavior elicited by a more innocuous stimulus, such as a tone, without an association having been established between the two stimuli. (Recall, for example, the phenomenon of dishabituation, discussed under "Characteristics of Habituation and Sensitization" in Chapter 2.) Therefore, increases in responding observed with repeated CS-US pairings can sometimes result from exposure to just the US. Instances in which exposure to just the US produces responses like the conditioned response are called **pseudoconditioning.** Control procedures are required to determine whether responses that develop to the CS represent an association between the CS and US rather than sensitization effects of exposure to the conditioned and unconditioned stimuli.

[handwritten margin note: what would be a good example of pseudo-conditioning]

Investigators have debated at length about the proper controls for classical conditioning. Ideally, a control procedure for the learning of an association would involve the same number and distribution of CS and US presentations as the experimental procedure, but with the CSs and USs arranged so that they would not become associated. One possibility is to present the CS and US at random during the course of an experimental session (Rescorla, 1967b). This is called the **random control** procedure. Unfortunately, evidence from a variety of sources indicates that the random control procedure can produce associative learning (see Papini & Bitterman, 1990; Rescorla, 2000)

A more successful control procedure involves presenting the conditioned and unconditioned stimuli on separate trials. Such a procedure is called the **explicitly unpaired control.** In the explicitly unpaired control, the CS and US are presented far enough apart to prevent their association. How much time has to elapse between them depends on the response system. In taste-aversion learning, much longer separation is necessary between the CS and US than in other forms of conditioning. In one variation of the explicitly unpaired control, only CSs are presented during one session and only USs are presented during a second session. (For a further discussion of control methodology, see Gormezano et al., 1983.)

Effectiveness of Common Conditioning Procedures

There has been considerable interest in determining which of the procedures depicted in Figure 3.7 produces the strongest evidence of learning. Traditionally, investigators followed Pavlov's lead in focusing on a single direct measure of learning. Learning laboratories were set up to conduct experiments using just one of the common conditioning preparations (fear conditioning, eyeblink conditioning, sign tracking, or taste aversion learning), and equipment was specially adapted to record only the particular response of interest for that laboratory. Fear conditioning laboratories, for example, measured only conditioned suppression or freezing; and eyeblink laboratories measured only the conditioned blink responses. After settling on a specific measure of learning, the investigator was ready to examine learning in delayed, simultaneous, trace, and backward conditioning procedures. The assumption was that Pavlovian conditioning would produce a CS-US association whose strength would be directly reflected in the vigor of the conditioned response.

The outcome of many early studies of the five conditioning procedures depicted in Figure 3.7 can be summarized by focusing on the interval between the start of the CS and the start of the US—the *interstimulus interval* or *CS-US interval.* In general, little conditioned responding was observed in simultaneous conditioning procedures, where the CS-US interval is zero (for example, Bitterman, 1964; Smith, Coleman, & Gormezano, 1969). Delaying the presentation of the US slightly after the CS often facilitated conditioned responding. However, this facilitation was fairly limited (Ost & Lauer, 1965; Schneiderman & Gormezano, 1964). If the CS-US interval was increased further, conditioned responding declined, as illustrated in Figure 3.8. Even in the taste-aversion conditioning procedure, where learning is possible with CS-US intervals of 1 or 2 hours, conditioned responding declines as the CS-US interval is increased (see Figure 3.6).

Trace conditioning procedures are interesting because they can have the same CS-US interval as delayed conditioning procedures. However, in trace procedures the CS is turned

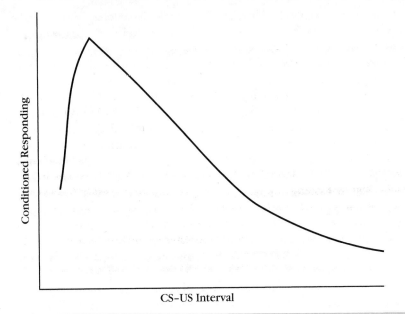

Figure 3.8 Traditional effects of the CS-US interval on the vigor of Pavlovian conditioned responding. (Idealized data.)

off a short time before the US occurs, resulting in a *trace interval.* Trace conditioning has traditionally been considered to be less effective than delayed conditioning (Ellison, 1964; Kamin, 1965) because of the trace interval (Kaplan & Hearst, 1982; Rescorla, 1982a). As with delayed conditioning, however, less conditioned responding is evident with a trace procedure if the interval between the CS and the US is increased (Kehoe, Cool, & Gormezano, 1991).

The above findings encouraged the conclusion that conditioning is most effective when the CS is a good signal that the US will soon occur. The signal value of the CS is best in the short-delayed procedure, where the US occurs shortly after the onset of the CS. The signal value of the CS decreases as the CS–US interval is increased. The CS is also a poor predictor of the US in simultaneous and trace procedures. In simultaneous conditioning, the US occurs at the same time as the CS and is therefore not signaled by the CS. In trace conditioning, the CS is followed by the trace interval rather than the US.

The one procedure whose results were difficult to interpret in terms of the CS-US interval and CS signal value is backward conditioning. Backward conditioning produced mixed results. Some investigators observed excitatory responding produced by backward pairings of a CS and a US (for example, Ayres, Haddad, & Albert, 1987; Hearst, 1989; Shurtleff & Ayres, 1981; Spetch, Wilkie, & Pinel, 1981). Others reported primarily inhibition of conditioned responding as a result of backward conditioning (for example, Maier, Rapaport, & Wheatley, 1976; Siegel & Domjan, 1971). To make matters even more confusing, in a rather remarkable experiment, Tait and Saladin (1986) found both excitatory and inhibitory conditioning effects resulting from the same backward conditioning procedure (see also McNish, Betts, Brandon, & Wagner, 1997).

The simple assumption that CS signal value determines whether a procedure will produce conditioned responding clearly cannot explain the complexity of findings that have been obtained in backward conditioning. The idea that there is a unitary hypothetical construct such as signal value or associative strength that varies as a function of the CS–US interval has also been challenged by the results of recent experiments that have employed

sophisticated and multiple measures of learning. These studies have documented that delayed, simultaneous, trace, and backward conditioning can all produce strong learning and
vigorous conditioned responding (for example, Albert & Ayres, 1997; Akins & Domjan,
1996; Marchand & Kamper, 2000; Romaniuk & Williams, 2000; Schreurs, 1998; Williams
& Hurlburt, 2000). The challenge is to formulate new theoretical ideas to explain these
diverse findings.

An entirely new conceptualization of the relative effectiveness of various Pavlovian conditioning procedures is beginning to emerge. According to contemporary views, delayed,
simultaneous, trace, and backward conditioning all produce robust learning, but these procedures differ in what the subject learns. Instead of learning just a CS-US association, the
subject is assumed to also learn when the US occurs in relation to the CS. Depending on
the specific conditioning procedure, the subject can learn that the US occurs at the same
time as the CS, before the CS, or with a short or a long delay after the CS. Thus, the subject
learns not only that the CS is associated with the US but exactly when the US occurs in
relation to the CS. This view is called the **temporal coding hypothesis** (Barnet, Cole, &
Miller, 1997; Brown, Hemmes, & de Vaca, 1997; Cole, Barnet, & Miller, 1995b; Savastano
& Miller, 1998). In Chapter 4, I describe in greater detail how the temporal information
the CS provides about the US is manifest in conditioned behavior. In brief, the idea is that
different types of conditioned responses occur depending on the temporal information the
CS provides about the US (for example, Akins, 2000; Silva & Timberlake, 2000; Silva,
Timberlake, & Cevik, 1998).

INHIBITORY PAVLOVIAN CONDITIONING

So far I have discussed Pavlovian conditioning in terms of learning to predict when a significant event or unconditioned stimulus will occur. But there is another type of Pavlovian
conditioning—one in which participants learn to predict the absence of the unconditioned
stimulus. Why would they want to predict the absence of something?

Consider being in an environment where bad things happen to you without warning.
A child in an abusive home experiences something like that. His parents may yell at him
and hit him unpredictably for no particular reason. Bad things can also happen with little
warning if you are driving in heavy traffic. Getting pushed and shoved in a crowd also
involves danger that arises without much warning and pretty much independent of what
you might be doing. Research with laboratory animals has shown that exposure to unpredictable aversive stimulation is highly aversive and results in stomach ulcers and other physiological symptoms of stress. Stressful work environments are similar in involving
unpredictable aversive events.

Another source of stress is a panic attack. A panic attack is a sudden sense of fear or
discomfort, accompanied by physical symptoms (for example, heart palpitations) and a
sense of impending doom. If such attacks are fairly frequent and become the source of
considerable anxiety, the individual is said to suffer from panic disorder. At some point in
their lives, 3.5% of the population experience panic disorder (Kessler et al., 1994). Individuals with panic disorder can sometimes predict the onset of a panic attack; at other times,
they may experience an attack without warning. In a study of individuals who experienced
both predictable and unpredictable panic attacks, Craske, Glover, and DeCola (1995) measured the general anxiety of the subjects before and after each type of attack. The results
are summarized in Figure 3.9. Before the attack, anxiety ratings were similar whether the
attack was predictable or not. Interestingly, however, anxiety significantly increased after an

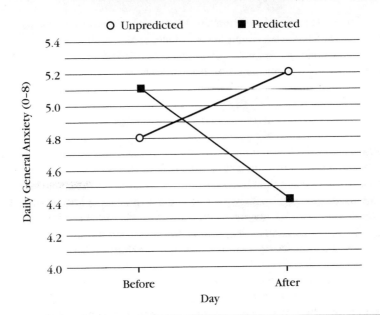

Figure 3.9 Ratings of general anxiety in individuals with panic disorder before and after predicted and unpredicted panic attacks. (From Craske, Glover, & DeCola, 1995.)

unpredicted panic attack and decreased after a predicted attack. Such results indicate that the anxiety generated by the experience of panic attacks occurs primarily because of the unpredictability of the attacks. Consistent with such findings, laboratory research with human and nonhuman subjects has shown that if one has to be exposed to aversive stimulation, predictable or signaled aversive stimuli are preferable to unpredictable aversive stimulation (Mineka & Henderson, 1985).

Why might predictable aversive stimuli be preferable to unpredicted events? A good possibility is that the ability to predict when an aversive event will occur also enables you to predict the absence of aversive stimulation. Being able to predict that absence may be the critical factor. Consistent with this reasoning, many effective stress-reduction techniques (such as relaxation training or meditation) involve creating a predictable period of safety or a time when you can be certain that aversive events will not occur. Stress management consultants recognize that it is often impossible to eliminate aversive events from one's life. for example, a teacher supervising a playground with 25 small children is bound to encounter unexpected and unpleasant events. One cannot entirely prevent accidents or avoid having one child hurt another. Eliminating aversive stimulation is often not a feasible stress management procedure. However, introducing even short periods of predictable safety (by allowing the teacher to take a break, for example) can substantially reduce stress.

Signals that predict the absence of an aversive stimulus are conditioned inhibitory stimuli. Although one can learn to predict the absence of a positive US just as well as a negative or aversive US, much of the research on conditioned inhibition has employed aversive stimulation.

Although Pavlov discovered inhibitory conditioning early in the twentieth century, this type of learning did not command the serious attention of psychologists until decades later (Boakes & Halliday, 1972; Rescorla, 1969b). The concept of conditioned inhibition was ignored because investigators thought evidence for inhibitory processes could be explained in other ways (for a historical discussion, see Williams, Overmier, & LoLordo, 1992). In contrast to excitatory conditioning, conditioned inhibition remains a controversial topic (for example, Miller & Matzel, 1988; Papini & Bitterman, 1993). Nevertheless, a considerable body of research has addressed problems related to conditioned inhibition (for reviews, see Fowler, Lysle, & DeVito, 1991; Miller & Spear, 1985; Savastano, Cole, Barnet, & Miller, 1999). The following section describes the major procedures used to produce conditioned inhibition as well as the special tests used to detect and measure conditioned inhibition.

Procedures for Inhibitory Conditioning

Unlike excitatory conditioning, which can proceed without special preconditions, conditioned inhibition has an important prerequisite. For the absence of a US to be a significant event, the US has to occur periodically in the situation. There are many signals for the absence of events in our daily lives. Signs such as "Closed," "Out of Order," and "No Entry" are all of this type, but they provide meaningful information and influence what we do only if they indicate the absence of something we otherwise expect to see. For example, if we encounter the sign "Out of Gas" at a service station, we may become frustrated and disappointed; the sign provides important information because service stations are expected to have gasoline. The same sign does not tell us anything of interest if it is in the window of a lumber yard, and it is not likely to discourage us from going to buy lumber.

The example I just gave illustrates the general rule that inhibitory conditioning and inhibitory control of behavior occur only if there is an excitatory context for the US in question (for example, Baker & Baker, 1985; Fowler, Kleiman, & Lysle, 1985; LoLordo & Fairless, 1985). This principle makes inhibitory conditioning very different from excitatory conditioning. Excitatory conditioning is not dependent on a special context in the same fashion.

Standard Procedure for Conditioned Inhibition.   Pavlov recognized the importance of an excitatory context for the conditioning of inhibition and was careful to provide such a context in his standard inhibitory training procedure (Pavlov, 1927). The procedure he used, diagrammed in Figure 3.10, involves two conditioned stimuli and two kinds of conditioning trials, one for excitatory conditioning and the other for inhibitory conditioning. The US is presented on excitatory conditioning trials (trial Type A in Figure 3.10), and whenever the US occurs, it is announced by the conditioned stimulus labeled CS+ (a tone, for example). Because of its pairings with the US, the CS+ becomes a signal for the US and can then provide the excitatory context for the development of conditioned inhibition.

During inhibitory conditioning trials (trial Type B in Figure 3.10), the CS+ is presented together with the second conditioned stimulus, the CS− (a light, for example), and the US does not occur. Thus, the CS− is presented in the excitatory context provided by the CS+, but the CS− is not paired with the US. This makes the CS− a conditioned inhibitor. During the course of training, A type and B type trials are alternated randomly. As the animal receives repeated trials of CS+ followed by the US and CS+/CS− followed by no US, the CS− gradually acquires inhibitory properties (Marchant, Mis, & Moore, 1972).

The standard conditioned inhibition procedure is analogous to a situation in which something is introduced that prevents an outcome that would occur otherwise. A red traffic light at a busy intersection is a signal (CS+) of potential danger (the US). However, if a police officer indicates that you should cross the intersection despite the red light (perhaps because the traffic lights are malfunctioning), you will probably not have an accident. The red light (CS+) together with the gestures of the officer (CS−) are not likely to be followed by danger. The gestures act like a CS− to inhibit, or block, your hesitation to cross the intersection because of the red light.

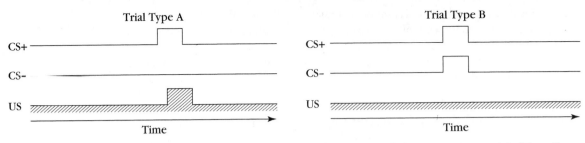

Figure 3.10 Standard procedure for conditioned inhibition. On some trials (Type A), the CS+ is paired with the US. On other trials (Type B), the CS+ is presented with the CS− and the US is omitted. The procedure is effective in conditioning inhibitory properties to the CS−.

Negative CS-US Contingency or Correlation Another common procedure for producing conditioned inhibition does not involve an explicit excitatory stimulus or CS+; rather, it involves only a CS− that is negatively correlated with the US. A negative correlation or contingency means that the US is less likely to occur after the CS than at other times. Thus, the CS signals a reduction in the probability that the US will occur. A sample arrangement that meets this requirement is diagrammed in Figure 3.11. The US is periodically presented by itself. However, each occurrence of the CS is followed by the predictable absence of the US for a while.

Consider a child who periodically gets picked on by her classmates when the teacher is out of the room. This is like periodically getting an aversive stimulus or US. When the teacher returns, the child can be sure she will not be bothered. Thus, the teacher serves as a CS− that signals a period free from harassment, or the absence of the US.

Conditioned inhibition is reliably observed in procedures in which the only explicit conditioned stimulus is negatively correlated with the US (Rescorla, 1969a). What provides the excitatory context for this inhibition? In this case, the environmental cues of the experimental chamber provide the excitatory context (Dweck & Wagner, 1970). Because the US occurs periodically in the experimental situation, the contextual cues of the experimental chamber acquire excitatory properties. This in turn permits the acquisition of inhibitory properties by the CS.

In a negative CS-US contingency procedure, the aversive US may occasionally occur shortly after the CS but this is unlikely. The aversive US is much more likely to occur in the absence of the CS, leading to the negative CS/US contingency. Even in the absence of the CS, however, the exact timing of the US cannot be predicted exactly. The US occurs probabilistically, in contrast to the standard procedure for conditioned inhibition. In the standard procedure, the US always occurs at the end of the CS+ and does not occur when the CS− is presented together with the CS+. Since the standard procedure permits predicting the exact timing of the US, it also permits predicting exactly when the US will *not* occur. (The US will not occur at the end of CS+ if the CS+ is presented with the CS−.) Thus, the standard procedure for conditioned inhibition permits temporal coding of the absence of the US (Denniston, Cole, & Miller, 1998; Denniston, Blaisdell, & Miller, 1998).

Measuring Conditioned Inhibition

How are conditioned inhibitory processes manifest in behavior? For conditioned excitation, the answer is straightforward. Conditioned excitatory stimuli come to elicit responses that

R. A. Rescorla

Courtesy of Donald A. Dewsbury

Figure 3.11   A negative CS-US contingency procedure for conditioning inhibitory properties to the CS. Notice that the CS is always followed by a period without the US.

were not evident before. Conditioned excitatory stimuli come to elicit new responses such as salivation, approach, or eyeblinking, depending on what was the unconditioned stimulus. One might expect that conditioned inhibitory stimuli would elicit the opposites of these reactions—namely, suppression of salivation, approach, or eyeblinking. But how can these response opposites be measured?

Bidirectional Response Systems.   Identification of opposing response tendencies is easy with response systems that can change in opposite directions from baseline or normal performance. This is characteristic of many physiological responses. Heart rate, respiration, and temperature, for example, can either increase or decrease from a baseline level. Certain behavioral responses are also bidirectional. For example, animals can either approach or withdraw from a stimulus, and their rate of lever pressing for a food reward can either increase or decrease. In these cases, conditioned excitation results in a change in behavior in one direction, and conditioned inhibition results in a change in behavior in the opposite direction.

The sign-tracking procedure, for example, has been used to provide evidence of inhibitory conditioning through bidirectional responses. As noted earlier, a pigeon will approach a key light associated with the forthcoming presentation of food. By contrast, if an inhibitory conditioning procedure is used, the pigeon will withdraw from the CS (Hearst & Franklin, 1977; Wasserman, Franklin, & Hearst, 1974; Janssen, Farley, & Hearst, 1995; see also Palya, 1993). Although bidirectional responses can provide evidence of conditioned inhibition, the technique is limited and has not come to be widely used. One limitation, of course, is that this approach works only with responses that can go in opposite directions. Another, less obvious, limitation is that this technique can show only the net effects of excitation and inhibition. The subject will approach the CS if the excitatory properties of the CS are greater than its inhibitory properties, and it will withdraw from the CS if the inhibitory properties exceed the excitatory properties. The pigeon cannot both approach and withdraw at the same time. This makes the procedure of little use in instances where a CS acquires both excitatory and inhibitory properties. (For further discussion of this point, see Savastano et al., 1999.)

The Compound-Stimulus, or Summation, Test.   How could researchers measure inhibition if the target behavior is not bidirectional? Consider, for example, the eyeblink response, which is frequently studied with rabbits. In the absence of an eliciting stimulus, rabbits rarely blink. If a stimulus had been conditioned to inhibit the eyeblink response, researchers would also not observe eyeblinks when this stimulus was presented. How could they tell whether the lack of responding reflected an active suppression of blinking or merely the low baseline level of this behavior? To conclude that a stimulus actively inhibits blinking, researchers have to use more sophisticated test procedures. One of these is the *compound-stimulus test.*

The **compound-stimulus** or **summation test** was particularly popular with Pavlov and is becoming the most acceptable procedure for the measurement of conditioned inhibition in contemporary research (see Miller & Spear, 1985). Difficulties created by low baseline levels of responding are overcome in the compound-stimulus test by presenting an excitatory conditioned stimulus that elicits the conditioned response. Conditioned inhibition is then measured in terms of the reduction or inhibition of this conditioned responding. Thus, the test involves observing the effects of an inhibitory CS in compound with an excitatory CS+. The procedure may also be conceptualized as one that involves observing the summation of the effects of the inhibitory stimulus (CS−) and an excitatory stimulus (CS+).

A particularly well-controlled demonstration of conditioned inhibition using the compound-stimulus or summation test was reported by Cole, Barnet, and Miller (1997). The experiment was conducted using the lick suppression procedure with laboratory rats. The subjects received inhibitory conditioning in which the presentation of a flashing light by itself always ended in a brief shock (A+), and the presentation of an auditory cue (X) together with the light ended without shock (AX−). Thus, the standard procedure for conditioned inhibition was used. Inhibitory conditioning was conducted over 7 sessions in which the subjects received a total of 28 A+ trials and 56 AX− trials. The subjects also received training with another auditory stimulus (B) in a different experimental chamber, and this stimulus always ended in the brief shock (B+). The intent of these procedures was to establish conditioned excitation to two different stimuli, A and B, and conditioned inhibition to X.

Cole et al. then asked whether the presumed inhibitor X would suppress responding to the excitatory stimuli A and B. The results of those tests are summarized in Figure 3.12. How long the subjects took to accumulate 5 seconds of uninterrupted drinking was measured. Notice that when the excitatory stimuli A and B were presented by themselves, the rats required substantial amounts of time to complete the 5-second drinking criterion. In contrast, when the excitatory stimuli were presented together with the conditioned inhibitor (AX and BX tests), the drinking requirement was completed much faster. Thus, presenting stimulus X with A and B reduced the drinking suppression that occurred when A and B were presented by themselves. Figure 3.12 includes yet another test condition, stimulus B tested with another auditory cue Y. Stimulus Y was not previously conditioned as an inhibitor and was presented in order to be sure that introducing a new stimulus with stimulus B would not cause disruption of the conditioned fear response. As Figure 3.12 illustrates, no such disruption occurred with stimulus Y. Thus, the inhibition of conditioned fear was limited to the stimulus (X) that had participated in the conditioned inhibition training. Another important aspect of these results is that X was able to inhibit conditioned fear not only to the exciter with which it was trained (A) but also to another exciter (B) that had never been presented with X during training.

The compound-stimulus test procedure for conditioned inhibition suggests that the presentation of a conditioned inhibitor or safety signal can reduce the stressful effects of an aversive experience. This prediction was tested with patients who were prone to experience panic attacks (Carter, Hollon, Carson, & Shelton, 1995). Panic attack patients were invited to the laboratory, accompanied by someone with whom they felt safe. Panic was experimentally induced in the participants by having them inhale a mixture of gas containing elevated levels of carbon dioxide. The participants were then asked to report on their perceived levels of anxiety and catastrophic ideation triggered by the carbon dioxide exposure. The experimental manipulation was the presence of another person with whom the participants felt safe. Half the participants were allowed to have their trusted acquaintance in the room with them during the experiment, whereas the remaining participants took part in the

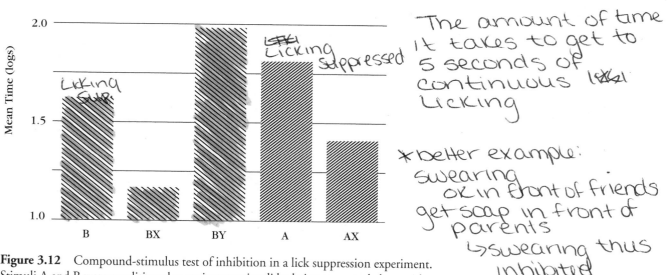

The amount of time it takes to get to 5 seconds of continuous licking

Licking Sup.

Licking suppressed

★better example: swearing ok in front of friends get soap in front of parents ↳ swearing thus inhibited

Figure 3.12 Compound-stimulus test of inhibition in a lick suppression experiment. Stimuli A and B were conditioned as excitatory stimuli by being presented alone with shock (A+ and B+). Stimulus X was conditioned as an inhibitor by being presented with stimulus A without shock (AX–). Stimulus Y was a control stimulus that had not participated in either excitatory or inhibitory conditioning. A was a flashing light. B, X, and Y were auditory cues (a clicker, white noise, and a buzzer, counterbalanced across subjects). A, and AX were tested in the original training context. B, BX, and BY were tested in a different context. (For additional details, see Cole, Barnet, & Miller, 1997, Experiment 1.)

experiment alone. The results indicated that the presence of a safe acquaintance reduced the anxiety and catastrophic ideation associated with the panic attack.

ex: minimized attacks w/ chuck → unless he's the cause 😊

The Retardation-of-Acquisition Test. Another frequently used indirect test of conditioned inhibition is the **retardation-of-acquisition test** (for example, Hammond, 1968; Rescorla, 1969a). The rationale for this test is also rather straightforward. If a stimulus actively inhibits a particular response, then it should be especially difficult to condition that stimulus to elicit the behavior. In other words, the rate of acquisition of an excitatory conditioned response should be retarded if the CS is a conditioned inhibitor. This prediction was tested by Cole et al. (1997) in an experiment very similar to their summation test study described earlier.

After the same kind of inhibitory conditioning that produced the results summarized in Figure 3.12, Cole et al. took stimulus X (which had been conditioned as an inhibitor) and stimulus Y (which had not been used in a conditioning procedure before) and conducted a retardation-of-acquisition test by pairing each stimulus with shock on three occasions. (This retardation-of-acquisition test was conducted in an experimental chamber different from the chamber in which the subjects previously received inhibitory training.)

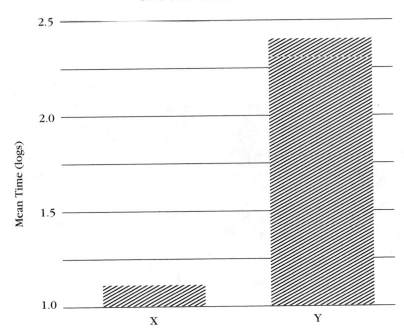

Figure 3.13 Effects of a retardation-of-acquisition test of inhibition in a lick suppression experiment after the same kind of inhibitory conditioning as was conducted to produce the results presented in Figure 3.12. Stimulus X was previously conditioned as an inhibitory stimulus, and stimulus Y previously received no training. (For additional details, see Cole, Barnet, & Miller, 1997, Experiment 2.)

After the three acquisition trials, each stimulus was tested to see which would cause a greater suppression of drinking. The results are presented in Figure 3.13. The time to complete a cumulative of 5 seconds drinking took much longer in the presence of the control stimulus Y than in the presence of stimulus X, which had previously been trained as a conditioned inhibitor. Thus, the initial inhibitory training of X retarded its acquisition of excitatory conditioned fear properties.

Conditioned inhibition can be difficult to distinguish from other behavioral processes. Therefore, the best strategy is to use more than one test and be sure that the different tests all point to the same conclusion. Rescorla (1969b) advocated using both the compound stimulus test and the retardation-of-acquisition test. This dual test strategy has remained popular ever since (Savastano et al., 1999; Williams et al., 1992).

PREVALENCE OF CLASSICAL CONDITIONING

Classical conditioning is typically investigated in laboratory situations. However, we do not have to know much about classical conditioning to realize that it also occurs in a wide range of situations outside the laboratory. Classical conditioning is most likely to develop when one event reliably precedes another in a short-delayed CS-US pairing. This occurs in many aspects of life. As I mentioned at the beginning of the chapter, stimuli in the environment occur in an orderly temporal sequence, largely because of the physical constraints of causation. Some events simply cannot happen before other things have occurred. Social institutions and customs also ensure that things happen in a predictable order. Whenever one stimulus reliably precedes another, classical conditioning may take place.

One area of research that has been of particular interest is how people come to judge one event as the cause of another. In studies of human causal judgment, participants are exposed to repeated occurrences of two events (pictures of a blooming flower and a water can briefly presented on a computer screen) in various temporal arrangements. In one condition, for example, the water can may always occur before the flower; in another, it may occur at random times relative to the flower. After observing numerous appearances of both objects, the subjects are asked to indicate their judgment about the strength of causal relation between them. Studies of human causal judgment are analogous to studies of Pavlovian conditioning in that both involve repeated experiences with two events and responses based on the extent to which those two events are related to one another. Given this correspondence, one might suspect that there is considerable commonality in the outcomes of causal judgment and Pavlovian conditioning experiments. That prediction has been borne out in numerous studies (Miller & Matute, 1996; Shanks & Dickinson, 1987; Wasserman, 1990), suggesting that Pavlovian associative mechanisms are not limited to Pavlov's dogs but may play a role in the numerous informal judgments of causality we all make during the course of our daily lives.

As I described earlier in the chapter, Pavlovian conditioning can result in the conditioning of food preferences and aversions. It can also result in the acquisition of fear. Conditioned fear responses have been of special interest because they may contribute significantly to anxiety disorders, phobias, and panic disorder (Bouton, 2001; Bouton, Mineka, & Barlow, 2001). As I discuss further in Chapter 4, Pavlovian conditioning is also involved in drug tolerance and addiction. Cues that reliably accompany drug administration can come to elicit drug-related responses through conditioning. In discussing this type of learning among crack addicts, Dr. Scott Lukas of McLean Hospital in Massachusetts described the effects of drug-conditioned stimuli by saying, "These cues turn on crack-related memories, and addicts respond like Pavlov's dogs" (*Newsweek*, February 12, 2001, p. 40).

Pavlovian conditioning is also involved in infant and maternal responses in nursing. Suckling involves mutual stimulation for the infant and the mother. To successfully nurse, the mother has to hold the baby in a particular position, which provides special tactile stimuli for both the infant and the mother. The tactile stimuli experienced by the infant may become conditioned to elicit orientation and suckling responses on the part of the baby (Blass, Ganchrow, & Steiner, 1984). The tactile stimuli experienced by the mother may also become conditioned, in this case to elicit the milk let-down response of the mother in anticipation of having the infant suckle. Mothers who nurse their babies frequently may experience the milk let-down reflex when the baby cries or when the usual time for breast-feeding arrives. All these stimuli (special tactile cues, the baby's crying, and the time of normal feedings) reliably precede suckling by the infant. Therefore, they may become conditioned by the suckling stimulation and come to elicit milk secretion as a conditioned response. The anticipatory conditioned orientation and suckling responses and the anticipatory conditioned milk let-down response make the nursing experience more successful for both the baby and the mother.

Pavlovian conditioning is also important in learning about sexual situations. Although clinical observations indicate that human sexual behavior can be shaped by learning experiences, the best experimental evidence of sexual conditioning has been obtained in studies

M. E. Bouton

Courtesy of Donald A. Dewsbury

Courtesy of Donald A. Dewsbury

K. L. Hollis

with laboratory animals (Domjan & Holloway, 1998). In these studies, males typically serve as participants, and the unconditioned stimulus is provided either by the sight of a sexually receptive female or by physical access to a female (Domjan, 1998). Subjects come to approach stimuli that signal the availability of a sexual partner (Burns & Domjan, 1996; Hollis, Cadieux, & Colbert, 1989). The presentation of a sexually conditioned stimulus also facilitates various aspects of reproductive behavior. Studies with rats, quail, and a fish species have shown that after exposure to a sexual CS, males are quicker to perform copulatory responses (Zamble, Hadad, Mitchell, & Cutmore, 1985), compete more successfully with other males for access to a female (Gutiérrez & Domjan, 1996), show more courtship behavior (Hollis et al., 1989), release greater quantities of sperm (Domjan, Blesbois, & Williams, 1998), and show increased levels of testosterone and leuteinizing hormone (Graham & Desjardins, 1980). Although these various manifestations of sexual conditioning are noteworthy, the ultimate payoff for sexual behavior is the numbers of offspring that are produced. In an important study with a fish species, Hollis, Pharr, Dumas, Britton, and Field (1997) found that the presentation of a Pavlovian CS+ before a sexual encounter greatly increased the numbers of offspring that resulted from the reproductive behavior. Similar findings are emerging in studies with domesticated quail (Domjan & Mahometa, 2001).

CONCLUDING COMMENTS

Chapter 3 continued the discussion of elicited behavior by turning attention from habituation and sensitization to classical conditioning. Classical conditioning is a bit more complex than habituation and sensitization in that it involves associatively mediated elicited behavior. Classical conditioning is one of the major techniques for investigating how associations are learned. As we have seen, classical conditioning may be involved in many different important aspects of behavior. Depending on the procedure used, the learning may occur quickly or slowly. With some procedures, excitatory response tendencies are learned; with other procedures, the organism learns to inhibit a particular response in the presence of the conditioned stimulus. Excitatory and inhibitory conditioning occur in many aspects of common experience and serve to increase how effectively we cope with significant biological events.

SAMPLE QUESTIONS

1. Describe similarities and differences between habituation, sensitization, and classical conditioning.
2. What is object learning, and how is it similar or different from conventional classical conditioning?
3. What is the most effective procedure for excitatory conditioning and how is it different from other possibilities?
4. What is a control procedure for excitatory conditioning, and what processes are the control procedure intended to rule out?
5. Are conditioned excitation and conditioned inhibition related, and if so how?
6. Describe procedures for conditioning and measuring conditioned inhibition.

autoshaping Same as *sign tracking.*

backward conditioning A procedure in which the conditioned stimulus is presented after the unconditioned stimulus on each trial.

CER Abreviation for *conditioned emotional response.*

compound-stimulus test A test procedure that identifies a stimulus as a conditioned inhibitor if that stimulus reduces the responding elicited by a conditioned excitatory stimulus. Also called *summation test.*

conditional or conditioned response The response that comes to be made to the conditioned stimulus as a result of classical conditioning. Abbreviated *CR.*

conditional or conditioned stimulus A stimulus that does not elicit a particular response initially, but comes to do so as a result of becoming associated with an unconditioned stimulus. Abbreviated *CS.*

conditioned emotional response Suppression of positively reinforced instrumental behavior (for example, lever pressing for food pellets) caused by the presentation of a stimulus that has become associated with an aversive stimulus. Abbreviation *CER.* Also called *conditioned suppression.*

conditioned suppression Same as *conditioned emotional response.*

conditioned lick suppression Similar to the conditioned emotional response (CER) or conditioned suppression procedure. However, instead of lever pressing for food serving as the behavior that is suppressed by conditioned fear, the baseline is licking a waterspout by thirsty rats. The presentation of a fear-conditioned CS slows down the rate of licking.

conditioning trial A training episode involving presentation of a conditioned stimulus with (or without) an unconditioned stimulus.

CR Abbreviation for *conditioned response.*

CS Abbreviation for *conditioned stimulus.*

CS-US interval Same as *interstimulus interval.*

explicitly unpaired control A procedure in which both conditioned and unconditioned stimuli are presented, but with sufficient time between them so that they do not become associated with each other.

interstimulus interval The amount of time that elapses between presentations of the conditioned stimulus (CS) and the unconditioned stimulus (US) during a classical conditioning trial. Also called the *CS-US interval.*

intertrial interval The amount of time that elapses between two successive trials.

latency The time elapsed between a stimulus (or the start of a trial) and the response that is made to the stimulus.

magnitude of a response A measure of the size, vigor, or extent of a response.

object learning Learning associations between different stimulus elements of an object.

probability of a response The likelihood of making the response, usually represented in terms of the percentage of trials on which the response occurs.

pseudoconditioning Increased responding that may occur to a stimulus whose presentations are intermixed with presentations of an unconditioned stimulus (US) in the absence of the establishment of an association between the stimulus and the US.

random control A procedure in which the conditioned and unconditioned stimuli are presented at random times with respect to each other.

retardation-of-acquisition test A test procedure that identifies a stimulus as a conditioned inhibitor if that stimulus is slower to acquire excitatory properties than a comparison stimulus.

short-delayed conditioning A classical conditioning procedure in which the conditioned stimulus is initiated shortly before the unconditioned stimulus on each conditioning trial.

sign tracking Movement toward and possibly contact with a stimulus that signals the availability of a positive reinforcer, such as food. Also called *autoshaping.*

simultaneous conditioning A classical conditioning procedure in which the conditioned stimulus and the unconditioned stimulus are presented simultaneously on each conditioning trial.

summation test Same as *compound-stimulus test*.

temporal coding hypothesis The idea that Pavlovian conditioning procedures lead not only to learning that the US happens but exactly when the US occurs in relation to the CS. The CS comes to represent (or code) the timing of the US.

test trial A trial in which the conditioned stimulus is presented without the unconditioned stimulus. This allows measurement of the conditioned response in the absence of the unconditioned response.

trace conditioning A classical conditioning procedure in which the unconditioned stimulus is presented after the conditioned stimulus has been terminated for a short period.

trace interval The interval between the end of the conditioned stimulus and the start of the unconditioned stimulus in trace-conditioning trials.

unconditional or unconditioned response A response that occurs to a stimulus without the necessity of prior training.

unconditional or unconditioned stimulus A stimulus that elicits a particular response without the necessity of prior training.

UR Abbreviation for *unconditioned response*.

US Abbreviation for *unconditioned stimulus*.

CHAPTER

4

CLASSICAL CONDITIONING: MECHANISMS

What Makes Effective Conditioned and Unconditioned Stimuli?

    Initial Response to the Stimuli

    The Novelty of Conditioned and Unconditioned Stimuli

    CS and US Intensity and Salience

    CS-US Relevance, or Belongingness

    The Concept of Biological Strength

What Determines the Nature of the Conditioned Response?

    The Stimulus Substitution Model

    Learning and Homeostasis:
      A Special Case of Stimulus Substitution

    The CS as a Determinant of the Form of the CR

    Conditioned Behavior and Behavior Systems

    S-R Versus S-S Learning

How Do Conditioned and Unconditioned Stimuli Become Associated?

    The Blocking Effect

    The Rescorla–Wagner Model

    Other Models of Classical Conditioning

Concluding Comments

C hapter 4 continues the discussion of classical conditioning, focusing on the mechanisms and outcomes of this type of learning. The discussion is organized around three key issues: (1) features of conditioned and unconditioned stimuli that influence their effectiveness in classical conditioning procedures, (2) factors that determine the types of responses that come to be made to conditioned stimuli, and (3) mechanisms involved in the formation of associations between conditioned and unconditioned stimuli and the mechanisms involved in the acquisition of conditioned behavior.

WHAT MAKES EFFECTIVE CONDITIONED AND UNCONDITIONED STIMULI?

This is perhaps the most basic question about classical conditioning. It was originally addressed by Pavlov and is also increasingly attracting the attention of contemporary researchers.

Initial Responses to the Stimuli

Pavlov addressed the effectiveness criteria for conditioned and unconditioned stimuli in his definitions of the terms *conditioned* and *unconditioned*. According to these definitions, the conditioned stimulus (CS) does not elicit the conditioned response initially, but comes to do so as a result of becoming associated with the unconditioned stimulus (US). By contrast, the US is effective in eliciting the target response from the outset without any special training.

Pavlov's definitions were stated in terms of the elicitation of a particular response—the one to be conditioned. Because of this, identifying potential CSs and USs requires comparing the responses elicited by each stimulus before conditioning. Such a comparison makes the identification of CSs and USs *relative*. A particular event may serve as a CS relative to one stimulus and as a US relative to another.

Consider, for example, a palatable saccharin solution for thirsty rats. The taste may serve as a CS in a taste-aversion experiment, with illness serving as the US. In this case, conditioning trials would consist of exposure to the saccharin flavor followed by injection of a drug that induces malaise, and the animals would learn to stop drinking the saccharin solution.

The same saccharin solution may also serve as a US—in a sign-tracking experiment, for example. The conditioning trials in this case would involve the illumination of a light just before each presentation of a small amount of saccharin. After a number of these trials, the animals would begin to approach the light CS. Thus, whether the saccharin solution is considered a US or a CS depends on its relation to other stimuli in the situation.

The Novelty of Conditioned and Unconditioned Stimuli

As studies of habituation show, the behavioral impact of a stimulus depends on its novelty. Highly familiar stimuli do not elicit as vigorous reactions as do novel stimuli. Novelty is also important in classical conditioning. If either the conditioned or the unconditioned stimulus is highly familiar, learning proceeds more slowly than if the CS and US are novel.

Investigations of the role of novelty in classical conditioning are usually conducted in two phases. Subjects are first given repeated presentations of the stimulus that is later to be used as the CS. During this initial phase of the experiment, the CS-to-be is always presented by itself. After the preexposure phase, the CS is paired with an unconditioned stimulus using conventional classical conditioning procedures. Initial familiarization with a stimulus presented by itself usually retards the subsequent conditioning of that stimulus. This phenomenon is called the **CS-preexposure effect** or the **latent-inhibition effect** (Hall, 1991; Lubow, 1989; Lubow & Gewirtz, 1995; for implications for psychopathology, see Lubow, 1998; Oberling, Gosselin, & Miller, 1997).

The function of the CS-preexposure effect is similar to the function of habituation. Both phenomena serve to limit processing and attention to stimuli that have proven to be inconsequential. Habituation serves to bias elicited behavior in favor of novel stimuli;

latent inhibition serves to bias learning in favor of novel stimuli. As Lubow and Gewirtz (1995) noted, latent inhibition "promotes the stimulus selectivity required for rapid learning" (p. 87).

Experiments on the importance of US novelty are similar in design to CS-preexposure experiments. Subjects are first given repeated exposures to the US presented by itself. The US is then paired with a CS, and the progress of learning is monitored. Subjects familiarized with a US before its pairings with a CS are slower to develop conditioned responding to the CS than participants for whom the US is novel during the CS-US pairings. This result is called the **US-preexposure effect** (Randich, 1981; Randich & LoLordo, 1979; Riley & Simpson, 2001; Saladin, ten Have, Saper, Labinsky, & Tait, 1989).

The mechanisms of CS- and US-preexposure effects have been the subject of extensive research and debate. No one theory has been successful in explaining all of the data. A reasonable conclusion at this time is that several mechanisms are involved (see Hall, 1991, for a discussion of this in relation to the CS-preexposure effect). One mechanism involves *associative interference*. According to the associative interference account, preconditioning exposures to the CS or US make these stimuli less able to enter into new associations (Lubow, Weiner, & Schnur, 1981; McPhee, Rauhut, & Ayres, 2001; Riley & Simpson, 2001).

The second explanation of CS- and US-preexposure effects is *memory interference*. According to the memory interference account, conditioned responding is disrupted because participants remember what happened in both phases of the experiment. They remember having received the CS (or US) by itself repeatedly during the preexposure phase and having received the CS paired with the US in the conditioning phase. The memory of the preexposure phase disrupts responding because the CS- and US-preexposure procedures do not stimulate the conditioned response. Consistent with this mechanism, procedures that reduce the memory of preexposure at the time of testing result in enhanced conditioned responding (for example, Graham, Barnet, Gunther, & Miller, 1994; Rosas & Bouton, 1997; Westbrook, Jones, Bailey, & Harris, 2000).

CS and US Intensity and Salience

Another important stimulus variable for classical conditioning is the intensity of the conditioned and unconditioned stimuli. Most biological and physiological effects of stimulation are related to the intensity of the stimulus input. This is also true of Pavlovian conditioning. More vigorous conditioned responding occurs when more intense conditioned and unconditioned stimuli are used (for example, Bevins, McPhee, Rauhut, & Ayres, 1997; Kamin & Brimer, 1963; Ploog & Zeigler, 1996; Scavio & Gormezano, 1974).

Stimulus intensity is one factor that contributes to what is more generally called **stimulus salience.** The term *salience* is not well defined, but it roughly corresponds to significance or noticeability. Theories of learning typically assume that learning will occur more rapidly with more salient stimuli (for example, McLaren & Mackintosh, 2000; Pearce & Hall, 1980). A stimulus can be made more salient, or significant, by making it more intense and hence more attention getting. Investigators can also make a stimulus more salient by making it more relevant to the biological needs of the organism. For example, animals become more attentive to the taste of salt if they suffer a nutritional salt deficiency (Kriekhaus, & Wolf, 1968). Consistent with this outcome, Sawa, Nakajima, and Imada (1999) found that sodium-deficient rats learn stronger aversions to the taste of salt than do nondeficient control subjects.

Another way to increase the salience of a CS is to make the laboratory CS more similar to the kinds of stimuli an animal is likely to encounter in its natural environment. Studies of sexual conditioning with domesticated quail provide an example. In the typical experiment, access to a female quail serves as the US for a male, and this sexual opportunity is signaled by the presentation of a CS. The CS can be an "arbitrary" cue such as a light or a terrycloth object. Alternatively, the CS can be made more natural or salient by adding partial cues of a female (see Figure 4.1). Studies have shown that more vigorous sexually conditioned responding occurs to a CS object that includes some of the stimulus features of a female quail (Cusato & Domjan, 1998, 2000; Domjan, 1998).

CS-US Relevance, or Belongingness

Another variable that governs the rate of classical conditioning is the extent to which the CS is relevant to, or belongs with, the US. The importance of stimulus relevance was first clearly demonstrated in a classic experiment by Garcia and Koelling (1966). The investigators compared learning about peripheral pain (induced by footshock) and learning about illness (induced by irradiation or a drug injection) in a study conducted with laboratory rats.

In their natural environment, rats are likely to get sick after eating a poisonous food. In contrast, they are likely to encounter peripheral pain after being chased and bitten by a predator that they can hear and see. To represent food-related cues, Garcia and Koelling used a flavored solution of water as the CS; to represent predator-related cues, they used an audiovisual CS.

The experiment, diagrammed in Figure 4.2, involved having the rats drink from a drinking tube before administration of one of the unconditioned stimuli. The drinking tube was filled with water flavored either salty or sweet. In addition, each lick on the tube activated a brief audiovisual stimulus (the click of a relay and a flash of light). Thus, the rats encountered the taste and audiovisual stimuli at the same time. After exposure to these conditioned stimuli, the animals either received a brief shock through the grid floor or were made sick.

Because the unconditioned stimuli used were aversive, the rats were expected to learn an aversion of some kind. The investigators measured the response of the animals to the taste and audiovisual CSs presented individually after conditioning. During tests of the taste CS, the water was flavored as before, but now licks did not activate the audiovisual cue. During tests of the audiovisual CS, the water was unflavored, but the audiovisual cue was briefly turned on each time the animal licked the spout. The degree of conditioned aversion to the taste or audiovisual CS was inferred from the suppression of drinking.

Figure 4.1 CS objects used as signals for copulatory opportunity in studies of sexual conditioning with male quail. The object on the left is "arbitrary" and made entirely of terrycloth. The object on the right includes limited female cues provided by the head and some neck feathers from a taxidermically prepared female bird. (From Cusato & Domjan, 1998.)

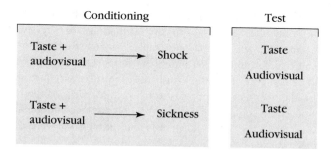

Conditioning		Test
Taste + audiovisual → Shock		Taste Audiovisual
Taste + audiovisual → Sickness		Taste Audiovisual

Figure 4.2 Diagram of Garcia and Koelling's (1966) experiment. A compound taste-audiovisual stimulus was first paired with either shock or sickness for separate groups of laboratory rats. The subjects were then tested with the taste and audiovisual stimuli separately.

The results of the experiment are summarized in Figure 4.3. Animals conditioned with shock subsequently suppressed their drinking much more when tested with the audiovisual stimulus than when tested with the taste CS. The opposite result occurred for animals that had been conditioned with sickness—these rats suppressed their drinking much more when the taste CS was presented than when drinking produced the audiovisual stimulus.

Garcia and Koelling's experiment demonstrates the principle of CS-US relevance, or belongingness. Learning depended on the relevance or appropriateness of the CS to the US that was administered. Taste became readily associated with illness, and audiovisual cues became readily associated with peripheral pain. Rapid learning occurred only if the CS was combined with the appropriate US. The audiovisual CS was not generally more effective than the taste CS. Rather, the audiovisual CS was more effective only when shock served as the US. Correspondingly, the shock US was not generally more effective than the sickness US. Rather, shock conditioned stronger aversions than sickness only when the audiovisual cue served as the CS.

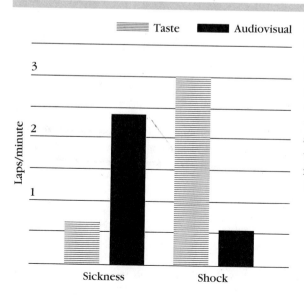

Figure 4.3 Results of Garcia and Koelling's (1966) experiment. Rats conditioned with sickness learned a stronger aversion to taste than to audiovisual cues. By contrast, rats conditioned with shock learned a stronger aversion to audiovisual than to taste cues. (Adapted from Garcia and Koelling, 1966.)

The CS-US relevance effect obtained by Garcia and Koelling was not readily accepted at first, but numerous subsequent studies have confirmed the original findings (for a review, see Domjan, 1983). Gemberling and Domjan (1982), for example, demonstrated that the effect occurs in rats 1 day after birth. This observation indicates that extensive experience with tastes and sickness (or audiovisual cues and peripheral pain) is not necessary for the stimulus relevance effect. Rather, the phenomenon appears to reflect a genetic predisposition for the selective association of certain combinations of conditioned and unconditioned stimuli. (For evidence of stimulus relevance in human food aversion learning, see Garb & Stunkard, 1974; Logue et al., 1981; Pelchat & Rozin, 1982).

Stimulus relevance effects have also been documented in other situations. For example, LoLordo and his associates investigated how pigeons learn about food as compared with peripheral pain. They found that pigeons associate visual cues with food much more easily than they associate auditory cues with food. By contrast, if the conditioning situation involves shock, auditory cues are more effective as the CS than are visual cues. These results suggest that, for pigeons, visual cues are relevant to feeding and auditory cues are relevant to defensive behavior (see LoLordo, Jacobs, & Foree, 1982; Kelly, 1986; Shapiro, Jacobs, & LoLordo, 1980; Shapiro & LoLordo, 1982).

Stimulus relevance effects are also evident in the acquisition of fear. Rhesus monkeys can become fearful of a live snake or a toy snake as a result of observing another monkey react with fear to the snakes. Cook and Mineka (1990) found that observational learning of fear was more likely if the demonstrator showed fear of a toy snake than if the demonstrator acted fearfully in the presence of artificial flowers. However, the artificial flower CS was just as effective as the toy snake in a learning task involving food. Thus, monkeys seem to be predisposed to learn to fear snakes.

People also exhibit stimulus selectivity in their learning of fear. They are more likely to report being afraid of snakes and spiders than of electric outlets or hammers that can also inflict severe pain (Seligman, 1971). Laboratory studies have shown that human participants associate pictures of snakes and spiders with shock more readily than pictures of flowers and houses (Öhman, Dimberg, & Öst, 1985). The mechanisms of these selective learning effects remain the subject of lively debate (Davey, 1995).

The Concept of Biological Strength

In all the examples of classical conditioning discussed so far, responses to the CS were not as strong as responses to the US prior to conditioning. The familiar example of salivary conditioning is a good case in point. In this situation, the conditioned stimulus (a tone) initially elicits only weak orientation movements. By contrast, the US (food) elicits vigorous approach, ingestion, salivation, chewing, swallowing, and so on. Pavlov was aware of this significant difference in the "biological strength" of the stimuli and considered the difference necessary for their effectiveness as conditioned and unconditioned stimuli (Pavlov, 1927). Pavlov suggested that for a stimulus to become conditioned, it had to be of weaker biological strength than the unconditioned stimulus with which it is paired. By "weaker biological strength," he meant that the CS initially had to elicit fewer and weaker responses than the US. (For a recent examination of the role of biological strength in the determination of CSs and USs, see Gunther, Miller, & Matute, 1997.)

Higher-Order Conditioning.   One implication of Pavlov's biological strength criterion is that a stimulus may serve in the role of a US after it has become strongly conditioned. Consider, for example, a tone that is repeatedly paired with food. After sufficient pairings, the tone will come to elicit salivation, as well as strong orientation and approach (sign tracking)

BOX **4.1**

BEHAVIORAL APPROACHES TO THE CONTROL OF SMOKING

A variety of aversion conditioning procedures have been developed to discourage cigarette smoking (Hall, Hall, & Ginsberg, 1990). Early efforts involved aversion therapy in which smoking was paired with pain induced by electric shock. More recent techniques have been based on findings indicating that the aversion conditioning is more effective if the aversive stimulus is "relevant" to the situation. In these procedures, cigarette smoking itself is used to provide the aversive stimulus. A frequently employed procedure is *rapid smoking* (USDHHS, 1996), which requires the subject to inhale every 6 seconds either for a fixed period or until nausea or dizziness develops. Such rapid smoking is aversive and serves to condition an aversion to smoking.

Aversion conditioning procedures are most effective in discouraging smoking when they are combined with other behavior modification techniques. Rapid smoking, for example, may be effectively combined with training in self-monitoring and self-management procedures. Individuals are first required to maintain an accurate record of the number of cigarettes they smoke, and the time, place, and circumstances of the smoking. Once the frequency and circumstances of a person's usual smoking behavior are known, two objectives are introduced with the goal of gradually reducing smoking: to reduce the total number of cigarettes smoked each day, and to reduce the number of situations in which the person is allowed to smoke. These objectives serve in combination to restrict smoking behavior. Compliance can be encouraged by setting up a contract system. For example, the person may deposit a sizable sum of money at the start of treatment and receive portions of this deposit back each time a specified objective is met.

responses. According to the concept of biological strength, at this point the tone should be effective in conditioning salivation to a novel light stimulus that does not initially elicit strong responses. Pairings of the previously conditioned tone with the novel light should gradually result in the conditioning of salivation to the light. Indeed, this effect is often observed and is called **higher-order conditioning**. Figure 4.4 summarizes the sequence of events that brings about higher-order conditioning.

As the term *higher order* implies, conditioning may be considered to operate at different levels. In the preceding example, pairings of the tone with food is considered *first-order conditioning*. Pairings of the light with the previously conditioned tone is considered *second-order conditioning*. If after becoming conditioned, the light were used to condition yet another stimulus—say, an odor—that would be *third-order conditioning*.

The procedure for second-order conditioning shown in Figure 4.4 is similar to the standard procedure for inhibitory conditioning described in Chapter 3 (see Figure 3.10). In both cases, one conditioned stimulus (CS_1 or the CS^+) is paired with the US ($CS_1 \rightarrow US$ or $CS^+ \rightarrow US$), and a second CS (CS_2 or CS^-) is paired with the first one without the unconditioned stimulus ($CS_1/CS_2 \rightarrow noUS$ or $CS^+/CS^- \rightarrow noUS$). Why does such a procedure produce conditioned inhibition in some cases and excitatory second-order conditioning under other circumstances? The critical factor appears to be the number of noUS trials. With a few nonreinforced trials, second-order excitatory conditioning occurs. With extensive training, conditioned inhibition develops (Yin, Barnet, & Miller, 1994).

Although second-order conditioning is a well-known robust phenomenon (Rescorla, 1980a), little research has been done to evaluate the mechanisms of third- and higher orders

Figure 4.4 Procedure for higher-order conditioning. CS_1 is first paired with the US and comes to elicit the conditioned response. A new stimulus (CS_2) is then paired with CS_1 and also comes to elicit the conditioned response.

of conditioning. However, even the existence of second-order conditioning is of considerable significance because it greatly increases the range of situations in which classical conditioning can take place. With higher-order conditioning, classical conditioning can occur without a primary unconditioned stimulus. The only requirement is that a previously conditioned stimulus be available.

Many instances of conditioning in human experience involve higher-order conditioning. For example, money is a powerful conditioned stimulus for human behavior because of its association with candy, toys, movies, and other things it can buy. A child may become fond of his uncle if the uncle gives him some money on each visit. The positive conditioned emotional response to the uncle develops because the child comes to associate the uncle with money, in a case of second-order conditioning.

Second-order conditioning is also of interest as a technique for confirming the occurrence of first-order conditioning. Sometimes, first-order conditioning is not evident in a clear conditioned response even though the first-order CS can support second-order conditioning (Barnet, Arnold, & Miller, 1991; Bevins, Delzer, & Bardo, 1996; Cole & Miller, 1999).

Counterconditioning. Many instances of association learning, including higher-order conditioning, satisfy the criterion of differential biological strength. However, this criterion is not met in all situations that permit the learning of associations between stimuli. In **counterconditioning,** two stimuli can become associated with each other even though both elicit strong responses initially. The response an animal makes to a CS is reversed, or "countered," by pairing this stimulus with a US that promotes the opposite type of reaction.

In one study of counterconditioning (Pearce & Dickinson, 1975), the aversive properties of brief shock were reduced or reversed by pairing the shock with food. In the first phase of the experiment, rats in the counterconditioned group received shock periodically, but each shock delivery ended in a food pellet. Animals in control groups received the shocks and food pellets unpaired, or they received only one or the other of the USs. How these treatments changed the aversiveness of shock was then measured by using the shock in a conditioned-suppression procedure. As expected, the animals that previously had shock paired with food showed less conditioned suppression than the control groups. This result indicates that the counterconditioning procedure had reduced the aversive properties of the shock. (For other examples of counterconditioning, see Dickinson & Dearing, 1979.)

Sensory Preconditioning. Associations can also be learned between two stimuli, each of which elicits only a mild orienting response before conditioning. Consider, for example, the flavors vanilla and cinnamon that you often encounter together in pastry without ill effects. Because of these pairings, the vanilla and cinnamon flavors may become associated with one another. What would happen if you then acquired an aversion to cinnamon through food

BOX **4.2**

HIGHER-ORDER CONDITIONING OF FEAR

Irrational fears sometimes develop through higher-order conditioning. For example, Wolpe (1990) describes the case of a woman who initially developed a fear of crowds. How this fear had been originally conditioned is unknown, but crowds had become fear-eliciting stimuli. To avoid arousing her fear, the woman would go to the movies only in the daytime when few people were present. On one such visit, the theater suddenly became crowded with students. The woman became extremely upset by this, and came to associate movie houses with crowds. Thus, one fear-conditioned stimulus (crowds) had conditioned fear to other stimuli (movie houses) that previously were innocuous, as in higher-order conditioning. The remarkable aspect of this experience was that an aversion became conditioned to movie-house stimuli even though those cues had not been directly paired with an aversive unconditioned stimulus.

After her frightening experience in the movie house, the woman avoided going to the movies even when she was unlikely to encounter many other people there. Furthermore, her newly acquired fear of movie houses generalized to other public places, such as restaurants, churches, and public buildings. She also avoided these, even if they were empty.

poisoning or illness? Chances are your acquired aversion to cinnamon would also lead you to now reject foods with the taste of vanilla because of the prior association of vanilla with cinnamon. This is an example of **sensory preconditioning.**

The basic procedure for sensory preconditioning is diagrammed in Figure 4.5. In a sensory preconditioning experiment, subjects first receive repeated pairings of two biologically weak stimuli or CSs. The stimuli may be two visual cues—a triangle $\triangle$ and a square $\square$, for example. No response conditioning is evident in this phase of training. Neither the triangle $\triangle$ nor the square $\square$ comes to elicit a conditioned response. Conditioned behavior is acquired in the second phase of the experiment, in which the triangle $\triangle$ is now paired with an unconditioned stimulus, such as shock. With shock as the US, a conditioned fear response comes to be elicited by the triangle $\triangle$.

Once the triangle $\triangle$ has come to elicit conditioned fear, an interesting thing happens: the square $\square$ now also elicits this response because of its prior association with the triangle $\triangle$. Thus, the square $\square$ comes to elicit conditioned fear not because of its own pairings with shock but because its associated stimulus (the triangle $\triangle$) became paired with shock. The

Figure 4.5 Procedure for sensory preconditioning. First, CS_2 is paired with CS_1 without a US in the situation. Then, CS_1 is paired with a US and comes to elicit a conditioned response (CR). In a later test session, CS_2 is also found to elicit the CR, even though CS_2 was never paired with the US.

association of the two innocuous visual cues with each other becomes evident when one of the stimuli is later conditioned to elicit a vigorous response. (For additional examples of sensory preconditioning, see Berridge & Schulkin, 1989; Lavin, 1976; Rescorla & Durlach, 1981; Ward-Robinson & Hall, 1996, 1998.)

WHAT DETERMINES THE NATURE OF THE CONDITIONED RESPONSE?

In this chapter and in Chapter 3, I describe numerous examples of classical conditioning. In each of these examples, conditioning is identified by the development of new responses to the conditioned stimulus. I describe a variety of responses that can become conditioned, including salivation, eyeblinking, fear, locomotor approach and withdrawal, and aversion responses. I now address why one set of responses becomes conditioned in one situation and other responses are learned in other circumstances.

The Stimulus Substitution Model

The first and most enduring explanation for the nature of the conditioned response (CR) is Pavlov's **stimulus substitution** model. According to this model, the association of the CS with the US turns the CS into a surrogate US. The CS comes to function much like the US did previously. Thus, the CS is assumed to activate neural circuits previously activated only by the US and to elicit responses similar to the US.

Pavlov suggested that conditioning results in the establishment of new functional neural pathways (see Figure 4.6). During the course of repeated pairings of the conditioned and unconditioned stimuli, a new connection develops between the neural circuits previously activated by the CS and the circuits previously activated only by the US. Once this new connection has been established, presentation of the CS results in activation of the US circuits, which in turn generate the unconditioned response. Therefore, according to Pavlov's model, conditioning enables the CS to elicit the unconditioned response. The CS becomes a *substitute* for the US.

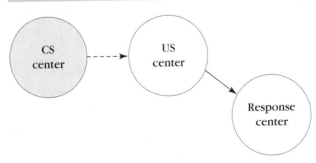

Figure 4.6 Diagram of Pavlov's stimulus substitution model. The solid arrow indicates preexisting neural connection. The dashed arrow indicates a learned neural connection. The CS comes to elicit a response by activating neural structures previously activated only by the US. Because of this, as conditioning progresses, the CS comes to elicit a response similar to the response to the US.

The US as a Determining Factor for the CR.   Different unconditioned stimuli elicit different unconditioned responses. Food elicits salivation and approach; shock elicits aversion and withdrawal. If conditioning turns a CS into a surrogate US, CSs conditioned with different USs should elicit different types of conditioned responses. This is obviously true. Animals learn to salivate when conditioned with food and to blink when conditioned with a puff of air to the eye. Salivation is not conditioned in eyeblink conditioning experiments, and eyeblink responses are not conditioned in salivary conditioning experiments.

Evidence that the nature of the conditioned response depends on the US is also available from more subtle comparisons. In one famous experiment, Jenkins and Moore (1973) compared Pavlovian conditioning in pigeons with food versus water as the US. A pigeon eating grain makes rapid, hard pecking movements directed at the grain with its beak open just before contact with the piece of grain. (The beak opening is related to the size of the grain about to be pecked.) By contrast, a pigeon drinks by lowering its beak into the water with the beak mostly closed. Once its beak is underwater, the bird opens it periodically to suck up the water (Klein, LaMon, & Zeigler, 1983). Thus, the unconditioned responses of eating and drinking differ in both speed and form. Jenkins and Moore (1973) were interested in whether responses conditioned with food and water would differ in a corresponding fashion.

The CS was illumination of a pecking key for 8 seconds. The CS was paired with either the presentation of grain or the access to water. Conditioning resulted in pecking of the key light in both cases. However, the form of the conditioned response differed depending on the US. When food was the US, the pigeons pecked the response key as if eating: the pecks were rapid, with the beak open at the moment of contact. With water as the US, the pecking movements were slower, made with the beak closed, and were often accompanied by swallowing. Thus, the form of the conditioned response resembled the form of the unconditioned response. Eating-like pecks occurred to the food-conditioned CS, and drinking-like responses occurred to the water-conditioned CS (see also Allan & Zeigler, 1994; Ploog & Zeigler, 1996; Ploog, 2001; Spetch, Wilkie, & Skelton, 1981; Stanhope, 1992). Similar findings have been obtained with food pellets and milk as unconditioned stimuli with laboratory rats (Davey & Cleland, 1982; Davey, Phillips, & Cleland, 1981).

Learning and Homeostasis: A Special Case of Stimulus Substitution

Proper functioning of the body requires that certain physiological parameters such as blood sugar, blood oxygen, and temperature be maintained within acceptable limits. For example, having a body temperature of 98.6 °F is so critical that substantial deviations from that value are considered symptoms of illness. The concept of **homeostasis** was introduced by Water Cannon to refer to physiological mechanisms that serve to maintain critical aspects of the body within acceptable limits.

How is a desired or homeostatic level achieved and defended against challenges? I described the concept of homeostasis in discussions of the opponent-process theory of motivation in Chapter 2. As I noted, maintaining any system within a desirable range requires that a disturbance that moves the system in one direction be met by opponent processes that counteract the disturbance. Thus, achieving homeostasis requires that a challenge to the homeostatic level trigger a compensatory reaction that will neutralize the disturbance. Consider, for example, homeostatic mechanisms of temperature regulation. In warm-blooded animals, any lowering of body temperature caused by exposure to cold reflexively triggers compensatory reactions that help to conserve and increase temperature. These compensatory reactions include peripheral vasoconstriction and shivering. The system operates through a *negative feedback loop*. A drop in body temperature is detected and this serves as a stimulus to activate compensatory responses.

Water Cannon lived from 1871 to 1945 and met Pavlov in 1923 when Pavlov visited the United States. They had considerable respect for each other's work, but it wasn't until more than half a century after both of them had died that Cannon's concept of homeostasis became integrated with studies of Pavlovian conditioning (Dworkin, 1993). Homeostatic mechanisms, as conceived by Cannon, operated by negative feedback processes that served to counteract a challenge after the disturbance had already caused a deviation from the homeostatic level. This can be rather inefficient, particularly if the corrective or compensatory process is slow to become activated. Dworkin (1993) pointed out that challenges to homeostasis can be met more effectively if those challenges are anticipated. Pavlovian conditioning provides the means for such feed-forward anticipation.

Consider, for example, exposure to cold. Feedback processes require that a drop in body temperature occur before compensatory shivering and vasoconstriction will occur to counteract the cold. However, if subjects can learn the cues that signal when they will get cold, they can make feed-forward compensatory adjustments in anticipation of the cold and thereby avoid suffering a drop in body temperature (Riccio, MacArdy, & Kissinger, 1991). According to this view, the conditioned response to a physiological challenge is the same as the reflexive compensatory response to the challenge. Thus, the conditioned response is the same as the unconditioned response, but the unconditioned response is considered to be the compensatory reaction to the physiological disturbance.

Conditioned homeostatic responses have been examined most extensively in studies of how organisms respond to the administration of a psychoactive drug (Poulos & Cappell, 1991; Ramsey & Woods, 1997; Siegel & Allan, 1998). (For studies of conditioned homeostatic mechanisms in color perception, see Siegel and Allan, 1998; for studies of Pavlovian feed-forward mechanisms in the control of social behavior, see Domjan, Cusato, & Villarreal, 2000.) Drugs often cause physiological challenges to homeostasis that trigger unconditioned compensatory reactions. Cues that become associated with the drug-induced physiological challenge can come to elicit these compensatory reactions as anticipatory or feed-forward conditioned responses. Drug craving in habitual drug users, for example, is a manifestation of these drug anticipatory conditioned responses.

It has been recognized for a long time that the administration of a drug constitutes a conditioning trial in which cues related to drug administration are paired with the pharmacological effects of the drug. Caffeine, for example, is a commonly used drug, whose pharmacological effects are typically preceded by the smell and taste of coffee. Thus, the taste and smell of coffee can serve as a conditioned stimulus that is predictive of the physiological effects of caffeine (for example, Flaten & Blumenthal, 1999). Studies of drug conditioning have been conducted with a wide range of pharmacological agents, including alcohol, heroin, morphine, and cocaine, and there has been considerable interest in how Pavlovian conditioning may contribute to drug tolerance, drug craving, and drug addiction (Baker & Tiffany, 1985; Cunningham, 1998; Siegel, 1983, 1989, 1999; Siegel, Baptista, Kim, McDonald, & Weise-Kelly, 2000).

Studies of drug conditioning have been conducted with both human and nonhuman animals and in laboratory and field settings. For example, in a study of naturally acquired drug-conditioned responses, Ehrman, Robbins, Childress, and O'Brien (1992) tested men with a history of freebasing and smoking cocaine (but no history of heroin use). A control group that had never used cocaine or heroin also provided data. The participants were observed under three test conditions. In one test, cues related to cocaine use were presented. The participants listened to an audiotape of people talking about their experiences freebasing and smoking cocaine, watched a videotape of people buying and using cocaine, and were asked to go through the motions of freebasing and smoking. In another test, cues related to heroin use were presented in the same manner as the cocaine stimuli. In the third

Courtesy of Donald A. Dewsbury

S. Seigel

test, control stimuli unrelated to drug use were presented. During each test, both physiological responses and self-reports of feelings were recorded.

Both the physiological measures and the self-reports of mood provided evidence that cocaine-related stimuli elicited conditioned responses. Figure 4.7 shows the results of measures of heart rate. Cocaine users exposed to cocaine-related stimuli experienced a significant increase in heart rate during the test. Furthermore, this increased heart rate response was specific to the cocaine-related stimuli. The heart rate of cocaine users did not change in response to heroin-related stimuli or nondrug stimuli. The increased heart rate response was also specific to the cocaine users. Participants in the control group did not show elevations in heart rate in any of the tests.

Participants with a history of cocaine use also reported feelings of cocaine craving and withdrawal elicited by the cocaine-related stimuli. They did not report these emotions in response to either the heroin-related or the nondrug stimuli. Feelings of cocaine craving and withdrawal were also not reported by participants in the control group. Thus, the results suggest that cocaine users acquired both physiological and emotional conditioned responses to cocaine-related stimuli during the course of their drug use.

The Conditioning Model of Drug Tolerance. The role of Pavlovian conditioning has been examined perhaps most extensively in relation to the development of **drug tolerance.** Tolerance to a drug is said to develop when repeated administrations of the drug have progressively less effect. Increasing doses are then required to produce the same drug effect. Drug tolerance has traditionally been considered to result from pharmacological processes. In contrast to this traditional approach, Shepard Siegel has proposed a model of drug tolerance based on classical conditioning.

The conditioning model takes advantage of the concepts of learned homeostasis. According to these concepts, the administration of a psychoactive drug causes physiological changes that disrupt homeostasis. Those physiological changes constitute the unconditioned stimulus that in turn triggers unconditioned compensatory adjustments to counteract the disturbance. These reflexive compensatory adjustments are the unconditioned

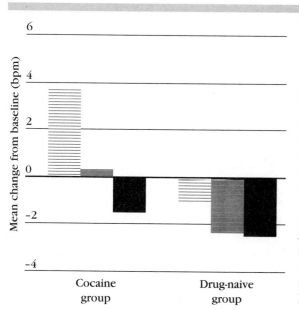

Figure 4.7 Mean change in heart rate from baseline levels for men with a history of cocaine use and a drug-naive control group during tests involving exposure to cocaine-related stimuli (light bars), heroin-related stimuli (medium bars), or nondrug stimuli (dark bars). (From "Conditioned Responses to Cocaine-Related Stimuli in Cocaine Abuse Patients," by R. N. Ehrman, S. J. Robbins, A. R. Childress, and C. P. O'Brien, 1992, *Psychopharmacology, 107,* pp. 523–529. Copyright © 1992 by Springer-Verlag. Reprinted by permission.)

response to the drug US. Through Pavlovian conditioning, stimuli that accompany the drug administration become associated with the drug US. These conditioned stimuli might be the time of day, the sensations involved in preparing a syringe, or the distinctiveness of the place where the drug is usually taken. As a result of association with the drug US, the drug administration cues come to elicit the drug compensatory responses that were previously triggered as unconditioned responses to the homeostatic challenge, and thereby come to attenuate the drug effects that were observed initially. Because the conditioned responses counteract the drug effects, the reaction otherwise elicited by the drug is reduced, resulting in drug tolerance (see Figure 4.8).

The conditioning model of drug tolerance attributes tolerance to compensatory responses conditioned to environmental stimuli paired with drug administration. A key prediction of the model is that drug tolerance will be attenuated if subjects receive the drug under novel circumstances or in the absence of the usual drug-predictive cues. The model also predicts that various factors (such as CS preexposure) that attenuate the development of conditioned responding should also attenuate the development of drug tolerance. These and other predictions of the conditioning model have been confirmed by Siegel and his colleagues, as well as by numerous other investigative teams in laboratory studies with opiates (morphine and heroin), alcohol, scopolamine, benzodiazepines, and amphetamine (see reviews by Siegel, 1989, 1999; Siegel & Allan, 1998; Stewart & Eikelboom, 1987).

When the conditioning model of drug tolerance was originally formulated, the assumption was that all drug-conditioned responses would be opposite the direct effects of the drug. However, as Siegel (1999) himself has acknowledged, this was an oversimplification. In the recently revised model (for example, Ramsey & Woods, 1997; Siegel, 1999), the initial effect of the drug is viewed as an unconditioned stimulus that triggers homeostatic compensatory reactions. The CS comes to elicit these compensatory URs. An important

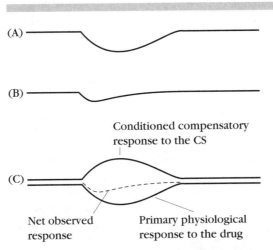

Figure 4.8 Diagram of the Pavlovian conditioning model of drug tolerance. The strength of the drug reaction is represented by deviations from the horizontal line. (A) Primary reaction to the drug before conditioning, illustrating the initial effects of the drug. (B) Attenuated reaction to the CS plus the drug after extensive experience with the drug, illustrating drug tolerance. (C) Components of the reaction after conditioning, showing that the net attenuated drug response is due to a conditioned compensatory response to the CS that counteracts the primary physiological change caused by the drug.

prediction of this view is that conditioned compensatory responses will develop only for physiological systems that are homeostatically controlled. Compensatory conditioned responses are not predicted in situations that lack homeostatic unconditioned responses.

The CS as a Determinant of the Form of the CR

The discussion thus far has considered how the form of the conditioned response is determined by the unconditioned stimulus. However, the US is not the only important factor. The form of the CR is also influenced by the nature of the CS. This was first illustrated by a rather unusual experiment by Timberlake and Grant (1975).

Timberlake and Grant investigated classical conditioning in rats with food as the US. Instead of a conventional light or tone, the CS was the presentation of another rat just before food delivery. One side of the experimental chamber was equipped with a sliding platform that could be moved in and out of the chamber through a flap door (see Figure 4.9). A live rat was gently restrained on the platform. Ten seconds before each delivery of food, the platform was moved into the experimental chamber, thereby transporting the stimulus rat through the flap door.

The stimulus-substitution model predicts that CS-US pairings will generate responses to the CS that are similar to responses elicited by the food US. Since the food US elicited gnawing and biting, these responses were also expected to be elicited by the CS. Contrary to prediction, the CS did not elicit gnawing and biting. Instead, as the CS rat was repeatedly paired with food, it came to elicit orientation, approach, and sniffing movements, as well as social contacts. Such responses did not develop if the CS rat was not paired with food or was presented at times unrelated to food.

The outcome of this experiment does not support any model that explains the form of the conditioned response solely in terms of the unconditioned stimulus that is used. The pattern of conditioned responses, particularly the social behavior elicited by the CS rat, was no doubt determined by the nature of the CS (see also Timberlake, 1983a). Other kinds of food-conditioned stimuli elicit different conditioned responses. For example, Peterson, Ackil, Frommer, and Hearst (1972) inserted an illuminated response lever into the experimental chamber immediately before presenting food to rats. With the protruding metal lever as the CS, the conditioned responses were "almost exclusively oral and consisted

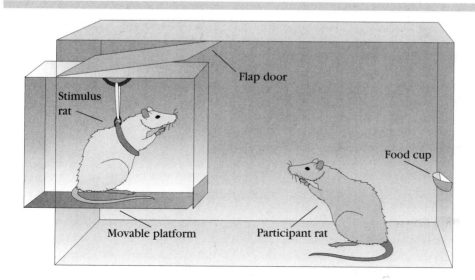

Figure 4.9 Diagram of the experiment by Timberlake and Grant (1975). The CS for food is presentation of a stimulus rat on a movable platform through a flap door on one side of the experimental chamber.

Flap door

Stimulus rat

Food cup

Movable platform

Participant rat

mainly of licking . . . and gnawing" (p. 1010). (For other investigations of how the CS determines the nature of the conditioned response, see Akins, 2000; Cusato & Domjan, 1998, 2000; Holland, 1977, 1980, 1984; Kim, Rivers, Bevins, & Ayres, 1996; Sigmundi & Bolles, 1983).

Conditioned Behavior and Behavior Systems

The approaches to the form of the conditioned response I have discussed so far have their intellectual roots in Pavlov's physiological model systems method for the study of learning. In this method, one or two responses are isolated for investigation and are used as indices of associative learning. This method continues to provide rich dividends in new knowledge, but it is becoming evident that complete understanding of the nature of conditioned behavior will require a broader perspective. Holland (1984), for example, has commented that the understanding of conditioned behavior will ultimately require "knowledge of the normal functions of behavior systems engaged by the various CSs, the natural, unlearned organization within those systems, and the ontogeny of those systems" (p. 164).

Different systems of behavior have evolved to enable animals to accomplish various critical tasks such as procuring and eating food, defending a territory, avoiding predation, producing and raising offspring, and so on. As I discussed in Chapter 2, each behavior system consists of a series of response modes, each with its own controlling stimuli and responses, arranged spatially and/or temporally. Consider, for example, the sexual behavior of male quail. When sexually motivated, the male will engage in a general search response to bring him into the vicinity of a female. Once there, he will engage in a more focal search response to actually locate her. Having found her, the male will then engage in courtship and copulatory responses. This sequence is illustrated in Figure 4.10.

Behavior systems theory assumes that the presentation of a US in a Pavlovian conditioning procedure activates the behavior system relevant to that US. Food unconditioned stimuli activate the foraging and feeding system. A sexual US, by contrast, will activate the sexual behavior system. Classical conditioning procedures involve superimposing a CS-US relationship on the behavioral system activated by the US. As a conditioned stimulus becomes associated with the US, it becomes integrated into the behavior system and comes to elicit component responses of that system. Thus, food-conditioned stimuli come to elicit components of the feeding system, and sexual conditioned stimuli come to elicit components of the sexual behavior system.

An especially provocative prediction of behavior systems theory is that the form of the CR will depend on the CS-US interval that is used. The CS-US interval is assumed to

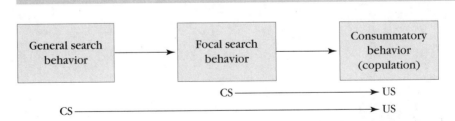

Figure 4.10 Sequence of responses, starting with general search and ending with copulatory behavior, that characterize the sexual behavior system. A conditioning procedure is superimposed on this behavior system. The CS-US interval determines where the CS becomes incorporated into the behavioral sequence.

determine where the CS becomes incorporated into the sequence of responses that makes up the behavior system.

Consider what might happen if a Pavlovian conditioning procedure were superimposed on the sexual behavior system. In the sexual conditioning of male quail, access to a female is the US. Access to the female activates the courtship and copulatory responses that characterize the end of the sexual behavior sequence. With a short CS-US interval, the CS occurs shortly before access to the female. If the CS becomes incorporated into the behavior system at this point, the CS should elicit focal search behavior: the male should approach and remain near the CS. The CR should be different if a long CS-US interval is used. In this case (see Figure 4.10), the CS should become incorporated into an earlier portion of the behavior system and elicit general search rather than focal search behavior. General search behavior should be manifest in increased nondirected locomotor behavior.

These predictions were recently tested in an experiment conducted with domesticated quail (Akins, 2000). Akins used a large rectangular experimental chamber. During each conditioning trial, a small visual CS was presented at one end either 1 minute before the male birds received access to a female or 20 minutes before the release of the female. Control groups were exposed to the CS and US in an unpaired fashion. To detect focal search behavior, Akins measured how much time the males spent close to the conditioned stimulus. To detect general search behavior, she measured pacing between one half of the experimental chamber and the other.

The results of the focal search and general search CR measures are presented in Figure 4.11. With a 1-minute CS-US interval, the conditioning procedure produced significant focal search but not general search behavior. In contrast, with the 20-minute CS-US interval, conditioning produced significant general search but not focal search responding. These results are precisely what is predicted by behavior systems theory. According to the theory,

C. K. Akins

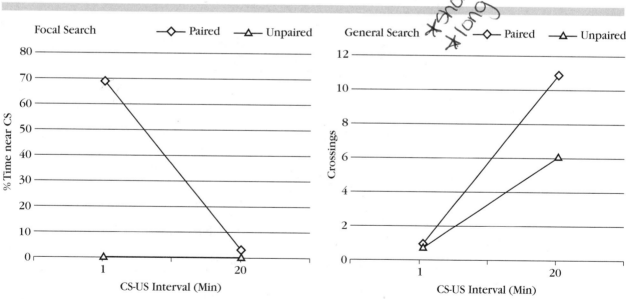

Figure 4.11 Effects of the CS-US interval on the conditioning of focal search and general search responses in male domesticated quail. When the CS-US interval was 1 minute, conditioning resulted in increased focal search behavior. When the CS-US interval was 20 minutes, conditioning resulted in increased general search behavior. (Adapted from Akins, 2000.)

the CS does not come to either substitute for or compensate for the US. Rather, the CS comes to substitute for a stimulus in the behavior system at a point that is determined by the CS-US interval. (For related studies, see Akins, Domjan, & Gutiérrez, 1994; Silva & Timberlake, 1997).

Behavior systems theory has been developed most extensively by William Timberlake (Timberlake, 1983a, 1983b, 2001; Timberlake & Lucas, 1989) and is consistent with much of what is known about the nature of classically conditioned behavioral responses. The theory is clearly consistent with the fact that the form of conditioned responses is determined by (1) the nature of the US, since different unconditioned stimuli activate different behavior systems; and (2) the nature of the conditioned stimulus. Certain types of stimuli are more effective than others in eliciting particular component responses of a behavior system. Therefore, the nature of the CS is expected to determine how the CS becomes incorporated into the behavior system (for example, Cusato & Domjan, 1998). Finally, behavior systems theory makes unique predictions about differences in conditioned behavior as a function of the CS-US interval.

S-R versus S-S Learning

I turn now to how a CS produces responding. Historically, conditioned behavior was viewed as a response elicited directly by the CS. According to **S-R learning,** conditioning establishes a new *stimulus-response* or S-R connection between the CS and the CR. A more contemporary alternative view is that subjects learn a new *stimulus-stimulus* or S-S connection between the CS and the US. According to the **S-S learning** view, subjects respond to the CS not because it elicits a CR directly but because the CS activates a representation of the US. In a sense, presentation of the CS makes the subject "think about" the US—these thoughts cause the conditioned behavior. Conditioned behavior is assumed to reflect the status of the US representation activated by the CS.

How might investigators decide between these two interpretations? One important research method used to decide between S-R and S-S learning involves the technique of **US devaluation,** which has been applied to a variety of issues in behavior theory. (I will describe applications of it in instrumental conditioning in Chapter 7.) Therefore, it is important to understand its rationale.

The basic strategy of a US devaluation experiment is illustrated in Figure 4.12. Holland and Rescorla (1975a), for example, first conditioned two groups of mildly food-deprived rats by repeatedly pairing a tone with pellets of food. This initial phase of the experiment was assumed to establish an association between the tone CS and the food US, as well as to get the rats to form a representation of the food US. Conditioned responding was evident in increased activity elicited by the tone.

In the next phase of the experiment, the experimental group received a treatment designed to make the US less valuable to them. This US devaluation was accomplished by giving the subjects sufficient free food to satisfy their hunger completely. Food satiation presumably reduces the value of food and thus devalues the US representation. The deprivation state of the control group was not changed in Phase 2; therefore, the US representation was assumed to remain intact for the control group (see Figure 4.12). Both groups then received a series of test trials with the tone-conditioned stimulus. During these tests, the experimental group showed significantly less conditioned responding than the control group. These results are indicative of S-S learning rather than S-R learning.

If conditioning had established a new reflex connection between the CS and the CR (an S-R connection), the CR would have been elicited whenever the CS occurred. That did

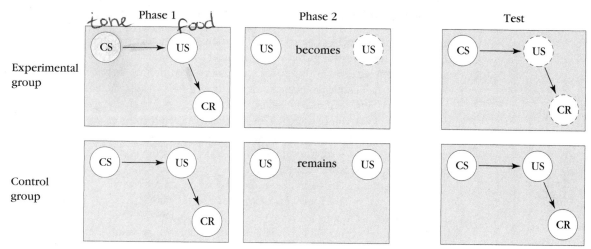

	Phase 1	Phase 2	Test
Experimental group	tone → food (CS → US → CR)	US becomes US	CS → US → CR
Control group	CS → US → CR	US remains US	CS → US → CR

Figure 4.12   Basic strategy and rationale involved in US-devaluation experiments. In Phase 1 the experimental and control groups receive conventional conditioning to establish an association between the CS and the US and to lead the participants to form a representation of the US. In Phase 2 the US representation is devalued for the experimental group but remains unchanged for the control group. If the CR is elicited by way of the US representation, devaluation of the US representation should reduce responding to the CS.

not happen. Instead, conditioning resulted in an association between the CS and a representation of the US (S-S learning). Presentation of the CS activated the US representation, and the CR depended on the status of that US representation.

Evidence of S-S learning is available from a variety of classical conditioning situations (for example, Cleland & Davey, 1982; Colwill & Motzkin, 1994; Holland & Straub, 1979; Holloway & Domjan, 1993; Kraemer, Hoffmann, Randall, & Spear, 1992; Rescorla, 1973; Hilliard, Domjan, Nguyen, & Cusato, 1998). However, not all instances of classical conditioning involve S-S learning. Participants in some cases appear to learn a direct association between the CS and the CR. Evidence for S-R learning comes from studies of second-order conditioning (for example, Holland & Rescorla, 1975a, 1975b). However, some instances of second-order conditioning involve S-S learning (Rashotte, Griffin, & Sisk, 1977; Rescorla, 1982b).

HOW DO CONDITIONED AND UNCONDITIONED STIMULI BECOME ASSOCIATED?

The issue of how conditioned and unconditioned stimuli become associated is a critical one. What are the mechanisms of association learning—the underlying processes that are activated by conditioning procedures to produce learning? This question has been the subject of intense scholarly work. The evolution of theories of classical conditioning continues today, as investigators strive to formulate comprehensive accounts of the mechanisms of association learning that can embrace all the diverse research results. (For recent reviews, see Pearce & Bouton, 2001; Hall, 1994; Mowrer & Klein, 2001; Wasserman & Miller, 1997).

The Blocking Effect

The modern era in theories of Pavlovian conditioning got under way about 35 years ago with the discovery of several provocative phenomena that stimulated the application of information processing ideas to the analysis of classical conditioning (for example, Rescorla, 1967b, 1968b; Wagner, Logan, Haberlandt, & Price, 1968). One of the most prominent of these phenomena was the **blocking effect.**

To get a sense of the blocking effect, consider the following scenario: Each Sunday afternoon you visit your grandmother, who always serves a rice pudding that slightly disagrees with you. Not wanting to upset her, you always eat the pudding, and you consequently acquire an aversion to rice pudding. One of the visits falls on a holiday, and to make the occasion a bit more festive, your grandmother serves tea cookies with the rice pudding. This time, as usual, you eat some of everything she serves, and as usual you get a bit sick to your stomach. Will you now learn an aversion to the tea cookies? Probably not. Knowing that rice pudding disagrees with you, you probably will attribute your illness to the proven culprit and not learn to dislike the tea cookies.

The blocking effect involves a similar sequence of events. First, an association is established between one conditioned stimulus (stimulus A) and the US. Once CS_A is well conditioned, a second stimulus (stimulus B) is added to stimulus A during the conditioning trials. The basic finding is that prior conditioning of stimulus A interferes with or blocks the development of conditioned responding to the added stimulus B.

The blocking effect was initially investigated using the conditioned suppression technique with rats (Kamin, 1968, 1969). Subsequently, the phenomenon has been demonstrated in various other conditioning preparations with both human and nonhuman animals (for example, Giftakis & Tait, 1998; Goddard, 1996; Khallad & Moore, 1996; Oades, Roepcke, & Schepker, 1996; Roberts & Pearce, 1999; Symonds & Hall, 1997). The basic procedure involves three phases and employs two conditioned stimuli, such as a tone and a light. In Phase 1 (see Figure 4.13), the experimental group receives repeated pairings of one of the stimuli (A) with the US. This phase of training is continued until a strong conditioned response develops to stimulus A. In Phase 2, stimulus B is presented together with stimulus A and paired with the US. After several such conditioning trials, stimulus B is presented alone in a test trial to see if it also elicits the conditioned response. Interestingly, very little responding occurs to stimulus B even though B was repeatedly paired with the US during Phase 2.

L. J. Kamin

Courtesy of L. J. Kamin

Figure 4.13 Diagram of the blocking procedure. During Phase 1, stimulus A is conditioned with the US in the experimental group, while the control group receives stimulus A presented unpaired with the US. During Phase 2, both experimental and control groups receive conditioning trials in which stimulus A is presented simultaneously with stimulus B and paired with the US. A later test of stimulus B alone shows that less conditioned responding occurs to stimulus B in the experimental group than in the control group.

BOX **4.3**

THE PICTURE-WORD PROBLEM
IN TEACHING READING:
A FORM OF BLOCKING

Early instruction in reading often involves showing children a written word, along with a picture of what that word represents. Thus, two stimuli are presented. The children have already learned what the picture is called (a "horse," for example). Therefore, the two stimuli in the picture-word compound include one that is already known (the picture) and one that is not (the word). This makes the picture-word compound much like the compound stimulus in a blocking experiment: a known stimulus is presented along with a new stimulus the child does not know. Research on the blocking effect predicts that the presence of the previously learned picture should disrupt learning about the word. Singh and Solman (1990) found that this occurs when using picture-word

compounds in teaching reading to mentally retarded students.

The children were taught to read words such as knife, lemon, radio, stamp, and chalk. Some of the words were taught using a variation of the blocking design in which the picture of the object was presented first and the student was asked to name it. The picture was then presented, together with its written word, and the student was asked, "What is that word?" In other conditions, the words were presented without corresponding pictures. All 8 students showed the slowest learning for the words that were taught in the blocking procedure. By contrast, 6 of the 8 students showed the fastest learning of the words that were taught without corresponding pictures. (The remaining 2 students learned most rapidly with a modified procedure.) These results suggest that processes akin to blocking may occur in learning to read. They also suggest that pictorial prompts should be used with caution in reading instruction because they may disrupt rather than facilitate learning. (See also Didden, Prinsen, & Sigafoos, 2000.)

The control group in the blocking design receives the same kind of conditioning trials with stimulus B as the experimental group (Phase 2 of Figure 4.13); that is, stimulus B is presented simultaneously with stimulus A. For the control group, however, stimulus A is not conditioned prior to these compound-stimulus trials. Rather, during Phase 1, the control group receives presentations of stimulus A and the US in an unpaired fashion. In many replications of this design, stimulus B invariably produced less conditioned responding in the experimental group than in the control group.

A recent study examined the blocking effect in a conditioned suppression procedure with college students in Spain (Acediano, Matute, & Miller, 1997). In the typical conditioned suppression procedure with laboratory rats, the subjects are periodically reinforced with food for pressing a response lever. In the study with college students, the task was a variation on a video game that required the students to repeatedly fire a "laser gun" to prevent invading Martians from landing. (The laser gun was the space bar.) To create suppression of this behavior, periodically an anti-laser shield was activated during which lots of Martians would land in large numbers if the subject continued to shoot. The presence of the anti-laser shield was indicated by a flashing light and constituted the unconditioned stimulus or US.

In Phase 1, presentations of the US were signaled by a visual CS that consisted of a change in the color of the background of the computer screen. In Phase 2, this visual CS was presented together with an auditory CS (a complex tone), and this stimulus compound ended with the US. For subjects in the experimental group, compound conditioning (in

Phase 2) was preceded by conditioning of the light alone (in Phase 1). In contrast, subjects in the control group received the light CS unpaired with the US in Phase 1. Subsequent tests of conditioned suppression to the tone CS after Phase 2 indicated that the experimental group showed significantly less conditioned suppression than the control group. The mean suppression ratio for the experimental group was 0.39 (standard error = .02). In contrast, the mean suppression ratio for the control group was 0.27 (standard error = .04). (Keep in mind that lower values of the suppression ratio indicate greater levels of conditioned suppression.)

Since the time of Aristotle, temporal contiguity has been considered the primary means by which stimuli become associated. The blocking effect has become a landmark phenomenon in classical conditioning because it called into question the assumption that temporal contiguity is sufficient for learning. The blocking effect clearly shows that pairings of a CS with a US are not enough for conditioned responding to develop. During Phase 2 of the blocking experiment, CS_B is paired with the US in an identical fashion for the experimental and the control groups. Nevertheless, CS_B comes to elicit vigorous conditioned responding only in the control group.

Why does the presence of the previously conditioned stimulus A block the acquisition of responding to the added cue B? Kamin, the originator of the blocking effect, explained the phenomenon by proposing that a US has to be surprising to be effective in producing learning. If the US is signaled by a previously conditioned stimulus (A), it will not be surprising and therefore will not function well in conditioning the added stimulus (B). Kamin reasoned that if the US is not surprising, it will not startle the animal and stimulate the "mental effort" needed for the formation of an association. Unexpected events are events to which the organism has not adjusted yet. Therefore, unexpected events activate processes leading to new learning. To be effective, the US has to be unexpected or surprising.

The Rescorla–Wagner Model

The idea that the effectiveness of an unconditioned stimulus is determined by how surprising it is forms the basis of a formal mathematical model of conditioning by Robert Rescorla and Allan Wagner (Rescorla & Wagner, 1972; Wagner & Rescorla, 1972). With the use of this model, the implications of the concept of US surprisingness were extended to a wide variety of conditioning phenomena. The Rescorla–Wagner model dominated research on classical conditioning for about 10 years after its formulation and continues to be used in a variety of areas of psychology (Siegel & Allan, 1996).

What does it mean to say that something is surprising? How might observers measure the surprisingness of an unconditioned stimulus? By definition, *an event is surprising if it is different from what is expected.* If you expect a small gift for your birthday and get a car, you will be very surprised. This is analogous to an unexpectedly large US. Correspondingly, if you expect a car and receive a box of candy, you will also be surprised. This is analogous to an unexpectedly small US. According to the Rescorla–Wagner model, an unexpectedly large US is the basis for excitatory conditioning or increases in associative value, and an unexpectedly small US is the basis for inhibitory conditioning or decreases in associative value.

Rescorla and Wagner assumed that the surprisingness, and hence the effectiveness, of a US depends on how different the US is from what the individual expects. They also assumed that expectation of the US is related to the conditioned or associative properties of the stimuli that precede the US. Strong conditioned responding indicates strong expectation that the US will occur; weak conditioned responding indicates a low expectation of the US.

These ideas can be expressed mathematically by using λ to represent the asymptote of learning possible with the US being used, and V to represent the associative value of the

A. R. Wagner

Courtesy of Donald A. Dewsbury

stimuli that precede the US. The surprisingness of the US will then be $(\lambda - V)$. The amount of learning on a given trial is assumed to be proportional to $(\lambda - V)$ or US surprisingness. The value of $(\lambda - V)$ is large at the start of learning (because V, the associative value of the stimuli preceding the US, is close to zero at this point). Hence, substantial increments in associative strength occur during early conditioning trials. Once the associative value of the cues that precede the US has increased, $(\lambda - V)$ will be small, and little additional learning will occur.

Learning on a given conditioning trial is the change in the associative value of a stimulus. That change can be represented as ΔV. Using these symbols, the idea that learning depends on the surprisingness of the US can be expressed as follows:

$$\Delta V = k(\lambda - V),$$

where "k" is a constant related to the salience of the CS and US. This is the fundamental equation of the Rescorla–Wagner model.

Application to the Blocking Effect. The basic ideas of the Rescorla–Wagner model clearly predict the blocking effect. In applying the model, it is important to keep in mind that expectations of the US are based on all of the cues available to the organism during the conditioning trial. As presented in Figure 4.13, the experimental group in the blocking design first receives extensive conditioning of stimulus A so that it acquires a perfect expectation that the US will occur whenever it encounters stimulus A. Therefore, V_A equals the asymptote of learning or λ ($V_A = \lambda$). In Phase 2, stimulus B is presented together with stimulus A, and the two CSs are followed by the US. According to the Rescorla–Wagner model, no conditioning of stimulus B will occur in Phase 2 because the US is now perfectly predicted by the presence of stimulus A: $(\lambda - V_{A+B}) = 0$.

The control group receives the identical training in Phase 2, but for them the presence of stimulus A does not lead to an expectation of the US. Therefore, the US in Phase 2 is surprising for the control group and produces new learning.

Loss of Associative Value Despite Pairings with the US. The Rescorla–Wagner model is consistent with fundamental facts of classical conditioning such as acquisition and the blocking effect. Much of the importance of the model, however, has come from its unusual predictions. One such prediction is that under certain circumstances the conditioned properties of stimuli will decline despite continued pairings with the US. How might this happen? Stimuli are predicted to lose associative value if they are presented together on a conditioning trial after having been trained separately. Such an experiment is outlined in Figure 4.14.

Figure 4.14 shows a 2-phase experiment. In Phase 1, stimuli A and B are paired with the same US (one pellet of food, for example) on separate trials. This continues until both A and B have been conditioned completely—until both stimuli predict perfectly the one-food-pellet US, or $V_A = V_B = \lambda$. Phase 2 is then initiated. In Phase 2, stimuli A and B are presented simultaneously for the first time, and this stimulus compound is followed by the same US—one food pellet. The question is, What happens to the conditioned properties of stimuli A and B as a result of the Phase 2 training?

Note that the same US that was used in Phase 1 continues to be presented in Phase 2. Given that there is no change in the US, informal reflection suggests that the conditioned properties of stimuli A and B should also remain unchanged during Phase 2. In contrast to this commonsense prediction, the Rescorla–Wagner model predicts that the conditioned properties of the individual stimuli A and B will decrease in Phase 2.

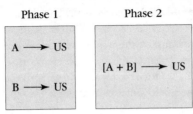

Figure 4.14 Loss of associative value despite continued presentations of the US. Stimuli A and B are conditioned separately to asymptote in Phase 1 so that each CS perfectly predicts the US. In Phase 2, stimuli A and B are presented simultaneously and paired with the same US that was used in Phase 1. This produces an overexpectation of the US. Because the delivered US is surprisingly small at the start of Phase 2, the conditioned properties of stimuli A and B decrease until the simultaneous presentation of the two CSs no longer produces the overexpectation.

As a result of training in Phase 1, stimuli A and B both come to predict the one-food-pellet US ($V_A = \lambda$; $V_B = \lambda$). When stimuli A and B are presented simultaneously for the first time, in Phase 2, the expectations based on the individual stimuli are assumed to add together, with the result that two food pellets are predicted as the US ($V_{A+B} = V_A + V_B = 2\lambda$). This is an overexpectation because the US remains only one food pellet. Thus, a discrepancy exists between what is expected (two pellets) and what occurs (one pellet). At the start of Phase 2, the participants find the US surprisingly small. To bring their expectations of the US in line with what actually occurs in Phase 2, the participants have to decrease their expectancy of the US based on stimuli A and B. Thus, stimuli A and B are predicted to lose associative value despite continued presentations of the same US. The loss in associative value is predicted to continue until the sum of the expectancies based on A and B equals one food pellet. The predicted loss of conditioned response to the individual stimuli A and B in this type of procedure is highly counterintuitive but has been verified experimentally (see Kremer, 1978; Khallad & Moore, 1996; Lattal & Nakajima, 1998; Rescorla, 1999b).

Conditioned Inhibition. How does the Rescorla–Wagner model explain the development of conditioned inhibition? Consider, for example, the standard inhibitory conditioning procedure (see Figure 3.10). This procedure involves two kinds of trials—trials on which the US is presented (reinforced trials), and trials on which the US is omitted (nonreinforced trials). On reinforced trials, a conditioned excitatory stimulus (CS+) is presented. On nonreinforced trials, the CS+ is presented together with the conditioned inhibitory stimulus, CS–.

Application of the Rescorla–Wagner model to such a procedure requires considering reinforced and nonreinforced trials separately. To accurately anticipate the US on reinforced trials, the CS+ has to gain excitatory properties. The development of such conditioned excitation is illustrated in the left-hand panel of Figure 4.15. Excitatory conditioning involves the acquisition of positive associative value and ceases once the organism predicts the US perfectly on each reinforced trial.

What happens on nonreinforced trials? Both the CS+ and the CS– occur. Once the CS+ has acquired some degree of conditioned excitation (because of its presentation on reinforced trials), the organism will expect the US whenever the CS+ occurs, including on nonreinforced trials. However, the US does not happen on nonreinforced trials. Therefore, this is a case of overexpectation, similar to the example illustrated in Figure 4.14. To accurately predict the absence of the US on nonreinforced trials, the associative value of the CS+ and the value of the CS– have to sum to zero (the value represented by no US). How can this be achieved? Given the positive associative value of the CS+, the only way to achieve a net zero expectation of the US on nonreinforced trials is to make the associative value of the CS– negative. Hence, the Rescorla–Wagner model explains conditioned inhibition by assuming that the CS– acquires negative associative value (see the left-hand panel of Figure 4.15).

Extinction of Excitation and Inhibition.   In an extinction procedure, the conditioned stimulus is presented repeatedly without the US. (I say more about extinction in Chapter 10.) Consider predictions of the Rescorla–Wagner model for extinction, illustrated in the right-hand panel of Figure 4.15. If a CS has acquired excitatory properties (see CS+ in Figure 4.15), there will be an overexpectation of the US the first time the CS is presented by itself in extinction. With continued CS-alone trials, the expectation elicited by the CS will be brought in line with the absence of the US by gradual reduction of the associative value of the CS+ to zero.

The Rescorla–Wagner model predicts an analogous scenario for extinction of conditioned inhibition. At the start of extinction, the CS– has negative associative value. This may be thought of as creating an underprediction of the US; the organism predicts less than the zero US that occurs on extinction trials. To bring expectations in line with the absence of the US, the negative associative value of the CS– is gradually lost and the CS– ends up with zero associative strength.

Figure 4.15   Predicted associative values of CS+ and CS– during the course of conditioned inhibition training (left) and extinction (right). During conditioned inhibition training, when the CS+ is presented alone, it is followed by the US; by contrast, when the CS+ is presented with the CS–, the US is omitted. The net associative value of CS+ and CS– is the sum of the associative values of the individual stimuli. During extinction, the conditioned stimuli are presented alone, and the US never occurs.

Problems with the Rescorla–Wagner Model. The Rescorla–Wagner model stimulated a great deal of research and led to the discovery of many new and important phenomena in classical conditioning (Siegel & Allan, 1996). Not unexpectedly, however, the model has also encountered some difficulties since it was proposed about 30 years ago (see Miller, Barnet, & Grahame, 1995).

One of the difficulties with the model that became evident early on is that its analysis of the extinction of conditioned inhibition is incorrect. The model (see Figure 4.15) predicts that repeated presentations of a conditioned inhibitor (CS−) by itself will lead to loss of conditioned inhibition, but this does not occur (Zimmer-Hart & Rescorla, 1974; Witcher & Ayres, 1984). On the contrary, some investigators have found that repeated nonreinforcement of a CS− can enhance its conditioned inhibitory properties (for example, DeVito & Fowler, 1987; Hallam, Grahame, Harris, & Miller, 1992). Curiously, an effective procedure for reducing the conditioned inhibitory properties of a CS− does not involve presenting the CS− at all. Rather, it involves extinguishing the excitatory properties of the CS+ with which the CS− was presented during inhibitory training (Best, Dunn, Batson, Meachum, & Nash, 1985; Lysle & Fowler, 1985). (For a more complete discussion of procedures for extinguishing conditioned inhibition, see Fowler et al., 1991.)

Another difficulty is that the Rescorla–Wagner model views extinction as the reverse of acquisition, or the return of the associative value of a CS to zero. A growing body of evidence indicates that extinction should not be viewed as simply the reverse of acquisition (see Chapter 10). Extinction appears to involve the learning of a new relationship between the CS and the US (namely, that the US no longer follows the CS).

Another puzzling finding that has been difficult to incorporate into the Rescorla–Wagner model is that under certain conditions, the same CS may have both excitatory and inhibitory properties (Barnet & Miller, 1996; Matzel, Gladstein, & Miller, 1988; McNish, Betts, Brandon, & Wagner, 1997; Robbins, 1990; Tait & Saladin, 1986; Williams & Overmier, 1988b). The Rescorla–Wagner model allows for conditioned stimuli to have only one associative value. That value can be excitatory or inhibitory, but not both.

Finally, the Rescorla–Wagner model has difficulty explaining recent findings obtained in taste- and odor-aversion learning. These experiments employed a 2-phase procedure very similar to the blocking design (Figure 4.13). In Phase 1, laboratory rats received one CS (taste or odor) paired with lithium-induced malaise to condition an aversion to that stimulus. In Phase 2, this previously conditioned stimulus was presented simultaneously with a new stimulus, and the compound was paired with lithium toxicosis. The CS added in Phase 2 was a novel odor for the taste-conditioned subjects and a novel taste for the odor-conditioned subjects. Thus, Phase 2 involved the presentation of an odor-taste compound, one component of which had been previously conditioned. Based on the blocking effect, researchers would expect that the presence of the previously conditioned CS would interfere with the conditioning of the CS that was added in Phase 2. Just the opposite result has been found—an **augmentation** or **contra-blocking effect** (Batsell, Paschall, Gleason, & Batson, 2001; Batsell & Batson, 1999; Batson & Batsell, 2000). Instead of disrupting conditioning of the added CS in Phase 2, the previously conditioned stimulus augmented the conditioning of the added CS. The augmentation, or contra-blocking effect, is a relatively new discovery and not much is known about its boundary conditions. However, it presents a serious challenge to the Rescorla–Wagner model, which was built on the opposite outcome, a blocking rather than a contra-blocking effect.

Other Models of Classical Conditioning

Devising a comprehensive theory of classical conditioning is a formidable challenge. Given the nearly 100 years of research on classical conditioning, a comprehensive theory must account for many diverse findings. No theory available today has been entirely successful in accomplishing that goal. Nevertheless, interesting new ideas about classical conditioning continue to be proposed and examined. Some of these proposals supplement the Rescorla–Wagner model; others are incompatible with it and move the theoretical debate in some startling new directions.

Attentional Models of Conditioning. In the Rescorla–Wagner model, how much is learned on a conditioning trial depends on the effectiveness of the unconditioned stimulus. Psychologists in North America have favored theories of learning that focus on changes in US effectiveness. In contrast, those in Great Britain have approached phenomena such as the blocking effect by postulating changes in how well the CS commands the subject's attention. The general assumption is that for conditioning to occur subjects have to pay attention to the CS. Procedures that disrupt attention to the CS are expected to also disrupt learning (Mackintosh, 1975; McLaren & Mackintosh, 2000; Pearce & Hall, 1980).

Attentional theories differ in their assumptions about what determines the salience, or noticeability, of the CS on a given trial. Pearce and Hall (1980), for example, assumed that how much attention an animal devotes to the CS on a given trial is determined by how surprising the US was on the preceding trial (see also Hall, Kaye, & Pearce, 1985; McLaren & Mackintosh, 2000). Animals to whom the US was surprising on the preceding trial have a lot to learn and will therefore pay closer attention to that CS on the next trial. In contrast, if a CS was followed by an expected US, the subject will pay less attention to that CS on the next trial. An expected US is assumed to decrease the salience or attention commanded by the CS.

Courtesy of Donald A. Dewsbury

N. J. Mackintosh

An important feature of attentional theories is that they assume that the surprisingness of the US on a given trial alters the degree of attention commanded by the CS on future trials. For example, if Trial 10 ends in a surprising US, that will increase the salience of the CS on Trial 11. Thus, US surprisingness is assumed to have only a *prospective* or *proactive* influence on attention and conditioning. This is an important contrast to US-reduction models such as the Rescorla–Wagner model, in which the surprisingness of the US on a given trial determines what is learned on that same trial.

The assumption that the US on a given trial influences only what is learned on the next trial has permitted attentional models to explain certain findings (for example, Mackintosh, Bygrave, & Picton, 1977). That assumption has made it difficult for the models to explain other results. In particular, the models cannot explain blocking that occurs on the first trial of Phase 2 of the blocking experiment (for example, Azorlosa & Cicala, 1986; Balaz, Kasprow, & Miller, 1982; Dickinson, Nicholas, & Mackintosh, 1983; Gillan & Domjan, 1977). According to attentional models, blocking occurs because in Phase 2 of the blocking experiment the lack of surprisingness of the US reduces attention to the added CS. Because that reduction in salience can occur only after the first Phase 2 trial, attentional models cannot explain the blocking that occurs on the first trial of Phase 2 of the blocking experiment.

Temporal Factors and Conditioned Responding. Neither the Rescorla–Wagner model nor CS modification models were designed to explain the effects of time in conditioning, although time is obviously a critical factor. One important temporal variable is the CS-US interval. As noted in Chapter 3, conditioned responding is inversely related to the CS-US interval or CS duration. Beyond an optimal point, procedures with longer CS-US intervals produce less responding (see Figure 3.8). This relation appears to be a characteristic primarily of responses closely related to the US (such as focal search). If behaviors that are ordinarily farther removed from the US are measured (such as general search), responding is greater with procedures that involve longer CS-US intervals (see Figure 4.11). Both types of

Courtesy of J. Gibbon

J. Gibbon

findings illustrate that the duration of the CS is an important factor in conditioning. (For other research on the importance of the CS-US interval in conditioning, see studies of the *temporal coding hypothesis,* Barnet, Cole, & Miller, 1997; Brown, Hemmes, & de Vaca, 1997; Cole, Barnet, & Miller, 1995; Savastano & Miller, 1998.)

Another important temporal variable is the interval between successive trials. In general, more conditioned responding is observed with procedures in which trials are spaced farther apart. Of greater interest, however, is the fact that the intertrial interval and the CS duration act in combination to determine responding. Numerous studies have shown that the critical factor is the relative duration of these two temporal variables rather than the absolute value of either one by itself (Gibbon & Balsam, 1981; Gallistel & Gibbon, 2000). A particularly clear example of this relationship was recently reported by Holland (2000).

Holland's experiment was conducted with laboratory rats. Food was presented periodically in a cup as the US, and presentations of the food were signaled by a CS that was white noise. Initially, the rats went to the food cup only when the food was delivered. As conditioning proceeded, they started going to the food cup as soon as they heard the noise CS. Thus, nosing of the food cup served as the anticipatory conditioned response. Each group was conditioned with one of two CS durations, either 10 seconds or 20 seconds, and one of six intertrial intervals (ranging from 15 seconds to 960 seconds). Each procedure could be characterized in terms of the ratio of the intertrial interval (I) and the CS duration, which Holland called the trial duration (T). The results of the experiment are summarized in Figure 4.16. Time spent nosing the food cup during the CS is shown as a function of the relative value of the intertrial interval (I) and the trial duration (T) for each group of subjects. Notice that conditioned responding was directly related to the I/T ratio. At each I/T ratio, the groups that received the 10-second CS responded similarly to those that received the 20-second CS. (For other recent studies of the role of the I/T ratio in conditioning, see Burns & Domjan, 2001; Kirkpatrick & Church, 2000; Lattal, 1999.)

Figure 4.16 Percent time rats spent nosing the food cup during an auditory CS in conditioning with either a 10-second or a 20-second trial duration (T) and various intertrial intervals (I) that created I/T ratios ranging from 1.5 to 48.0. Data are shown in relation to responding during baseline periods when the CS was absent. (From Figure 2, p. 125, P. C. Holland, in *Animal Learning & Behavior,* Vol. 28, Copyright 2000 Psychonomic Society, Inc. Reprinted with permission.)

Various interpretations have been offered for why conditioned responding is so strongly determined by the I/T ratio. An early explanation was the **relative waiting time hypothesis** (Jenkins, Barnes, & Barrera, 1981; see also scalar expectancy theory, Gibbon & Balsam 1981). This hypothesis was built on the assumption that a CS is informative about the occurrence of the US only if the subject has to spend less time waiting for the US when the CS is present than in the experimental situation irrespective of the CS. With a low I/T ratio, the CS waiting time is similar to the context waiting time. In this case, the CS provides little new information about when the US will occur, and not much conditioned responding will develop. In contrast, with a high I/T ratio, the CS waiting time is much shorter than the context waiting time. This makes the CS highly informative about when the US will occur, and conditioned responding will be more vigorous.

More recently, these ideas have been elaborated within the context of a comprehensive theory of temporal factors and conditioning in what is called *rate expectancy theory* (Gallistel & Gibbon, 2000). I discuss timing further in Chapter 12. It is now well accepted that organisms perceive and remember temporal aspects of a conditioning procedure (such as the intertrial interval and the CS duration) and that conditioned responding depends on decision processes that involve comparing these temporal variables. Originally, these temporal variables were considered to be performance factors that just influenced the behavioral manifestations of learning. It is now clear that they are directly involved in the basic learning processes themselves (Holland, 2000; Lattal, 1999).

The Comparator Hypothesis. The relative waiting time hypothesis and related theories were developed to explain certain temporal features of excitatory conditioning and manipulations of CS-US contingency. One of their important contributions was to emphasize that conditioned responding depends not only on what happens during the CS but also on what happens in the experimental situation in general. The idea that both of these factors influence many learning phenomena has been developed in greater detail by R. Miller and his collaborators in the **comparator hypothesis** (Denniston, Savastano, & Miller, 2001; Miller & Matzel, 1988, 1989).

The comparator hypothesis is similar to the relative waiting time hypothesis in assuming that conditioned responding depends not only on associations between a target CS and the US but also on possible associations that may be learned between contextual cues and the US. The associative strength of other cues present during training with the target CS is especially important. Another restriction of the comparator hypothesis is that it only allows for the formation of excitatory associations with the US. Whether conditioned responding reflects excitation or inhibition is assumed to be determined by the relative strengths of excitation conditioned to the target CS as compared to the excitatory value of the contextual cues that were present with the target CS during training.

The comparator process is represented by the balance in Figure 4.17. As Figure 4.17 illustrates, a comparison is made between the excitatory value of the target CS and the excitatory value of the other cues that are present during the training of the CS. If CS excitation exceeds the excitatory value of the contextual cues, the balance of the comparison will be tipped in favor of excitatory responding to the target CS. As the excitatory value of the other cues becomes stronger, the balance of the comparison will become less favorable for excitatory responding. If the excitatory value of the contextual cues becomes sufficiently strong, the balance may become tipped in favor of inhibitory responding to the target CS.

Unlike the relative waiting time hypothesis, the comparator hypothesis emphasizes associations rather than time. It assumes that organisms learn three associations during the course of conditioning (see Figure 4.18). The first association (Link 1 in Figure 4.18) is between the target CS (X) and the US. The second association (Link 2) is between the

M. Burns

P. D. Balsam

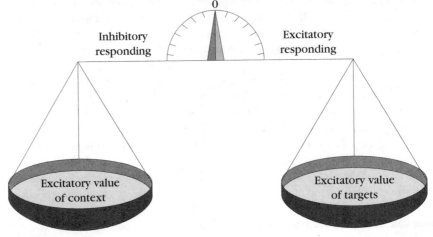

Figure 4.17 Illustration of the comparator hypothesis. Responding to the target CS is represented by the reading on the balance. If the excitatory value of the target CS exceeds the excitatory value of the other cues present during training of the target CS, the balance tips in favor of excitatory responding to the CS. As the associative value of the contextual cues increases, the comparison becomes less favorable for excitatory responding and may tip in favor of inhibitory responding.

R. R. Miller

target CS (X) and the comparator contextual cues. Finally, there is an association between the comparator stimuli and the US (Link 3). With all three links in place, once the CS is presented, it activates the US representation directly (through Link 1) and indirectly (through Links 2 and 3). A comparison of the direct and indirect activations determines the degree of excitatory or inhibitory responding that occurs.

It is important to note that the comparator hypothesis makes no assumptions about how associations become established. Rather, it describes how CS-US and context-US associations determine responding to the target CS. Thus, unlike US-modification and attentional models, the comparator hypothesis is a theory of *performance,* not a theory of learning.

An important corollary to the comparator hypothesis is that the comparison of CS-US and context-US associations is made at the time of testing for conditioned responding. Because of this assumption, the comparator hypothesis makes the unusual prediction that extinction of context-US associations following training of a target CS will enhance responding to that target CS. This prediction has been repeatedly confirmed (for example, Blaisdell, Gunther, & Miller, 1999; Cole, Oberling, & Miller, 1999; Miller, Barnet, & Grahame, 1992). US-modification and attentional theories of learning cannot explain such results.

The comparator hypothesis has also been tested in studies of conditioned inhibition (see Friedman, Blaisdell, Escobar, & Miller, 1998; Kasprow, Schachtman, & Miller, 1987; Schachtman, Brown, Gordon, Catterson, & Miller, 1987). The hypothesis attributes inhibitory responding to situations in which the association of the target CS with the US is weaker than the association of contextual cues with the US. The contextual cues in this case are the stimuli that provide the excitatory context for inhibitory conditioning. Interestingly, the hypothesis predicts that extinction of these conditioned excitatory stimuli following inhibitory conditioning will reduce inhibitory responding. Thus, the comparator hypothe-

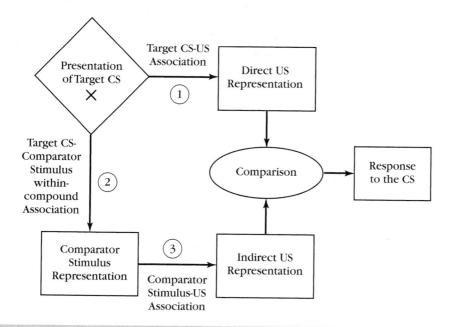

Figure 4.18 The associative structure of the comparator hypothesis. The target CS is represented as X. Excitatory associations result in activation of the US representation, either directly by the target (Link 1) or indirectly (through Links 2 and 3). (From Friedman et al., 1998.)

sis is unique in predicting that extinction of conditioned inhibition is best accomplished not by presenting the CS– alone but by extinguishing the CS+ cues that provided the excitatory context for inhibitory conditioning. As I noted earlier in the discussion of the extinction of conditioned inhibition, this unusual prediction has been confirmed (Best et al., 1985; Lysle & Fowler, 1985).

Although the comparator hypothesis has accurately predicted the results of studies involving extinction of contextual and other comparator cues after training, efforts to obtain the opposite effect have been less successful. The model predicts that increasing the excitatory value of contextual cues after training (Link 3 in Figure 4.18) will reduce conditioned responding to the target CS. A number of experiments have failed to find this outcome (Miller, Hallam, & Grahame, 1990; Robbins, 1988), but this failure is not universal. Furthermore, the negative findings are not entirely unexpected since increasing the excitatory value of the contextual cues may weaken the association between the target stimulus and the comparator (Link 2 in Figure 4.18) (see Denniston et al., 2001).

On balance, the comparator hypothesis has identified some important contextual constraints on conditioned responding. One of its major contributions has been to emphasize that differences in conditioned responding may reflect differences in performance rather than learning. In fact, it views even a robust phenomenon such as the blocking effect as a failure of performance rather than learning. It predicts, for example, that postconditioning extinction of a blocking stimulus will elevate conditioned responding to the blocked CS. Recent studies have verified this unusual prediction (Blaisdell et al., 1999). Given these successes, other theories of learning will have to address such postconditioning modulations of responding more successfully to be viable. Rate estimation theory (Gallistel & Gibbon, 2001) has risen to this challenge.

Overview of Theoretical Alternatives. Each of the new models I have described emphasizes a different aspect of classical conditioning. The relative waiting time hypothesis addresses a fairly small range of phenomena involving the temporal distribution of conditioned and unconditioned stimuli, although its successor (rate expectancy theory) is much more far-reaching. The comparator hypothesis is also ambitious, but it is a theory of performance rather than learning and therefore does not provide an explanation of how associations are acquired. Attentional models attempt to address the same wide range of phenomena as does the Rescorla–Wagner model, but they have some of the same difficulties as the Rescorla–Wagner model. All of these models have been important in directing attention to previously ignored aspects of classical conditioning. None of them has come to dominate the study of classical conditioning as the Rescorla–Wagner model did in the 1970s.

CONCLUDING COMMENTS

Initially, some psychologists regarded classical conditioning as a relatively simple and primitive type of learning that is involved in the regulation of only glandular and visceral responses, such as salivation. The establishment of CS-US associations was assumed to occur fairly automatically with the pairing of a CS and a US. Given the simple and automatic nature of the conditioning and its limitation to glandular and visceral responses, it was not viewed as important in explaining the complexity and richness of human experience. Clearly, this view of classical conditioning is no longer tenable.

The research reviewed in Chapters 3 and 4 has shown that classical conditioning involves numerous complex processes and is involved in the control of a wide variety of responses, including emotional behavior and approach-and-withdrawal responses. The learning does not occur automatically with the pairing of a CS with a US. It depends on the organism's prior experience with each of these stimuli, the presence of other stimuli during the conditioning trial, and the extent to which the CS and the US are relevant to each other. Furthermore, the processes of classical conditioning are not limited to CS-US pairings. Learned associations can occur between two biologically weak stimuli (sensory preconditioning), in the absence of an unconditioned stimulus (higher-order conditioning), or in the absence of conventional conditioned stimuli (counterconditioning).

Given these and other complexities of classical conditioning processes, it is a mistake to disregard classical conditioning in attempts to explain complex forms of behavior. The richness of classical conditioning mechanisms makes them relevant to the richness and complexity of human experience.

SAMPLE QUESTIONS

1. What, if any, limits are there on the kinds of stimuli that can serve as conditioned and unconditioned stimuli in Pavlovian conditioning?

2. How can Pavlovian conditioning mechanisms explain drug tolerance, and what are some of the implications of these mechanisms?

3. How can you distinguish between S-R and S-S learning experimentally?

4. Describe the basic idea of the Rescorla–Wagner model. What aspect of the model allows it to explain the blocking effect and make some unusual predictions?

5. In what respects are attentional theories of learning different from other theories?

6. How would the comparator hypothesis explain the blocking effect?

augmentation Facilitation of the conditioning of a novel stimulus because of the presence of a previously conditioned stimulus. Also called the *contra-blocking effect.*

blocking effect Interference with the conditioning of a novel stimulus because of the presence of a previously conditioned stimulus.

comparator hypothesis The idea that conditioned responding depends on a comparison between the associative strength of the conditioned stimulus (CS) and the associative strength of other cues present during training of the target CS.

conditioned homeostatic-response A conditioned response that is similar to the unconditioned homeostatic reactions that are elicited by some unconditioned stimuli.

contra-blocking effect Same as *augmentation.*

counterconditioning A conditioning procedure that reverses the organism's previous response to a stimulus. For example, an animal may be conditioned to approach a stimulus that initially elicited withdrawal reactions.

CS-preexposure effect Interference with conditioning produced by repeated exposures to the conditioned stimulus before the conditioning trials. Also called *latent-inhibition effect.*

drug tolerance Reduction in the effectiveness of a drug as a result of repeated use of the drug.

higher-order conditioning A procedure in which a previously conditioned stimulus (CS_1) is used to condition a new stimulus (CS_2).

homeostasis A concept introduced by Water Cannon to refer to physiological mechanisms that serve to maintain critical aspects of the body (such as blood sugar level and temperature) within acceptable limits. The homeostatic level is typically achieved by the operation of negative feedback mechanisms that serve to counteract the effects of challenges to the homeostatic level.

latent-inhibition effect Same as *CS-preexposure effect.*

relative waiting time hypothesis The idea that conditioned responding depends on how long the organism has to wait for the unconditioned stimulus (US) in the presence of the conditioned stimulus (CS), as compared to how long the organism has to wait for the US in the experimental situation irrespective of the CS.

S-R learning The learning of an association between a stimulus and a response, with the result that the stimulus comes to elicit the response. Same as *stimulus-response learning.*

S-S learning The learning of an association between two stimuli, with the result that exposure to one of the stimuli comes to activate a representation, or "mental image," of the other stimulus. Same as *stimulus-stimulus learning.*

sensory preconditioning A procedure in which one biologically weak stimulus (CS_2) is repeatedly paired with another biologically weak stimulus (CS_1). Then, CS_1 is conditioned with an unconditioned stimulus. In a later test trial, CS_2 also will elicit the conditioned response, even though CS_2 was never directly paired with the unconditioned stimulus.

stimulus-response learning Same as *S-R learning.*

stimulus-stimulus learning Same as *S-S learning.*

stimulus salience The significance or noticeability of a stimulus to the organism. In general, conditioning proceeds more rapidly with more salient conditioned and unconditioned stimuli.

stimulus substitution The theoretical idea that the outcome of classical conditioning is that organisms come to respond to the conditioned stimulus in much the same way that they respond to the unconditioned stimulus.

US-preexposure effect Interference with conditioning produced by repeated exposures to the unconditioned stimulus before the conditioning trials.

US devaluation Reduction in the attractiveness of an unconditioned stimulus, usually achieved by aversion conditioning or satiation.

INSTRUMENTAL CONDITIONING: FOUNDATIONS

 hapter 5 begins a discussion of instrumental conditioning and goal-directed behavior. In this type of conditioning, presentations of stimuli depend on the prior occurrence of designated responses. First, I describe the origins of research on instrumental conditioning and the investigative methods used in contemporary research. This discussion lays the groundwork for the section following, in which the four basic types of instrumental conditioning procedures are described. I conclude the chapter with a discussion of three fundamental elements of the instrumental conditioning paradigm: the instrumental response, the goal event, and the relation between the instrumental response and the goal event.

In the preceding chapters I described various aspects of how responses are elicited by discrete stimuli. Studies of habituation, sensitization, and classical conditioning are all concerned with analyses of the mechanisms of elicited behavior. Because of this emphasis, experiments on habituation, sensitization, and classical conditioning use procedures in which the organism has no control over the stimuli to which it is exposed. In this chapter, I turn to the analysis of learning situations in which the stimuli an organism encounters are a direct result of its behavior. Such behavior is commonly referred to as "goal-directed."

By studying hard, a student can earn a better grade in a class; by turning the car key in the ignition, a driver can start the engine; by putting a coin in a vending machine, a child can obtain a piece of candy. In all these instances, some aspect of the person's behavior is instrumental in producing a significant stimulus or outcome. Furthermore, the behavior occurs because similar actions produced the same type of outcome in the past. Students would not study if studying did not yield better grades; drivers would not turn the ignition key if this did not start the engine; and children would not put coins in a candy machine if they did not get candy in return. Behavior that occurs because it was previously instrumental in producing certain consequences is called **instrumental behavior.**

The fact that the consequences of an action can determine future occurrences of that action is obvious to everyone. If you happen to find a dollar bill when you glance down, you will keep looking at the ground as you walk. How such consequences influence future behavior is not so readily apparent. Much of the remainder of this text is devoted to a discussion of the mechanisms responsible for the control of behavior by its consequences. In this chapter, I describe some of the history, basic techniques, procedures, and issues in the experimental analysis of instrumental, or goal-directed, behavior.

How might instrumental behavior be investigated? One way would be to look for examples of goal-directed behavior in the natural environment. This approach, however, is not likely to lead to definitive results because factors responsible for goal-directed behavior are difficult to isolate without experimental manipulation.

Consider, for example, a dog sitting comfortably in its yard. When an intruder approaches, the dog starts to bark vigorously, with the result that the intruder goes away. Because the dog's barking has a clear consequence (departure of the intruder), it is tempting to conclude that the dog barked in order to produce this consequence—that barking was goal-directed. An equally likely possibility is that barking was elicited by the novelty of the intruder and persisted as long as the eliciting stimulus was present. The response consequence—departure of the intruder—may have been incidental to the dog's barking. Deciding between such alternatives is difficult without experimental manipulations of the relation between barking and its consequences. (For an experimental analysis of a similar situation in a fish species, see Losey & Sevenster, 1995).

The type of research I discuss in this chapter brings instrumental behavior into the laboratory. The idea, as with elicited behaviors, is to study representative instrumental responses in the hope of discovering general principles.

EARLY INVESTIGATIONS OF INSTRUMENTAL CONDITIONING

Laboratory and theoretical analyses of instrumental conditioning began in earnest with the work of E. L. Thorndike. Thorndike's original intent was to study animal intelligence (Thorndike, 1898, 1911; for recent commentaries, see Catania, 1999; Dewsbury, 1998;

Figure 5.1 Two of
Thorndike's puzzle boxes,
A and I. In Box A, the subject had to pull a loop to
elease the door. In Box I,
pressing down on a lever
eleased a latch on the other
side. *Left:* Chance (1999).
*ournal of Experimental
Analysis of Behavior, 72,*
433–440. Copyright 1999
by the Society for the
Experimental Analysis
of Behavior, Inc. *Right:*
Thorndike (1898). *Animal
ntelligence: Experimental
Studies.*

Lattal, 1998). As I noted in Chapter 1, the publication of Darwin's theory of evolution stimulated people to speculate about the extent to which human intellectual capacities were
present in animals. Thorndike pursued this question through empirical research. He devised
a series of puzzle boxes for his experiments. His training procedure consisted of placing a
hungry cat (or dog or chicken) in the puzzle box with some food left outside in plain view of
the animal. The task for the cat was to learn how to get out of the box and obtain the food.

Different puzzle boxes required different responses to get out, and some were easier
than others. Figure 5.1 illustrates two of the easier puzzle boxes. In Box A, the required
response was to pull a ring to release a latch that blocked the door on the outside. In Box I,
the required response was to press down on a lever, which released a latch. Initially, the subjects were slow to make the correct response, but with continued practice on the task, their
latencies became shorter and shorter. Figure 5.2 shows the latencies of a cat to get out of
Box A on successive trials. The cat took 160 seconds to get out of Box A on the first trial. Its
shortest latency later on was 6 seconds (Chance, 1999).

Thorndike's careful empirical approach was a significant advance in the study of "animal intelligence." Another important contribution was his strict avoidance of anthropo-
morphic interpretations of the behavior he observed. Although Thorndike titled his treatise
"Animal Intelligence," he thought many aspects of his subjects' behavior seemed rather
unintelligent. He did not think that the subjects got faster in escaping from a puzzle box
because they gained insight into the task or figured out how the release mechanism was
designed. Rather, Thorndike interpreted the results of his studies as reflecting the learning
of an S-R association. When a cat was initially placed in a box, it displayed a variety of
responses typical of a confined animal. Some of these responses eventually resulted in opening the door. Thorndike believed that such successful escapes led to the learning of an
association between the stimuli inside the puzzle box and the escape response. As the association, or connection, between the box cues and the successful response became stronger,

Box I

Box A

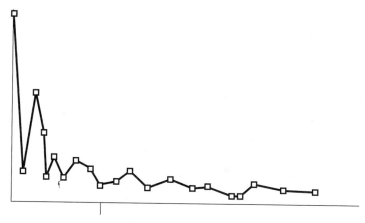

Figure 5.2 Latencies to escape from Box A during successive trials. The longest latency was 160 seconds; the shortest was 6 seconds. (Notice that the axes are not labeled, as in Thorndike's original report.)

the cat came to make that response more quickly. The consequence of the successful response—escaping the box—strengthened the association between the box stimuli and that response.

On the basis of his research, Thorndike formulated the **law of effect.** This law states that if a response in the presence of a stimulus is followed by a *satisfying event,* the association between the stimulus (S) and the response (R) is strengthened. If the response is followed by an *annoying event,* the S-R association is weakened. It is important to stress that according to the law of effect, animals learn an association between the response and the stimuli present at the time of the response. Notice that the consequence of the response is not one of the elements in the association. The satisfying or annoying consequence simply serves to strengthen or weaken the association, or bond, between the response and the stimulus situation. Thus, Thorndike's law of effect involves *S-R learning.*

MODERN APPROACHES TO THE STUDY OF INSTRUMENTAL CONDITIONING

Thorndike used 15 different puzzle boxes in his investigations. Each box required different manipulations for the cat to get out. As more scientists became involved in studying instrumental learning, the range of tasks they used became much smaller. A few of these became "standard" and have been used repeatedly to facilitate comparison of results obtained in different laboratories.

Discrete-Trial Procedures

Discrete-trial procedures are similar to the method Thorndike used in that each training trial ends with removal of the animal from the apparatus, and the instrumental response is performed only once during each trial. Discrete-trial investigations of instrumental behavior are often conducted in some type of maze. The use of mazes in investigations of learning was introduced at the turn of the twentieth century by the American psychologist W. S.

BOX **5.1**

E. L. THORNDIKE: BIOGRAPHICAL SKETCH

As an undergraduate at Wesleyan University, Edward Lee Thorndike (1874–1949) became interested in the work of William James, then at Harvard. Thorndike himself entered Harvard as a graduate student in 1895, where he began his research on instrumental behavior, at first using chicks. Having no laboratory space at Harvard, he set up his project in William James's cellar. He was soon offered a fellowship at Columbia University, where he located his laboratory in the attic of psychologist James Cattell.

Thorndike received his Ph.D. from Columbia in 1898, for his work entitled "Animal Intelligence: An Experimental Analysis of Associative Processes in Animals." This included the famous puzzle-box experiments. After a short stint at Western Reserve University in Cleveland, Thorndike returned to Columbia, where for many years he served as professor of educational psychology in the Teachers College. Among other things, he attempted to apply to children the principles of trial-and-error learning he had uncovered with animals. He also became interested in psychological testing and became a leader in this newly formed field. By the time of his retirement, he had written 507 scholarly works, about 50 of them books (Cumming, 1999). Several years before his death, Thorndike returned to Harvard as the William James Lecturer—a fitting honor considering the origins of his interests in psychology.

Small (1899, 1900). Small was interested in studying rats and decided to use a maze after reading an article in *Scientific American* that described the complex system of underground burrows that kangaroo rats build in their natural habitat. He reasoned that a maze would take advantage of the rats' "propensity for small winding passages."

Figure 5.3 shows two mazes frequently used in contemporary research. The runway or straight-alley maze contains a start box at one end and a goal box at the other. The rat is placed in the start box at the beginning of each trial. The movable barrier separating the start box from the main section of the runway is then lifted. The rat is allowed to make its way down the runway until it reaches the goal box, which usually contains a reinforcer, such as food or water.

Another frequently used maze is the T-maze, shown on the right in Figure 5.3. The T-maze consists of a start box and alleys arranged in the shape of a T. A goal box is located at the end of each arm of the T. Because it has two goal boxes, the T maze is well suited to studying choice behavior. For example, one goal box may be baited with plain food and the other with food flavored with artificial sweetener. By seeing which arm the rat chooses over a series of trials, the experimenter can measure preference for one food over the other.

Behavior in a maze can be quantified by measuring the **running speed**—how fast the animal gets from the start box to the goal box. The running speed typically increases with repeated training trials. Another common measure of behavior in runways is the **latency**—the time it takes the animal to leave the start box and begin moving down the alley. Typically, latencies become shorter as training progresses.

Free-Operant Procedures

In a runway or a T-maze, after reaching the goal box, the animal is removed from the apparatus for a while before being returned to the start box for its next trial. The animal conse-

Removable
barrier

Figure 5.3   Top view of a runway and a T-maze. S is the start box; G is the goal box.

quently has limited opportunities to respond, and those opportunities are scheduled by the experimenter. By contrast, **free-operant** procedures allow the animal to repeat the instrumental response over and over again without constraint. The free-operant method was devised by B. F. Skinner (1938) to study behavior in a more continuous manner than is possible with mazes.

Skinner (Figure 5.4) was interested in analyzing in the laboratory a form of behavior that would be representative of all naturally occurring ongoing activity. He recognized, however, that before behavior can be experimentally analyzed, a measurable unit of behavior must be defined. Casual observation suggests that ongoing behavior is continuous; one activity leads to another. Behavior does not fall neatly into units as do molecules of a chemical solution. Skinner proposed the concept of the operant as a way of dividing behavior into meaningful measurable units.

Figure 5.5 shows a typical Skinner box used to study free-operant behavior in rats. (A Skinner box used to study pecking in pigeons is presented in Figure 1.5.) The box is a small chamber that contains a lever that the rat can push down repeatedly. The chamber also has a mechanism that can deliver a reinforcer, such as food or water. In the simplest experiment, a hungry rat is placed in the chamber. The lever is electronically connected to the food-delivery system. When the rat depresses the lever, a pellet of food automatically falls into the food cup.

An **operant response,** such as the lever press, is defined in terms of the effect that it has on the environment. Activities that have the same environmental effect are considered to be instances of the same operant response. The critical thing is not the muscles involved in the behavior but the way in which the behavior "operates" on the environment. For example, the lever-press operant in rats is typically defined as sufficient depression of the lever to cause the closure of a microswitch. The rat may press the lever with its right paw, its left paw, or its tail. These different muscle responses constitute the same operant if they all

Figure 5.4 B. F. Skinner
(1904–1990)

depress the lever the required amount. Various ways of pressing the lever are assumed to be functionally equivalent because they all have the same effect on the environment—namely, closing the microswitch.

Magazine Training and Shaping. Most rats, when placed in a Skinner box, do not press the lever frequently. There are some preliminary steps for establishing the lever-press behavior. First, the animals have to learn when food is available in the food cup. This involves classical conditioning: the sound of the food-delivery device is repeatedly paired with the delivery of a food pellet into the cup. The food-delivery device is called the *food magazine.* After enough pairings of the sound of the food magazine with the food delivery, the sound comes to elicit a sign tracking response: the animal goes to the food cup and picks up the food pellet. This preliminary phase of conditioning is called **magazine training.**

After magazine training, the organism is ready to learn the required instrumental response. If the response is not something the animal already does occasionally, it may never happen on the response that produces the reinforcer on its own. To facilitate the acquisition of a new operant response, experimenters employ a strategy that has been used by animal trainers for centuries. At first, food is given if the animal does anything remotely related to the desired response. For example, at first a rat may be given a food pellet each time it gets up on its hind legs anywhere in the experimental chamber. Once the rearing response has been established, the food pellet may be given only if the rat makes the rearing response over the response lever. Rearing in other parts of the chamber would no longer be reinforced. Once rearing over the lever has been established, the food pellet may be given only after the rat actually depresses the lever. Such a sequence of training steps is called **shaping.** Shaping

Omikron/Photo Researchers, Inc.

Figure 5.5 A Skinner box equipped with a response lever and a food-delivery device. Electronic equipment is used to program procedures and record responses automatically.

involves two complementary tactics: *reinforcement of successive approximations* to the required response and *nonreinforcement of earlier response forms.*

As illustrated in the preceding example, the shaping of a new operant requires training response components or approximations to the final behavior. Once an operant response such as lever pressing has become established, the manner in which the organism accomplishes the required operation on the environment does not matter. Nevertheless, the steps used in shaping the behavior continue to influence how the response is made. For example, if rearing was one of the reinforced approximations during shaping, the rat is likely to continue to rear as it presses the lever (Stokes & Balsam, 1991). With extensive training, responding becomes more efficient and comes to involve less energy expenditure (Brener & Mitchell, 1989; Mitchell & Brener, 1991).

Shaping and New Behavior. Shaping procedures are often used to generate new behavior, but exactly how new are those responses? Consider, for example, a rat's lever-press response. To press the bar, the rat has to approach the bar, stop in front of it, raise its front paws, and then bring the paws down on the bar with sufficient force to push it down. All of these response components are things the rat is likely to have done at one time or another in other situations (while exploring its cage, interacting with another rat, or handling pieces of food). In teaching the rat to press the bar, the investigator is not teaching new response components. He or she is teaching the rat how to combine familiar responses into a new activity. Instrumental conditioning often involves the construction or synthesis of a new behavioral unit from preexisting response components that already occur in the subject's repertoire (Balsam, Deich, Ohyama, & Stokes, 1998; Reid, Chadwick, Dunham, & Miller, 2001; Schwartz, 1981).

Instrumental conditioning can also be used to produce responses unlike anything the individual is likely to do without training. Consider, for example, throwing a football 60 yards down the field. It takes more than putting familiar behavioral components together to achieve such a feat. The force, speed, and coordination involved in throwing a

131

football 60 yards is unlike anything an untrained individual might do. It is an entirely new response. Expert performance in sports, in playing a musical instrument, or in ballet involves novel response forms. Such novel responses are also created by shaping.

In a laboratory study, for example, Deich, Allan, and Zeigler (1988) shaped the gape response of pigeons pecking for food reinforcement. As I pointed out in Chapter 4, pigeons peck for food with their beaks opened a bit. Deich et al. used a special transducer to measure how far the birds opened their beaks as they pecked a response key. In a baseline phase, the pigeons were reinforced for pecking irrespective of the size of their gape. In another phase of the experiment, food was provided only if their beaks were opened wider than a criterion value. The criterion was chosen based on the previous day's performance so that at least 20% of the birds' pecks would be reinforced. As the birds met each new criterion, the criterion was made more stringent, thereby shaping the birds to peck with increasingly wider gapes. In a comparable manner, decreases in the gape response were shaped in another phase of the experiment.

Figure 5.6 shows the results for one pigeon. During the baseline phase, when reinforcement was independent of the bird's gape, the pigeon made intermediate gape responses. After the shaping procedure in which the criterion for reinforcement required progressively wider gapes, the pigeon learned to peck with its beak opened wider. By contrast, after shaping in which the criterion for reinforcement involved progressively smaller gapes, the pigeon learned to peck with its beak more tightly closed. These changes occurred fairly rapidly. The data in the middle panel of Figure 5.6 were obtained during the 5th

Figure 5.6   Ilustration of the shaping of gape size in pigeons. Each panel shows the relative frequency of gapes of various sizes observed in the pecking behavior of a pigeon. During the baseline phase (top panel), pecking was reinforced with food irrespective of the size of the gape. In the other phases, pecking was reinforced only if it occurred with gapes that either exceeded a progressively increasing criterion (middle panel) or were less than a progressively decreasing criterion (bottom panel). (From "Conjunctive Differentiation of Gape During Food-Reinforced Keypecking in the Pigeon," by J. D. Deich, R. W. Allan, and H. P. Zeigler, 1988, *Animal Learning & Behavior, 16,* pp. 268–276. Copyright © 1988 by the Psychonomic Society. Reprinted by permission.)

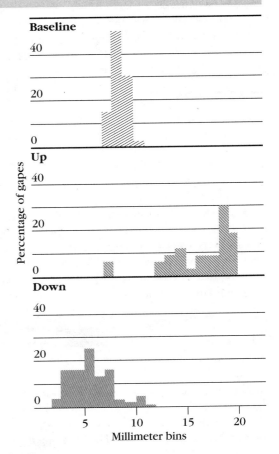

training session, and the data in the bottom panel came from the 7th session of that condition. (Each session had 32 trials.)

The results presented in Figure 5.6 illustrate several important aspects of the process of shaping. Most responses are like the gape response in that they occur with some variability. The gape response was most uniform during the baseline phase. However, even then, the pigeon pecked with gapes of 7 to 10 mm. This variability in responding helps to ensure that at least a few responses occur that are in the direction you may want to shape the behavior. Thus, *shaping takes advantage of the inherent variability of behavior.* Without such variability, shaping procedures could not succeed. (For a recent study of response variability and shaping, see Stokes, Mechner, & Balsam, 1999.)

When a gape-size criterion was introduced, the distribution of gape sizes shifted in the direction of the reinforcement criterion. Presenting food only if the gape exceeded a certain size, for example, served to shift the distribution of gape sizes to higher values. It was important to set each new criterion so that at least some of the pigeon's existing responses could be reinforced. For example, the first shaping criterion could not have been set at 15 mm because during the baseline phase the pigeon never made a peck with its beak more than 10 mm apart.

As the criterion for reinforcement was gradually shifted during shaping, the pigeon's responses shifted correspondingly. Eventually, the pigeon started making responses that it had never displayed prior to training. For example, after the pigeon was trained to peck with progressively larger gapes, it pecked with its beak opened 20 mm some of the time. By contrast, during the baseline phase, gapes had never exceeded 10 mm. In an analogous fashion, shaping of small gapes produced pecks with gapes as small as 4 mm, which had never been observed during the baseline phase. These aspects of the results illustrate that *shaping can produce new response forms,* forms never before performed by the organism. (For additional discussions of shaping, see Galbicka, 1988; Midgley, Lea, & Kirby, 1989; Pear & Legris, 1987; Platt, 1973.)

Response Rate as a Measure of Operant Behavior. In contrast to discrete-trial techniques for studying instrumental behavior, free-operant methods permit continuous observation of behavior over long periods. With continuous opportunity to respond, the organism rather than the experimenter determines the frequency of its instrumental response. Hence, free-operant techniques provide a special opportunity to observe changes in the likelihood of behavior over time.

How might a researcher take advantage of this opportunity and measure the probability of an operant response? Measures of response latency and speed that are commonly used in discrete-trial procedures do not characterize the likelihood of repetitions of a response. Skinner proposed that the *rate of occurrence* of operant behavior (frequency of the response per minute, for example) be used as a measure of response probability. Highly likely responses occur frequently and have a high rate. In contrast, unlikely responses occur seldom and have a low rate.

INSTRUMENTAL CONDITIONING PROCEDURES

In all instrumental conditioning situations, the subject makes a response and thereby produces an outcome. Paying the boy next door for mowing the lawn, yelling at a cat for getting on the kitchen counter, closing a window to prevent the rain from coming in, and canceling a teenager's driving privileges for staying out late are all forms of instrumental

test question

TABLE 5.1	TYPES OF INSTRUMENTAL CONDITIONING PROCEDURES	
NAME OF PROCEDURE	**RESPONSE-OUTCOME CONTINGENCY**	**RESULT**
Positive reinforcement	*Positive:* Response produces an appetitive stimulus	*Reinforcement* or increase in response rate
Punishment (positive punishment)	*Positive:* Response produces an aversive stimulus	*Supression* or decrease in response rate
Negative reinforcement (escape or avoidance)	*Negative:* Response eliminates or prevents the occurrence of an aversive stimulus	*Reinforcement* or increase in response rate
Omission training (DRO)	*Negative:* Response eliminates or prevents the occurrence of an appetitive stimulus	*Supression* or decrease in response rate

conditioning. Two of these examples involve pleasant events (getting paid, driving a car) whereas the other two involve unpleasant stimuli (the sound of yelling, and rain coming in the window). A pleasant outcome is technically called an **appetitive stimulus.** An unpleasant outcome is technically called an **aversive stimulus.** The instrumental response may turn on the stimulus, as when the boy next door gets paid for mowing the lawn. In this case a *positive contingency* is said to be in effect between the response and its stimulus outcome. Alternatively, the instrumental response may turn off or eliminate a stimulus, as in closing a window to stop the incoming rain. In that case a *negative contingency* is said to be in effect between the response and its outcome. Whether the result of a conditioning procedure is an increase or a decrease in the rate of responding depends both on response-outcome contingency and on the nature of the outcome.

Table 5.1 describes four common instrumental conditioning procedures. The procedures differ in what type of stimulus (appetitive or aversive) is controlled by the instrumental response and whether the response produces or eliminates the stimulus.

Positive Reinforcement. A father gives his daughter a cookie when she puts her toys away; a teacher praises a student when the student hands in a good report; an employee receives a bonus check when he performs well on the job. These are all examples of **positive reinforcement.** Positive reinforcement is a procedure in which the instrumental response turns on or produces an appetitive stimulus. If the response occurs, the appetitive stimulus is presented; if the response does not occur, the appetitive stimulus is not presented. Thus, a positive contingency exists between the instrumental response and the appetitive stimulus. Positive reinforcement produces an increase in the rate of responding. Giving a hungry rat a food pellet whenever it presses a response lever but not when it does not press the lever is a common laboratory example of positive reinforcement.

Punishment. A mother reprimands her child for running into the street; your boss criticizes you for being late to a meeting; your teacher gives you a failing grade for answering too many test questions incorrectly. These are examples of **punishment.** In a *punishment* procedure, the instrumental response produces or turns on an unpleasant, or aversive, stimulus.

There is a positive contingency between the instrumental response and the stimulus outcome, but the outcome is an aversive stimulus. Effective punishment procedures produce a decline in the instrumental response.

Negative Reinforcement.   Both positive reinforcement and punishment involve a positive contingency between the instrumental response and the stimulus outcome. I now turn to procedures that involve a *negative contingency* between the instrumental response and an environmental event. In a negative contingency, the response turns off or prevents the presentation of the environmental event. A procedure in which the instrumental response terminates or prevents the delivery of an *aversive* stimulus is called **negative reinforcement.**

There are two types of negative reinforcement procedures: escape and avoidance. In **escape,** the aversive stimulus is present but can be terminated by the instrumental response. You may escape the unpleasant static of a radio by turning it off. People may leave a movie theater to escape the experience of a bad movie. In the laboratory, a rat may be exposed to a continuous loud noise at the beginning of a trial. By jumping over a barrier or pressing a lever, the rat can escape the noise. In all these cases, the presence of the aversive stimulus sets the occasion for the instrumental response. The instrumental response is then reinforced by termination of the aversive stimulus.

Avoidance involves an aversive stimulus that is scheduled to be presented sometime in the future. In this case the instrumental response prevents delivery of the aversive stimulus. People do many things to prevent the occurrence of something bad. Students study before an examination to avoid receiving a bad grade; factory workers may avoid injury by responding to a fire alarm; people get their cars tuned up regularly to avoid unexpected breakdowns. In the laboratory, a rat may be scheduled to receive shock at the end of a warning stimulus. However, if the rat makes the instrumental response during the warning stimulus, the shock will not be delivered. I have more to say about avoidance behavior in Chapter 10.

Omission Training.   Another type of procedure that involves a negative contingency between the instrumental response and an environmental event is called **omission training.** In this case, the instrumental response prevents the delivery of a pleasant or an appetitive stimulus. Omission training is often a preferred method of discouraging human behavior because, unlike punishment, it does not involve delivering an aversive stimulus. Omission training is being used when a child is told to go to his room after doing something bad. The child does not receive an aversive stimulus when he is told to go to his room. There is nothing aversive about the child's room. Rather, by sending the child to the room, the parent is withdrawing sources of positive reinforcement, such as playing with friends or watching television. Suspending a person's driver's license for drunken driving also constitutes omission training (withdrawal of the pleasure and convenience of driving).

Omission training procedures are sometimes called **differential reinforcement of other behavior,** or **DRO.** This term highlights the fact that the individual periodically receives the appetitive stimulus provided he is engaged in behavior other than the response specified by the procedure. Making the target response results in omission of the reward that would have been delivered had the individual performed some "other" behavior. Thus, omission training involves the reinforcement of "other" behavior.

The terms used to describe instrumental conditioning procedures are a bit confusing. For example, people tend to confuse negative reinforcement and punishment. Although an aversive stimulus is used in both procedures, the relation of the instrumental response to the aversive stimulus in each is drastically different. In what is commonly called punishment, a positive contingency exists between the instrumental response and the aversive stimulus.

BOX **5.2**

OMISSION TRAINING AS A THERAPEUTIC PROCEDURE

Omission training, or differential reinforcement of other behavior (DRO), involves the delivery of an appetitive stimulus when the individual fails to perform the target response. Therefore, such procedures can be used to discourage undesired responses. In one study (Barton, Brulle, & Repp, 1986), omission training was used with mentally retarded students of elementary school age. The reinforcers were things like apples, raisins, grapes, and juice. One student engaged in recurrent handflapping (moving the hand up and down or back and forth). The rate of this behavior was first observed under baseline conditions (in the absence of special intervention) for 12 days. Then, an omission training (DRO) procedure was introduced for the next 29 days. Omission training consisted of providing a reinforcer whenever a 1-minute period elapsed without any handflapping. The omission training phase was then followed by return to the baseline condition, followed by reintroduction of omission training.

The results of the study are summarized in Figure 5.7. During the first baseline phase, the student engaged in handflapping about once a minute. This rate of responding declined to near zero during the first omission training (DRO) phase. Removal of the omission procedure resulted in recovery of the handflapping response. Reintroduction of omission training at the end of the study produced another decline in responding. Interestingly, responding dropped to close to zero faster the second time the omission contingency (DRO) was introduced. These results indicate that omission training is an effective procedure for suppressing responding. Omission training or DRO procedures have also been used successfully to suppress self-injurious behavior and aggression in individuals diagnosed with mental retardation (Lindberg et al., 1999; Progar et al., 2001).

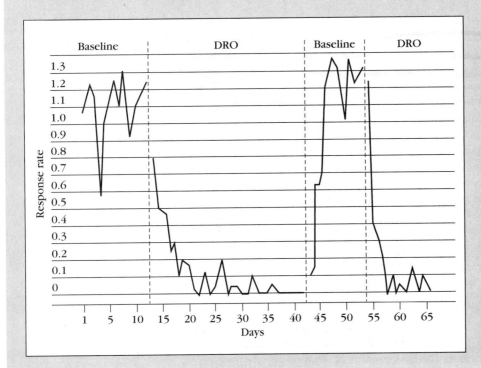

Figure 5.7 Rate of handflapping (responses per minute) by a mentally retarded student during baseline conditions, when reinforcement was not provided, and during omission training phases (DRO), when reinforcement was provided for 1-minute periods without handflapping. (From "Maintenance of Therapeutic Change by Momentary DRO," by L. E. Barton, A. R. Brulle, and A. C. Repp, 1986, *Journal of Applied Behavior Analysis, 19,* 277–282. Copyright © 1986 by the *Journal of Applied Behavior Analysis.* Reprinted by permission.)

(The response results in delivery of the aversive stimulus.) By contrast, in negative rein-forcement, there is a negative response-outcome contingency. (The response either termi-nates or prevents the delivery of the aversive stimulus.) This difference in the contingencies produces very different outcomes. The instrumental response is decreased by punishment and increased by negative reinforcement.

FUNDAMENTAL ELEMENTS OF INSTRUMENTAL CONDITIONING

As I show in the coming chapters, analysis of instrumental conditioning involves numerous factors and variables. However, the essence of instrumental behavior is that it is controlled by its consequences. Instrumental conditioning involves three key elements: a response, an outcome (the reinforcer), and a relation, or contingency, between the response and the out-come. In the remainder of this chapter, I describe how each of these elements influences the course of instrumental conditioning.

The Instrumental Response

The outcome of instrumental conditioning procedures depends in part on the nature of the response being conditioned. Some responses are more easily modified than others. In Chap-ter 10, I describe how the nature of the response influences the outcome of negative rein-forcement (avoidance) and punishment procedures. The following section describes how the nature of the response determines the results of positive reinforcement procedures.

Behavioral Variability versus Stereotypy.   Thorndike described instrumental behavior as involving the "stamping in" of an S-R association. Skinner wrote about behavior being "re-inforced" or strengthened. Both pioneers emphasized that reinforcement increases the like-lihood that the instrumental response will be repeated in the future. This emphasis encouraged the belief that instrumental conditioning produces repetitions of the same re-sponse—that it produces uniformity or stereotypy in behavior. Increasingly stereotyped re-sponding does develop if that is allowed or required by the instrumental conditioning procedure (for example, Pisacreta, 1982; Schwartz, 1980, 1985, 1988.) However, that does not mean that instrumental conditioning cannot also be involved in producing creative or variable responses.

We are accustomed to thinking about the requirement for reinforcement being an observable action, such as movement of an individual's leg, torso, or hand. Interestingly, however, the criteria for reinforcement can also be defined in terms of more abstract dimen-sions of behavior, such as its variability. For example, organisms can learn to obtain rein-forcement in a situation where they are required to do something new, something unlike what they did on the preceding four or five trials. *Response variability* can be the basis for instrumental reinforcement.

In one study of the instrumental conditioning of response variability (Page & Neuringer, 1985), pigeons had to peck two response keys eight times to obtain food. The eight pecks could be distributed between the two keys in any manner. All the pecks could be on the left or the right key, or the pigeons could alternate between the keys in various ways (two pecks on the left, followed by one on the right, one on the left, three on the right, and one on the left, for example). However, to obtain food on a given trial, the

Courtesy of A. Neuringer

A. Neuringer

sequence of left-right pecks had to be different from the pattern of left-right pecks the bird made on the preceding 50 trials. Thus, the pigeons had to generate novel patterns of left-right pecks and not repeat any pattern for 50 trials. In a control condition, food was provided at the same frequency for eight pecks distributed between the two keys, but now the sequence of right and left pecks did not matter. The pigeons did not have to generate novel response sequences in the control condition.

Sample results of the experiment are presented in Figure 5.8 in terms of the percentage of response sequences performed during each session that were different from each other. Results for the first and last 5 days on each procedure are presented separately. About 50% of the response sequences performed were different from each other during the first five sessions of each procedure. When the instrumental conditioning procedure required response variability, variability in responding increased to about 75%. By contrast, in the control condition, when the pigeons were reinforced regardless of the sequence of left-right pecks they made, variability in performed sequences dropped to less than 20%.

This study illustrates two interesting facts about instrumental conditioning. First, it shows that variability in responding can be maintained and increased by reinforcement. Thus, response variability can be established as an operant (see also Machado, 1989, 1992; Morgan & Neuringer, 1990; Morris, 1987; Neuringer, 1991, 1992, 1993; Neuringer, Deiss, & Olson, 2000). The results also show that in the absence of explicit reinforcement

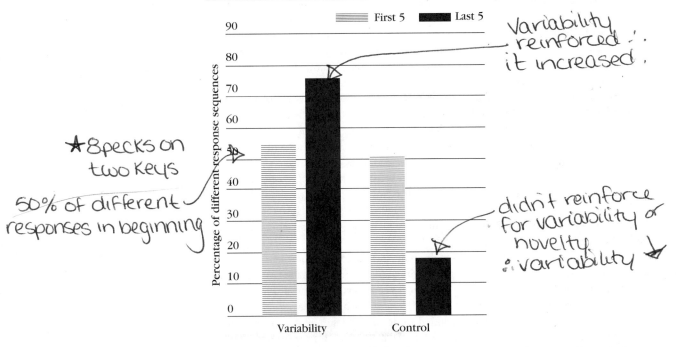

Figure 5.8 Percentage of novel left-right response sequences pigeons performed when variability in response sequences was required for food reinforcement (left) and when food reinforcement was provided regardless of the response sequence performed (right). Data are presented separately for the first five and last five sessions of each procedure. (After "Variability as an Operant," by S. Page and A. Neuringer, 1985, *Journal of Experimental Psychology: Animal Behavior Process, 11,* 429–452. Copyright © 1985 by the American Psychological Association).

[handwritten note at top:] rewarding children diminishes it's intrinsic value: not always true. But will if reinforcers are given irrespective of behavior
*rewarding everyone @ Bingo

BOX 5.3

DETRIMENTAL EFFECTS OF REWARD: MORE MYTH THAN REALITY

Reinforcement procedures have become commonplace in educational settings as a way to encourage students to read and do their assignments. However, some have been concerned that reinforcement may actually undermine a child's intrinsic interest and willingness to perform a task once the reinforcement procedure is removed (for example, Lepper, Greene, & Nisbett, 1973). Similar concerns have been expressed about possible detrimental effects of reinforcement on creativity or originality. Extensive research on these questions has produced inconsistent results. However, a meta-analysis of nearly 100 studies indicated that overall there is little evidence to support the claim that reinforcement undermines intrinsic motivation or performance (Cameron & Pierce, 1994). The only circumstance in which reinforcement consistently undermined performance was if the reward was given irrespective of behavior. Research with children also indicated that reinforcement makes children respond with less originality only under special circumstances (see Eisenberger & Cameron, 1996). Reinforcement can increase or decrease originality, depending on the criterion for reinforcement. If highly original responding is required to obtain reinforcement, originality increases, provided that the reinforcer is not so salient as to distract the participant from the task. (For a discussion of how such contingencies and other task constraints promote creativity in gifted children and artists, see Stokes, 2001.)

[handwritten note:] *being rewarded on effort alone

of variability, responding becomes more stereotyped with continued instrumental conditioning. Pigeons in the control condition decreased the range of different response sequences they performed as training progressed. Thus, the typical consequence of instrumental reinforcement is a decrease in response variability. (For other conditions that decrease response variability, see Cherot, Jones, & Neuringer, 1996.)

Relevance or Belongingness in Instrumental Conditioning.   As the preceding section showed, instrumental conditioning can act on overt response components or on abstract dimensions of behavior (such as variability). How far do these principles extend? Are there any limits on the types of new behavioral units or response dimensions that may be modified by instrumental conditioning? A growing body of evidence indicates that there are important limitations.

In Chapter 4, I described how classical conditioning occurs at different rates depending on the combination of CS and US that is used. Rats readily learn to associate tastes with sickness, for example, whereas associations between tastes and shock are not so easily learned. For conditioning to occur rapidly, the CS has to "belong" with the US, or be "relevant" to the US. Analogous belongingness, or relevance, relations occur in instrumental conditioning.

Thorndike was the first to observe differences in the ease of conditioning of various responses. In many of the puzzle-box experiments, the cat had to manipulate a latch or a string to escape from the box. Thorndike also tried to condition scratching and yawning as instrumental responses. The cats could learn to make these responses, but, interestingly, the form of the responses changed as training proceeded. At first, the cat would scratch itself vigorously to be let out of the box. On later trials, it would only make "aborted" scratching movements. It might put its leg to its body but would not make a true scratch response.

Similar results were obtained in attempts to condition yawning. As training progressed, the animal would open its mouth to be let out of the box, but it would not give a bona fide yawn.

Thorndike proposed the concept of **belongingness** to explain the failures to train scratching and yawning. According to this concept, certain responses naturally "belong with" the reinforcer because of the animal's evolutionary history. Operating a latch and pulling a string are manipulatory responses that are naturally related to release from confinement. By contrast, scratching and yawning characteristically do not help animals escape from confinement and therefore do not "belong with" release from a puzzle box. Presumably, this is why scratching and yawning do not persist as vigorous bona fide instrumental responses when reinforced by release from the box.

The concept of belongingness in instrumental conditioning is well illustrated by a more recent study involving a small fish species, the three-spined stickleback (*Gasterosteus aculeatus*). During the mating season each spring, male sticklebacks establish territories from which they court females but chase away and fight other males. Sevenster (1973) used the presentation of another male or a female as a reinforcer in instrumental conditioning of male sticklebacks. One group of fish was required to bite a rod to obtain access to the reinforcer. Biting is a component of the aggressive behavior that occurs when a resident male encounters an intruder male. When the reinforcer was another male, biting behavior increased; access to another male was an effective reinforcer for the biting response. By contrast, biting did not increase when it was reinforced with courtship opportunity. However, courtship opportunity was an effective reinforcer for other responses, such as swimming through a ring. A belongingness relation evidently exists between biting and the consequent presentation of another male, but biting does not "belong with" presentation of a female, which typically elicits courtship rather than aggression.

Various limitations on instrumental conditioning were also observed by Breland and Breland (1961) in attempts to condition instrumental responses with food reinforcement in several species. Their goal was to train animals to perform entertaining response chains for displays to be used in amusement parks and zoos. During the course of this work, they observed dramatic behavior changes that were not consistent with the reinforcement procedures they were using. For example, they describe a raccoon that was reinforced for picking up a coin and depositing it in a coin bank.

> We started out by reinforcing him for picking up a single coin. Then the metal container was introduced, with the requirement that he drop the coin into the container. Here we ran into the first bit of difficulty: he seemed to have a great deal of trouble letting go of the coin. He would rub it up against the inside of the container, pull it back out, and clutch it firmly for several seconds. However, he would finally turn it loose and receive his food reinforcement. Then the final contingency: we [required] that he pick up [two] coins and put them in the container.
>
> Now the raccoon really had problems (and so did we). Not only could he not let go of the coins, but he spent seconds, even minutes, rubbing them together (in a most miserly fashion), and dipping them into the container. He carried on this behavior to such an extent that the practical application we had in mind—a display featuring a raccoon putting money in a piggy bank—simply was not feasible. The rubbing behavior became worse and worse as time went on, in spite of nonreinforcement. (p. 682)

From "The Misbehavior of Organisms," by K. Breland and M. Breland, 1961. In *American Psychologist, 16,* 682.

The Brelands had similar difficulties with other species. Pigs, for example, also could not learn to put coins in a piggy bank. After initial training, they began rooting the coins

M. Breland-Bailey

Courtesy of Donald A. Dewsbury

Raccoons are adept at doing some things, like tearing up a package, but it is difficult to condition them to drop coins into a container for food reinforcement.

along the ground. The Brelands called the development of such responses as rooting in the pigs and rubbing coins together in the raccoons **instinctive drift.** As the term implies, the extra responses that developed in these food reinforcement situations were activities the animals instinctively perform when obtaining food. Pigs root along the ground in connection with feeding, and raccoons rub and dunk food-related objects. These natural food-related responses were apparently very strong and competed with the responses required by the experimenter. The Brelands emphasized that such instinctive response tendencies have to be taken into account in the analysis of behavior.

Behavior Systems and Constraints on Instrumental Conditioning. The response limitations on instrumental conditioning I have described are consistent with behavior systems theory, which I described in Chapter 4, in discussions of the nature of the conditioned response (see Timberlake, 1983a, 2001; Timberlake & Lucas, 1989). According to behavior systems theory, when an animal is food-deprived and is in a situation where it might encounter food, its feeding system becomes activated, and it begins to engage in foraging and other food-related activities. An instrumental conditioning procedure is superimposed on this behavior system. The effectiveness of the procedure in increasing an instrumental response will depend on the compatibility of that response with the preexisting organization of the feeding system. Furthermore, the nature of other responses that emerge during the course of training (or instinctive drift) will depend on the behavioral components of the feeding system that become activated by the instrumental conditioning procedure.

According to the behavior systems approach, we should be able to predict which responses will increase with food reinforcement by studying what animals do when their feeding system is activated in the absence of instrumental conditioning. This prediction has been confirmed. In a study of hamsters, Shettleworth (1975) found that food deprivation decreases the probability of self-care responses, such as face washing and scratching, but increases the probability of environment-directed activities, such as digging, scratching at a wall (scrabbling), and rearing on the hind legs. These results suggest that self-care responses (face washing and scratching) are not part of the feeding system activated by hunger,

S. J. Shettleworth

whereas environment-directed activities (digging, scrabbling, and rearing) are part of the feeding system. Given these findings, behavior systems theory predicts that food reinforcement should produce increases in digging, scrabbling, and rearing but not increases in face washing and scratching. This pattern of results is precisely what has been observed in studies of instrumental conditioning (Shettleworth, 1975). Thus, the susceptibility of various responses to food reinforcement can be predicted from how those responses are altered by food deprivation, which presumably reflects their compatibility with the feeding system.

As discussed in Chapter 4, another way to diagnose whether a response is a part of a behavior system is to perform a classical conditioning experiment. Through classical conditioning, a CS comes to elicit components of the behavior system activated by the US. If instinctive drift reflects responses of the behavior system, responses akin to instinctive drift should be evident in a classical conditioning experiment. Timberlake and his associates (see Timberlake, 1983b; Timberlake, Wahl, & King, 1982) tested this prediction with rats in a modification of the coin-handling studies conducted by Breland and Breland.

The apparatus used by Timberlake et al. (1982) delivered a ball bearing into the experimental chamber at the start of each trial. The floor of the chamber was tilted so that the ball bearing would roll from one end of the chamber to the other and exit through a hole. In one experimental condition, the rats were required to make contact with the ball bearing to obtain food reinforcement. Other conditions employed a classical conditioning procedure: food was provided after the ball bearing rolled across the chamber whether or not the rat touched the ball bearing. Consistent with the behavior systems view, in both procedures the rats came to touch and extensively handle the ball bearings instead of letting them roll into the hole. (Some animals picked up the bearing, put it in their mouth, carried it to the other end of the chamber, and sat and chewed it.) Such instinctive drift developed with both instrumental and classical conditioning procedures. These results indicate that touching and handling the ball bearing are manifestations of the feeding behavior system in rats. Thus, instinctive drift represents the intrusion of responses appropriate to the behavior system activated during the course of instrumental conditioning. (For additional research on the implications of behavior systems for instrumental conditioning, see Timberlake, 1983b; Timberlake & Washburne, 1989).

The Instrumental Reinforcer

Several aspects of a reinforcer determine its effects on the learning and performance of instrumental behavior. I first discuss the direct effects of the quantity and quality of a reinforcer on instrumental behavior. I then describe how responding to a particular reward amount and type depends on the organism's past experience with other reinforcers.

Quantity and Quality of the Reinforcer. Although the quantity and quality of the reinforcer are logically different characteristics, sometimes it is difficult to separate them experimentally. A change in the quantity of the reinforcer may also make the reinforcer qualitatively different. In a systematic study, Hutt (1954) tried to isolate the effects of the quantity and quality of a liquid food reinforcer by systematically varying both features. Independent groups of rats were trained to press a response lever to receive either small, medium, or large amounts of a fluid mixture of water, milk, and flour. Some of the rats were tested with the basic mixture; others were given a mixture that had been improved by adding saccharin. For yet other groups of rats, the quality of the fluid was reduced by adding a small amount of citric acid. Figure 5.9 shows the average rate of bar pressing for each group. Increases in either the quality or the quantity of the reinforcer produced higher rates of responding.

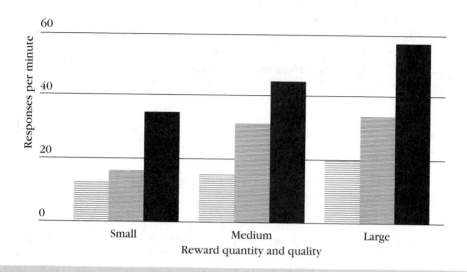

Figure 5.9 Average rates of responding in groups of rats for which responding was reinforced with reinforcers varying in quantity and quality. (From "Rate of Bar Pressing as a Function of Quality and Quantity of Food Reward," by P. J. Hutt, 1954, *Journal of Comparative and Physiological Psychology, 47,* pp. 235–239.)

Results similar to the findings of Hutt are typically obtained in runway experiments (see Mackintosh, 1974, for a review). Rats, for example, run faster for larger and more palatable reinforcers. In free-operant situations, however, the effects of reinforcer magnitude are more complex and depend on the schedule of reinforcement used and other factors (for example, Bizo, Kettle, & Killeen, 2001; Collier, Johnson, & Morgan, 1992; Leslie, Boyle, & Shaw, 2000; Reed, 1991; Reed & Wright, 1989). (I discuss schedules of reinforcement in Chapter 6.)

Shifts in Reinforcer Quality or Quantity. In the study by Hutt (1954), a given group of rats received only one particular quantity and quality of liquid food throughout the experiment. What would happen if the quantity or quality of the reinforcer were shifted from one value to another for the same individual? This is an interesting question because it raises the possibility that the effectiveness of a reinforcer depends not only on its own properties but also on how that reinforcer compares with others the individual has experienced.

I noted in Chapter 4 that the effectiveness of an unconditioned stimulus in classical conditioning depends on how the US compares with the individual's expectations based on prior experience. This idea serves as the foundation of the Rescorla–Wagner model. If the US is larger (or more intense) than expected, it will support excitatory conditioning. By contrast, if the US is smaller (or weaker) than expected, it will support inhibitory conditioning. Are there analogous effects in instrumental conditioning? Common experience suggests definitely yes. If you have been working for $9.50 per hour for the past 6 months, getting that rate of pay will not be too exciting. However, if you have been working for $7.50/hr, an increase to $9.50/hr will be especially attractive. Experimental evidence confirms these impressions. Numerous studies have shown that the effects of a particular amount and type of reinforcer depend on the quantity and quality of the reinforcers the individual experienced previously. (For reviews, see Flaherty, 1982, 1991, 1996.) Speaking loosely, a favorable reward is treated as especially good after reinforcement with a poor

Courtesy of Donald A. Dewsbury

R. L. Mellgren

reward, and an unfavorable reward is treated as especially poor after reinforcement with a good reward.

Effects of a shift in the quantity of reward were first described by Crespi (1942). The basic results are also nicely illustrated by a more recent study by Mellgren (1972), in which four groups of rats served in a runway experiment. During Phase 1, two of the groups received a small reward (S: 2 food pellets) each time they reached the end of the runway. The other two groups received a large reward (L: 22 pellets) for each trip down the runway. (Delivery of the food was always delayed for 20 seconds after the rats reached the end of the runway so that they would not run at their maximum speed.) After 11 trials of training in Phase 1, one group of rats with each reward quantity was shifted to the alternate quantity. Thus, some rats were shifted from small to large reward (S-L), and others were shifted from large to small reward (L-S). The remaining two groups continued to receive the same amount of reward in Phase 2 as they had received in Phase 1. (These groups were designated as L-L and S-S.)

Figure 5.10 summarizes the results. At the end of Phase 1, the animals that received the large reward ran slightly, but not significantly, faster than the rats that received the small reward. For groups that continued to receive the same amount of reward in Phase 2 as in Phase 1 (groups L-L and S-S), instrumental performance did not change much during Phase 2. By contrast, significant deviations from these baselines of running were observed in groups that received shifts in reward magnitude. Rats shifted from large to small reward (group L-S) rapidly decreased their running speeds, and rats shifted from small to large reward (group S-L) soon increased their running speeds.

The most significant finding was that following a shift in reward magnitude, running speed was not entirely determined by the new reward magnitude. Rather, the effects of the

Figure 5.10 Running speeds of four groups of rats in blocks of 3 trials. Block "Pre" represents running speeds at the end of Phase 1. Blocks 1–4 represent running speeds in Phase 2. At the start of Phase 2, groups S-L and L-S experienced a shift in amount of reward from small to large and large to small, respectively. Groups S-S and L-L received small and large rewards, respectively, throughout the experiment. (From "Positive and Negative Contrast Effects Using Delayed Reinforcement," by R. L. Mellgren, 1972, *Learning and Motivation, 3,* pp. 185–193. Copyright © 1972 by Academic Press. Reprinted by permission.)

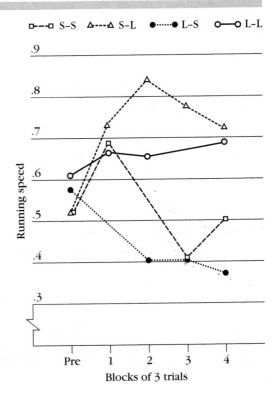

new reward were enhanced by previous experience with a contrasting reward magnitude. Rats shifted from a small to a large reward (group S-L) ran faster for the large reward than rats that always received the large reward (group L-L). Correspondingly, animals shifted from a large to a small reward (group L-S) ran more slowly for the small reward than animals that always received the small reward (group S-S).

The results Mellgren obtained illustrate the phenomena of successive positive and negative contrast. **Positive contrast** refers to elevated responding for a favorable reward resulting from prior experience with a less attractive outcome. More informally, the favorable reward looks especially good to individuals who experienced a worse outcome previously. **Negative contrast** refers to depressed responding for an unfavorable reward because of prior experience with a better outcome. In this case, the unfavorable reward looks especially bad to individuals who experienced a better reward previously.

In Mellgren's study, the two reward conditions were presented in different phases of the experiment, and only one shift in reward magnitude occurred for the shifted groups. Because of this, the results are called *successive* positive and negative contrast. Contrast effects also occur if reward conditions are shifted back and forth frequently, with a different cue signaling each reward condition (for example, McSweeney & Melville, 1993; Williams, 1983, 1990, 1992b, 1997b). These effects are examples of **simultaneous behavioral contrast.**

Different contrast effects are mediated by different mechanisms (see Flaherty, 1996; Williams, 1997b). However, all contrast effects illustrate that the effectiveness of a reinforcer in one situation is determined in part by the organism's experiences with reinforcers in other situations. For reasons that are not entirely clear, negative contrast has been obtained more readily than positive contrast. Negative contrast has traditionally been attributed to the aversive or frustrative effects of getting an unexpectedly small reward (Amsel, 1992). Studies with anti-anxiety drugs, however, suggest that the emotional effects of a downshift in reward value do not occur immediately (Flaherty, Grigson, & Lind, 1990). Current thinking is that a downshift in reward magnitude activates a series of cognitive and behavioral changes (Flaherty, 1996). The initial encounter with the unexpectedly small reward activates exploratory and search responses that might result in finding a better source of food (Flaherty, Greenwood, Martin, & Leszczuk, 1998; Pecoraro, Timberlake, & Tinsley, 1999). Emotional disappointment sets in when the search responses are unsuccessful and the subject has to contend with the small reward. This is then followed by an accommodation to the continued availability of only the small reward.

C. F. Flaherty

The Response-Reinforcer Relation

As I have said, instrumental behavior produces and is controlled by its consequences. In some cases, there is a strong relation between what a person does and the consequence that follows. If you put 75¢ into a soda machine, you will get a can of soda. As long as the machine is working, you will get a can of soda every time you put in the required 75¢. In other cases, there is no relation between behavior and an outcome. You may wear a red shirt to an examination and receive a good grade, but the grade would not be related to your having worn the red shirt. The relation between behavior and its consequences can also be probabilistic. For example, you might have to make several phone calls before finding someone who is willing to help you with a problem.

Human and nonhuman animals perform a continual stream of responses and experience all kinds of environmental events. You are always doing something, even if it is just sitting around, and things are continually happening in your environment. An organism must organize its behavior to meet various challenges, and it must do so in a way that makes the best use of its time and energy. There is no point in working hard to make the sun rise each morning, because that will happen anyway. It makes more sense to devote energy to fixing breakfast or working for a paycheck—things that do not become available without your effort. To be efficient, you have to know when you have to do something to obtain a reinforcer and when the reinforcer is likely to be delivered independent of your actions. Efficient instrumental behavior requires sensitivity to the response-reinforcer relation.

Two types of relationships exist between a response and a reinforcer. One is the *temporal relation,* which refers to the time between the response and the reinforcer. A special type of the temporal relation is the **temporal contiguity,** which refers to the delivery of the reinforcer immediately after the response. The second type of relation between a response and the reinforcer is the *causal relation* or **response-reinforcer contingency.** The response-reinforcer contingency refers to the extent to which the instrumental response is necessary and sufficient for the occurrence of the reinforcer.

Temporal and causal factors are independent of each other. A strong temporal relation does not require a strong causal relation, and vice versa. For example, there is strong causal relation between submitting an application for admission to college and getting accepted. (If you don't apply, you are guaranteed not to be accepted.) However, the temporal relation between applying and getting admitted is weak. You may not hear about the acceptance for several weeks (or months) after submitting your application.

Effects of Temporal Contiguity. Both conventional wisdom and experimental evidence tell us that immediate reinforcement is preferable to delayed reinforcement (McDevitt & Williams, 2001). In addition, since the early work of Grice (1948), learning psychologists have emphasized that instrumental conditioning requires providing the reinforcer immediately after the occurrence of the instrumental response. Grice reported that instrumental learning can be disrupted by delays as short as 0.5 seconds. More recent research has indicated that instrumental conditioning is possible with delays as long as 30 seconds (Critchfield & Lattal, 1993; Lattal & Gleeson, 1990; Lattal & Metzger, 1994; Sutphin, Byrne, & Poling, 1998; Williams & Lattal, 1999). The fact remains that instrumental learning is disrupted by delaying the delivery of the reinforcer after the occurrence of the instrumental response.

The effects of delayed reinforcement on learning to press a response lever is shown in Figure 5.11 (Dickinson, Watt, & Griffiths, 1992). Each time a rat pressed the lever, a food pellet was delivered after a fixed delay. For some subjects, the delay was short (2–4 seconds); for others, the delay was considerable (64 seconds). In this study, if the subject pressed the lever again during the delay interval, the new response resulted in another food pellet after the specified delay. (In other studies, such "extra" responses are programmed to reset the delay interval.) In Figure 5.11, response rates are shown as a function of the mean delay of reinforcement experienced by each group. The results indicate that responding dropped off fairly rapidly with increases in the delay of reinforcement. No learning was evident with a 64-second delay of reinforcement in this experiment.

Why is instrumental conditioning so sensitive to a delay of reinforcement? There are several contributing factors. One stems from the fact that a delay makes it difficult to figure out which response deserves the credit for the reinforcer that is delivered. As I pointed out earlier, behavior consists of an ongoing, continual stream of activities. When reinforcement is delayed after performance of a specified response, R1, the organism does not stop doing things. After performing R1, the organism may perform R2, R3, R4, and so on. If the reinforcer is set up by R1 but not delivered until some time later, the reinforcer may occur immediately after some other response, say, R6. To associate R1 with the reinforcer, the organism has to have some way to distinguish R1 from the other responses it performs during the delay interval.

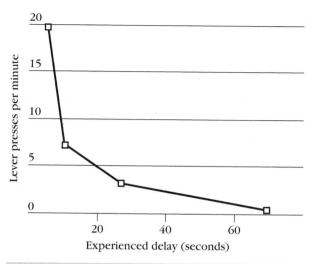

Figure 5.11 Effects of delay of reinforcement on acquisition of lever pressing in rats. (From "Free-Operant Acquisition with Delayed Reinforcement," by A. Dickinson, A. Watt, and W. J. H. Griffiths, 1992, *The Quarterly Journal of Experimental Psychology, 45B,* pp. 241–258. Copyright © 1992 by The Experimental Psychology Society. Reprinted by permission.)

There are a couple of ways to overcome this problem. The first technique, used by animal trainers and coaches for centuries, is to provide a secondary or conditioned reinforcer immediately after the instrumental response, even if the primary reinforcer cannot occur until some time later. A **secondary** or **conditioned reinforcer** is a conditioned stimulus that was previously associated with the reinforcer. Verbal prompts in coaching, such as "good" and "that's the way," are conditioned reinforcers that can provide immediate reinforcement for appropriate behavior. Good coaches are constantly providing such immediate verbal feedback or conditioned reinforcement. Conditioned reinforcers can serve to "bridge" a delay between the instrumental response and the delivery of the primary reinforcer (Cronin, 1980; Winter & Perkins, 1982; Williams, 1991, 1993; for an analogous outcome in human judgments of causality, see Reed, 1999).

Another technique that facilitates learning with delayed reinforcement is to *mark* the target instrumental response in some way to make it distinguishable from the other activities of the organism. The effectiveness of a **marking procedure** was first demonstrated by Lieberman, McIntosh, and Thomas (1979). Rats served in the experiment, and the apparatus was a special maze, shown at the top in Figure 5.12. After release from the start box, the rats had a choice between entering a white or a black side arm. Entering the white arm was designated as the correct instrumental response and was reinforced with access to food in the goal box after a delay of 60 seconds.

Two groups of animals were tested, and they were differentiated by what happened to them immediately after making the correct choice. Rats in the "marked" group were picked up by the experimenter and placed in the delay box. By contrast, the animals in the "unmarked" group were undisturbed. After they made the correct response, the door at the end of the choice alley was opened for them, and they were allowed to walk into the delay box without being handled. Sixty seconds after the instrumental response, both groups were placed in the goal box to obtain the reinforcer. The same sequence of events occurred when the rats made an incorrect response, except that in this case they were not reinforced at the end of the delay interval. Because the same marking stimulus (handling) occurred on both reinforced and nonreinforced trials, the marking stimulus was not specifically correlated with reinforcement.

Results of the experiment are shown in the graph in Figure 5.12. Rats in the marked group learned the instrumental response with the 60-second delay of reinforcement much

D. A. Lieberman

Courtesy of D. A. Lieberman

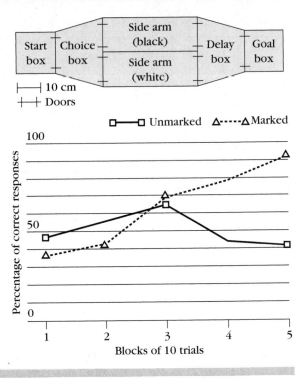

Figure 5.12 Top view of apparatus and results of an experiment to test the effects of marking an instrumental response on instrumental conditioning with reinforcement delayed 60 seconds. Choosing the white side arm was designated as the correct response. Rats spent the delay interval in the delay box. Those in the "Marked" group were placed in the delay box after each choice response. Those in the "Unmarked" group were allowed to walk into the delay box undisturbed. (From "Learning When Reward Is Delayed: A Marking Hypothesis," by D. A. Lieberman, D. C. McIntosh, and G. V. Thomas, 1979, *Journal of Experimental Psychology: Animal Behavior Processes, 5,* pp. 224–242. Copyright © 1979 by the American Psychological Association. Reprinted by permission.)

better than animals in the unmarked group. At the end of 50 training trials, the marking procedure resulted in the correct choice 90% of the time. By contrast, without the marking procedure, the correct choice occurred about 50% of the time, which is chance performance.

In another experiment, Lieberman and his colleagues demonstrated successful learning with delayed reinforcement when the instrumental response was marked by a brief, intense light or noise (Lieberman et al., 1979). These effects of marking cannot be explained in terms of secondary or conditioned reinforcement, because the marking stimulus was presented after both correct and incorrect choices. Any conditioned reinforcement effects would have increased both correct and incorrect choices and thus cannot be responsible for the preponderance of correct responses that was observed (see also Lieberman, Davidson, & Thomas, 1985; Lieberman & Thomas, 1986; Ploog, 2001; Thomas & Lieberman, 1990; Urcuioli & Kasprow, 1988).

Secondary reinforcement and marking procedures both focus on better connecting the target instrumental response to the delayed reinforcer. Another way to think about this issue is that when reinforcement is delayed, it is treated as if the reinforcer occurred independent of behavior. What are the consequences of response-independent reinforcement that could contribute to the deleterious effects of delayed reinforcement? When a reinforcer is presented independent of behavior, the subject cannot easily tell when it will get reinforced. Not being able to predict when it will get fed, the subject may look into the food hopper more frequently, and these hopper-observing responses will interfere with the target instrumental response. Experiments with pigeons have provided data in support of this interpretation (Schaal, Shahan, Kovera, & Reilly, 1998; see also Lattal & Abreu-Rodrigues, 1997).

Another consequence of response-independent reinforcement is the conditioning of contextual cues. If there is a delay between the target response and the delivery of the reinforcer, the reinforcer will occur in the experimental context without being signaled by the response. This will permit conditioning of the contextual cues. By becoming associated with the reinforcer, these contextual cues can then block the formation of an association between the target response and the reinforcer. Consistent with this interpretation, Dickinson, Watt, and Varga (1996) found that procedures that disrupt the conditioning of contextual cues help to overcome the deleterious effects of delayed reinforcement on instrumental conditioning.

The Response-Reinforcer Contingency.   As I noted earlier, the response-reinforcer contingency refers to the extent to which the delivery of the reinforcer is dependent on the prior occurrence of the instrumental response. In studies of delay of reinforcement, there is a perfect causal relation between the response and the reinforcer. Although the reinforcer is delayed, it is only provided if the organism makes the instrumental response. Studies of delay of reinforcement show that a perfect causal relation between the response and the reinforcer is not sufficient to produce vigorous instrumental responding. Even with a perfect causal relation, conditioning does not occur if reinforcement is delayed too long. Such data encouraged early investigators to conclude that response-reinforcer contiguity rather than contingency was the critical factor producing instrumental learning. However, this view has turned out to be unjustified by subsequent research. The response-reinforcer contingency is also important.

Skinner's Superstition Experiment.   A landmark experiment in the debate about the role of contiguity versus contingency in instrumental learning was Skinner's superstition experiment (Skinner, 1948). Skinner placed pigeons in separate experimental chambers and set the equipment to deliver a bit of food every 15 seconds irrespective of what the pigeons were doing. The birds were not required to peck a key or perform any other specified response to get the food. After some time, Skinner returned to see what his birds were doing. He described some of what he saw as follows:

> In six out of eight cases the resulting responses were so clearly defined that two observers could agree perfectly in counting instances. One bird was conditioned to turn counterclockwise about the cage, making two or three turns between reinforcements. Another repeatedly thrust its head into one of the upper corners of the cage. A third developed a "tossing" response, as if placing its head beneath an invisible bar and lifting it repeatedly. (p. 168)

The pigeons appeared to be responding as if their behavior controlled the delivery of the reinforcer, when, in fact, food was provided independently of behavior. Accordingly, Skinner called this **superstitious behavior.**

Skinner's explanation of superstitious behavior rests on the idea of **accidental, or adventitious, reinforcement.** Adventitious reinforcement refers to the accidental pairing of a response with delivery of the reinforcer. Animals are always doing something, even if no particular responses are required to obtain food. Skinner suggested that whatever response a subject happened to make just before it got free food became strengthened and subsequently increased in frequency because of adventitious reinforcement. One accidental pairing of a response with food increases the chance that the same response will occur just before the next delivery of the food. A second accidental response-reinforcer pairing further increases the probability of the response. In this way, each accidental pairing helps to "stamp in" a particular response. After a while, the response will occur frequently enough to be identified as superstitious behavior.

Skinner's interpretation of his experiment was appealing and consistent with views of reinforcement that were widely held at the time. Impressed by studies of delay of reinforcement, theoreticians thought that temporal contiguity was the main factor responsible for

don't have to do any specific behavior

J. E. R. Staddon

learning. Skinner's experiment appeared to support this view and suggested that a positive response-reinforcer contingency is not necessary for instrumental conditioning.

1. *Reinterpretation of the Superstition Experiment.* Skinner's bold claim that response-reinforcer contiguity rather than contingency is most important for instrumental conditioning has been challenged by subsequent empirical evidence. In a landmark study, Staddon and Simmelhag (1971) attempted to replicate Skinner's experiment. However, Staddon and Simmelhag made much more extensive and systematic observations. They defined and measured the occurrence of many responses, such as orienting to the food hopper, pecking the response key, wing flapping, turning in quarter circles, and preening. They then recorded the frequency of each response according to when it occurred during the interval between successive free deliveries of food.

Figure 5.13 shows the data obtained by Staddon and Simmelhag for several responses for one pigeon. Clearly, some of the responses occurred predominantly toward the end of the interval between successive reinforcers. For example, R1 and R7 (orienting to the food magazine and pecking at something on the magazine wall) were much more likely to occur at the end of the food-food interval than at other times. Staddon and Simmelhag called these **terminal responses.** Other activities increased in frequency after the delivery of food and then decreased as the time for the next food delivery drew closer. The pigeons were most likely to engage in R8 and R4 (moving along the magazine wall and making a quarter turn) somewhere near the middle of the interval between food deliveries. These activities were called **interim responses.**

Which actions were terminal responses and which were interim responses did not vary much from one pigeon to another. Furthermore, Staddon and Simmelhag failed to find evi-

Figure 5.13 Probability of several responses as a function of time between successive deliveries of a food reinforcer. R1 (orienting toward the food magazine wall) and R7 (pecking at something on the magazine wall) are terminal responses, having their highest probabilities at the end of the interval between food deliveries. R3 (pecking at something on the floor), R4 (a quarter turn), and R8 (moving along the magazine wall) are interim responses, having their highest probabilities somewhere near the middle of the interval between food deliveries. (From "The 'Superstition' Experiment: A Reexamination of Its Implications for the Principles of Adaptive Behavior," by J. E. R. Staddon and V. L. Simmelhag, 1971, *Psychological Review, 78*, pp. 3–43. Copyright © 1971 by the American Psychological Association. Reprinted by permission.)

*most commonly reinforced behavior related to food

dence for accidental reinforcement effects. Responses did not always increase in frequency merely because they occurred coincidentally with food delivery. Food delivery appeared to influence only the strength of terminal responses, even in the initial phases of training.

Subsequent research has provided much additional evidence that periodic presentations of a reinforcer produce behavioral regularities, with certain responses predominating late in the interval between successive food presentations, and other responses predominating earlier in the food-food interval (Anderson & Shettleworth, 1977; Innis, Simmelhag-Grant, & Staddon, 1983; Silva & Timberlake, 1998). It is not clear why Skinner failed to observe such regularities in his experiment. One possibility is that he focused on different aspects of the behavior of different birds in an effort to document that each bird responded in a unique fashion. For example, he may have focused on the terminal response of one bird and interim responses in other birds. Subsequent investigators have also noted some variations in behavior between individuals but have emphasized what are even more striking similarities among animals that are given food periodically, independent of their behavior.

2. *Explanation of the Periodicity of Interim and Terminal Responses.* What is responsible for the development of similar terminal and interim responses in animals exposed to the same schedule of response-independent food presentations? Staddon and Simmelhag (1971) suggested that terminal responses are species-typical responses that reflect the anticipation of food as time draws nearer to the next food presentation. By contrast, they viewed interim responses as reflecting other sources of motivation that become prominent early in the interfood interval, when food presentation is unlikely. In contrast, subsequent investigators have favored approaches in which terminal and interim responses are considered to be different manifestations of the same motivational system (for example, Innis, Reberg, Mann, Jacobson, & Turton, 1983; Matthews, Bordi, & Depollo, 1990; but see Lawler & Cohen, 1992). The best developed of these alternative formulations is behavior systems theory (Lucas, Timberlake, & Gawley, 1988; Timberlake & Lucas, 1985, 1991; Silva & Timberlake, 1998).

According to behavior systems theory, the feeding system (and its accompanying foraging responses) is activated in food-deprived animals that are periodically given small portions of food. Behavior under these circumstances is assumed to be a reflection of preorganized species-typical foraging and feeding behavior. Different behaviors occur depending on when food was last delivered and when food is going to occur again. Just after the delivery of food, the organism is assumed to display *post-food focal search* responses that involve activities near the food cup. In the middle of the interval between food deliveries (when the subjects are least likely to get food), *general search* responses are evident that take the subject away from the food cup. As time for the next food delivery approaches, subjects exhibit *focal search* responses that are again concentrated near the food cup. In Figure 5.13, the terminal responses, R1 and R7 were distributed in time in the manner expected of focal search behavior, and R4 and R8 were distributed in the manner expected of general search responses. (For studies examining these issues in greater detail, see Timberlake & Lucas, 1985; Matthews et al., 1990; Silva & Timberlake, 1998.)

Consistent with behavior systems theory, the distribution of activities that develops with periodic deliveries of a reinforcer depend on the nature of that reinforcer. For example, different patterns of behavior develop with food versus water presentations (Innis et al., 1983; Papadouka & Matthews, 1995; Reberg, Innis, Mann, & Eizenga, 1978; Timberlake & Lucas, 1991), presumably because food and water activate different foraging patterns.

Effects of the Controllability of Reinforcers. A strong contingency between an instrumental response and a reinforcer essentially means that the response controls the reinforcer. With a strong contingency, whether the reinforcer occurs depends on whether the instrumental response has occurred. Studies of the effects of control over reinforcers have provided the most extensive body of evidence on the sensitivity of behavior to response-reinforcer contingencies. Although some of these studies have involved positive reinforcement (for example, Caspy & Lubow, 1981; Ferguson & Job, 1997; Job, 1987, 1989), most of the research has focused on the effects of control over aversive stimulation (see reviews by LoLordo & Taylor, 2001; Overmier & LoLordo, 1998; Maier & Jackson, 1979; Peterson, Maier, & Seligman, 1993).

Contemporary research on the effects of the controllability of aversive stimulation on learning originated with the pioneering studies of Seligman, Overmier, and Maier (Overmier & Seligman, 1967; Seligman & Maier, 1967), who investigated the effects of exposure to uncontrollable shock on subsequent escape-avoidance learning in dogs. The major finding was that exposure to uncontrollable shock disrupted subsequent learning. This phenomenon has come to be called the **learned-helplessness effect.**

The learned-helplessness effect continues to be the focus of a great deal of research, but dogs are no longer used in the experiments. Instead, most of the research is now done with laboratory rats and human participants. The results of the research with humans has turned out to be more relevant to issues in social and clinical psychology than behavior theory (see Mikulincer, 1994, for a review); consequently, I mention that work only briefly.

1. *The Triadic Design.* Learned-helplessness experiments are usually conducted using the *triadic design* presented in Table 5.2. The design involves two phases: exposure and conditioning. During the exposure phase, one group of rats (E, for *e*scape) is exposed to periodic shocks that can be terminated by performing an escape response (rotating a small wheel or tumbler, for example). Each subject in the second group (Y, for *y*oked) is yoked to an animal in Group E and receives the same shocks as its Group E partner. However, animals in Group Y cannot do anything to turn off the shocks. The third group (R, for *r*estricted) receives no shocks during the exposure phase but is restricted to the apparatus for as long as the other groups. During the conditioning phase, all three groups receive escape-avoidance training. This is usually conducted in a shuttle apparatus that has two adjacent compartments (see Figure 10.4). The animals have to go back and forth between the two compartments to avoid shock (or escape any shocks that they did not avoid).

The remarkable finding in experiments on the learned-helplessness effect is that the effects of aversive stimulation during the exposure phase depend on whether or not shock is escapable. Exposure to uncontrollable shock (Group Y) produces a severe disruption in subsequent escape-avoidance learning. In the conditioning phase of the experiment, Group Y typically shows much poorer escape-avoidance performance than both Group E and Group R. By contrast, little or no deleterious effects are observed after exposure to escapable shock. In fact, Group E often learns the subsequent escape-avoidance task as rapidly as Group R, which received no shock during the exposure phase. Similar detrimental effects of exposure to yoked inescapable shock have been reported on subsequent responding for food reinforcement (for example, Rosellini & DeCola, 1981; Rosellini, DeCola, & Shapiro, 1982; see also DeCola & Rosellini, 1990).

The fact that Group Y shows a deficit in subsequent learning in comparison to Group E indicates that the animals are sensitive to the procedural differences between escapable and yoked inescapable shock. The primary procedural difference between Groups E and Y is the presence of a response-reinforcer contingency for Group E but not for Group Y. Therefore, the difference in the rate of learning between these two groups shows that the animals are sensitive to the response-reinforcer contingency.

2. *The Learned-Helplessness Hypothesis.* The first major explanation of studies employing the triadic design—the **learned-helplessness hypothesis**—was based on the conclusion that

TABLE 5.2	**THE TRIADIC DESIGN USED IN STUDIES OF THE LEARNED-HELPLESSNESS EFFECT**		
GROUP	**EXPOSURE PHASE**	**CONDITIONING PHASE**	**RESULT**
Group E	Escapable shock	Escape-avoidance	Rapid avoidance learning
Group Y	Yoked inescapable shock	Escape-avoidance	Slow avoidance learning
Group R	Restricted to apparatus	Escape-avoidance	Rapid avoidance learning

animals can perceive the contingency between their behavior and the delivery of a reinforcer (Maier & Seligman, 1976; Maier, Seligman, & Solomon, 1969). The learned-helplessness hypothesis assumes that during exposure to uncontrollable shocks, animals learn that the shocks are independent of their behavior—that they can do nothing to control the shocks. Furthermore, they come to expect that reinforcers will continue to be independent of their behavior in the future. This expectation of future lack of control undermines their ability to learn a new instrumental response. The learning deficit occurs for two reasons. First, the expectation of lack of control reduces the motivation of the subjects to perform an instrumental response. Second, even if they make the response and get reinforced in the conditioning phase, the previously learned expectation of lack of control makes it more difficult for the subjects to learn that their behavior is now effective in producing reinforcement.

It is important to distinguish the learned-helplessness *hypothesis* from the learned-helplessness *effect.* The learned-helplessness effect is the pattern of results obtained with the triadic design (poorer learning in Group Y than in Groups E and R). The learned-helplessness effect has been replicated in numerous studies and is a well-established finding. By contrast, the learned-helplessness hypothesis has been a provocative and controversial explanation of the learned-helplessness effect since its introduction (see Black, 1977; Levis, 1976; LoLordo & Taylor, 2001; Overmier & LoLordo, 1998).

3. *Activity Deficits.* Early in the history of research on the learned-helplessness effect, investigators became concerned that the learning deficit observed in Group Y was a result of these animals learning to be inactive in response to shock during the exposure phase. Consistent with this hypothesis, in some situations, inescapable shock produces a decrease in motor movement, or response perseveration, and this is responsible for subsequent performance deficits (Anderson, Crowell, Cunningham, & Lupo, 1979; Anisman, de Catanzaro, & Remington, 1978; Anisman, Hamilton, & Zacharko, 1984; Irwin, Suissa, & Anisman, 1980). There are also situations in which effects on learning are not likely to be due to the suppression of movement caused by inescapable shock (for example, Jackson, Alexander, & Maier, 1980; Rosellini, DeCola, Plonsky, Warren, & Stilman, 1984). Therefore, a learned inactivity hypothesis cannot explain all instances of learned-helplessness effects (Maier & Jackson, 1979).

4. *Attentional Deficits.* Why might lack of control over reinforcers produce a deficit in learning if the effect is not due to a deficit in activity? One interesting possibility is that inescapable shock causes animals to pay less attention to their actions. If an animal fails to pay attention to its behavior, it will have difficulty associating its actions with reinforcers in escape-avoidance or other forms of instrumental conditioning.

S. F. Maier

M. E. P. Seligman

The fact that a history of lack of control over reinforcers can severely disrupt subsequent instrumental performance has important implications for human behavior. The concept of helplessness has been extended and elaborated to many areas of human concern, including aging, athletic performance, chronic pain, academic achievement, susceptibility to heart attacks, and victimization and bereave-

ment (see Garber & Seligman, 1980; Peterson, Maier, & Seligman, 1993). Perhaps the most prominent area to which the concept of helplessness has been applied is depression (Seligman, 1975; see also Abramson, Metalsky, & Alloy, 1989; Peterson & Seligman, 1984).

Animal research on uncontrollability and unpredictability has also been used to gain insights into human posttraumatic stress disorder (Foa, Zinbarg, & Rothbaum, 1992). Victims of rape, assault, or combat stress have symptoms that correspond to the effects of chronic uncontrollable and unpredictable shock in animals. Recognition of these similarities promises to provide new insights into the origin and treatment of posttraumatic stress disorder.

In a fascinating experiment, Maier, Jackson, and Tomie (1987) tested this attention-deficit hypothesis with rats. They reasoned that an animal that fails to pay attention to its behavior because of exposure to inescapable shock is faced with the same problem as an animal that receives delayed reinforcement. In both cases, the animals have difficulty figuring out which of their actions causes the delivery of the reinforcer. This analogy suggested to Maier and his colleagues that manipulations that facilitate learning with delayed reinforcement might also help animals exposed to inescapable shock.

As I described earlier in this chapter, the problem of identifying which response is responsible for delayed reinforcement can be solved by marking the target response with an immediate external feedback stimulus of some sort. Maier and his colleagues reasoned that reduced attention to instrumental behavior also may be alleviated by introducing an external response feedback cue or marking stimulus. Thus, they predicted that rats given inescapable shock will not be disrupted in their subsequent escape learning if each instrumental response is marked by an external stimulus.

The relevant results of their experiment are presented in Figure 5.14. The figure shows the latency of escape responses performed by various groups during conditioning—the second phase of the experiment. Higher values indicate slower escape responses, and hence poorer escape learning. Groups E, Y, and R were the standard groups of the triadic design and yielded the usual learned-helplessness effect. Group E, which received escapable shocks during the exposure phase, performed with as short latencies as Group R, which was not given shock during the exposure phase. By contrast, Group Y, which received inescapable shocks at first, had significantly longer escape latencies.

The fourth group, Group Y-M (yoked-marker) received the same type of shocks as Group Y during the exposure phase. During the conditioning phase, Group Y-M received a marking stimulus after each escape response. The marker consisted of turning off the house lights for 0.75 second and having the floor tilt slightly as the rat crossed from one side of the shuttle box to the other. The presence of this marker completely eliminated the deficit in learning that was otherwise produced by prior exposure to inescapable shock. Group Y-M performed much better than Group Y and as well as Groups R and E. (Other aspects of the experiment ruled out nonspecific effects of the marking stimulus.) Thus, as predicted, mark-

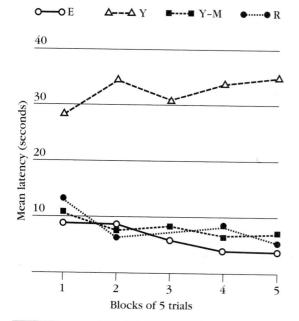

Figure 5.14 Mean escape latency during the conditioning phase for four groups of rats in a learned-helplessness experiment. During the exposure phase, Group E received escapable shocks, Groups Y and Y-M received yoked inescapable shocks, and Group R received no shock. During the conditioning phase, a brief marking stimulus was presented after each escape response for subjects in Group Y-M. (From "Potentiation, Overshadowing, and Prior Exposure to Inescapable Shock," by S. F. Maier, R. L. Jackson, and A. Tomie, 1987, *Journal of Experimental Psychology: Animal Behavior Processes, 13,* pp. 260–270. Copyright © 1987 by the American Psychological Association. Reprinted by permission.)

ing the instrumental response overcame the learned-helplessness deficit. This outcome suggests that one of the sources of the learning deficit is a reduction in attention to the responses the animal performs (see also Lee & Maier, 1988; Rodd, Rosellini, Stock, & Gallup, 1997).

5.   *Stimulus Relations in Escape Conditioning.* The interpretations of the learned-helplessness effect I have described so far have focused on the deleterious effects of exposure to inescapable shock. An equally important question is why exposure to shock is not as harmful if the animal can perform a response to escape the shock (Minor, Dess, & Overmier, 1991). This question has stimulated a closer look at what happens when animals are permitted to escape shock in the exposure phase of the triadic design. It is apparent that escape training is more complex than was previously thought.

The defining feature of escape behavior is that the instrumental response results in the termination of an aversive stimulus. However, there are also special stimulus relations in an escape procedure that are potentially very important. These are illustrated in Figure 5.15. Making the escape response results in internal response feedback cues. Some of these response-produced stimuli are experienced at the start of the escape response, just before the shock is turned off, and are called *shock-cessation feedback cues.* Other response-produced stimuli are experienced as the animal completes the response, just after the shock has been turned off at the start of the intertrial interval. These are called *safety-signal feedback cues.*

At first, investigations of stimulus factors involved with escapable shock centered on the possible significance of safety-signal feedback cues. Safety-signal feedback cues are reliably followed by the intertrial interval, and hence by the absence of shock. Therefore, such feedback cues can become conditioned inhibitors of fear and limit or inhibit fear elicited by contextual cues of the experimental chamber. No such safety signals exist for animals given yoked inescapable shock because, for them, shocks and shock-free periods are not predictable. Therefore, contextual cues of the chamber in which shocks are delivered are more likely to become conditioned to elicit fear with inescapable shock. These considerations have encouraged analyzing the triadic design in terms of group differences in signals for safety rather than in terms of differences in response-reinforcer contingencies.

N. K. Dess

Courtesy of N. K. Dess

155

Shock

Escape response

Shock-cessation
feedback cues

Safety-signal
feedback cues

Time

Figure 5.15 Stimulus relations in an escape conditioning trial. Shock-cessation feedback cues are experienced at the start of the escape response, just before the termination of shock. Safety-signal feedback cues are experienced just after the termination of shock, at the start of the intertrial interval.

Courtesy of UCLA Department of Psychology

T. R. Minor

Although some studies have indicated that group differences in signals for safety can account for the learned-helplessness effect (Jackson & Minor, 1988), findings from other experiments have not supported this conclusion (DeCola, Rosellini, & Warren, 1988; Maier, 1990; Maier & Warren, 1988; Rosellini, Warren, & DeCola, 1987). These considerations have encouraged focusing on other aspects of escape responding that may protect animals from the deleterious effects of exposure to shock. One study suggests, for example, that the critical aspect of an escape response may be that it indicates that the shock is being terminated (Minor, Trauner, Lee, & Dess, 1990). Thus, cessation signals may mimic critical features of an escape response more effectively than safety signals.

Focusing on stimulus factors in escape conditioning rather than on response-reinforcer contingencies has not yet yielded a comprehensive account of the results of all experiments with the triadic design. However, the available evidence indicates that significant differences in how animals cope with aversive stimulation can result from differences in signal relations. The more restricted focus of the learned-helplessness hypothesis cannot explain such findings. On balance, the triadic design has been invaluable in focusing attention on the possible importance of response-reinforcer contingencies. Recent research, however, has uncovered important factors other than the response-reinforcer contingency that also determine the effects of exposure to uncontrollable aversive stimulation (for reviews, see LoLordo & Taylor, 2001; Overmier & LoLordo, 1998).

CONTIGUITY AND CONTINGENCY: CONCLUDING COMMENTS

As I have described, organisms are sensitive to the contiguity as well as the contingency between an instrumental response and a reinforcer. Typically, these two aspects of the relation between response and reinforcer act jointly to produce learning (Davis & Platt, 1983). Both

BOX **5.5**

HELPLESSNESS WITHIN THE SPINAL CORD

If someone asks you where learning occurs, you would likely give a quick response accompanied by an expression of disbelief. Everyone knows that learning occurs within the brain. But what about the neural tissue that lies below the brain, the cylinder of axons and gray matter that is protected by the bones of the vertebrate column? Can it learn? Recent work suggests that neurons within this region are sensitive to environmental relations and can exhibit some simple forms of learning (for a review, see Patterson & Grau, 2001).

The spinal cord is composed of two regions (see Figure 5.16A). The inner region (the central gray) is composed of neurons that form a network that can modulate signals and organize some simple behaviors. The central gray is surrounded by a band of axons (the white matter) that carry neural signals up and down the spinal cord, relaying information between the periphery and the brain. When an individual has an accident that causes paralysis below the waist (paraplegia), the loss of sensory and motor function is due to disruption in the relay cable formed by the axons of the white matter.

Spinal injury does not eliminate neural control of reflex responses. Below the point of injury, the neurons of the central gray retain the capacity to organize some simple behaviors. These spinal reflexes can be studied in non-human subjects such as rats by surgically cutting the spinal cord, disconnecting the lower region of the spinal cord (the lumbar-sacral region) from the brain. After the spinal injury, pressure applied to the rear paw will still elicit an upward movement of the paw (a flexion response). This protective reflex is designed to move the limb away from noxious stimuli that might cause damage to the skin. The reflex is mediated by neurons within the lumbosacral region of the spinal cord. The flexion response does not require the brain.

Groves and Thompson (1990) have shown that the vigor of a spinal reflex can change with experience. Repeated stimulation produces habituation while an intense stimulus can induce sensitization. These observations formed the cornerstone of the dual-process theory of nonassociative learning that was described in Chapter 2 (Groves & Thompson, 1970).

More recently, Grau and his colleagues have shown that neurons within the spinal cord can also support a simple form of instrumental learning (reviewed in Grau & Joynes, 2001). In these studies, the spinal cord was cut and subjects were trained using a shock that elicited a hindlimb flexion response. One group (the master rats) received legshock whenever the leg was extended. Subjects in a yoked group were experimentally coupled to the master subjects. Each time a master rat received shock, its yoked partner did, too. Master rats quickly learned to hold the leg up, effectively minimizing net shock exposure (Figure 5.16B). In contrast, the yoked rats, which received shock independent of leg position, failed to learn. This difference between master and yoked rats indicates that neurons within the spinal cord are sensitive to an instrumental (response-reinforcer) relation (for additional evidence, see Grau & Joynes, 2001).

Master and yoked rats were then tested under common conditions with controllable shock. As you would expect, master rats learned faster than control subjects that previously had not received shock. In contrast, the yoked rats failed to learn. Their behavioral deficit resembles the phenomenon of learned helplessness (Maier & Seligman, 1976). Crown and Grau (2001) have gone on to show that prior exposure to controllable shock has an immunizing effect that can protect the spinal cord from becoming helpless. Other experiments demonstrated that a combination of behavioral and drug treatments can restore the spinal cord's capacity for learning.

Across a range of behavioral manipulations, the spinal cord has yielded a pattern of results remarkably similar to those derived from brain-mediated behaviors. These results indicate that learning theorists have identified some very

(continued)

Box 5.5 (continued)

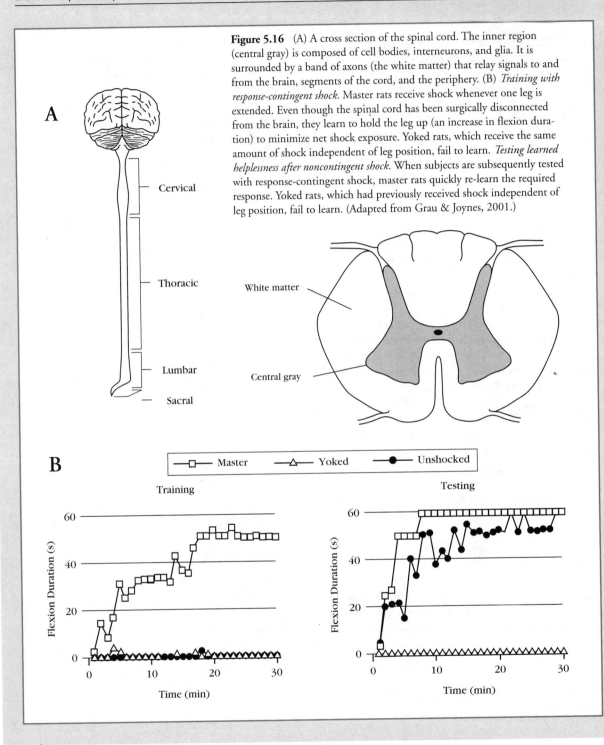

Figure 5.16 (A) A cross section of the spinal cord. The inner region (central gray) is composed of cell bodies, interneurons, and glia. It is surrounded by a band of axons (the white matter) that relay signals to and from the brain, segments of the cord, and the periphery. (B) *Training with response-contingent shock.* Master rats receive shock whenever one leg is extended. Even though the spinal cord has been surgically disconnected from the brain, they learn to hold the leg up (an increase in flexion duration) to minimize net shock exposure. Yoked rats, which receive the same amount of shock independent of leg position, fail to learn. *Testing learned helplessness after noncontingent shock.* When subjects are subsequently tested with response-contingent shock, master rats quickly re-learn the required response. Yoked rats, which had previously received shock independent of leg position, fail to learn. (Adapted from Grau & Joynes, 2001.)

general principles of learning, principles that apply across a range of species (from *Aplysia* to humans) and across different levels of the neural axis (from spinal cord to forebrain). Of course, higher neural systems enable more complex functional capacity. However, there appear to be some core principles of neural plasticity that are evident in all learning situations.

Other researchers have shown that spinal cord neurons can also support stepping behavior (Edgerton, Roy, & de Leon, 2001). In these studies, the spinal cord was cut and the animal's hindlegs were suspended over a treadmill. The movement of the treadmill against the paws engaged a neural circuit that organizes stepping behavior. With experience, and some shaping of the response, an animal can recover the capacity to step over a range of treadmill speeds. Moreover, this system can be modified by experience. If an obstacle is placed in the path of the paw so that the paw hits it while the leg swings forward, the spinal cord will learn to lift the paw higher to minimize contact with the obstacle.

On the basis of these observations, Anton Wernig (Wernig, Muller, Nanassy, & Cagol, 1995) attempted to shape locomotive behavior in humans who were paraplegic. The participants were suspended over a treadmill and step training was conducted over a period of 12 weeks. Over the course of this experience, the spinal cord appeared to regain the capacity to organize stepping. The participants regained additional leg support and learned to engage the stepping circuit, allowing them to walk forward using a wheeled walker (rollator). The results were remarkable. At the start of training, 86% of the participants were confined to a wheelchair. By the end, 86% were able to move about using a walker or rollator. Very few (7%) of the subjects in a comparison group that received conventional therapy exhibited any improvement. These studies were conducted in the mid-1990s. Today, step training is a common behavioral treatment available across the country. For other examples of how animal research has benefited society, see Carroll & Overmier (2001).

—J. W. Grau

factors serve to focus the effects of reinforcement on the instrumental response. The causal relation, or contingency, ensures that the reinforcer is delivered only after occurrence of the specified instrumental response. The contiguity relation ensures that other activities do not intrude between the specified response and the reinforcer to interfere with conditioning of the target response.

SAMPLE QUESTIONS

1. Compare and contrast free-operant and discrete-trial methods for the study of instrumental behavior.

2. What are the similarities and differences between positive and negative reinforcement?

3. What is the current thinking about instrumental reinforcement and creativity, and what is the relevant experimental evidence?

4. What are the effects of a delay of reinforcement on instrumental learning, and what causes these effects?

5. What was the purpose of Skinner's superstition experiment? What were the results, and how have those results been reinterpreted?

6. Describe alternative explanations of the learned-helplessness effect.

KEY TERMS

accidental reinforcement An instance in which the delivery of a reinforcer happens to coincide with a particular response even though that response was not responsible for the reinforcer presentation. Also called *adventitious reinforcement.*

adventitious reinforcement Same as *accidental reinforcement.*

appetitive stimulus A pleasant or satisfying stimulus that can be used to positively reinforce an instrumental response.

aversive stimulus An unpleasant or annoying stimulus than can be used to punish an instrumental response.

avoidance An instrumental conditioning procedure in which the instrumental response prevents the delivery of an aversive stimulus.

belongingness The theoretical idea, originally proposed by Thorndike, that an organism's evolutionary history makes certain responses fit or belong with certain reinforcers. Belongingness facilitates learning.

conditioned reinforcer A stimulus that becomes an effective reinforcer because of its association with a primary or an unconditioned reinforcer. Also called *secondary reinforcer.*

contiguity The simultaneous (or almost simultaneous) occurrence of two events, such as a response and a reinforcer. Also called *temporal contiguity.*

differential reinforcement of other behavior An instrumental conditioning procedure in which a positive reinforcer is periodically delivered only if the participant fails to perform a particular response. Abbreviated *DRO.*

discrete-trial method A method of instrumental conditioning in which the participant can perform the instrumental response only during specified periods usually determined either by placement of the participant in an experimental chamber or by the presentation of a stimulus.

DRO Abbreviation for *differential reinforcement of other behavior.*

escape An instrumental conditioning procedure in which the instrumental response terminates an aversive stimulus. (See also *negative reinforcement.*)

free-operant method A method of instrumental conditioning that permits repeated performance of the instrumental response without the participant being removed from the experimental chamber. (Compare with *discrete-trial method.*)

instinctive drift A gradual drift of instrumental behavior away from the responses required for reinforcement to species-typical or "instinctive" responses related to the reinforcer and to other stimuli in the experimental situation.

instrumental behavior An activity that occurs because it is effective in producing a particular consequence or reinforcer.

interim response A response that increases in frequency after the delivery of a periodic reinforcer and then declines as time for the the next reinforcer approaches.

latency The time between the start of a trial (or the start of a stimulus) and the instrumental response.

law of effect A rule for instrumental behavior, proposed by Thorndike, which states that if a response in the presence of a stimulus is followed by a satisfying event, the association between the stimulus and the response will be strengthened; if the response is followed by an annoying event, the association will be weakened.

learned-helplessness effect Interference with the learning of new instrumental responses as a result of exposure to inescapable and unavoidable aversive stimulation.

learned-helplessness hypothesis A theoretical idea that assumes that during exposure to inescapable and unavoidable aversive stimulation, participants learn that their behavior does not control environmental events.

magazine training A preliminary stage of instrumental conditioning in which a stimulus is repeatedly paired with the reinforcer to enable the participant to learn to go and get the reinforcer when it is presented. The sound of the food-delivery device, for example, may be repeatedly paired with food so that the animal will learn to go to the food cup when food is delivered.

marking procedure A procedure in which the instrumental response is immediately followed by a distinctive event (the participant is picked up or a flash of light is presented) that makes the instrumental response more memorable and helps overcome the deleterious effects of delayed reinforcement.

negative contrast Less responding for an unfavorable reinforcer following previous experience with a more desired reinforcer than in the absence of such prior experience.

negative reinforcement An instrumental conditioning procedure in which there is a negative contingency between the instrumental response and an aversive stimulus. If the instrumental response is performed, the aversive stimulus is terminated or prevented from occurring; if the instrumental response is not performed, the aversive stimulus is presented.

omission training An instrumental conditioning procedure in which the instrumental response prevents the delivery of a reinforcing stimulus. (See also *differential reinforcement of other behavior.*)

operant response A response that is defined by the effect it produces in the environment. Examples include pressing a lever and opening a door. Any sequence of movements that depresses the lever or opens the door constitutes an instance of that particular operant.

positive contrast Greater responding for a favorable reinforcer following previous experience with a less desired reinforcer than in the absence of such prior experience.

positive reinforcement An instrumental conditioning procedure in which there is a positive contingency between the instrumental response and a reinforcing stimulus. If the participant performs the response, it receives the reinforcing stimulus; if the participant does not perform the response, it does not receive the reinforcing stimulus.

punishment An instrumental conditioning procedure in which there is a positive contingency between the instrumental response and an aversive stimulus. If the participant performs the instrumental response, it receives the aversive stimulus; if the participant does not perform the instrumental response, it does not receive the aversive stimulus.

response-reinforcer contingency The causal relation between a response and a reinforcer, measured in terms of the probability of getting reinforced for making the response as compared to the probability of getting reinforced in the absence of the response.

running speed How fast (in feet per second, for example) an animal moves in a runway.

secondary reinforcer Same as *conditioned reinforcer.*

shaping Reinforcement of successive approximations to a desired instrumental response.

simultaneous behavioral contrast Behavioral contrast effects (positive and negative contrast) that are produced by frequent shifts between a favorable and an unfavorable reward condition, with each reward condition associated with its own distinctive stimulus.

superstitious behavior Behavior that increases in frequency because of accidental pairings of the delivery of a reinforcer with occurrences of the behavior.

temporal contiguity Same as *contiguity.*

terminal response A response that is most likely at the end of the interval between successive reinforcements that are presented at fixed intervals.

SCHEDULES OF REINFORCEMENT AND CHOICE BEHAVIOR

hapter 6 continues the discussion of the importance of the response-reinforcer relation in instrumental behavior by describing the effects of various schedules of reinforcement. A schedule of reinforcement is a program or rule that determines how presentations of the reinforcer are related to occurrences of the instrumental response. Schedules of reinforcement are important because they determine the rate and pattern of instrumental responses. I first describe simple fixed and variable ratio and fixed and variable interval schedules, and the patterns of instrumental responding produced by these schedules. I then describe response-rate schedules of reinforcement, before moving on to discuss choice behavior. A great deal of research has dealt with how schedules of reinforcement determine choice between different response alternatives. Concurrent and concurrent-chain schedules of reinforcement are techniques used in the empirical and theoretical analyses of choice. A particularly interesting form of choice is between modest short-term gains versus larger long-term gains, because these alternatives represent the dilemma of self-control.

In describing various instrumental conditioning procedures in Chapter 5, I may have given the impression that every occurrence of the instrumental response invariably results in delivery of the reinforcer in these procedures. Casual reflection suggests that such a perfect contingency between response and reinforcement is rare in the real world. You do not get a high grade on a test every time you spend many hours studying. You cannot get on a bus every time you go to the bus stop. Inviting someone over for dinner does not always result in a pleasant evening. In fact, in most cases the relation between instrumental responses and consequent reinforcement is rather complex. Attempts to study how these complex relations control the occurrence of instrumental responses have led to laboratory investigations of schedules of reinforcement.

A **schedule of reinforcement** is a program, or rule, that determines how and when the occurrence of a response will be followed by a reinforcer. Such a program could be set up in an infinite number of ways. The delivery of a reinforcer could depend on the occurrence of a certain number of responses, the passage of time, the presence of certain stimuli, the occurrence of other responses of the animal, or any number of other things. Cataloging the behavioral effects produced by the various possible schedules of reinforcement might seem to be a difficult task, but research has shown that the job is quite manageable. Reinforcement schedules that involve similar relations among stimuli, responses, and reinforcers usually produce similar patterns of behavior. The exact rate of responding may differ from one situation to another, but the pattern of results is highly predictable. This regularity has made the study of reinforcement schedules both interesting and fruitful.

Schedules of reinforcement influence both how an instrumental response is learned and how it is then maintained by reinforcement. Traditionally, however, investigators of schedule effects have been concerned primarily with the maintenance of behavior. Reinforcement schedules are typically investigated in Skinner boxes that permit continuous observation of behavior so that changes in the rate of responding can be readily observed and analyzed (Ferster & Skinner, 1957). The manner in which the operant response is initially shaped and conditioned is rarely of interest. Thus, investigations of reinforcement schedules have provided a great deal of information about the factors that control the maintenance and repetitive performance of instrumental behavior rather than its original acquisition.

Schedules of reinforcement are important for managers who have to make sure their employees continue to perform a job after having learned it. Even teachers are often concerned with encouraging the occurrence of already learned responses rather than teaching new ones. Many students who do poorly in school know how to do their homework and how to study, but simply choose not to. Schedules of reinforcement can be used to motivate more frequent studying behavior.

The study of schedules of reinforcement is critical to the understanding of instrumental behavior because of what such studies tell us about the reinforcement process and because "they serve as useful baselines for the study of other behavioral processes" (Lattal & Neef, 1996, p. 214). The influence of drugs, changes in motivation, and other manipulations often depend on the schedule of reinforcement that is in effect at the time. This makes the understanding of schedule performance critical to the study of a variety of other issues in behavior theory and behavioral neuroscience. Because of their pervasive importance, Zeiler (1984) called reinforcement schedules the "sleeping giant" in the analysis of behavior.

SIMPLE SCHEDULES OF INTERMITTENT REINFORCEMENT

Processes that organize and direct instrumental performance are activated in different ways by different schedules of reinforcement. In "simple" schedules, a single factor determines which occurrence of the instrumental response is reinforced.

Ratio Schedules

The defining characteristic of a **ratio schedule** is that reinforcement depends only on the number of responses the organism has performed. A ratio schedule requires merely counting the number of responses that have occurred and delivering the reinforcer each time the required number is reached. If the required number is one, every occurrence of the instrumental response results in delivery of the reinforcer. Such a schedule is technically called **continuous reinforcement** (abbreviated CRF).

Continuous reinforcement rarely occurs outside the laboratory because the world is not perfect. Pushing an elevator button usually brings the elevator, but all elevators occasionally malfunction so that nothing may happen when you push the button. Other forms of instrumental behavior also may result in reinforcement only some of the time. Situations in which responding is reinforced only some of the time are said to involve **partial** or **intermittent reinforcement.**

Fixed Ratio. Consider, for example, delivering the reinforcer after every 10th lever-press response in a study with laboratory rats. In such a schedule, there would be a fixed ratio between the number of responses the rat made and the number of reinforcers it got. (There would always be 10 responses per reinforcer.) This makes the procedure a **fixed ratio schedule.** More specifically, the procedure would be called a *fixed ratio 10* schedule of reinforcement (abbreviated FR 10).

Fixed ratio schedules are found in daily life wherever a fixed number of responses are always required for reinforcement. The delivery person who always has to visit the same number of houses to complete his route is working on a fixed ratio schedule. Checking class attendance by reading the roll involves a fixed ratio schedule, set by the number of students on the class roster. Piecework in factories is usually set up on a fixed ratio schedule: workers get paid for every so many "widgets" they put together. Making a phone call involves a fixed ratio schedule: you have to dial a fixed number of digits to complete each call.

A continuous reinforcement schedule is also a fixed ratio schedule. Continuous reinforcement involves a fixed ratio of one response per reinforcer. On a continuous reinforcement schedule, organisms typically respond at a steady but moderate rate. Only brief and unpredictable pauses occur. On a CRF schedule, a pigeon, for example, will peck a key for food steadily at first and will then slow down as it satisfies its hunger.

A very different pattern of responding occurs when an intermittent fixed ratio schedule of reinforcement is in effect. You are not likely to pause in the middle of dialing a phone number, but you may take a while before starting to make the call. This is the typical pattern for fixed ratio schedules. A steady and high rate of responding exists once the behavior gets under way, but there may be a pause before the start of the required number of responses. These features of responding are clearly evident in a **cumulative record** of the behavior.

A cumulative record is a special way of representing how a response is repeated over time. It shows the total (or cumulative) number of responses that have occurred up to a particular point in time. Before computers became common, cumulative records were obtained

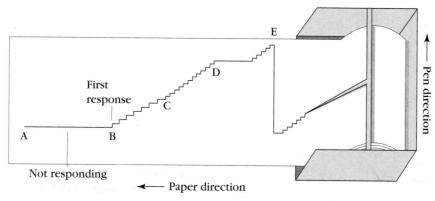

Figure 6.1 The construction of a cumulative record by a cumulative recorder for the continuous recording of behavior. The paper moves out of the machine toward the left at a constant speed. Each response causes the pen to move up the paper one step. No responses occurred between points A and B. A moderate rate of responding occurred between points B and C, and a rapid rate occurred between points C and D. At point E, the pen reset to the bottom of the page.

with the use of a chart recorder (see Figure 6.1). The recorder consisted of a rotating drum that pulled paper out of the recorder at a constant speed. A pen rested on the surface of the paper. If no responses occurred, the pen remained stationary and made a horizontal line as the paper came out of the machine. If the subject performed a lever-press response, the pen moved one step vertically on the paper. Since each lever-press response caused the pen to move one step up the paper, the total vertical distance traveled by the pen represented the cumulative (or total) number of responses the subject made. Because the paper came out of the recorder at a constant speed, the horizontal distance on the cumulative record provided a measure of how much time had elapsed in the session. The slope of the line made by the cumulative recorder represents the subject's *rate of responding.*

The cumulative record provides a complete visual representation of when and how frequently the subject responds during a session. In the record of Figure 6.1, for example, the subject did not perform the response between points A and B, and a slow rate of responding occurred between points B and C. Responses occurred more frequently between points C and D, but the subject paused at D. After responding resumed, the pen reached the top of the page (at point E) and reset to the bottom for additional responses.

Figure 6.2 shows the cumulative record of a pigeon whose responding had stabilized on a reinforcement schedule that required 120 pecks for each delivery of the reinforcer (an FR 120 schedule). Each food delivery is indicated by the small downward deflections of the recorder pen. The bird stopped responding after each food delivery; when it resumed pecking, it responded at a high and steady rate. The zero rate of responding that occurs just after reinforcement is called the **postreinforcement pause.** The high and steady rate of responding that completes each ratio requirement is called the **ratio run.**

If the ratio requirement is increased a little (from FR 120 to FR 150, for example), the rate of responding during the ratio run may remain the same. With higher ratio requirements, longer postreinforcement pauses tend to occur (for example, Baron & Herpolsheimer, 1999; Felton & Lyon, 1966). If the ratio requirement undergoes a sudden and significant increase (from FR 120 to FR 500, for example), the animal is likely to pause periodically before the completion of the ratio requirement (for example, Stafford & Branch,

[handwritten margin notes:]
variable ratio +
interval > Slot
machine

FI & FR : Post reinforcement
pauses
FR & FI : Produce high
response just
before.

Start a behavior
you want a
continuous
reinforcer
To maintain it, you
want to use a
VI or VR.

[handwritten notes above figure:] high responding just before present of next reinforcers

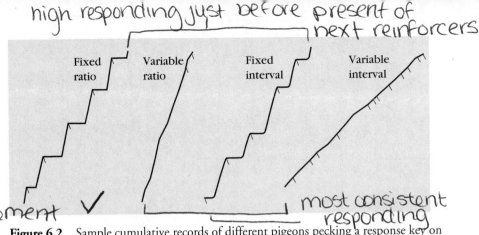

[handwritten: ✓] *[handwritten: most consistent responding]*

Figure 6.2 Sample cumulative records of different pigeons pecking a response key on four simple schedules of food reinforcement: fixed ratio 120, variable ratio 360, fixed interval 4 minute, and variable interval 2 minute. (From *Schedules of Reinforcement*, by C. B. Ferster and B. F. Skinner, 1957, Appleton-Century-Crofts.)

1998). This effect is called **ratio strain.** In extreme cases, ratio strain may be so great that the animal stops responding altogether. In using ratio schedules, an investigator must be careful not to raise the ratio requirement (or, more generally, the difficulty of a task) too quickly, because ratio strain may occur and the organism may give up altogether.

Although the pause that occurs before a ratio run in fixed ratio schedules is historically called the *postreinforcement pause,* research has shown that the length of the pause is controlled by the upcoming ratio requirement (for example, Baron & Herpolsheimer, 1999). If you procrastinate before starting a ratio task such as washing your car, it is because you are not quite ready to tackle the job, not because you are "resting" from the previous time you did the work. Thus, the postreinforcement pause would be more correctly labeled the *pre-ratio pause.*

Variable Ratio. In a fixed ratio schedule, a predictable number of responses is required for each reinforcer. This predictability can be disrupted by varying the number of responses required for reinforcement from one occasion to the next. Such a procedure is still a ratio schedule because reinforcement still depends on how many responses the organism makes. A procedure in which a different number of responses is required for the delivery of each reward is called a **variable ratio schedule** (abbreviated VR). Investigators may, for example, require a pigeon to make 10 responses to earn the first reward, 13 to earn the second reward, 7 for the next one, and so on. The numerical value of a variable ratio schedule indicates the average number of responses required per reinforcer. Thus, the procedure in this case would be a variable ratio 10 schedule (abbreviated VR 10).

Variable ratio schedules are found in daily life whenever an unpredictable amount of effort is required to obtain a reinforcer. For example, each time a custodian goes into a room on his rounds, he knows that some amount of cleaning will be necessary, but he does not know exactly how dirty the room will be. Gamblers playing a slot machine are responding on a VR schedule. They have to play the machine to win, but they never know how many plays will produce the winning combination. Variable ratio schedules are also common in sports. A certain number of strokes are always required to finish a hole in golf, but players cannot be sure how many strokes they will need when they start.

Because the number of responses required for reinforcement is not predictable, predictable pauses in the rate of responding are less likely with VR schedules than with FR

BOX 6.1

THE POSTREINFORCEMENT PAUSE AND PROCRASTINATION

The postreinforcement pause that occurs in fixed ratio schedules in the laboratory is also evident in common human experience. In FR schedules, the pause occurs because a predictably large number of responses are always required to produce the next reward. Such procrastination is legendary in human behavior. Consider, for example, a semester in which you have several term papers to write. You are likely to work on one term paper at a time. When you have completed one, however, you probably will not start working on the next one right away. There will be a postreinforcement pause. After completing a large project, people tend to take some time off before starting the next

one. Procrastination between tasks or before the start of a new job is the rule rather than the exception.

Laboratory results provide a suggestion for overcoming procrastination. Fixed ratio schedule performance in the laboratory indicates that once animals begin to respond on a ratio run, they respond at a high and steady rate until they complete the ratio requirement. This suggests that if somehow you got yourself to start on a job, chances are you would not find it difficult to keep going. Only the beginning is hard. One technique that works pretty well in getting started is to tell yourself that you will start by just doing a little bit of the job. If you are trying to write a paper, tell yourself that you will write only one paragraph to start with. Once you have completed the first paragraph, you may find it easier to write the second one, then the one after that, and so on. If you are procrastinating about spring cleaning, try not to think about doing the entire job. Start with a small part of it, such as washing the kitchen floor. The rest will then come more easily.

schedules. Rather, organisms respond at a fairly steady rate on VR schedules. Figure 6.2 shows a cumulative record for a pigeon whose pecking behavior was maintained on a VR 360 schedule of reinforcement. Notice that even though the VR 360 schedule required, on average, many more pecks for each reinforcer than the FR 120 schedule, the VR 360 schedule maintained a much steadier pattern of responding.

Although postreinforcement pauses can occur on variable ratio schedules (see Blakely & Schlinger, 1988; Schlinger, Blakely, & Kaczor, 1990), such pauses are longer and more prominent with fixed ratio schedules. The overall response rate on FR and VR schedules is similar provided that, on average, similar numbers of responses are required. However, the overall response rate tends to be distributed in a pause-run pattern with FR schedules, whereas a steadier pattern of responding is observed with VR schedules (for example, Crossman, Bonem, & Phelps, 1987). (For additional analyses of ratio schedules, see Bizo & Killeen, 1997.)

Interval Schedules

In ratio schedules, reinforcement depends only on the number of responses the organism has performed. In **interval schedules,** responses are reinforced only if the responses occur after a certain amount of time has passed.

Fixed Interval.   In a simple interval schedule, a response is reinforced only if it occurs more than a set amount of time after the last delivery of the reinforcer. In a **fixed interval schedule** (abbreviated FI), the set time is constant from one occasion to the next. Fixed interval schedules are found in situations where a fixed amount of time is required to prepare or set up the reinforcer. For example, washing clothes in a washing machine requires a certain amount of time to complete the wash cycle. No matter how many times you open the washing machine before the required amount of time has passed, you will not be reinforced with clean clothes. Once the cycle is finished, the reinforcer becomes available, and you can take out your clean clothes any time after that.

Similar contingencies can be set up in the laboratory. Consider, for example, a fixed interval 4-minute schedule (FI 4 min) for pecking in pigeons. A bird on this schedule would get reinforced for the first peck it made after 4 minutes have passed since the last food delivery (or the beginning of the schedule cycle). Because pecks made less than 4 minutes after each food delivery are never reinforced, the subjects learn to wait to respond until the end of the FI (see Figure 6.2). As the time for the availability of the next reinforcer draws closer, the response rate increases. This increase in response rate is evident as an acceleration in the cumulative record toward the end of the FI. The pattern of responding that develops with FI reinforcement schedules is accordingly called the **fixed interval scallop.**

Performance on an FI schedule reflects the subject's accuracy in telling time. If the subject were entirely incapable of telling time, it would respond equally throughout the FI cycle. The postreinforcement pause and the subsequent acceleration toward the end of the interval reflect a rudimentary ability to tell time. How could this ability be improved? Common experience suggests that having a clock of some sort makes it much easier to judge time intervals. The same thing happens with pigeons on an FI schedule. In one study, the clock consisted of a spot of light that grew into a slit as time passed during the FI cycle. Introduction of this clock stimulus increased the duration of the postreinforcement pause and caused responding to shift closer to the end of the FI cycle (Ferster & Skinner, 1957). As expected, the clock stimulus increased the efficiency of performance on the FI schedule.

It is important to realize that an FI schedule does not guarantee that the reinforcer will be provided at a certain point in time. Pigeons on an FI 4-min schedule do not automatically receive access to grain every 4 minutes. Instrumental responses are required for the reinforcer in interval schedules, just as in ratio schedules. The interval determines only when the reinforcer *becomes available,* not when it is delivered. In order to receive the reinforcer after it has become available, the subject still has to make the instrumental response. (For recent analyses of FI schedule performance, see Baron & Leinenweber, 1994; Hoyert, 1992; Lejeune & Wearden, 1991; Machado, 1997b; Wynne, Staddon, & Delius, 1996).

The scheduling of tests in college courses has important similarities to the basic FI schedule. Usually, each course has only two or three tests, and they are evenly distributed during the term. There may be only a midterm and a final exam. Such a schedule encourages a pattern of studying that is very similar to what is observed with an FI schedule in the laboratory. Students spend little effort studying at the beginning of the semester or just after the midterm exam. Instead, they begin to study a week or so before each exam, and the rate of studying rapidly increases as the day of the exam approaches.

Variable Interval. In fixed interval schedules, responses are reinforced if they occur after a fixed amount of time has passed since the delivery of the previous reinforcer (or the beginning of the schedule cycle). Interval schedules also can be unpredictable. With a **variable interval schedule** (abbreviated VI), responses are reinforced if they occur after a variable interval since the delivery of the previous reinforcer (or the beginning of the schedule cycle).

Variable interval schedules are found in situations where an unpredictable amount of time is required to prepare or set up the reinforcer. A mechanic who cannot tell you how long it will take to fix your car has imposed a VI schedule on you. The car will not be ready for some time, during which attempts to get it will not be reinforced. How much time has to pass before the car will be ready is unpredictable. A sales clerk at a bakery is also on a VI schedule of reinforcement. Some time has to pass after waiting on a customer before another will enter the store to buy something. The interval between customers is unpredictable.

In a laboratory study, a VI schedule could be set up in which the first reinforcer became available when at least 1 minute has passed since the beginning of the session, the second reinforcer became available when at least 3 minutes have passed since the first reward, and the third reinforcer became available when at least 2 minutes have passed since the second reward. In this procedure, the average interval that has to pass before successive rewards become available is 2 minutes. Therefore, the procedure would be called a variable interval 2-minute schedule, or VI 2 min.

As in fixed interval schedules, the subject in VI schedules has to perform the instrumental response to obtain the reinforcer. Reinforcers are not given "free"; they are given only if the organism responds after the variable interval. Like variable ratio schedules, VI schedules maintain steady and stable rates of responding without regular pauses (see Figure 6.2).

Interval Schedules and Limited Hold.   In simple interval schedules, once the reinforcer becomes available, it remains available until the required response is made, no matter how long that may take. On an FI 2-min schedule, for example, the reinforcer becomes available 2 minutes after the start of the schedule cycle. If the animal responds at exactly this time, it will be reinforced. If it waits and responds 90 minutes later, it will still get reinforced. Once the reinforcer has been set up, it remains available until the response occurs.

With interval schedules outside the laboratory, it is more common for reinforcers to become available only for limited periods. Consider, for example, a dormitory cafeteria. Meals are served only at fixed intervals; therefore, going to the cafeteria is reinforced only after a certain amount of time has passed since the last meal. Once a meal becomes available, however, you have a limited amount of time in which to get it. This kind of restriction on how long the reinforcer remains available is called a **limited hold.** Limited hold restrictions can be added to both fixed interval and variable interval schedules.

Comparison of Ratio and Interval Schedules

There are striking similarities between the patterns of responding maintained by simple ratio and interval schedules. As I have described, both fixed ratio and fixed interval schedules have a postreinforcement pause after each delivery of the reinforcer. In addition, both FR and FI schedules produce high rates of responding just before the delivery of the next reinforcer. By contrast, variable ratio and variable interval schedules maintain steady rates of responding, without predictable pauses. Does this mean that interval and ratio schedules motivate behavior in the same way? Hardly! The surface similarities hide fundamental differences in underlying mechanisms between interval and ratio schedules.

Ratio and interval schedules activate different neurochemical changes in the brain (Barrett & Hoffmann, 1991). As might be expected, behavior maintained by interval schedules is mediated by the organism's sense of time, whereas timing mechanisms are not involved with ratio performance (Staddon, Wynne, & Higa, 1991). (I discuss mechanisms of timing in greater detail in Chapter 12.)

Early evidence of fundamental differences between ratio and interval schedules was provided by an important experiment by Reynolds (1975). Reynolds compared the rate of key pecking in pigeons reinforced on variable ratio and variable interval schedules. Two pigeons were trained to peck the response key for food reinforcement. One bird was reinforced on a VR schedule—the frequency of reinforcement was entirely determined by the bird's rate of responding. The other bird was reinforced on a VI schedule. To make sure that the opportunities for reinforcement would be identical for the two birds, the VI schedule was controlled by the behavior of the bird reinforced on the VR schedule. Each time the VR pigeon was just one response short of the requirement for reinforcement on that trial, the experimenter set up the reinforcer for the VI bird. With this arrangement, the next response made by each bird was reinforced. Thus, the frequency of reinforcement was virtually identical for the two animals.

Figure 6.3 shows the cumulative record of pecking exhibited by each bird. Even though the two pigeons received the same frequency and distribution of reinforcers, they behaved very differently. The pigeon reinforced on the VR schedule responded at a much higher rate than the pigeon reinforced on the VI schedule. The VR schedule motivated much more vigorous instrumental behavior (see also Baum, 1993; Cole, 1994).

Similar results have been found in a study of schedule effects with undergraduate students (Raia, Shillingford, Miller, & Baier, 2000). The task was akin to a video game. A target appeared on a computer screen, and the students had to maneuver a spaceship and "fire" at the target with a joystick as the instrumental response. Following a direct hit of the target, the subjects received 5 cents. However, not every "hit" was reinforced. Which occurrence of the instrumental response was reinforced depended on the schedule of reinforcement programmed into the software. The students were assigned to pairs, but each worked in a separate cubicle and didn't know that he or she had a partner. One member of each pair received reinforcement on a variable ratio schedule. The other member of the pair was reinforced on a variable interval schedule that was yoked to the VR schedule. Thus, as in the pigeon experiment, reinforcers became available to both subjects at the same time, but one controlled access to the reinforcer through a VR schedule and the other did not.

Raia et al. (2000) studied the effects of response shaping, instructions, and the presence of a consummatory response on performance on the VR-VI yoking procedure. (The consummatory response was being required to pick up the 5-cent reinforcer each time it was delivered and put it into a piggy bank.) One set of conditions was quite similar to the pigeon studies: the students were shaped to make the instrumental response, they received

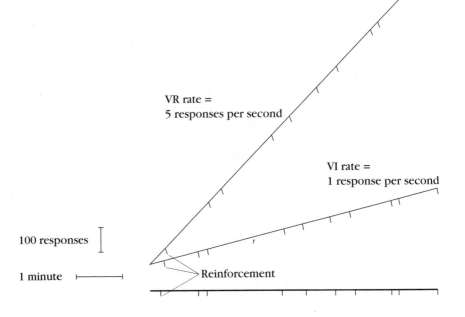

Figure 6.3 Cumulative records for two pigeons, one reinforced on a variable ratio (VR) schedule and the other yoked to it on a variable interval (VI) schedule. Although the two pigeons received the same rate of reinforcement, the VR bird responded five times as fast as the VI bird. (From *A Primer of Operant Conditioning*, 2nd ed., by G. S. Reynolds. Copyright © 1975 by Scott, Foresman. Reprinted by permission.)

VR rate =
5 responses per second

VI rate =
1 response per second

100 responses

1 minute

Reinforcement

minimal instructions, and they were required to make the consummatory response. Interestingly, under these conditions, the college students performed just like the pigeons. Higher rates of responding occurred for the individual of each pair who was reinforced on the variable ratio schedule.

Differential Reinforcement of Interresponse Times. Why might ratio schedules produce higher rates of responding than interval schedules? The answer has not been easy to find, but research is converging on the idea that what is critical is the spacing between responses just before reinforcement. The interval between one response and the next is called the **interresponse time** or **IRT.** I noted in Chapter 5 that a variety of different features of behavior can be increased in probability by reinforcement. The interval between successive responses is also a behavioral parameter than can be shaped by reinforcement. If short IRTs are reinforced, the subject becomes more likely to make short IRTs. If long IRTs are reinforced, the subject becomes more likely to make long IRTs. A subject that shows mostly short interresponse times will be responding at a high rate. By contrast, a subject that shows mostly long interresponse times will be responding at a low rate.

How do ratio and interval schedules determine the reinforcement of interresponse times? With a ratio schedule, there are no constraints on when responses count toward obtaining the reinforcer. In fact, the faster the subject completes the ratio requirement, the faster it will receive the reinforcer. Thus, a ratio schedule favors not waiting long between responses. It favors short interresponse times.

In contrast, interval schedules provide little advantage for short interresponse times; they favor the performance of long IRTs. Consider, for example, an FI 2-min schedule of food reinforcement. Each food pellet becomes available 2 minutes after the last one was delivered. If the subject responds frequently before the food pellet is set up, those responses and short IRTs will not be reinforced. On the other hand, if the subject waits a long time between responses (emitting long IRTs), its response is more likely to occur after the reinforcer has been set up, and it is more likely to be reinforced. Thus, interval schedules differentially reinforce long IRTs, and this results in lower rates of responding than what is observed with ratio schedules (Cole, 1999; Reed, Soh, Hildebrandt, DeJongh, & Shek, 2000; see also Baum, 1993; Cole, 1994; Dawson & Dickinson, 1990; McDowell & Wixted, 1988; Wearden & Clark, 1988; see also Lattal, Reilly, & Kohn, 1998).

Response-Rate Schedules of Reinforcement

Although ratio schedules produce higher rates of responding than comparable interval schedules, neither type of schedule requires a specific rate of responding for reinforcement. By contrast, **response-rate schedules** specifically require that the organism respond at a particular rate to get reinforced.

In response-rate schedules, whether a response is reinforced depends on how soon it occurs after the preceding response. A reinforcement schedule can be set up, for example, in which a response is reinforced only if it occurs within 5 seconds following the preceding response. If the animal makes a response every 5 seconds, its rate of response will be 12 per minute. Thus, the schedule provides reinforcement if the rate of response is 12 per minute or greater. The organism will not be reinforced if its rate of response falls below 12 per minute. As you might suspect, this procedure encourages responding at high rates. It is called **differential reinforcement of high rates,** or DRH.

In DRH schedules, a response is reinforced only if it occurs *before* a certain amount of time has elapsed following the preceding response. The opposite result is achieved if a response is reinforced only if it occurs *after* a certain amount of time has elapsed following

BOX **6.2**

WAGE SCALES AND SCHEDULES OF REINFORCEMENT

The basis for determining the wages paid for work performed in a company constitutes a schedule of reinforcement. Laboratory research indicates that different schedules of reinforcement maintain different patterns and rates of responding. We may expect different wage systems to produce different rates of responding in work situations as well. A study of productivity among servers at three family restaurants illustrates such effects (George & Hopkins, 1989).

As is customary, the servers were paid an hourly wage. Most earned $1.90 plus tips, and a few earned more based on seniority. The employees complained that they were underpaid. The owners decided that they could not increase wages without an increase in productivity because the restaurants were already losing money. The servers claimed that because of their low wages, they had no incentive to increase productivity. The two sides thus found themselves stuck in a common labor–management dispute.

Following the advice of behavioral consultants, the owners adopted a performance-contingent pay scale. Such a system is a variant of a fixed ratio schedule in which rate of reinforcement is directly related to rate of responding. In a performance-contingent pay scale, each server is paid a fixed proportion of his or her gross sales. The proportion was set at 7%. Servers could easily make at least $1.90 per hour at 7% of gross sales, and 7% seemed to be the break-even point for profitability of the restaurant.

Introduction of the performance-contingent pay scale increased the hourly earning of the servers 24–30% in the three restaurants. The new schedule of reinforcement also increased productivity. Gross sales per labor hour increased 18–36%. This increase occurred primarily because of increases of 18–26% in the number of customers served per labor hour, rather than because of how much was purchased by each customer.

---

the previous response. This type of procedure is called **differential reinforcement of low rates,** abbreviated DRL. As you might suspect, DRL schedules encourage subjects to respond slowly.

Response-rate schedules are found outside the laboratory in situations that require particular rates of responding. DRH schedules are in effect in sports where speed is of the essence. For example, running from home plate to first base in a baseball game is reinforced only if it occurs faster than the time it takes to throw the ball to first base. In other circumstances, responding is reinforced only if it occurs at a specified rate. This is typically the case in dancing and music. Response-rate schedules are also in effect on an assembly line, where the speed of movement of the line dictates the rate of response for the workers. If an employee responds more slowly than the specified rate, he or she will not be reinforced and may, in fact, get fired. However, workers must be careful not to work too fast. Those who work faster than the accepted norm may be disliked by their peers.

CHOICE BEHAVIOR: CONCURRENT SCHEDULES

The reinforcement schedules I have described thus far involve a single response and reinforcement of that response. However, experiments in which only one response is being measured are not likely to provide a complete account of behavior. Behavior involves more than the repetition of individual responses. Even in a simple situation such as a Skinner box, organisms engage in a variety of activities and are continually choosing among possible alternatives. People are also constantly having to make choices about what to do. Should you go to the movies or stay at home and study? Should you go shopping tonight or watch television and go shopping tomorrow? Understanding the mechanisms of choice is fundamental to the understanding of behavior because the choices organisms make determine the occurrence of individual responses.

Choice situations can be rather complicated. For example, a person may have a choice of 12 different activities (reading the newspaper, watching television, going for a walk, playing with the dog, and the like), each of which produces a different type of reinforcer according to a different reinforcement schedule. Analyzing all the factors that control the individual's behavior in such a situation is a formidable task, if not an impossible one. Therefore, psychologists have begun experimental investigations of the mechanisms of choice by studying simpler situations. The simplest choice situation has two response alternatives, with each response followed by a reinforcer according to its own schedule of reinforcement.

Historically, research on choice behavior was conducted using mazes, particularly the T maze (see Woodworth & Schlosberg, 1954). Recent approaches to the study of choice use Skinner boxes equipped with two manipulanda, such as two pecking keys. In the typical experiment, responding on each key is reinforced on some schedule of reinforcement. The two schedules are in effect at the same time (or concurrently), and the subject is free to switch from one response key to the other. This type of procedure is called a **concurrent schedule.** It allows for continuous measurement of choice because the organism is free to change back and forth between the response alternatives at any time.

Figure 6.4 shows an example of a concurrent schedule. If the pigeon pecks the left key, it receives food according to a VI 60-sec schedule. Pecks on the right-hand key produce food according to an FR 10 schedule. The subject is free to peck on either key at any time. The point of the experiment is to see how the pigeon distributes its pecks on the two keys and how the schedule of reinforcement on each key influences its choices.

Measures of Choice Behavior

The individual's choice in a concurrent schedule is reflected in the distribution of its behavior between the two response alternatives. This can be measured in several ways. One common technique is to calculate the *relative rate of responding* on each alternative. The relative

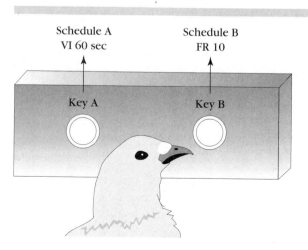

Schedule A
VI 60 sec

Schedule B
FR 10

Key A

Key B

Figure 6.4 Diagram of a concurrent schedule. Pecks on key A are reinforced according to a VI 60-sec schedule of reinforcement. Pecks on key B are reinforced according to an FR 10 schedule of reinforcement.

Know formulas:

✗

rate of responding on key A, for example, is calculated by dividing the response rate on key A by the total rate of responding (rate on key A plus rate on key B):

$$R_A/(R_A + R_B) \qquad\qquad (6.1)$$

where R_A is the rate of responding on key A and R_B is the rate on key B. If the pigeon pecks equally often on the two response keys, this ratio will be 0.5. If the rate of responding on key A is greater than on key B, the ratio will be greater than 0.5. On the other hand, if the rate of responding on key A is less than on key B, the ratio will be less than 0.5. The relative rate of responding on key B can be calculated in a comparable manner.

As you might suspect, how an organism distributes its behavior between the two response alternatives is greatly influenced by the reinforcement schedule in effect for each response. For example, if the same variable interval reinforcement schedule is available for each response alternative, as in a concurrent VI 60-sec VI 60-sec procedure, the pigeon will peck the two keys equally often. The relative rate of responding for pecks on each side will be 0.5. This result is intuitively reasonable. If the pigeon spent all its time pecking on one side, it would receive only the reinforcers programmed for that side. The bird can get more reinforcers by pecking on both sides. Since the VI schedule available on each side is the same, there is no advantage in responding more on one side than on the other.

By responding equally often on each side of a concurrent VI 60-sec VI 60-sec schedule, the pigeon will also earn reinforcers equally often on each side. The relative rate of reinforcement earned for each response alternative can be calculated in a manner comparable to the relative rate of response. For example, the relative rate of reinforcement for alternative A is the rate of reinforcement of response A divided by the total rate of reinforcement (the sum of the rate of reward earned on side A plus the rate of reward earned on side B). This is expressed in the formula

$$r_A/(r_A + r_B) \qquad\qquad (6.2)$$

✗ where r_A and r_B represent the rates of reinforcement earned on each response alternative. On a concurrent VI 60-sec VI 60-sec schedule, the relative rate of reinforcement for each response alternative will be 0.5 because the subject earns rewards equally often on each side.

The Matching Law

As I have described, with a concurrent VI 60-sec VI 60-sec schedule, both the relative rate of responding and the relative rate of reinforcement for each response alternative are 0.5. Thus, the relative rate of responding is equal to the relative rate of reinforcement. Will this equality also occur if the two response alternatives are not reinforced according to the same schedule?

To answer this important question, Herrnstein (1961) studied the distribution of responses on various concurrent VI-VI schedules in which the maximum total rate of reinforcement the pigeons could earn was fixed at 40 per hour. Depending on the exact value of each VI schedule, different proportions of the 40 reinforcers could be obtained by pecking the left and right keys. For example, with a concurrent VI 6-min VI 2-min schedule, a maximum of 10 reinforcers per hour could be obtained by responding on the VI 6-min alternative, and a maximum of 30 reinforcers per hour could be obtained by responding on the VI 2-min alternative.

Herrnstein studied the effects of a variety of concurrent VI-VI schedules. There was no constraint on which side the pigeons could peck. They could respond exclusively on one side or the other, or they could distribute their pecks between the two sides in some manner.

Courtesy of Donald A. Dewsbury

R. J. Herrnstein

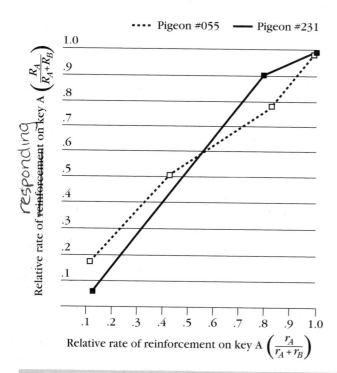

Figure 6.5 Various combinations of VI schedules were tested whose combined reinforcement rate was 40 reinforcements per hour. Note that throughout the range of schedules, the relative rate of responding nearly equals (matches) the relative rate of reinforcement. (From "Relative and Absolute Strength of Response as a Function of Frequency of Reinforcement," by R. J. Herrnstein, 1961, *Journal of the Experimental Analysis of Behavior, 4,* pp. 267–272. Copyright © 1961 by the Society for the Experimental Analysis of Behavior, Inc. Reprinted by permission.)

★relative rate of responding = relative rate of reinforcement

As it turned out, the pigeons distributed their responses in a highly predictable fashion. The results, summarized in Figure 6.5, indicate that the relative rate of responding on a given alternative was always very nearly equal to the relative rate of reinforcement earned on that alternative. If the pigeons earned a greater proportion of their reinforcers on alternative A, they made a correspondingly greater proportion of their responses on alternative A. Thus, the relative rate of responding on an alternative *matched* the relative rate of reinforcement on that alternative. Similar findings have been obtained in a variety of situations, which encouraged Herrnstein to state the relation as a law of behavior, the **matching law.** (For an anthology of Herrnstein's papers on this topic, see Herrnstein, 1997.)

There are two common mathematical expressions of the matching law. In one formulation, rates of responding and reinforcement on one alternative are expressed as a proportion of total response and reinforcement rates, as follows:

$$R_A/(R_A + R_B) = r_A/(r_A + r_B) \qquad (6.3)$$

As before, R_A and R_B in this equation represent the rates of responding on keys A and B, and r_A and r_B represent the rates of reinforcement earned on each response alternative.

The second formulation of the matching law is simpler but mathematically equivalent to equation 6.3. In the second version, the rates of responding and reinforcement on one alternative are expressed as a proportion of the rates of responding and reinforcement on the other alternative, as follows:

$$R_A/R_B = r_A/r_B \qquad (6.4)$$

Both mathematical expressions of the matching law represent the same basic principle, namely, that *relative rates of responding match relative rates of reinforcement.* (For an example

W. M. Baum

of matching involving a drug reinforcer in monkeys, see Meisch & Spiga, 1998. For an extension of the matching law to how pigeons distribute themselves between patches of food, see Baum & Kraft, 1998.)

Undermatching, Overmatching, and Response Bias. The matching law clearly indicates that choices are not made capriciously—they are an orderly function of rates of reinforcement. The precise characterization of the function is the subject of continuing research (see reviews by Baum, 1979; Davison & McCarthy, 1988; Nevin, 1998; Wearden & Burgess, 1982; Williams, 1988, 1994). Although the matching law has enjoyed considerable success and has guided much research over the past 30 years, relative rates of responding do not always exactly match relative rates of reinforcement.

Most instances in which choice behavior does not correspond perfectly to the matching relation can be accommodated by adding two parameters, *b* and *s*, to equation 6.4. This generalized form of the matching law (Baum, 1974) is as follows:

$$R_A/R_B = b(r_A/r_B)^s \tag{6.5}$$

The parameter *s* represents *sensitivity* of the choice behavior to the relative rates of reinforcement for the response alternatives. When perfect matching occurs, *s* is equal to 1.0, in which case relative response rates are a direct function of relative rates of reinforcement.

One type of deviation from perfect matching involves reduced sensitivity of the choice behavior to the relative rates of reinforcement. Such results are referred to as **undermatching** and can be accommodated by equation 6.5 by making the exponent *s* less than 1.0. Notice that if the exponent *s* is less than 1.0, the value of the term representing relative reinforcer rates—$(r_A/r_B)^s$—becomes smaller, indicating the reduced sensitivity to the relative rate of reinforcement.

In other instances, the relative rate of responding is more sensitive to the relative rate of reinforcement than what is predicted by perfect matching. Such outcomes are called **overmatching** and can be accommodated by equation 6.5 by making the exponent greater than 1.0. In this case, the value of the term representing the relative rate of reinforcement—$r_A/r_B)^s$—is increased, indicating the increased sensitivity to this factor.

Choices are more likely to exhibit reduced sensitivity to relative reinforcement rates than they are to exhibit enhanced sensitivity to reinforcement rates. Consequently, undermatching is found more often than overmatching. The sensitivity parameter can be influenced by numerous variables, including the species tested, the effort or difficulty involved in switching from one alternative to the other, and the details of how the schedule alternatives are constructed (for example, see Aparicio, 2001; Davison, 1991a; Davison & Jones, 1995; Dreyfus, DePorto-Callan, & Pesillo, 1993; Elliffe & Alslop, 1996; Foster, Temple, Robertson, Nair, & Poling, 1996). In general, making it more difficult to switch from one response alternative to the other increases the sensitivity parameter; when switching is more difficult, organisms are more sensitive to the relative rates of reinforcement for the response alternatives.

The parameter *b* in equation 6.5 represents response *bias*. In Herrnstein's original experiment (and in most others that have followed), animals chose between two responses of the same type (pecking a response key), and each response was reinforced by the same type of reinforcer (a short period of access to food). Response bias influences choice when the response alternatives are different (for example, pecking a key and stepping on a treadle). Parameter *b* is also important when the reinforcer provided for the two responses is different. In the case of pigeons, one reinforcer may be buckwheat and the other hemp seed. A preference (or bias) for one response or one reinforcer over the other influences the bias parameter *b* (see Hanson & Green, 1986; Miller, 1976; Sumpter, Temple, & Foster, 1998).

In the absence of bias, b is equal to 1.0. Depending on the nature of the bias or preference, b will be greater or less than 1.0.

The Matching Law and Reinforcer Value.   The matching relation has been extended to aspects of reinforcers other than their rate of occurrence. For example, the relative rate of responding has been found to be a function of the relative amount of each reinforcer, as well as the relative delay of reinforcement (for example, Gibbon & Fairhurst, 1994; Grace, 1995; see also Ho, Wogar, Bradshaw, & Szabadi, 1997). Relative rates of responding have also been found to be determined by the palatability of the reinforcers (Shah, Bradshaw, & Szabadi, 1991). Features of a reinforcer such as its amount, palatability, and delay can be considered to be aspects of its general value. Larger, more palatable, and more immediate reinforcers presumably are of greater value. However, it is not yet clear exactly how various features of a reinforcer combine to determine reinforcer value. (For further discussion of this issue, see McLean & Blampied, 2001; Nevin, 1998; Williams, 1994b.)

The Matching Law and Simple Reinforcement Schedules.   If the matching law represents a fundamental fact about behavior, then it should also characterize responding on simple schedules of reinforcement. But simple schedules have only one response manipulandum. How can a law that describes the distribution of responses among several alternatives be applied to single response?

As Herrnstein (1970) pointed out, even single-response situations can involve a choice. The choice is between making the specified response (bar pressing or pecking a key, for example) and engaging in other possible activities (grooming, walking around, pecking the floor, sniffing holes in the experimental chamber). On a simple schedule, the subject receives not only explicit reinforcement for making a specific operant response but also intrinsic rewards for the other activities in which it may engage. Hence, the total reinforcement includes the programmed extrinsic rewards as well as the unprogrammed sources of reinforcement. This type of analysis permits application of the matching law to single-response reinforcement schedules.

Assume that R_A represents the rate of the specified operant response in the schedule, R_O represents the rate of the animal's other activities, r_A is the rate of the explicit programmed reinforcement, and r_O is the rate of the intrinsic reinforcement for the other activities. With these values substituted into equation 6.3, the matching law for single-response situations can be stated as follows:

$$R_A/(R_A + R_O) = r_A/(r_A + r_O) \qquad (6.6)$$

Solving this equation for R_A provides the following:

$$R_A = (R_A + R_O)r_A/(r_A + r_O) \qquad (6.7)$$

This equation can be solved if the investigator assumes that $(R_A + R_O)$ is equal to a constant irrespective of the reinforcer that is employed. If this constant is labeled k, equation 6.7 can be rewritten as

$$R_A = kr_A/(r_A + r_O)$$

This equation predicts that the rate of responding (R_A) will be directly related to the rate of reinforcement for that response in a negatively accelerating fashion. Another implication of the equation, of particular clinical interest, is that the rate of responding will decline as the rate of alternative sources of reinforcement (r_O) is increased. Thus, equation 6.8 provides two ways of changing the rate of a response (by changing its rate of reinforcement or by changing the rate of other sources of reinforcement).

BOX 6.3
THE MATCHING LAW, HUMAN BEHAVIOR, AND BEHAVIOR THERAPY

The matching law and its implications have been found to apply to a wide range of human behavior (see, for example, Baum, 1975; Conger & Killeen, 1974; Martens, Lochner, & Kelly, 1992; McDowell, 1982). In an interesting study, Vollmer and Bourret (2000) examined the choices that college basketball players made during the course of intercollegiate games. A basketball player can elect to shoot at the basket from an area close to the basket and thereby get 2 points, or from farther away and get 3 points. Teams compile statistics on the number of 2- and 3-point shots attempted and made by individual players. These data provide information about the relative rates of selecting each response alternative. The team data also include information about the success of each attempt and can be used to calculate the rate of reinforcement for each response alternative. Vollmer and Bourret examined the data for 13 players on the men's team and 13 players on the women's team of a large university and found that the relative choice of the different types of shots was proportional to the relative rates of reinforcement for those shots. Thus, the choice behavior of these athletes during regular games followed the matching law.

The matching law has important implications for behavior therapy (McDowell, 1982; Noll, 1995). According to this law, the tendency to make a particular response depends not only on the rate of reinforcement for that response but also on the rates of reinforcement available for alternative activities. This implies that analysis of a problematic behavior (truancy from school, for example) has to include not only consideration of the rewards available for that particular behavior but also the rewards the person can obtain in other ways. Thus, the matching law suggests that accurate assessment of a behavior problem requires consideration of the individual's full range of activities and sources of reinforcement.

The matching law also suggests novel techniques for decreasing undesired responses and increasing desired responses. According to the matching law, an undesired response can be decreased by providing more reinforcement for other activities or by simply providing more "free" reinforcers. Conversely, a desired response can be increased by withdrawing reinforcement for other activities.

The extension of the matching law to single-response situations has enjoyed considerable success (for example, Belke & Heyman, 1994a, 1994b; Heyman & Monaghan, 1994; Petry & Heyman, 1994). It is now well established that responding in single-response situations is a negatively accelerating function of the rate of reinforcement for that response. However, recent studies varying the reinforcer but not the instrumental response have called into question the assumption that $(R_A + R_O)$ is constant for a particular instrumental situation. Because of that, the usefulness of matching as a theory of behavior in single-operant situations is currently in doubt (Belke, 1998; Dallery, McDowell, & Lancaster, 2000; McDowell & Dallery, 1999).

Mechanisms of the Matching Law

The matching law describes how organisms distribute their responses in a choice situation but does not explain what mechanisms are responsible for this response distribution. It is a descriptive law of nature rather than a mechanistic law. Factors that may be responsible for matching in choice situations have been the subject of continuing experimentation and theoretical debate (see Commons, Herrnstein, & Rachlin, 1982; Davison & McCarthy, 1988; Herrnstein, 1997; Williams, 1988, 1994b).

The matching law is stated in terms of rates of responding and reinforcement averaged over the entire duration of experimental sessions. It ignores when individual responses are made. Similarly, *molar theories* of matching ignore what might occur at the level of individual responses. Molar theories explain aggregates of responses and deal with the overall distribution of responses and reinforcers in choice situations.

In contrast to molar theories, *molecular theories* focus on what happens at the level of individual responses and view the matching relation as the net result of these individual choices. Yet other theories provide characterizations of behavior that are neither molar nor molecular but somewhere in between; one such theory is *melioration*. The following is a discussion of molecular, molar, and melioration theories of choice. (For a theoretical treatment that takes both long-term and short-term factors into account, see Dragoi & Staddon, 1999.)

B. A. Williams

Matching and Maximizing Rates of Reinforcement. The most extensively investigated explanations of choice behavior are based on the intuitively reasonable idea that organisms distribute their actions among response alternatives in order to receive the maximum amount of reinforcement possible in the situation (for a good overview, see Baum & Aparicio, 1999). According to this idea, animals switch back and forth between response alternatives so as to receive as many reinforcers as they possibly can. The idea that organisms maximize reinforcement has been used to explain choice behavior at both molecular and molar levels of analysis.

1. *Molecular Maximizing.* According to molecular theories of maximizing, organisms always choose whichever response alternative is most likely to be reinforced at the time (Hinson & Staddon, 1983a, 1983b). Shimp (1966, 1969) proposed an early version of molecular matching. He suggested that when two schedules (A and B) are in effect simultaneously, the subject switches from schedule A to schedule B as the probability of reinforcement for schedule B increases. Consider, for example, a pigeon working on a concurrent VI-VI schedule. As the pigeon pecks key A, the timer controlling reinforcement for key B is still operating. The longer the pigeon stays on key A, the greater the probability that the requisite interval for key B will elapse and reinforcement will become available for pecking key B. By switching, the pigeon can pick up the reinforcer on key B. Now, the longer it continues to peck key B, the more likely key A will become set for reinforcement. Shimp proposed that the matching relation is a by-product of prudent switching when the probability of reinforcement on the alternative response key becomes greater than the probability of reinforcement on the current response key.

Detailed studies of the patterns of switching from one to another response alternative have not always supported the molecular maximizing theory proposed by Shimp. In fact, some studies have shown that matching is possible in the absence of momentary maximizing (for example, Nevin, 1969, 1979; see also Machado, 1994; Williams, 1991, 1992a). However, recent approaches to molecular analyses of choice behavior have met with more success.

One approach has emphasized analyzing a two-alternative choice in terms of reinforcement for staying with a particular alternative and reinforcement for switching to the other option. For example, a situation in which a laboratory rat has two response levers available can be analyzed as involving four different options: staying on the right lever, switching from the right lever to the left one, staying on the left lever, and switching from the left lever to the right one. Each of these four options has its own reinforcement contingency by virtue of the schedule of reinforcement that is programmed on each lever. The relative distribution of right and left responses is presumed to depend on the relative rate of reinforcement for staying on each lever versus switching to the other lever (MacDonall, 1998, 1999, 2000). The success of these analyses suggests that such molecular mechanisms can contribute to the performance that is observed on concurrent schedules, but the extent to which such molecular processes are responsible for (or necessary for) matching remains in dispute (Machado & Keen, 1999). (For other recent molecular accounts of choice in concurrent schedules, see Cleaveland, 1999; Gallistel & Gibbon, 2000.)

2. *Molar Maximizing.* Molar theories of maximizing assume that organisms distribute their responses among various alternatives in order to maximize the amount of reinforcement they earn over the long run (for example, Rachlin, Battalio, Kagel, & Green, 1981; Rachlin, Green, Kagel, & Battalio, 1976). What is long enough to be considered a "long run" is not clearly specified. In contrast to molecular theories, however, molar theories focus on aggregates of behavior over some period of time rather than on individual choice responses.

Molar maximizing theory was originally formulated to explain choice on concurrent schedules made up of ratio components. In concurrent ratio schedules, animals rarely switch back and forth between response alternatives; instead, they respond exclusively on the ratio component that requires the fewest responses. On a concurrent FR 20–FR 10 schedule, for example, the organism is likely to respond only on the FR 10 alternative. In this way it maximizes its rate of reinforcement with the least effort.

In many situations, molar maximizing accurately predicts the results of choice procedures, but certain findings present difficulties. One difficulty arises from the results of concurrent VI-VI schedules of reinforcement in which organisms can earn close to all of the available rewards on both schedules, provided they occasionally sample each alternative. The total amount of reinforcement obtained on a concurrent VI-VI schedule can therefore be close to the same despite wide variations in how responding is distributed between the two alternatives. The matching relation is only one of many different possibilities that yield close to maximal rates of reinforcement. Because other response distributions can yield similar amounts of total reward, molar maximizing cannot explain why choice behavior is distributed so close to the matching relation on concurrent VI-VI schedules and not in other equally effective ways (Heyman, 1983).

Another challenge for molar matching is provided by results of studies in which there is a choice between a variable ratio and a variable interval schedule. On a variable ratio schedule, the organism can obtain reinforcement at any time by making the required number of responses. By contrast, on a variable interval schedule, the subject has to respond only occasionally to obtain close to the maximum number of rewards possible. Given these differences, for maximum return on a concurrent VR-VI schedule, subjects should concentrate their responses on the variable ratio alternative and respond only occasionally on the variable interval component. Evidence shows that animals do favor the VR component but not as strongly as molar maximizing predicts (Baum, 1981; DeCarlo, 1985; Herrnstein & Heyman, 1979; Heyman & Herrnstein, 1986; see also Vyse & Belke, 1992; but see Baum & Aparicio, 1999). Human participants also respond much more on the VI alternative than is prudent if they are trying to maximize their rate of reinforcement (Savastano & Fantino, 1994).

3. *Melioration.* The third major mechanism of choice, melioration, is neither a molecular nor a molar mechanism. Melioration mechanisms operate on a timescale that is between the timescale of molar and molecular theories.

Many aspects of behavior are not optimal in the long run. People make choices that result in their being overweight, being addicted to cigarettes or other drugs, or being without close friends. No one chooses these end points. As Herrnstein (1997) has pointed out,

"A person does not normally make a once-and-for-all decision to become an exercise junkie, a miser, a glutton, a profligate, or a gambler; rather he slips into the pattern through a myriad of innocent, or almost innocent choices, each of which carries little weight" (p. 285). It is these "innocent choices" that meliation is intended to characterize.

The term *melioration* refers to making something better. Notice that melioration does not refer to selecting the best alternative at the moment (molecular maximizing) or making something as good as it can be in the long run (molar maximizing). Melioration refers to the more modest (or "innocent") goal of just making the situation better. Better than what? Better than how that situation has been in the recent past. The benefits are assessed specific to a limited situation—not overall or in the long run.

An important term in translating these ideas to testable experimental predictions is the *local rate* of responding and reinforcement. Molar theories focus on overall rates of responding and reinforcement, which are calculated over the entire duration of an experimental session. In contrast, local rates are calculated only over the time period that a subject devotes to a particular choice alternative. For example, if the situation involves two options (A and B), the local rate of responding on A is calculated by dividing the frequency of responses on A by the time the subject devoted to responding on A.

The local rate of a response is always higher than its overall rate. If the subject responds 75 times in an hour on alternative A, the overall rate for response A will be 75/hour. However, those 75 responses might be made during just 20 minutes of the session, with the subject working on response B the rest of the time. Therefore, the local rate of response A will be 75/20 minutes, or 225/hour.

Melioration theory assumes that organisms change from one response alternative to another to improve on the local rate of reinforcement they are receiving (Herrnstein, 1997; Herrnstein & Vaughan, 1980; Vaughan, 1981, 1985). Adjustments in the distribution of behavior between alternatives are assumed to continue until the organism is obtaining the same local rate of reward on all alternatives. It can be shown mathematically that when subjects distribute their responses to obtain the same local rate of reinforcement on each response alternative, they are behaving in accordance with the matching law. Therefore, the mechanism of melioration results in matching.

To see how melioration works, consider a concurrent VI 1-min VI 3-min schedule. During the first hour of exposure to this schedule, a pigeon will switch back and forth between the two alternatives and may end up accumulating a total of 30 minutes responding on each component, earning all of the available reinforcers. On a VI 1-min schedule, at most 60 reinforcers are available in 1 hour. The pigeon could get all of these during the course of spending 30 minutes on the VI 1-min schedule, provided it distributed its responses appropriately. If the pigeon received all 60 reinforcers during the course of accumulating 30 minutes on the VI 1-min schedule, its local rate of reinforcement will be 60 reinforcers in 30 minutes, or *120 per hour*. On a VI 3-min schedule, at most 20 reinforcers are available in 1 hour. If the pigeon got all of these during the course of accumulating a total of 30 minutes on the VI 3-min schedule, its local rate of reinforcement on the VI 3-min component will be 20 reinforcers in 30 minutes, or *40 per hour*.

According to melioration theory, the pigeon will shift its preference in favor of the response alternative that yields the higher local rate of reinforcement. Since the local rate of reinforcement on the VI 1-min schedule (120/hr) was much higher than on the VI 3-min schedule (40/hr), the pigeon will shift its behavior in favor of the VI 1-min alternative. However, if it begins to spend too much time on the VI 1-min schedule and samples the VI 3-min schedule only rarely, it may be reinforced every time it pecks the VI 3-min key. This will make the local rate of reinforcement on the VI 3-min key higher than the local rate of reinforcement on the VI 1-min alternative. That in turn would produce a shift in favor of the VI 3-min schedule. According to melioration theory, such shifts back and forth will continue until the local rates of reinforcement earned on the two alternatives are equal.

Although tests of the melioration hypothesis have yielded confirmatory evidence (for example, McSweeney, Melville, Buck, & Whipple, 1983), the hypothesis has also encountered some difficulties (for example, Belke, 1992; Williams, 1993). Given the complexity of choice behavior, it is not surprising that investigators are continuing their exploration of alternative approaches to explaining how organisms choose between different sources of reinforcement (for example, Davis, Staddon, Machado, & Palmer, 1993; Dragoi & Staddon, 1999; Gallistel & Gibbon, 2000; Grace, 1994; Mazur, 2001).

CHOICE WITH COMMITMENT

In a standard concurrent schedule of reinforcement, two (or more) response alternatives are available at the same time, and switching from one to the other can occur at any time. Many choice situations outside the laboratory are of this type. If you have a plate of roast beef, vegetables, and mashed potatoes, you can switch from one food to another at any time during the meal. You can similarly switch back and forth among television channels or parts of a newspaper. In some cases, however, choosing one alternative makes other alternatives unavailable, and the choice may involve assessing complex, long-range goals.

Should you go to college and get a degree in engineering or start in a full-time job without a college degree? You cannot switch back and forth between such alternatives. Furthermore, to make the decision, you need to consider long-range goals. A degree in engineering may enable you to get a higher paying job eventually, but it may require significant economic sacrifices initially. Getting a job without a college degree would enable you to make money sooner, but in the long run you would not earn as much.

Important choices in life often involve a short-term small benefit versus a more delayed but larger benefit. This is fundamentally the problem of self-control. People are said to lack self-control if they choose a small short-term reward instead of waiting for a larger but more delayed benefit. The student who talks with a friend instead of studying is selecting a small short-term reward over the more delayed but larger reward of successfully completing college. The heroin addict who uses a friend's needle instead of getting a clean one is similarly selecting the smaller, quicker reward, as is the drunk who elects to drive home now instead of waiting to sober up.

Concurrent-Chain Schedules

Obviously, investigators cannot conduct experiments that directly involve choosing between college and a job after high school, or driving while intoxicated versus waiting to sober up. However, simplified analogous questions may be posed in laboratory experiments. Many such studies have been done with pigeons, rats, and monkeys, and these experiments have stimulated analogous studies with human subjects (see, for example, studies by Forzano & Corry, 1998; Ito & Nakamura, 1998; Logue, Forzano, & Ackerman, 1996). The basic technique in this area of research is the **concurrent-chain schedule** of reinforcement.

We have all heard that variety is the spice of life. How could investigators determine whether this is true? One implication may be that subjects will prefer a variable ratio schedule of reinforcement (which provides variety in the number of responses required for successive reinforcers) over a fixed ratio schedule (which requires the same number of responses per reinforcer). A concurrent-chain schedule is ideal for answering such questions.

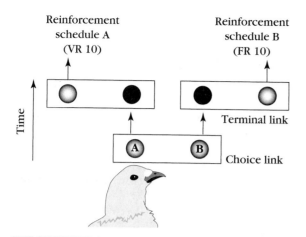

Figure 6.6 Diagram of a concurrent-chain schedule. Pecking the left key in the choice link puts into effect reinforcement schedule A in the terminal link. Pecking the right key in the choice link puts into effect reinforcement schedule B in the terminal link.

A concurrent-chain schedule of reinforcement involves at least two stages or links (see Figure 6.6). During the first stage, the *choice link,* the participant is allowed to choose between two schedule alternatives by making one of two responses. In the example diagrammed in Figure 6.6, the pigeon makes its choice by pecking either the left or the right response key. Pecking the left key produces alternative A, the opportunity to peck the left key for 10 minutes on a VR 10 schedule of reinforcement. If the pigeon pecks the right key in the choice link, it produces alternative B, which is the opportunity to peck the right key for 10 minutes on an FR 10 schedule. Responding on either key during the choice link does not yield food. The opportunity for reinforcement occurs only after the initial choice has been made and the pigeon has entered the *terminal link.* Another important feature of the concurrent-chain schedule is that once the participant has made a choice, it is stuck with that choice until the end of the terminal link of the schedule (10 minutes in the hypothetical example). Thus, concurrent-chain schedules involve *choice with commitment.*

The pattern of responding that occurs in the terminal component of a concurrent-chain schedule is characteristic of whatever schedule of reinforcement is in effect during that component. In the example, if the pigeon selects alternative A, its pattern of pecking during the terminal component will be similar to the usual response pattern for a VR 10 schedule. If the pigeon selects alternative B, its pattern of pecking during the terminal component will be characteristic of an FR 10 schedule.

Studies of this sort have shown that subjects do prefer the variable ratio alternative. In fact, pigeons favor the VR alternative even if it requires, on average, more responses per reinforcer than the FR alternative. To this extent, variety does seem to be the spice of life. The preference for the VR schedule is driven by the fact that occasionally a VR schedule provides reinforcement for relatively few responses (Field, Tonneau, Ahearn, & Hineline, 1996). (For other studies of preference for a schedule in which reinforcers are unpredictable over one that provides reinforcement in a predictable fashion, see Belke & Spetch, 1994; Bruner, Gibbon, & Fairhurst, 1994; Mazur, 1991; Mazur & Romano, 1992; Spetch, Mondloch, Belke, & Dunn, 1994).

As I noted, the consequence of responding during the initial (choice) link of a concurrent schedule is not the primary reinforcer (food). It is entry into one of the terminal links, each of which is typically designated by a particular color on the pecking key. Thus, the immediate consequence of an initial link response is a stimulus that is associated with the terminal link that was chosen. Since that stimulus is present when the primary reinforcer is

E. Fantino

L. Green

provided, the terminal link stimulus becomes a *conditioned reinforcer.* Thus, one may regard a concurrent schedule as one in which the initial link responses are reinforced by the presentation of a conditioned reinforcer. Differences in the value of the conditioned reinforcer will then determine the relative rate of each choice response in the initial link. Because of this, concurrent-chain schedules are often used in modern studies of conditioned reinforcement (Goldshmidt, Lattal, & Fantino, 1998; Mazur, 1998; Savastano & Fantino, 1996; Williams, 1997a). They have been also used to study some unusual and interesting questions about behavior. Cerutti and Catania (1997), for example, examined whether pigeons prefer a situation in which they have a choice of where to peck versus one in which there is only one place where pecking will yield food.

Although many studies of concurrent-chain schedules were carried out to determine how organisms select between different situations represented by the terminal links, the consensus of opinion is that choice behavior is governed by both the terminal link schedules and whatever schedule is in effect in the initial link. Several different models have been proposed to explain how variables related to the initial and terminal links act in concert to determine concurrent choice performance (for an excellent review, see Mazur, 2000, 2001).

Studies of "Self-Control"

Self-control is often a matter of choosing a large delayed reward over an immediate small reward. For example, self-control in eating involves selecting the large delayed reward of being thin over the immediate small reward of eating a piece of cake. When a piece of cake is in plain view, it is very difficult to choose the delayed reward; it is difficult to pass up the piece of cake in favor of being thin. Self-control is easier if the tempting alternative is not as readily available. It is easier to pass up a piece of cake if you are deciding on what to eat at the next meal. Rachlin and Green (1972) set up a laboratory analog of self-control with pigeons based on these ideas.

The basic concurrent-chain schedule used by Rachlin and Green is shown in Figure 6.7. In the terminal components of the schedule, responding was rewarded by either immediate access to a small amount of grain (alternative A) or access to a large amount of grain that was delayed by 4 seconds (alternative B). The pigeons could choose between these two alternatives by pecking either key A or key B during the initial component of the schedule.

Rachlin and Green tested the choice behavior of the pigeons under two different conditions. In one case ("direct-choice procedure" in Figure 6.7), the small immediate reward and the delayed large reward were available as soon as the pigeons pecked the corresponding choice key once. Under these conditions, the pigeons lacked self-control. They predominantly selected the small immediate reward. In the second case ("concurrent-chain procedure" in Figure 6.7), the terminal components of the concurrent-chain schedule were delayed after the pigeons made their initial choice. If a sufficient delay was imposed before the terminal components, the pigeons showed self-control; they primarily selected the large delayed reward.

The phenomenon of self-control as illustrated by the Rachlin and Green experiment has stimulated much research and theorizing. Many investigators have found, in agreement with Rachlin and Green, that preferences shift in favor of the delayed large reward as participants are required to wait longer to receive either reward after making their choice. If rewards are delivered shortly after a choice response, subjects generally favor an immediate small reward over a delayed large reward. However, if a constant delay is added to the delivery of both rewards, individuals are more likely to show self-control and favor the delayed large reward. This crossover in preference has been obtained in laboratory experiments with both human and nonhuman animals and thus represents a general property of choice

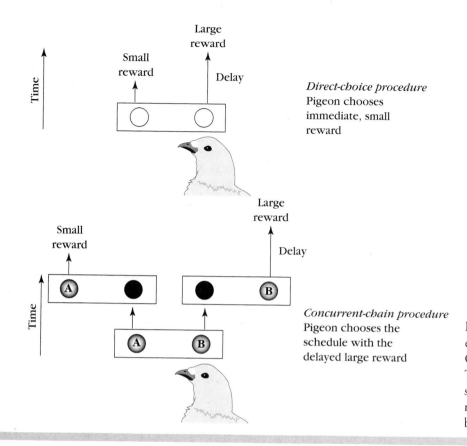

Large
reward

Small
reward

Delay

Direct-choice procedure
Pigeon chooses
immediate, small
reward

Large
reward

Small
reward

Delay

A

B

A B

Concurrent-chain procedure
Pigeon chooses the
schedule with the
delayed large reward

Figure 6.7 Diagram of the
experiment by Rachlin and
Green (1972) on self-control.
The direct-choice procedure is
shown at the top; the concurrent-chain procedure, at the
bottom.

behavior. (For applications of these concepts to university administration, see Logue, 1998a;
For more comprehensive reviews of self-control, see Logue, 1988b, 1995, 1998b.)

Explanations of Self-Control. Which would you prefer, $1,000 today or $1,000 next
year? For most people, the answer is obvious: $1,000 today would be of much greater value.
How about $1,000 next week, or next month? Most people would agree that the longer one
has to wait for the $1,000, the less exciting is the prospect of getting the money. This illus-
trates a general principle that is the key to behavioral explanations of self-control, namely,
that the value of a reinforcer is reduced by how long you have to wait to get it. The mathematical function describing this decrease in value is called the **value discounting function**.
The exact mathematical form of the value discounting function has taken a bit of empirical
effort to pin down. But the current consensus is that the value of a reinforcer (V) is directly
related to reward magnitude (M) and inversely related to reward delay (D), according to the
formula,

$$V = M/(1 + KD)$$

(6.9)

A. W. Logue

Courtesy of A. W. Logue

where K is the discounting rate parameter (Mazur, 1987). Equation 6.9 is called the *hyperbolic decay function*. (For a generalized version of the hyperbolic decay function, see Grace,
1999.) According to this equation, if the reinforcer is delivered with no delay (D=0), the
value of the reinforcer is directly related to its magnitude (larger reinforcers have larger values). The longer the reinforcer is delayed, the smaller its value.

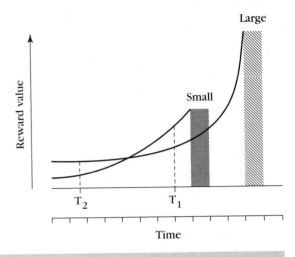

Figure 6.8 Hypothetical relations between reward value and waiting time to reward delivery for a small reward and a large reward presented some time later.

How can the discounting function explain the problem of self-control, which involves a small reward available soon versus a large reward available after a longer delay? Consider Figure 6.8. Time in this figure is represented by distance on the horizontal axis, and reward value is represented by the y axis. The figure represents the value of a large and a small reward as a function of how long participants have to wait to receive the reward. Two different points in time are identified, T_1 and T_2. The usual self-control dilemma involves considering the reward values at T_1, where there is a very short wait for the small reward and a longer wait for the large reward. Waiting for each reward reduces its value. Because reward value decreases rapidly at first, given the delays involved at T_1 the value of the large reward is smaller than the value of the small reward. Hence, the model predicts that if the choice occurs at T_1, participants will select the small reward (the impulsive option). However, the discounting functions cross over with further delays. The value of both rewards is less at T_2 than at T_1 because T_2 involves longer delays. Notice, however, that at T_2 the value of the large reward is now greater than that of the small reward. Therefore, a choice at T_2 would have participants select the large reward (the self-control option).

The value discounting functions illustrated in Figure 6.8 predict the results of Rachlin and Green (1972) described earlier, as well as numerous other studies of self-control. Increasing the delay to both small and large rewards makes it easier to exhibit self-control by selecting the larger but more delayed reinforcer.

Discounting Functions and the Problems of Self-Control in Drug Addiction. As I have noted, the parameter K in equation 6.8 indicates how rapidly reward value declines as a function of delay. The steeper a person's delay discounting function, the more difficulty he or she will have in exhibiting self-control (electing the larger delayed reward) rather than impulsivity (electing the smaller, quicker reward). A team of investigators at the University of Vermont led by Warren Bickel and Gregory Madden has been using the delay discounting function to study how problems of self-control are involved in drug addiction.

Madden, Petry, Badger, and Bickel (1997) noted that "substance abuse frequently reflects a series of impulsive choices" (p. 256). Addicts will choose the relatively quick small reward of drug intoxication at the risk of more delayed negative consequences of interpersonal problems, and loss of social support, steady employment, and good health. Such choices suggest discounting the value (or threat) of long-term consequences. If this is true,

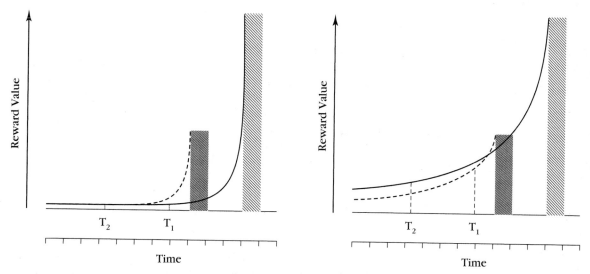

Figure 6.9 Reward discount functions for a large and smaller monetary reward. The left panel shows the discount functions obtained with a group of heroin-dependent subjects. The right panel shows data from a control group. (From "Impulsive and Self-Control Choices in Opioid-Dependent Patients and Non-Drug-Using Control Participants: Drug and Monetary Rewards," by G. J. Madden, N. M. Petry, G. J. Badger, and W. K. Bickel, 1997, *Experimental and Clinical Psychopharmacology, 5,* pp. 256–262. Reprinted by permission.)

then drug addicts should show steeper reward discount functions than other individuals. Madden et al. (1997) tested this prediction with a group of heroin-dependent patients enrolled in a substance abuse program and a group of nondependent individuals matched for age, gender, education, and IQ.

The procedure was a variant of the adjusting-delay procedure developed by Mazur (1987) in studies with pigeons. On each trial, the subjects were asked to choose between two hypothetical scenarios: getting $1,000 sometime in the future or a smaller amount of money right away. In different repetitions of the task, the $1,000 was to be received at one of seven future times ranging from 1 week to 25 years. For each delay period, the magnitude of the smaller immediate alternative was varied across trials until the investigators determined how much money obtained immediately was as attractive as the $1,000 sometime in the future. Using these data, Madden et al. (1997) were able to construct reward discount functions for both heroin-dependent and control subjects.

The results are summarized in Figure 6.9. Keep in mind that these are reward discount functions for hypothetical choices between different amounts of money to be received soon (T_1) or after a substantial delay (T_2). The data for the heroin addicts are presented in the left panel, and the data for the control subjects appear in the right panel. One striking finding was that the reward discount functions were much steeper for the heroin addicts; that is, for heroin-dependent subjects the value of money dropped very quickly if receipt of the money was to be delayed. This steep reward discounting function is indicative of lack of control and impulsivity. Madden et al. (1997) speculated that because drug-dependent subjects showed more rapid discounting of reward value, "heroin-addicted individuals may be more likely to engage in criminal and dangerous activities to obtain immediate rewards (e.g., theft, prostitution, drug sales)" (p. 261). It is also possible that heroin use induces more rapid discounting of future consequences. Whether cause or effect, these results implicate self-control mechanisms in drug abuse and illustrate how techniques developed to study self-control in nonhuman subjects can be used to provide precise quantitative estimates of reward discounting relevant to important human problems.

Subsequent work extended this type of analysis to cigarette smokers and the problem of needle sharing among heroin addicts. Bickel, Odum, and Madden (1999) found that the reward discounting function for hypothetical monetary choices is much steeper for current smokers than it is for nonsmokers and ex-smokers. This suggests that the same kind of self-control deficits that are involved in heroin addiction are also evident among cigarette addicts.

The sharing of needles among heroin addicts may also reflect lack of self-control due to rapid reward discounting. Needle sharing is a highly risky behavior because it increases the chance of getting various infectious diseases (AIDS and hepatitis, for example). Odum, Madden, Badger, and Bickel (2000) measured the reward discounting functions of heroin-dependent patients in a substance abuse program using hypothetical monetary choices. They then asked the subjects to select between two hypothetical scenarios: using a friend's needle right away or waiting a week to obtain a new sterile needle. Interestingly, the subjects who expressed a willingness to share a needle had much steeper reward discount functions than subjects who preferred to wait for a new needle. This difference, however, was observed only when the task involved hypothetical monetary amounts. When the subjects were asked to judge the relative value of a small amount of heroin now or a larger amount later, the two groups of patients showed similarly rapid discount functions. (For related work, see Kirby, Petry, & Bickel, 1999; Madden, Bickel, & Jacobs, 1999.)

Can Self-Control Be Trained?   A person who cannot tolerate the waiting time required for large rewards has to forgo obtaining those reinforcers. Self-control, or the preference for a large delayed reward over a small immediate reward, is often a sensible strategy. In fact, some have suggested that self-control is a critical component of socialization and emotional adjustment. This raises an interesting question: Can self-control be trained? Fortunately for society, the answer is yes.

Training people with delayed reward appears to have generalized effects in increasing their tolerance for delayed reward. In one study (Eisenberger & Adornetto, 1986), second- and third-grade students in a public elementary school were first tested for self-control by being asked whether they wanted to get 2¢ immediately or 3¢ at the end of the day. Children who elected the immediate reward were given 2¢; for those who elected the delayed reward, 3¢ was placed in a cup to be given to the child later. The procedure was repeated eight times to complete the pretest. The children then received three sessions of training with either immediate or delayed reward.

During each training session, various problems were presented: one involved counting objects on a card, another was a picture–memory task, and the third was a shape-matching task. For half the students, correct responding was reinforced immediately with 2¢. For the remaining students, correct responses resulted in 3¢ being placed in a cup that was given to the child at the end of the day. After the third training session, preference for small immediate reward versus larger delayed reward was measured as in the pretest. Provided that the training tasks involved low effort, training with delayed reward increased preference for the larger delayed reward during the posttest. Thus, training with delayed reinforcement produced generalized self-control. (For other approaches to increasing self-control, see Logue, 1998b; Schweitzer & Sulzer-Azaroff, 1988).

CONCLUDING COMMENTS

The basic principle of instrumental conditioning is very simple: reinforcement increases (and punishment decreases) the future probability of an instrumental response. However, as I have described, the experimental analysis of instrumental behavior can be rather intricate. Many important aspects of instrumental behavior are determined by the schedule of reinforcement. There are numerous schedules by which responses can be reinforced. Reinforcement can depend on how many responses have occurred, the passage of time, or the rate of responding. Furthermore, more than one reinforcement schedule may be available to the organism at the same time. The pattern of instrumental behavior, as well as choices between various response alternatives, is strongly determined by the schedule of reinforcement that is in effect. These various findings have revealed a great deal about how reinforcement controls behavior in a variety of circumstances and have encouraged many powerful applications of reinforcement principles to human behavior.

SAMPLE QUESTIONS

1. Compare and contrast ratio and interval schedules in terms of how the contingencies of reinforcement are set up and the effects they have on the instrumental response.
2. Describe how response rate schedules are designed and what their effects are.
3. Describe the generalized matching law equation, and explain each of its parameters.
4. Describe various theoretical explanations of the matching law.
5. How are concurrent-chain schedules different from concurrent schedules, and what kinds of research questions require the use of concurrent-chain schedules?
6. What is a reward discounting function, and how is it related to the problem of self-control?

KEY TERMS

concurrent-chain schedule A complex reinforcement procedure in which the participant is permitted to choose which of several simple reinforcement schedules will be in effect. Once a choice has been made, the rejected alternatives become unavailable for some time.

concurrent schedule A complex reinforcement procedure in which the participant can choose any one of two or more simple reinforcement schedules that are available simultaneously. Concurrent schedules allow for the measurement of choice between simple schedule alternatives.

continuous reinforcement A schedule of reinforcement in which every occurrence of the instrumental response produces the reinforcer. Abbreviated CRF.

cumulative record A graphical representation of how a response is repeated over time, with the passage of time represented by the horizontal distance (or x axis), and the total or cumulative number of responses that have occurred up to a particular point in time represented by the vertical distance (or y axis).

differential reinforcement of high rate A reinforcement schedule in which a response is reinforced only if it occurs *before* a specified amount of time has elapsed following the preceding response. Abbreviated DRH.

differential reinforcement of low rate A reinforcement schedule in which a response is reinforced only if it occurs *after* a specified amount of time has elapsed following the preceding response. Abbreviated DRL.

fixed interval scallop The gradually increasing rate of responding that occurs between successive reinforcements on a fixed interval schedule.

fixed interval schedule A reinforcement schedule in which the reinforcer is delivered for the first response that occurs after a fixed amount of time following the last reinforcer. Abbreviated FI.

fixed ratio schedule A reinforcement schedule in which a fixed number of responses must occur in order for the next response to be reinforced. Abbreviated FR.

intermittent reinforcement A schedule of reinforcement in which only some of the occurrences of the instrumental response are reinforced. The instrumental response is reinforced occasionally, or intermittently. Also called *partial reinforcement.*

interresponse time or IRT The interval between one response and the next. IRTs can be differentially reinforced in the same fashion as other aspects of behavior, such as response force or variability.

interval schedule A reinforcement schedule in which a response is reinforced only if it occurs after a set amount of time following the last reinforcement.

limited hold A restriction on how long reinforcement remains available. In order for a response to be reinforced, it must occur during the limited-hold period.

matching law A rule for instrumental behavior, proposed by R. J. Herrnstein, which states that the relative rate of responding on a particular response alternative equals the relative rate of reinforcement for that response alternative.

melioration A mechanism for achieving matching by responding so as to improve the local rates of reinforcement for response alternatives.

overmatching Greater sensitivity to the relative rate of reinforcement than predicted by perfect matching.

partial reinforcement Same as *intermittent reinforcement.*

postreinforcement pause A pause in responding that typically occurs after the delivery of the reinforcer on fixed ratio and fixed interval schedules of reinforcement.

ratio run The high and invariant rate of responding observed after the postreinforcement pause on fixed ratio reinforcement schedules. The ratio run ends when the necessary number of responses have been performed, and the participant is reinforced.

ratio schedule A reinforcement schedule in which reinforcement depends only on the number of responses the participant performs, irrespective of when those responses occur.

ratio strain Disruption of responding that occurs when a fixed ratio response requirement is increased too rapidly.

response-rate schedule A reinforcement schedule in which a response is reinforced depending on how soon that response is made after the previous occurrence of the behavior.

schedule of reinforcement A program, or rule, that determines how and when the occurrence of a response will be followed by the delivery of the reinforcer.

undermatching Less sensitivity to the relative rate of reinforcement than predicted by perfect matching.

value discounting function The mathematical function that describes how reinforcer value decreases as a function of how long a participant has to wait for delivery of the reinforcer.

variable interval schedule A reinforcement schedule in which reinforcement is provided for the first response that occurs after a variable amount of time from the last reinforcement. Abbreviated VI.

variable ratio schedule A reinforcement schedule in which the number of responses necessary to produce reinforcement varies from trial to trial. The value of the schedule refers to the average number of responses needed for reinforcement. Abbreviated VR.

hapter 7 is devoted to a discussion of processes that motivate and direct instrumental behavior. Two distinctively different approaches have been pursued in an effort to understand why instrumental behavior occurs. One of these originated in the work of Thorndike and Pavlov and focuses on identifying the associative structure of instrumental conditioning. The other approach originated in the work of Skinner and focuses on how behavior is regulated in the face of limitations or restrictions created by an instrumental conditioning procedure. Behavior regulation theories describe reinforcement effects within the broader context of an organism's behavioral repertoire, using concepts from several areas of inquiry, including behavioral economics and behavioral ecology. The associationist approach considers molecular mechanisms and is not concerned with the long-range goal or function of instrumental behavior. In contrast, the behavioral regulation approach considers molar aspects of behavior and regards instrumental conditioning effects as manifestations of maximization or optimization processes. These two approaches provide an exciting illustration of the sometimes turbulent course of scientific inquiry. Investigators studying the motivational substrates of instrumental behavior have moved boldly to explore radically new conceptions when older ideas did not meet the challenges posed by new empirical findings.

In Chapters 5 and 6 I defined instrumental behavior, pointed out how it is investigated, and described how such behavior is influenced by various experimental manipulations, including schedules of reinforcement. I did not say much about what motivates instrumental responding, perhaps because the answer seemed obvious. Informal reflection suggests that instrumental behavior occurs because the subject is motivated to obtain the reinforcer and can do so only by performing the instrumental response. But what does it mean to be "motivated" to obtain the reinforcer? And what is the full impact of setting up a situation so that the reinforcer is accessible only by making the required instrumental response? Answers to these questions have occupied scientists for more than a century and have encompassed some of the most important and interesting research in the analysis of behavior.

The motivation of instrumental behavior has been considered from two radically different perspectives. The first originated with Thorndike and involves analysis of the *associative structure of instrumental conditioning*. As the label implies, this approach relies heavily on the concept of associations and hence is compatible with the theoretical tradition of Pavlovian conditioning. In fact, much of the research relevant to the associative structure of instrumental conditioning was stimulated by efforts to identify the role of Pavlovian mechanisms in instrumental learning. In addition, some of the investigative tactics that were developed to study Pavlovian conditioning were imported to the problem of instrumental learning.

The associative approach takes a molecular perspective. It focuses on individual responses and their specific stimulus antecedents and outcomes. To achieve this level of detail, the associative approach examines instrumental learning in isolated behavioral preparations, not unlike studying something in a test tube or a petri dish. Because associations can be substantiated in the nervous system, the associative approach provides a convenient framework for studying the neural mechanisms of instrumental conditioning.

The alternative approach to motivational processes in instrumental learning is *behavioral regulation*. This approach developed within the Skinnerian tradition and involves considering instrumental conditioning within the broader context of the numerous things organisms are constantly doing. In particular, the behavioral regulation approach is concerned with how an instrumental conditioning procedure sets limits on the organism's free flow of activities and the behavioral consequences of such constraints. Unlike the associative approach, behavioral regulation considers the motivation of instrumental behavior from a more molar perspective. It considers "goals" and how organisms take advantage of the complexities of their environment and their multiple behavioral options in achieving their goals. Thus, the behavioral regulation theory views instrumental behavior from a more functional perspective. Because it takes a molar approach, behavioral regulation does not provide a convenient framework for studying the neural mechanisms of instrumental learning.

The associative and behavioral regulation approaches have thus far proceeded nearly independently of each other. Each approach has identified important issues, but neither can stand alone. The hope is that at some point the molecular analyses of the associative approach will make sufficient contact with the more molar functional analyses of behavioral regulation to provide a comprehensive integrated account of the motivation of instrumental behavior.

THE ASSOCIATIVE STRUCTURE OF INSTRUMENTAL CONDITIONING

Edward Thorndike was the first to recognize that instrumental conditioning involves more than just a response and a reinforcer. The instrumental response occurs in the presence of particular stimuli. Three events must be considered in an analysis of instrumental

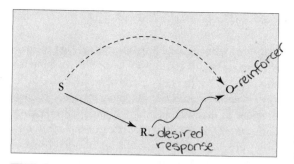

Figure 7.1 Diagram of instrumental conditioning. The instrumental response (R) occurs in the presence of distinctive stimuli (S) and results in delivery of the reinforcer outcome (O). This allows for the establishment of several different types of associations.

conditioning: the stimulus context (S), the instrumental response (R), and the response outcome (O), or reinforcer. Skinner also subscribed to the three-event notion and described instrumental conditioning in terms of a *three-term contingency* involving S, R, and O. (For a contemporary treatment, see Davison & Nevin, 1999.) The traditional conception of how these three terms are related is presented in Figure 7.1.

The S-R Association and the Law of Effect

The basic structure of an instrumental conditioning procedure permits the development of several different types of associations. The first of these is an association between the contextual stimuli S and the instrumental response R, the *S-R association*. The S-R association was postulated by Thorndike to be the key to instrumental learning in his *Law of Effect*. According to the Law of Effect, the role of the reinforcer or response outcome is to establish or "stamp in" an association between the contextual cues S and the instrumental response R. Thorndike thought that once established, this S-R association was solely responsible for the occurrence of the instrumental response. Thus, the basic impetus or motivation for the instrumental response was the activation of the S-R association by exposing the subject to the stimuli in the presence of which the instrumental response was previously reinforced. (For a discussion of the role of S-R associations in contemporary theorizing, see Donahoe, Palmer, & Burgos, 1997, and following commentary.)

An important implication of the Law of Effect is that instrumental conditioning does not involve learning about the reinforcer (O) or the relation between the response and the reinforcing outcome (the R-O association). The Law of Effect assumes that the only role of the reinforcer is to create the S-R association, that the reinforcer itself is not a party or participant in this association. This is a rather counterintuitive assumption, and perhaps because of that, it is not always appreciated. It is tempting to think that instrumental conditioning involves learning to expect the reinforcer or learning to expect that the response will produce the reinforcer. Rigorous formulations or tests of these ideas were unavailable at the turn of the twentieth century, and therefore Thorndike and Skinner shied away from the cognitive notion of an expectancy. The idea that reward expectancy may motivate instrumental behavior had to await modern developments in Pavlovian conditioning, and the integration of those developments into a consideration of instrumental behavior.

Expectancy of Reward and the S-O Association

How might we capture the notion that subjects learn to expect the reinforcer during the course of instrumental conditioning? Both human and nonhuman animals come to expect that something important will happen when they encounter a stimulus that signals a significant event or allows them to predict that the event will occur. Pavlovian conditioning is the basic process of signal learning. Hence, one way to look for reward expectancy is to consider how Pavlovian processes may be involved in instrumental learning.

As Figure 7.1 illustrates, specification of an instrumental response ensures that the participant will always experience certain distinctive stimuli (S) in connection with making the response. These stimuli may involve the place where the response is to be performed, the texture of the object the participant is to manipulate, or distinctive olfactory or visual cues. Whatever the stimuli may be, reinforcement of the instrumental response will inevitably result in a pairing between S and the reinforcer or response outcome (O). Such pairings provide the potential for classical conditioning and the establishment of an association between S and O. This S-O association is represented by the dashed line in Figure 7.1 and is the basis for reward expectancy in instrumental conditioning.

One of the earliest and most influential accounts of the role of classical conditioning in instrumental behavior was proposed by Clark Hull (1930, 1931) and later elaborated by Kenneth Spence (1956). Their basic assumption was that during the course of instrumental conditioning, the instrumental response comes to be instigated or motivated by two factors. First, the presence of S comes to evoke the instrumental response directly by association with R, through the Thorndikian S-R association. Second, the instrumental activity also comes to be made in response to the expectancy of reward because of the establishment of an S-O association. Exactly how the S-O association comes to motivate instrumental behavior has been the subject of considerable debate and experimental investigation (see review by Black, 1971). A particularly influential formulation was *modern two-process theory* (Rescorla & Solomon, 1967).

Modern Two-Process Theory.   Modern two-process theory assumes that there are two distinct types of learning, Pavlovian and instrumental conditioning. (Nothing too radical there.) The theory further assumes that these two learning processes are related in a special way. In particular, during the course of instrumental conditioning, the stimuli (S)—in the presence of which the instrumental response is reinforced—are presumed to become associated with the response outcome (O) through Pavlovian conditioning to establish an S-O association. Through the S-O association, stimulus S comes to motivate the instrumental behavior by activating a *central emotional state.* The nature of that emotional state or motivation will depend on the nature of the reinforcer. For example, in an instrumental conditioning procedure in which the response is reinforced by the presentation of food (or other appetitive reinforcers), the S-O association activates the expectancy of food, or what Mowrer (1960) more generally called "hope." (For a contemporary discussion of these ideas, see Berridge, 2001.)

How could investigators test the notion that "hope" or some other Pavlovian expectancy motivates instrumental behavior? Rescorla and Solomon (1967) pointed out that if a Pavlovian expectancy motivates instrumental behavior, then the presentation of a Pavlovian conditioned stimulus should alter the course of instrumentally reinforced responding. Thus, the basic implication of modern two-process theory is that *the rate of an instrumental response will be modified by the presentation of a classically conditioned stimulus.* This prediction is based on the following considerations. During instrumental conditioning, a conditioned central emotional state is assumed to develop to motivate the instrumental response. Reinforcing a lever-press response with food, for example, creates the expectancy of food and the emotion of "hope." Classically conditioned stimuli also are assumed to elicit central emotional states. A CS+ for food will also elicit "hope" of getting food. Therefore, presentation of a classically conditioned CS+ for food during performance of a food-reinforced response should enhance the "hope" that was created by the instrumental contingency and increase responding.

Results Consistent with Modern Two-Process Theory. Studies that evaluate modern two-process theory typically employ an experimental design called the **transfer-of-control experiment.** Such experiments basically consist of three phases. Phase 1 involves instrumental conditioning of an operant response using some schedule of positive or negative reinforcement. In Phase 2 the participants are given classical conditioning in which an explicit CS is associated with either the presence or the absence of an unconditioned stimulus. The instrumental conditioning procedure need not be in effect during the Pavlovian conditioning phase. Phase 3 is the critical *transfer phase.* Here the participants are allowed to engage in the instrumental response, and the CS from Phase 2 is periodically presented to observe its effect on the rate of the instrumental behavior.

Modern two-process theory has stimulated a great deal of research using the transfer-of-control design. We have already seen an example of this in the conditioned emotional response (CER) procedure described in Chapter 3. In that procedure, animals are first trained to press a response lever for food reinforcement; then a discrete stimulus, such as a light or a tone, is repeatedly paired with shock. This classically conditioned fear stimulus is then presented while the subjects are lever pressing for food. Presentation of the CS+ for shock produces a decrease in the rate of the lever-press response (Blackman, 1977; Davis, 1968; Lyon, 1968). This occurs because the Pavlovian CS elicits an emotional state (fear) that is contrary to the emotion or expectancy (hope) that is established in instrumental conditioning with food.

How would these same subjects respond if they were presented with a Pavlovian CS that had been paired with food (and presumably elicited "hope")? The emotion elicited by the Pavlovian CS would be compatible with the emotion established during instrumental conditioning, and an increase in responding should occur during the Pavlovian signal. Evidence consistent with this prediction has been obtained (for example, Estes, 1943, 1948; LoLordo, 1971; Lovibond, 1983). (For a more detailed discussion of other predictions of modern two-process theory, see Domjan, 1993.)

Response Interactions in Transfer-of-Control Experiments. Classically conditioned stimuli elicit not only emotional states but also overt responses. Consequently, a classically conditioned stimulus may influence instrumental behavior through the overt responses it elicits. Consider a hypothetical situation in which the classically conditioned stimulus makes the animal remain still, and the instrumental response is shuttling back and forth in a shuttle box. In this example, presentation of the CS will decrease the instrumental response simply because the tendency to stop moving elicited by the CS will interfere with the shuttle behavior. An appeal to central emotional states is not necessary to understand such an outcome. An appeal to central emotional states is also unnecessary if a classically conditioned stimulus elicited overt responses that were similar to the instrumental behavior. In this case, presentation of the CS would increase responding because responses elicited by the CS would be added to the responses being performed by the animal to receive instrumental reinforcement.

Investigators have been very concerned with the possibility that the results of transfer-of-control experiments are due to Pavlovian CSs eliciting overt responses that either interfere with or facilitate the behavior required for instrumental reinforcement. A number of experimental strategies have been designed to rule out such response interactions (for a review, see Overmier & Lawry, 1979). These strategies have generally been successful in showing that many transfer-of-control effects are not produced by interactions between overt responses. However, overt classically conditioned responses have been important in some transfer-of-control experiments (for example, Karpicke, 1978; LoLordo, McMillan, & Riley, 1974; Schwartz, 1976).

Conditioned Central Emotional States or Reward-Specific Expectancies? Modern two-process theory assumes that classical conditioning mediates instrumental behavior through the conditioning of central emotional states such as hope (in the case of positive reinforcement) or fear (in the case of negative reinforcement). However, animals also acquire specific reward expectancies instead of more general central emotional states during instrumental and classical conditioning (Peterson & Trapold, 1980).

In one study, for example, solid food pellets and a sugar solution were used as USs in the classical and instrumental conditioning of rats (Kruse, Overmier, Konz, & Rokke, 1983). A CS+ for food facilitated instrumental responding reinforced with food much more than instrumental behavior reinforced with the sugar solution. Correspondingly, a CS+ for sugar increased instrumental behavior reinforced with sugar more than instrumental behavior reinforced with food pellets. Thus, expectancies for specific rewards rather than a general central emotional state of hope determined the results.

This study as well as similar experiments clearly indicate that under some circumstances, animals acquire reinforcer-specific expectancies rather than the more general emotional state of "hope" during instrumental and classical conditioning. (For additional evidence of reinforcer-specific expectancies, see Baxter & Zamble, 1982; DeMarse & Urcuioli, 1993; Henderson, Patterson, & Jackson, 1980; Urcuioli & DeMarse, 1996; Sherburne & Zentall, 1998.) Reinforcer-specific expectancy learning is a challenging alternative to modern two-process theory in explaining certain types of results. This alternative is, however, based on the assumption that instrumental conditioning involves the learning of an S-O association.

S-O associations appear to be fundamental to the motivation of instrumental behavior. In a recent analysis, Berridge (2001) pointed out that the S-O association is the basis for the core process of "wanting" the reinforcer. Through the S-O association, S becomes an incentive stimulus; S itself becomes attractive. This acquired incentive motivation contributes significantly to the motivation of the instrumental response.

R-O and S(R-O) Relations in Instrumental Conditioning

So far I have explained two different associations that can motivate instrumental behavior, Thorndike's S-R association and the S-O association, which activates a reward-specific expectancy or emotional state. For a couple of reasons, it would be odd to explain all of the motivation of instrumental behavior in terms of these two associations (see Colwill & Rescorla, 1986). First, notice that neither the S-R nor the S-O association involves a direct link between the response R and the reinforcer, or response outcome, O. The response outcome O is not directly represented in the S-R association, or otherwise associated with the response. This is counterintuitive. If you ask someone why she is performing an instrumental response, her reply would be that she expected the response (R) to result in the reinforcer (O). Intuition suggests that instrumental behavior involves R-O associations. You comb your hair because you expect that doing so will improve your appearance; you go to see a movie because you expect that watching the movie will be entertaining; and you open the refrigerator because you anticipate that doing so will enable you to get something to eat. Although informal explanations of instrumental behavior emphasize R-O associations, such associations do not exist in two-process models.

Another peculiarity of the associative structure of instrumental conditioning assumed by two-process theories is that S is assumed to become associated directly with O on the assumption that the pairing of S with O is sufficient for the occurrence of classical conditioning. However, as I explained in Chapter 4, CS-US pairings are not sufficient for the development of Pavlovian associations. The CS must also provide information about the US, or in some way be related to the US. In an instrumental conditioning situation, the reinforcer O cannot be predicted from S alone. Rather, O occurs if the participant makes response R in the presence of S. Thus, instrumental conditioning involves a conditional relation in which S is followed by O only if R occurs. This conditionality in the relation of S to O is ignored in two-process theories.

Evidence of R-O Associations.   A number of investigators have suggested that instrumental conditioning leads to the learning of response-outcome associations (for example, Bolles, 1972b; Mackintosh & Dickinson, 1979), and several different types of evidence have been obtained in support of this possibility. A common technique involves devaluing the reinforcer after conditioning to see if this decreases the instrumental response. (For reviews, see Dickinson & Balleine, 1994; Colwill, 1994; Colwill & Rescorla, 1986; Rescorla, 1991.) This strategy is analogous to the strategy of US devaluation in studies of Pavlovian conditioning (see Chapter 4). In Pavlovian conditioning, US devaluation is used to determine whether the conditioned response is mediated by a CS-US association. If US devaluation after conditioning disrupts the CR, investigators may conclude that the CR was mediated by the CS-US association. In a corresponding fashion, reinforcer devaluation has been used to determine if an instrumental response is mediated by an association between the response and its reinforcer outcome.

In one definitive demonstration, Colwill and Rescorla (1986) first reinforced rats for pushing a vertical rod to either the right or the left. Responding in either direction was reinforced on a variable interval 1-minute schedule of reinforcement. Both response alternatives were always available during training sessions. The only difference was that responses in one direction were reinforced with food pellets, and responses in the opposite direction were always reinforced with a bit of sugar solution (sucrose).

After both responses had become well established, the rod was removed and the reinforcer devaluation procedure was introduced. One of the reinforcers (either food pellets or sugar solution) was periodically presented in the experimental chamber, followed by an injection of lithium chloride to condition an aversion to that reinforcer. After an aversion to the selected reinforcer had been conditioned, the vertical rod was returned, and the rats received a test during which they were free to push the rod either to the left or to the right but neither food nor sucrose was provided.

The results of the test are presented in Figure 7.2. The important finding was that the rats were less likely to make the response whose reinforcer had been made aversive by pairings with lithium chloride. For example, if sucrose was used to reinforce responses to the left and an aversion was then conditioned to sucrose, the rats were less likely to push the rod to the left than to the right.

The selective response suppression that was obtained is difficult to explain in terms of the S-O or S-R associations that are assumed to be learned according to two-process theory. S-R associations cannot produce the results because the reinforcer is not included in an S-R association. Therefore, changes in the value of the reinforcer cannot alter behavior mediated by an S-R association. The results cannot be explained in terms of S-O associations because the two responses, pushing the vertical rod left or right, were made in the same place, with the same manipulandum, and therefore in the presence of the same external S stimuli. If devaluation of one of the reinforcers had altered the properties of S, that should have changed the two responses equally. Instead, devaluation of a reinforcer selectively depressed the particular response that had been trained with that reinforcer. This finding indicates that each response was associated separately with its own reinforcer. The participants evidently

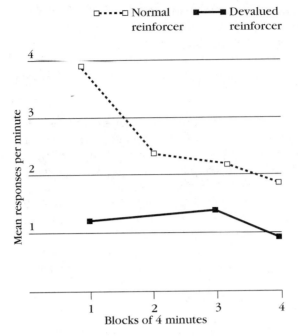

Figure 7.2 Effects of reinforcer devaluation on instrumental behavior. Devaluation of a reinforcer selectively reduces the response that was previously reinforced with that reinforcer. (From "Associative Structures in Instrumental Learning," by R. M. Colwill and R. A. Rescorla, in G. H. Bower [Ed.], 1986, *The Psychology of Learning and Motivation*, Vol. 20, pp. 55–104. Copyright © 1986 Academic Press. Reprinted by permission.)

learned separate R-O associations. (For further consideration of the role of R-O associations and the motivation of instrumental behavior, see Balleine, 2001; Dickinson & Balleine, 1994. For an alternative perspective on the effects of reinforcer devaluation, see Donahoe & Burgos, 2000.)

Evidence of the Learning of a Hierarchical S-(R-O) Relation. The evidence cited earlier clearly shows that organisms learn to associate an instrumental response with its outcome. However, R-O associations cannot act alone to produce instrumental behavior. As Mackintosh and Dickinson (1979) point out, the fact that the instrumental response activates an expectancy of the reinforcer is not sufficient to tell us what causes the response. An additional factor is required to activate the R-O association. One possibility is that the R-O association is activated by the stimuli S that are present when the response is reinforced. According to this view, S does not activate R directly, but rather it activates the R-O association. The subject comes to think of the R-O association when it encounters S, and that motivates it to make the instrumental response.

Skinner (1938) suggested many years ago that S, R, and O in instrumental conditioning are connected through a conditional S-(R-O) relation. This suggestion has been vigorously pursued in recent years. A variety of direct and indirect lines of evidence have been developed that point to the learning of S-(R-O) relations in instrumental conditioning (Colwill & Rescorla, 1990; Davidson, Aparicio, & Rescorla, 1988; Holman & Mackintosh, 1981; Goodall & Mackintosh, 1987; Rescorla, 1990a, 1990b). Most of these studies have involved rather complicated discrimination training procedures that are beyond the scope of this book. (For an especially good example, see Colwill & Delamater, 1995, Experiment 2.)

BEHAVIORAL REGULATION

Although contemporary associative analyses of instrumental motivation go far beyond Thorndike's S-R mechanisms, they are a part of the Thorndikian and Pavlovian tradition that views the world of behavior in terms of stimuli, responses, and associations. Behavioral regulation analyses are based on a radically different worldview. Instead of considering instrumental conditioning in terms of the reinforcement of a response in the presence of certain stimuli, behavioral regulation analyses focus on how instrumental contingencies put limitation on an organism's activities.

Antecedents of Behavioral Regulation

Reinforcers were initially considered to be special kinds of stimuli. Thorndike, for example, characterized a reinforcer as a stimulus that produces a "satisfying state of affairs." Various proposals were made about the special characteristics a stimulus must have for it to serve as a reinforcer. Although there were differences of opinion, for about a half century after Thorndike's Law of Effect, theoreticians agreed that reinforcers were special stimuli that "strengthened" instrumental behavior.

Consummatory Response Theory. The first challenge to the idea that reinforcers are stimuli came from Fred Sheffield and his colleagues, who formulated the **consummatory response theory.** Many reinforcers, such as food and water, elicit species-typical unconditioned responses, such as chewing, licking, and swallowing. The consummatory response theory attributes reinforcement to these species-typical behaviors. It asserts that species-typical consummatory responses—eating, drinking, and the like—are themselves the critical feature of reinforcers. In support of this idea, Sheffield, Roby, and Campbell (1954) showed that saccharin, an artificial sweetener, can serve as an effective reinforcer, even though it has no nutritive value and hence cannot satisfy a biological need. The reinforcing properties of artificial sweeteners now provide the foundations of a flourishing diet drink industry. Apart from their commercial value, however, artificial sweeteners were important in advancing scientific thinking about instrumental motivation.

The consummatory response theory was a radical innovation because it moved the search for reinforcers from special kinds of stimuli to special types of responses. Reinforcer responses were assumed to be special because they involved the consummation or completion of an instinctive behavior sequence. (See discussion of consummatory behavior in Chapter 2.) The theory assumed that consummatory responses (chewing and swallowing, for example) are fundamentally different from various potential instrumental responses, such as running, jumping, or pressing a lever. David Premack took issue with this theory and suggested that reinforcer responses are special only because they are more likely to occur than the instrumental responses they follow.

The Premack Principle. Premack pointed out that responses involved with commonly used reinforcers are activities that animals are highly likely to perform. For example, animals in a food reinforcement experiment are typically food deprived and therefore are highly likely to engage in eating behavior. By contrast, instrumental responses are typically low-probability activities. An experimentally naive rat, for example, is much less likely to press a response lever than it is to eat. Premack (1965) proposed that this difference in response probabilities is critical for reinforcement. Formally, the **Premack principle** can be stated as follows:

> Given two responses of the different likelihood, H and L, the opportunity to perform the higher probability response H after the lower probability response L will result in reinforcement of response L. (L→H reinforces L.) The opportunity to perform the lower probability response L after the higher probability response H will not result in reinforcement of response H. (H→L does not reinforce H.)

The Premack principle focuses on the difference in the likelihood of the instrumental and reinforcer responses; therefore, it is also called the **differential probability principle.**

Eating will reinforce bar pressing because eating is typically more likely than bar pressing. Under ordinary circumstances, bar pressing cannot reinforce eating. Premack's theory suggests, however, that if for some reason bar pressing became more probable than eating, it would reinforce eating. Premack's theory denies that a fundamental distinction exists between reinforcers and instrumental responses. There is nothing inherently unique about reinforcers; rather, the effectiveness of a reinforcer is a relative matter. The reinforcing response is simply more likely to occur at the outset than the instrumental response. This relative property of reinforcers makes it possible to use a wide variety of responses as reinforcers.

Premack and his colleagues conducted many experiments to test his theory (see Premack, 1965, 1971a). One of the early studies was conducted with young children. Premack first gave the children two response alternatives (eating candy and playing a pinball machine) and measured which response was more probable for each child. Some of the children preferred eating candy over playing pinball; others preferred the pinball machine. In the second phase of the experiment (see Figure 7.3), the children were tested with one of two procedures. In one procedure, eating was specified as the reinforcing response, and playing pinball was the instrumental response—that is, the children had to play the pinball machine in order to get access to candy. The question was whether all the children would increase their pinball playing. Consistent with Premack's theory, only those

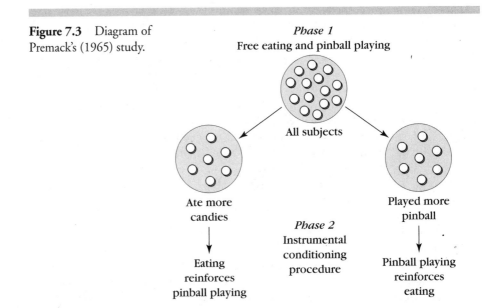

Figure 7.3   Diagram of Premack's (1965) study.

Phase 1
Free eating and pinball playing

All subjects

Ate more
candies

Played more
pinball

Phase 2
Instrumental
conditioning
procedure

Eating
reinforces
pinball playing

Pinball playing
reinforces
eating

children who preferred eating to playing pinball showed a reinforcement effect under these circumstances.

In another test, the roles of the two responses were reversed: eating was the instrumental response, and playing pinball was the reinforcing response. The children had to eat candy to get access to the pinball machine. In this situation, only those children who preferred playing pinball to eating showed a reinforcement effect.

Premack (1962) also tested his theory in studies of drinking and wheel running in laboratory rats (see Figure 7.4). Premack altered the probabilities of the drinking and wheel running by changing deprivation conditions. In one procedure, the rats were deprived of water but not of the opportunity to run in the wheel. Under these circumstances drinking was more probable than running, and the opportunity to drink was effective in reinforcing running. In the second procedure, the rats were not deprived of water. Under these circumstances, they were more likely to run in the wheel than to drink. Now the opportunity to run in the wheel could reinforce drinking, but drinking could no longer be used to reinforce running. This study shows that running and drinking could be used interchangeably as instrumental and reinforcing responses, depending on the animal's state of water deprivation. Nothing inherent to one response or the other made it a reinforcer.

The Premack principle advanced scientific thinking about reinforcement in significant ways. It encouraged thinking about reinforcers as responses rather than as stimuli, and it

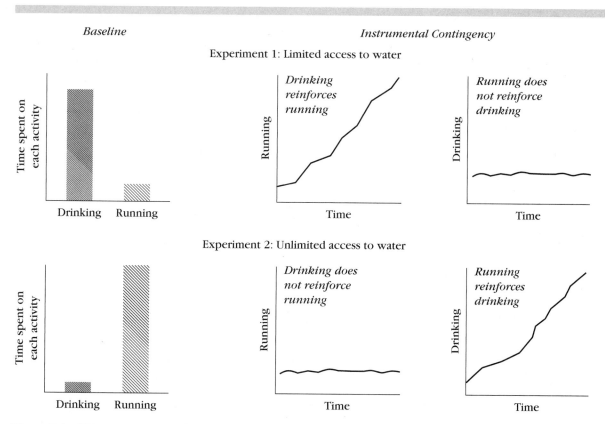

Figure 7.4 When a rat is water-deprived (Experiment 1), it drinks more than it runs. Therefore, drinking reinforces running, but running does not reinforce drinking. When a rat is not water-deprived (Experiment 2), it runs more than it drinks. This time running reinforces drinking, but drinking does not reinforce running.

BOX **7.1**

Using reinforcement procedures to encourage appropriate behavior in children requires identifying an effective reinforcer. Food is often a good choice, but practical and ethical considerations have encouraged investigators to identify other forms of reinforcement. The Premack principle has been a great help in this regard because it suggests that any activity that is more likely than the response to be reinforced can serve as an effective reinforcer.

Children, like adults, vary in their preferred activities. Some prefer playing ball after school; others prefer talking to friends on the phone. By measuring the relative probability of different activities for each child, reinforcement procedures can be personalized to take advantage of each individual's unique response preferences. This may result in some rather unusual responses serving as reinforcers.

Children with autism often engage in repetitive aberrant behaviors. One such behavior, called *delayed echolalia,* involves repeating words. For example, one autistic child was heard to say over and over again, "Ding! ding! ding! You win again," and "Match Game 83." Another form of aberrant behavior, *perseverative behavior,* involves persistent manipulation of an object. For example, the child may repeatedly handle only certain plastic toys.

The high probability of echolalia and perseverative behavior in children with autism suggests that these responses may be effectively used as reinforcers in treatment procedures. This possibility has been explored by several investigators. In a study by Charlop, Kurtz, and Casey (1990), the effectiveness of different forms of reinforcement was compared in training various academic-related skills in autistic children. The tasks included identifying which of several objects was the same or different from the one held up by the teacher, adding up coins, and correctly responding to sentences designed to teach receptive pronouns or prepositions. In one experimental condition, a preferred food (such as a small piece of chocolate, cereal, or a cookie) served as the reinforcer, in the absence of programmed food deprivation. In another condition, the opportunity to perform an aberrant response for 3 to 5 seconds served as the reinforcer.

Some results of the study are illustrated in Figure 7.5. Each panel represents the data for a different student. Notice that in each case, the opportunity to engage in a prevalent aberrant response resulted in better performance on the training tasks than food reinforcement. Both delayed echolalia and perseverative behavior served to increase task performance above what was observed with food reinforcement. These results indicate that high-probability responses can serve to reinforce lower-probability responses, even if the reinforcer responses are not characteristic of normal behavior.

greatly expanded the range of things investigators started to use as reinforcers. With the Premack principle, any activity could serve as a reinforcer provided that it was more likely than the instrumental response. Differential probability as the key to reinforcement paved the way for applications of reinforcement procedures to all sorts of human problems. However, problems with the measurement of response probability, and a closer look at instrumental conditioning procedures, moved subsequent theoretical developments away from the Premack principle.

The Response Deprivation Hypothesis. In most instrumental conditioning procedures, the momentary probability of the reinforcer response is kept at a high level by restricting access to the reinforcing response. A rat lever pressing for food, for example, typically comes into the experimental situation not having eaten much and does not receive a whole meal for each lever-press response. These limitations on the reinforcing response are very impor-

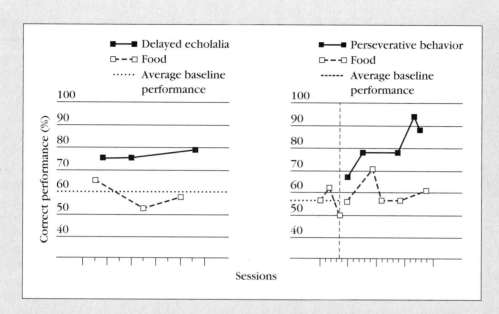

Figure 7.5 Task performance data for two children with autism. One student's behavior was reinforced with food or the opportunity to engage in delayed echolalia. Another student's behavior was reinforced with food or the opportunity to engage in perseverative responding. (Responding during baseline periods was also reinforced with food.) (From "Using Aberrant Behaviors as Reinforcers for Autistic Children," by M. H. Charlop, P. F. Kurtz, & F. G. Casey, *Journal of Applied Behavior Analysis, 23,* pp. 163–181. Copyright © 1990 by the Society for the Experimental Analysis of Behavior, Inc. Reprinted by permission.)

tant. If an investigator were to give the rat a full meal for pressing the lever once, chances are it would not increase its rate of responding very much. Restrictions on the opportunity to engage in the reinforcing response serve to increase its effectiveness as a reinforcer.

Premack (1965) recognized the importance of restricting access to the reinforcer response for instrumental conditioning. He regarded response deprivation as not only a necessary condition for reinforcement but also an adjunct to the differential probability principle. In his view, the reinforcer response still had to be a more likely behavior than the instrumental response. By contrast, Timberlake and Allison (1974; see also Allison, 1993) abandoned the differential probability principle altogether and argued that restriction of the reinforcer response was the critical factor for instrumental reinforcement. This proposal is called the **response deprivation hypothesis.**

In particularly decisive tests of the response deprivation hypothesis, several investigators found that even access to a low-probability response can serve as a reinforcer, provided that

Courtesy of W. Timberlake

W. Timberlake

Courtesy of J. Allison

J. Allison

subjects are restricted from making this response (Timberlake & Allison, 1974; Eisenberger, Karpman, & Trattner, 1967). Thus, with response deprivation, even a low-probability response can be used to reinforce a higher-probability response. This set of conditions seriously violates the Premack principle and shows that response deprivation is more basic to the motivation of instrumental behavior than differential response probability.

The response deprivation hypothesis provides a new principle for predicting what will serve as an effective reinforcer. It also provides a new procedure for creating reinforcers—restricting access to the reinforcer response. It is interesting to note that restricting access to the reinforcer response is inherent in all instrumental conditioning procedures—the reinforcer is withheld until the specified instrumental response has been performed. The response deprivation hypothesis points out that this definitional feature of instrumental conditioning is critical for producing a reinforcement effect.

Traditional views of reinforcement assume that a reinforcer is something that exists independent of an instrumental conditioning procedure. Stimulus views of reinforcement and the consummatory response theory all assume that reinforcers exist whether or not they are used in an instrumental conditioning procedure. The response deprivation hypothesis makes explicit the radically different idea that a reinforcer is produced by the instrumental contingency itself. The Premack principle was the first theory to suggest that reinforcers do not exist in an absolute sense. In the Premack principle, whether a response was a reinforcer depended on how its likelihood of occurrence compared with that of the instrumental response, but the principle did not imply that the instrumental conditioning procedure itself was responsible for the creation of a reinforcer. How instrumental contingencies create reinforcers and reinforcement effects has been developed further in behavioral regulation theories.

Behavioral Regulation and the Behavioral Bliss Point

Regulation is a recurrent theme in learning theory. I discussed regulatory processes in Chapter 2 in connection with the opponent-process theory of motivation, and in Chapter 4 in connection with the role of learning in physiological homeostasis. Physiological homeostasis refers to mechanisms that serve to maintain critical aspects of the body (such as blood sugar level and temperature) within acceptable limits. A shift away from the physiologically optimal or homeostatic level triggers changes that serve to return the system to the homeostatic level.

Behavioral regulation theories assume that analogous homeostatic mechanisms exist with respect to behavior. Within the framework of behavioral regulation, organisms are presumed to have a preferred or an optimal distribution of activities that they work to maintain in the face of challenges or disruptions. Behavioral regulation theories focus on the extent to which an instrumental response-reinforcer contingency disrupts behavioral stability and forces the individual away from its preferred or optimal distribution of activities (see Allison, 1983, 1989; Hanson & Timberlake, 1983; Tierney, 1995; Timberlake, 1980, 1984, 1995).

An individual has to eat, breathe, drink, keep warm, exercise, entertain itself, and so on. All these activities have to occur in particular proportions—an individual should not eat too much or too little, or exercise too much or too little. If the preferred or optimal balance of activities is upset, behavior is assumed to change so as to correct the deviation from the homeostatic level. This basic assumption of behavioral regulation is fairly simple. However, numerous factors (some of which are a bit complicated) can influence how organisms meet challenges to their preferred or optimal distribution of responses.

The Behavioral Bliss Point.   Every situation provides various response opportunities. In an experimental chamber, for example, an animal may run in a wheel, drink, eat, scratch itself, sniff holes, or manipulate a response lever. Behavioral regulation theory assumes that if organisms are free to distribute their responses among the available alternatives, they will do so in a way that is most comfortable or in some sense "optimal" for them. This response distribution defines the **behavioral bliss point.**

The particular distribution of activities that constitutes the bliss point will vary from one situation to another. For example, if the running wheel is made very difficult to turn or the participant is severely deprived of water, the relative likelihood of running and drinking will change. However, for a given circumstance, the behavioral bliss point, as revealed in unconstrained choices among response alternatives, is assumed to be stable across time.

The behavioral bliss point can be identified by the relative frequency of occurrence of all the responses of an organism in an unconstrained situation. To simplify analysis, I focus on just two responses. Consider how a high school student may distribute his activities between studying and watching TV. Figure 7.6 represents time spent watching TV on the vertical axis and time spent studying on the horizontal axis. If no restrictions are placed on the student's behavior, he will probably spend a lot more time watching TV than studying. This is represented by the open circle in Figure 7.6 and is the *behavioral bliss point* in this situation. At the bliss point, the student watches TV for 60 minutes for every 15 minutes that he spends studying.

Imposing an Instrumental Contingency.   How would the introduction of an instrumental contingency between studying and watching TV disrupt the student's behavioral bliss? That depends on the nature of the contingency. Figure 7.6 shows a schedule line starting at

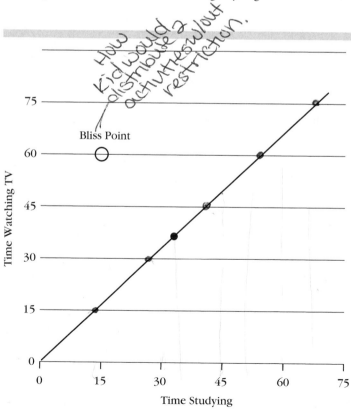

Figure 7.6   Allocation of behavior between watching TV and studying. The open circle shows the optimal allocation, or behavioral bliss point, obtained when there are no constraints on either activity. The schedule line represents a schedule of reinforcement in which the student is required to study for the same amount of time that he or she gets to watch TV. Notice that once this schedule of reinforcement is imposed, it is no longer possible for the student to achieve the behavioral bliss point. The schedule deprives the student of access to the TV and forces or motivates an increase in studying.

BOX 7.2

THE BLISS POINT APPROACH AND BEHAVIOR THERAPY

Behavior regulation theories of reinforcement not only provide new insights into age-old theoretical issues concerning reinforcement but also suggest new approaches to behavior therapy (Timberlake & Farmer-Dougan, 1991). The bliss point approach, for example, forces investigators to consider the behavioral context in which an instrumental contingency is introduced. Depending on that behavioral context, a reinforcement procedure may increase or decrease the target response. The bliss point approach can therefore provide insights into situations in which a reinforcement procedure produces an unexpected decrease in the instrumental response.

One area of behavior therapy in which reinforcement procedures are surprisingly ineffective is the use of parental social reinforcement to increase a child's prosocial behavior. A parent whose child frequently misbehaves is encouraged to provide more social reinforcement for positive behavior on the assumption that low rates of parental reinforcement are responsible for the child's misbehavior.

Viken and McFall (1994) have pointed out that the common failure of such reinforcement procedures is predictable when the behavioral bliss point of the child is considered.

Figure 7.7 shows the behavioral space for parental social reinforcement and positive child behavior. The open circle represents the child's presumed bliss point. Left to her own devices, the child prefers a lot of social reinforcement while emitting few positive behaviors. The dashed line represents the low rate of parental reinforcement in effect before a therapeutic intervention. According to this schedule line, the child has to perform two positive responses to receive each social reinforcer from her parent. The filled circle on the line indicates the equilibrium point, where positive responses by the child and social reinforcers earned are equally far from their respective bliss point values.

The therapeutic procedure involves increasing the rate of social reinforcement, say, to a ratio of 1:1. This is illustrated by the solid line in Figure 7.7. Now the child receives one social reinforcer for each positive behavior. The equilibrium point is again illustrated by the filled data point. Notice that with the increased social reinforcement, the child can get more of the social reinforcers she wants without having to make more positive responses. In fact,

the origin and increasing at a 45° angle. This line defines a schedule of reinforcement, according to which the student is required to study for the same amount of time that he wants to watch TV. If the student studies for 10 minutes, he will get to watch TV for 10 minutes; if he studies for 1 hour, he will get to watch TV for 1 hour. What might be the consequences of disrupting the free choice of studying and TV watching by imposing such a schedule constraint?

Behavioral regulation theory states that organisms will defend against challenges to the behavioral bliss point, just as physiological regulation involves defense against challenges to a physiological set point. The interesting thing is that the free-baseline behavioral bliss point cannot always be reestablished after an instrumental contingency has been introduced. In my example, the behavioral bliss point is 60 minutes of watching TV for 15 minutes of studying. Once the instrumental contingency is imposed, there is no way the student can watch TV for 60 minutes and study for only 15. If he insists on watching TV for 60 minutes, he will have to tolerate adding 45 minutes to his studying time. On the other hand, if he insists on spending only the 15 minutes on his studies (as at the bliss point), he will have to make do with 45 minutes less than his optimal 60 minutes of TV watching. Defending the bliss amount of studying or the bliss amount of TV watching both have their disadvan-

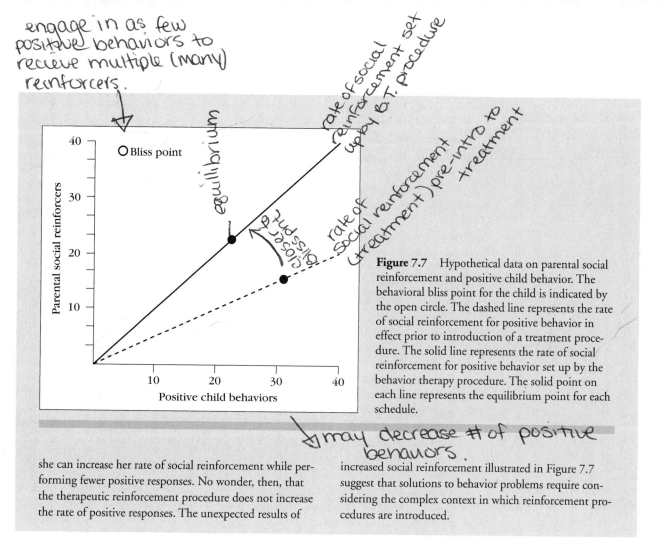

(handwritten annotations)

engage in as few positive behaviors to recieve multiple (many) reinforcers.

equilibrium

bliss point

rate of social reinforcement set up by B.T. procedure

rate of social reinforcement (treatment) pre-intro to treatment

may decrease # of positive behaviors.

Figure 7.7 Hypothetical data on parental social reinforcement and positive child behavior. The behavioral bliss point for the child is indicated by the open circle. The dashed line represents the rate of social reinforcement for positive behavior in effect prior to introduction of a treatment procedure. The solid line represents the rate of social reinforcement for positive behavior set up by the behavior therapy procedure. The solid point on each line represents the equilibrium point for each schedule.

she can increase her rate of social reinforcement while performing fewer positive responses. No wonder, then, that the therapeutic reinforcement procedure does not increase the rate of positive responses. The unexpected results of increased social reinforcement illustrated in Figure 7.7 suggest that solutions to behavior problems require considering the complex context in which reinforcement procedures are introduced.

tages. That is often the dilemma posed by an instrumental contingency. It does not permit getting back to the bliss point.

Although the instrumental contingency shown in Figure 7.6 makes it impossible to return to the behavioral bliss point, this does not mean that the bliss point becomes irrelevant. To the contrary. The bliss point still provides the motivation for instrumental behavior. Behavioral regulation theory assumes that returning to the behavioral set point remains a goal of response allocation. When this goal cannot be reached, the redistribution of responses between the instrumental and contingent behaviors becomes a matter of compromise. The rate of one response is brought as close as possible to its preferred level without moving the other response too far away from its preferred level.

Staddon, for example, proposed a **minimum deviation model** of behavioral regulation to solve the dilemma of schedule constraints (Staddon, 1979; see also Staddon, 1983). According to this model, introduction of a response-reinforcer contingency causes organisms to redistribute their behavior between the instrumental and contingent responses in a way that minimizes the total deviation of the two responses from the optimal or bliss point. The minimum deviation point is shown by the filled circle on the schedule line in Figure 7.6. For situations in which the free-baseline behavioral bliss point cannot be achieved, the minimum deviation model provides one view of how organisms settle for the next best thing.

Explanation of Reinforcement Effects.   How are reinforcement effects produced by behavioral regulation? Behavioral regulation involves the defense of a behavioral bliss point in the face of restrictions on responding imposed by a response-reinforcer contingency. As noted earlier, this defense may require settling for something close to but not exactly at the free-baseline bliss point. How do these mechanisms lead to increases in instrumental behavior in typical instrumental conditioning procedures?

A reinforcement effect is identified by an increase in the occurrence of an instrumental response above the level of that behavior in the absence of the response-reinforcer contingency. The schedule line shown in Figure 7.6 involves restricting access to TV watching below the level specified by the bliss point. To move toward the behavioral bliss point, the student has to increase his studying in order to gain more opportunity to watch TV. This is precisely what occurs in typical instrumental conditioning procedures. Access to the reinforcer is restricted; to gain more opportunity to engage in the reinforcer response, the individual has to perform more of the instrumental response. Thus, increased performance of the instrumental response (a reinforcement effect) results from behavioral regulatory mechanisms that function to minimize deviations from the behavioral bliss point.

Viewing Reinforcement Contingencies in a Broader Behavioral Context.   The earlier explanation of how schedule constraints produce reinforcement effects considers only the instrumental and reinforcer responses (studying and watching TV). A student's environment most likely provides a much greater range of options. Instrumental contingencies do not occur in a behavioral vacuum or test tube. They occur in the context of a variety of responses and reinforcers the subject may obtain. Furthermore, that broader behavioral context can significantly influence how the subject adjusts to a schedule constraint. For example, if the student enjoys listening to the radio as much as watching TV, restrictions on access to the TV may not increase studying behavior. The student may switch to listening to the radio, or he may switch to reading comic books or going to the movies. Any of these options will undermine the instrumental contingency. If the student opts for listening to the radio or going to the movies in place of watching TV, he will not increase his studying behavior to obtain his preferred amount of TV time.

This example illustrates that accurate prediction of the effects of an instrumental conditioning procedure requires considering the broader context of the organism's response options. Focusing on just the instrumental response and its antecedent and consequent stimuli (that is, the associative structure of instrumental behavior) ignores the broader behavioral context in which instrumental contingencies operate. It is important to consider that broader behavioral context because it can significantly influence the outcome of particular instrumental conditioning procedures. The effect of a particular instrumental conditioning procedure may depend on what alternative sources of reinforcement are available to the organism, how those other reinforcers are related to the particular reinforcer involved in the instrumental contingency, and the costs of obtaining those alternative reinforcers. These issues have been systematically considered with the application of economic concepts to the problem of response allocation.

Economic Concepts and Response Allocation

The bliss point approach redefined the fundamental issue in the analysis of instrumental motivation. It shifted attention away from the notion that reinforcers are special stimuli that enter into special associative relations with the instrumental response and its antecedents.

With the bliss point approach, the fundamental question in instrumental motivation became, "How do the constraints of an instrumental conditioning procedure produce changes in behavior?"

Students who have studied economics may recognize a similarity here to problems addressed by economists. Economists, like psychologists, strive to understand changes in behavior in terms of preexisting preferences and restrictions on fulfilling those preferences. As Bickel, Green, and Vuchinich (1995) noted, "economics is the study of the allocation of behavior within a system of constraint" (p. 258). In the economic arena, the restrictions on behavior are imposed by an individual's income and the price of the goods that he or she wants to purchase. In instrumental conditioning situations, the restrictions are provided by the number of responses an organism is able to make and the number of responses required to obtain each reinforcer.

Psychologists have become interested in the similarities between economic restrictions in the marketplace and schedule constraints in instrumental conditioning. In the following section, I discuss how economic ideas have influenced behavior regulation theories of reinforcement. For the sake of simplicity, I concentrate on the basic ideas that have had the most impact on understanding reinforcement. (For further details, see Allison, 1983, 1993; Green & Freed, 1998; Hursh, 1984; Lea, 1978; Rachlin, 1989; Rachlin et al., 1976.)

Consumer Demand.   Fundamental to the application of economic concepts to the problem of reinforcement is the relation between the price of a commodity and how much of it is purchased. This relation is called the **demand curve.** Figure 7.8 shows three examples of demand curves. Curve A illustrates a situation in which the consumption of a commodity is very easily influenced by its price, such as is the case with candy. If the price of candy increases substantially, the amount purchased quickly drops. Other commodities are less responsive to price changes (Curve C in Figure 7.8). The purchase of gasoline, for example, is not as easily discouraged by increases in price. People continue to purchase gas for their cars even if the price increases substantially.

The degree to which price influences consumption is called **elasticity of demand.** Demand for candy is highly elastic. The more candy costs, the less people will buy. In contrast, demand for gasoline is much less elastic. People continue to purchase gas even if the price increases a great deal.

Figure 7.8   Hypothetical consumer demand curves illustrating high sensitivity to price (Curve A), intermediate sensitivity (Curve B), and low sensitivity (Curve C).

The concept of consumer demand can be used to analyze instrumental reinforcement by considering the number of responses performed (or time spent responding) to be analogous to money. The "price" of a reinforcer is the time or number of responses required to obtain the reinforcer. Thus, the "price" of the reinforcer is determined by the schedule of reinforcement. The goal is to understand how instrumental behavior ("spending") is controlled by instrumental contingencies ("prices").

Madden and Bickel (1999) investigated the elasticity of demand for cigarettes in smokers who were not trying to quit. Subjects used a special apparatus that had two plungers they could pull. One of the plungers was designated as the instrumental response, and pulling this plunger was reinforced with 10¢ each time a subject completed 100 responses (an FR 100). After a subject had accumulated enough money, he or she could pull the second plunger and obtain two puffs on a lit cigarette. The price for the two puffs varied from one session to the next in random order, ranging from 2¢ to 120¢. The subjects went through the test series twice. In the abstinence condition, they were required to go without cigarettes for 5–6 hours before coming to the laboratory. In the nonabstinence condition, they were allowed to smoke normally before coming to the laboratory. The goal of the experiment was to see if working for access to a cigarette would be a function of price (elasticity of demand), and if the demand curve would be influenced by abstinence.

The results of the experiment are summarized in Figure 7.9. As might be expected, subjects who were abstinent when they started each session worked to obtain more puffs on the cigarette than did subjects who had been allowed to smoke as usual before the session. However, regardless of whether the participants abstained before coming to the lab, they showed considerable sensitivity to price (elasticity of demand). Smoking significantly decreased with increases in price. (For additional studies of the behavioral economics of smoking, see Bickel, DeGrandpre, Hughes, & Higgins, 1991; Bickel, Madden, & DeGrandpre, 1997; Madden, Bickel, & Jacobs, 2000. For recent studies of price effects in research with nonhuman animals, see Collier & Johnson, 1997, 2000; Sumpter, Temple, & Foster, 1999.)

Determinants of the Elasticity of Demand. The application of economic concepts to the analysis of instrumental conditioning would be of little value if the application did not provide new insights into the mechanisms of reinforcement. As it turns out, economic concepts have helped to identify three major factors that influence how schedule constraints shape

Figure 7.9 Number of cigarette puffs obtained as a function of price for cigarette smokers who were not planning to quit. Data for subjects who abstained from smoking for 5–6 hours before the session are shown by the open circles. Data for subjects who did not abstain from smoking before the session are shown by the filled circles. (After Madden & Bickel, 1999. Only data from the first half of each session are presented.)

the reallocation of behavior. Each of these factors determines the degree of elasticity of demand, or the extent to which increases in price cause a decrease in consumption.

1. *Availability of Substitutes.* Perhaps the most important factor that influences the elasticity of demand is the availability of substitutes. Whether increases in the price of one item cause a decline in consumption depends on the availability (and price) of other goods that can be used in place of the original item. The availability of substitutes increases the sensitivity of the original item to higher prices.

Coffee and tea are good examples of substitutes. Both are common sources of caffeine. Furthermore, many people find tea a good substitute for coffee. Therefore, if the price of coffee increases substantially, they will switch to tea. The elasticity of the demand for coffee is influenced by the availability of tea as a substitute for coffee. In contrast to coffee, how much gasoline people buy is not highly influenced by price, because there are no readily available substitutes for gasoline to fuel a car.

The availability of drug substitutes on elasticity of demand for food was recently examined by Foltin (1999) in an experiment conducted with baboons. The subjects had to press a response lever to obtain food pellets. The "price" of the pellets was varied by requiring different numbers of lever presses for each pellet (using fixed ratio schedules). Foltin was interested in whether food intake would decrease as the price of food was increased, and whether the availability of alternative reinforcers would influence this function. In different experimental conditions, responses on a second lever produced either nothing, a sugar solution, or solutions with different concentrations of cocaine. The availability of these alternative reinforcers always required two presses (FR 2) on the alternate lever. In general, increases in the "price" of food resulted in fewer pellets being obtained. More interesting, the availability of cocaine on the alternate response lever increased the elasticity of demand for food. This effect was particularly striking in baboon #3.

The results for baboon #3 are shown in Figure 7.10. Notice that for this subject increasing the price of food had little effect if the alternate response lever produced either nothing or dextrose (a sugar solution). However, when the alternate response lever yielded cocaine, increases in the price of food resulted in a precipitous decline in food-reinforced responding. The largest effect was obtained with the intermediate cocaine concentration. With this concentration, availability of cocaine on the alternate lever dramatically increased the elasticity of demand for food. This study illustrates a powerful example of substitutability on the elasticity of demand. In addition, it shows how the methodology provided by behavioral economic concepts can be used to identify substitutable reinforcers. For baboon #3 an intermediate concentration of cocaine was an excellent substitute for food.

One source of substitutable reinforcers is the availability of the reinforcer outside the experimental session. When food is used as the reinforcer in experiments with laboratory animals, the subjects are typically given a certain amount of food each day. Any part of this ration that they fail to earn during an experimental session is given to them later as "free" food in the home cage. Such a situation is called an *open economy.* This is contrasted with a *closed economy,* in which subjects do not receive supplemental feedings. In a closed economy, if the subjects fail to obtain their daily food ration during the experimental session, they have to wait until the next session to make up the deficit. In general, elasticity of demand is greater in open economy situations than in closed economies (Hursh, 1991; see also Foster, Blackman, & Temple, 1997). (For additional studies of substitutability with laboratory animals, see Collier & Johnson, 2000; Foltin, 1997; Green & Freed, 1993; Schultz, Collier, & Johnson, 1999. For a recent study of substitutability among heroin addicts who also use other drugs, see Petry & Bickel, 1998.)

2. *Price Range.* Another important determinant of the elasticity of demand is the price range of the commodity. Generally, an increase in price has less effect at low prices than at

Figure 7.10 Number of food pellets obtained as a function of increases in the response requirement for food for a baboon that could also press an alternate response lever that produced either nothing, a solution of dextrose (a type of sugar), or different concentrations of cocaine. Notice that the elasticity of demand for food dramatically changed with the availability of cocaine. (After Foltin, 1999.)

high prices. Consider, for example, the cost of candy. A 10% increase in the price from 50¢ to 55¢ is not likely to discourage consumption. But if the candy costs $5.00, a 10% increase to $6.00 might well discourage purchases.

Price effects on elasticity of demand are evident in Figures 7.9 and 7.10. Notice that at low prices, there is little change in the number of reinforcers obtained as the price increases a bit. However, dramatic declines occur in the number of reinforcers obtained in the high range of prices. Price effects on the elasticity of demand for food have also been documented in studies with laboratory rats and baboons (Hursh, Raslear, Shurtleff, Bauman, & Simmons, 1988; Foltin, 1991, 1994). In these experiments, the price of food was increased by increasing the number of responses required for reinforcement, using fixed ratio schedules. As the price of food increased, the animals at first increased their responding correspondingly to obtain the same amount of food as before. Thus, over a range of low prices, demand for food was inelastic. Responding failed, however, to keep up with further increases in price, and at the high FR schedules, food consumption declined.

3. *Income Level.* A third factor that determines elasticity of demand is the level of income. In general, the higher the income, the less deterred a consumer will be by increases in price. This is also true for reinforcers obtained on schedules of reinforcement. In studies of instrumental conditioning, the number of responses or amount of time available for responding corresponds to income. These are resources an organism can use to respond to a schedule

BOX **7.3**

CONCEPTS OF CONSUMER DEMAND IN THE ANALYSIS OF DRUG ABUSE

The use of illicit drugs such as heroin and cocaine is instrumental behavior. Going to obtain an illicit drug and paying for it provides the opportunity to use it. Government efforts to reduce the use of illicit drugs have involved manipulating various aspects of its cost or "price." Confiscating shipments limits the availability of a drug and increases its monetary cost, as shortages drive up the price. Severe penalties for drug possession also impose a "cost," but only after the drug has been obtained.

Laboratory studies of rats, monkeys, and people self-administering drugs under various schedules of reinforcement have shown that the concepts of consumer demand are useful in the analysis of instrumental drug-seeking be-

havior (for example, Bickel et al., 1991; Carroll, Carmona, & May, 1991; English, Rowlett, & Woolverton, 1995; Petry & Heyman, 1995). The results of experimental studies of consumer demand have also been extended to analyses of drug abuse policy (Hursh, 1991).

The effectiveness of policies intended to curb drug use depend on the drug's elasticity of demand. As I have described, increasing the cost of a commodity fails to reduce its consumption if the price remains relatively low, if there are no substitutes for the item, or if the consumer has a high income level. These considerations suggest that to discourage drug use, more than the cost of the drug needs to be considered. A highly effective technique for increasing the elasticity of demand for an item involves making available an effective substitute. Interestingly, under certain circumstances, nondrug reinforcers can serve as effective substitutes for a drug reinforcer (for example, Carroll et al., 1991).

constraint. The more responses or time animals have available, the less their behavior is influenced by increases in the cost of the reinforcer (Hastjarjo, Silberberg, & Hursh, 1990; Silberberg, Warren-Bouton, & Asano, 1987; see also Hastjarjo & Silberberg, 1992; De-Grandpre, Bickel, Rizvi, & Hughes, 1993).

Problems with Behavioral Regulation Approaches

Behavioral regulation theories have done much to change the way we think about reinforcement and instrumental conditioning, but several major shortcomings have emerged.

Behavioral regulation approaches are based on the assumption that individuals seek to defend an "optimal" or preferred combination of activities, or bliss point. This bliss point is defended by reallocating behavior between insrumental and reinforcer responses or by opting for substitute reinforcers. The bliss point is a molar characteristic of behavior. It is based on a measure of each response totaled over a large block of time (such as an entire free-baseline session). A given molar bliss point can be achieved in a variety of ways. In the hypothetical example in Figure 7.6, the student was allowed to choose between watching TV and studying during the free-baseline period and ended up watching TV for 60 minutes and studying for 15. This could have been achieved by doing all the TV watching before any studying or by switching back and forth between the two activities. According to the behavioral bliss point approach, such differences in response patterns should not matter. But experimental evidence indicates that how the molar bliss point is achieved is important (for example, Gawley, Timberlake, & Lucas, 1987; Tierney, Smith, & Gannon, 1987). Therefore, an adequate characterization of "behavioral bliss" requires information about molecular choice patterns.

Another, and perhaps more serious, difficulty is that responses during a free-operant baseline period do not always have the same "value" as responses that occur as a part of an arranged instrumental contingency. In behavioral regulation approaches, the outcome of instrumental contingencies is predicted from the free-baseline distribution of responses. For such predictions to work, an investigator has to assume that responses performed in the absence of experimenter-imposed constraints are basically the same as the responses that occur when an instrumental contingency is imposed. For example, studying in the absence of an externally imposed response constraint has to be of the same "value" as studying in order to gain access to the TV. This assumption has been found to be incorrect in several experiments (Allison, Buxton, & Moore, 1987; Gawley et al., 1987; Tierney et al., 1987). Doing something when there are no externally imposed requirements (jogging for pleasure, for example) appears to be different from doing the same thing when it is required by an imposed instrumental contingency (jogging in a physical education class, for example).

Finally, because behavioral regulation and economic approaches to instrumental behavior do not deal with molecular behavioral processes, they say nothing about how organisms manage to defend a preferred combination of goods or activities. As Killeen (1995) pointed out, economics "provides an approach to understanding the trade-offs animals make between alternate packages of goods" (p. 426), but it does not tell us the processes that are involved in making those trade-offs.

Contributions of Behavioral Regulation

The behavioral regulation approach emerged from the theoretical developments that originated with Premack and his differential probability principle. Although this line of theorizing encountered some serious difficulties, it has also made major contributions to how we think about the motivation of instrumental behavior (see Tierney, 1995). It is instructive to review some of these contributions.

1. Behavioral regulation and the Premack principle moved us away from thinking about reinforcers as special kinds of stimuli or as special kinds of responses. We are now encouraged to look for the causes of reinforcement in how instrumental contingencies constrain the free flow of behavior. Reinforcement effects are seen as produced by schedule constraints on an organism's ongoing activities.

2. Instrumental conditioning procedures are no longer considered to "stamp in" or to "strengthen" instrumental behavior. Rather, instrumental conditioning is seen as creating a new distribution, or allocation, of responses. Typically, the reallocation of behavior involves an increase in the instrumental response and a decrease in the reinforcer response. These two changes are viewed as equally important features of the redistribution of behavior.

3. There is no fundamental distinction between instrumental and reinforcer responses. Reinforcer responses are not assumed to be more likely than instrumental responses. They are not assumed to provide any special physiological benefits or to have any inherent characteristics that make them different from instrumental responses. Rather, instrumental and reinforcer responses are distinguished only by the roles assigned to them by an instrumental conditioning procedure.

4. Behavioral regulation and behavioral economics embrace the assumption that organisms respond in order to maximize benefits. The idea of optimization or maximization is not original with behavioral regulation. I introduced the idea (maximizing rates of reinforcement) earlier in discussions of concurrent schedules. The bliss point approach suggests

that the optimal distribution of activities is determined not only by physiological needs but also by the organism's ecological niche and natural or phylogenetically determined response tendencies. It is not always clear what is being maximized. In fact, studies of behavior can be used to identify what organisms value and work to conserve (Rachlin, 1995).

5. Behavioral regulation and behavioral economics have provided new and precise ways of describing constraints that various instrumental conditioning procedures impose on an organism's repertoire of behavior. More important, they have emphasized that instrumental behavior cannot be studied in a vacuum or behavioral test tube. All of the organism's response options at a given time must be considered as a system. Changes in one part of the system influence changes in other parts. Constraints imposed by instrumental procedures are more or less effective depending on the nature of the constraint, the availability of substitutes, and the organism's level of "income."

CONCLUDING COMMENTS

Motivational processes in instrumental behavior have been addressed from two radically different perspectives and intellectual traditions: the associationist perspective rooted in Thorndike's Law of Effect and Pavovian conditioning, and the behavioral regulation perspective rooted in Skinnerian behavioral analysis. These two approaches differ in more ways than they are similar, making it difficult to imagine how they might be integrated. For example, the fundamental concept in the associationist approach (the concept of an association) is entirely ignored in behavioral regulation. Correspondingly, the critical concepts of behavioral regulation (bliss points and schedule constraints) have no correspondence in the associationist approach. The associationist approach readily lends itself to explorations of the neural circuitry of instrumental conditioning. On the other hand, it is difficult to see how the behavioral regulation approach could be used to guide neurophysiological research.

The two approaches appear to be focused on entirely different things, but both have contributed significantly to our understanding of the motivation of instrumental behavior. It is obvious that one approach cannot be ignored in favor of the other, but how does each approach contribute to our complete understanding of instrumental motivation?

One way to think about the two approaches is that they involve different levels of analysis. The associationist approach involves the molecular level where the focus is on specific stimuli, responses, and their connections. In contrast, as I have described, behavioral regulation operates at a molar level of aggregates of behavior and the broader behavioral context in which instrumental contingencies operate. Thus, the behavioral regulation approach makes better contact with the complexities of an organism's ecology.

Another way to think about the relation between the two approaches is that one is concerned with processes and the other is more concerned with functions or long-range goals. The associationist approach describes specific processes [S-R, S-O, R-O, and S-(R-O) associations] that serve to generate and direct instrumental behavior, but it ignores the long-range "purpose" or function of instrumental learning. That is the purview of behavioral regulation and behavioral economics, which assumes that organisms work to defend an optimal distribution of activities. The defense of the behavioral bliss point is achieved through the molecular mechanisms of associations. (For a formal discussion of the relations between processes, ecology, and function, see Killeen, 1995.)

The conceptual developments in the study of the motivation of instrumental behavior provide an exciting illustration of the course of scientific inquiry. This inquiry has spanned intellectual developments from simple stimulus-response formulations to comprehensive considerations of how the organism's repertoire is constrained by instrumental contingencies and how organisms solve complex ecological problems. In this aspect of the study of conditioning and learning, perhaps more than in any other, investigators have moved boldly to explore radically new conceptions when older ideas did not meet the challenges posed by new empirical findings.

SAMPLE QUESTIONS

1. What is an S-O association, and what research tactic provides the best evidence for it?
2. What investigative techniques are used to provide evidence of R-O associations? Why is it not possible to explain instrumental behavior by assuming only R-O association learning?
3. Describe similarities and differences between the Premack principle and subsequent behavioral regulation theory.
4. What are the primary contributions of economic concepts to the understanding of the motivational bases of instrumental behavior?
5. What are the shortcomings of behavioral regulation theory?
6. Describe implications of modern concepts of reinforcement for behavior therapy.

KEY TERMS

behavioral bliss point The preferred distribution of an organism's activities before an instrumental conditioning procedure is introduced that sets constraints and limitations on response allocation.

consummatory response theory A theory that assumes that species-typical consummatory responses (eating, drinking, and the like) are the critical features of reinforcers.

demand curve The relation between how much of a commodity is purchased and the price of the commodity.

differential probability principle A principle that assumes that reinforcement depends on how much more likely the organism is to perform the reinforcer response than the instrumental response before an instrumental conditioning procedure is introduced. The greater the differential probability of the reinforcer and instrumental responses during baseline conditions, the greater will be the reinforcement effect of providing opportunity to engage in the reinforcer response after performance of the instrumental response. Also known as the *Premack principle*.

elasticity of demand The degree to which price influences the consumption or purchase of a commodity. If price has a large effect on consumption, elasticity of demand is high. If price has a small effect on consumption, elasticity of demand is low.

minimum deviation model A model of instrumental behavior, according to which participants respond to a response-reinforcer contingency in a manner that gets them as close as possible to their behavioral bliss point.

Premack principle Same as *differential probability principle*.

response deprivation hypothesis An explanation of reinforcement according to which restricting access to a response below its baseline rate of occurrence (response deprivation) is sufficient to make the opportunity to perform that response an effective positive reinforcer.

transfer-of-control experiment An experiment that assesses the effects of a classically conditioned stimulus (CS) on the performance of instrumental behavior. The CS and the instrumental response are first conditioned in independent phases of the experiment. The effects of the CS on instrumental reponding are then determined in the transfer phase.

STIMULUS CONTROL OF BEHAVIOR

hapter 8 is organized around the principles of stimulus control. Although most of the chapter deals with the ways in which instrumental behavior comes under the control of particular stimuli that are present when the response is reinforced, the concepts are equally applicable to classical conditioning. The chapter begins with a definition of stimulus control and the basic concepts of stimulus discrimination and generalization. I then discuss factors that determine the extent to which behavior comes to be restricted to particular stimulus values. Along the way, I describe special forms of stimulus control (intradimensional discrimination) and control by special categories of stimuli (compound stimuli and contextual cues). The chapter concludes with a discussion of the learning of conditional relations in both instrumental and classical conditioning.

As I pointed out in earlier chapters, both Thorndike and Skinner recognized that instrumental responses and reinforcers occur not in a vacuum, but in the presence of particular stimuli. As I described in Chapter 7, research on the associative structure of instrumental conditioning emphasized that these stimuli can come to determine whether the instrumental response is performed. The importance of antecedent stimuli has been examined further in studies of the stimulus control of instrumental behavior, which is the topic of this chapter.

The stimulus control of instrumental behavior is evident in many aspects of life. Studying, for example, is under the strong control of school-related stimuli. College students who have fallen behind in their work may resolve to study a lot when they return home for the holidays, but they rarely carry out such good intentions. Holiday stimuli are very different from the stimuli students experience when classes are in session and consequently do not engender effective studying behavior.

The proper fit between an instrumental response and the stimulus context in which the response is performed is so important that the failure of appropriate stimulus control is often considered abnormal. Getting undressed, for example, is acceptable instrumental behavior in the privacy of your bedroom, but doing so on a public street will get you arrested. Staring at a television set is considered appropriate if the TV is turned on, whereas staring at a blank television screen may be a symptom of behavior pathology. If you respond in a loving manner in the presence of your spouse or other family members, your behavior is welcomed. Directing the same behavior toward strangers is likely to be greeted with far less acceptance.

The stimulus control of behavior is an important aspect of how organisms adjust to their environment. The survival of both human and nonhuman animals depends on their ability to perform responses that are appropriate to the situation. With seasonal changes in food supply, for example, animals have to change how they forage for food. Within the same season, they have to respond one way in the presence of predators or intruders and in other ways in the absence of nearby danger. In cold weather, animals may seek comfort by going to uncovered areas warmed by the sun; on rainy days, they may seek covered areas sheltered from the rain. To effectively obtain comfort and avoid pain, animals have to behave in ways that are appropriate to their changing circumstances.

IDENTIFICATION AND MEASUREMENT OF STIMULUS CONTROL

To investigate the stimulus control of behavior, a researcher first has to figure out how to identify and measure it. How can he or she tell that an instrumental response has come under the control of certain stimuli?

Differential Responding and Stimulus Discrimination

Consider, for example, an experiment by Reynolds (1961). Two pigeons were reinforced on a variable interval schedule for pecking a circular response key. Reinforcement for pecking was available whenever the response key was illuminated by a visual pattern consisting of a white triangle on a red background (see Figure 8.1). Thus the stimulus on the key had two components—the white triangle and the red color of the background. Reynolds was interested in which of these stimulus components gained control over the pecking behavior.

After the pigeons learned to peck steadily at the triangle on the red background, Reynolds measured the amount of pecking that occurred when only one of the stimuli was presented. On some of the test trials, the white triangle was projected on the response key without the red color; on others, the red background color was projected on the response key without the white triangle.

The results are summarized in Figure 8.1. One of the pigeons pecked a great deal more when the response key was illuminated with the red light than when it was illuminated with the white triangle. This outcome shows that the bird's pecking behavior was much more strongly controlled by the red color than by the white triangle. By contrast, the other pigeon pecked a great deal more when the white triangle was projected on the response key than when the key was illuminated by the red light. Thus, for the second bird, the pecking behavior was more strongly controlled by the triangle. (For a more recent similar study, see Cheng & Spetch, 1995.)

This experiment illustrates several important ideas. First, it shows researchers how to determine whether instrumental behavior has come under the control of a particular stimulus. *The stimulus control of instrumental behavior is demonstrated by variations in responding (differential responding) related to variations in stimuli.* If an organism responds one way in the presence of one stimulus, and a different way in the presence of another stimulus, its behavior has come under the control of those stimuli. Such differential responding was evident in the behavior of both pigeons Reynolds tested.

Differential responding to two stimuli also indicates that the pigeons were treating each stimulus as different from the other. This is called **stimulus discrimination.** *An organism is said to exhibit stimulus discrimination if it responds differently to two or more stimuli.* Stimulus discrimination and stimulus control are two ways to consider the same phenomenon: one does not exist without the other. If an organism does not discriminate between two stimuli, its behavior is not under the control of those cues.

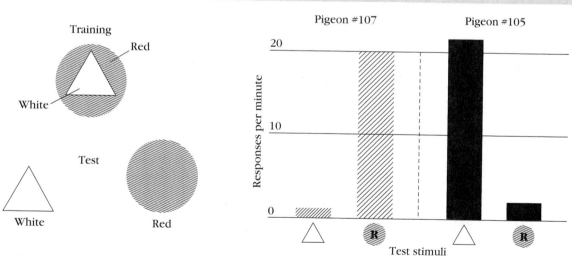

Figure 8.1 Summary of procedure and results of an experiment by Reynolds (1961). Two pigeons were first reinforced for pecking whenever a compound stimulus consisting of a white triangle on a red background was projected on the response key. The rate of pecking was then observed with each pigeon when the white triangle and the red background stimuli were presented separately.

Another interesting aspect of the results of Reynolds's experiment was that the pecking behavior of each bird came under the control of a different stimulus. The behavior of bird 107 came under the control of the red color, whereas the behavior of bird 105 came under the control of the triangle. The procedure used by Reynolds did not direct attention to one of the stimuli at the expense of the other. Therefore, it is not surprising that each bird came to respond to a different aspect of the situation. The experiment was comparable to showing a group of children a picture of a cowboy grooming a horse. Some of the children may focus on the cowboy; others may find the horse more interesting. In the absence of special procedures (that I describe later in the chapter), investigators cannot always predict which of the various stimuli an organism experiences will gain control over its instrumental behavior.

Stimulus Generalization

Identifying and differentiating various stimuli is not a simple matter (Fetterman, 1996). Stimuli may be defined in all kinds of ways. Sometimes widely different objects or events are considered instances of the same stimulus because they all share the same function. A wheel, for example, may be small or large, spoked or not spoked, and made of wood, rubber, or metal, but it is still a wheel. By contrast, stimuli in other cases are identified and distinguished in terms of precise physical features, such as the wavelength of light or the frequency of radio waves. For example, to listen to a particular FM radio station, you have to tune your radio within a very small range of the FM band. Small variations in tuning will significantly change the quality of the reception.

Psychologists and physiologists have long been concerned with how organisms identify and distinguish different stimuli. Some have suggested that this is the single most important question in psychology (Stevens, 1951). The problem is central to the analysis of stimulus control. As this chapter shows, numerous factors are involved in the identification and differentiation of stimuli. Experimental analyses of the problem have depended mainly on the phenomenon of **stimulus generalization,** which in a sense is the opposite of differential responding, or stimulus discrimination. *An organism is said to show stimulus generalization if it responds in a similar fashion to two or more stimuli*—if the same level of behavior is observed in the presence of different stimuli.

The phenomenon of stimulus generalization was first observed by Pavlov. He found that after one stimulus was used as a CS, his dogs would also make the conditioned response to other, similar stimuli. That is, they failed to respond differentially to stimuli that were similar to the original conditioned stimulus.

Stimulus generalization has also been investigated in instrumental conditioning. In a landmark experiment, Guttman and Kalish (1956) first reinforced pigeons on a variable interval schedule for pecking a response key illuminated by a yellowish-orange light with a wavelength of 580 nanometers (nm). After training, the birds were tested with a variety of other colors presented in a random order without reinforcement, and the rate of responding in the presence of each color was recorded.

The results of the experiment are summarized in Figure 8.2. The highest rate of pecking occurred in response to the original 580-nm color. But the birds also made substantial numbers of pecks when lights of 570-nm and 590-nm wavelength were tested, which indicates that responding generalized to the 570-nm and 590-nm stimuli. However, as the color of the test stimuli became increasingly different from the color of the original training stimulus, progressively fewer responses occurred. The results showed a gradient of responding as a function of how similar each test stimulus was to the original training stimulus. This is an example of a **stimulus generalization gradient.**

Stimulus Generalization Gradients as Measures of Stimulus Control

Stimulus generalization gradients are often used to measure stimulus control because they provide information about how sensitive the organism's behavior is to variations in a particular aspect of the environment (for a review of this technology, see Honig & Urcuioli, 1981). With the use of stimulus generalization gradients, investigators can determine exactly how much a stimulus has to be altered to produce a change in behavior.

Consider, for example, the gradient in Figure 8.2. The pigeons responded much more when the original 580-nm training stimulus was presented than when the response key was illuminated by lights whose wavelengths were 520, 540, 620, and 640 nm. Differences in color controlled different levels of responding, but this control was not very precise. Responding to the 580-nm color generalized to the 570-nm and 590-nm stimuli. The wavelength of the 580-nm training stimulus had to be changed by more than 10 nm before a decrement in performance was observed. This aspect of the stimulus generalization gradient provides precise information about how much the stimulus has to be changed for the pigeons to respond to the change.

How do you suppose color-blind pigeons would have responded? They could not have distinguished lights on the basis of color or wavelength and therefore would have responded in much the same way regardless of what color was projected on the response key. Figure 8.3 presents hypothetical results of an experiment of this sort. If the pigeons did not respond on the basis of the color of the key light, similar high rates of responding would have occurred as different colors were projected on the key. Thus, the stimulus generalization gradient would have been flat.

A comparison of the results obtained by Guttman and Kalish (1956) and the hypothetical experiment with color-blind pigeons indicates that *the steepness of a stimulus generalization gradient provides a precise measure of the degree of stimulus control.* A flat generalization gradient (Figure 8.3) is obtained if the organism responds in a similar fashion to all the test stimuli. Such lack of differential responding shows that the stimulus feature that is varied in the generalization test does not control the instrumental behavior. By contrast, a steep generalization gradient (Figure 8.2) is obtained if the organism responds more to some of the test stimuli than to others. Such differential responding is evidence that the instrumental behavior is under the control of the stimulus feature that is varied among the test stimuli.

Figure 8.2 Stimulus generalization gradient for pigeons that were trained to peck in the presence of a colored light of 580-nm wavelength and were then tested in the presence of other colors. (From "Discriminability and Stimulus Generalization," by N. Guttman and H. I. Kalish, 1956, *Journal of Experimental Psychology, 51,* pp. 79–88.)

Figure 8.3 Hypothetical stimulus generalization gradient for color-blind pigeons trained to peck in the presence of a colored light of 580-nm wavelength and then tested in the presence of other colors.

Generalization and differential responding are opposites. If a great deal of generalization occurs, there is little differential responding. If responding is highly differential to stimuli, little generalization is obtained.

STIMULUS AND RESPONSE FACTORS IN STIMULUS CONTROL

In the experiment by Reynolds (1961) described at the outset of this chapter, pigeons pecked a response key that had a white triangle on a red background. Such a stimulus obviously has two features: the color of the background and the shape of the triangle. Perhaps less obvious is the fact that all stimulus situations can be analyzed in terms of multiple features. Even if the response key had only the red background, it could be characterized in terms of its brightness, shape, or location in the experimental chamber, in addition to its color. (For a more complete discussion of approaches to stimulus analysis, see Fetterman, 1996.)

Situations outside the laboratory are even more complex. During a football game, for example, cheering is reinforced by social approval if you and the people near you are all rooting for the same team, and if that team is doing well. The cues that accompany appropriate cheering include your team making a good play on the field, the announcer describing the play, cheerleaders dancing exuberantly, and the people around you cheering.

The central issue in the analysis of the stimulus control is, What determines which of the many features of a stimulus situation gains control over the instrumental behavior? Stimuli as complex as those found at a football game are difficult to analyze experimentally. Laboratory studies are typically conducted with stimuli that consist of more easily identified features. In the present section, I describe stimulus and response factors that determine which cues come to control behavior. I discuss learning factors in the section beginning on page 230.

BOX **8.1**

GENERALIZATION OF TREATMENT OUTCOMES

Stimulus generalization is critical to the success of behavior therapy. Behavior therapy, like other forms of therapy, is typically conducted under specific circumstances (in a therapist's office, for example). For the treatment to be maximally useful, what is learned during treatment should generalize outside the training situation. An autistic child, for example, who is taught certain communicative responses in interactions with a particular therapist should also exhibit those responses in interactions with other people. The following, sometimes contradictory, techniques have been proposed to facilitate generalization of treatment outcomes (for example, Schreibman, Koegel, Charlop, & Egel, 1990; Stokes & Baer, 1977):

1. The treatment situation should be made as similar as possible to the natural environment of the client. For example, if the natural environment provides reinforcement only intermittently, it is a good idea to reduce the frequency of reinforcement during treatment sessions as well. It is also best to use the same reinforcers the client is likely to encounter in the natural environment.
2. Conduct the treatment procedure in new settings. This strategy is called *sequential modification*. After a behav-

ior has been conditioned in one situation (a classroom), training is conducted in a new situation (the playground). If that does not result in sufficient generalization, training can be extended to a third environment (the school cafeteria, for example).
3. Use numerous exemplars during training. In trying to extinguish fear of elevators, for example, conduct training with various types of elevators.
4. Condition the new responses to stimuli that are common to various situations. Language provides effective mediating stimuli. Responses conditioned to verbal or instructional cues are likely to generalize to new situations in which those instructional stimuli are encountered.
5. Make the training procedure indiscriminable or incidental to other activities. In one study (McGee, Krantz, & McClannahan, 1986), for example, the investigators took advantage of the interest that autistic children showed in specific toys during a play session to teach the children how to read the names of the toys.
6. Generalization outside a training situation is achieved if the training helps bring the individual into contact with contingencies of reinforcement available in the natural environment (Baer & Wolf, 1970). Once a response is acquired through special training, the behavior often can be maintained by naturally available reinforcers. Reading, calculating simple arithmetic problems, and riding a bicycle are all responses that are maintained by natural reinforcers once the responses have been acquired through special training.

Sensory Capacity and Orientation

The most obvious factor that determines whether a particular stimulus feature comes to control responding is the organism's sensory capacity and orientation. The range of stimuli that potentially can control behavior is determined by the organism's sensory world—the world of sensations experienced by a particular individual. Sensory capacity and orientation determine which stimuli are included in an organism's sensory world. Presentation of stimuli with certain features of interest to one organism does not guarantee that another organism will respond to the same features. The individual's own (and possibly unique) point of view or sensory world must always be considered.

Figure 8.4 An infant looking up at a mobile.

Photo courtesy of the author

Events outside the range of what an organism can detect with its sense organs simply do not exist for that individual unless the stimuli are amplified or transduced into something the individual can detect. People, for example, cannot hear sounds above about 20,000 cps. Such stimuli are called "ultrasounds" because they are outside the range of human hearing. Because ultrasounds are inaudible to people, such sounds cannot come to control human behavior. Other species, however, are able to hear ultrasounds. Dogs, for example, can hear whistles outside the range of human hearing and therefore can be trained to respond to such sounds.

Limitations on the stimuli that can come to control behavior are also set by whether the individual comes into contact with the stimulus. Consider, for example, a child's crib. Parents often place mobiles and other decorations on and around the crib to provide interesting stimuli for the child to look at; for example, the mobile shown in Figure 8.4 consists of several animal figures (a giraffe, a seal, and a lion) made of thin needlework.

Which aspects of the mobile in the crib in Figure 8.4 can potentially control the child's behavior? To answer this question, first consider what the child sees about the mobile rather than what the mobile looks like to adults. From the child's vantage point under the mobile, only the bottom edges of the animal figures are visible. The shapes of the animals and their surface decorations cannot be seen from below and thus are not likely to gain control of the child's looking behavior. (For findings illustrating the importance of orientation for the acquisition of stimulus control in laboratory animals, see, for example, Gillette, Martin, & Bellingham, 1980.)

Relative Ease of Conditioning Various Stimuli

Having the necessary sense organs and the appropriate sensory orientation does not guarantee that the organism's behavior will come under the control of a particular stimulus. Whether a stimulus comes to control behavior also depends on the presence of other cues in the situation. In particular, how strongly organisms learn about one stimulus depends on how easily other cues in the situations can become conditioned. This phenomenon is called **overshadowing,** which illustrates competition among stimuli for access to the processes of learning.

Consider, for example, trying to teach a child to read by having her follow along as you read a children's book that has a big picture and a short sentence on each page. Learning about pictures is easier than learning words; therefore, the pictures may well overshadow the words. The child will quickly memorize the story based on the pictures rather than the words and will soon appear to be "reading" without error.

Pavlov (1927) was the first to observe that if two stimuli are presented at the same time, the presence of the more easily trained stimulus may hinder learning about the other one. In many of his experiments, the two stimuli differed in intensity. In general, the more intense stimulus became conditioned more rapidly and overshadowed learning about the weaker stimulus. Pavlov found that the weak stimulus could become conditioned (somewhat slowly) if it was presented by itself. Less conditioning occurred if the weak stimulus was presented simultaneously with a more intense stimulus. (For more recent studies of overshadowing, see March, Chamizo, & Mackintosh, 1992; Schachtman, Kasprow, Meyer, Bourne, & Hart, 1992; Spetch, 1995)

Type of Reinforcement

The development of stimulus control also depends on the type of reinforcement that is used. Certain types of stimuli are more likely to gain control over the instrumental behavior with positive reinforcement than with negative reinforcement. This relation has been extensively investigated in experiments with pigeons (see LoLordo, 1979).

V. M. LoLordo

In one study (Foree & LoLordo, 1973), two groups of pigeons were trained to press a foot treadle in the presence of a compound stimulus consisting of a red light and a tone whose pitch was 440 cps. When the light/tone compound was absent, responses were not reinforced. For one group of pigeons, reinforcement for treadle pressing was provided by food. For the other group, treadle pressing was reinforced by the avoidance of shock. If the avoidance group pressed the treadle in the presence of the light/tone stimulus, no shock was delivered on that trial; if they failed to respond during the light/tone stimulus, a brief shock was periodically applied until a response occurred.

Both groups of pigeons learned to respond during the light/tone compound. Foree and LoLordo then sought to determine which of the two elements of the compound stimulus was primarily responsible for the treadle-press behavior. Test trials were conducted during which the light and tone stimuli were presented one at a time. The results are summarized in Figure 8.5.

Pigeons that were trained with food reinforcement responded much more when tested with the light stimulus alone than when tested with the tone alone. In fact, their rate of treadle pressing in response to the isolated presentation of the red light was nearly as high as when the light was presented simultaneously with the tone. Therefore, the investigators concluded that the behavior of these birds was nearly exclusively controlled by the red light.

A contrasting pattern of results occurred with the pigeons trained with shock-avoidance reinforcement. These birds responded much more when tested with the tone alone than when tested with the light alone. Thus, with shock-avoidance reinforcement the tone acquired more control over the treadle response than did the red light.

Similar results have been obtained in a variety of other experiments conducted with both pigeons and rats (for example, Kelly, 1986; Kraemer & Roberts, 1985; Schindler & Weiss, 1982; Shapiro et al., 1980; Shapiro & LoLordo, 1982; Weiss & Panlilio, 1999).

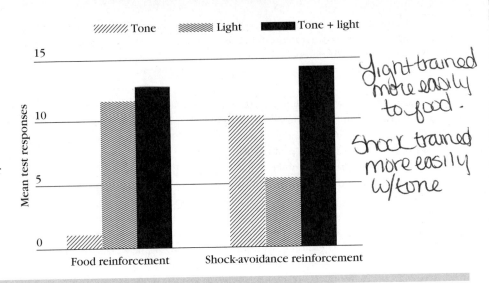

Figure 8.5 Effects of type of reinforcement on stimulus control. A treadle-press response in pigeons was reinforced in the presence of a compound stimulus consisting of a tone and a red light. With food reinforcement, the light gained much more control over the behavior than the tone. With shock-avoidance reinforcement, the tone gained more control over behavior than the light. (Adapted from Foree & LoLordo, 1973.)

light trained more easily to food.

Shock trained more easily w/ tone

 # belongingness

These findings indicate that stimulus control of instrumental behavior is determined in part by the type of reinforcement used. Although the mechanisms responsible for this effect are still being worked out (Weiss, Panlilio, & Schindler, 1993a, 1993b), the results are clear. Visual stimuli are more likely to gain control over behavior in appetitive situations than are auditory cues, whereas auditory cues are more likely to gain control in aversive situations.

The dominance of visual control in appetitive situations and auditory control in aversive situations is probably related to the behavior systems that are activated in the two cases. Food-reinforcement procedures activate the feeding system. Food eaten by pigeons and rats is more likely to be identified by visual cues than by auditory cues. Therefore, activation of the feeding system may involve increased sensitivity to visual stimuli. In contrast, shock-avoidance procedures activate the defensive behavior system. Responding to auditory cues may be particularly adaptive in avoiding danger.

Unfortunately, we do not know enough about the evolutionary history of pigeons or rats to be able to calculate the adaptive value of different types of stimulus control in feeding versus defensive behavior. We also do not know much about how stimulus control varies as a function of the type of reinforcement in other species. This issue remains a fertile area for future research.

Type of Instrumental Response

Another factor that can determine which of several features of a compound stimulus gains control over behavior is the nature of the response required for reinforcement. The importance of the instrumental response for stimulus control is illustrated by an experiment by Dobrzecka, Szwejkowska, and Konorski (1966). These investigators studied the control of instrumental behavior by auditory stimuli in dogs. The dogs were gently restrained in a harness, with a metronome placed in front of them and a buzzer placed behind them. The metronome and buzzer provided qualitatively different types of sounds, a periodic beat versus a continuous rattle. The two stimuli also differed in spatial location, one in front of the animal and the other behind it. The investigators were interested in which of these two stimulus characteristics (sound quality or location) would come to control behavior.

Two groups of dogs served in the experiment (see Figure 8.6). Each group differed in what responses were required for reinforcement in the presence of the buzzer and the met-

Group 1
(right/left discrimination)

Group 2
(go/no-go discrimination)

Training

Testing

Figure 8.6 Diagram of the experiment by Dobrzecka, Szwejkowska, and Konorski (1966). Dogs were trained on a left/right or go/no-go task (Groups 1 and 2, respectively) with auditory stimuli that differed both in location (in front or in back of the animals) and in quality (the sound of a buzzer or a metronome). During testing, the location of the two sounds was reversed. The results showed that the left/right differential response was controlled mainly by the location of the sounds, whereas the go/no-go differential response was controlled mainly by the quality of the sounds.

ronome stimuli. Group 1 received training in a right/left task. When the metronome was sounded, dogs in this group were reinforced for raising the right leg; when the buzzer was sounded, they were reinforced for raising the left leg. Thus, the location of the response (right/left) was important for reinforcement in this group.

Group 2 received training on a go/no-go task. In this case, the dogs had to raise the right leg when the buzzer sounded and not raise the leg when the metronome sounded. Thus, the quality of the response (go/no-go) rather than its location was important for reinforcement for this group.

What aspect of the auditory cues—quality or location—gained control over the instrumental behavior in the two groups? To answer this question, investigators reversed the positions of the metronome and the buzzer—the buzzer was placed in front of the dogs and the metronome behind them (see Figure 8.6). This manipulation produced different test results in the two groups.

Dogs trained on the right/left task responded mainly on the basis of the location of the auditory cues rather than their quality. The participants in Group 1 raised the right leg in response to sound from the front, regardless of whether the sound was made by the metronome or the buzzer. When the sound came from the back, they raised the left leg, again regardless of whether it was the metronome or the buzzer. Thus, their behavior was more strongly controlled by the location of the sounds than their quality.

The opposite outcome was observed in the animals trained on the go/no-go task. These dogs responded more on the basis of the quality of the sounds rather than their location. They raised a leg in response to the buzzer whether the sound came from the front or the back, and they did not raise a leg when the metronome was sounded, again irrespective of the location of the metronome.

These results indicate that responses differentiated by location (right/left) are more likely to come under the control of the spatial feature of auditory cues. By contrast, responses differentiated by quality (go/no-go) are more likely to come under the control of the quality of auditory cues (see also Bowe, Miller, & Green, 1987; Williams, Butler, & Overmier, 1990). The phenomenon is called the *quality–location effect.*

The quality–location effect is a form of selective association. The appetitive–aversive reinforcement effect on stimulus control described earlier in this chapter is another example of a selective association. In that case, there was greater learning about visual features with appetitive reinforcement and about auditory features with negative reinforcement. Another example of a selective association was described in Chapter 4, where I pointed out that taste cues are more readily associated with illness than are audiovisual cues, whereas audiovisual cues are more readily associated with footshock than are taste cues. It is important to keep in mind that these selective associations are typically not all or none. As is the case with other examples of selective associations, the quality–location effect reflects the relative ease of establishing control by different features of an auditory stimulus rather than all-or-none effects. That is, the quality–location effect does not mean that subjects can never learn about the quality of sounds when spatially differentiated responses are involved or that they can never learn about the location of sounds in a go/no-go task. With judicious placement of the sound sources (one much closer to the response than the other), subjects can come to respond to location features of sounds in a go/no-go task (Neill & Harrison, 1987).

Stimulus Elements versus Configural Cues in Compound Stimuli

In the discussion so far of control of behavior by various stimulus elements, I have assumed that organisms treat these stimulus elements as distinct and separate features of the environment. This is called the **stimulus-element approach.** Thus, in the quality–location effect, the quality and location of an auditory stimulus were considered to be separate features of the auditory cues. The assumption was that a particular stimulus feature (sound quality) was perceived the same way regardless of the status of the other feature (sound location). An important alternative theoretical approach assumes that organisms treat a complex stimulus as an integral whole that is not divided into parts or elements. This is called the **configural-cue approach.**

According to the configural-cue approach, individuals respond to a compound stimulus in terms of the unique configuration of its elements. It is assumed that the elements are not treated as separate entities. In fact, they may not even be identifiable when the stimulus compound is presented. In the configural-cue approach, stimulus elements are important not because of their individuality but because of the way they contribute to the entire configuration of stimulation provided by the compound.

The concept of a configural cue may be illustrated by considering the sound made by a symphony orchestra. The orchestral sound originates from the sounds of the individual instruments. The sound of the entire orchestra, however, is very different from the sound of any of the individual instruments, some of which are difficult to identify when the entire orchestra is playing. We primarily hear the configuration of the sounds made by the individual instruments.

TABLE 8.1	**CONFIGURAL EXPLANATION OF OVERSHADOWING**		
GROUP	**TRAINING STIMULI**	**TEST STIMULUS**	**GENERALIZATION FROM TRAINING TO TEST**
Overshadowing group	aB	a	Decrement
Control group	a	a	No decrement

The configural-cue approach has been encouraged by the theoretical work of John Pearce (1987, 1994), who showed that many learning phenomena are consistent with this framework. Consider, for example, the overshadowing effect (see Table 8.1). An overshadowing experiment involves two groups of subjects and two stimulus elements, one of low intensity (*a*) and the other of high intensity (*B*). For the overshadowing group, the two stimuli are presented together (*aB*) as a compound cue and paired with reinforcement during conditioning. For the control group, only the low-intensity stimulus (*a*) is presented during conditioning. Tests are then conducted for each group with the weaker stimulus element (*a*) presented alone. These tests show less responding to *a* in the overshadowing group than in the control group. Thus, the presence of *B* during conditioning disrupts control of behavior by the weaker stimulus *a*.

According to the configural-cue approach, overshadowing reflects different degrees of generalization decrement from training to testing for the overshadowing and the control groups (Pearce, 1987). There is no generalization decrement for the control group when it is tested with the weak stimulus *a* because that is the same as the stimulus it received during conditioning. In contrast, considerable generalization decrement occurs when the overshadowing group is tested with stimulus *a* after conditioning with the compound *aB*. For the overshadowing group, responding becomes conditioned to the *aB* compound, which is very different from *a* presented alone during testing. Therefore, responding conditioned to *aB* suffers considerable generalization decrement. According to the configural-cue approach, this greater generalization decrement is responsible for the overshadowing effect.

The configural-cue approach has enjoyed considerable success (see Pearce & Bouton, 2001, for a review). Under certain conditions, organisms clearly respond to compound stimuli primarily in terms of the configuration of the elements that make up the compound (for recent examples, see Nakajima, 1997, 1998; Nakajima & Urushihara, 1999; Pearce, Aydin, & Redhead, 1997). However, some experimental results favor analyses of stimulus control in terms of stimulus elements (for example, Myers, Vogel, Shin, & Wagner, 2001; Rescorla, 1997e, 1999a). In addition, the configural-cue approach is incompatible with the various examples of selective associations that I described earlier. For example, the configural-cue approach does not explain why stimulus control is a function of the type of reinforcement used or the type of response that is required. The most prudent conclusion at this point is that organisms respond to stimulus compounds both in terms of the stimulus elements that make up the compound and in terms of unique stimulus configurations created by the stimulus elements. Under certain circumstances elemental control predominates, whereas under other conditions control by configural features of stimulus compounds predominates. What is required is a comprehensive theory that deals successfully with both types of phenomena.

The structure of such a unified theory was recently described by Wagner and Brandon (2001). According to the Wagner–Brandon theory, stimuli such as the sound of a tone

Courtesy of Donald A. Dewsbury

J. M. Pearce

consist of distinctive features (pitch, loudness, and location). When one stimulus is combined with another (a tone combined with a clicker, for example), new configural stimulus elements that are unique to this new stimulus combination are created. In addition, some of the individual features of the original stimuli are lost in the combination. This biases stimulus control in favor of the configural elements and produces results consistent with the configural-cue approach.

LEARNING FACTORS IN STIMULUS CONTROL

The stimulus and response factors described in the preceding section set the preconditions for how human and nonhuman animals learn about the environmental stimuli they encounter. Stimulus and response factors are the starting points for stimulus control. The fact that certain stimuli can be perceived does not ensure that those stimuli will come to control behavior. A child, for example, may see Ford and Chevy pickups but may not be able to distinguish between them. A novice chess player may be able to look at two different patterns on a chess board without being able to identify which represents the more favorable configuration. Whether certain stimuli come to control behavior often depends on what the organism has learned about those stimuli—not just whether the stimuli can be detected.

The suggestion that experience with stimuli may determine the extent to which those stimuli come to control behavior originated in efforts to explain the phenomenon of stimulus generalization. As I noted earlier, stimulus generalization refers to the fact that a response conditioned to one stimulus will also occur when other stimuli similar to the original cue are presented. Pavlov suggested that stimulus generalization occurs because learning about a CS becomes transferred to other stimuli on the basis of the physical similarity of those test stimuli to the original CS.

In a spirited attack, Lashley and Wade (1946) took exception to Pavlov's proposal. They rejected the idea that stimulus generalization reflects the transfer of learning and argued that it reflects the *absence* of learning. In particular, they proposed that stimulus generalization occurs if organisms have not learned to distinguish differences among the stimuli. Lashley and Wade proposed that animals have to learn to treat stimuli as different from one another. Thus, in contrast to Pavlov, Lashley and Wade considered the shape of a stimulus generalization gradient to be determined primarily by the organism's previous learning experiences rather than by the physical properties of the stimuli tested.

Stimulus Discrimination Training

Lashley and Wade were closer to the truth than Pavlov. Numerous studies have shown that stimulus control can be dramatically altered by learning experiences. Perhaps the most powerful procedure for bringing behavior under the control of a stimulus is stimulus discrimination training. In a **stimulus discrimination procedure,** the participants are exposed to at least two different stimuli—a red and a green light, for example—but reinforcement for performing the instrumental response is available only in the presence of one of the colors. The participants could be reinforced for responding when the red light is on but not when the green light is on. In this procedure, diagrammed in Figure 8.7, the red light signals the availability of reinforcement for responding. The green light signals that responding will not be reinforced. The stimulus that signals the availability of reinforcement is called the S+ or

S^D (pronounced "ess dee"). By contrast, the stimulus that signals the lack of reinforcement is called the S− or S^Δ (pronounced "ess delta").

With sufficient exposure to a discrimination procedure, participants will come to respond during S+ and withhold responding during S−. The acquisition of this pattern of responding is illustrated in the cumulative record in Figure 8.7. Initially, organisms respond similarly in the presence of the S+ and the S−. As training progresses, responding in the presence of the S+ persists, and responding in the presence of the S− declines. The emergence of greater responding to the S+ than to the S− indicates differential responding to these stimuli. Thus, *stimulus discrimination procedures establish control by the stimuli that signal when reinforcement is and is not available.* Once the S+ and S− have gained control over the organism's behavior, they are called **discriminative stimuli.** The S+ is a discriminative stimulus for performing the instrumental response, and the S− is a discriminative stimulus for not performing the response.

The procedure diagrammed in Figure 8.7 is the standard procedure for stimulus discrimination training in instrumental conditioning. Stimulus discriminations can also be established with the use of classical conditioning procedures: one stimulus (the CS+) is paired with the unconditioned stimulus and another (the CS−) is presented in the absence of the US. With repeated pairings of the CS+ with the US, and presentations of the CS− by itself, conditioned responding comes to be elicited by the CS+ but not by the CS−. (In fact, the CS− might become a conditioned inhibitor.)

Instrumental stimulus discrimination procedures are different from classical conditioning procedures only in that the reinforcer is presented contingent on responding during the S+. Responding is not required for pairings of the CS+ with the US in classical conditioning. Unlike a CS+, an S+ does not signal that the reinforcer will inevitably occur. Rather, the S+ indicates that the instrumental response will be reinforced.

The stimulus discrimination procedure shown in Figure 8.7 is a special case of a **multiple schedule of reinforcement.** In a multiple schedule, different schedules of reinforcement

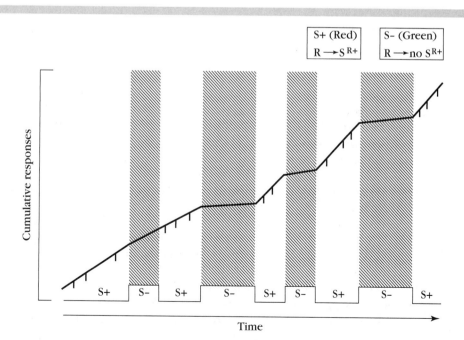

Figure 8.7 Procedure and hypothetical results (presented as a cumulative record) of stimulus discrimination training. Responding is reinforced on a variable interval schedule in the presence of the S+ (a red light) and is not reinforced in the presence of the S− (a green light). Differential responding gradually develops to the two stimuli. (Hatch marks on the cumulative record indicate reinforcements.)

BOX 8.2

STIMULUS CONTROL
OF SLEEPING IN CHILDREN

Getting young children to go to sleep in the evening and remain asleep during the night can be difficult. Night wakings by young children can be stressful for parents and have been linked to increased maternal malaise, marital discord, and child abuse. Behavioral approaches to the treatment of night waking have stressed the concepts of stimulus control and extinction.

In the absence of special intervention, a child may wake up at night and cry or call a parent. The parent visits with the child and tries to put him back to sleep either in the child's own bed or in the parent's bed, where the child eventually falls asleep. This scenario may serve to maintain the sleep disturbance in two ways. First, parental attention upon waking may serve to reinforce the child for waking up. Second, special efforts the parent makes to encourage the child to go back to sleep (taking the child into the parent's bed, for example) may introduce special discriminative stimuli for getting back to sleep. In the absence of those cues, getting back to sleep may be especially difficult.

In a study of behavioral treatment of night waking in infants from 8 to 20 months old, France and Hudson (1990) gave parents the following instructions:

> At bedtime, carry out the usual bed-time routine (story, song, etc.). Then place (*child's name*) in bed. Bid him or her "Good night" and immediately leave the room. Do not return unless absolutely necessary. If absolutely necessary, check your child (when illness or danger is suspected), but do so in silence and with a minimum of light." (p. 93)

This procedure was intended to minimize reinforcement of the child for waking up. The procedure was also intended to make the child's own bed in the absence of parental interaction a discriminative stimulus for getting back to sleep should the child wake up at night. With the introduction of these procedures, all seven infants in the study were reported to decrease the number of times they woke up and cried or called for their parents during the night. Before introduction of the procedure, the mean number of nightly awakenings was 3.3. After the treatment procedure, this declined to 0.8. These gains were maintained during follow-up tests conducted 3 months and 2 years later.

are in effect during different stimuli. For example, a VI schedule of reinforcement may be in effect when a light is turned on, and an FR schedule may be in effect when a tone is presented. With sufficient exposure to such a procedure, the pattern of responding during each stimulus will correspond to the schedule of reinforcement in effect during that stimulus. The participants will show a steady rate of responding during the VI stimulus and a stop-run pattern during the FR stimulus. (For a recent study of multiple schedule performance with cocaine reinforcement, see Weiss, Kearns, Cohn, Schindler, & Panlilio, in press.)

Stimulus discrimination and multiple schedules are common outside the laboratory. Nearly all reinforcement schedules that exist outside the laboratory are in effect only in the presence of particular stimuli. Playing a game yields reinforcement only in the presence of enjoyable or challenging partners. Driving rapidly is reinforced when you are on a freeway but not when you are on a crowded city street. Loud and boisterous discussions with your friends are reinforced at a party but frowned upon during a church service. Eating with your fingers is reinforced when you are on a picnic but not when you are in a fine restaurant. Daily activities typically consist of going from one situation to another (to the kitchen to get breakfast, to the bus stop, to your office, to the grocery store, and so on), and each situation has its own schedule of reinforcement.

Discrimination training brings the instrumental response under the control of the S+ and S−. How precise is the control that S+ acquires over the instrumental behavior, and what factors determine the precision of the stimulus control that is achieved? To answer these questions, it is not enough to observe differential responding to S+ versus S−. Investigators must also find out how steep the generalization gradient is when the participants are tested with stimuli that systematically vary from the S+. Furthermore, it must be determined which aspect of the discrimination training procedure is responsible for the type of stimulus generalization gradient that is obtained. These issues were first addressed in classic experiments by Jenkins and Harrison (1960, 1962).

Jenkins and Harrison examined how auditory stimuli that differed in pitch came to control the pecking behavior of pigeons reinforced with food. They measured how pigeons responded to tones of various frequencies after three types of training procedures. One group of birds was reinforced for pecking in the presence of a 1,000-cps tone and received no reinforcement when the tone was off. The 1,000-cps tone served as the S+ and the absence of tones served as the S−.

For the second group, the 1,000-cps tone again served as the S+, but the S− was a 950-cps tone. The third group of pigeons served as a control and did not receive discrimination training. The 1,000-cps tone was continuously turned on for these animals, and they could always receive reinforcement for pecking in the experimental chamber.

Upon completion of the three different training procedures, each group was tested for pecking in the presence of tones of various frequencies to see how precisely pecking was controlled by pitch. Figure 8.8 shows the generalization gradients that were obtained. The control group, which had not received discrimination training, responded nearly equally in the presence of all the test stimuli: the pitch of the tones did not control their behavior. Each of the other two training procedures produced more stimulus control by pitch. The steepest generalization gradient, and hence the strongest stimulus control, was observed in birds that had been trained with the 1,000-cps tone as S+ and the 950-cps tone as S−. Pigeons that previously received discrimination training between the 1,000-cps tone (S+) and the absence of tones (S−) showed an intermediate degree of stimulus control by tonal frequency.

The Jenkins and Harrison experiment provided two important principles: (1) discrimination training increases the stimulus control of instrumental behavior, and (2) a particular stimulus dimension (such as tonal frequency) is most likely to gain control over responding if the S+ and S− differ along that stimulus dimension. The most precise control by tonal frequency was observed after discrimination training in which the S+ was a tone of one frequency (1,000 cps) and the S− was a tone of another frequency (950 cps). Discrimination training did not produce as strong control by pitch if the S+ was a 1,000-cps tone and the S− was the absence of tones. The discrimination between the presence and absence of the 1,000-cps tone could have been based on the loudness or timbre of the tone in addition to its frequency. Hence, tonal frequency did not gain as much control in this case. (For further discussion of these and related issues, see Balsam, 1988; Dinsmoor, 1995; Hinson & Cannon, 1999; Hinson, Cannon, & Tennison, 1999.)

Range of Possible Discriminative Stimuli

Discrimination procedures can be used to bring an organism's instrumental behavior under the control of a wide variety of stimuli. D'Amato and Salmon (1982), for example, used two different tunes as discriminative stimuli for rats and monkeys. Porter and Neuringer

Figure 8.8 Generalization gradients of response to tones of different frequencies after various types of training. One group received discrimination training in which a 1,000-cps tone served as the S+ and the absence of tones served as the S−. Another group received training in which a 1,000-cps tone served as the S+ and a 950-cps tone served as the S−. The control group did not receive discrimination training before the generalization test. (From "Effects of Discrimination Training on Auditory Generalization," by H. M. Jenkins and R. H. Harrison, 1960, *Journal of Experimental Psychology, 59,* pp. 246–253; also from "Generalization Gradients of Inhibition Following Auditory Discrimination Learning," by H. M. Jenkins and R. H. Harrison, 1962, *Journal of Experimental Analysis of Behavior, 5,* pp. 435–441.

(1984) showed that pigeons are able to discriminate music by Bach from music by Stravinsky and generalize this discrimination to music of other composers from the same periods in musical history. In another study, pigeons learned to distinguish color slides of paintings by Monet from paintings of Picasso (Watanabe, Sakamoto, & Wakita, 1995). Discrimination procedures used with laboratory rats and pigeons have also been based on internal cues related to level of hunger (Davidson, Flynn, & Jarrard, 1992), number of stimuli in a visual array (Emmerton, 1998), the relative frequency of events (Keen & Machado, 1999; Machado & Cevik, 1997), time of day (morning versus afternoon; Budzynski & Bingman, 1999), or video images of different pigeons or their actions (Jitsumori, Natori, & Okuyama, 1999).

Discrimination training procedures are often used to evaluate the sensory capacity of animals. Schusterman and his colleagues, for example, have used discrimination training to determine the visual and hearing thresholds of several species of pinniped (sea lions, harbor seals, and elephant seals) (Levenson & Schusterman, 1999; Kastak & Schusterman, 1998). The pinnipeds in these studies were first reinforced (with a piece of fish) for resting the chin on a piece of PVC pipe. This was done so that the head of the subject would be in a standard position at the start of each trial. Trials then consisted of the presentation of a visual or an auditory cue (the S+) or no stimulus (the S−). In the presence of the S+, the subject had to move the head to one side to press on a paddle or ball to obtain a piece of fish. Responses during the S− were not reinforced. After the discrimination was well learned, the intensity of the visual or auditory S+ was systematically varied to obtain estimates of the visual and auditory thresholds of the subject (see also Kastak, Schusterman, Southall, & Reichmuth, 1999).

Investigators have also been interested in studying whether animals can detect the internal sensations created by a drug state. Can a pigeon, for example, tell when it is under the influence of pentobarbital (a sedative), and do other drugs (chlordiazepoxide, alcohol, and methamphetamine, for example) produce sensations similar those of pentobarbital? Discrimination training with drug stimuli and tests of stimulus generalization can provide answers to such questions (for recent examples, see McMillan & Li, 1999, 2000; McMillan, Li, & Hardwick, 1997; Snodgrass & McMillan, 1996; Zarcone & Ator, 2000).

This research has shown that the mechanisms of stimulus control by drug stimuli are remarkably similar to the mechanisms identified by Jenkins and Harrison (1960, 1962) for the control of key pecking by visual cues in pigeons.

Schaal and his colleagues, for example, compared the extent of stimulus control by drug stimuli before and after discrimination training (Schaal, McDonald, Miller, & Reilly, 1996). Pigeons were reinforced for pecking a response key on a variable interval 2-minute schedule of reinforcement. In the first phase of the experiment (no discrimination training), the birds were injected with 3.0 mg/kg cocaine before each session. After responding stabilized, generalization tests were periodically interspersed between training sessions. During these tests, the subjects received no drug (saline) or various doses of cocaine ranging from 0.3 to 5.6 mg/kg. (Responding was not reinforced during the test sessions.) The results obtained with one of the birds (P1) are presented in the left panel of Figure 8.9. Notice that the generalization gradient as a function of drug dose is fairly flat, indicative of weak stimulus control.

Figure 8.9 Responding as a function of cocaine dose for a pigeon before (left panel) and after (right panel) discrimination training in which 3.0 mg/kg of cocaine was present during S+ sessions and a saline injection (no drug) was given prior to S− sessions. (After Schaal et al., 1996.)

Before discrimination training

After discrimination training

During the next phase of the experiment, a discrimination procedure was introduced. During this phase, some sessions were preceded with an injection of cocaine as before, and pecking was reinforced. In addition, the subjects received sessions without the drug during which pecking was not reinforced. Thus, cocaine in the bird's system served as the S+. The subjects learned the discrimination, responding strongly during S+ sessions and much less during S- sessions. Once the discrimination was established, generalization tests were conducted as before. The results of those tests are shown in the right panel of Figure 8.9. Notice that now the generalization gradient was much steeper, indicating much stronger control by the drug stimuli. The greatest level of responding occurred when the pigeon was tested with the 3.0 mg/kg of cocaine that had been used during reinforced sessions. Virtually no responding occurred during sessions with no drug or with just 0.3 or 1.0 mg/kg of cocaine. Interestingly, responding also declined a bit when the test dose was 5.6 mg/kg, which exceeded the training dose. Thus, as was the case with stimulus control of behavior by tonal frequency (Figure 8.8), discrimination training increased stimulus control by the internal sensations created by cocaine.

The fact that stimulus discrimination procedures can be used to bring behavior under the control of a wide variety of stimuli makes these procedures powerful tools for the investigation of how animals process information. Some impressive results of this research are presented in discussions of animal cognition in Chapters 11 and 12.

What Is Learned in Discrimination Training?

Investigators have been interested in what is learned during discrimination training because of the profound effect it has on stimulus control. Consider the following relatively simple situation: Responses are reinforced whenever a red light is turned on (S+) and not reinforced whenever a loud tone is presented (S−). What strategies could a subject use to make sure that most of its responses were reinforced in this situation? One possibility is to learn to respond whenever the S+ is present and not learn anything about the S−. If an organism adopted this strategy, it would end up responding much more to S+ than to S− and could obtain all of the available reinforcers. Another possibility is to learn to suppress responding during S− but not learn anything about S+. This would constitute following the rule, "Suppress responding only when S− is present." This strategy would also lead to more responding during S+ than during S−. A third possibility is to learn the significance of both S+ and S−, to learn both to respond to S+ and to suppress responding to S−.

Spence's Theory of Discrimination Learning. One of the first and most influential theories of discrimination learning, proposed by Kenneth Spence (1936), is based on the last of the possibilities described above. According to this theory, reinforcement of a response in the presence of the S+ conditions excitatory response tendencies to S+. By contrast, nonreinforcement of responding during S− conditions inhibitory properties to S− that serve to suppress the instrumental behavior. Differential responding to S+ and S− is assumed to reflect both the excitation of responding to S+ and the inhibition of responding to S−.

How can the excitation-inhibition theory of discrimination learning be experimentally evaluated? The mere observation that organisms respond more to S+ than to S− is not sufficient to prove that they have learned something about both of these stimuli. More sophisticated experimental tests are required. One possibility is to use stimulus generalization gradients.

If an excitatory tendency has become conditioned to S+, then stimuli that increasingly differ from S+ should be progressively less effective in evoking the instrumental response. In other words, a steep generalization gradient, with the greatest amount of responding occurring to S+ should be observed. Such an outcome is called an **excitatory stimulus general-ization gradient.** Conversely, if an inhibitory tendency has become conditioned to S−, then stimuli that increasingly differ from S− should be progressively less effective in inhibit-ing the instrumental response. Such an outcome is called an **inhibitory stimulus general-ization gradient.**

When Spence proposed his theory, behavioral techniques were not sufficiently sophis-ticated to allow direct observation of the excitatory and inhibitory generalization gradients assumed in his theory. Experimental tests conducted decades later, however, proved that his ideas were substantially correct. In a landmark experiment, two groups of pigeons received discrimination training with visual stimuli before tests of stimulus generalization (Honig, Boneau, Burstein, & Pennypacker, 1963). One group was reinforced for pecking when the response key was illuminated by a white light that had a black vertical bar superimposed on it (S+) and was not reinforced when the white light was presented without the vertical bar (S−). The second group of animals received the same type of discrimination training, but with the S+ and S− stimuli reversed—the black vertical bar served as the S−, and the white key without the bar served as the S+. After both groups had learned to respond much more to S+ than to S−, tests of stimulus generalization were conducted to see how much control the vertical bar had gained over the instrumental behavior in the two groups. The test stim-uli consisted of the black bar on a white background, with the bar tilted at various angles away from the vertical position during the test trials.

The results of the experiment are summarized in Figure 8.10. First, consider the out-come for Group 1, which received the vertical bar as the S+ during discrimination training. These birds came to respond in the presence of the vertical bar. During the generalization test, the highest rate of responding occurred when the bar was presented in the original

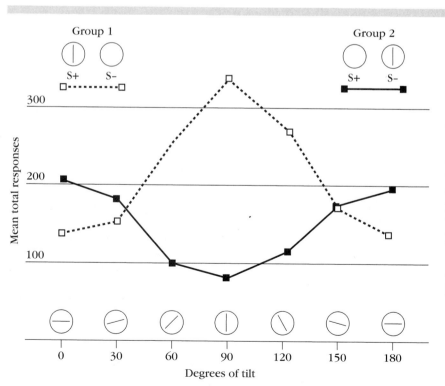

Figure 8.10 Stimulus generaliza-tion gradients for line-tilt stimuli in two groups of pigeons after discrimi-nation training. For Group1, a verti-cal black bar on a white background served as the S+, and the white light without the bar served as the S−. For Group 2, the functions of the stimuli were reversed. (From "Posi-tive and Negative Generalization Gradients Obtained Under Equiva-lent Training Conditions," by W. K. Honig, C. A. Boneau, K. R. Burstein, and H. S. Pennypacker, 1963, *Journal of Comparative and Physiological Psychology,* 56, p. 111–116.)

vertical position, and progressively less responding was observed when the bar was tilted more and more away from the vertical. These results illustrate an excitatory stimulus generalization gradient around S+.

Group 2, which received the vertical bar as the S− during discrimination training, did not peck when the vertical bar was projected on the response key. Results of the generalization test indicated that this failure to respond to the vertical bar was due to active inhibition of the pecking behavior in response to the position of the vertical bar. As the bar was tilted away from the original vertical position, progressively more pecking occurred. Stimuli that were increasingly different from the original S− produced progressively less inhibition of the pecking behavior, illustrating an inhibitory stimulus generalization gradient.

This experiment shows that discrimination training can produce both excitatory conditioning to S+ and inhibitory conditioning to S−. The excitatory gradient had an inverted-U shape, with greatest responding occurring to the original S+. The inhibitory gradient had the opposite shape, with the least responding occurring to the original S−. The fact that gradients of excitation and inhibition can occur around S+ and S− provides strong support for Spence's theory of discrimination learning.

The choice of the stimuli that served as S+ and S− was very important for the success of this experiment. Consider, for example, Group 2, which received the vertical bar on a white background as the S− and the white background without a bar as the S+. Responding in the inhibitory generalization gradient increased as the bar was tilted away from vertical. This outcome cannot be explained by claiming that tilting the black bar made the test stimuli more similar to the S+. Changing the orientation of the black bar does not make a bar more or less similar to the white background that served as the S+. The bar stimuli are qualitatively different from the background alone. As I point out in the following section, different results occur if the S+ and S− stimuli differ quantitatively in one feature rather than qualitatively (involving many features).

Interactions between S+ and S−: Peak Shift

So far I have described general characteristics of stimulus discrimination training under the assumption that what subjects learn about S+ is pretty much independent of what they learn about S−. This assumption is too simplistic. Learning is not so neatly compartmentalized. What is learned about S+ can influence the response to S− and vice versa. Such interactions are particularly likely if S+ and S− are related in some way.

One way that S+ and S− may be related is if they are similar except for one feature or attribute. A training procedure in which the S+ and S− differ only in terms of the value of one stimulus feature is called an **intradimensional discrimination.**

Intradimensional discriminations are of particular interest because they are related to the problem of expert performance. Expert performance typically involves making subtle distinctions. Distinguishing stimuli that differ only in a single feature is more difficult than distinguishing stimuli that differ in many respects. It does not require much expertise to tell the difference between a compact car and a bus. In contrast, a fairly sophisticated knowledge of cars is needed to tell the difference between one version of the Honda Civic and another. The fewer distinguishing features there are between two stimuli, the more difficult it is to tell them apart, and the greater is the expertise required to make the distinction. Two championship skaters may perform with equal skill as far as most people can tell, but expert judges are able to detect subtle but important distinctions that result in one performer getting higher marks than the other. Intradimensional discrimination requires detecting a single differentiating feature between S+ and S− and therefore is a form of expert performance.

An important characteristic of intradimensional discriminations is that sometimes they result in an interesting interaction between S+ and S− performance. This was illustrated by Hanson (1959) in a landmark experiment that examined the effects of intradimensional discrimination training on the extent to which various colors controlled the pecking behavior of pigeons. All the participants in the experiment were reinforced for pecking in the presence of a light whose wavelength was 550 nm. Thus, the S+ was the same for all of the subjects. The groups differed in how similar the S− was to the S+ (how expert the pigeons had to become in telling the colors apart). One group received discrimination training in which the S− was a color of 590-nm wavelength, 40 nm away from the S+. For another group, the wavelength of the S− was 555 nm, only 5 nm away from the S+. The performance of these pigeons was compared with the behavior of a control group that did not receive discrimination training but was also reinforced for pecking in the presence of the 550-nm stimulus.

After their different training experiences, all of the birds were tested for their rate of pecking in the presence of stimuli of various colors. The results are shown in Figure 8.11. The control group showed the highest rates of response to the S+ stimulus, and progressively lower rates of responding occurred as the pigeons were tested with stimuli increasingly different from the S+. Thus, the control group showed the usual excitatory stimulus generalization gradient centered around the S+.

Different results were obtained after discrimination training with the 590-nm color as S−. These pigeons also responded at high rates to the 550-nm color that had served as the S+, but they showed much more generalization of the pecking response to the 540-nm color. Their rate of response was slightly higher to the 540-nm color than to the original 550-nm S+. This shift of the peak responding away from the original S+ was even more dramatic after discrimination training with the 555-nm color as S−. These birds showed much lower rates of responding to the original S+ (550 nm) than either of the other two groups. Furthermore, their highest response rates occurred to colors of 540- and 530-nm wavelength. This shift of the peak of the generalization gradient away from the original S+ is remarkable because in the earlier phase of discrimination training, responding was never reinforced in the presence of the 540-nm or the 530-nm stimuli. Thus, the highest rates of pecking occurred to stimuli that had never been presented during original training.

The shift of the peak of the generalization gradient away from the original S+ is called the **peak-shift** phenomenon. The peak-shift effect is a result of intradimensional discrimination training. A peak shift did not occur in the control group, which had not received discrimination training. The peak-shift effect was a function of the similarity of the S− to the S+ used in discrimination training. The biggest peak shift occurred after training in which the S− was very similar to the S+ (555 nm and 550 nm, respectively). Less peak shift occurred after discrimination training with more widely different colors (590 nm compared with 550 nm). It is interesting to note that a small peak-shift effect is also evident in Figure 8.8 for pigeons that received discrimination training with the 1,000-cps tone as S+ and the 950-cps tone as S−.

The peak-shift effect can result from any intradimensional discrimination, not just pitch and color. The S+ and S− may be lines of different orientations, tones of different loudness, squares of different size, or different positions on a computer screen (see Cheng, Spetch, & Johnson, 1997; Dougherty & Lewis, 1991; Moye & Thomas, 1982; Weiss & Schindler, 1981; Weiss & Weissman, 1992; Wills & Mackintosh, 1998).

Spence's Explanation of Peak Shift. The peak-shift effect is remarkable because it shows that the only stimulus in whose presence responding is reinforced (the S+) is not necessarily the stimulus that evokes the highest response rate. How can this be? Excitatory stimulus generalization gradients are supposed to peak at the S+. Can the peak shift effect be

M. E. Rilling

explained in terms of standard excitatory and inhibitory gradients such as those shown in Figure 8.10? In an ingenious analysis, Spence (1937) suggested that excitatory and inhibitory gradients may produce the peak-shift phenomenon. His analysis is particularly remarkable because it was proposed more than 20 years before the peak-shift effect and gradients of excitation and inhibition were experimentally demonstrated.

Spence assumed that intradimensional discrimination training produces excitatory and inhibitory stimulus generalization gradients centered at S+ and S−, respectively, in the usual fashion. However, because the S+ and S− are similar in intradimensional discrimination tasks (both being colors, for example), the generalization gradients of excitation and inhibition will overlap. Furthermore, the degree of overlap will depend on the degree of similarity between S+ and S−. Because of this overlap, generalized inhibition from S− will suppress responding to S+, resulting in a peak-shift effect. More inhibition from S− to S+ will occur if S− is closer to S+, and this will result in a greater peak-shift effect, just as Hanson (1959) found (see Figure 8.11). (For other evidence in support of Spence's theory, see Hearst, 1968, 1969; Klein & Rilling, 1974; Marsh, 1972).

Alternative Accounts of Peak Shift. As I noted earlier, studies of stimulus control can reveal a great deal about how human and nonhuman animals view the world. An important question that has been a source of debate for decades is whether we view stimuli in terms of their individual and absolute properties or in terms of their relation to other stimuli that we experience (for example, Köhler, 1939). Evidence consistent with each of these approaches to the analysis of stimulus control is available, suggesting that both types of mechanisms are involved in how organisms respond (for example, Hulse, Page, & Braaten, 1990).

Spence's model of discrimination learning is an absolute stimulus learning model. It predicts behavior based on the net excitatory properties of individual stimuli. An alternative approach assumes that organisms learn to respond to a stimulus based on the relation of that stimulus to other cues in the situation. An interesting prediction of this approach is

Figure 8.11 Effects of intradimensional discrimination training on stimulus control. All three groups of pigeons were reinforced for pecking in the presence of a 550-nm light (S+). One group received discrimination training in which the S− was a 590-nm light. For another group, the S− was a 555-nm light. The third group served as a control and did not receive discrimination training before the test for stimulus generalization. (From "Effects of Discrimination Training on Stimulus Generalization," by H. M. Hanson, 1959, *Journal of Experimental Psychology, 58,* pp. 321–333.)

that the shape of a generalization gradient will change as a function of the range of test stimuli that are presented during the generalization test session. These and other predictions of the relational approach have been confirmed in studies with human participants (see Thomas, 1993).

Stimulus Equivalence Training

The peak-shift effect is a curious and counterintuitive outcome of intradimensional discrimination training. However, as the studies of Jenkins and Harrison showed (see Figure 8.8), even with this effect, discrimination training dramatically increases the stimulus control of behavior. It limits the generalization of behavior from S+ to other cues and increases the steepness of generalization gradients. This raises questions: Are there learning procedures that have the opposite effect? Are there learning procedures that increase stimulus generalization? How might we construct such procedures?

In a discrimination procedure, stimuli are treated differently—they have different consequences. One stimulus is associated with reinforcement, whereas the other is not. The differential treatment or significance of the stimuli leads organisms to respond to them as distinct from each other. What would happen if two stimuli were treated in the same or equivalent fashion? Would such a procedure lead organisms to respond to the stimuli as similar or equivalent? The answer seems to be yes. Just as discrimination training encourages differential responding, equivalence training encourages generalized responding or **stimulus equivalence.**

Several approaches are available to promote generalization rather than discrimination among stimuli. In Chapter 12, I describe research on perceptual concept learning that involves learning to treat various physically different instances of a perceptual concept in the same manner. For example, pigeons can be trained to respond in a similar fashion to different photographs, all of which include water in some form (ocean, lake, puddle, stream) (Herrnstein, Loveland, & Cable, 1976). The basic training strategy is to reinforce the same response (pecking a response key) in the presence of various pictures containing water, and to not reinforce that response when photographs without water appear. Herrnstein et al. trained such a discrimination using 500–700 photographs of various scenes in New England. Once the pigeons learned the water/no-water discrimination, their behavior generalized to novel photographs that had not been presented during training. (For additional discussion of perceptual concept learning, see Chapter 12.)

Investigators have also explored the possibility that functional equivalence between two different stimuli might be established by linking each of the distinct cues with a common third stimulus (Saunders & Green, 1999; Zentall, 1998; Zentall & Smeets, 1996). In an experiment by Honey and Hall (1989), for example, rats first received presentations of two different auditory cues, a noise and a clicker. For one group of animals, both the noise and the clicker were paired with food. The common food outcome was expected to create functional equivalence between the noise and the clicker stimuli. The control group also received presentations of the noise and the clicker, but for that group only the clicker was paired with food. Both groups then had the noise paired with mild footshock, resulting in the conditioning of fear to the noise. The investigators were interested in the extent to which this conditioned fear of the noise would generalize to the clicker. Significantly more generalization occurred in the equivalence-trained animals than in the control group. The equivalence-trained animals were more apt to treat the clicker and the noise similarly than was the control group. (For additional research along these lines, see Bonardi, Rey, Richmond, & Hall, 1993; Hall, 1991; Hall, Ray, & Bonardi, 1993; Honey & Hall, 1991; Honey & Watt, 1998, 1999; Ward-Robinson & Hall, 1999.)

Pairing different stimuli with the same outcome creates *functional equivalence* among those stimuli, with the consequence that a response conditioned to one of the stimuli generalizes to the others. A more formal definition of *equivalence class* has been proposed by Sidman and his colleagues (Sidman, 1990, 1994, 2000; Sidman & Tailby, 1982; see also Tierney & Bracken, 1998). An equivalence class is said to exist if its members possess three mathematical properties: (1) reflexivity or sameness, (2) symmetry, and (3) transitivity. Consider, for example, an equivalence class consisting of the three stimuli A, B, and C. *Reflexivity* or sameness refers to the relation A=A, B=B, and C=C. *Symmetry* is said to exist if a relationship is bidirectional. For example, if A leads to B (A→B), then symmetry requires that B leads to A (B→A). Finally, *transitivity* refers to the integration of two relationships into a third one. For example, given the relations A→B and B→C, transitivity requires that A→C.

The concept of equivalence class has been particularly important in analyses of language. The word *apple,* for example, derives its meaning from the fact that the word is in an equivalence class that includes other items that we call "apple," such as an actual apple and a photograph or drawing of an apple. These physically different objects have the property of reflexivity (apple = apple). They also have the property of symmetry. If you learned to say the word apple when you saw a picture of one, you will be able to pick out the picture if asked to identify what the word apple signifies. Finally, these items exhibit transitivity. If you learned that the word refers to the picture (A→B), and the picture refers to the physical apple object (B→C), you will be able to identify the object when given the word (A→C).

In general, individuals with good verbal skills learn equivalence classes more easily than those with poor verbal skills. This has encouraged some investigators to suggest that verbal skill and the formation of equivalence classes are integrally related (see Horne & Lowe, 1996, 1997, and related commentary). Consistent with this view, Zentall (1998) concluded that the "evidence for the emergence of the component relations presumed to underlie stimulus equivalence in [nonhuman] animals has not been overwhelming. Nor has there been extensive evidence for equivalence (as defined by Sidman, 1990) in animals" (p. 373). (See also Dugdale & Lowe, 2000.) The ability to use verbal labels facilitates equivalence class formation (for example, Randell & Remington, 1999). However, the ability to name stimuli and objects may not be essential for the acquisition of stimulus equivalence (Carr & Blackman, 2001; Carr, Wilkinson, Blackman, & McIlvane, 2000). Given the potential of equivalence classes to produce emergent stimulus relations that need not be specifically trained (such as symmetry and transitivity), this promises to be an exciting area for continued research.

CONTEXTUAL CUES AND CONDITIONAL RELATIONS

So far I have been discussing the control of behavior by discrete stimuli, such as a tone or a light, presented individually or in combination with one another. A stimulus is said to be *discrete* if it is presented for a brief period and has a clear beginning and end. Although studies with discrete stimuli have provided much information about the stimulus control of instrumental behavior, such studies do not tell the whole story. A more comprehensive analysis of the stimuli organisms experience during the course of instrumental conditioning indicates that discrete discriminative stimuli occur in the presence of background contextual cues. The contextual cues may be visual, auditory, or olfactory cues of the room or place where the discrete discriminative stimuli are presented. Recent research indicates that contextual cues can provide an important additional source of control of learned behavior.

Control by Contextual Cues

Several examples of stimulus control described at the beginning of this chapter involved the control of behavior by contextual cues. It is easier to concentrate on studying in the school library than at home during holidays because of contextual control of studying behavior by stimuli experienced in the library. Cheering at a football game but not during a church sermon also illustrates the power of contextual cues.

Contextual cues can come to control behavior in a variety of ways (see Balsam, 1985; Balsam & Tomie, 1985). In a study of sexual conditioning, for example, Akins (1998, Experiment 1) used contextual cues as a signal for sexual reinforcement, in much the same way that discrete stimuli might be used. Male domesticated quail served as subjects, and the apparatus consisted of two large compartments that were distinctively different. One compartment had sand on the floor, and the walls and ceiling were colored orange. The other compartment had a wire-mesh floor and green walls and ceiling. Before the start of the conditioning trials, the subjects were allowed to move back and forth between the two compartments during a 10-minute preference test to determine their baseline preference. The nonpreferred compartment was then designated as the CS. Conditioning trials consisted of placing the male subject in its CS context for 5 minutes, at which point a sexually receptive female was placed with them for another 5 minutes. Thus, these subjects received exposure to the CS context paired with the sexual US. Subjects in a control group received access to a female in their home cages 2 hours before being exposed to the CS context. Thus, the CS and US were unpaired for the control subjects.

In addition to the preference test conducted before the start of conditioning, tests were conducted after the 5th and 10th conditioning trials. The results of these tests are presented in Figure 8.12. Notice that the Paired and Unpaired groups showed similar low preferences for the CS compartment at the outset of the experiment. This low preference persisted in the control group. In contrast, subjects that received the CS context paired with sexual reinforcement came to prefer that context. Thus, the association of contextual cues with sexual reinforcement increased preference for those cues.

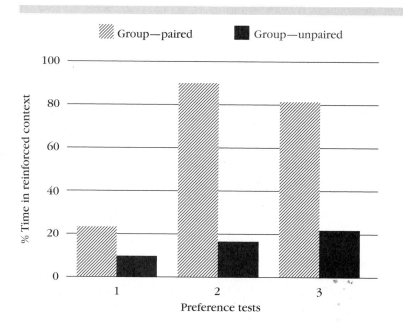

Figure 8.12 Development of a preference for a distinctive context paired (or unpaired) with sexual reinforcement in male domesticated quail. Five conditioning trials were conducted between successive tests for the subjects in the Paired group. (From Figure 1, p. 419, C. K. Akins in *Animal Learning & Behavior*, Vol. 26. Copyright 1998 Psychonomic Society, Inc. Reprinted with permission.)

Experiments like the one by Akins illustrate that contextual cues can come to control behavior if they serve as a signal for a US or a reinforcer. Do contextual cues come to control behavior when they do not signal reinforcement—when they are truly "background" stimuli that the organism is not specifically required to pay attention to? This is a major issue in the stimulus control of instrumental behavior. Much work has been devoted to it, and the answer is clearly yes.

In one experiment, for example, Thomas, McKelvie, and Mah (1985) first trained pigeons on a line-orientation discrimination in which a vertical line (90°) served as the S+ and a horizontal line (0°) served as the S−. The pigeons were periodically reinforced with food for pecking on S+ trials and were not reinforced on S− trials. The training took place in a standard Skinner box (Context 1), but the availability of reinforcement was signaled by the line-orientation S+ and S− stimuli rather than by contextual cues.

After the discrimination was well learned, the contextual cues of the experimental chamber were changed by altering both the lighting and the type of noise in the chamber. In the presence of these new contextual cues (Context 2), the discrimination training contingencies were reversed. Now, the horizontal line (0°) served as the S+ and the vertical line (90°) served as the S−. Notice that the pigeons were not specifically required to pay attention to the contextual cues. They were only required to learn a new discrimination problem. (They could have learned this new problem had the contextual cues not been changed.)

After mastery of the reversal problem, the birds received generalization tests in which lines of various orientations between 0° and 90° were presented. One such generalization test was conducted in Context 1, and another was conducted in Context 2. The results of these tests are presented in Figure 8.13. Remarkably, the shape of the generalization gradient in each context was appropriate to the discrimination problem that was in effect in that context. Thus, in Context 1, the birds responded most to the 90° stimulus, which had served as the S+ in that context, and least to the 0° stimulus, which had served as the S−. The opposite pattern of results occurred in Context 2. Here, the pigeons responded most to the 0° stimulus and least to the 90° stimulus, appropriate to the reverse discrimination contingencies that had been in effect in Context 2.

These results clearly illustrate that contextual cues can come to control instrumental behavior. The results also illustrate that contextual stimulus control can occur without one context being more strongly associated with reinforcement than another. In both Context 1 and Context 2, the pigeons received reinforced (S+) and nonreinforced (S−) trials. Therefore, one context could not have become a better signal for the availability of reinforcement than the other context. (See also Hall & Honey, 1989; Honey, Willis, & Hall, 1990; Swartzentruber, 1993.)

How did Context 1 and Context 2 come to produce different types of responding? Since one context was not a better signal for reinforcement than the other, direct associations of each context with food cannot explain the results. A different kind of mechanism must have been involved. One possibility is that each context activated a different memory. Context 1 activated the memory of reinforcement with 90° and nonreinforcement with 0°. In contrast, Context 2 activated the memory of reinforcement with 0° and nonreinforcement with 90°. Instead of being associated with a particular stimulus, each context appeared to be associated with a different S+ /S− contingency. Such associations are called conditional relations.

Control by Conditional Relations

In many of the earlier chapters, I have emphasized relations that involved just two events: a CS and a US, or a response and a reinforcer. Relations between two events are called *binary*

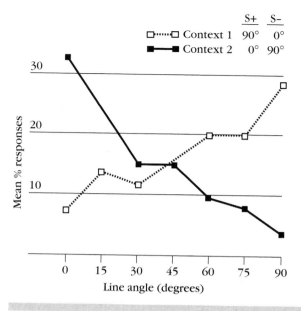

Figure 8.13 Generalization gradients obtained with various line-angle stimuli following training in two different contexts. In Context 1, the 90° stimulus served as the S+ and the 0° stimulus served as the S−. In Context 2, the 0° stimulus served as the S+ and the 90° stimulus served as the S−. (From "Context as a Conditional Cue in Operant Discrimination Reversal Learning," by D. R. Thomas, A. R. McKelvie, & W. L. Mah, 1985, *Journal of Experimental Psychology: Animal Behavior Processes, 11,* pp. 317–330. Copyright © 1985 by the American Psychological Association. Reprinted by permission.)

relations. Under certain circumstances, the nature of a binary relation is determined by a third event, called a **modulator.** In the experiment by Thomas et al. (1985), each context was a modulator. Whether a particular line-angle stimulus was associated with reinforcement depended on which contextual cues were present. The relation of a modulator to the binary relation that it signals is called a **conditional relation.** Numerous experiments have indicated that animals can learn to use modulators to tell when a particular binary relation is in effect (see reviews by Holland, 1984, 1992; Schmajuk & Holland, 1998; Swartzentruber, 1995).

I have already described some conditional relations without having identified them as such. One example is instrumental stimulus discrimination training, a procedure in which the organism is reinforced for responding during S+ but is not reinforced during S−. The discriminative stimuli S+ and S− are modulators that signal the relation between the response and the reinforcer. One response-reinforcer relation exists during S+ (positive reinforcement), and a different relation exists during S− (nonreinforcement). Thus, instrumental discrimination procedures involve conditional control of the relation between the response and the reinforcer (Davidson, Aparicio, & Rescorla, 1988; Goodall & Mackintosh, 1987; Holman & Mackintosh, 1981; Jenkins, 1977; Skinner, 1938).

Conditional Control in Pavlovian Conditioning. Conditional relations have been extensively investigated using Pavlovian conditioning procedures. The fundamental concept of conditional control is that one event signals the relation between two other events. Classical conditioning is typically conceived as involving a binary relation between a conditioned and an unconditioned stimulus. The CS may be brief illumination of a localized response key with an orange light, and the US may be food. A strong relation exists between the CS and the US if food is presented immediately after each occurrence of the CS but not at other times. How could conditional control be established over such a CS-US relation?

Establishing a conditional relation requires introducing a third event (the modulator) that indicates when presentation of the key light will end in food. For example, a noise stimulus could be introduced, in the presence of which the key light would be followed by food. In the absence of the noise stimulus, the key light would not end with food. This procedure

Reinforced trials	Nonreinforced trials
Noise	No noise
Key light → food	Key light → no food

Figure 8.14 Procedure for establishing conditional stimulus control in classical conditioning. On reinforced trials, a noise stimulus (the modulator) is presented, and a key-light CS is paired with food. On nonreinforced trials, the noise stimulus is absent, and the key-light CS is presented without food.

is diagrammed in Figure 8.14. As in instrumental discrimination procedures, the participants receive both reinforced and nonreinforced trials. During reinforced trials, the noise stimulus is turned on for 15 seconds. Ten seconds later, the orange key-light CS is turned on for 5 seconds and is immediately followed by the food US. During nonreinforced trials, the noise stimulus is not presented. The key-light CS is turned on alone for 5 seconds without the food US.

The procedure I just described is similar to one investigated in a sign tracking experiment with pigeons by Rescorla, Durlach, and Grau (1985). A noise stimulus was used as the modulator on reinforced trials for half the pigeons. For the rest of the birds, a diffuse flashing light was used in place of the noise. The measured conditioned response was pecking the response key when it was illuminated with the orange key-light CS. Since pecking is not elicited by diffuse auditory or visual stimuli, the key-peck behavior could be interpreted as a response only to the orange key-light CS.

The results of the experiment are illustrated in Figure 8.15. The birds pecked the orange key much more when it was presented after presentation of the modulator than when it was presented as an isolated element. Thus, the presence of the modulator facilitated responding to the key-light CS. It is important to keep in mind that the modulator itself did not elicit pecking, because pigeons do not peck in response to diffuse auditory and visual stimuli. Rather, the modulator increased the ability of the orange key-light CS to elicit pecking. The diffuse modulator gained conditional control over the effectiveness of the key-light CS in eliciting the conditioned response. Just as a discriminative stimulus facilitates instrumental behavior, the modulator facilitated CS-elicited responding in the present study. (See also Boakes, Westbrook, Elliott, & Swinbourne, 1997; Parker, Serdikoff, Kaminski, & Critchfield, 1991.)

In instrumental discrimination procedures, modulators (S+ and S−) are called "discriminative stimuli." In Pavlovian conditioning, some investigators have called conditional control of responding **facilitation** because the modulator facilitates responding to the CS (Rescorla, 1985; Rescorla et al., 1985). In this terminology, the modulator is called a *facilitator*. More commonly, conditional control in classical conditioning is called **occasion setting** because the modulator sets the occasion for pairings of the CS with the US (Holland, 1985; Ross, 1983; Ross & Holland, 1981). In this terminology, the modulator is called an *occasion setter*.

Note that the procedure outlined in Figure 8.14 is the converse of the standard procedure for inhibitory conditioning (see Figure 3.10). To turn the procedure outlined in Figure 8.14 into one that will result in the conditioning of inhibitory properties to the noise, all the investigator has to do is to reverse the type of trial on which the noise is presented. Instead of being presented on reinforced trials, the noise would be presented on nonreinforced trials.

As I noted in Chapter 3, conditioned inhibition develops if a stimulus signals the absence of the US that is otherwise expected to occur. Presenting the noise stimulus on non-

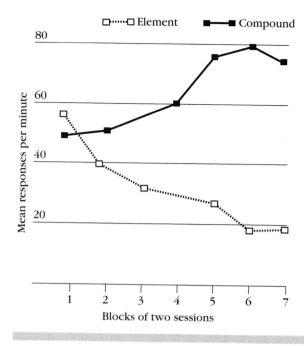

Figure 8.15 Acquisition of pecking to an orange key light in a study of conditional stimulus control of Pavlovian conditioned key pecking in pigeons. An orange key-light CS was paired with food in the presence of a modulator (compound trials) and was presented without food in the absence of the modulator (element trials). (From "Contextual Learning in Pavlovian Conditioning" by R. A. Rescorla, P. J. Durlach, & J. W. Grau. In P. Balsam & A. Tomie [Eds.], *Context and Learning.* Copyright © 1985, Lawrence Erlbaum and Associates. Reprinted by permission.)

reinforced trials would make the noise a signal for nonreinforcement of the key light, and would make the noise a conditioned inhibitor. This illustrates that the procedure for inhibitory Pavlovian conditioning involves a conditional relation, just as positive occasion setting and facilitation procedures do. This argument also suggests that conditioned inhibition may be the conceptual opposite of facilitation or occasion setting rather than the opposite of conditioned excitation. In certain circumstances, this indeed appears to be the case (Rescorla, 1987, 1988a).

Distinction between Excitation and Modulation. Occasion setting is an important aspect of classical conditioning not only because it illustrates that classical conditioning is subject to conditional control, but also because it appears to involve different mechanisms of learning from those considered previously. As discussed in Chapter 4, pairings of a CS with a US result in an association between the two events such that presentation of the CS comes to activate a representation of the US. I have referred to this kind of learning as the conditioning of excitation to the CS. Modulatory properties of stimuli are different from conditioned excitation.

In several studies, attempts to obtain evidence of conditioned excitatory properties of modulators failed to reveal such evidence (for example, Bouton & Swartzentruber, 1986; Puente, Cannon, Best, & Carrell, 1988). These experiments indicate that a stimulus can set the occasion for conditioned responding elicited by another cue without itself eliciting visible conditioned responding. Other studies have shown that conditioning simple excitatory properties to a stimulus does not make that stimulus function as a modulator (see Holland, 1985; Rescorla, 1985; but see Gewirtz, Brandon, & Wagner, 1998; Swartzentruber, 1997).

Additional evidence for a distinction between modulation and conditioned excitation is based on the effects of extinction procedures. *Extinction* refers to a procedure in which a previously conditioned stimulus is presented repeatedly but now without the US. I describe extinction in greater detail in Chapter 9. The typical outcome of extinction is that conditioned responding declines. Interestingly, the same procedure (repeated nonreinforced

247

stimulus presentations) carried out with an occasion setter often has no effect. Once a stimulus has become established to set the occasion for a CS-US relation, repeated presentations of the stimulus by itself do not reduce its ability to facilitate conditioned responding to the CS (for example, Holland, 1989a; Rescorla, 1985; Ross, 1983).

The difference in the effects of an extinction procedure on conditioned excitatory stimuli and occasion setters may be related to what is signaled. A conditioned excitatory stimulus signals the forthcoming presentation of the US. The absence of the US following presentation of the CS during extinction is a violation of that expectancy. Hence, the signal value of the CS has to be readjusted in extinction to bring it in line with the new reality. Such a readjustment is not required by an extinction procedure for an occasion setter.

An occasion setter signals a relation between a CS and a US. The absence of the US when the occasion setter is presented alone in extinction does not mean that the relation between the CS and the US has changed. The information signaled by an occasion setter is not proved incorrect by presenting the modulator by itself during extinction. Therefore, the ability of the modulator to promote responding elicited by the CS remains intact during extinction. However, a modulator's effectiveness is reduced if the CS-US relation signaled by the modulator is altered (Rescorla, 1986).

Another line of evidence that supports the conclusion that occasion setting is distinct from conventional excitation has been obtained from transfer tests. These tests were conducted to determine whether a stimulus that has been conditioned to set the occasion for responding to a particular target CS will also increase responding to other CSs. Evidence of successful transfer of the effects of a modulator to new target CSs has been obtained. Of particular interest is the type of properties the targets must have in order to be subject to the influence of a modulator. Transfer effects are most likely to be obtained if the new target stimuli had previously served as targets of other modulator stimuli (Holland, 1992; Swartzentruber, 1995). Little transfer is obtained if the new target previously served as a conditioned excitatory stimulus, or if it had a history of reinforcement and nonreinforcement but was not a part of a conditional relation. Such limitations on transfer effects would not occur if a modulator increased responding to a target stimulus because the excitatory properties of the modulator summated with the excitatory properties of the target. Therefore, limitations on transfer provide additional evidence that modulators have their effects by some mechanism other than conventional excitation. (For further evidence of limitations on transfer of occasion setting, see Bonardi, 1996; Goddard & Holland, 1996; Nakajima, 1997; Skinner, 2000.)

Modulation versus Configural Conditioning.   Not all conditional discrimination procedures of the type illustrated in Figure 8.14 result in the learning of a conditional relation between the stimuli involved. On reinforced trials in this procedure, a compound stimulus consisting of the noise and the key light was presented. As I noted earlier, organisms can respond to a compound stimulus either in terms of the elements that make up the compound, or in terms of the unique stimulus configuration produced by the elements. For the noise to serve as a signal that the key light will be paired with food, the noise and key light have to be treated as independent events rather than as a combined configural cue. Thus, modulatory effects require responding to the stimulus compound as consisting of independent stimulus elements (Holland, 1992).

To encourage organisms to treat stimulus compounds as consisting of independent elements, investigators have presented the elements one after the other, rather than simultaneously, in what is called a *serial compound.* On reinforced trials, the occasion setter is usually presented first, followed by the target CS and reinforcement. For example, in many of his experiments on occasion setting, Holland has even inserted a 5-second gap between the modulator and the target CS. Such procedures discourage the perception of a stimulus configuration based on the occasion setter and the target CS. In numerous studies, Holland and his associates have found that organisms respond to conditional discriminations involving serial compounds in terms of conditional relations. By contrast, the use of simultaneous compounds in conditional discriminations often does not result in modulatory effects (for example, Holland, 1986, 1989a, 1989c, 1991; Ross & Holland, 1981; see also Holland, 1989b; Thomas, Cook, & Terrones, 1990; Thomas, Curran, & Russell, 1988).

CONCLUDING COMMENTS

Stimulus control refers to how precisely tuned an organism's behavior is to specific features of the environment. Therefore, issues concerning the stimulus control of behavior are critical for understanding how an organism interacts with its environment. Stimulus control is measured in terms of the steepness of generalization gradients. A steep generalization gradient indicates that small variations in a stimulus produce large differences in responding. Weaker stimulus control is indicated by flatter generalization gradients.

The degree of stimulus control is determined by numerous factors, including the sensory capacity and sensory orientation of the organism, the relative salience of other cues in the situations, the type of reinforcement used, and the type of response required for reinforcement. Stimulus control is also a function of learning. Discrimination training increases the stimulus control of behavior whether that training involves stimuli that differ in several respects or stimuli that differ in only one respect. Discrimination training with stimuli that differ in only one dimension produces more precise stimulus control and may lead to the counterintuitive outcome that the peak level of responding is shifted away from the reinforced stimulus. The converse of discrimination training is equivalence training, which increases the generalization of behavior.

Not only discrete stimuli but also background contextual cues can come to control behavior. Stimulus control by contextual cues can develop even if attention to contextual cues is not required to optimize reinforcement. Contextual cues can become associated with a US directly or can serve to modulate the relation between a discrete CS and a US.

SAMPLE QUESTIONS

1. Describe the relationship between stimulus discrimination and stimulus generalization.
2. Describe the phenomenon of overshadowing, and describe how it may be explained by elemental and configural approaches to stimulus control.
3. Describe how the steepness of a generalization gradient may be altered by experience and learning.
4. Describe the difference between intradimensional and interdimensional discrimination training.
5. Describe the peak-shift effect and its determinants.
6. Compare and contrast conditioned excitation and occasion setting or facilitation.

KEY TERMS

conditional relation A relation in which the significance of one stimulus or event depends on the status of another stimulus.

configural-cue approach An approach to the analysis of control by compound stimuli that assumes that organisms respond to a compound stimulus as an integral whole rather than a collection of separate and independent stimulus elements. (Compare with *stimulus element approach*.)

discriminative stimulus A stimulus that controls the performance of instrumental behavior because it signals the availability (or nonavailability) of reinforcement.

excitatory stimulus generalization gradient A gradient of responding that is observed when organisms are tested with the S+ from a discrimination procedure and with stimuli that increasingly differ from the S+. The highest level of responding occurs to stimuli similar to the S+; progressively less responding occurs to stimuli that increasingly differ from the S+ . Thus, the gradient has an inverted-U shape.

facilitation A procedure in which one cue designates when another cue will be reinforced. Also called *occasion setting*.

inhibitory stimulus generalization gradient A gradient of responding observed when organisms are tested with the S− from a discrimination procedure and with stimuli that increasingly differ from the S−. The lowest level of responding occurs to stimuli similar to the S−; progressively more responding occurs to stimuli that increasingly differ from S−. Thus, the gradient has a U shape.

intradimensional discrimination A discrimination between stimuli that differ only in terms of the value of one stimulus feature, such as color, brightness, or pitch.

modulator A stimulus that signals the relation between two other events. The nature of a binary relation is determined by the modulator.

multiple schedule of reinforcement A procedure in which different reinforcement schedules are in effect in the presence of different stimuli presented in succession. Generally, each stimulus comes to evoke a pattern of responding that corresponds to whatever reinforcement schedule is in effect during that stimulus.

occasion setting Same as *facilitation*.

overshadowing Interference with the conditioning of a stimulus because of the simultaneous presence of another stimulus that is easier to condition.

peak shift A displacement of the highest rate of responding in a stimulus generalization gradient away from the S+ in a direction opposite the S− after intradimensional discrimination training.

stimulus discrimination Differential responding in the presence of two or more stimuli.

stimulus discrimination procedure (in classical conditioning) A classical conditioning procedure in which one stimulus (the CS+) is paired with the unconditioned stimulus on some trials and another stimulus (the CS−) is presented without the unconditioned stimulus on other trials. As a result of this procedure, the CS+ comes to elicit a conditioned response, and the CS− comes to inhibit this response. (Also called *differential inhibition*.)

stimulus discrimination procedure (in instrumental conditioning) A procedure in which reinforcement for responding is available whenever one stimulus (the S+, or S^D) is present and not available whenever another stimulus (the S−, or S$^\Delta$) is present.

stimulus-element approach An approach to the analysis of control by compound stimuli that assumes that participants respond to a compound stimulus in terms of the stimulus elements that make up the compound. (Compare with *configural-cue approach*.)

stimulus equivalence Responding to physically distinct stimuli as if they were the same because of common prior experiences with the stimuli.

stimulus generalization The occurrence of behavior learned through habituation or conditioning in the presence of stimuli that are different from the stimuli used during training.

stimulus generalization gradient A gradient of responding that is observed if participants are tested with stimuli that increasingly differ from the stimulus that was present during training. (See also *excitatory stimulus generalization gradient* and *inhibitory stimulus generalization gradient*.)

EXTINCTION OF CONDITIONED BEHAVIOR

hapter 9 represents a departure from previous chapters in that it focuses on extinction, a procedure that produces a decline in responding. Extinction can be conducted only after a response or association has been established using Pavlovian or instrumental conditioning. Often the goal is to reverse the effects of acquisition, but a true reversal is rarely achieved and may not be possible. Phenomena such as spontaneous recovery, renewal, and reinstatement all show that extinction does not erase what was learned originally. Studies of reinforcer devaluation suggest that extinction has virtually no measurable impact on S-O and R-O associations. Rather, extinction seems to involve the new learning of an inhibitory S-R association that is superimposed on what was learned earlier. The inhibition arises from the frustrative effects of the unexpected absence of reward. The frustration produced by nonreward is responsible for a number of "paradoxical" reward effects, including the partial reinforcement extinction effect. Intermittent or partial reinforcement permits organisms to learn about nonreward in ways that serve to immunize them against the effects of extinction. This kind of resistance to change is also the subject of studies of behavioral momentum that are described at the end of the chapter.

So far, my descriptions of classical and instrumental conditioning have centered on various aspects of the acquisition and maintenance of new associations and new responses. Learning mechanisms are important because they provide needed flexibility in how individuals interact with their environment. Learning mechanisms are more useful than unconditioned response processes because the behavioral plasticity that they enable promotes adjustments to a changing environment. But if learned behavior is an adaptation to a changing environment, then the loss of conditioned behavior should be just as prevalent as its acquisition. Not many reinforcement schedules remain in effect throughout an organism's lifetime. Responses that are successful at one stage may cease to be effective as circumstances change. Children, for example, are praised for drawing crude representations of people and objects in nursery school, but the same type of drawing is not considered good if made in sixth grade. Dating someone may be extremely pleasant and rewarding at first, but stops being reinforcing when that person falls in love with someone else.

Acquisition of conditioned behavior involves procedures in which a reinforcing outcome is presented. In Pavlovian conditioning, the reinforcing outcome or unconditioned stimulus is presented as a consequence of a conditioned stimulus. In instrumental conditioning, the reinforcing outcome is presented as a consequence of the instrumental response. **Extinction** involves omitting the US or reinforcer. Thus, extinction in classical conditioning involves repeated presentations of the conditioned stimulus by itself. Extinction in instrumental conditioning involves no longer presenting the reinforcer as a consequence of the instrumental response. The typical result is that conditioned responding, be it classical or instrumental, declines. Thus, the behavioral change that occurs in extinction is the reverse of what was observed in acquisition. Because this reverse behavioral change is produced by omitting the reinforcer or US that motivated the original learning, extinction appears to be the opposite of acquisition. Indeed, that is how extinction has been characterized in traditional theories of learning, such as the Rescorla–Wagner model (see Chapter 4). However, as the evidence described in the present chapter shows, this view of extinction is incorrect.

It is important to point out that the loss of the conditioned response that occurs as a result of extinction is not the same as the loss of behavior that may occur because of **forgetting.** Extinction is produced by omitting the US following presentations of the CS or omitting the reinforcer following occurrences of the instrumental response. Forgetting, by contrast, is a decline in conditioned responding that may occur simply because of the passage of time. Extinction occurs as a consequence of repeated presentations of the CS by itself or repeated instances of the instrumental response by itself. Forgetting occurs with prolonged absence of experience with the conditioned stimulus or the instrumental response.

Understanding extinction is important for both behavior theory and behavior therapy (Bouton & Nelson, 1998; Falls, 1998). Individuals seek therapy when some aspect of their behavior is creating a problem for them. One approach to alleviating the difficulty is to extinguish the problematic response. Presumably, if a problematic behavior developed because of Pavlovian or instrumental conditioning, the behavior should be susceptible to extinction. However, extinction does not always work in behavior therapy. An observer may be tempted to conclude that in these cases the original behavioral problem was not acquired through conditioning. However, recent advances in the understanding of extinction suggest that failures of extinction reflect the normal limitations of extinction. Extinction does not reverse the effects of acquisition. Rather, it involves learning something new that is superimposed on what was learned earlier (without the loss of that earlier learning).

What would you do if you unexpectedly did not succeed in opening the door to your apartment with your key? Chances are you would not give up after the first attempt but would try several more times, perhaps jiggling the key in different ways each time. But, if none of those response variations worked, you would eventually quit trying. This illustrates two basic behavioral effects of extinction. The most obvious behavioral effect is that responding decreases when the response no longer results in reinforcement. This is the primary behavioral effect of extinction, the one that scientists have given the most attention. Investigations of extinction have focused on the rate or probability of the instrumental response during the course of extinction and have been concerned with how rapidly responding decreases. If the key to your apartment no longer opens the door, you will give up trying. Notice, however, that before you give up entirely, you are likely to jiggle the key in various ways in an effort to make it work. This illustrates the second basic behavioral effect of extinction, namely, that it increases response variability.

The two basic behavioral effects of extinction are illustrated in a recent study by Neuringer, Kornell, and Olufs (2001). Two groups of rats served in the experiment. During the first phase, both groups were reinforced for making instrumental responses, but only one group was required to vary its instrumental behavior. The two groups were then observed in extinction, to see how the rate and variability of their responses would be altered by nonreinforcement. As I described in Chapter 5, reinforcement can increase the probability of response variability if variation in responding is required for reinforcement. The study by Neuringer et al. was designed to examine the effects of extinction on this phenomenon.

The experimental chamber had two response levers on one wall and a round response key on the opposite wall. During the reinforcement phase, the rats had to make three responses in a row to obtain a food pellet. For example, they could press the left lever three times (LLL), press each lever and the response key once (RLK), or press the left lever twice and the key once (LLK). For the subjects in Group 1, a sequence of three responses was reinforced only if this sequence was different from 95% of the previous response sequences the subjects performed (adjusted for recency). Thus, Group 1 had to vary their response sequences to obtain reinforcement. Each subject in the Group 2 was yoked to a subject in the variability group (Group 1) and received reinforcement on a particular trial only if its yoked partner got reinforced. Subjects in the yoked group also had to make three responses to get reinforced, but whether they got a food pellet did not depend on the variability of their response sequences. After behavior was well established by the reinforcement contingencies, both groups were shifted to a phase of extinction.

Figure 9.1 shows the results of the experiment for the last four sessions of the reinforcement phase and the first four sessions of the extinction phase. The left panel represents the variability in the response sequences each group performed; the right panel represents their rates of responding. Notice that reinforcement produced the expected difference between the two groups in terms of the variability of their response sequences. Subjects reinforced for varying their responses (Group 1) showed much more variability than the yoked subjects (Group 2), which did not have to vary their behavior. Interestingly, the yoked subjects responded somewhat faster, perhaps because they did not have to move as frequently from one response lever to the other.

As expected, extinction produced a decline in the rate of responding in both groups (see right panel of Figure 9.1). Interestingly, this decline in responding occurred in the face

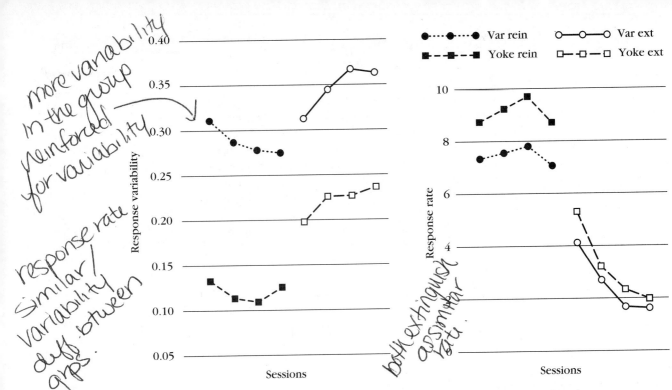

Figure 9.1 Effects of extinction on response variability (left panel) and response rate (right panel) for a group of rats that was required to perform variable response sequences for reinforcement (Var) or received reinforcement regardless of their response sequences (Yoke). The filled symbols represent the last four sessions of the reinforcement phase. The open symbols represent the first four sessions of the extinction phase. (Response variability was measured in terms of the probability of meeting the variability criterion. Response rate was measured in terms of the number of three-response sequences that were completed per minute.) (After Neuringer, Kornell, & Olufs, 2001.)

of an increase in the variability of the response sequences the subjects performed (see left panel of Figure 9.1). Both groups showed a significant increase in the variability of the response sequences they performed during extinction. The increase in response variability was evident during the first extinction session and increased during subsequent sessions. Thus, extinction produced a decline in the number of response sequences the subjects performed, but it increased the variability of those sequences. (For another example of increased response variability due to nonreinforcement, see Gharib, Derby, & Roberts, 2001.)

Another interesting finding in the study by Neuringer et al. (2001) was that the increase in response variability that occurred during extinction did not come at the expense of the subjects repeating response sequences that they had performed during the reinforcement phase. Response sequences that were highly likely to occur during the reinforcement phase continued to occur during extinction but were supplemented by sequences that the subjects had rarely tried previously. This last outcome confirms previous conclusions that the basic structure of instrumental behavior is altered very little by the introduction of extinction (Machado & Cevik, 1998; Schwartz, 1981; for similar evidence in Pavlovian conditioning, see Ohyama, Gibbon, Deich, & Balsam, 1999). Extinction decreases the rate of responding and increases response variability, but otherwise does not alter the structure of behavior.

In addition to the behavioral effects illustrated in Figure 9.1, extinction procedures may produce strong emotional effects (see Papini & Dudley, 1997, for a recent review). If an organism has become accustomed to receiving reinforcement for a particular response, it may become upset when reinforcers are no longer delivered. The emotional reaction induced by withdrawal of an expected reinforcer is called **frustration.** Frustrative nonreward energizes behavior (for carefully controlled studies, see Dudley & Papini, 1995, 1997; Thomas & Papini, 2001). Under certain conditions, frustration may be sufficiently severe to include aggressive reactions. When a vending machine breaks down and no longer delivers a soft drink or candy after you put in your money, you may become abusive and pound and kick the machine. If your spouse has coffee ready for you every morning, you are likely to get angry the first time the coffee is not ready when you get up. If your partner takes you on a date every Saturday evening, you will surely be very upset if your partner unexpectedly calls one Saturday afternoon to cancel the date.

Frustrative aggression induced by extinction is dramatically demonstrated by experiments in which two animals—pigeons, for example—are placed in the same Skinner box (Azrin, Hutchinson, & Hake, 1966). One pigeon is initially reinforced for pecking a response key, while the other animal is restrained in a corner of the experimental chamber. The key-pecking bird largely ignores the other one as long as reinforcers are provided. However, when extinction is introduced and reinforcement ceases, the previously rewarded bird is likely to attack its innocent partner. Similar aggression occurs if a stuffed model instead of a real animal is placed in the Skinner box. Extinction-induced aggression has also been investigated in studies with rats and with people (for example, Lewis, Alessandri, & Sullivan, 1990; Nation & Cooney, 1982; Tomie, Carelli, & Wagner, 1993) and can be a problem when extinction is used as a therapeutic procedure (Lerman, Iwata, & Wallace, 1999).

EXTINCTION AND ORIGINAL LEARNING

Although extinction produces important behavioral and emotional effects, it does not reverse the effects of acquisition. Evidence that extinction does not erase what was originally learned has been obtained through studies of spontaneous recovery, renewal, reinstatement, and reinforcer devaluation effects.

Spontaneous Recovery

Spontaneous Recovery following Pavlovian Conditioning. One of the hallmark features of extinction is that it dissipates with time. The consequence of this loss of the extinction effect over time is that the originally conditioned response returns if the subject is tested after a delay following the extinction procedure. In a recent study with laboratory rats as subjects, for example, Rescorla (1997b) used two appetitive unconditioned stimuli, sucrose and a solid food pellet, delivered into cups recessed in one wall of the experimental chamber. Infrared detectors identified each time the rat poked its head into the food cups. This magazine entry behavior is a form of goal tracking (see Chapter 3). The experimental chamber was usually dark. During the initial acquisition phase, one of the unconditioned stimuli was signaled by a noise CS and the other was signaled by a light CS. As conditioning progressed, each CS quickly came to elicit the goal tracking conditioned response, with the two CSs eliciting similar levels of responding. The mean number of magazine entries per minute at the end of acquisition was 15.6 during the CSs (and 4.6 during the intertrial intervals).

Two extinction sessions (of 16 trials each) were then conducted with each CS, followed by a series of 4 test trials. The experimental manipulation of primary interest was that for one of the CSs (CS-No rest), the extinction trials immediately preceded the test trials. In contrast, an 8-day rest period separated extinction and testing for the other CS (CS-Rest). Responses to both of the stimuli during the test trials are shown in Figure 9.2. Both CSs elicited very little responding at the end of the extinction phase. (Mean response rates were below 2 per minute.) This low level of responding persisted during the test session for the stimulus (CS-No rest) that was tested immediately after extinction. In contrast, for the stimulus that was tested 8 days after extinction (CS-Rest), responding was substantially higher, especially during the first trial. This represents *spontaneous recovery*. Notice, however, that the recovery was not complete. At the end of the acquisition phase, the rate of magazine entries had been 15.6 responses/min. During the first trial after the rest period, the mean response rate was about 6.2 responses/min. (For other studies of spontaneous recovery of Pavlovian conditioned responding after extinction, see Brooks & Bouton, 1993; Robbins, 1990; Rosas & Bouton, 1996.)

Spontaneous Recovery after Instrumental Conditioning. Spontaneous recovery is also a prominent phenomenon in extinction after instrumental conditioning. A particularly clear demonstration of the phenomenon was provided by a study with laboratory rats (Rescorla, 1996c). The rats were first trained to make two different instrumental responses for food reinforcement (pressing a response lever and poking their nose into a small opening). Separate training sessions were conducted with each response, and reinforcement was provided on a variable interval 1-min schedule. This instrumental conditioning resulted in mean response rates of about 17 per minute for each response.

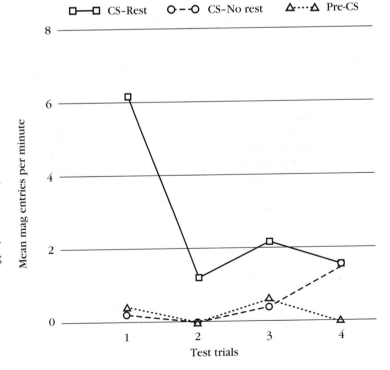

Figure 9.2 Rate of goal tracking for two different CSs during a test session for spontaneous recovery. Both CSs were initially conditioned by pairing them with food reinforcement. Each CS was then extinguished. For CS-Rest, the test session occurred 8 days after the extinction phase. For CS-No Rest, the test session occurred immediately after the extinction phase. Notice that the 8-day rest period caused a substantial recovery in the rate of responding. (From "Spontaneous recovery after Pavlovian conditioning with multiple outcomes" by R. A. Rescorla, in *Animal Learning & Behavior*, Vol. 25, p. 101. Copyright 1997 Psychonomic Society, Inc. Reprinted with permission.)

Figure 9.3 Instrumental responding during a recovery test to demonstrate spontaneous recovery. At first, laboratory rats were trained to make two different instrumental responses for food reinforcement (a lever press and a nose-poke response). One response was then extinguished shortly before the recovery test (R-No rest), and the other was extinguished 7 days before the test (R-Rest). Notice that much more responding occurred during the recovery test if extinction was followed by the 7-day rest period. (From Figure 2, p. 13, in R. A. Rescorla, in *Animal Learning & Behavior,* Copyright 1996 Psychonomic Society, Inc. Reprinted with permission.)

After the acquisition phase, two 20-minute extinction sessions were conducted with each response. For one of the responses (counterbalanced across subjects), the extinction phase occurred shortly before a recovery test. For the other response, the extinction phase occurred 7 days before the recovery test. By the end of the extinction phase, mean response rates did not exceed 2 per minute for either response. The results of the test sessions conducted with each response are displayed in Figure 9.3. Notice that the response whose recovery was tested after a rest period after extinction (R-Rest) occurred at a much higher rate than the response whose recovery was tested without a rest period after extinction (R-No rest). Introducing a period of rest after extinction produced a substantial recovery in responding, illustrating the phenomenon of spontaneous recovery. (For other examples of spontaneous recovery of instrumental and more complex forms of behavior, see Devenport, 1998; Rescorla, 1997c.)

Renewal of Original Excitatory Conditioning

Another strong piece of evidence that extinction does not result in unlearning is the phenomenon of **renewal** identified by Mark Bouton and his colleagues. Renewal refers to a recovery of acquisition performance when the contextual cues that were present during extinction are changed. The change can be a return to the context of original acquisition or a shift to a "neutral" context. Renewal is particularly troublesome for behavior therapy because it means that irrational fears that are extinguished in the context of a therapist's office can easily return when the subject moves to a different context.

The phenomenon of renewal is clearly demonstrated by a study of conditioned fear conducted with the conditioned suppression technique (Bouton & King, 1983). Laboratory rats were first trained to press a response lever for food reinforcement, and then a tone CS was repeatedly paired with footshock. The training occurred in one of two experimental chambers that provided distinctively different contextual cues. Which context was used for training was counterbalanced across subjects and labeled Context A. As usual, excitatory conditioning resulted in a conditioned suppression of lever pressing during presentations of the CS. For the next phase of the experiment, the subjects were divided into three groups. Two of the groups received 20 extinction trials consisting of presentations of the tone CS without shock. For Group A, these extinction trials occurred in the same context (A) as original excitatory conditioning. For Group B, extinction occurred in the alternate context (B). A third group (NE) did not receive extinction.

The results of the extinction trials are shown on the left side of Figure 9.4. Recall that in a conditioned suppression procedure, greater levels of conditioned fear are represented by smaller values of the suppression ratio (see Chapter 3). Groups A and B showed similarly strong levels of suppression to the tone at the start of the extinction trials. This shows that the fear that had been conditioned in Context A easily generalized when the tone was presented in Context B for Group B. As the tone was repeatedly presented during the extinction phase, conditioned suppression gradually dissipated, and did so in a similar fashion for subjects extinguished in Context A or Context B.

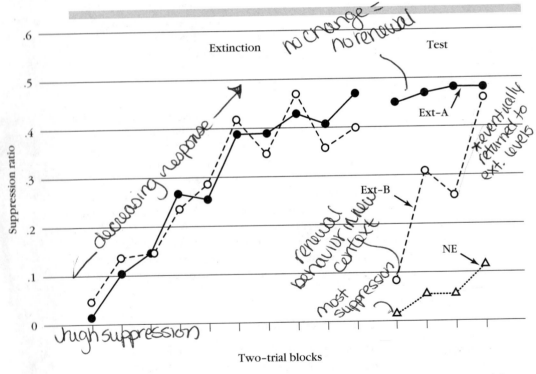

Figure 9.4 Demonstration of the renewal effect in conditioned suppression. All of the subjects first received pairings of a tone with footshock in Context A (data not shown). Groups A and B then received extinction trials either in Context A or Context B. Group NE did not receive extinction. Test sessions were then conducted in Context A for all subjects. (From Bouton & King, 1983.)

Following extinction in either Context A or Context B, all subjects received a series of test trials in Context A, where they had been trained originally. The results of these test trials are presented on the right side of Figure 9.4. Group NE, which did not receive extinction, showed the strongest degree of suppression to the tone during the test trials. The least suppression was evident in Group A, which received extinction in the same context as the context of testing. Group B, which also received extinction but in Context B, showed substantial levels of suppression when first returned to Context A. Group B's conditioned fear during the first three test trials was substantially greater than it had been at the end of the extinction phase. Thus, conditioned fear was *renewed* when Group B was removed from the extinction context and returned to the context of original training.

The difference in the degree of conditioned fear in Groups A and B evident during the test sessions is significant because these two groups showed similar losses of conditioned fear during the extinction phase. The fact that conditioned fear was renewed in Group B indicates that the loss of suppression evident during the extinction phase did not reflect the unlearning of the conditioned fear response. (For more recent studies of the renewal effect in aversive Pavlovian conditioning, see Harris, Jones, Bailey, & Westbrook, 2000; Rosas & Bouton, 1997; Williams & Sly, 1999.)

Since its original demonstration, the renewal effect has been observed not only in Pavlovian fear conditioning but also in Pavlovian appetitive conditioning (for example, Bouton & Peck, 1989; Goddard, 1999), in conditioned inhibition (Fiori, Barnet, & Miller, 1994), and in various instrumental conditioning situations (for example, Nakajima, Tanaka, Urushihara, & Imada, 2000). Interestingly, the phenomenon is evident not just with external contextual cues but with contextual cues created by drug states (for example, Bouton, Kenney, & Rosengard, 1990; Cunningham, 1979). Renewal can also occur if the subject is removed from the context of extinction to an alternate context that is not the context of original acquisition (Bouton & Ricker, 1994). However, this type of renewal is not as robust as the renewal that occurs when the context of original acquisition is reinstated.

A simple and rather uninteresting explanation of the renewal effect is that it is due to excitatory properties conditioned to the renewal context. This interpretation readily comes to mind if original acquisition is conducted in one context (A), extinction is conducted in another context (B), and the subjects are then returned to Context A. Because the US was presented in Context A during acquisition, Context A presumably acquired excitatory properties. If these excitatory properties summate with any residual excitation remaining to the CS, responding to the CS will be greater in Context A than Context B. A number of control experiments, however, have ruled out this kind of simple summation explanation of the renewal effect. In one study (Harris et al., 2000, Experiment 1), for example, original acquisition with two different conditioned stimuli was conducted in Context C. One CS was then extinguished in Context A and the other was extinguished in Context B. Subsequent tests revealed that responding to the CS extinguished in Context A was renewed if this CS was tested in Context B. This outcome cannot be attributed to possible excitatory properties of the Context B because the US was never presented in Context B. (For additional experiments that rule out context excitation, see Bouton & Ricker, 1994.)

The preponderance of evidence indicates that the renewal effect occurs because the memory of extinction is specific to the cues that were present during the extinction phase. Therefore, a shift away from the context of extinction disrupts retrieval of the memory of extinction, with the result that extinction performance is lost. But why should this restore behavior characteristic of the original acquisition? To account for that, one has to make the added assumption that original acquisition performance generalizes from one context to another more easily than does extinction performance. This is indeed the case. For example, in the experiment by Bouton and King (1983) I described earlier, acquisition for all subjects occurred in Context A. Half the subjects were then shifted to Context B for extinction. Figure 9.4 shows that these subjects performed the same way during the extinction phase as subjects that remained in Context A during extinction. Thus, a shift in context did not disrupt the originally acquired conditioned suppression.

Why is it that original acquisition is less disrupted (if at all) by a change in context when extinction performance is highly context-specific? Bouton (1993, 1994) has suggested that contextual cues serve to disambiguate the significance of a conditioned stimulus. This function is similar to the function of semantic context in disambiguating the meaning of a word. Consider the word *cut*. Cut could refer to the physical procedure of creating two pieces, as in "The chef cut the carrots." Alternatively, it could refer to dropping a player from a team, as in "Johnny was cut from the team after the first game." The meaning of the word cut depends on the semantic context. A CS that has undergone excitatory conditioning and then extinction also has an ambiguous meaning, in that the CS could signify an impending US (acquisition) or the absence of the US (extinction). This ambiguity allows the CS to come under contextual control more easily. After acquisition training alone, the CS is not ambiguous because it signifies only one thing (impending US delivery). Therefore, such a CS is not as susceptible to contextual control.

The renewal effect has important implications for behavior therapy, and unfortunately these implications are rather troubling. It suggests that even if a therapeutic procedure is effective in extinguishing a pathological fear or phobia in the relative safety of a therapist's office, the conditioned fear may easily return when the client encounters the fear CS in a different context. Equally problematic is the fact that the effects of excitatory conditioning readily generalize from one context to another (see, for example, the left panel of Figure 9.4). Thus, if you acquire a pathological fear in one situation, the fear is likely to plague you in a variety of other contexts. But if you overcome your fear in a particular context, that benefit will not generalize as readily. The renewal effect suggests that problems created by conditioning will have much more widespread effects than the solutions or remedies for those problems.

Troubled by the above dilemma, investigators have explored ways to reduce the renewal effect. One procedure that shows promise is to conduct extinction in a variety of different contexts. Extinction performance is less context-specific if extinction training is carried out in several different alternative contexts (Chelonis, Calton, Hart, & Schachtman, 1999; Gunther, Denniston, & Miller, 1998). Other techniques for reducing the renewal effect involve conditioned inhibition training, differential conditioning, and presenting the CS explicitly paired with the US (Rauhut, Thomas, & Ayres, 2001). (For further discussion of the implications of the renewal effect for behavior therapy, see Bouton, 1988; Bouton & Nelson, 1998.)

Restoration of Extinction Performance

The renewal effect involves reactivating the memory of original excitatory conditioning by shifting the subject out of contextual cues that were present during extinction. More generally, this represents reactivating a previously learned behavior by changing the context to better approximate conditions present when that behavior was previously acquired. This general strategy has been applied to a variety of situations in which something learned is then altered by a second learning experience (Bouton, 1991, 1993). In particular, the strategy can be applied to extinction—that is, extinction performance can be restored by introducing contextual cues that reactivate the memory of extinction. This has been examined within the framework of the phenomenon of spontaneous recovery.

As I described earlier, spontaneous recovery involves the recovery of originally conditioned behavior following extinction if a sufficient period of time passes after the extinction phase. Extinction-like behavior can be restored (thus counteracting spontaneous recovery) by presenting cues that were present during the extinction phase. Such renewal of extinction has been observed in taste-aversion learning (Brooks, Palmatier, Garcia, & Johnson, 1999) as well as in appetitive conditioning preparations (Brooks, 2000; Brooks & Bouton, 1993). Various control experiments have encouraged the conclusion that extinction cues counteract spontaneous recovery because they reactivate the memory of extinction. These results are consistent with the hypothesis that spontaneous recovery is due to a deterioration of the contextual cues of extinction with the passage of time (Bouton, 1993).

Reinstatement of Conditioned Excitation

Another procedure that serves to restore responding to an extinguished conditioned stimulus is called **reinstatement.** Reinstatement refers to the recovery of excitatory responding to an extinguished stimulus produced by exposures to the unconditioned stimulus. Consider, for example, learning an aversion to french fries because you got sick after eating some on a trip. Your aversion is then extinguished by nibbling on french fries without getting sick on a number of occasions. You may actually regain your enjoyment of french fries because of this extinction experience. The phenomenon of reinstatement suggests that if you were to become sick again for some reason, your aversion to french fries would return even if your illness had nothing to do with eating this particular food. (For an analogous study with laboratory rats, see Schachtman, Brown, & Miller, 1985.)

As with renewal, reinstatement is a troublesome phenomenon for behavior therapy. Behavior therapy often involves trying to get clients to stop doing things that are problematic for them. Extinction may be one of the techniques for reducing behavior. Because of reinstatement, responses that are successfully extinguished during the course of therapeutic intervention can recur if the individual encounters the unconditioned stimulus again. Fear and anxiety that are acquired during the course of being in an abusive relationship or living with an abusive parent can return even after years of therapy if the individual encounters similar forms of abuse later in life.

In the initial experiments on the reinstatement effect (for example, Rescorla & Heth, 1975), excitatory conditioning, extinction, and subsequent reinstatement US exposures were all conducted in the same experimental context. As was the case with the renewal effect, it is important to consider whether the reinstatement effect may be a result of context conditioning. Context conditioning is a possible contributor because the US presentations that occurred during the reinstatement phase can result in conditioning of the contextual cues of the experimental situation. That context conditioning could then summate with any excitation remaining to the CS at the end of extinction, to produce the reinstatement of conditioned responding.

A great deal of research has been done on the reinstatement effect in the past 20 years (see Bouton, 1993, 1994; Bouton & Nelson, 1998). The results have indicated that contextual conditioning is important but not because it permits summation of excitation. Furthermore, as was the case with renewal, the role of context is to disambiguate the significance of a stimulus that has a mixed history of conditioning and extinction. Context has relatively little effect on stimuli that have a history of only conditioning.

These conclusions are supported by the results of an early study by Bouton (1984). The experiment was conducted in the conditioned suppression preparation with rats. The procedure is summarized in Table 9.1. For half the subjects, reinstatement was conducted after conditioning a CS with a weak shock that produced only moderate levels of conditioned

TABLE 9.1	EFFECTS OF REINSTATEMENT AFTER ACQUISITION ALONE OR AFTER BOTH ACQUISITION AND EXTINCTION (Bouton, 1984)			
PHASE 1	**PHASE 2**	**REINSTATEMENT**	**TEST**	
CS → Weak shock	No treatment	Shock same	CS	
CS → Weak shock	No treatment	Shock different	CS	
CS → Strong shock	Extinction	Shock same	CS	
CS → Strong shock	Extinction	Shock different	CS	

suppression. The remaining subjects were initially conditioned with a strong shock that resulted in substantially more conditioned suppression. However, extinction was then provided so that by the time the reinstatement procedure was introduced, the level of suppression in these subjects was similar to the suppression in the first group. Thus, reinstatement was introduced when responding to the CS was similar in all subjects; but some of them got to that point by receiving only conditioning, whereas for the others the CS was both conditioned and extinguished. Reinstatement consisted of delivering four unsignaled shocks either in the context of testing or in an alternate context. The results of tests conducted after the reinstatement USs are presented in Figure 9.5.

For subjects that did not receive extinction (left side of Figure 9.5), it did not make any difference whether the reinstatement shocks occurred in the test context (shock same) or elsewhere (shock different). This outcome shows that contextual conditioning did not summate with the suppression elicited by the target CS. In contrast, for subjects that received extinction (right side of Figure 9.5), reinstatement shocks given in the same context as test-

Figure 9.5 Demonstration of reinstatement of conditioned suppression. Four reinstatement shocks were delivered either in the training and test context (Shock same) or in a different context (Shock different) after just excitatory conditioning (Conditioned only CS) or after conditioning and extinction (Conditioned and extinguished CS). (From William O'Donohue, ed., *Learning and Behavior Therapy.* Copyright 1998 by Allyn & Bacon. Reprinted by permission.)

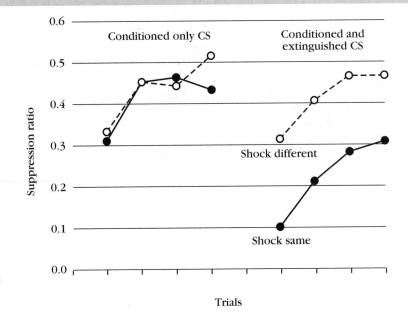

ing produced significantly more response suppression than shocks given in a different context. This outcome shows that context conditioning facilitates the reinstatement effect. (For additional research on the role of context conditioning in the reinstatement effect, see Richardson, Duffield, Bailey, & Westbrook, 1999.)

Results such as those presented in Figure 9.5 have encouraged Bouton to think about reinstatement as a form of renewal. According to this interpretation, conditioned contextual cues provide some of the contextual cues for excitatory responding under ordinary circumstances. These contextual cues become extinguished when the CS is presented by itself during extinction. Reinstatement US presentations in the test context serve to restore the excitatory properties of the contextual cues and thereby enable those cues to be more effective in reactivating the memory of excitatory conditioning of the CS.

Sensitivity to Reinforcer Devaluation

The persistence of original learning despite extinction can also be examined by evaluating the effects of reinforcer devaluation. As I described in Chapter 4, reinforcer or US devaluation in Pavlovian conditioning disrupts performance of the conditioned response if the CR was the product of S-S rather than S-R learning. Rescorla has used the US devaluation technique to determine whether the CS-US association established through Pavlovian conditioning persists through extinction. If extinction does not disrupt a CS-US association, then US devaluation will disrupt responding to an extinguished CS, just as it disrupts responding to a CS that has not undergone extinction.

The outline of one experiment (Rescorla, 1996a, Experiment 2) is presented in Table 9.2. Rats received appetitive conditioning with food and sucrose as the US. For each subject a light was paired with one of the USs and a tone was paired with the other. Which CS was paired with which US was counterbalanced across subjects, and each CS was always paired only with its own US. As conditioning progressed, each subject came to insert its head in

| TABLE 9.2 | EFFECTS OF US DEVALUATION ON A PAVLOVIAN CS FOLLOWING EXTINCTION (Rescorla 1996a, Experiment 2) | | |

PHASE 1	PHASE 2	US DEVALUATION	TEST
Group Ext			
CS → US1	CS1 Ext		CS1
and	and	US1 → LiCl	and
CS2 → US2	CS2 Ext		CS2
Group NotExt			
CS → US1			CS1
and		US1 → LiCl	and
CS2 → US2			CS2

CS1 and CS2 were a light and a tone (counterbalanced across subjects). US1 and US2 were sucrose and food pellets (counterbalanced across subjects and CSs). Before the US Devaluation phase, both CS1 and CS2 were conditioned with a third US (polycose).

the food magazine as the conditioned response (goal tracking). The rate of goal tracking during each CS was about 20 responses/minute at the end of the acquisition phase. Following acquisition, group Ext received extinction trials with both CS1 and CS2. This reduced their responding to CS1 and CS2 to about 1 response/minute. The control group (NotExt) was placed in the experimental chamber during the extinction phase but did not get either CS1 or CS2 trials.

The extinction phase was followed by training in which all subjects had CS1 and CS2 paired with a new US (US3: polycose). This was done to make sure all subjects would show some responding to the CSs during the final test session. US3 was deliberately selected for retraining to be sure that retraining would not influence whatever associations each CS still had with US1 and US2. All of the subjects then had the value of US1 reduced by taste-aversion conditioning. Presentations of US1 in the experimental chamber were followed by an injection of lithium chloride that served to make the rats feel sick. After US devaluation, each subject was tested with CS1 and CS2.

The results of the first two presentations of CS1 and CS2 during the test session are summarized in Figure 9.6. Despite retraining with polycose as the US, responding to CS1 and CS2 in the extinction group was a bit lower than responding in the control group (NotExt). Nevertheless, the two groups showed equal sensitivity to US devaluation. In each group, responding to the CS whose associated US had been devalued was lower than responding to the CS whose associated US had not been devalued. This pattern of results could have occurred only if extinction allowed the original CS-US associations to remain intact. Thus, this pattern of results indicates that a CS-US association remains intact despite extinction of the CS.

One might argue that the conditioned stimuli in this experiment remained sensitive to devaluation of their associated US because not enough extinction trials had been conducted. Six extinction sessions were conducted, with each CS presented eight times during each ses-

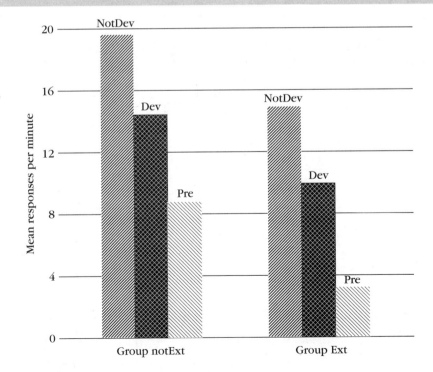

Figure 9.6 Susceptibility of a Pavlovian conditioned stimulus to the effects of US devaluation as a function of whether the CS had (or had not) undergone extinction previously. (Procedures are summarized in Table 9.2. Adapted from Rescorla, 1996a.)

sion. This was clearly enough to produce a major extinction effect because, as I noted above, responding declined from about 20 responses/minute to about 1 response/minute. Thus, extinction had a large impact. It is remarkable that despite this large effect of extinction on conditioned responding, the extinction manipulation did not reduce the sensitivity of the subjects to US devaluation, indicating that the CS-US association remained intact. (For additional related studies, see Delamater, 1996; Rescorla, 2001a.)

Experiments similar to the above study of US devaluation have also been conducted using instrumental conditioning procedures, in which subjects have to perform a specified response to obtain a reinforcer outcome (R → O). As I discussed in Chapter 7, if the instrumental conditioning procedure results in the learning of an R-O association, then devaluation of the reinforcer will produce a decline in the instrumental response. Rescorla has examined whether this susceptibility of instrumental behavior to reinforcer devaluation remains intact through extinction. The procedure for one experiment is summarized in Table 9.3.

Rats were trained to make four different instrumental responses (pressing a lever, pulling a chain, pulling a handle below the grid floor, and nosing a response key) with two different types of food (sucrose and food pellets) serving as the reinforcers. Training procedures were arranged so that within each of a pair of responses, one response (R1 or R3) was reinforced by one of the food types (O1) and the other response (R2 or R4) was reinforced by the second reinforcer (O2), as indicated in Table 9.3. One pair of responses (R1 and R2) was then extinguished. This was then followed by devaluation of the first food type (O1) using a taste-aversion conditioning procedure. As in the Pavlovian conditioning study, the extinguished responses (R1 and R2) were retrained with a third reinforcer (polycose) before the devaluation procedure to make sure that some responding would be evident during the final test.

The results of the experiment are summarized in Figure 9.7. The usual finding with responses that have not been extinguished is that devaluation of a reinforcer reduces the rate of its associated response. This was indeed the case when the subjects were tested with the two responses (R3 and R4) that had not undergone extinction. When given a choice between R3 and R4, the subjects exhibited fewer of the responses whose reinforcer had been devalued (see left panel of Figure 9.7). The primary question in the study was whether this effect would also occur with responses R1 and R2 that had undergone extinction. This was indeed the case (see right panel of Figure 9.7). Although the overall level of responding was

---

TABLE 9.3   **EFFECTS OF REINFORCER DEVALUATION ON INSTRUMENTAL RESPONDING FOLLOWING EXTINCTION** (Rescorla 1993a, Experiment 3)

PHASE 1	PHASE 2	US DEVALUATION	TEST
R1 → O1	R1 Ext		R1 vs. R2
R2 → O2	R2 Ext	O1 → LiCl	and
R3 → O1			R3 vs. R4
R4 → O2			

R1, R2, R3, and R4 were four different instrumental responses (counterbalanced across subjects). O1 and O2 were sucrose and food pellets (counterbalanced across subjects and responses). Before the US Devaluation phase both R1 and R2 were reconditioned with a third reinforcer (O3: polycose).

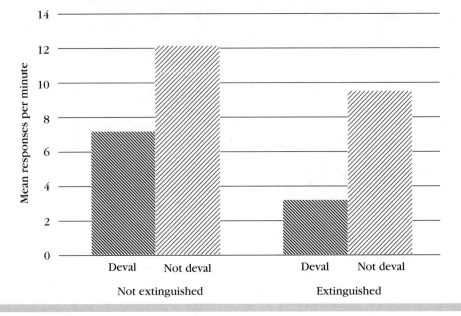

Figure 9.7 Effects of reinforcer devaluation (Deval) evaluated with two responses that have not been extinguished and two responses that previously underwent extinction. (From Figure 4, p. 242, in R. A. Rescorla, *Animal Learning & Behavior*, Vol. 21a. Copyright 1993 Psychonomic Society, Inc. Reprinted with permission.)

less for the responses that had undergone extinction, the devaluation effect was still very much in evidence.

The findings presented in Figure 9.7 and other similar studies have encouraged the conclusion that extinction does not eliminate the R-O and S-O associations that are learned during the course of instrumental conditioning. Rescorla (1993a), for example, has commented that "R-O associations, once trained, are relatively impervious to modification" (p. 244). (For related studies, see Rescorla, 1992, 1993b, 1996, 2001a.)

WHAT IS LEARNED IN EXTINCTION?

The evidence reviewed in the preceding section emphasized that extinction does not involve "unlearning" and that extinction leaves R-O and S-O associations pretty much intact. If these critical associations remain intact, why does responding decline in extinction procedures? In discussing Pavlovian conditioning, I reviewed evidence indicating that S-S associations or S-S learning is more important than S-R learning (see Chapter 4). In discussing instrumental conditioning, I reviewed evidence indicating that S-O and R-O associations are more important than the S-R association that Thorndike emphasized (see Chapter 7). These discussions reflected the major shift away from S-R mechanisms that has occurred in contemporary learning theory during the last quarter of the twentieth century. But this emphasis on S-S and R-O associations creates a dilemma for theories of extinction.

Inhibitory S-R Associations

If conditioned behavior is supported primarily by S-S and R-O associations and these associations are not degraded during the course of extinction, why does extinction produce a decline in responding? In trying to answer this question, investigators have resurrected the importance of S-R associations. However, instead of focusing on excitatory S-R associations, as Thorndike originally did, contemporary investigators have come to the conclusion that nonreinforcement produces an inhibitory S-R association. That is, nonreinforcement of a response in the presence of a specific stimulus produces an inhibitory S-R association that serves to suppress that response whenever S is present. Consistent with the renewal effect, this hypothesis predicts that the effects of extinction will be highly specific to the context in which the response was extinguished.

Why should nonreinforcement produce an inhibitory S-R association? In answering this question, it is important to keep in mind that extinction involves a special type of nonreinforcement. It involves nonreinforcement after a history of reinforcement. Nonreinforcement without such a prior history is not extinction but more akin to habituation. This is an important distinction because nonreinforcement is aversive only after a history of reinforcement. Thus, the emotional effects of nonreinforcement depend critically on the subject's prior history. If your partner never made you coffee in the morning, you will not be disappointed if the coffee is not ready when you get up. If you never received an allowance, you will not be disappointed when you don't get one. It is only the omission of an expected reward that creates disappointment or frustration. Furthermore, these emotional effects are presumed to play a critical role in the behavioral decline that occurs in extinction.

As I mentioned at the outset of the chapter, extinction involves both behavioral and emotional effects. The emotional effects stem from the frustration that is triggered when an expected reinforcer is not forthcoming. Nonreinforcement in the face of the expectation of reward is assumed to trigger an unconditioned aversive frustrative reaction (Amsel, 1958). This aversive emotion serves to discourage responding during the course of extinction through the establishment of an inhibitory S-R association (Rescorla, 2001a).

The establishment of an inhibitory S-R association during the course of extinction is illustrated by an experiment whose procedures are outlined in Table 9.4. The subjects first received discrimination training in which a common response (Rc) was reinforced with food pellets whenever a light or noise stimulus (L or N) was present. This training was conducted so that nonreinforcement in the presence of L or N would elicit frustration when extinction was introduced. The targets of extinction were a lever press and a chain pull response (designated as R1 and R2, counterbalanced across subjects). To allow extinction of these responses, they were first reinforced, again with food pellets. Notice that the reinforcement of R1 and R2 did not occur in the presence of the light and noise stimuli. Therefore, this reinforcement training was not expected to establish any S-R associations involving the light and noise stimuli.

Extinction was conducted in the third phase and consisted of presentations of L and N (to create the expectancy of reward) with either R1 or R2 available but nonreinforced. The

TABLE 9.4	DEVELOPMENT OF AN INHIBITORY S-R ASSOCIATION IN INSTRUMENTAL EXTINCTION (Rescorla 1993b, Experiment 3)		
PHASE 1	PHASE 2	EXTINCTION	TEST
N: Rc → P	R1 → P	N: R1–	N: R1, R2
L: Rc → P	R2 → P	L: R2–	L: R1, R2

N and L were noise and light discriminative stimuli. Rc was a common response (nose poking) for all subjects, P represents the food pellet reinforcer, R1 and R2 were lever press and chain pull, counterbalanced across subjects.

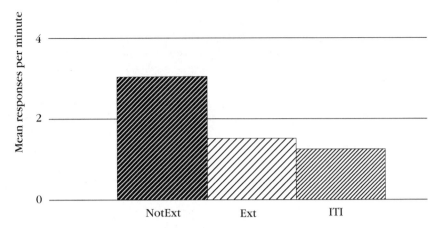

Figure 9.8 Demonstration that extinction involves the acquisition of an inhibitory S-R association that is specific to the stimulus in the presence of which the response is nonreinforced (see procedure summarized in Table 9.4). A particular response occurred less often during the stimulus with which the response had been extinguished than during an alternate stimulus. (From Rescorla, 1993b.)

extinction phase presumably established inhibitory S-R associations involving N-R1 and L-R2. The presence of these associations was tested by measuring the rate of R1 and R2 in the presence of the L and N stimuli. If an inhibitory N-R1 association was established during extinction, the subjects were predicted to make fewer R1 than R2 responses when tested with N. In a corresponding fashion, they were expected to make fewer R2 than R1 responses when tested with L. Notice that this differential response outcome cannot be explained in terms of changes in R-O or S-O associations because such changes should have affected R1 and R2 equally.

The results of the experiment are presented in Figure 9.8. Responding is shown for the intertrial interval (ITI) and in the presence of the stimulus (L or N) with which the response had been extinguished or not. Responding during the stimulus with which the response had been extinguished was significantly less than responding during the alternate stimulus. Furthermore, the extinction stimulus produced responding not significantly higher than what occurred during the intertrial interval. These results indicate that the extinction procedure produced an inhibitory S-R association that was specific to a particular stimulus and response. (For related studies, see Rescorla, 1997a, 1997c.)

The proposition that extinction involves the learning of an inhibitory association is contrary to conventional wisdom that considered conditioned inhibition and extinction to be different phenomena. In previous editions of this text, for example, I emphasized that extinction should not be considered a case of conditioned inhibition because an extinguished stimulus does not pass the conventional summation and retardation-of-acquisition tests for conditioned inhibition (for example, Domjan & Burkhard, 1982, 1986; Domjan, 1993, 1998). However, the distinction between extinction and inhibition is becoming increasingly difficult to maintain in light of data such as those presented in Figure 9.8. Some studies have also demonstrated that extinguished stimuli can pass both of the conventional tests for conditioned inhibition. For example, Carlton, Mitchell, and Schachtman (1996) reported that in a taste-aversion conditioning preparation, an extinguished CS is slower to reacquire excitatory properties than a novel flavor. In addition, an extinguished CS can attenuate responding to a previously established excitatory stimulus, in a summation test (see also Schachtman, Threlkeld, & Meyer, 2000). Evidence that an extinguished CS passes the retardation-of-acquisition test of inhibition has also been reported by Bouton (1986) and Bouton and Swartzentruber (1989). (For additional consideration of retardation of acquisition following extinction, see Bouton & Nelson, 1998; Hart, Bourne, & Schachtman, 1995; Ricker & Bouton, 1996; Rescorla, 2001b). Few published studies of the summation test following extinction are available, and it remains to be seen whether the type of inhibition that is involved in extinction is the same as more traditional forms of Pavlovian conditioned inhibition.

"Paradoxical" Reward Effects

If the decline in responding in extinction is due to the frustrative effects of an unexpected absence of reinforcement, then one would expect more rapid extinction following training that establishes greater expectations of reward. This is indeed the case and has led to a number of paradoxical effects. For example, the more training that is provided with reinforcement, the stronger will be the expectancy of reward, and therefore the stronger will be the frustration that occurs when extinction is introduced. If the decline in responding is due to the frustrative effects of nonreward, more extensive reinforcement training should produce more rapid extinction. This prediction has been confirmed and is called the **overtraining extinction effect** (Ishida & Papini, 1997; Senkowski, 1978; Theios & Brelsford, 1964).

The overtraining extinction effect is "paradoxical" because it represents fewer responses in extinction after more extensive reinforcement training. Thinking casually, an observer might think that more extensive training should create a "stronger" response that would be more resistant to extinction. But the opposite is the case, especially when training involves continuous reinforcement.

Another paradoxical reward effect that reflects similar mechanisms is the **magnitude reinforcement extinction effect.** This phenomenon refers to the fact that responding declines more rapidly in extinction following reinforcement with a larger reinforcer. This phenomenon is also most commonly observed if training involves continuous reinforcement (Hulse, 1958; Wagner, 1961), and is readily accounted for in terms of the frustrative effects of nonreward. Nonreinforcement is apt to be more frustrative if the individual has come to expect a large reward than if the individual has come to expect a small reward. Consider two scenarios: In one, you receive $100/month from your parents to help with incidental expenses at college; in the other, you get only $20/month. In both cases, your parents stop the payments when you drop out of school for a semester. This nonreinforcement will be more aversive if you had come to expect the larger monthly allowance.

The most extensively investigated paradoxical reward effect is the **partial reinforcement extinction effect.** A key factor that determines the magnitude of both the behavioral and the emotional effects of an extinction procedure is the schedule of reinforcement that was in effect before the extinction procedure was introduced. Various subtle features of reinforcement schedules can influence the extinction of instrumental responses. But the dominant schedule characteristic that determines extinction effects is whether the instrumental response was reinforced every time it occurred (**continuous reinforcement**) or only some of the times it occurred (**intermittent,** or *partial,* **reinforcement**). The general finding is that extinction is much slower and involves fewer frustration reactions if partial reinforcement rather than continuous reinforcement was in effect before introduction of the extinction procedure. This phenomenon is called the *partial reinforcement extinction effect,* or PREE.

In one interesting study, the emergence of the PREE during the course of infant development was examined with infant rats serving as subjects (Chen & Amsel, 1980). The rat pups were permitted to run down an alley for a chance to suckle, and they obtained milk as the reinforcer. Some pups were reinforced each time (continuous reinforcement), whereas others were reinforced only some of the time (partial reinforcement). Following training, all of the subjects were tested under conditions of extinction. The experiment was repeated with rat pups of two different ages. In one replication, the experiment began when the pups were 10 days of age. In another, the experiment began when the subjects were 12 days old— just 2 days later. The results are presented in Figure 9.9.

All of the rat pups acquired the runway instrumental response. As might be expected, the 12-day-old pups ran faster than the 10-day-olds, but the 10-day-olds also increased their running speeds with training. This increase in the speed of running was due to the instrumental reinforcement, not to getting older, because when extinction was introduced, all of the subjects slowed down. However, a difference in extinction between continuous reinforcement and partial reinforcement developed only for the pups that began the experiment at 12 days of age. Thus, the PREE was evident in 12-day-old rat pups but not in 10-day-old pups. On the basis of a variety of different lines of evidence, Amsel (1992) has concluded that this developmental difference in the emergence of the PREE is related to the rapid maturation of the hippocampus during this stage of life in rat pups.

The persistence in responding that is created by intermittent reinforcement can be remarkable. Habitual gamblers are at the mercy of intermittent reinforcement. Occasional winnings encourage them to continue gambling during long strings of losses. Intermittent reinforcement can also have undesirable consequences in parenting. Consider, for example, a child riding in a grocery cart while the parent is shopping. The child asks the parent to buy a piece of candy for him. The parent says no. The child asks again and again and then begins to throw a temper tantrum because the parent continues to say no. At this point, the parent is likely to give in to avoid public embarrassment. By finally buying the candy, the parent will have provided intermittent reinforcement for the repeated demands for candy. The parent will also have reinforced the tantrum behavior. The intermittent reinforcement of the requests for candy will make the child very persistent in asking for candy during future shopping trips.

Although most studies of the partial reinforcement extinction have employed instrumental conditioning procedures, the PREE has also been demonstrated in Pavlovian conditioning (for recent examples, see Pearce, Redhead, & Aydin, 1997; Rescorla, 1999). In early studies, the PREE was found only in studies that compared the effects of continuous and partial reinforcement training in different groups of subjects. Recent studies have demonstrated that the PREE can also occur in the same subjects if they experience continuous reinforcement in the presence of one set of cues and intermittent reinforcement in the presence of other stimuli (for example, Pearce, Redhead, & Aydin, 1997; Rescorla, 1999c; Svartdal, 2000; Zarcone, Branch, Hughes, & Pennypacker, 1997). This within-subject PREE presents theoretical challenges that so far have not been completely worked out.

Mechanisms of the Partial Reinforcement Extinction Effect

Perhaps the most obvious explanation of the PREE is that the introduction of extinction is easier to detect after continuous reinforcement than after partial reinforcement. If you don't receive the reinforcer after each response during training, you may not immediately notice when reinforcers are omitted altogether. The absence of reinforcement is presumably much

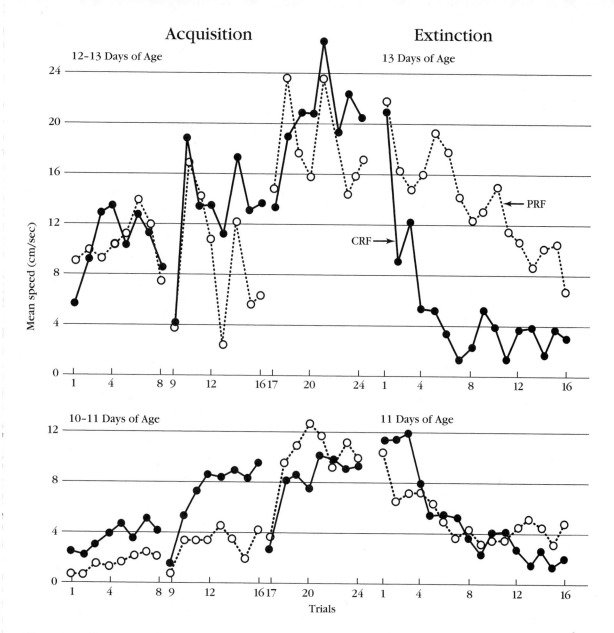

Figure 9.9 Emergence of the partial reinforcement extinction effect between the 10th and 12th day of life in infant rat pups. During acquisition, the pups were reinforced with a chance to suckle milk after running down an alley on either a continuous or a partial reinforcement schedule. Extinction was introduced after 3 sessions of reinforcement training. (From Figure 1, p. 484, J. S. Chen & A. Amsel, in *Developmental Psychobiology*, Vol. 13. © John Wiley & Sons. Reprinted by permission of John Wiley & Sons, Inc.)

easier to detect after continuous reinforcement. This explanation of the partial reinforcement extinction effect is called the **discrimination hypothesis.**

Although the discrimination hypothesis provides an intuitively reasonable explanation, the partial reinforcement extinction effect is not so straightforward. In an ingenious test of the discrimination hypothesis, Jenkins (1962) and Theios (1962) first trained one group of animals with partial reinforcement and another with continuous reinforcement. Both groups then received a phase of continuous reinforcement before extinction was introduced. Because the extinction procedure was introduced immediately after continuous reinforcement training for both groups, extinction was presumably equally noticeable or discriminable for both. Nevertheless, Jenkins and Theios found that the subjects that initially received partial reinforcement training responded more in extinction. These results indicate that the response persistence produced by partial reinforcement does not come from greater difficulty in detecting the start of extinction. Rather, it seems that subjects learn something long-lasting from partial reinforcement that is carried over if they receive a period of continuous reinforcement before extinction. Partial reinforcement seems to teach subjects to not give up in the face of failure, and this learned persistence is retained even if subjects subsequently experience an unbroken string of successes.

What do subjects learn during partial reinforcement that makes them more persistent in the face of a run of bad luck or failure? Numerous complicated experiments have been performed in attempts to answer this question. These studies indicate that partial reinforcement promotes persistence in two different ways. One explanation, **frustration theory,** is based on what subjects learn about the emotional effects of nonreward during partial reinforcement training. The other explanation, **sequential theory,** is based on what subjects learn about the memory of nonreward.

A. Amsel

Frustration Theory. Frustration theory was developed by Abram Amsel (for example, 1958, 1962, 1967, 1992). According to frustration theory, persistence in extinction results from learning something paradoxical, namely, to continue responding when you expect to be nonreinforced or frustrated. Frustration theory assumes that intermittent reinforcement results in learning to respond in the face of expected nonreinforcement. However, this learning requires considerable experience with intermittent reinforcement.

Frustration theory characterizes the learning that occurs during the course of intermittent reinforcement in terms of stages. Intermittent reinforcement involves both rewarded and nonrewarded trials. Rewarded trials lead individuals to expect reinforcement, and nonrewarded trials lead them to expect the absence of reward. Consequently, intermittent reinforcement leads to the learning of expectations of both reward and nonreward. At first, the expectation of reward encourages subjects to respond, and the anticipation of nonreinforcement discourages responding. Thus, early in training, subjects trained with intermittent reinforcement are in a conflict about what to do. Their expectations encourage opposite response tendencies. As training continues, however, this conflict is resolved in favor of responding.

The resolution of the conflict occurs because reinforcement is not predictable in the typical partial reinforcement schedule. The instrumental response ends up being reinforced some of the times when the subject expects nonreward. Because of such experiences, the instrumental response becomes conditioned to the expectation of nonreward. According to frustration theory, this is the key to persistent responding in extinction. With sufficient training, *intermittent reinforcement results in learning to make the instrumental response as a reaction to the expectation of nonreward.* Once the response has become conditioned to the expectation of nonreward, responding persists when extinction is introduced. By contrast, there is nothing about the experience of continuous reinforcement that encourages subjects to respond when they expect nonreward. Continuous reinforcement does not produce persistence in extinction.

Sequential Theory. Sequential theory was proposed by Capaldi (for example, 1967, 1971) and is stated in terms of memory concepts. It assumes that subjects can remember whether they were reinforced for performing the instrumental response in the recent past. They remember both recent rewarded and nonrewarded trials. The theory assumes further that during intermittent reinforcement training, the memory of nonreward becomes a cue for performing the instrumental response. According to sequential theory, this produces persistence in extinction. Precisely how this happens depends greatly on the sequence of rewarded (R) and nonrewarded (N) trials that are administered in the intermittent reinforcement schedule. That is why the theory is labeled "sequential."

Consider the following sequence of trials: RNN<u>R</u>RN<u>R</u>. The subject is rewarded on the first trial, not rewarded on the next two trials, then rewarded twice, then not rewarded, and then rewarded again. The fourth and last trials are critical in this schedule and are therefore underlined. On the fourth trial, the subject is reinforced after receiving nonreward on the preceding two trials. It is assumed that the subject remembers the two nonrewarded trials when it is reinforced on the fourth trial. Because of this, the memory of two nonrewarded trials becomes a cue for responding. Responding in the face of the memory of nonreward is again reinforced on the last trial. On the last trial, the animal is reinforced for responding during the memory of one nonreinforced trials. With enough experiences of this type, the subject learns to respond whenever it remembers not having been reinforced on the preceding trials. This learning creates persistence of the instrumental response in extinction. (For more recent studies of this mechanism, see Capaldi, Alptekin, & Birmingham, 1996; Capaldi, Alptekin, Miller, & Barry, 1992; Haggbloom, Lovelace, Brewer, Levins, & Owens, 1990.)

Some have regarded frustration theory and sequential theory as competing explanations of the partial reinforcement extinction effect. However, since the two mechanisms were originally proposed, a large and impressive body of evidence has been obtained in support of each theory. Therefore, neither theory can be regarded as correct and the other as incorrect. Rather, the two theories point out two different ways in which partial reinforcement can promote responding during extinction. Memory mechanisms may make more of a contribution when training trials are not separated by long intertrial intervals (thus, reducing the difficulty of remembering the outcome of the preceding trial). In contrast, the emotional learning described by frustration theory is less sensitive to intertrial intervals and thus provides a better explanation of the PREE when widely spaced training trials are used. The prudent conclusion is that both mechanisms contribute to persistence in most situations.

E. J. Capaldi

RESISTANCE TO CHANGE AND BEHAVIORAL MOMENTUM

Another way to think about response persistence in extinction is that it represents resistance to the change in reinforcement contingencies that occurs when the extinction procedure is introduced. Nevin and his colleagues have focused on resistance to change more generally and have proposed the concept of **behavioral momentum** to characterize the susceptibility of behavior to disruptions (Nevin, 1992, 1998; Nevin & Grace, 2000). The term *behavioral momentum* is based on the concept of momentum in Newtonian physics. The momentum of a physical object is the product of its weight (or mass) and its speed. A fast-moving bullet and a slow-moving freight train both have tremendous momentum, and because of that both are hard to stop. The bullet is not heavy but it moves very fast, making the product of its weight and speed high. A freight train moves slower than a bullet but is much heavier. As a consequence, the product of its weight and speed is also high. By analogy (and a detailed mathematical model), the behavioral momentum hypothesis predicts that behavior that has a great deal of momentum will also be hard to "stop" or disrupt by various manipulations.

Research on behavioral momentum has been conducted using multiple schedules of reinforcement. As I described in Chapter 8, a multiple schedule has two (or more) components. Each component is identified by a distinctive stimulus and its accompanying schedule of reinforcement. Multiple schedules are popular in studies of behavioral momentum because they enable investigators to compare the susceptibility of behavior to disruption under two different conditions in the same session. One observer may be interested, for example, in whether responding maintained by a continuous reinforcement schedule is more (or less) susceptible to disruption than responding maintained on a variable ratio schedule. Such a question can be answered by using a multiple CRF-VR schedule.

A number of different sources of disruption have been examined in studies of behavioral momentum. These have included providing extra food before the experimental session, providing extra food during intervals between components of the multiple schedule, and extinction. Although most of the research has employed laboratory animals, experiments have also been conducted with human subjects (for example, Mace, Lalli, Shea, Lalli, West, Roberts, & Nevin, 1990).

The basic behavioral momentum experiment is illustrated by a recent study that was conducted with two individuals who had severe mental retardation (Dube & McIlvane, 2001). One of the participants, HCB, was a 17-year-old woman whose mental age score was lower than 3 years. Two different instrumental tasks (A and B) were presented on a computer monitor, and pieces of food served as the reinforcer. In one task, a white square with a black cross appeared in one of the four corners of the computer screen, and HCB had to touch the square to get reinforced. In the other task, HCB had to touch one of two pictures that was the same as a picture that had been presented briefly at the start of the trial. The two tasks were alternated in blocks of 15 trials (either ABAB or BABA), with a 3-second pause between components. In the first phase of the experiment, responding on task A was reinforced on a CRF schedule, and responding on task B was reinforced on a variable ratio 4 schedule (VR4). After responding stabilized in each component (the baseline condition), tests of behavioral momentum were conducted. During the momentum test sessions, the CRF and VR4 components remained in effect, but HCB received some food before the session as well as during the pause between task components. In addition, HCB could see Disney cartoons on a TV screen near by, play with a toy displaying colored patterns, and hear an audiotape with various sound effects.

The results obtained in the first phase of the experiment are presented in the left panel of Figure 9.10. The rate of responding during the momentum test is shown as a proportion of the rate of responding during the baseline sessions when the disruptors were not presented. As expected, introducing the various sources of distraction during the test sessions resulted in a decrease in responding. More important, responding during the VR component was disrupted much more than responding during the CRF component. These results suggest that VR responding had less behavioral momentum than CRF responding.

During the second phase of the experiment, responding in each component of the multiple schedule was reinforced on a CRF schedule. The momentum test conducted with this multiple schedule is shown in the middle panel. This time, responding was equally disrupted in each of the components of the multiple schedule. The right panel of Figure 9.10 shows data from a third phase of the experiment, in which the multiple CRF-VR4 schedule was reintroduced. As in Phase 1, responding on the CRF component was less susceptible to disruption than responding on the VR4 component.

The results obtained with HCB illustrate two of the common (but not universal) outcomes of studies of behavioral momentum (see Nevin & Grace, 2000). The first is that

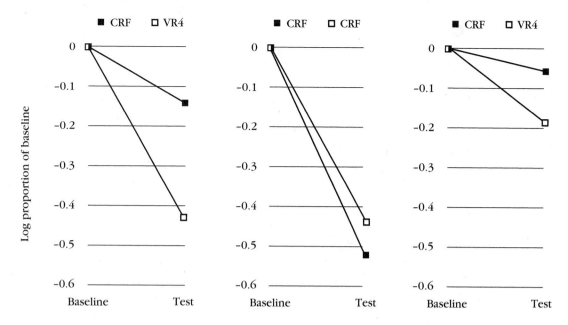

Figure 9.10 Responding on a multiple schedule by a mentally retarded individual (HCB) during baseline and behavioral momentum tests. In Phase 1, responding on components of the multiple schedule was reinforced on CRF and VR4 schedules. In Phase 2, responding in both components was reinforced on a CRF schedule. Phase 3 involved return to the CRF-VR4 multiple schedule. (After Dube & McIlvane, 2001.)

behavioral momentum is directly related to the rate of reinforcement. A higher rate of reinforcement produces behavior that has greater momentum and is less susceptible to disruption. Analyses of rates of reinforcement obtained by HCB indicated that she received a higher rate of reinforcement during the CRF component of the multiple schedule than during the VR component in Phases 1 and 3 of the experiment. In accordance with the generalization that behavioral momentum is directly related to rate of reinforcement, HCB's responding during the CRF component displayed greater momentum in Phases 1 and 3. When both components of the multiple schedule involved CRF (Phase 2), rates of reinforcement were similar in the two components, and measures of behavioral momentum were also similar.

Another common (but not universal) finding is that behavioral momentum is unrelated to response rate. Although this is not shown in Figure 9.10, HCB responded at similar rates on the CRF and VR4 components of the multiple schedule on Phases 1 and 3 of the experiment. Nevertheless, she showed differences in behavioral momentum in those two components. Thus, two behaviors that occur at similar rates do not necessarily have similar degrees of behavioral momentum (for example, Nevin, Mandell, & Atak, 1983). Nevin (1998; see also Nevin & Grace, 2000) has emphasized reinforcement rate rather than response rate as the primary determinant of behavioral momentum. This conclusion is further confirmed by studies showing that schedules that provide similar rates of reinforcement but different rates of responding have similar momentum or resistance to change (for example, Fath, Fields, Malott, & Grossett, 1983).

The primacy of reinforcement rate rather than response rate as the determinant of behavioral momentum has encouraged Nevin and Grace (2000) to attribute behavioral momentum primarily to Pavlovian conditioning or S-O associations (for example, McLean,

Campbell-Tie, & Nevin, 1996). How Pavlovian S-O associations serve to promote behavioral momentum has not been spelled out. In addition, some instances of behavioral momentum do not support the conclusion that stimulus-outcome associations or stimulus-reinforcer contingencies are the primary determining factor (Bell, 1999).

The behavioral momentum hypothesis has helped to characterize data from a variety of multiple schedule situations. (For recent examples, see Cohen, 1998; Grace & Nevin, 2000; Nevin & Grace, 1999.) The generality of the effects and their underlying mechanisms remain controversial. Perhaps the most serious challenge to the basic proposition that behavioral momentum is directly related to rate of reinforcement is the partial reinforcement extinction effect, or PREE. The PREE is a case in which resistance to extinction is greater following a lower rate or probability of reinforcement. The PREE is a commonly observed phenomenon, especially in discrete-trial studies conducted in runways. The challenge to the behavioral momentum hypothesis posed by the PREE has been recognized for more than a decade (for example, Nevin, 1988; see also Harper & McLean, 1992) without adequate resolution. Nevin and Grace (2000) have suggested that the PREE can be explained by assuming that extinction is less discriminable after intermittent rather than continuous reinforcement. This is essentially the discrimination hypothesis of the PREE. However, as I described earlier, this hypothesis is difficult to reconcile with the fact that partial reinforcement increases resistance to extinction even if a stage of continuous reinforcement is provided before the extinction procedure (Jenkins, 1962; Theios, 1962).

The idea of behavioral momentum is intriguing because it attempts to capture in a single concept the resistance of behavior to a variety of sources of change. A related overarching concept that has been entertained periodically is "response strength" (see Killeen & Hall, 2001, for a recent discussion). It remains to be seen whether a single concept can characterize behavioral persistence in the face of various sources of disruption. Some have suggested that the concept of behavioral momentum be applied only to sources of disruption that cause changes in performance rather than to ones that also produce new learning. This restriction is promising because it includes manipulations such as satiation and pre-session feeding, whose effects appear to be consistent with the behavioral momentum hypothesis. At the same time, the restriction excludes manipulations such as extinction, which produce data that are difficult to explain in terms of behavioral momentum.

CONCLUDING COMMENTS

In many ways, studies of extinction illustrate the enduring nature of certain issues in behavior theory. Early studies of extinction focused on the partial reinforcement extinction effect and other "paradoxical" reward effects and were conducted in the Hullian tradition that emphasized S-R learning. S-R mechanisms fell in disrepute with growing evidence that Pavlovian and instrumental conditioning involve S-O and R-O associations and are controlled or modulated by contextual cues. This body of evidence was part of the "cognitive revolution" that swept over psychology in the last quarter of the twentieth century. It gave us a better understanding of spontaneous recovery and led to the discovery of new phenomena such as renewal and reinstatement. However, these phenomena represent the failures of extinction rather than extinction itself. As I have described, understanding extinction itself has required a return to S-R concepts, this time in the form of inhibitory S-R associations. Investigators remain interested in what makes behavior resistant to change. Such resistance or behavioral momentum creates special challenges for behavior therapy.

SAMPLE QUESTIONS

1. Describe the basic behavioral and emotional consequences of extinction.
2. Describe the various ways in which control of behavior by contextual cues is relevant to the behavioral effects of extinction.
3. Describe evidence that identifies the development of inhibitory S-R associations in extinction.
4. Describe the partial reinforcement extinction effect and major explanations of the phenomenon.
5. Describe the concept of behavioral momentum. What are the advantages and disadvantages of the concept?

KEY TERMS

behavioral momentum The susceptibility of responding to disruption by manipulations such as pre-session feeding, delivery of free food, or a change in the schedule of reinforcement.

continuous reinforcement A schedule of reinforcement in which every occurrence of the instrumental response produces the reinforcer. Abbreviated CRF.

discrimination hypothesis An explanation of the partial reinforcement extinction effect, according to which extinction is slower after partial reinforcement than continuous reinforcement because the onset of extinction is more difficult to detect following partial reinforcement.

extinction (in classical conditioning) Reduction of a learned response that occurs because the conditioned stimulus is no longer paired with the unconditioned stimulus. Also, the procedure of repeatedly presenting a conditioned stimulus without the unconditioned stimulus.

extinction (in instrumental conditioning) Reduction of the instrumental response that occurs because the response is no longer followed by the reinforcer. Also, the procedure of no longer reinforcing the instrumental response.

forgetting A reduction of a learned response that occurs because of the passage of time, not because of particular experiences.

frustration An aversive emotional reaction that results from the unexpected absence of reinforcement.

frustration theory A theory of the partial reinforcement extinction effect, according to which extinction is retarded after partial reinforcement because the instrumental response becomes conditioned to the anticipation of frustrative nonreward.

intermittent reinforcement A schedule of reinforcement in which only some of the occurrences of the instrumental response are reinforced. The instrumental response is reinforced occasionally, or intermittently. Also called *partial reinforcement.*

magnitude reinforcement extinction effect Less persistence of instrumental behavior in extinction following training with a large reinforcer than following training with a small or moderate reinforcer.

overtraining extinction effect Less persistence of instrumental behavior in extinction following extensive training with reinforcement (overtraining) than following only moderate levels of reinforcement training.

partial reinforcement extinction effect The term used to describe greater persistence in instrumental responding in extinction after partial (intermittent) reinforcement training than after continuous reinforcement training. Abbreviated PREE.

reinstatement Recovery of excitatory responding to an extinguished stimulus produced by exposures to the unconditioned stimulus.

renewal Recovery of excitatory responding to an extinguished stimulus produced by a shift away from the contextual cues that were present during extinction.

sequential theory A theory of the partial reinforcement extinction effect according to which extinction is retarded after partial reinforcement because the instrumental response becomes conditioned to the memory of nonreward.

10

AVERSIVE CONTROL:
AVOIDANCE
AND PUNISHMENT

Avoidance Behavior

Origins of the Study of Avoidance Behavior

The Discriminated Avoidance Procedure

Two-Process Theory of Avoidance

Experimental Analysis of Avoidance Behavior

Alternative Theoretical Accounts of Avoidance Behavior

The Avoidance Puzzle: Concluding Comments

Punishment

Experimental Analysis of Punishment

Theories of Punishment

Punishment outside the Laboratory

hapter 10 deals with how behavior can be controlled by aversive stimulation. The discussion focuses on two types of instrumental aversive control—avoidance and punishment. Avoidance conditioning increases the performance of a target behavior, and punishment decreases the target response. In both cases, individuals learn to minimize their exposure to aversive stimulation. Because of this similarity, theoretical analyses of avoidance and punishment share some of the same concepts. Nevertheless, experimental analyses of avoidance and punishment have, for the most part, proceeded independently of each other. In this chapter, I describe the major theoretical puzzles and empirical findings in both areas of research.

Aversive stimulation is a fact of life and influences much of what we do. Fear, pain, and disappointment are an inevitable part of living. It is therefore understandable that we should be interested in how behavior is controlled by aversive stimuli. Two procedures have been extensively investigated in studies of aversive control—avoidance and punishment. In an avoidance procedure, the individual has to make a specific response to prevent an aversive stimulus from occurring. For example, grabbing a handrail to avoid slipping on the stairs is an avoidance response. An avoidance procedure involves a negative contingency between an instrumental response and the aversive stimulus. If the response occurs, the aversive stimulus is not presented. If you grab the handrail, you will not suffer the pain of falling. By contrast, a punishment procedure involves a positive contingency between the response and the aversive stimulus. In punishment, the aversive stimulus occurs if the specified response is made. For example, if you cut in line at a ticket window, you are likely to be reprimanded by others waiting in the line.

Avoidance procedures increase the occurrence of instrumental behavior, whereas punishment procedures suppress instrumental responding. With both procedures, the behavior that develops serves to minimize contact with the aversive stimulus. The critical difference is that, in avoidance, taking specific action prevents the aversive stimulus whereas, in punishment, refraining from action minimizes contact with the aversive stimulus. Because of this, avoidance behavior is sometimes referred to as *active avoidance* and punishment is sometimes referred to as *passive avoidance*. Both terms emphasize the fact that both avoidance and punishment involve minimizing contact with an aversive stimulus.

Despite the similarities between them, avoidance and punishment have been the subjects of different investigative approaches. Research on avoidance behavior has focused primarily on theoretical issues. Investigators focused on avoidance behavior have been working hard to determine what mechanisms are responsible for behavior whose primary consequence is the absence of aversive stimulation. By contrast, investigators interested in punishment have focused on practical and ethical considerations, such as what procedures are effective in suppressing behavior, and under what circumstances is it justified to use these procedures?

AVOIDANCE BEHAVIOR

Origins of the Study of Avoidance Behavior

One cannot understand the study of avoidance behavior without understanding its historical roots. Experimental investigations of avoidance behavior originated in studies of classical conditioning. The first avoidance conditioning experiments were conducted by the Russian psychologist Vladimir Bechterev (1913) as an extension of Pavlov's research. Unlike Pavlov, however, Bechterev was interested in studying associative learning in human subjects. In one situation, participants were instructed to place a finger on a metal plate. A warning stimulus (the CS) was then presented, followed by a brief shock (the US) through the metal plate. As you might predict, the participants quickly lifted their finger off the plate upon being shocked. After a few trials, they also learned to make this response to the warning stimulus.

Although Bechterev's experiment was viewed as a standard example of classical conditioning, the participants themselves determined whether or not they were exposed to the US. If they lifted their finger in response to the CS, they did not experience the shock delivered through the metal plate on that trial. This aspect of the procedure constitutes a signifi-

Figure 10.1   Modern running wheel for rodents.

cant departure from Pavlov's methods, because in standard classical conditioning exposure to the US does not depend on the participant's behavior.

The fact that Bechterev did not use a standard classical conditioning procedure went unnoticed for many years. However, starting in the 1930s, several investigations focused attention on the difference between a standard classical conditioning procedure and a procedure that had an instrumental avoidance component added (for example, Schlosberg, 1934, 1936). One of the most influential of these studies was performed by Brogden, Lipman, and Culler (1938).

Brogden et al. tested two groups of guinea pigs in a rotating wheel apparatus (see Figure 10.1). A tone served as the CS, and a shock served as the US. The shock stimulated the guinea pigs to run and thereby rotate the wheel. For the classical conditioning group, the shock was always presented 2 seconds after the beginning of the tone. For the avoidance conditioning group, the shock also followed the tone when the animals did not make the conditioned response (a small movement of the wheel). However, if the avoidance animals moved the wheel during the tone CS before the shock occurred, the scheduled shock was omitted. Figure 10.2 shows the percentage of trials on which each group made the conditioned response. The avoidance group quickly learned to make the conditioned response and was responding on 100% of the trials within 8 days of training. In contrast, the classical conditioning group never achieved this high level of performance.

The results obtained by Brogden and his collaborators proved that avoidance conditioning is different from standard classical conditioning and ushered in several decades of active research on avoidance learning.

The Discriminated Avoidance Procedure

Although avoidance behavior is not just another case of classical conditioning, the classical conditioning heritage of the study of avoidance behavior has greatly influenced its experimental and theoretical analysis to the present day (for example, Ayres, 1998). Investigators have been concerned with the importance of the warning signal in avoidance procedures and with how such warning signals are related to the aversive US and the instrumental response. Experimental issues of this type have been extensively investigated with procedures similar to that used by Brogden and his colleagues. This method is called **discriminated,** or **signaled, avoidance.** The standard features of the discriminated avoidance procedure are diagrammed in Figure 10.3.

Figure 10.2 Percentage of trials with a conditioned response on successive days of training. The conditioned response prevented shock delivery for the avoidance group but not for the classical group. (From "The Role of Incentive in Conditioning and Extinction," by W. J. Brogden, E. A. Lipman, and E. Culler, 1938. *American Journal of Psychology, 51*, pp. 109–117.)

The first thing to note about the discriminated avoidance procedure is that it involves discrete trials. Each trial is initiated by the CS or warning stimulus. The events that occur after that depend on what the participant does. There are two possibilities. If the subject makes the response required for avoidance during the CS but before the shock is delivered, the CS is turned off and the US is omitted on that trial. This is a successful **avoidance trial.** If the subject fails to make the required response during the CS-US interval, the scheduled shock is presented and remains on until the response occurs, whereupon both the CS and the US are terminated. In this case, the instrumental response results in escape from the shock; hence, this type of trial is called an **escape trial.** During early stages of training, most of the trials are escape trials; but as training progresses and the subject starts making the avoidance response, avoidance trials come to predominate.

Discriminated avoidance procedures are often conducted in a shuttle box like that shown in Figure 10.4. The shuttle box consists of two compartments separated by an open-

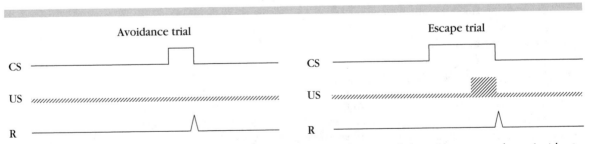

Figure 10.3 Diagram of the discriminated, or signaled, avoidance procedure. *Avoidance trial:* If the participant makes the response required for avoidance during the CS (the signal) but before the US (for example, shock) is scheduled, the CS is turned off, and the US is omitted on that trial. *Escape trial:* If the participant fails to make the required response during the CS-US interval, the scheduled shock is presented and remains on until the response occurs, whereupon both the CS and the US are terminated.

Figure 10.4 A shuttle box. The box has a metal grid floor and is separated into two compartments by an archway. The instrumental response consists of crossing back and forth (shuttling) from one side of the box to the other.

ing at floor level. The animal is placed on one side of the apparatus. At the start of a trial, the CS is presented (a light or a tone, for example). If the subject crosses over to the other side before the shock occurs, no shock is delivered and the CS is turned off. At the end of the intertrial interval, the next trial can be administered starting with the animal in the second compartment. With this procedure, the animal shuttles back and forth between the two sides on successive trials. The response is therefore called **shuttle avoidance.**

There are two types of shuttle avoidance procedures: In the one just described, the animal moves from left to right on the first trial, and from right to left on the second trial. This type is technically called *two-way shuttle avoidance,* because the animal moves in different directions on successive trials. In *one-way shuttle avoidance,* the animal starts each trial on the same side of the apparatus and always moves in the same direction, to the other side. One-way avoidance is generally easier to learn than the two-way procedure.

Two-Process Theory of Avoidance

Avoidance procedures involve a negative contingency between a response and an aversive stimulus. If you make the appropriate avoidance responses, you will not fall, bump into things, or drive off the road. No particular pleasure is derived from these experiences. You simply do not get hurt. The absence of the aversive stimulus is presumably the reason that avoidance responses are made. However, how can the absence of something provide reinforcement for instrumental behavior? This is the fundamental question in the study of avoidance.

Mowrer and Lamoreaux (1942) pointed out more than a half century ago that "not getting something can hardly, in and of itself, qualify as rewarding" (p. 6). Since then, much intellectual effort has been devoted to figuring out what subjects "get" in avoidance conditioning procedures that might provide reinforcement for the avoidance response. In fact, the investigation of avoidance behavior has been dominated by this theoretical problem. The first and most influential solution to the puzzle, proposed by Mowrer (1947) and elaborated by Miller (for example, 1951) and others, is known as the **two-process theory of avoidance.**

In one form or another, two-process theory has been the dominant theoretical viewpoint on avoidance learning for many years and continues to enjoy success and support (Levis, 1989; Levis & Brewer, 2001; D. E. McAllister & W. R. McAllister, 1991; W. R.

N. E. Miller

Courtesy of Donald A. Dewsbury

McAllister & D. E. McAllister, 1995; Zhuikov, Couvillon, & Bitterman, 1994). Because other approaches deal more directly with certain findings, two-process theory is no longer viewed as a complete explanation of avoidance learning. Nevertheless, the theory remains the standard against which all other explanations of avoidance behavior are always measured.

As the name implies, two-process theory assumes that two mechanisms are involved in avoidance learning. The first is a classical conditioning process activated by pairings of the warning stimulus (CS) with the aversive event (US) on trials when the organism fails to make the avoidance response. Because the US is an aversive stimulus, through classical conditioning the CS also becomes aversive. Mowrer (1947) assumed that because it is aversive, it comes to elicit fear. Thus, the first component of two-process theory is the *classical conditioning of fear to the CS.*

Fear is an emotionally arousing unpleasant state. As I noted in Chapter 5, the termination of an unpleasant or aversive event provides negative reinforcement for instrumental behavior. Since fear is elicited by the CS, termination of the CS presumably results in a reduction in the level of fear, and this can be a source of negative reinforcement. The second process in two-process theory is based on this negative reinforcement. Mowrer assumed that learning of the instrumental avoidance response occurs because the response terminates the CS and thereby reduces the conditioned fear elicited by the CS. Thus, the second component in two-process theory is *instrumental reinforcement of the avoidance response through fear reduction.*

There are several noteworthy aspects of two-process theory. First, and perhaps most important, the classical and instrumental processes are assumed to depend on each other. Instrumental reinforcement through fear reduction is not possible until fear has become conditioned to the CS. Therefore, the classical conditioning process has to occur first. After that, the instrumental conditioning process may create extinction trials for the classical conditioning process. This occurs because each successful avoidance response prevents the occurrence of the US. Thus, two-process theory predicts repeated interplay between classical and instrumental processes.

Another important aspect of two-process theory is that it explains avoidance behavior in terms of escape from conditioned fear rather than in terms of the prevention of shock. The fact that the avoidance response prevents shock is seen as a by-product in two-process theory, not as the critical event that motivates avoidance behavior. Escape from conditioned fear provides the critical reinforcement for avoidance behavior. Thus, according to two-process theory, the instrumental response is reinforced by a tangible event (fear reduction) rather than merely the absence of something (aversive stimulation).

Experimental Analysis of Avoidance Behavior

Avoidance learning has been the subject of many experiments. Much of the research has been stimulated by efforts to prove or disprove two-process theory. Space does not permit reviewing all the evidence. However, several important findings must be considered in any effort to fully understand the mechanisms of avoidance behavior.

Acquired-Drive Experiments. In the typical avoidance procedure, classical conditioning of fear and instrumental reinforcement through fear reduction occur intermixed in a series of trials. If these two processes make separate contributions to avoidance learning, it should be possible to demonstrate their operation in a situation where the two types of conditioning are not intermixed. This is the goal of *acquired-drive experiments.*

The basic strategy is to first condition fear to a CS with a "pure" classical conditioning procedure in which the CS is paired with the US regardless of what the subject does. In the

BOX **10.1**

FEAR AND THE AMYGDALA

Much of what we do is motivated by fear. Because fear serves a defensive and protective function, organisms seem biologically prepared to learn about stimuli that signal danger (for example, snakes, heights). While such learning is generally adaptive, fear can grow out of proportion to the danger, producing a phobic response that undermines the person's ability to function.

Neuroscientists have discovered that a small region of the brain, the amygdala, plays a central role in fear-mediated behavior (for a review, see Fendt & Fanselow, 1999; LeDoux, 1996). The amygdala (Latin for "almond") is part of the limbic system, a subcortical region of the brain that has been implicated in the processing of emotional stimuli. In humans, brain scans have revealed that processing fear-related stimuli (for example, pictures of a fearful expression) activates the amygdala. Damage to the amygdala disrupts a person's ability to recognize signs of fear, and electrical stimulation of this region produces feelings of fear and apprehension.

The neural circuit that underlies conditioned fear has been explored in laboratory animals using a variety of physiological techniques, including selective lesions, localized stimulation, and physiological recording (see Box 3.2). In animals, electrical stimulation of the amygdala produces a range of behavioral and physiological responses indicative of fear, including freezing, enhanced startle to a loud acoustic stimulus, and a change in heart rate. Conversely, lesioning the amygdala produces a fearless creature that no longer avoids dangerous situations. Rats normally show signs of fear in the presence of a predator (for example, a cat). After having the amygdala lesioned, a rat will approach a cat as if it's a long-lost friend.

Lesioning the amygdala also disrupts learning about cues (CSs) that have been paired with an aversive event (for example, a shock US) in a Pavlovian paradigm. As discussed earlier, animals can associate many different types of stimuli with shock. In some cases, the cue may be relatively simple, such as a discrete light or tone; in others, a constellation of cues, such as the context in which shock occurs, may be associated with shock. In both cases, pairing the stimulus with shock produces conditioned fear, as indicated by a CS-induced increase in freezing and startle.

Evidence suggests that in fear conditioning, the neural signals elicited by the CS and US converge within the amygdala (see Figure 10.5). Information about the US is provided by two distinct neural circuits, each of which is sufficient to support conditioning (Shi & Davis, 1999). Information about the CS is provided by three functionally distinct systems, each of which may represent a distinct type of stimulus quality. One CS path to the amygdala is fairly direct, a path that sacrifices stimulus detail for speed. This pathway allows for a rapid response and primes neural activity. Additional CS inputs arrive from the cortex and likely provide a slower, but more precise, representation of the CS features. In the absence of this cortical input, subjects can acquire a conditioned response to a discrete cue (for example, a tone). They cannot, however, learn to discriminate two auditory cues in a differential conditioning paradigm, where only one of the stimuli is paired with shock. Normally, rats will freeze only during the cue that has been paired with shock. Rats with lesions of the auditory cortex do not respond differentially, but instead show signs of fear to both the paired and the unpaired tones.

The third CS pathway conveys information that has been processed within the hippocampus, a structure that binds together unique sets of stimuli (Fanselow, 1999). For example, in everyday life, we associate the cues that occur together with a temporal code, providing a unique memory that encodes a particular episode in time (for example, what you had for breakfast yesterday). A similar type of learning is required to encode the constellation of cues that distinguish environmental contexts. Both types of memory are disrupted by damage to the hippocampus, a deficit that contributes to the memory dysfunction observed with Alzheimer's and Korsakoff's disease. In animal subjects, hippocampal lesions have no effect on a rat's ability to learn and remember that a discrete cue (for example, tone) predicts shock. But this same rat appears unable to associate a distinct context with shock. It seems that the

(continued)

Box 10.1 (continued)

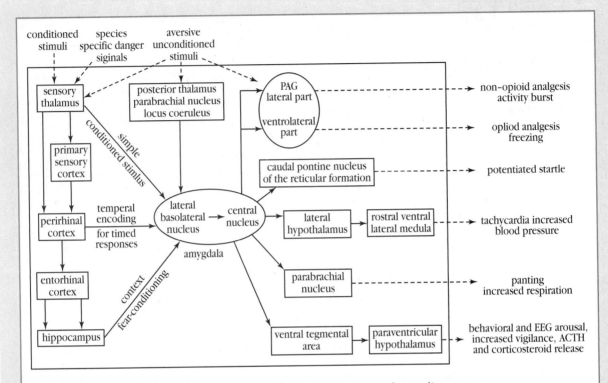

Figure 10.5 A block diagram illustrating some of the neural components that mediate fear and defensive behavior. An aversive US engages parallel pathways that project to the lateral/basolateral amygdala. Information about the CS is conveyed from the sensory thalamus, the cortex, or by means of a hippocampal-dependent process. Output is channeled through the central nucleus of the amygdala, which organizes the expression of fear-mediated behavior. Distinct behavioral outcomes are produced by projections to various brain structures. (Adapted from Fendt and Fanselow, 1989.)

hippocampus plays an essential role in processing complex stimuli. Somehow, the hippocampus helps package the components of a stimulus together, producing a kind of configural representation that can be associated with shock.

Interestingly, the role of the hippocampus changes over time. When the organism is first exposed to a complex stimulus, the hippocampus appears to be necessary to process the interrelated features of the stimulus. Over time, however, the new representation seems to be consolidated and stored elsewhere, presumably within the cortex. Once the configural nature of a stimulus has been established, which takes about a month in rats, the new representation

can function on its own without the hippocampal. As a result, lesion of the hippocampus has less effect if the lesion is administered during later stages of learning. If the lesion is conducted within a few days of context exposure, it eliminates the animal's ability to associate the context with shock. In contrast, if rats are exposed to a novel context a month earlier, an enduring memory trace is established that survives the hippocampal lesion. These rats can associate the previously experienced context with shock, but are unable to learn about new contexts. It seems that the hippocampal lesion has eliminated the animal's ability to form a lasting configural representation.

The neural circuits activated by the CS and US converge within the amygdala in the lateral (toward the sides) and basal (lower) lateral region. Here, stimulus inputs may compete for association with the US, with the most predictive cues laying down a form of long-term potentiation (LTP) that helps encode the CS-US relation (Fanselow, 1999). LTP is thought to underlie information storage in other brain regions (see Box 11.1) and depends on the activation of the NMDA receptor. Microinjecting into the basolateral amygdala a drug that blocks the NMDA receptor disrupts the acquisition of conditioned fear. In addition, LTP-like changes have been observed in the CS-input pathways, suggesting that multiple sources of synaptic plasticity contribute to the development of a conditioned response (LeDoux, 1996).

The output of the fear circuit is channeled through the central nucleus of the amygdala, which organizes the expression of conditioned fear. This structure produces a wide range of behavioral and physiological effects, the outcome of which depends on the neural system engaged. For example, enhanced startle is mediated by a neural projection to a region of the brainstem reticular formation (the pontine nucleus). Slightly above this brainstem structure, in the midbrain, is a region known as the periaqueductral gray (PAG). This structure plays a crucial role in organiz-

ing defensive behavior. The portion that lies along the upper sides (dorsolateral) organizes active defensive behaviors needed for fight and flight. These circa-strike behaviors are engaged by direct, or inevitable, contact with a noxious, or life-threatening, stimulus. The lower (ventral) portion of the PAG mediates CS-elicited freezing behavior. Rats that have received lesions limited to the ventral PAG appear afraid on a variety of measures but do not freeze.

A CS that predicts shock also elicits a reduction in pain reactivity. This conditioned analgesia is thought to help the organism cope with a painful US. The analgesia is mediated by an internally manufactured (endogenous) opioid that, like morphine, decreases behavioral reactivity to noxious stimuli. Like freezing, this physiological response depends on neurons within the ventral PAG. This conditioned analgesia could provide a form of negative feedback that decreases the effectiveness of an expected aversive US. It is well established that learning that one cue predicts an aversive event can block learning about other cues. This blocking effect can be eliminated by the administration of a drug (an opioid antagonist) that prevents the opioid analgesia, providing a physiological explanation for why an expected US receives less processing (Bolles & Fanselow, 1980; Fanselow, 1999).

—J. W. Grau

next phase of the experiment, the subjects are periodically exposed to the fear-eliciting CS and allowed to perform an instrumental response that is effective in terminating the CS (and thereby reducing fear). No shocks are scheduled in this phase. Therefore, the instrumental response is not required to avoid shock. If escape from a fear-eliciting CS can reinforce instrumental behavior, then the instrumental response should become conditioned in the second phase of the experiment. This type of experiment is called an **acquired-drive** study because the drive to perform the instrumental response (fear) is learned through classical conditioning. (It is not an innate drive, such as hunger or thirst.)

One of the first definitive acquired-drive experiments was performed by Brown and Jacobs (1949), who tested rats in a shuttle box. During the first phase of the experiment, the opening between the two shuttle compartments was blocked. The rats were individually placed on one side of the apparatus and a pulsating light/tone CS was presented, ending in shock through the grid floor. Twenty-two such Pavlovian conditioning trials were conducted, with the rats confined on the right and left sides of the apparatus on alternate trials. The control group received the same training except that no shocks were delivered.

Instrumental conditioning was conducted during the next phase of the experiment. Each animal was placed on one side of the shuttle box, and the center barrier was removed. The CS was then presented and remained on until the rat turned it off by crossing to the other side. The animal was then removed from the apparatus until the next trial. No shocks were delivered during the instrumental conditioning phase. Brown and Jacobs wanted to determine whether the rats would learn to cross rapidly from one side to the other when the only reinforcement for crossing was termination of the previously conditioned light/tone CS.

How long the rats took to cross the shuttle box and turn off the CS was measured for each trial in the instrumental conditioning phase. Figure 10.6 summarizes these response latencies for both the shock-conditioned group and the control group. The two groups had similar response latencies at the beginning of instrumental training. As training progressed, the shock-conditioned animals learned to cross the shuttle box faster (and thus turn off the CS sooner) than the control group. This outcome shows that termination of a fear-conditioned stimulus is sufficient to provide reinforcement for an instrumental response. This basic finding has since been replicated in a variety of experimental situations (for example, Dinsmoor, 1962; McAllister & McAllister, 1971; see also Delprato, 1969; Israel, Devine, O'Dea, & Hamdi, 1974; Katzev, 1967, 1972). These results provide strong support for two-process theory.

Independent Measurement of Fear during Acquisition of Avoidance Behavior. Another important strategy that has been used in investigations of avoidance behavior involves independent measurement of fear and instrumental avoidance responding. This approach is based on the assumption that if fear motivates and reinforces avoidance responding, then the conditioning of fear and the conditioning of instrumental avoidance behavior should go hand in hand. Contrary to this prediction, however, conditioned fear and avoidance responding are not always highly correlated (Mineka, 1979).

Fairly early in the investigation of avoidance learning, it was noted that animals become less fearful as they become more proficient in performing the avoidance response (Solomon, Kamin, & Wynne, 1953; Solomon & Wynne, 1953). Since then, more systematic measurements of fear have been used. One popular behavioral technique for measuring fear involves the conditioned suppression procedure described in Chapter 3. In this technique, animals are first conditioned to press a response lever for food reinforcement. A shock-conditioned CS is then presented while the animals are responding to obtain food. In general, the CS

S. Mineka

Courtesy of Donald A. Dewsbury

Figure 10.6 Mean latencies to cross from one side to the other in the shuttle box for control and experimental groups. The shuttle crossing resulted in termination of the CS on that trial. For the experimental group, the CS was previously conditioned with shock. Such conditioning was not conducted with the control group. (From "The Role of Fear in the Motivation and Acquisition of Responses," by J. S. Brown and A. Jacobs, 1949, *Journal of Experimental Psychology, 39,* pp. 747–759.)

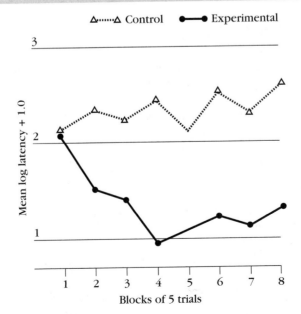

produces suppression of the lever-press behavior, and the extent of this response suppression is assumed to reflect the amount of fear elicited by the CS.

If the warning signal in an avoidance procedure comes to elicit fear, then presentation of that warning stimulus in a conditioned suppression procedure should result in suppression of food-reinforced behavior. This prediction was tested for the first time in a famous experiment by Kamin, Brimer, and Black (1963). The rats in the experiment were initially trained to press a response lever for food reinforcement on a variable interval schedule. The animals were then trained to avoid shock in response to an auditory CS in a shuttle box. Training was continued for independent groups of animals until they successfully avoided shock on 1, 3, 9, or 27 consecutive trials. The animals were then returned to the Skinner box for lever pressing. The auditory CS that had been used in the shuttle box was periodically presented to see how much suppression of lever pressing it would produce.

The results are summarized in Figure 10.7. Lower values of the suppression index indicate greater disruptions of lever pressing by the shock-avoidance CS. Increasing degrees of response suppression were observed among groups of rats that had received avoidance training until they successfully avoided shock on 1 to 9 successive trials. With more extensive avoidance training, however, response suppression declined. Animals trained until they avoided shock on 27 consecutive trials showed less conditioned suppression to the avoidance CS than those trained to a criterion of 9 consecutive avoidances. This outcome indicates that fear, as measured by conditioned suppression, decreases during extended avoidance training and is at a minimal level after extensive training (see also Cook, Mineka, & Trumble, 1987; Neuenschwander, Fabrigoule, & Mackintosh, 1987; Starr & Mineka, 1977). Interestingly, however, the decrease in fear is not accompanied by a decrease in the strength of the avoidance response (Mineka & Gino, 1980).

The decline in fear to the CS with extended avoidance training presents a puzzle for two-process theory. However, recent evidence and theoretical argument suggest that the scope of two-process theory can accommodate this finding. Although it is well accepted

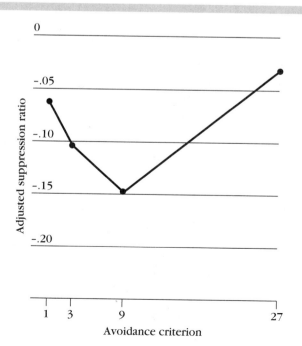

Figure 10.7 Suppression of lever pressing for food during a CS that was previously conditioned in a shock-avoidance procedure. Independent groups received avoidance training until they met a criterion of 1, 3, 9, or 27 consecutive avoidance responses. The suppression scores were adjusted for the degree of suppression produced by the CS before avoidance conditioning. Lower values of the adjusted ratio indicate greater suppression of lever pressing. (From "Conditioned Suppression as a Monitor of Fear of the CS in the Course of Avoidance Training," by L. J. Kamin, C. J. Brimer, and A. H. Black, 1963, *Journal of Comparative and Physiological Psychology, 56*, pp. 497–501.)

that fear declines as avoidance conditioning proceeds, the CS continues to elicit some fear—that is, fear does not decline to zero. D. E. McAllister and W. R. McAllister (1991) pointed out that as long as the CS elicits some degree of fear, CS termination can result in fear reduction and hence reinforcement of the avoidance behavior. Furthermore, as the avoidance response becomes well learned, a small degree of fear reduction may be sufficient to maintain the response. (For additional factors that can lead to a dissociation between avoidance responding and fear elicited by the warning stimulus, see Levis, 1989; Levis & Brewer, 2001; McAllister & McAllister, 1995.)

Asymptotic Avoidance Performance. Two-process theory not only specifies mechanisms responsible for the acquisition of avoidance behavior but also makes predictions about the nature of performance once the response has been well learned. More specifically, it predicts that the strength of the avoidance response will fluctuate in cycles.

Whenever a successful avoidance response occurs, the shock is omitted on that trial. This is an extinction trial for the conditioned fear response. Repetition of the avoidance response (and thus the CS-alone extinction trials) should lead to extinction of fear. As the CS becomes extinguished, there will be less reinforcement resulting from the reduction of fear, and the avoidance response should also become extinguished. However, when shock is not avoided, the CS is paired with the US. This pairing should reinstate fear to the CS and reestablish the potential for reinforcement through fear reduction, thereby reconditioning the avoidance response. Thus, the theory predicts that after initial acquisition, the avoidance response will go through cycles of extinction and reacquisition.

Although evidence of cyclic avoidance responding at asymptote has been obtained (for example, Sheffield, 1948), such findings are not always observed. Some researchers have argued that one of the hallmarks of avoidance behavior is its persistence. Avoidance responding may continue for many trials after shocks are discontinued, as long as the response continues to be effective in terminating the CS. In one experiment (Solomon et al., 1953), for example, a dog was reported to have performed the avoidance response on 650 successive trials after only a few shocks.

In terms of two-process theory, there are several approaches to explaining instances in which avoidance behavior persists after the unconditioned aversive stimulus is no longer delivered. One approach is based on the observation that once an avoidance response has been well learned, it occurs with a short latency. Because the animal responds quickly to turn off the CS, later segments of the CS are never experienced and therefore do not have the opportunity to undergo extinction. The short latency of well-learned avoidance responses serves to protect later segments of the CS from becoming extinguished and thereby contributes to the persistence of avoidance behavior. This mechanism, first proposed by Solomon and Wynne (1953), is called **conservation of fear.** (For elaborations on this idea, see Levis, 1981, 1989, 1991; Levis & Brewer, 2001. For additional factors involved in the persistence of avoidance behavior, see Soltysik, Wolfe, Nicholas, Wilson, & Garcia-Sanchez, 1983.)

Extinction of Avoidance Behavior through Response-Blocking and CS-Alone Exposure. As I have noted, if the avoidance response is effective in terminating the CS and no shocks are presented, avoidance responding may persist for a long time. How might avoidance behavior be extinguished? The answer to this question is very important not only for theoretical analyses of avoidance behavior but also for forms of behavior therapy whose goal is to extinguish maladaptive or pathological avoidance responses.

An effective and extensively investigated extinction procedure for avoidance behavior is called **flooding,** or **response prevention** (Baum, 1970). It involves presenting the CS in the avoidance situation without the US, but with the apparatus altered in such a way that the participant is prevented from making the avoidance response. Thus, the organism is exposed to the CS without being permitted to terminate it. In a sense, it is "flooded" with the CS. (For discussion of a related procedure, called *implosive therapy,* see Levis, 1995; Levis & Brewer, 2001.)

One of the most important variables determining the effects of a flooding procedure is the duration of the forced exposure to the CS. This was convincingly illustrated in an experiment by Schiff, Smith, and Prochaska (1972). Rats were trained to avoid shock in response to an auditory CS by going to a safe compartment. After acquisition, the safe compartment was blocked off by a barrier and the rats received various amounts of exposure to the CS without shock. Different groups received 1, 5, or 12 blocked trials, and on each of these trials the CS was presented for 1, 5, 10, 50, or 120 seconds. The barrier blocking the avoidance response was then removed, and the animals were tested for extinction. At the start of each extinction trial, the animal was placed in the apparatus and the CS was presented until it crossed into the safe compartment. Shocks never occurred during the extinction trials, and each animal was tested until it took at least 120 seconds to cross into the safe compartment on 3 consecutive trials. The strength of the avoidance response was measured by the number of trials required to reach this extinction criterion.

The results of the experiment are summarized in Figure 10.8. As expected, blocked exposure to the CS facilitated extinction of the avoidance response. Furthermore, this effect was determined mainly by the total duration of exposure to the CS. The number of flooding trials administered (1, 5, or 12) facilitated extinction only because each trial added to the total amount of inescapable exposure to the CS. Increases in the total duration of blocked exposure to the CS resulted in more rapid extinction (see also Baum, 1969; Weinberger, 1965).

Two-process theory predicts that flooding will extinguish avoidance behavior because exposure to the CS without the US will produce extinction of fear. The fact that more extensive exposure to the CS results in more rapid extinction is consistent with this view.

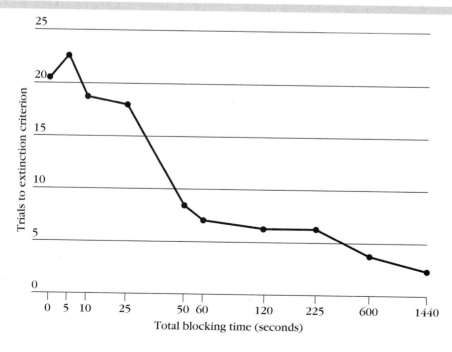

Figure 10.8 Trials to extinction criterion for independent groups of animals that previously received various durations of blocked exposure to the CS. (From "Extinction of Avoidance in Rats as a Function of Duration and Number of Blocked Trials," by R. Schiff, N. Smith, and J. Prochaska, 1972, *Journal of Comparative and Physiological Psychology, 81,* pp. 356–359. Copyright © 1972 by the American Psychological Association. Reprinted by permission.)

However, detailed investigations of the role of fear in flooding procedures have also provided evidence contrary to two-process theory. Independent measurements of fear (with the conditioned suppression technique, for example) have shown that in some situations flooding extinguishes avoidance behavior more rapidly than it extinguishes fear, whereas in other situations the reverse holds (see, for example, Coulter, Riccio, & Page, 1969; Mineka & Gino, 1979; Mineka, Miller, Gino, & Giencke, 1981). These results suggest that extinction of fear is only one factor responsible for the effects of flooding procedures. Other variables may be related to the fact that, during flooding, organisms not only receive forced exposure to the CS but are prevented from making the avoidance response. (For further discussion, see Baum, 1970; Katzev & Berman, 1974; Mineka, 1979.)

Nondiscriminated (Free-Operant) Avoidance. As I have described, two-process theory places great emphasis on the role of the warning signal, or CS, in avoidance learning. Can individuals also learn to avoid shock if there is no external warning stimulus in the situation? Within the context of two-factor theory, this is a heretical question. However, progress in science requires posing bold questions, and Sidman (1953a, 1953b) did just that. He devised an avoidance conditioning procedure that did not involve a warning stimulus. The procedure has come to be called **nondiscriminated**, or **free-operant, avoidance.**

In a free-operant avoidance procedure, a brief shock is scheduled to occur periodically without warning—say, every 3 seconds. Each time the participant makes the avoidance response, it obtains a period of safety—say, 10 seconds—during which shocks do not occur. Repetition of the avoidance response before the end of the shock-free period serves to start the safe period over again.

A free-operant avoidance procedure is constructed from two time intervals (see Figure 10.9). One of these is the interval between shocks in the absence of a response. This is called the **S-S (shock-shock) interval.** The other critical time period is the interval between the avoidance response and the next scheduled shock. This is called the **R-S (response-shock) interval.** The R-S interval is the period of safety created by each response. In my example, the S-S interval was 3 seconds and the R-S interval was 10 seconds.

In addition to lacking a warning stimulus, the free-operant avoidance procedure differs from discriminated avoidance in allowing for avoidance responses to occur at any time. In discriminated avoidance procedures, the avoidance response is effective in preventing the delivery of shock only if it is made during the CS. Responses in the absence of the CS (the intertrial interval) have no effect. In fact, in some experiments (particularly those involving one-way avoidance), the subject is removed from the apparatus between trials. By contrast, in the free-operant procedure, an avoidance response occurring at any time will reset the R-S interval. If the R-S interval is 10 seconds, shock is scheduled 10 seconds after each response. By always responding just before this R-S interval is over, the subject can always reset the R-S interval and thereby prolong its period of safety indefinitely.

Figure 10.9 Diagram of the nondiscriminated, or free-operant, avoidance procedure. Each occurrence of the response initiates a period without shock, as set by the R-S interval. In the absence of a response, the next shock occurs a fixed period after the last shock, as set by the S-S interval. Shocks are not signaled by an exteroceptive stimulus and are usually brief and inescapable

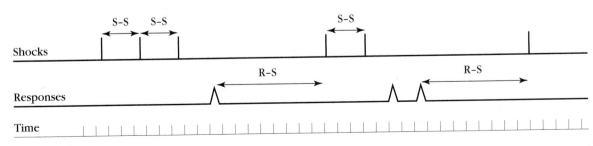

Demonstrations of Free-Operant Avoidance Learning. Most research on free-operant avoidance learning has been conducted with laboratory rats and has used brief footshock as the aversive stimulus. Experiments have also been conducted with human participants and more "natural" aversive stimuli. In one study, for example, four college students served as subjects, and exposure to carbon dioxide (CO_2) was used as the aversive stimulus (Lejuez, O'Donnell, Wirth, Zvolensky, & Eifert, 1998). CO_2 rather than shock was used because the investigators wanted to produced symptoms related to panic attacks. CO_2 inhalation produces respiratory distress, increased heart rate (tachycardia), and dizziness similar to what is experienced during a panic attack.

Potential subjects for the experiment were first screened to make sure they did not have a history of respiratory problems. During the experiment, the students were asked to wear a mask that usually provided room air. To deliver the aversive stimulus, the room air was switched to 20% CO_2 for 25 seconds. Each CO_2 delivery was followed by a 65-second rest period to permit resumption of normal breathing. The instrumental response was operating a plunger. Three seconds after the rest period, a hit of CO_2 was provided without warning if the subject did not pull the plunger (S-S interval = 3 seconds). Following a response, the next CO_2 delivery was scheduled 10 seconds later (R-S interval = 10 seconds). Furthermore, each occurrence of the avoidance response reset the R-S interval. If the subjects never responded, they could get as many as 22 CO_2 deliveries in each avoidance conditioning session. If they responded before the end of the first S-S interval and then before the end of each R-S interval, they could avoid all CO_2 deliveries. Sessions during which the avoidance contingency was in effect were alternated with control sessions during which responding had no effect and the subjects received a CO_2 delivery on average every 6 minutes.

The results of the experiment are summarized in Figure 10.10. The left side of the figure shows the response rates of the four students during the avoidance and control sessions. The right side of the figure shows the number of CO_2 deliveries the subjects received during the two types of sessions. Notice that response rates were higher during the avoidance sessions than during the control sessions. Furthermore, as the subjects acquired the avoidance response, the number of CO_2 presentations they received declined. And these behavior changes (and consequences) occurred even though the CO_2 presentations were not signaled by an explicit warning stimulus.

No explicit instructions about the response plunger were provided at the beginning of the experiment. Subjects S1 and S2 "discovered" the avoidance contingency without much difficulty on their own. In contrast, subjects S3 and S4 had a bit of trouble at first and were given a hint before their 6th and 7th sessions, respectively. The hint was, "The only thing that you can do by pulling the plunger is sometimes change the number of times you receive carbon-dioxide-enriched air. It is even possible for you to sometimes receive no deliveries of carbon dioxide." This hint was enough to get subjects S3 and S4 to respond effectively during subsequent avoidance sessions. Notice, however, that the instructions did not provide clues about the difference between the avoidance and control sessions. Nevertheless, subjects S3 and S4 responded more vigorously during the avoidance sessions than during the control sessions by the end of the experiment. Thus, the difference in response levels (and CO_2 presentations) that occurred during avoidance versus control sessions cannot be attributed to "following instructions" for any of the subjects. They all had to discover without help when the avoidance contingency was in effect when it was not in effect.

Free-operant avoidance behavior has been investigated in numerous other studies, primarily with rats serving as subjects and brief shock as the aversive stimulus (see Hineline, 1977; Sidman, 1966). Because nonverbal subjects were used, observers did not have to worry about the possible role of instructions. These experiments have shown that the rate of responding is controlled by the length of the S-S and R-S intervals. The more frequently

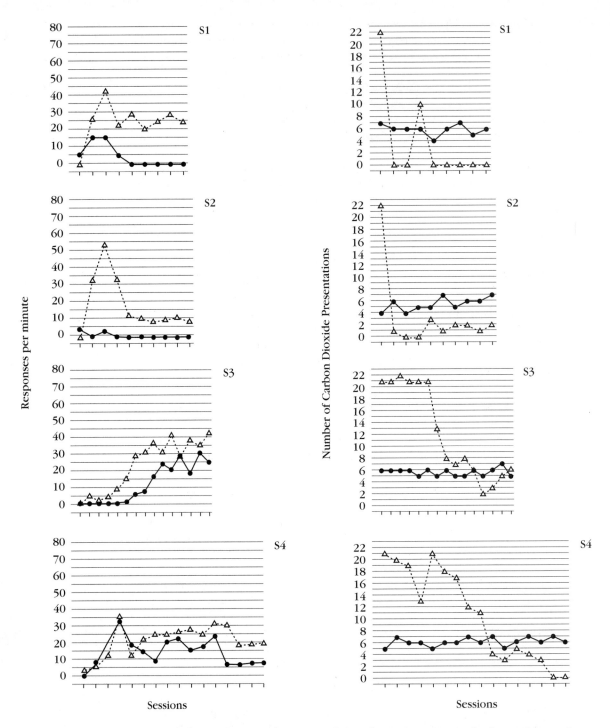

Figure 10.10 Rate of responding and rate of CO_2 presentations for four college students in a study of free-operant avoidance. Open symbols represent data obtained during sessions when the avoidance contingency was in effect. Closed symbols represent data obtained during control sessions when the avoidance response was not effective and the subjects received a CO_2 delivery every 6 minutes. (After Lejuez et al., 1998.)

shocks are scheduled in the absence of responding (the S-S interval), the more likely the subject is to learn the avoidance response. Increasing the periods of safety produced by the response (the R-S interval) also promotes the avoidance behavior. In addition, the relative value of the S-S and R-S intervals is important. Responding is not likely to develop if the R-S interval is shorter than the S-S interval.

Free-Operant Avoidance and Two-Process Theory. Free-operant avoidance behavior presents a challenge for two-process theory because there is no explicit CS to elicit conditioned fear and it is not clear how the avoidance response reduces fear. However, two-process theory has not been entirely abandoned in attempts to explain free-operant avoidance (see Anger, 1963). The S-S and R-S intervals used in effective procedures are usually rather short (less than 1 minute). Furthermore, they remain fixed during an experiment, so that the intervals are highly predictable. It is not unreasonable to suggest that the animals might learn to respond to the passage of time as a signal for shock. This assumption of temporal conditioning permits application of the mechanisms of two-process theory to free-operant avoidance procedures.

According to the two-process explanation of free-operant avoidance, the passage of time after the last shock (in the case of the S-S interval) or after the last response (in the case of the R-S interval) becomes conditioned to elicit fear. Since the timing starts over again with each avoidance response, the response effectively removes the fear-eliciting temporal cues. Termination of these time signals can then reinforce the avoidance response through fear reduction. Thus, the temporal cues that predict shock are assumed to have the same role in free-operant avoidance procedures as the explicit CS has in discriminative avoidance.

The preceding analysis predicts that organisms will not distribute their responses randomly in a free-operant avoidance procedure. They will concentrate their responses at the end of the R-S interval because it is here that the temporal cues presumably elicit the greatest amount of fear. Results consistent with this prediction have been obtained. However, many animals successfully avoid a great many shocks without distributing their responses in the manner predicted by two-process theory. Furthermore, the predicted distribution of responses often develops only after extensive training—after the participants are avoiding a great many of the scheduled shocks (see Sidman, 1966). In addition, avoidance behavior has been successfully conditioned with the use of free-operant procedures in which the S-S and R-S intervals are varied throughout the experiment (for example, Herrnstein & Hineline, 1966). Making the S-S and R-S intervals unpredictable makes it more difficult to use the passage of time as a signal for shock. These types of results have discouraged some investigators from accepting two-process theory as an explanation of free-operant avoidance learning. (For further discussion, see Herrnstein, 1969; Hineline, 1977, 1981.)

Alternative Theoretical Accounts of Avoidance Behavior

In the preceding discussion of experimental investigations of avoidance behavior, I used two-process theory to provide the conceptual framework. This was reasonable because many of the research questions were stimulated in one way or another by two-process theory. However, alternative approaches to the analysis of avoidance learning also have been proposed, as investigators have gradually moved away from using traditional discrete-trial discriminated avoidance procedures. I will now discuss some of the more important of these alternative theories.

In two-process theory, reinforcement for the avoidance response is assumed to be provided by the reduction of fear. This is a case of negative reinforcement—reinforcement due

P. N. Hineline

Courtesy of Donald A. Dewsbury

to removal of an aversive stimulus. Several subsequent theoretical treatments have proposed that avoidance procedures also provide for positive reinforcement of the avoidance response, whereas others have suggested that neither negative reinforcement nor positive reinforcement is important in avoidance learning.

Positive Reinforcement through Conditioned Inhibition of Fear or Conditioned Safety Signals. Performance of an avoidance response always results in distinctive feedback stimuli, such as spatial cues involved in going from one side to the other in a shuttle box or tactile and other external stimuli involved in pressing a response lever. Because the avoidance response produces a period of safety in all avoidance conditioning procedures, response feedback stimuli may acquire conditioned inhibitory properties and become signals for the absence of aversive stimulation. Such stimuli are called **safety signals.** Because a shock-free period is desirable, a conditioned inhibitory stimulus for shock may serve as a positive reinforcer. Thus, according to the *safety-signal hypothesis,* the stimuli that accompany avoidance responses may provide positive reinforcement for avoidance behavior.

In most avoidance experiments, no special steps are taken to ensure that the avoidance response is accompanied by vivid feedback stimuli that could acquire conditioned inhibitory properties. Spatial, tactile, and proprioceptive stimuli that are not specifically programmed but inevitably accompany the avoidance response serve this function (Dinsmoor, 2001a). However, any avoidance procedure can easily be modified to provide a distinctive stimulus, such as a brief light or tone, after each occurrence of the avoidance response. The safety-signal hypothesis predicts that introducing an explicit feedback stimulus will facilitate the learning of an avoidance response. Numerous experiments have found this to be true (for example, Bolles & Grossen, 1969; Cándido, Maldonado, & Vila, 1991; D'Amato, Fazzaro, & Etkin, 1968; Keehn & Nakkash, 1959; see also McAllister & McAllister, 1992).

Other studies have shown that during the course of avoidance training, a response feedback stimulus becomes a conditioned inhibitor of fear (for example, Morris, 1974; Rescorla, 1968a). There is also direct evidence that a feedback stimulus that has been conditioned to inhibit fear during avoidance training is an effective positive reinforcer for new responses (Morris, 1975; Weisman & Litner, 1972; see also Dinsmoor & Sears, 1973). Thus, there is considerable evidence for safety signals as sources of positive reinforcement in avoidance learning. (For a review, see Dinsmoor, 2001b, and ensuing commentary.)

There are important similarities and differences between positive reinforcement of avoidance behavior through conditioned inhibition and the negative reinforcement process assumed by two-process theory. Both mechanisms involve a reduction of fear, but the manner in which this occurs is different in the two cases. Whereas a conditioned inhibitor actively inhibits fear, CS termination is assumed to lead to the passive dissipation of fear. Because both mechanisms involve fear reduction, the operation of both processes depends on the existence of fear. However, the conditioned inhibition reinforcement process is less restrictive about the source of the fear. The fear may be elicited by an explicit warning stimulus or by contextual cues or cues of the environment in which the avoidance procedure is conducted.

The fact that fear elicited by situational cues can provide the basis for conditioned inhibition reinforcement makes the safety-signal hypothesis particularly well suited to explain free-operant avoidance behavior. Participants often experience numerous shocks during acquisition of free-operant avoidance behavior. This and the absence of an exteroceptive warning stimulus make it highly likely that the entire experimental situation becomes conditioned to elicit fear. Because shocks never occur for the duration of the R-S interval after a response is made, the proprioceptive and tactile stimuli that accompany the response can become conditioned inhibitors of fear. Thus, response-associated feedback cues can come to

BOX 10.2

OBSERVATIONAL LEARNING OF FEARS AND PHOBIAS

Excessive fears and phobias can be debilitating and may require therapeutic intervention. Some of the most successful treatment procedures, such as flooding and systematic desensitization, were designed on the basis of conditioning principles. A persistent problem for theoretical analyses of such fears is that people with clinically significant fear and anxiety often have no known history of conditioning with traumatic events. Many people, for example, have an intense fear of snakes even though they have never been bitten by a snake.

How might an individual who has no known experience with traumatic events have acquired a fear or phobia? Research with rhesus monkeys (*Macaca mulatta*) suggests that significant fears may be acquired through observational learning (Mineka & Cook, 1988). Rhesus monkeys reared in the wild have an intense fear of snakes. In response to the sight of a snake, they exhibit a variety of fear responses, including fear grimacing, ear flapping, clutching the cage, averting their eyes, and piloerection (erection of the hair follicles). Fear is also evident in their reluctance to reach over the snake to obtain a food treat. By contrast, monkeys reared in the laboratory do not show these behaviors. Mineka and Cook investigated whether laboratory-reared monkeys could acquire a fear of snakes by observing the fear reactions of wild-reared monkeys in response to a snake.

A discriminative observational conditioning procedure was used. During preliminary training, the demonstrator monkeys were taught to reach over a clear plastic container to obtain a food treat. Observer monkeys were then given the opportunity to watch the reactions of the demonstrator monkeys. On some trials, a live or toy snake was placed in the plastic container. During other trials, the plastic container held a neutral object (a block of wood, for example). The demonstrators showed intense fear of the snake stimuli but not of the neutral objects. After as few as two fear-observation trials, most of the observer monkeys showed similar fear reactions to the snake stimuli. The level of fear they acquired was closely related to the level of fear shown by the demonstrator monkeys. Furthermore, once the observers became fearful of the snakes, they could serve effectively as demonstrators in the observational conditioning of other rhesus monkeys. These results indicate that observational learning could be the basis for wide social transmission of fear among members of a monkey troupe or other social group (see also Cook & Mineka, 1990).

---

provide positive reinforcement for the free-operant avoidance response (Dinsmoor, 1977, 2001a, 2001b; Rescorla, 1968a).

It is important to realize that the conditioned inhibition reinforcement mechanism is not incompatible with or necessarily a substitute for the negative reinforcement process assumed by two-process theory. That is, negative reinforcement through CS termination and positive reinforcement through conditioned inhibitory feedback cues could well be operative simultaneously, both processes contributing to the strength of the avoidance behavior (see Cicala & Owen, 1976; Owen, Cicala, & Herdegen, 1978).

Reinforcement of Avoidance through Reduction of Shock Frequency. As I have described, positive reinforcement through conditioned inhibition can occur alongside the negative reinforcement mechanism of two-process theory. In contrast, another reinforcement mechanism, **shock-frequency reduction,** has been proposed as an alternative to two-process theory (deVilliers, 1974; Herrnstein, 1969; Herrnstein & Hineline, 1966; Hineline, 1981). By definition, avoidance responses prevent the delivery of shock and

R. C. Bolles

Courtesy of Donald A. Dewsbury

thereby reduce the frequency of shocks an organism receives. The theories of avoidance I have discussed so far have viewed the reduction of shocks almost as an incidental by-product of avoidance responses rather than as a primary cause of avoidance behavior. By contrast, the shock-frequency reduction hypothesis views the avoidance of shock as critical to the reinforcement of avoidance behavior.

Shock-frequency reduction as the cause of avoidance behavior was first entertained by Sidman (1962) to explain results he obtained in a concurrent free-operant avoidance experiment. Rats were exposed to two free-operant avoidance schedules at the same time. Responses on one response lever prevented shocks on one of the schedules, and responses on the other lever prevented shocks on the second schedule. Sidman concluded that the animals distributed their responses between the two levers in order to reduce the overall frequency of shocks they received. The idea that shock frequency reduction can serve to reinforce avoidance behavior was later encouraged by evidence of learning in a free-operant avoidance procedure specifically designed to minimize the role of fear-conditioned temporal cues (Herrnstein & Hineline, 1966). Studies of the relative importance of various components of the discriminated avoidance procedure have also shown that the avoidance component significantly contributes to the learning (for example, Bolles, Stokes, & Younger, 1966; see also Bolles, 1972a; Kamin, 1956).

Although the evidence just cited clearly indicates that avoidance of shock is important, the mechanisms responsible for these results are debatable. Several experiments have shown that animals can learn to make an avoidance response even if the response does not reduce the frequency of shocks delivered (Gardner & Lewis, 1976; Hineline, 1970; see also Hineline, 1981). Responding in these studies delayed the onset of the next scheduled shock but did not prevent its delivery. Thus, overall shock frequency was unchanged by the instrumental response. Such results can be explained in terms of the shock-frequency reduction hypothesis by assuming that organisms calculate shock frequencies over only a limited period following an avoidance response. However, once this possibility is allowed, the shock-frequency reduction hypothesis becomes difficult to differentiate from conditioned inhibition reinforcement. If a response reduces the frequency of shocks in the short term, external and proprioceptive stimuli involved in making the response will come to signal this shock reduction and become conditioned inhibitors of fear. The conditioned inhibitory properties of these stimuli can then reinforce the avoidance behavior (Dinsmoor, 2001a, 2001b).

Avoidance and Species-Specific Defense Reactions (SSDRs). In the theories discussed so far, the main emphasis has been on how the events that precede and follow the avoidance response control avoidance behavior. The exact nature or form of the response itself was not a concern to these theories. In addition, the reinforcement mechanisms assumed by the theories all required some time to develop. Before fear reduction can be an effective reinforcer, fear first must be conditioned to the CS; before response feedback cues can come to serve as reinforcers, they must become signals for the absence of shock; and before shock-frequency reduction can work, organisms must experience enough shocks to be able to "calculate" shock frequencies. Therefore, these theories tell us little about what determines the organism's behavior during the first few trials of avoidance training.

Lack of concern with what an organism does during the first few trials of avoidance conditioning is a serious weakness. For an avoidance mechanism to be useful under natural conditions, the mechanism has to generate successful avoidance responses quickly. Consider, for example, an animal trying to avoid a predator. An avoidance mechanism that requires numerous training trials is of no use in this case. If the animal fails to avoid being eaten by the predator during its initial encounter, it will not be around for future training trials. Bolles (1970, 1971) recognized this problem and focused on what controls an organism's behavior during the early stages of avoidance training.

Bolles assumed that aversive stimuli and situations elicit strong unconditioned, or innate, responses. These innate responses are assumed to have evolved because they are successful in defense against pain and injury. Therefore, Bolles called these **species-specific defense reactions (SSDRs).** In rats, for example, prominent SSDRs include flight (running), freezing (remaining vigilant but motionless, except for breathing), and defensive fighting. Other reactions to danger include thigmotaxis (approaching walls), defensive burying (covering up the source of aversive stimulation), and seeking out dark areas.

Bolles proposed that the configuration of the environment determines which particular SSDR occurs. For example, flight may predominate when an obvious escape route is available, and freezing may predominate if there is no way out of the situation. This is indeed the case (Blanchard, 1997; Sigmundi, 1997). Defensive fighting, for example, is not possible without an opponent; and defensive burying is not possible unless a medium, such as sand, is available in which to bury the source of danger. Even freezing, a response that you might think does not require stimulus supports, occurs only in relatively safe places (near a wall or in a corner) rather than in the middle of an arena. If a rat finds itself in the middle of an arena when it encounters danger, it will move to a wall or a corner before freezing.

The SSDR theory of avoidance behavior states that species-specific defense reactions predominate during the initial stages of avoidance training. If the most likely SSDR is successful in preventing shocks, this behavior will persist as long as the avoidance procedure is in effect. If the first SSDR is not effective, it will be followed by shock, which will suppress the behavior through punishment. The animal will then make the next most likely SSDR. If shocks persist, this second SSDR will also become suppressed by punishment, and the organism will make the third most likely SSDR.

The response-selection process is assumed to end when a response is found that is effective in avoiding shocks, so that the behavior will not be suppressed by punishment. Thus, according to the SSDR account, *punishment is responsible for the selection of the instrumental avoidance response* from other activities of the organism. Reinforcement, be it positive or negative, is assumed to have a minor role, if any, in avoidance learning. According to SSDR theory, the correct avoidance response is not strengthened by reinforcement; rather, it occurs because other SSDRs are suppressed by punishment.

One obvious prediction of the SSDR theory is that some types of responses will be more easily learned in avoidance experiments than others. Consistent with this prediction, Bolles (1969) found that rats can rapidly learn to run in a running wheel to avoid shock. By contrast, their performance of a rearing response (standing on the hind legs) did not improve much during the course of avoidance training. Presumably, running was learned faster because it was closer to the rat's species-specific defense reactions in the running wheel (see also Grossen & Kelley, 1972).

SSDR theory made significant contributions to the understanding of avoidance learning by calling attention to the importance of species-typical behavior in aversive situations. However, it has not been entirely successful in explaining experimental findings. For example, contrary to SSDR theory, defensive responses that are ineffective in avoiding aversive stimulation are not necessarily suppressed by punishment. Instead, punishment sometimes facilitates the occurrence of species-specific defense responses (for example, Bolles & Riley, 1973; Melvin & Ervey, 1973; Walters & Glazer, 1971).

Predatory Imminence and the Distinction between Defensive and Recuperative Behavior. Shortcomings of SSDR theory have stimulated alternative formulations that have introduced the concept of predatory imminence (Fanselow & Lester, 1988; Fanselow,

M. S. Fanselow

1989, 1997). These formulations also make a distinction between defensive responses that presumably reflect the anticipation of a painful event or injury and recuperative responses that are assumed to be performed after the aversive or injurious stimulus (Bolles & Fanselow, 1980).

The concept of **predatory imminence** can be illustrated by considering the circumstances faced by a small rodent (a rat, for example) that is a potential source of food for cats, coyotes, snakes, and other predators. The rat is presumably safest in its nest in a burrow, but it has to go out periodically to forage for food. When it is out foraging, it is not in much danger as long as no cats or snakes are around. When a snake appears, the rat's level of danger increases, but not by much if the snake is far away. As the snake gets closer, the level of danger rises. The situation is very dangerous when the snake is about to strike, and maximally dangerous when the strike actually occurs. This progression of increasing levels of danger is called the predatory-imminence continuum and is illustrated in Figure 10.11.

Different species-typical defense responses are assumed to occur at different levels of predatory imminence. If a rat is forced to forage for food in a location where it periodically encounters snakes, it is likely to leave its burrow to get food less often but eat larger meals during each excursion (Fanselow, Lester, & Helmstetter, 1988). Thus, the response to a low level of predatory imminence is an adjustment in meal patterns. When a snake appears but is not yet about to strike, the rat's defensive behavior is likely to change to freezing. Freezing will reduce the chance that a predator will see or hear the rat. Many predators will strike only at moving prey. Freezing by the prey also may result in the predator shifting its attention to something else (Suarez & Gallup, 1981).

When the snake actually touches the rat, the rat is likely to leap into the air. It is as if the rat's prior freezing behavior prepares it to explode into the air when it is touched. This is called the *circa strike response*. If the rat does not successfully escape the predator at this point, it is likely to engage in defensive aggressive activities. If the defensive behavior is successful and the rat manages to get away from the snake, the rat is likely to engage in grooming and other recuperative responses that should promote healing from its injuries.

The predatory-imminence hypothesis differs from the SSDR theory in two important respects. First, as the scenario illustrates, species-specific defense responses such as freezing, fleeing, and aggression are most likely to occur in anticipation of injury rather than in response to the injury itself. The actual injury stimulates recuperative responses. Thus, unlike the SSDR theory, the predatory-imminence hypothesis makes a distinction between defensive and recuperative responses to aversive stimulation. Second, in the predatory-imminence hypothesis, the primary determinant of the particular defense response that is

Figure 10.11   The predatory-imminence continuum. (From "A Functional Behavioristic Approach to Aversively Motivated Behavior: Predatory Imminence as a Determinant of the Topography of Defensive Behavior," by M. S. Fanselow and L. S. Lester. In R. C. Bolles and M. D. Beecher [Eds.], 1988, *Evolution and Learning,* pp. 185– 212. Copyright © 1988 by Lawrence Erlbaum and Associates. Reprinted by permission.)

Status of the predator	Status of the prey
Predator cannot appear	Nonaversively motivated behavior and recuperative behavior due to a previous attack
Predator could appear	Preencounter defensive behavior (e.g., modification of foraging patterns)
Predator detected	Postencounter defensive behavior (e.g., freezing)
Predator makes contact	Strike-defensive behavior (leap-jump, defensive aggression)

observed is assumed to be the level of predatory imminence rather than the configuration of the environment. Thus, selection among possible SSDRs is not through suppression of ineffective SSDRs by punishment, as the SSDR theory proposes, but by different levels of perceived danger.

Despite these differences, both the SSDR theory and the predatory-imminence hypothesis assume that defensive behavior initially occurs as unconditioned responding. Stimuli that become associated with an aversive event can come to elicit a defensive response as well. The available evidence suggests that in rats the defensive response that comes to be elicited by a conditioned stimulus is usually one level lower on the predatory-imminence scale than the response elicited by the unconditioned stimulus (Fanselow, 1989). Thus, if the unconditioned stimulus elicits the leap and jump (circa strike) characteristic of peak predatory imminence, the conditioned stimulus is likely to elicit the freezing behavior of the level just below.

Another important similarity between the predatory-imminence hypothesis and the SSDR theory is that neither of them assumes that positive reinforcement is involved in the development of avoidance behavior. The predatory-imminence hypothesis takes a more radical position than the SSDR theory in rejecting the importance of instrumental conditioning altogether, since it does not even include a punishment mechanism. However, the predatory-imminence hypothesis was developed as an explanation of defensive behavior—not as an explanation of the diverse findings that have been obtained in avoidance learning experiments. Therefore, it was not intended to serve as a complete account of what happens in avoidance conditioning experiments.

The Avoidance Puzzle: Concluding Comments

We have learned a great deal about avoidance behavior since Mowrer and Lamoreaux (1942) puzzled about how "not getting something" can motivate avoidance responses. As I described, numerous ingenious answers to this puzzle have been provided. Two-process theory, conditioned inhibition reinforcement, and shock-frequency reduction reinforcement all provide different views of how the avoidance response may be reinforced. By contrast, the SSDR account focuses on unconditioned aspects of defensive behavior, a theme that is further elaborated through the concept of predatory imminence.

None of the major theories can explain everything that occurs in aversive conditioning situations, but each provides ideas that are useful for understanding various aspects of avoidance behavior. For example, two-process theory is uniquely suited to explain the results of the acquired-drive experiments. The safety-signal theory is particularly useful in explaining free-operant avoidance learning, the role of response feedback stimuli in avoidance conditioning, and the maintenance of avoidance behavior in the absence of an explicit warning stimulus. The concept of predatory imminence provides the most useful account of what happens during early stages of avoidance training. Given the complexities of the various avoidance learning paradigms, it is not surprising that several conceptual frameworks are needed to explain all of the available data.

PUNISHMENT

Although most of us engage in avoidance behavior of one sort or another every day, there is little public awareness of it. As a society, we are not particularly concerned about what is involved in making avoidance responses. This may be because procedures that generate active

N. H. Azrin

avoidance are rarely used in organized efforts to change or control someone's behavior. By contrast, **punishment** has always been of great concern to people. Sometimes punishment is used as a form of retribution or as a price extracted for undesirable behavior. Punishment is also frequently used to encourage adherence to religious and civil codes of conduct. Many institutions and rules have evolved to ensure that punishment will be administered in ways that are deemed ethical and acceptable to society. What constitutes acceptable punishment in the criminal justice system, in childrearing, in schools, or in the treatment of individuals with psychiatric disorders or mental retardation is a matter of continual debate.

Despite long-standing societal concerns about punishment, for many years experimental psychologists devoted little attention to the topic. On the basis of a few experiments, Thorndike (1932) and Skinner (1938, 1953) concluded that punishment was not a very effective method for controlling behavior and that it had only temporary effects at best (see also Estes, 1944). This claim was not seriously challenged until the 1960s, when punishment processes began to be investigated more extensively (Azrin & Holz, 1966; Campbell & Church, 1969; Church, 1963; Solomon, 1964). We now know that punishment can be an effective technique for modifying behavior (Dinsmoor, 1998). Given several behavioral options, punishment produces a response bias away from the punished behavior (McAdie, Foster, & Temple, 1996). With appropriate procedural parameters, responding can be suppressed nearly totally in just one or two trials. With less severe parameters, the suppression of behavior may be incomplete, and responding may recover.

Experimental Analysis of Punishment

The basic punishment procedure involves presenting an aversive stimulus after a specified response. If the procedure is effective, the specified response becomes suppressed. By not making the punished response, the organism avoids the aversive stimulation. Because punishment involves the suppression of behavior, it can be observed only with responses that are likely to occur in the absence of punishment. To ensure occurrence of the behavior, experimental studies of punishment usually also involve reinforcement of the punished response with something such as food or water. This sets up a conflict between responding to obtain positive reinforcement and withholding responding to avoid punishment. The degree of response suppression that occurs is determined by variables related both to presentation of the aversive stimulus and to the availability of positive reinforcement.

Characteristics of the Aversive Stimulus and Its Method of Introduction. A great variety of aversive stimuli have been used in punishment experiments, including electric shock, a sudden burst of air, loud noise, verbal reprimands, a physical slap, a squirt of lemon juice in the mouth, and a cue previously conditioned with shock (Azrin, 1958; Hake & Azrin, 1965; Hall, Axelrod, Foundopoulos, Shellman, Campbell, & Cranston, 1971; Masserman, 1946; Sajwaj, Libet, & Agras, 1974; Skinner, 1938). Other response-suppression procedures have involved the loss of positive reinforcement, time out from positive reinforcement, overcorrection, and manual restraint (Foxx & Azrin, 1973; Lerman, Iwata, Shore, & DeLeon, 1997; Thomas, 1968; Trenholme & Baron, 1975).

Time out refers to removal of the opportunity to obtain positive reinforcement. Time out is often used to punish children, as when a child is told "Go to your room" after doing something bad. **Overcorrection** involves requiring a person not only to rectify what was done badly but to overcorrect for the mistake. For example, a child who has placed an object in his mouth may be asked to remove the object and also to wash out his mouth with an antiseptic solution.

A convenient aversive stimulus in human studies of punishment is point loss. In one recent study (O'Donnell, Crosbie, Williams, & Saunders, 2000), college students were reinforced for pressing a response lever by points that could be exchanged for money at the end of the experiment. Two discriminative stimuli (lines of different lengths) were used. During the baseline phase, only the S^D was presented, and responses were reinforced on a variable interval schedule. After that, the S^D was alternated with the other discriminative stimulus, the S^D_p. Responding continued to be reinforced according to the VI schedule during the S^D_p, but now a point-loss punishment contingency was also in effect. With each response, a certain number of points was subtracted from the total the subject had obtained.

The results of the experiment are summarized in Figure 10.12. Responding was well maintained during S^D in the baseline phase. In the subsequent punishment phase, responding continued at substantial levels during S^D but was suppressed during S^D_p.

The response suppression produced by punishment depends in part on features of the aversive stimulus. The effects of various characteristics of the aversive event have been most extensively investigated with shock because the duration and intensity of shock can be precisely controlled. The general finding has been that more intense and longer shocks are

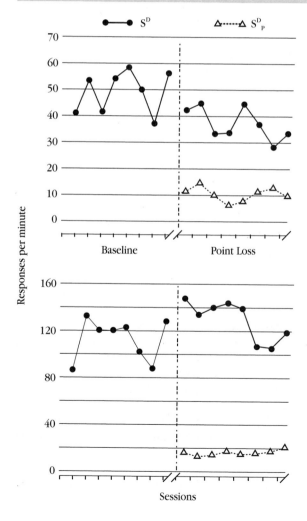

Figure 10.12 Lever-press responding of college students reinforced on a variable interval schedule with points that could be exchanged for money at the end of the experiment. During the baseline phase only the reinforced discriminative stimulus (S^D) was presented. During the next phase the S^D was presented in alternation with a punishment stimulus (S^D_p), during which the VI schedule remained in effect but each response was also punished by point loss. The top and bottom panels present data for different students. (After O'Donnell et al., 2000.)

more effective in suppressing responding (see reviews by Azrin & Holz, 1966; Church, 1969; Walters & Grusec, 1977). Low-intensity aversive stimulation produces only moderate suppression of responding, and responding may recover with continued exposure to the mild punishment procedure (for example, Azrin, 1960). By contrast, if the aversive stimulus is sufficiently intense, responding will be completely suppressed for a long time. In one experiment, for example, high-intensity punishment completely suppressed the instrumental response for 6 days (Azrin, 1960).

Another very important factor in punishment is how the aversive stimulus is introduced. If a high intensity of shock is used from the outset of punishment, the instrumental response will be severely suppressed. Much less suppression of behavior will occur if the shock intensity is gradually increased during the course of continued punishment training (Azrin, Holz, & Hake, 1963; Miller, 1960; see also Banks, 1976). This finding is very important because it shows that an organism becomes resistant to the effects of intense punishment if it is first exposed to lower levels of shock that do not produce much response suppression. Spending two weeks in jail is not a disturbing experience for someone who has become accustomed to shorter periods of incarceration.

The preceding findings suggest that how organisms respond during their *initial exposure* to punishment determines how they will respond to subsequent punishment (Church, 1969). This idea has an interesting implication. Suppose an individual is first exposed to intense shock that results in a very low level of responding. If the shock intensity is subsequently reduced, the severe suppression of behavior should persist. Thus, after exposure to intense shock, mild shock should be more effective in suppressing behavior than if the mild shock had been used from the beginning. Such findings have been obtained by Raymond (reported in Church, 1969). Taken together, the evidence indicates that initial exposure to mild aversive stimulation that does not disrupt behavior reduces the effects of later intense punishment. By contrast, initial exposure to intense aversive stimulation increases the suppressive effects of later mild punishment.

Response-Contingent versus Response-Independent Aversive Stimulation.   Another important variable that determines the extent to which aversive stimulation suppresses behavior is whether the aversive stimulus is presented contingent on a specified response or independently of behavior. Response-independent aversive stimulation can result in some suppression of instrumental behavior. However, the general finding is that significantly more suppression of behavior occurs if the aversive stimulus is produced by the instrumental response (for example, Azrin, 1956; Bolles, Holtz, Dunn, & Hill, 1980; Camp, Raymond, & Church, 1967; Frankel, 1975).

In one study demonstrating the importance of the response contingency in punishment, Goodall (1984) compared a CER, or conditioned suppression, procedure (in which footshock during a CS was delivered independent of behavior) and a discriminative punishment procedure (in which shock during the CS was delivered contingent on lever pressing). One group of rats was trained initially to press a lever for food reinforcement on a VI 60-sec schedule. After responding stabilized, two conditioned stimuli were introduced, a tone and a light. One of the stimuli (let's say the tone) was designated as the punishment cue, and the other stimulus (the light) was designated as the cue for response-independent aversive stimulation. Two trials with each of the CSs were presented each day in alternation, starting with the punishment cue. During the punishment stimulus, the rats received a brief shock after every third lever-press response. Thus, punishment was delivered on an FR 3 schedule. Each CER trial was yoked to the preceding punishment trial, so that the rats received the same number and distribution of shocks during the CER cue as they had received during the

Figure 10.13 Suppression of lever pressing during punishment and CER stimuli during 10 successive sessions. During the punishment cue, lever pressing was punished on an FR 3 schedule. During the CER cue, the same number and distribution of shocks was delivered independent of behavior. (From "Learning Due to the Response-Shock Contingency in Signalled Punishment," by G. Goodall, 1984, *The Quarterly Journal of Experimental Psychology, 36B,* pp. 259–279. Copyright © 1984 by Lawrence Erlbaum and Associates. Reprinted by permission.)

immediately preceding punishment trial. However, shocks during the CER cue were always delivered independent of the lever-press behavior.

The results of the experiment are presented in Figure 10.13 in terms of suppression of lever pressing during the CER and punishment cues. Given the brief and mild shocks that were used (0.5 mA, 0.5 sec), not much suppression of behavior was evident during the CER stimulus. By contrast, the same number and distribution of shocks substantially suppressed responding during the punishment stimulus. This difference illustrates that delivering shocks contingent on an instrumental response is more effective in suppressing that response than delivering aversive stimulation independent of behavior.

Effects of Delay of Punishment. Another important factor in punishment is the interval between the instrumental behavior and the aversive stimulation. The general finding is that increasing the delay of punishment results in less suppression of behavior (for example, Baron, 1965; Camp et al., 1967). This relation is particularly important in practical applications of punishment. Inadvertent delays may occur if the undesired response is not detected right away, if it takes time to investigate who is actually at fault for an error, or if preparing the aversive stimulus requires time. Such delays can make punishment totally ineffective in modifying the undesired behavior.

Effects of Schedules of Punishment. Just as positive reinforcement does not have to be provided for each occurrence of the instrumental response, punishment may also be delivered only intermittently. This was the case in the experiment by Goodall. In the Goodall study, punishment was delivered on an FR 3 schedule. More systematic studies have shown that the degree of response suppression produced by punishment depends on the proportion of responses that are punished.

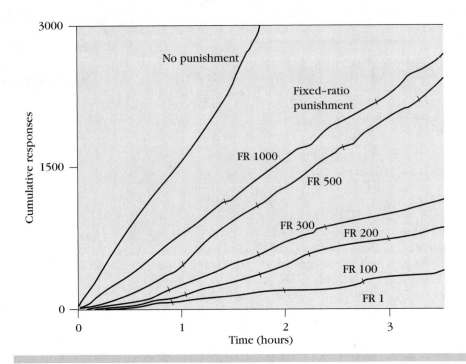

Figure 10.14 Cumulative record of pecking when the response was not punished and when the response was punished according to various fixed-ratio schedules of punishment. The oblique slashes indicate the delivery of punishment. Responding was reinforced on a variable interval 3-min schedule. (From "Fixed-Ratio Punishment," by N. H. Azrin, W. C. Holz, and D. R. Hake, 1963, *Journal of the Experimental Analysis of Behavior, 6,* pp. 141–148.)

In a study of fixed ratio punishment by Azrin and his colleagues (1963), pigeons were first reinforced with food on a variable interval schedule for pecking a response key. Punishment was then introduced. Various fixed ratio punishment procedures were tested while food reinforcement continued to be provided for the pecking behavior. The results are summarized in Figure 10.14. When every response was shocked (FR 1 punishment), key pecking ceased entirely. With the other punishment schedules, the rate of responding depended on the frequency of punishment. Higher fixed ratio schedules allowed more responses to go unpunished. Not surprisingly, therefore, higher rates of responding occurred when higher fixed ratio punishment schedules were used. However, some suppression of behavior was observed even when only every thousandth response was followed by shock.

Effects of Schedules of Positive Reinforcement. As I noted earlier, in most studies of punishment the instrumental response is simultaneously maintained by a positive reinforcement schedule so that some level of responding is available to be punished. The effects of a punishment procedure are in part determined by this positive reinforcement. When behavior is maintained by either a fixed or a variable interval schedule of positive reinforcement, punishment produces a decrease in the overall rate of responding. However, the temporal distribution of the behavior is not disturbed. That is, during the punishment procedure, variable interval positive reinforcement produces a suppressed but stable rate of responding (see Figure 10.14), whereas fixed interval positive reinforcement produces the typical scalloped pattern of responding (for example, Azrin & Holz, 1961).

The outcome is different if the behavior is maintained by a fixed ratio schedule of positive reinforcement. As noted in Chapter 6, fixed ratio schedules produce a pause in responding just after reinforcement (the postreinforcement pause), followed by a high and steady rate of responding to complete the number of responses necessary for the next reinforcer (the ratio run). Punishment usually increases the length of the postreinforcement pause but has little effect on the ratio run (Azrin, 1959; see also Church, 1969; Dardano & Sauerbrunn, 1964).

Availability of Alternative Sources of Positive Reinforcement.   Punishment has dramatically different outcomes depending on whether the subject is able to obtain reinforcement by engaging in some other activity. This is particularly important in practical applications of punishment. If the punished response is the only activity available to the subject for obtaining reinforcement, punishment will be much less effective than if an alternative source of reinforcement is provided along with punishment.

The importance of alternative sources of reinforcement was demonstrated by an early study of adult male smokers conducted by Herman and Azrin (1964). The subjects were seated facing two response levers. Pressing either lever was reinforced with a cigarette on a variable interval schedule. After the behavior was occurring at a stable rate, responding on one of the levers was punished by a brief obnoxious noise. In one experimental condition, only one response lever was available during the punishment phase. In another condition, both response levers were available, but responding on one of the levers was punished with the loud noise. Figure 10.15 shows the results. When the punished response was the only way to obtain cigarettes, punishment produced a moderate suppression of behavior. By contrast, when the alternative response lever was available, responding on the punished lever ceased altogether. Thus, the availability of an alternative response for obtaining positive reinforcement greatly increased the suppressive effects of punishment. Similar results have been obtained in other situations. For example, children punished for playing with certain toys are much less likely to play with these if they are allowed to play with other toys instead (Perry & Parke, 1975). Reinforcement for alternative behavior also increases the effectiveness of mild punishment in suppressing self-injurious behavior in individuals with profound mental retardation (Thompson, Iwata, Conners, & Roscoe, 1999).

Effects of a Discriminative Stimulus for Punishment.   As discussed in Chapter 8, if positive reinforcement is available for responding in the presence of a distinctive stimulus but is not available in its absence, the organism will learn to respond only when the stimulus is present. The suppressive effects of punishment can also be brought under stimulus control.

Figure 10.15   Cumulative record of responding when responses are not punished, when responses are punished and there is no alternative source of reinforcement, and when responses are punished but an alternative reinforced response is available. (From "Punishment," by N. H. Azrin and W. C. Holz. In W. K. Honig [Ed.], 1966, *Operant Behavior.* Copyright © 1966 by Prentice-Hall.)

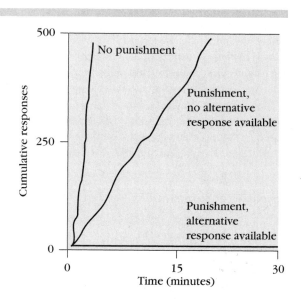

This occurs if responding is punished in the presence of a discriminative stimulus but is not punished when the stimulus is absent. Such a procedure is called **discriminative punishment.** With continued exposure to discriminative punishment, the suppressive effects of punishment will come to be limited to the presence of the discriminative stimulus (Dinsmoor, 1952).

Discriminative punishment was used in the study whose results were summarized in Figure 10.12. The college students who served in this experiment could earn points for responding during one discriminative stimulus, the S^D. In the presence of another discriminative stimulus, the $S^D{}_P$, responding was also punished by loss of points. As Figure 10.12 illustrates, the suppressive effects of punishment were largely limited to the $S^D{}_P$.

The fact that the suppressive effects of punishment can be limited to the presence of a discriminative stimulus is often problematic in applications of punishment. In many situations, the person who administers the punishment also serves as a discriminative stimulus for punishment, with the result that the undesired behavior is suppressed only as long as the monitor is present. For example, children learn which teachers are strict about discipline and learn to suppress their rambunctious behavior in those classes more than in other classes. As another example, a highway patrol car is a discriminative stimulus for punishment for speeding. Drivers are more likely to obey speed laws in areas where they see patrol cars than in unpatrolled stretches of highway.

Punishment as a Signal for the Availability of Positive Reinforcement. Punishment does not always suppress behavior. In fact, in certain situations people seem to seek out punishment. Does this represent a breakdown of the normal mechanisms of behavior, or can such behavior be explained by the principles I have discussed so far? Experimental evidence suggests that conventional behavioral mechanisms may lead to such seemingly abnormal behavior. Punishment seeking can result if positive reinforcement is available only when the instrumental response is also punished. In such circumstances, punishment may become a signal, or discriminative stimulus, for the availability of positive reinforcement. If this occurs, punishment will increase rather than suppress responding.

In one demonstration of the discriminative stimulus properties of punishment, pigeons were first trained to peck a response key for food reinforcement on a variable interval schedule (Holz & Azrin, 1961). Each response was then punished by a mild shock sufficient to reduce the response rate by about 50%. In the next phase of the experiment, periods in which the punishment procedure was in effect were alternated with periods in which punishment was not scheduled. In addition, the pecking response was reinforced with food only during the punishment periods. The punishment and safe periods were not signaled by an environmental stimulus, such as a light or a tone. Therefore, the only way for the pigeons to tell whether reinforcement was available was to see whether they were punished for pecking. Under these circumstances, higher rates of pecking occurred during punishment periods than during safe periods. Punishment became a discriminative stimulus for food reinforcement. (For other examples of self-punitive behavior, see Brown, 1969; Brown & Cunningham, 1981; Dean & Pittman, 1991; Melvin, 1971.)

Theories of Punishment

In contrast to the study of avoidance behavior, investigations of punishment, by and large, have not been motivated by theoretical considerations. Most of the evidence available about the effects of punishment has been the product of empirical curiosity. The investigators were interested in finding out how punishment is influenced by various manipulations rather than in testing specific theoretical formulations. In fact, few systematic theories of punish-

BOX 10.3

WHEN PUNISHMENT DOESN'T WORK

Sometimes children are brought to a therapist because their behavior is out of control. A child may be unruly and unresponsive to the disciplinary practices of parents or teachers. Punishment may be tried as a procedure of last resort, but without much success. The parents or teachers may note that punishing the child only makes the behavior worse. It is not uncommon for children with a severe problem of this type to be diagnosed as hyperactive or emotionally disturbed. These labels suggest there is something fundamentally wrong with the child. Behavior therapists, however, have found that in some cases the problem may be nothing more than the result of mismanaged discipline. The parents or teachers may have inadvertently established punishment as a discriminative stimulus for positive reinforcement. Instead of decreasing some undesirable behavior, punishment increases it. How can this happen?

Take the hypothetical situation of Johnny, who lives in a home with two busy parents. Johnny, like most children, is rather active. If he is quietly playing in his room, the parents are likely to ignore him and engage in activities of their own. By contrast, if Johnny behaves badly or makes demands, the parents are forced to pay attention to him. The parents may be giving Johnny attention only when he is misbehaving or making demands. Any time he is not being a problem, the parents may be thankfully relieved to have a moment's peace. Thus, rather than reinforcing cooperative or peaceful behavior, the parents may be ignoring Johnny at these times. What we have then is a vicious circle. The more Johnny misbehaves, the less attention he is given for nondisruptive behavior, because the parents increasingly come to cherish quiet moments as a chance to do something on their own. Misbehavior becomes Johnny's main means of obtaining attention. The punishments and reprimands that go with the behavior signal to him that his parents are caring and attending.

In actuality, the therapist does not have the opportunity to observe how behavior problems of this type originate. The "discriminative value of punishment" explanation is supported by the outcome of attempts to change the situation. The hypothesis suggests that if one changes the attention patterns, the behavior problem can be alleviated. Indeed, clinical psychologists often show parents how to attend to appropriate and constructive activities and how to administer punishment with a minimum of attention directed toward the child. In many cases dramatic improvement ensues when parents are able to positively reinforce cooperative behavior with their attentions and ignore disruptive activities as much as possible.

ment exist, and most were formulated in some form about 50 years ago. I will describe three of the most prominent theories.

The Conditioned Emotional Response Theory of Punishment. One of the first theories of punishment was proposed by Estes (1944) and is based on the observation by Estes and Skinner (1941) that a conditioned stimulus that has been paired with shock will suppress the performance of food-reinforced instrumental behavior. I discussed this conditioned suppression, or conditioned emotional response, procedure earlier in this chapter as well as in Chapters 3. Conditioned suppression involves a suppression of ongoing behavior elicited by a stimulus that has been associated with aversive stimulation. The behavioral suppression occurs primarily because a fear-conditioned stimulus elicits freezing, which then interferes with other activities.

Estes (1944) proposed that punishment suppresses behavior through the same mechanism that produces response suppression to a fear-conditioned stimulus (see also Estes, 1969). In contrast to the usual conditioned suppression experiment, however, punishment procedures usually do not involve an explicit CS that signals the impending delivery of an aversive stimulus. Estes suggested that the various stimuli an individual experiences just before making the punished response serve this function. Consider for example, how an "invisible" fence works to keep a dog in its yard. An invisible or electronic fence detects when the dog goes to the edge of its yard and administers a brief shock to the dog through a remote sensing collar if the dog steps beyond this boundary. The punished response (going too far) is associated with various cues of the boundary of the yard. When the dog is punished, the various visual and other spatial cues of the yard boundary become paired with shock. With repetition of the punishment episode, the boundary stimuli become strongly conditioned by the shock. According to the conditioned emotional response theory, as these cues acquire conditioned aversive properties, they will come to elicit freezing, which is incompatible with the punished behavior. Thus, the punished response will become suppressed.

The conditioned emotional response theory can explain many punishment effects. For example, the fact that more intense and longer duration shocks produce more response suppression can be explained by assuming that the stimuli conditioned by these aversive events elicit more vigorous conditioned emotional responses. The theory can also explain why response-contingent aversive stimulation produces more response suppression than response-independent delivery of shock. If shock is produced by the instrumental response, the stimuli that become conditioned by the shock are more likely to be closely related to performance of this behavior. Therefore, the conditioned emotional responses are more likely to interfere with the punished response.

The Avoidance Theory of Punishment.   An alternative to the conditioned emotional response theory regards punishment as a form of avoidance behavior. This theory is most closely associated with Dinsmoor (1954, 1977, 1998) and follows the tradition of two-process theory of avoidance. Dinsmoor accepted the idea that the stimuli that accompany the instrumental response acquire aversive properties when the response is punished. Dinsmoor went on to propose that organisms learn to escape from the conditioned aversive stimuli related to the punished response by engaging in some other behavior that is incompatible with the punished activity. Since this other behavior is incompatible with the punished response, performance of the alternative activity results in suppression of the punished behavior. Thus, the avoidance theory explains punishment in terms of the acquisition of incompatible avoidance responses.

The avoidance theory of punishment is an ingenious proposal. It suggests that all changes produced by aversive instrumental conditioning, be they increases or decreases in the likelihood of a response, can be explained by the same avoidance learning mechanisms. Suppression of behavior is not viewed as reflecting the weakening of the punished response. Rather, it is explained in terms of the strengthening of competing avoidance responses.

Despite its cleverness and parsimony, the avoidance theory of punishment has been controversial. Because it explains punishment in terms of avoidance mechanisms, all the theoretical problems that have been troublesome in the analysis of avoidance behavior become problems in the analysis of punishment as well. Another challenge for the theory is that its critical elements are not stated in a way that makes them easily accessible to experimental proof (Rachlin & Herrnstein, 1969; Schuster & Rachlin, 1968). The stimuli that are assumed to acquire conditioned aversive properties are not under the direct control of the experimenter. Rather, they are events that an organism is assumed to experience when it is about to make the punished response. The avoidance responses that are presumably acquired are also ill specified. The theory does not tell us what these responses will be in a given situation or how one might look for them.

Punishment and the Negative Law of Effect. This third and last explanation of punishment is also the oldest. Thorndike (1911) originally proposed that positive reinforcement and punishment involve symmetrically opposite processes. Just as positive reinforcement strengthens behavior, so punishment weakens it. In later years Thorndike abandoned the idea that punishment weakens behavior because he failed to find supporting evidence in some of his experiments (Thorndike, 1932). However, the belief that there is a negative law of effect that is comparable to but the opposite of a positive law of effect has retained favor with some investigators (for example, Azrin & Holz, 1966; Rachlin & Herrnstein, 1969).

One approach to the analysis of the negative law of effect was initiated by Premack and his colleagues. As I discussed in Chapter 7, Premack proposed that positive reinforcement occurs when the opportunity to engage in a highly valued activity is made to depend on the prior performance of an activity of lower value. According to Premack, the punishment contingency reverses this relation. In punishment, a low-valued activity is made to occur contingent on the performance of a higher-valued behavior. Exposing oneself to shock, for example, has a much lower probability than pressing a lever for food. Hence, shock can punish lever pressing. (For further discussion, see Premack, 1971a; Weisman & Premack, 1966.)

With a reinforcement procedure, the instrumental response is increased and the reinforcing response is decreased relative to a baseline free-responding situation. With a punishment procedure, the instrumental response is decreased and the reinforcing or punishing response is increased relative to a baseline condition. Moreover, in both cases the response that increases is the low-valued behavior and the one that decreases is the higher-valued behavior (see Table 10.1). Viewed in this way, the procedures of reinforcement and punishment produce the same effects. Operationally, there is only one significant difference. In punishment, the individual must be forced to engage in the lower-valued activity. Individuals do not ordinarily expose themselves to aversive stimuli. In reinforcement, the individual is "induced" to engage in the lower-valued activity by the contingency itself.

The similarity between punishment and reinforcement assumed by the Premack was tested in an interesting experiment involving toy-playing behavior in children (Burkhard, Rachlin, & Schrader, 1978). In a baseline phase, the children were observed playing with three toys. The toys were ranked high, medium, and low on the basis of how much time the children spent with each one. The children were assigned to reinforcement and punishment groups. For the reinforcement group, 1 minute of playing with the high-ranked toy was allowed after 1 minute of play with the low-ranked toy. For the punishment group, 1 minute of play with the low-ranked toy was required after 1 minute of play with the

TABLE 10.1	COMPARISON OF RESPONSE REALLOCATION IN POSITIVE REINFORCEMENT AND PUNISHMENT	

PROCEDURE	RESPONSE-REINFORCER CONTINGENCY	RESULTANT BEHAVIOR CHANGE
Positive reinforcement	L → H	L increases H decreases
Punishment	H → L	L increases H decreases

(L = low-valued activity; H = high-valued activity)

high-ranked toy. In both cases, the toy ranked as medium provided background activity and could be used freely. If Premack's punishment hypothesis is correct, the reinforcement and punishment procedures should have produced the same new distribution of time among the three toys. This, in fact, was the result. The reinforcement and punishment groups were indistinguishable in how much time they ended up playing with each toy. Playing with the low-ranked toy increased and playing with the high-ranked toy decreased to comparable levels for the two groups.

Premack's perspective suggests that punishment is similar to positive reinforcement in that it imposes a restriction against which behavior has to be adjusted. The negative law of effect is a statement of the way behavior changes under these restrictions: a low-valued activity produces a decrease in a higher-valued activity. Economically minded theorists propose, as in the case of positive reinforcement (see Chapter 7), that organisms respond so as to maximize overall value. The maximization process, with both reinforcement and punishment procedures, involves an increase in a low-valued activity balanced against a decrease in a high-valued activity.

Punishment outside the Laboratory

As I have described, punishment can be a highly effective procedure for rapidly suppressing behavior. However, the effectiveness of punishment in laboratory studies is not sufficient to justify its application outside the laboratory. Punishment procedures are easily misused, and even if the procedures are administered appropriately, there are serious ethical constraints on their application and they can have troublesome side effects.

Punishment is typically not applied in an effective manner. Often, punishment is first introduced at low intensities (a reprimand for the first offense, for example). The aversive stimulus may not be administered rapidly after the target response but delayed until it is convenient to administer it ("Wait until I tell your parents about this"). Punishment is usually administered on an intermittent schedule, and the chances of getting "caught" may not be high. Appropriate alternative behavior may not be recognized and positively reinforced at the same time that transgressions are punished. Often, there are clear discriminative stimuli for punishment. The undesired behavior may be monitored only at particular times or by a particular person, making it likely that the punished response will be suppressed only at those times. Finally, punishment may be the only source of attention for someone, making punishment a discriminative stimulus for positive reinforcement.

The preceding problems with the uses of punishment outside the laboratory can be overcome, but it is difficult to guard against these pitfalls in common interpersonal interactions. People who punish others may do so because they are frustrated and angry. A frustrative act of punishment is likely to violate many of the guidelines for effective use of punishment. Punishing someone in an act of anger and frustration is a form of abuse—not a form of systematic training.

The use of punishment in parenting has been the subject of extensive research. Consistent with the implications of laboratory research, a recent review of the literature on parental corporal punishment concluded that punishment is strongly associated with increased immediate compliance on the part of a child. The same analysis showed, however, that corporal punishment is also associated with increases in aggression and delinquent and anti-social behavior on the part of the children (Gershoff, 2002). In addition, parental punishment is associated with deterioration in the relationship between the parent and the child, poorer child mental health, and increased incidence of aggressive behavior in adulthood. Precise conclusions about the causal role of parental punishment in these effects are difficult to justify because the data were provided by correlational studies.

Parental use of corporal punishment has been outlawed in Austria, Croatia, Cyprus, Denmark, Finland, Germany, Israel, Italy, Latvia, Norway, and Sweden. Although corporal punishment by parents is not against the law in the United States, 27 states have adopted laws limiting the use of corporal punishment by teachers and guardians. Corporal punishment is sometimes used as a procedure of last resort in the treatment of severe behavior problems when other procedures have been unsuccessful.

In one study, for example, punishment was used to suppress recurrent vomiting by a 9-month-old infant (Linscheid & Cunningham, 1977). The recurrent vomiting had resulted in excessive weight loss and malnutrition. Without treatment, the infant risked potentially fatal medical complications. Brief (0.5-second) shocks sufficient to elicit a startle response, but not sufficient to elicit crying, were used as the aversive stimulus. Within 3 days, vomiting was nearly totally suppressed by the punishment procedure. The suppression of vomiting persisted after discharge from the hospital. The infant started gaining weight again and was soon within normal range.

Cases such as the preceding one illustrate that punishment can be beneficial, but even in such instances, serious ethical dilemmas have to be resolved. There is an ongoing debate about when, if ever, punishment is justified as a treatment procedure, and therapists are continuing their search for alternative ways to deal with potentially life-threatening behavior problems (see Repp & Singh, 1990.) Many states have adopted stringent procedures to review and monitor the use of aversive control procedures in therapeutic settings and have banned certain forms of aversive control altogether. Professional and patient rights organizations also have adopted detailed and restrictive guidelines for the therapeutic uses of aversive control. Fewer restrictions apply to punishment involving time out from reinforcement rather than the administration of a physically painful aversive stimulus.

SAMPLE QUESTIONS

1. What is the fundamental problem in the analysis of avoidance behavior, and how is this problem resolved by two-process theory?

2. Compare and contrast discriminated and free-operant avoidance procedures.

3. How can the concept of a safety signal be used to explain free-operant avoidance learning?

4. Describe factors that enhance the effectiveness of punishment in suppressing behavior.

5. In what ways is punishment similar to positive reinforcement; in what ways is it different?

KEY TERMS

acquired-drive A source of motivation for instrumental behavior caused by the presentation of a stimulus that was previously conditioned with a primary, or unconditioned, reinforcer.

avoidance An instrumental conditioning procedure in which the participant's behavior prevents the delivery of an aversive stimulus.

avoidance trial A trial in a discriminated avoidance procedure in which the occurrence of the avoidance response prevents the delivery of the aversive stimulus.

conservation of fear The assumption that conditioned fear is maintained in a signaled avoidance procedure if participants respond rapidly to turn off the CS because later segments of the CS are not experienced.

discriminated avoidance An avoidance conditioning procedure in which occurrences of the aversive stimulus are signaled by a conditioned stimulus. Responding during the conditioned stimulus terminates the CS and prevents the delivery of the aversive unconditioned stimulus. Also called *signaled avoidance*.

discriminative punishment A procedure in which responding is punished in the presence of a particular stimulus and not punished in the absence of that stimulus.

escape trial A type of trial during avoidance training in which the required avoidance response is not made and the aversive unconditioned stimulus is presented. Performance of the instrumental response during the aversive stimulus results in termination of the aversive stimulus. Thus, the organism is able to escape from the aversive stimulus.

flooding A procedure for extinguishing avoidance behavior in which the conditioned stimulus is presented while the participant is prevented from making the avoidance response. Also called *response prevention*.

free-operant avoidance Same as *nondiscriminated avoidance*.

nondiscriminated avoidance An avoidance conditioning procedure in which occurrences of the aversive stimulus are not signaled by an external stimulus. In the absence of avoidance behavior, the aversive stimulus is presented periodically, as set by the S-S interval. Each occurrence of the avoidance response prevents delivery of aversive stimulation for a fixed period (the R-S interval). Also called *free-operant avoidance*; originally called *Sidman avoidance*.

overcorrection A procedure for discouraging behavior in which the participant is required not only to correct or rectify a mistake but to go beyond that by, for example, extensively practicing the correct response alternative.

predatory imminence The perceived likelihood of being attacked by a predator. Different species-typical defense responses are assumed to be performed in the face of different degrees of predatory imminence.

punishment An instrumental conditioning procedure in which there is a positive contingency between the instrumental response and an aversive stimulus. If the participant performs the instrumental response, it receives the aversive stimulus; if the participant does not perform the instrumental response, it does not receive the aversive stimulus.

R-S interval The interval between the occurrence of an avoidance response and the next scheduled presentation of the aversive stimulus in a nondiscriminated avoidance procedure.

response prevention Same as *flooding*.

safety signal A stimulus that signals the absence of an aversive event.

shock-frequency reduction A hypothesis according to which reduction in the frequency of shock serves to reinforce avoidance behavior.

shuttle avoidance A type of avoidance conditioning procedure in which the required instrumental response consists in going back and forth (shuttling) between two sides of an experimental apparatus.

signaled avoidance Same as *discriminated avoidance*.

species-specific defense reactions (SSDRs) Species-typical responses that animals perform in an aversive situation. The responses may involve freezing, fleeing, or fighting.

S-S interval The interval between successive presentations of the aversive stimulus in a nondiscriminated avoidance procedure when the avoidance response is not performed.

time out A period during which the opportunity to obtain reinforcement is removed. This may involve removal of the participant from the situation where reinforcers may be obtained.

two-process theory of avoidance A theory originally developed to explain discriminated avoidance learning that presumes the operation of two mechanisms: (1) classical conditioning of fear to the warning signal, and (2) instrumental reinforcement of the avoidance response through termination of the warning signal and consequent fear reduction.

ANIMAL COGNITION I: MEMORY MECHANISMS

In Chapter 11, I turn to a more focused consideration of animal cognition. The study of animal cognition dates back to Darwin's writings about the evolution of intelligence and the subsequent research on learning in nonhuman animals. However, the best research on animal cognition has been done in the past 30 years. Chapter 11 begins with a definition of animal cognition and a brief discussion of some cognitive effects I have already described in earlier sections of this book. The rest of the chapter is devoted to one of the most important cognitive processes—memory. I describe the relationship between learning and memory and the distinction between working memory and reference memory. I then discuss several prominent paradigms for the study of working memory in nonhuman animals and describe research relevant to three different stages of memory—acquisition, retention, and retrieval. The chapter ends with a discussion of different sources of forgetting or memory failure.

As I noted in Chapter 1, interest in animal cognition dates back to the founding of the field of animal learning in the second half of the nineteenth century. Early experimental efforts to study animal cognition employed animal learning paradigms. Studies of animal learning soon came to have a life of their own. Through much of the twentieth century, learning processes in animals have been investigated for what they told us about behavior in general rather than about animal cognition or animal intelligence in particular. However, the past 30 years have witnessed a resurgence of interest in animal cognition and animal intelligence (for example, Griffin, 1976; Hulse, Fowler, & Honig, 1978; Ristau, 1991; Roitblat, Bever, & Terrace, 1984; Shettleworth, 1998; Spear & Riccio, 1994; Zentall, 1993).

The renewed focus on issues relevant to animal cognition is part of the "cognitive revolution" that has swept many areas of psychology. These developments have stimulated considerable theoretical debate (for example, Amsel, 1989; Hintzman, 1991). Regardless of that debate, an important consequence of contemporary interest in animal cognition has been the extension of the study of animal learning to numerous new paradigms. These extensions have raised many new and interesting questions about behavior—questions that were not explored in conventional studies of classical and instrumental conditioning. I describe some of these developments in this chapter and in Chapter 12.

In addition to providing important new information about learning and memory processes, studies of animal cognition address the kind of theoretical questions about the evolution of intelligence that captivated Darwin. Exploring the cognitive skills of animals tells us about the uniqueness of various human cognitive skills, just as exploring other planets can reveal the uniqueness of our terrestrial habitat. As Wasserman (1993, p. 211) put it, "comparing the intelligence of many species of animals may help us know better what it means to be human." Studies of animal cognition are also important because they provide model systems for the investigation of the neurophysiological bases of cognitive functions. Memory-enhancing drugs, for example, cannot be developed without first developing animal model systems for the study of memory mechanisms. Studies of the mechanisms of cognition in animals may also help us in designing intelligent machines and robots (Meyer, Berthoz, Floreano, Roitblat, & Wilson, 2000; Meyer & Wilson, 1991; Roitblat & Meyer, 1995).

WHAT IS ANIMAL COGNITION?

The word *cognition* comes from the Latin meaning "knowledge or thinking" and is commonly used to refer to thought processes. In casual discourse, we regard thinking as voluntary, deliberate, and conscious reflection on some topic, usually involving language. When we "think out loud," we say the words loud enough for someone else to hear. The casual inference is that silent thinking involves similar verbal behavior.

The second prominent characteristic of thinking is that it can lead to actions that cannot be explained on the basis of the external stimuli a person experiences at the time. For example, on your way to work, you may start thinking that you did not lock the door to your apartment when you left home. This thought may stimulate you to return home to check whether the door is locked. Your returning cannot be explained by the external stimuli to which you are exposed on your way to work. You encounter these same stimuli every day, but usually they do not make you return home. Rather, your behavior is attributed to the thought of the unlocked door.

There is some controversy about what the domain of animal cognition should be. Advocates of **cognitive ethology** claim that animals are capable of conscious thought and intentionality (Griffin, 1992; Ristau, 1991). According to cognitive ethologists, animal cognition should encompass the full range of issues that are included in considerations of human cognition. The claim that nonhuman animals are capable of consciousness and intentionality is based on the complexity, flexibility, and cleverness of various examples of animal behavior. The argument is that conscious intent is the likely source of such complex, flexible, and apparently clever behavior. This is basically an argument from design, an argument that has been debated and rejected by philosophers for centuries (Blumberg & Wasserman, 1995). In addition to such philosophical arguments, it is also important to consider recent studies showing the limitations of conscious intent as an adequate explanation of human behavior (Bargh & Chartrand, 1999; Wegner & Wheatley, 1999). If conscious intent cannot adequately characterize important features of human behavior, why should we assume that the concept will be useful in explaining the behavior of nonhuman organisms?

In contrast to cognitive ethologists, experimental psychologists use the term *animal cognition* in a more restricted sense. They follow H. S. Jennings (1904–1976) who argued a century ago that "objective evidence cannot give a demonstration either of the existence or of the non-existence of consciousness, for consciousness is precisely that which cannot be perceived objectively." Jennings went on to say that "no statement concerning consciousness in animals is open to refutation by observation and experiment." To make sure that their cognitive concepts can be refuted by observation, contemporary experimental psychologists tie cognitive mechanisms closely to behavioral predictions. Experimental psychologists make inferences about the internal or cognitive machinery that mediates behavior in cases where simple S-R or reflex mechanisms are insufficient. They are careful, however, to accept only those hypothesized cognitive processes that lead to unambiguous behavioral predictions (Zentall, 2001). Thus, for experimental psychologists, animal cognition does not imply anything about awareness, consciousness, or verbal reasoning. As Terrace (1984) pointed out nearly 20 years ago, "The rationale for the study of cognitive processes in animals requires no reference to animal consciousness" (p. 8). Rather **animal cognition** refers to theoretical constructs and models used to explain aspects of behavior that cannot be readily characterized in terms of simple S-R or reflex mechanisms.

A common feature of cognitive mechanisms is that they involve an internal representation or "mental" record of something and rules for manipulating these mental records. Internal representations may encode various types of information, such as particular features of stimuli or relations between stimuli. Internal representations and their manipulations cannot be investigated directly by looking into the brain. Rather, they have to be inferred from behavior. Thus, a cognitive mechanism is a theoretical construct inferred from behavior, just as gravity is a theoretical construct inferred from the behavior of falling objects.

Research on animal cognition is concerned with questions like how representations are formed, what aspects of experience they encode, how the information is stored, and how it is used later to guide behavior. I have already discussed research relevant to such questions in analyses of classical and instrumental conditioning. For example, I noted in Chapter 4 that classical conditioning involves the learning of an association between a CS and a US. As a result of this association, presentation of the CS activates a representation ("mental image") of the US, and the conditioned response is performed because of this representation. In Chapter 7, I noted that instrumental conditioning results in the establishment of S-O and R-O associations. Because of these associations, an internal representation of the reinforcer O is activated by the stimuli of the conditioning situation (S) as well as by the instrumental response (R). Additional evidence suggests that S can also activate the R-O association. Another area that clearly involves cognitive processes is the study of memory (Spear & Riccio, 1994).

ANIMAL MEMORY PARADIGMS

The term **memory** is commonly used to refer to the ability to respond to or recount information that was experienced earlier. We are said to remember what happened in our childhood if we talk about our childhood experiences, and we are said to remember someone's name if we call that person by the correct name. Unfortunately, such tests of memory are impractical with nonhuman animals. We cannot ask a pigeon to tell us what it did last week. Instead, we have to use the bird's nonverbal responses as clues to its memory.

If your cat goes down the street but finds its way back to your house, you might conclude that it remembers where you live. If your dog greets you with unusual exuberance after a long vacation, you might conclude that it remembers you. These and similar examples illustrate that the existence of memory in animals is identified by the fact that *their current behavior is based on some aspect of their earlier experiences.* Any time an animal's behavior is determined by past events, we can conclude that some type of memory is involved.

This definition of memory is very similar to the definition of learning stated in Chapter 1. There, learning was defined as an enduring change in how an organism might respond to a particular situation because of prior experience with that type of situation. Evidence of learning is also identified on the basis of changes in behavior due to earlier experiences. Indeed, learning is not possible without memory.

How, then, are studies of memory to be distinguished from studies of learning? The differences may be clarified by considering the components that are common to both learning and memory experiments (see Table 11.1). The first thing that happens in both types of experiments is that the participants are exposed to certain kinds of stimuli or information. This phase is termed **acquisition.** The information that was acquired is then retained for a period called the **retention interval.** At the end of the retention interval, the participants are tested for their memory of the original experience, which requires **retrieval** or reactivation of the information encountered during acquisition. Thus, studies of learning and studies of memory all involve three basic phases: acquisition, retention, and retrieval.

Consider, for example, riding a bicycle. Skilled bicyclists initially had to be trained to balance, pedal, and steer the bike (acquisition). They have to hold onto the information they acquired (retention). And when they get on a bicycle again, they have to reactivate their knowledge of bike riding (retrieval).

In studies of learning, the focus is on the acquisition phase. Learning experiments deal with the kind of information we acquire and the ways in which we acquire it. Thus, *learning experiments involve manipulations of the conditions of acquisition.* The retention interval is always fairly long (a day or longer), because short-term changes in behavior are not considered to be instances of learning. Furthermore, the retention interval typically is not varied within the experiment. Because the emphasis is on the conditions of acquisition, the conditions of retrieval are also kept constant. All participants in a given experiment are tested for their knowledge using the same test procedures.

In contrast, *studies of memory focus on the retention and retrieval phases.* Acquisition is of interest only to the extent that it is relevant to retention and retrieval. The retention interval is often varied to determine how the availability of the acquired information changes with time. Unlike studies of learning, which employ only long retention intervals, studies of memory can employ retention intervals of any duration. In fact, many studies of animal memory involve short retention intervals.

Studies of memory also focus on the circumstances of retrieval. Consider, for example, taking a vocabulary test on a set of technical terms in a college course. You may miss many items if the test consists of a series of fill-in-the-blank questions for which you have to pro-

TABLE 11.1	COMPARISON OF LEARNING AND MEMORY EXPERIMENTS	
PHASE	**STUDIES OF LEARNING**	**STUDIES OF MEMORY**
Acquisition	Varied	Constant
Retention	Constant (long)	Varied (short and long)
Retrieval	Constant	Varied

vide the technical terms. In contrast, you are likely to do much better if you are provided with a list of the technical terms and are merely required to match up each term with its definition. These different forms of the test involve different conditions of retrieval.

Memory mechanisms have been classified in various ways depending on what is remembered (the contents of memory), how long the memory lasts (the retention interval), and the mechanisms involved in the memory. Schachter and Tulving (1994), for example, identified five types of human learning and memory: *procedural memory, perceptual memory, semantic memory, primary or working memory,* and *episodic or declarative memory.* Not all these forms of memory have their counterparts in research with nonhuman subjects.

Much of the research on classical and instrumental conditioning that I described in earlier chapters corresponds to **procedural memory.** This type of memory often reflects knowledge about invariant relationships in the environment and mediates the learning of behavioral and cognitive skills that are performed automatically, without the requirement of conscious control. However, investigators of memory in nonhuman animals have not emphasized the distinction between procedural and other forms of memory. Rather, they have emphasized the distinction between working memory and reference memory.

Working Memory and Reference Memory

One of the earliest experimental investigations of animal memory was conducted by the American psychologist Walter S. Hunter (1913). Hunter tested rats, dogs, and raccoons in a simple memory task. The apparatus consisted of a start area from which the animals could enter any one of three goal compartments. Only one of the goal compartments was baited with a piece of food on each trial, and the baited compartment was marked by turning on a light above that compartment at the start of the trial. Which compartment was baited (and marked by the light) was varied from trial to trial.

After the animals learned to always choose the compartment whose light was turned on, Hunter made the task a bit more difficult. Now the light marking the baited goal compartment remained on for only a short time. After the signal was turned off, the animal was detained in the start area for various lengths of time before being allowed to choose among the three compartments. The animal had to somehow remember which light had been on in order to find the food. The longer the animals were delayed before being allowed to make a choice, the less likely they were to go to the correct compartment. The maximum delay rats could handle was about 10 seconds. The performance of dogs did not deteriorate until the delay interval was extended past 5 minutes. Raccoons performed well as long as the delay was no more than 25 seconds.

The species also differed in what they did during the delay interval. Rats and dogs were observed to maintain a postural orientation toward the correct compartment during the delay interval. No such postural orientations were observed in the raccoons. Since the raccoons did not maintain a postural orientation during the delay interval, their behavior required some type of internal memory mechanism.

With the delay procedure, the animals had to remember which compartment had been illuminated at the start of that trial. Once the trial was finished, however, this information was no longer useful because the food could be in any of the three goal compartments on the next trial. Thus, memory for which compartment had been recently illuminated was required only to complete the work during a given trial. This type of memory is called **working memory.**

Working memory is operative when information has to be retained only long enough to complete a particular task, after which the information is best discarded because it is not needed or (as in Hunter's experiment) because it may interfere with successful completion of the next trial. A mechanic changing the oil and lubricating a car has to remember which steps of the job he has finished, but only as long as he is servicing that particular car. In cooking a good stew, you have to remember which spices you have already put in before adding others, but once the stew is finished, you can forget this information. All these illustrate instances of working memory.

Working memory is often short-lasting. In Hunter's experiment, the memory lasted for only 10 seconds in rats and for 25 seconds in raccoons. In some situations, working memory may last for several hours or days.

Examples of working memory illustrate the retention, for a limited duration, of recently acquired information. However, such information is useful only in the context of more enduring knowledge. In Hunter's experiment, for example, remembering which compartment had been illuminated at the start of a trial was not enough to obtain food. This information was useful only in the context of the knowledge that the light marked the baited compartment. In contrast to information in working memory that was disposed of after each trial, information about the relation between the light and food had to be remembered on all trials. Such memory is called **reference memory** (Honig, 1978).

Reference memory is *long-term retention of information necessary for successful use of incoming and recently acquired information.* Information about what a mechanic has done recently is useless without more general knowledge about cars and lubrication procedures. Knowing which spices you have already added to a stew is useful only if you know the basics of cooking and flavoring food. All successful uses of working memory require appropriate reference memories.

Since Hunter's research, increasingly sophisticated techniques have been developed for the study of working memory, such as the two I now describe. The first procedure, delayed matching to sample, is a laboratory procedure that was developed without much regard for the behavioral predispositions of animals and can be adapted to the study of how animals remember a variety of different events. The second technique, the radial maze, tests spatial memory or memory for particular locations.

Delayed Matching to Sample

The delayed-matching-to-sample procedure is perhaps the most versatile technique available for the study of working memory and is a substantial refinement of Hunter's original procedure. As in Hunter's procedure, the participant is exposed to a cue that identifies the correct response on a particular trial. This stimulus is then removed before the animal is permitted to perform the designated behavior. In the typical experiment with pigeons, for ex-

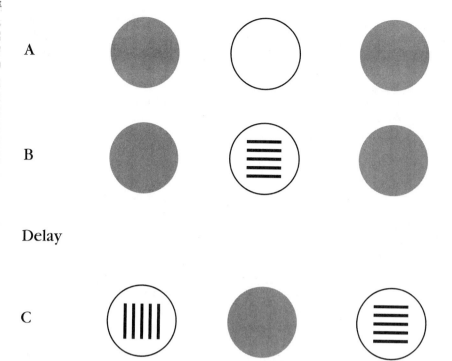

A

B

Delay

C

Figure 11.1   Diagram of the delayed-matching-to-sample procedure for pigeons. The experimental chamber has three response keys arranged in a row. At the start of a trial, the center key is illuminated with a white light, the start cue (row A). After the pigeon pecks the start cue, the sample stimulus (horizontal) is projected on the center key (row B). This stimulus is then removed, and after a delay two choice stimuli (horizontal and vertical) are presented on the side keys (row C). Pecks at the choice stimulus that matches the sample are reinforced.

ample, the experimental chamber contains three response keys arranged in a row, as in Figure 11.1. The cue that identifies the correct response is called the *sample* and is presented on the center key. After a delay, the pigeon is given a choice between the sample and an alternative stimulus, and pecks on the test stimulus that matches the sample are reinforced.

The stimuli used in an experiment might include arrays of horizontal and vertical lines projected on the response keys from the rear. The start of a trial is signaled by illumination of the center key with a white light, the start cue (see row A in Figure 11.1). The pigeon is first required to peck the start cue, to make sure it is facing the pecking keys. Then, the sample for that trial—the horizontal array, for example—is projected on the center key (row B in Figure 11.1). Usually several pecks at the sample stimulus are required, after which the sample is turned off and the two side keys are lit up. One of the side keys is illuminated with the sample for that trial (horizontal), and the other key is illuminated with the alternative pattern (vertical) (row C in Figure 11.1). If the pigeon pecks the test stimulus that matches the sample (in this case horizontal), it is reinforced with access to grain. If it pecks the other stimulus, no reinforcement is provided. Thus, to obtain reinforcement, the pigeon has to select the test stimulus that matches what was the sample on that trial—hence the term *matching to sample.*

Whether the horizontal or vertical grid pattern serves as the sample is randomly varied from one trial to the next. In addition, the matching stimulus is equally likely to be presented on the right or left key during the choice component of the trial. Therefore, the pigeon cannot predict which stimulus will be the sample on a given trial or where the matching stimulus will appear during the choice test.

During the initial stages of matching-to-sample training, the sample stimulus remains visible until the pigeon has made the correct choice. Thus, in my example, the horizontal pattern on the center key would remain illuminated until the bird correctly pecked the horizontal side key. Such a procedure is called **simultaneous matching to sample.** It does not require working memory because the cue for the correct response is visible when the choice response is made. Once a bird has mastered the simultaneous matching procedure, the sample stimulus can be presented just briefly and removed before the choice stimuli are provided. Introduction of a delay between exposure to the sample stimulus and availability of the choice cues changes the procedure to **delayed matching to sample,** which requires working memory.

As I mentioned, the matching stimulus is equally likely to appear on the left or the right choice key at the end of a trial. Because of this, the participant cannot make the correct response merely by orienting to the right or left when the sample appears on the center key and holding this body posture until the choice stimuli are presented. In contrast to Hunter's procedure, simple postural orientations do not help in making the correct choice. The participants are forced to use more sophisticated memory processes. (For an especially effective matching-to-sample procedure for use with pigeons, see Wright & Delius, 1994.)

Procedural Determinants of Delayed Matching to Sample.   The delayed-matching-to-sample procedure has been used extensively with a variety of species, including monkeys, pigeons, dolphins, sea lions, goldfish, rats, and humans (Baron & Menich, 1985; Blough, 1959; D'Amato, 1973; D'Amato & Colombo, 1985; Forestell & Herman, 1988; Jarrard & Moise, 1971; Iversen, 1993a; Kastak & Schusterman, 1994; Roberts & Grant, 1976; Steinert, Fallon, & Wallace, 1976). In addition, the procedure has been adapted to investigate how animals remember a variety of stimuli, including visual shapes, numbers of responses performed, presence or absence of reward, the spatial location of stimuli, the order of two successively presented events, or which particular response the subject recently performed (for example, D'Amato, 1973; Maki, Moe, & Bierley, 1977; MacDonald, 1993; Mercado, Murray, Uyeyama, Pack, & Herman, 1998; Wilkie & Summers, 1982).

Several aspects of the matching-to-sample procedure are critical in determining the accuracy of performance. One of these is the nature of the stimulus that serves as the sample. Some types of stimuli are more effective than others (for example, Wilkie & Summers, 1982). Other important factors are the duration of exposure to the sample stimulus at the start of the trial and the delay interval after the sample. In one experiment, for example, Grant (1976) tested pigeons in a standard three-key apparatus after they had received extensive training on delayed matching to sample with visual stimuli. Two pairs of colors— red/green and blue/yellow—served as sample and comparison stimuli on alternate trials. At the start of each trial, the center key was illuminated with a white light. After the pigeon pecked the start cue, the sample color for that trial was presented on the center key for 1, 4, 8, or 14 seconds. This was followed by delay intervals of 0, 20, 40, or 60 seconds, after which the two side keys were illuminated, one with the sample-matching color and the other with the paired alternative color. After the bird made its choice, all the keys were turned off for a 2-minute intertrial interval.

The results of the experiment are summarized in Figure 11.2. If pigeons had pecked the choice keys randomly, they would have been correct 50% of the time. Better than chance performance indicates the use of working memory. For each sample duration, the accuracy of matching decreased as longer delays were introduced between exposure to the sample and opportunity to make the choice response. In fact, if the sample was presented for only 1 second and the opportunity to make a choice was delayed 40 seconds or more, the pigeons responded at chance level. Performance improved if the birds were exposed to the sample for longer periods. When the sample was presented for 4, 8, or 14 seconds, the birds performed above chance levels even when the delay interval was as long as 60 seconds. Thus, accuracy in the delayed-matching-to-sample procedure decreased as a function of the

D. S. Grant

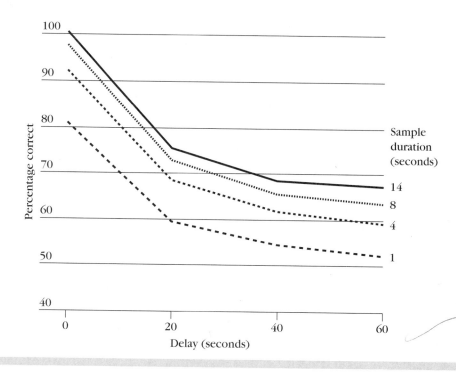

Figure 11.2 Percentage of correct responses in a delayed-matching-to-sample task as a function of the duration of the sample stimulus (1–14 seconds) and the delay between the sample and the choice stimuli (0–60 seconds). (From "Effect of Sample Presentation Time on Long Delay Matching in the Pigeon," by D. S. Grant, 1976, *Learning and Motivation, 7,* pp. 580–590. Copyright © 1976 by Academic Press. Reprinted by permission.)

delay interval and increased as a function of the duration of exposure to the sample stimulus (see also Blough, 1996; Hunt, Parr, & Smith, 1999; Guttenberger & Wasserman, 1985).

Results such as those in Figure 11.2 can be explained by the **trace decay hypothesis,** the oldest and simplest account of memory (and memory loss) (Roberts & Grant, 1976). This hypothesis assumes that presentation of a stimulus produces changes in the nervous system that gradually dissipate, or decay, after the stimulus has been removed. The initial strength of the stimulus trace is assumed to reflect the physical energy of the stimulus. Thus, longer or more intense stimuli are presumed to result in stronger stimulus traces. No matter what the initial strength of the trace, it is assumed to decay at the same rate after the stimulus ends.

According to the trace decay hypothesis, the extent to which the memory of an event controls behavior depends on the strength of the stimulus trace at that moment. The stronger the trace, the stronger is the effect of the past stimulus on the organism's behavior. The trace decay model predicts results exactly like those summarized in Figure 11.2. Increasing the delay interval in the matching-to-sample procedure reduces the accuracy of performance presumably because the trace of the sample stimulus is weaker after longer delays. By contrast, increasing the duration of exposure to the sample improves performance presumably because longer stimulus exposures establish stronger stimulus traces.

The trace decay hypothesis assumes that forgetting functions like those presented in Figure 11.2 reflect fairly directly the strength of memory for the sample stimulus at different delay intervals. Unfortunately, no behavioral test permits a "direct" readout of the strength of memory. Performance on memory tests also depends a great deal on the conditions of training. In a key recent experiment, Sargisson and White (2001) asked whether the forgetting function would be influenced by the delay between the sample and the choice stimuli that was in effect during training.

Sargisson and White trained separate groups of pigeons on a matching-to-sample procedure with different sample-choice delays. For one group, the delay between the sample

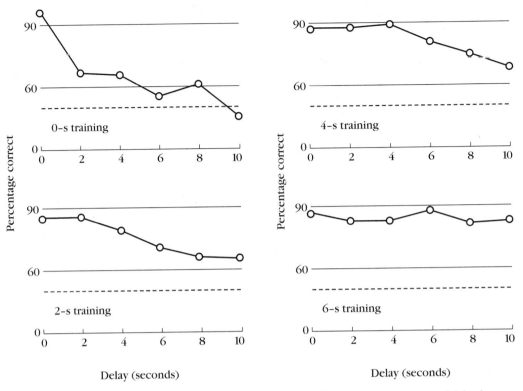

Figure 11.3 Accuracy of matching-to-sample performance as a function of delay between the sample and choice stimuli for independent groups of pigeons that were previously trained with delays of 0, 2, 4, or 6 seconds. (After Sargisson & White, 2001.)

M. Spetch

and choice stimuli was always 0 seconds during training. For other groups, this delay was 2, 4, or 6 seconds. Training was continued until each group performed correctly on at least 80% of the trials. All of the birds were then tested with delays ranging from 0 to 10 seconds to determine the forgetting function. The results of these tests are presented in Figure 11.3.

The group that had been trained with a 0-second sample-choice delay showed the standard forgetting function. They made more errors as the delay between the sample and choice stimuli was increased from 0 to 10 seconds. In contrast, no such decline was evident in pigeons that had been trained with a 6-second delay between the sample and choice stimuli. These birds performed equally well at all test delays. The other groups showed results between these two extremes. It is important to note that for all groups the most accurate performance occurred when the delay used in the test was the same as the delay that they received during training. These results clearly show that forgetting functions do not directly reflect the decay or fading of memory for the sample stimulus as a function of time. Rather, test performance depends on the similarity between the conditions of testing and the conditions of training (see also Spetch, 1987). The common finding that memory gets worse with the passage of time may simply reflect the fact that subjects are unfamiliar with long delay intervals.

The delay interval used in training is just one training variable that influences delayed-matching-to-sample performance. Matching is basically instrumental behavior motivated by the reinforcer provided at the end of the trial. Therefore, it should not be surprising that matching behavior is also influenced by the relation between the sample stimulus and the reinforcer. In general, subjects perform more accurately on a matching task under conditions in which the sample stimulus is a better signal for reinforcement. Matching accuracy is greater when the interval between the sample stimulus and the reinforcer is shorter (Weavers, Foster, & Temple, 1998). Matching accuracy is also improved if the sample stimulus signals a greater reduction in delay to reinforcement (Hartl, Dougherty, & Wixted, 1996; Urcuioli, DeMarse, & Lionello, 1999). Both of these factors presumably make the sample stimulus a better signal for reinforcement or a more effective conditioned reinforcer. (For a discussion of additional reinforcement variables that influence accuracy in delayed matching memory tasks, see White & Wixted, 1999.)

Response Strategies in Matching to Sample. The matching-to-sample procedure is analogous to a discrimination problem in that the participant has to respond to the correct stimulus and refrain from responding to the incorrect one to get reinforced. As I described in discussions of what is learned in discrimination training in Chapter 8, such a two-alternative task can be solved in several ways. The participant can make the correct choice by focusing on the correct stimulus, by inhibiting behavior to the incorrect stimulus, or by using both these response strategies. In discrimination learning (which establishes a reference memory), participants appear to use the combined response strategy. By contrast, participants in matching to sample appear to focus primarily on the correct choice.

One interesting experiment supporting this conclusion used a three-key apparatus for pigeons that was specially constructed so that the stimulus projected on a response key was visible only if the pigeon was standing directly in front of that key (Wright & Sands, 1981). This apparatus enabled the experimenters to determine which response keys the pigeons looked at before making their choice. The results showed that the birds focused on the correct alternative. If they saw the matching stimulus, they pecked it without bothering to check what stimulus was presented on the other side (see also Roitblat, Penner, & Nachtigall, 1990; Wright, 1990, 1992; Zentall, Edwards, Moore, & Hogan, 1981).

A. A. Wright

General versus Specific Rule Learning. The evidence just reviewed indicates that animals focus on the correct choice in matching to sample. What leads them to identify a stimulus as correct? One possibility is that they learn a general "same as" rule. The rule may be, "Choose the choice stimulus that is the same as the sample." Another possibility is that the animals learn a series of specific rules or stimulus-response relations. In the experiment by Grant (1976), for example, pairs of colors were used—red/green and blue/yellow. The pigeons may have learned a series of specific stimulus-response relations: "Select red after exposure to red," "Select green after exposure to green," and so on. Most matching-to-sample procedures can be solved either by learning a general "same as" rule or by learning a series of specific stimulus-response relations.

The two alternative strategies can be evaluated by testing transfer of matching performance to new stimuli. After training with one set of stimuli, another matching problem is presented with a new set of stimuli. Specific stimulus-response learning predicts little positive (or negative) transfer of matching behavior to the new stimuli because the new task requires learning a new set of stimulus-response relations. By contrast, general-rule learning predicts considerable positive carryover, because the general "same as" rule can be used to solve any matching-to-sample problem. Thus, in tests of transfer from one matching-to-sample problem to another, general-rule learning should produce better performance than specific-rule learning.

In a study with infant chimpanzees, Oden, Thompson, and Premack (1988) first provided training on a matching-to-sample task with just one pair of stimulus objects, a stainless steel measuring cup and a brass bolt lock. One of the objects was presented at the start of the trial, followed by a choice of both objects. If the chimp selected the matching object, it was reinforced with effusive praise, tickling, cuddling, or an edible treat, depending on its preference. After the animals learned the task with the two training stimuli, they were tested with a variety of other stimulus objects. Remarkably, with most of the test objects, the transfer performance was better than 80% accurate. Thus, the chimps seemed to have learned a general "same as" rule with just two training stimuli.

Chimpanzees are more likely to show evidence of generalized matching than pigeons and other species. However, the preponderance of evidence suggests that both general-rule learning and specific stimulus-response learning can occur as a result of matching-to-sample training in a variety of species. Which type of learning predominates appears to be related to the size of the stimulus set used in the matching-to-sample procedure. A study such as Grant's (1976), in which sample and comparison stimuli were selected from two pairs of colors, is likely to favor the learning of specific stimulus-response relations. By contrast, procedures that employ a wide range of stimuli are more likely to favor the learning of a general rule. The extreme of a procedure of this type is the **trials-unique procedure.**

In a trials-unique procedure, a different stimulus serves as the sample on each trial and is paired with another stimulus during the choice phase. Because a given sample stimulus is not presented on more than one trial, accurate performance with a trials-unique procedure is possible only if the participant learns to respond on the basis of a general "same as" rule. Successful learning of the "same as" concept has been obtained with the trials-unique procedure with visual stimuli in pigeons and auditory stimuli in monkeys (Wright, Cook, Rivera, Sands, & Delius, 1988; Wright, Shyan, & Jitsumori, 1990). (For another approach to learning the concept "same as," see Wright, 1997.)

Spatial Memory in a Radial Maze

The matching-to-sample procedure can be adapted to investigate how animals remember a variety of stimuli. The next technique I describe has more limited applicability but focuses on a very important type of memory—memory for places.

To move about their habitat efficiently, animals have to remember how their environment is laid out—where open spaces, sheltered areas, and potential food sources are located. In many environments, once food has been eaten at one location, it is not available there again for some time until it is replenished. Therefore, animals have to remember where they last found food and avoid that location for a while. For example, the amakihi (*Loxops virens*), a species of Hawaiian honeycreeper, feeds on the nectar of mamane flowers (Kamil, 1978). After feeding on a cluster of flowers, these birds have to avoid returning to the same flowers for about an hour. By delaying their return to clusters they have recently visited, the birds increase the chance that they will find nectar in the flowers they search. They appear to remember the spatial location of recently visited flower clusters (see also Healy & Hurly, 1995).

Memory for locations in space—spatial memory—has been studied in the laboratory with the use of complex mazes (for example, Olton, 1979). One popular technique uses an elevated radial arm maze (see Figure 11.4). Olton and Samuelson (1976) tested rats in an elevated maze that had eight arms radiating from a central choice area, with a food cup at the end of each arm. Before the start of each trial, a pellet of food was placed in each food cup. The rat was then placed in the center of the maze and was allowed to go from one arm

Courtesy of Donald A. Dewsbury

D. S. Olton

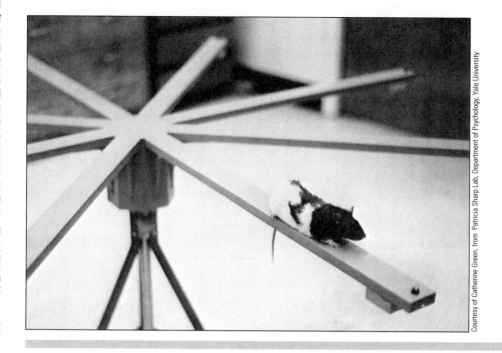

Courtesy of Catherine Green, from Patricia Sharp Lab, Department of Psychology, Yale University

Figure 11.4 Rat foraging on an elevated radial maze.

to another and pick up all the food. Once a food pellet had been consumed, that arm of the maze remained without food for the rest of the trial.

How could the rat have gone about finding food in this situation? It could have randomly selected which alley to enter each time. Thus, the rat might have entered an alley, eaten the food there, returned to the center area and then randomly selected another arm of the maze to enter next. With such a strategy, however, the rat would have ended up going down alleys from which it had already removed the food. A more efficient strategy would have been to enter only those arms of the maze that had not yet been visited and therefore still had food. This is in fact what the animals learned to do.

The results of the experiment are summarized in Figure 11.5. Entering an arm that had not been visited previously was considered to be a correct choice. Figure 11.5 summarizes the number of correct choices the rats made during the first eight choices of successive tests. During the first five test runs after familiarization with the maze, the rats made a mean of nearly seven correct choices during each test. With continued practice, the mean number of correct choices was consistently above seven, indicating that the animals rarely entered an arm they had previously chosen on that trial.

Rats do not require much training to perform efficiently in the radial maze. The radial maze task appears to take advantage of a preexisting tendency of rats to move about without returning to recently visited places. This tendency is so strong that the failure of rats to return to a place where they recently have obtained food may not be related to having obtained food there (Gaffan & Davies, 1981). Several investigators have found that rats tend to stay away from recently visited arms in a radial maze whether or not the maze arms are baited with food (FitzGerald, Isler, Rosenberg, Oettinger, & Battig, 1985; Timberlake & White, 1990; see also Maki, 1987).

There are several mechanisms by which rats could choose to enter only previously unchosen arms of a maze without necessarily remembering which arms they had already

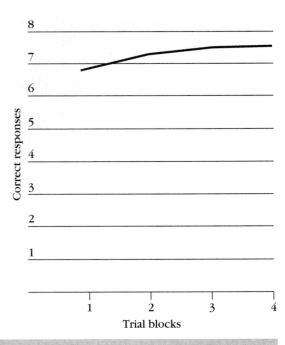

Figure 11.5 Mean number of correct responses rats made in the first eight choices during blocks of five test trials in the eight-arm radial maze. (Adapted from Olton, 1978.)

visited. For example, they could mark each arm they visit with a drop of urine, and then avoid maze arms that had this odor marker. Alternatively, they could select arms in a fixed sequence, such as always entering successive arms in a clockwise order. However, they do not appear to use either of these tactics.

Various procedures have convincingly ruled out the use of odor cues in the selection of maze arms (for example, Olton, Collison, & Werz, 1977; Olton & Samuelson, 1976; Zoladek & Roberts, 1978). The available evidence also indicates that rats in a radial maze experiment can perform efficiently without using response chains or entering maze arms in a fixed order from one trial to the next. As long as the central choice area is small enough for the rats to reach all the arms easily from anywhere in the central area, they do not choose arms in a fixed order (Olton & Samuelson, 1976; see also Olton et al., 1977). Furthermore, rats select previously unvisited arms even if procedures are introduced that should disrupt response chains (for example, Beatty & Shavalia, 1980a, 1980b).

The studies cited have been important in ruling out various potential cues for radial maze performance and suggest that spatial stimuli are critical. What are spatial cues and how are they identified? Spatial cues are stimuli that identify the location of an object in the environment. Rats appear to use distinctive features of the environment, such as a window, a door, a corner of the room, or a poster on the wall, as landmarks and locate maze arms relative to these landmarks. Movement of landmarks relative to the maze causes the rats to treat the maze arms as being in new locations (Suzuki, Augerinos, & Black, 1980). Thus, under ordinary circumstances, spatial location is identified relative to distal room cues, not to local stimuli inside the maze (see also Morris, 1981). However, rats are able to use intra-maze cues to guide their choices if access to extra-maze cues is blocked (Brown & Bing, 1997; Brown & Moore, 1997).

Because radial maze performance usually depends on memory for recently visited locations, the radial maze procedure has become a popular technique for the study of memory processes, both at the behavioral level and the physiological level. The memory capacity

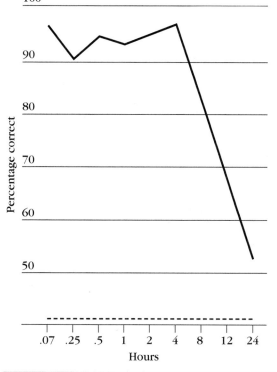

Figure 11.6 Percentage correct responses on choices 5–8 in an eight-arm radial maze. Between choices 4 and 5 the animals were returned to their home cages for varying intervals ranging from .07 to 24 hours. The dashed line indicates chance performance (41%). (From "Rat Spatial Memory: Resistance to Retroactive Interference at Long Retention Intervals," by W. W. Beatty and D A. Shavalia, 1980, *Animal Learning & Behavior, 8,* pp. 550–552. Copyright © 1980 by the Psychonomic Society. Reprinted by permission.)

revealed by the technique is impressive. For example, rats and gerbils have been observed to perform well in radial mazes with as many as 17 arms (Olton et al., 1977; Wilkie & Slobin, 1983), and this probably does not represent the limit of their spatial memory (Roberts, 1979). The duration of spatial working memory is also remarkable.

In a test of the limits of spatial memory, Beatty and Shavalia (1980b) allowed rats to make four choices in the eight-arm radial maze in the usual manner. The subjects were then detained in their home cages for various periods up to 24 hours. After the delay interval, they were returned to the maze and allowed to make choices 5–8. As usual, an entry into an alley they had not previously visited was considered a correct choice.

Figure 11.6 shows the percentage of correct choices as a function of the delay interval between the first four and last four choices. Delays of up to 4 hours after the first four choices did not disrupt performance. Longer periods of confinement in the home cage produced progressively more errors. These data show that spatial memory is not permanent. However, the memory can last for several hours (see also Maki, Beatty, Hoffman, Bierley, & Clouse, 1984; Spetch, 1990; Strijkstra & Bolhuis, 1987; Willson & Wilkie, 1991).

Results such as those presented in Figure 11.6 illustrate that rats have excellent spatial memory. How do they use this memory to guide their search responses? On an elevated maze, the rats have little choice but to run along the arms of the maze. There are no other places to go. In a highly creative experiment, Hoffman, Timberlake, Leffel, and Gont (1999) repeated the radial-arm maze experiment, but instead of having the maze raised off the floor to restrict the rats to the maze arms, they put the maze on the floor so that the rats could easily step off and go from one food cup to another without returning to the central choice area. Hoffman et al. used a six-arm maze. With the maze on the floor, the rats could

BOX 11.1

LEARNING AS SYNAPTIC PLASTICITY: LONG-TERM POTENTIATION (LTP) AND LONG-TERM DEPRESSION (LTD)

It is estimated that the human brain contains more than a 100 billion neurons. Each neuron may be coupled through a chemical synapse to thousands of other neurons, forming a complex neural network. If we assume that each of these connections can store just one bit of information, the brain can hold the computer equivalent of 100,000 gigs!

How can experience bring about a change within this network? Many assume that experience modifies the strength of the synaptic connections. If this is true, when are the connections modified, and what are the molecular mechanisms that mediate this synaptic plasticity?

An answer to the first question was suggested by Donald Hebb a half century ago (Hebb, 1949). He argued that neural connections are strengthened when two cells are active at the same time, an idea that is sometimes summarized with the mnemonic "cells that fire together wire together." Modern theorists have extended this notion to address decreases in synaptic strength, arguing that this will occur when cellular activity is uncorrelated.

In a classic experiment, Bliss and Lomo (1973) provided neural evidence for Hebb's hypothesis. They examined how neural activity within the hippocampus alters the strength of synaptic connections. To induce neural activity, they lowered an electrode into a bundle of neurons known as the perforant path and applied an electrical current (see Figure 11.7). The cells that form the perforant path synapse on neurons are called mossy fibers. By recording neural activity through electrodes placed near the mossy fiber cell bodies, Bliss and Lomo obtained a measure of synaptic strength. As we would expect, applying a moderate electrical stimulus to the perforant path elicited moderate neural activity in the mossy fibers, and this response changed little over time. But if a strong input was provided—one that caused a very strong response in the mossy fibers—subsequent inputs produced a much larger response. This phenomenon is called *long-term potentiation* (LTP). It appears that a strong input can effectively strengthen synaptic connections. The

converse phenomenon, *long-term depression* (LTD), can weaken synaptic connections. Both LTP and LTD can last for days to weeks. This enduring feature of LTP and LTD has encouraged researchers to suggest that these phenomena may represent a kind of neurobiological memory—a way in which cells can store the consequences of experience (for a recent review, see Martin, Grimwood, & Morris, 2000).

Cells communicate at a synapse through the release of neurotransmitters that engage a response in the adjoining (postsynaptic) neuron by activating specialized receptors. A strong input could alter the strength of a chemical synapse by increasing either the amount of transmitter released or the responsiveness of the postsynaptic cell. Research suggests that LTP is largely due to the latter possibility. One of the most important ways in which a postsynaptic cell can become more responsive involves specialized receptors (NMDA receptors) that lie on the surface of the cell. NMDA receptors act as coincidence detectors. Their activation depends on both the release of transmitter and a strong response in the postsynaptic cell. If these two conditions are met, the NMDA receptors initiate a biochemical cascade that awakens silent AMPA receptors. The AMPA receptors mediate the propagation of the neural signal from one neuron to the next. Awakening more of these receptors increases the magnitude of the response elicited in the postsynaptic cell. As a result, the postsynaptic cell exhibits a stronger response even though the amount of neurotransmitter released has not changed.

LTP has a number of properties that suggest it plays a role in learning and memory. The most obvious is *its enduring nature*. Another important quality is *input specificity*—the modification is limited to those synapses that are concurrently active. LTP also exhibits a kind of *cooperativity*. The induction of LTP requires a strong response in the postsynaptic cell. This strong response does not have to come from just one input. A number of inputs can work together to drive the postsynaptic cell to the threshold for learning, and all the contributing inputs can benefit. A variation of this cooperativity yields the final, and most interesting, property—*associativity* (Figure 11.7). If a weak input is paired with a strong input; the latter will be sufficient to engage LTP at both connections. As a result, the weak input will acquire the capacity to drive a response in

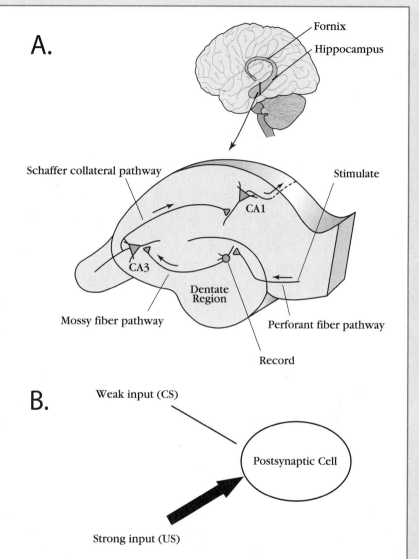

A.

Fornix

Hippocampus

Schaffer collateral pathway

Stimulate

CA1

CA3

Dentate Region

Mossy fiber pathway

Perforant fiber pathway

Record

B.

Weak input (CS)

Postsynaptic Cell

Strong input (US)

Figure 11.7 (A) A slice of the hippocampus. Bliss and Lomo (1973) stimulated the axons of the perforant path and recorded the response observed in the mossy fibers. They found that a strong input produced a long-lasting increase in the response elicited in the cells of the mossy fiber pathway. (B) A schematic of the neural relations that could support associativity. One cell has weak input (the CS) while another has a strong connection (the US). The weak connection can be strengthened through paired presentation of both weak and strong inputs. (Adapted from Kandel, Schwartz, & Jessel, 2000.)

the postsynaptic cell, in much the same way that a CS acquires the ability to generate a CR as a result of being paired with a US.

To explore whether hippocampal LTP plays a role in learning and memory, researchers have used a number of behavioral tasks that are known to depend on the hippocampus. One of the most popular involves learning about spatial cues. R. G. Morris developed a simple way

to study such learning using a water maze. The maze consists of a large tank filled with a milky liquid. Just under the surface of the liquid lies a hidden platform on which the rat can stand. Subjects are gently lowered into the pool from various locations along the edge of the tank. Normally, rats quickly learn to swim to the location of the

(continued)

Box 11.1 (continued)

platform, which they climb upon to rest. Rats with lesions to the hippocampus do not remember where the platform is located from one test to the next and take far longer to find the hidden platform. Lesioned rats do not have any problem swimming to a visible platform, which suggests that their sensory and motor functions are not impaired. Rather, hippocampal lesions produce a more selective deficit that interferes with the capacity to learn about spatial cues.

Developing a behavioral assay that is sensitive to hippocampal lesions gives us a tool to explore whether synaptic modification (NMDA-mediated plasticity) is involved in learning. To explore this issue, researchers have tested the impact of drugs that disrupt NMDA receptor activity (for example, APV and MK-801). These drugs bind to the NMDA receptor and prevent it from working normally. Physiological studies have shown that pretreatment with an NMDA antagonist blocks the induction of LTP. Significantly, the same drug manipulation also disrupts spatial

learning in the water maze (Morris, Anderson, Lynch, & Baudry, 1986).

Similar experiments conducted in other learning paradigms have indicated that synaptic plasticity mediated by the NMDA receptor is not limited to spatial learning. For example, encoding the cues that represent a context, a new object, or a new conspecific (a form of social learning) all depend on the hippocampus, and evidence suggests that each of these forms of learning depends on NMDA-mediated plasticity (Martin et al., 2000).

Researchers have also shown that LTP occurs in many other regions of the brain. Even neurons within the spinal cord exhibit LTP. When you get a sunburn, neurons within the spinal cord become sensitized (Willis, 2001). This increases the level of pain you feel when the skin is stimulated. This heightened pain appears to reflect a form of LTP, a cellular memory within the spinal cord that heightens the pain signal sent to the brain.

—J. W. Grau

adopt one of four strategies to visit all of the food cups. These are illustrated in Figure 11.8. The most efficient strategy, illustrated in Panel "a" of Figure 11.8, minimizes travel distance and involves going directly from the first food cup to the next by stepping off the maze. Panel "b" illustrates the path the rats would take if they used the arms of the maze as guides to following a trail. Panel "c" represents the path the rats might take if they walked about randomly. Panel "d" represents the path the rats might take if they followed the walls of the experimental chamber (thigmotaxis).

Interestingly, even though the rats could have easily stepped off the maze arms and gone directly from one food cup to the next (and thereby minimized travel distance), they rarely did. Rather, they followed the maze arms, with only occasional forays off the maze. This type of behavior resembles the trail-following behavior of rats in the wild. Rat colonies typically establish clear trails above ground and go from place to place by following those trails. Evidently, the radial-arm maze takes advantage of this propensity for trail-following behavior in rats. The rats treat the arms of the maze as trails even if the maze is on the floor so that the rats are not confined to the maze arms (see also Timberlake, Leffel, & Hoffman, 1999). Rats may show rapid learning and impressive memory on a radial-arm maze because this experimental paradigm is particularly well suited to their behavioral propensities.

MEMORY MECHANISMS

In the preceding section I described several prominent techniques for the study of memory processes in animals and some results of that research. I now discuss factors that determine what we remember and how well we remember it. As I noted earlier, memory processes in-

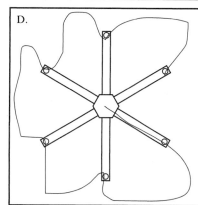

Figure 11.8 Possible routes a rat might take to obtain food from food cups at the ends of a radial-arm maze that is placed on the floor. Panel "a" shows route that minimizes travel distance. Panel "b" shows trail following behavior. Panel "c" shows random search. Panel "d" shows travel along the walls or thigmotaxis. (From Hoffman, Timberlake, Leffel, & Gont, 1999.)

volve three phases: acquisition, retention, and retrieval (see Table 11.1). What we remember and how well we remember it depend on all three of these phases, often in combination with each other. In this part of the chapter, I also discuss research with nonhuman animals relevant to each of the three phases of memory processes.

Acquisition and the Problem of Stimulus Coding

Obviously, we cannot remember something (the winning play in a championship game, for example) if we were not exposed to it in the first place. Memory depends on our having experienced an event and having made some kind of record of that experience. However, even when our memory is excellent, it is not because we have retained a perfect or literal record of the earlier experience.

Experiences cannot be recorded in a literal sense, even by machines. A movie camera can do an excellent job recording the sights and sounds of the winning play in a championship game. The visual aspects of the event are recorded in a series of stationary images; the auditory aspects are recorded in a pattern of magnetized particles on the film. The winning play is coded in terms of still photographs and magnetic patterns for the purposes of retention, but the coded record (a strip of film with a soundtrack) bears little resemblance to the actual event.

In a similar fashion, we do not have a literal record of a past experience in memory. The experience is coded in the nervous system in some way for the purposes of retention, and our memory is based on how the experience was coded and how that code is retrieved at a later time. Thus, **stimulus coding** is a critical feature of the acquisition phase of memory.

Investigators have been interested in several aspects of the problem of coding (Zentall, 1993). Consider, for example, rats foraging for food in a radial maze (see Figure 11.4). The animals have to enter the various arms of the maze to obtain the food located at the end of each arm. So as not to waste effort, they have to select only the arms they have not yet tried that day. As we have seen, rats rely on their memory to do this. But what do they keep in mind? How is memory coded?

Cognitive Maps and Other Navigational Codes. One possibility is that the animals make a serial list of the maze arms they visit, adding an item to the list with each new arm visited. Given the excellent performance of rats on mazes with 17 arms or more (Olton et al., 1977; Roberts, 1979; Wilkie & Slobin, 1983), this would involve a rather long list. Such extensive list learning seems unlikely, since even humans have difficulty maintaining 17 items or more in working memory at one time. Another possibility is that the animals form a mental map or mental representation of how the maze and the food cups are arranged and then use this "cognitive map" to decide which arm of the maze to enter next (Roberts, 1984).

The idea that animals form a cognitive map that guides their spatial navigation has been an attractive hypothesis, but it calls for further specification. Potentially, maps can represent many different types of information (distance, height or topography, presence of particular landmarks, compass direction, etc.). To claim that animals form a cognitive map does not tell us precisely what kinds of information are contained in such a map and how animals use this information. Such questions have led investigators to focus on more specific mechanisms that enable subjects to find a particular location in space (see reviews by Biegler, 2000; Cheng, 2000; Gallistel, 1990; Roberts, 1998; Shettleworth, 1998). Shettleworth (1998), for example, advocated that "discussion of cognitive mapping should be abandoned in favor of more operational discussion of how animals get from place to place" (p. 311). A number of mechanisms have been examined.

Figure 11.9 illustrates three possible navigational mechanisms. The goal is located near a rock. There is a tree to the left of the rock and a bush to the right. An animal could find the goal location by looking at the rock and aiming for it. This represents *beacon following*. The rock serves as a beacon that marks the location of the goal object. Beacon following is a fairly simple navigational tactic, requiring little more than the formation of an association between the beacon and the goal object. Sign tracking behavior described in Chapter 3 is an example of beacon following (see especially Figure 3.5). Given the cues present in Figure 11.9, the animal could also find the goal by going to the right of the tree or to the left of the bush. In these cases, it would be using the tree and the bush as landmarks to guide its navigation. A *landmark* is a distinctive stimulus that is not at the goal location but has a fixed relation to the goal ("to the left of" or "to the right of"). A third navigation tactic is to find the goal by using the *relation between the landmarks*. The goal is located midway between the tree and bush landmarks.

Animals can encode spatial information by using beacons, landmarks, and the relation between landmarks. Depending on the demands of a particular spatial task, animals may use one or another spatial coding mechanism, or may rely on several mechanisms at the same time.

Retrospective and Prospective Coding. So far I have discussed the kinds of spatial information animals may use in finding particular food locations. Another interesting question is which food locations are encoded as a rat goes about foraging on a radial-arm maze. Perhaps the most obvious possibility is that the animals keep in mind where they have al-

D. Wilkie

Courtesy of Dr. D. M. Wilkie

Figure 11.9 Diagram of a spatial task in which the goal (a patch of food, for example) is located near a rock, with a tree to the left of the goal and a bush to the right. An animal can find the goal by going to the rock (beacon following), or by responding to the tree and bush as landmarks.

Food Patch

ready been. This is called **retrospective memory,** or *retrospective coding.* An equally effective memory strategy is for the animals to keep in mind which maze arms they have yet to visit. This strategy is called **prospective memory,** or *prospective coding.* Because animal memory paradigms typically have a limited range of outcomes, they can be solved successfully either by remembering a past event (retrospection) or by remembering a plan for future action (prospection). This distinction has become a major focus of research (Honig & Thompson, 1982; Wasserman, 1986; Grant, 1993).

Consider going shopping at a mall. Let's assume that to complete your shopping, you have to visit six stores: a shoe store, a record store, a bookstore, a bakery, a clothing store, and a pharmacy. What memory strategy could you use to avoid going to the same place twice? One possibility would be to form a memory code for each store after visiting that store. This would be a retrospective code. You could then decide whether to enter the next store on the list based on whether you remembered already having gone there. With such a retrospective strategy, the contents of your working memory would increase by one item with each store you visit. Thus, how much you have to remember (the memory load) would increase as you progressed through the task (see Figure 11.10).

An alternative would be to memorize a list of all the stores you intended to visit before you start your trip. Such memory would involve prospection, because it would be memory for what you intended to do. After visiting a particular store, you could delete that store from your memory. Thus, in this scheme, a visit to a store would be "recorded" by having that store removed from the prospective memory list. Because you would be keeping in

retro – have been
prospect – yet to go

335

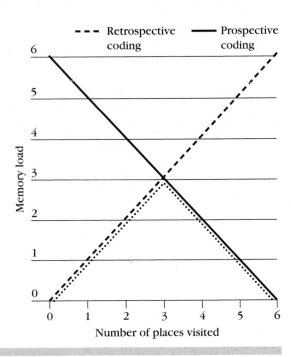

Figure 11.10 Memory load following different numbers of places visited, out of a possible total of six, given retrospective and prospective coding strategies. The dotted line represents memory load when the coding strategy is changed from retrospection to prospection halfway through the task. (Based on Cook, Brown, & Riley, 1985.)

P. Urcuioli

mind only which stores you still had to visit, the memory load would decrease as you progressed through your shopping, as shown in Figure 11.10.

Numerous ingenious experiments have been conducted to determine whether animals use retrospective or prospective memory. Many of these have involved variations of the matching-to-sample procedure with pigeons. The experiments have demonstrated that animals use both retrospective and prospective memory, but under different circumstances (Santi, Musgrave, & Bradford, 1988; Zentall, Jagielo, Jackson-Smith, & Urcuioli, 1987; Zentall, Urcuioli, Jagielo, & Jackson-Smith, 1989). Such experiments illustrate that coding strategies are flexible, with different strategies adopted in response to different task demands. (For other evidence of coding flexibility, see Ducharme & Santi, 1993; Grant, 1991; Grant & Spetch, 1993.)

Coding Strategies and Task Demands. To illustrate how coding strategies might change as a function of task demands, return to the example of having to shop in six different stores in a mall. As I have noted, with a retrospective coding strategy the demands on working memory increase as you progress through the shopping trip. In contrast, with a prospective coding strategy the demands on working memory decrease as you progress through the six stores (see Figure 11.10). How might you minimize the demands on your memory? Is there a way to keep the demands on working memory to three items or fewer throughout the shopping trip? There is, if you change your memory strategy halfway through the task.

At the start of the shopping trip, memory load is least if you use a retrospective strategy. Therefore, you should start with retrospective coding. Remembering where you have been works well for the first three stores you visit. After that, the memory load for retrospection begins to exceed the memory load for prospection (see Figure 11.10). Therefore, after having visited three stores, you should switch to a prospective code and keep in mind only which stores remain to be visited. By switching coding strategies halfway through, you minimize how much you have to remember at any one time. If you use retrospection followed by prospection, memory load will at first increase and then decrease as you complete the task, as illustrated by the dashed line in Figure 11.10.

Do animals (including people) use coding strategies so flexibly, and if so how could researchers prove that? The results of several experiments indicate that coding strategies change from retrospection to prospection as one goes through a list of places or items. Early in the list, individuals keep in mind what has already happened. Later, they remember what remains to be done (Cook, Brown, & Riley, 1985; Zentall, Steirn, & Jackson-Smith, 1990; see also Brown, Wheeler, & Riley, 1989).

In one study, Kesner and DeSpain (1988) compared the coding strategies of rats and college students in spatial memory tasks. If individuals switch from retrospection to prospection in the course of remembering a series of places, memory load should first increase and then decrease. Memory load was estimated from the rate of errors the participants made on a test that was conducted after they had visited different numbers of places (see Figure 11.11).

The rats in Kesner and DeSpain's study were first trained to forage for food on a 12-arm radial maze in the standard manner. Once they had become proficient at obtaining food by going to each maze arm, a series of test trials was conducted. On each test trial, the rats were allowed to make a certain number of arm entries. They were then removed from the maze for 15 minutes. At the end of the delay, they were returned to the maze and allowed to enter one of two alleys selected by the experimenter. One was an alley they had entered earlier; the other was a previously unchosen alley. Selecting the new alley was judged to be the correct response. The rate of errors the rats made during the test phase is presented in the left graph of Figure 11.11. As the number of visited locations before the test increased from 2 to 8 arms of the maze, the error rate increased. This finding is consistent with the hypothesis that the rats were using a retrospective coding strategy during the first 8 arm entries. Interestingly, however, when the rats were tested after having entered 10 arms, they

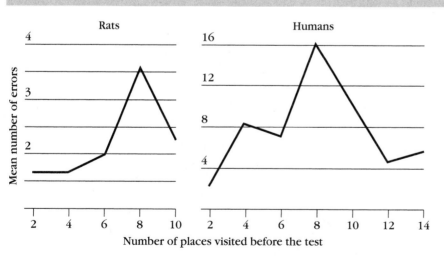

Figure 11.11 Error rate of rats (left) and college students (right) on spatial memory tasks requiring identification of a new place after a delay. The delay was imposed after the participants had "visited" various numbers of locations. (From "Correspondence Between Rats and Humans in the Utilization of Retrospective and Prospective Codes," by R. P. Kesner and M. J. DeSpain, 1988, *Animal Learning and Behavior, 16,* pp. 299–302. Copyright © 1988 by the Psychonomic Society. Reprinted by permission.)

made fewer errors. This improvement in performance toward the end of the series suggests that the animals switched to a prospective coding strategy.

The college students in the study were presented with a grid with 16 squares (corresponding to 16 places in a maze). During the course of a trial, the symbol X traveled from one square to another in an irregular order, simulating movement from one place to another in a maze. After the X had been presented at various locations, a delay of 5 seconds was introduced, followed by a test of two test locations. One test location was a place where the X had been; the other was a new square. The participants had to identify which was the new square.

The rate of errors the young adults made is presented in the right graph of Figure 11.11 as a function of the number of places the X had been before the test. The results were strikingly similar to the pattern of errors obtained with the rats. The error rate initially increased, consistent with a retrospective coding strategy. After the target stimulus had been in 8 places, however, the error rate decreased, consistent with a prospective coding strategy.

These results illustrate that memory performance is a function of coding strategies and that coding strategies may vary as a function of task demands. Given alternative possible coding strategies, participants switch from one to another so as to reduce memory load and thereby improve response accuracy. (For evidence of the flexibility of coding strategies in a matching-to-sample task, see Clement & Zentall, 2000b.)

Retention and the Problem of Rehearsal

The second phase of memory processes is retention. With working-memory tasks, a prominent issue involving retention is **rehearsal.** Rehearsal refers to keeping information in an active state, readily available for use. If someone tells you a phone number, you may rehearse the number by repeating it to yourself over and over again until you get to a phone. If someone is giving you directions for getting to the post office, you may try to create a mental image of the route and imagine yourself following the route a number of times. Such rehearsal strategies facilitate keeping newly acquired information readily at hand, available to guide behavior.

Rehearsal processes were first investigated in animal memory as they relate to the learning or establishment of new associations. Models of learning and memory typically assume that associations are formed between two events (a conditioned and an unconditioned stimulus, for example) provided that the two events are rehearsed at the same time (for example, Wagner, 1976, 1981). Given this assumption, learning should be disrupted by manipulations that disrupt rehearsal. Early studies of rehearsal processes in animal memory focused on such manipulations and their effects on the learning of new associations (for example, Wagner, Rudy, & Whitlow, 1973). More recent research has been on the role of rehearsal in working-memory paradigms. An important line of evidence for rehearsal processes in working memory comes from studies of **directed forgetting.**

Studies of human memory have shown that the accuracy of recall can be modified by cues or instructions indicating that something should (or should not) be remembered (for example, Bjork, 1972; Johnson, 1994). In this research, participants are first exposed to a list of items. Some of the items are accompanied by a remember cue (R-cue), indicating that the item will appear later in a test of memory. Other items are accompanied by a forget cue (F-cue) indicating that the item will not be included in the memory test. Occasionally, probe trials are included in which memory is tested for an item that was accompanied by the F-cue. The results of these probe trials indicate that memory is disrupted by the forget cues.

T. Zentall

Demonstrations of directed forgetting are important because they provide evidence that memory is an active process that can be brought under stimulus control. Research on directed forgetting in people has sparked interest in finding analogous effects with non-human animals (Rilling, Kendrick, & Stonebraker, 1984.) How might researchers devise a procedure to study directed forgetting in animals?

One possibility is to use a variation of the delayed-matching-to-sample procedure. In a matching task, each trial begins with exposure to a sample stimulus (a horizontal grid, for example). The animal is then presented with both the sample (horizontal grid) and a distracter stimulus (vertical grid). Responses to the sample are reinforced; responses to the distracter stimulus do not produce reinforcement. In this paradigm, cues to remember or forget can be introduced into the matching task after the sample stimulus, as is shown in Figure 11.12. On R-cue trials, the animals are tested for their memory of the sample; on F-cue trials, such a memory test is not conducted; the F-cue ends the trial and nothing else happens until the next trial begins.

Early research on directed forgetting in animals used procedures similar to that outlined in Figure 11.12. After extensive training on such a procedure, probe trials were introduced that tested for memory of the sample after an F-cue. As in the human research, these probe trials indicated that memory was disrupted by the F-cue. Why might such a disruption occur? One possibility is that the F-cue disrupts rehearsal and thereby leads to poorer memory performance. Unfortunately, however, the procedure outlined in Figure 11.12 allows other possibilities as well (see Roper & Zentall, 1993; Zentall, Roper, Kaiser, & Sherburne, 1997). Notice, for example, that during training, the animals cannot earn reinforcement on F-cue trials. Therefore, the F-cue may become a signal for nonreinforcement and may elicit

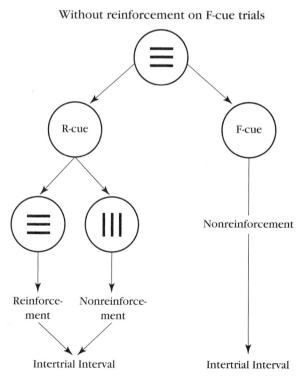

Without reinforcement on F-cue trials

Figure 11.12 A simple but inadequate procedure for studying directed forgetting in the context of delayed matching to sample. Each trial begins with a sample stimulus. This is then followed by either a remember cue (R-cue) or a forget cue (F-cue). Subjects are tested with the sample versus a distracter stimulus at the end of R-cue trials but not at the end of F-cue trials.

R-cue

F-cue

Nonreinforcement

Reinforcement

Nonreinforcement

Intertrial Interval

Intertrial Interval

negative emotions or frustration. Poor performance on F-cue probe trials may be due to the expectation of nonreward elicited by the F-cue rather than to poor memory (Zentall, Roper, & Sherburne, 1995).

Poor performance on F-cue probe trials may also be due to attentional factors. During training, the subjects may learn that once they have seen the F-cue, there is no reason to pay attention to anything else that happens on that trial. This lack of attention may result in low accuracy on F-cue probe trials.

To overcome the problems identified above, the procedure should permit subjects to obtain reinforcement on F-cue trials and should also maintain attention. These goals are met by the procedure outlined in Figure 11.13. Devised by Roper, Kaiser, and Zentall (1995), it involves two remember cues (White and Blue) and two forget cues (filled circle and open circle). At the end of R-cue trials, the subjects are asked to chose between the sam-

Figure 11.13 Procedures used by Roper, Kaiser, and Zentall (1995) to demonstrate directed forgetting in pigeons. On R-cue training (and test) trials, a color sample (Red) was followed by one of two remember cues (Blue or White). At the end of a 4-second delay interval, the subjects were presented with the sample (Red) and a distracter (Green) stimulus, and responding to the sample was reinforced. On F-cue training trials, the sample was followed by one of two forget cues, which in turn were followed by vertical and horizontal lines. If the forget cue was a filled circle, responding to the vertical lines was reinforced. If the forget cue was an open circle, responding to the horizontal lines was reinforced. On F-cue probe trials, the sample and distractor color stimuli (Red and Green) appeared after the forget cues.

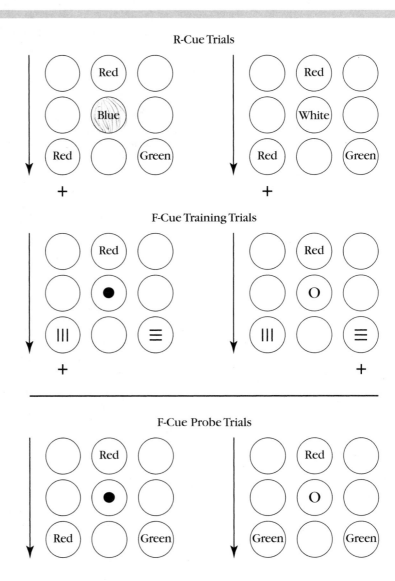

ple stimulus (Red) and a distractor (Green). In contrast, the sample stimulus (and its distractor) do not appear at the end of F-cue trials during training. Rather, the subjects are given a choice between vertical and horizontal lines. If the F-cue was the filled circle, pecking the vertical lines is reinforced. If the F-cue was the open circle, pecking the horizontal lines is reinforced. Thus, the subjects can earn reinforcement on both R-cue and F-cue trials. In addition, they cannot afford to stop paying attention as soon as they have seen the F-cue because they have to select between the vertical and horizontal lines on F-cue trials. On F-cue probe trials, the subjects are tested with the color sample stimuli instead of the vertical or horizontal lines following presentation of the F-cue.

Roper et al. (1995) tested six pigeons with the procedures outlined in Figure 11.13. All of the pigeons showed evidence of directed forgetting on the F-cue probe trials. On R-cue trials, the mean accuracy for selecting the sample stimulus at the end of the 4-sec delay was 86%. In contrast, mean accuracy on F-cue probe trials was just 73%. Furthermore, each of the six pigeons tested in the experiment responded more accurately on R-cue trials than on F-cue probe trials (see also Kaiser, Sherburne, & Zentall, 1997).

Retrieval

In the third phase of memory processes, retrieval, stored information is recovered so that it can be used to guide behavior. Whereas problems of coding and rehearsal are primarily being investigated in working-memory paradigms, research on retrieval has focused on reference memory and, more specifically, on memory for learned associations. Retrieval processes are of special interest because many instances of memory failure reflect deficits in the recovery of information—**retrieval failure**—rather than loss of the information from the memory store.

During the course of our daily lives, we learn many things, all of which are somehow stored in the brain. Which aspect of our extensive knowledge we think of at a particular time depends on which pieces of information are retrieved from our long-term memory store. At any moment, we recall only a minute proportion of what we know. Retrieval processes are triggered by reminders, or **retrieval cues.** If you are discussing summer camp experiences with your friends, the things they say will serve as retrieval cues to remind you of things you did at summer camp.

Retrieval cues are effective in reminding you of a past experience because they are associated with the memory for that experience. A song may remind you of the concert you attended on your first date. Balancing on a bicycle will remind you of what you have to do to ride a bicycle. The sensations of sinking in a swimming pool will remind you of what you learned about swimming, and the voice of a friend you have not seen for a long time will stimulate retrieval of memories for the things you used to do together.

Retrieval Cues and Memory for Instrumental Behavior in Human Infants. Various stimuli that are present during acquisition of a memory can come to serve as retrieval cues for that memory. Borovsky and Rovee-Collier (1990), for example, investigated retrieval of the memory for instrumental conditioning in 6-month-old infants. The infants were trained in their own homes in playpens whose sides were covered with a cloth liner. Some of these liners were striped and others had a square pattern. The investigators were interested in whether the cloth liner might serve as a retrieval cue for the instrumental response.

A mobile was mounted above the playpen. Each infant was seated in the playpen in a reclining baby seat so that he or she could see the mobile. One end of a satin ribbon was

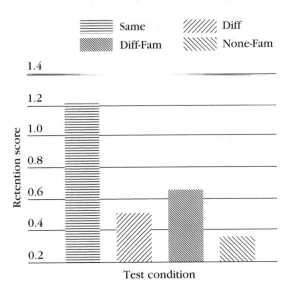

Figure 11.14 Retention scores of 6-month-old infants in a test of instrumental conditioning. Group Same was tested in a playpen with the same cloth liner that had been present during conditioning. Group Diff was tested with a new cloth liner. Group Diff-Fam was tested with a familiar cloth liner that was different from the one in the playpen during conditioning. Group None-Fam was tested without a cloth liner but in a familiar playpen in a familiar room. (From "Contextual Constraints on Memory Retrieval at Six Months," by D. Borovsky and C. Rovee-Collier, 1990, *Child Development, 61,* pp. 1569–1583. Copyright © 1990 by University of Chicago Press. Reprinted by permission.)

Courtesy of Donald A. Dewsbury

C. Rovee-Collier

looped around the infant's ankle and the other end was attached to the stand that supported the mobile. With this arrangement, each kick by the infant made the mobile move. The instrumental response was kicking the leg, and the reinforcer was movement of the mobile. The kicking response first was conditioned in two short training sessions. The infants then received a test session 24 hours later.

The cues present during the test session were varied for different groups of infants. Some of the babies were tested in a crib with the same cloth liner that had been present during the training sessions (Group Same). Others were tested with the alternate cloth liner that was new to them (Group Diff). For a third group, the alternate cloth liner was familiar, but it had not been present during the training trials (Group Diff-Fam). A fourth group of babies was tested without a liner and could look around their familiar playroom (None-Fam).

The results of the experiment are summarized in Figure 11.14. The best retention performance was evident in the group that was tested with the same playpen liner that had been present during conditioning. Each of the other groups showed significantly poorer memory performance. Infants tested with a novel liner (Group Diff) may have shown poor performance because novelty somehow disrupted their behavior (Thomas & Empedocles, 1992). However, the poor performance of Group Diff-Fam indicates that novelty was not entirely responsible for the disruptions of memory that occurred. A change in the crib liner from conditioning to testing resulted in poor performance even if the liner used during testing was familiar. The inferior performance of Group Diff-Fam as compared to group

Same provides strong evidence that the cloth liner served as a retrieval cue for the instrumental kicking behavior. (For related research with human infants, see Bhatt, Rovee-Collier, & Shyi, 1994; Rovee-Collier & Bhatt, 1993; Hartshorn & Rovee-Collier, 1997. For other examples of context effects in memory retrieval, see Smith & Vela, 2001; Zhou & Riccio, 1996.)

Contextual Cues and the Retrieval of Conflicting Memories.   Changing the cloth pattern on the playpen liner changed the contextual cues of the playpen. Thus, the study by Borovsky and Rovee-Collier was a study of the role of contextual cues in memory retrieval. I described other examples of contextual cues in memory retrieval in the discussion of contextual stimulus control in Chapter 8 and in connection with extinction, in Chapter 9. A particularly striking example was presented in Figure 8.13, which showed data from an experiment by Thomas, McKelvie, and Mah (1985). Pigeons in this experiment first learned to peck when a vertical line (S+ = 90°) was projected on the response key and to not peck when a horizontal line (S− = 0°) appeared. The contextual cues were then changed (by altering the sounds and lighting in the chamber), and the pigeons were trained on the reversal of the original discrimination. Now, the horizontal line (0°) was S+ and the vertical line (90°) was S−.

Subsequent generalization tests in each context indicated that responding to the vertical and horizontal lines depended on the context in which the lines were tested. Which discrimination was retrieved depended on which set of contextual cues was presented. The study illustrates that organisms can retain memories of diametrically opposing response tendencies. (For other examples of involving the retrieval of conflicting memories, see Bouton, 1993, 1994; Dekeyne & Deweer, 1990; Fiori, Barnet, & Miller, 1994; Haggbloom & Morris, 1994.)

The Generality of Reminder Treatments.   Much has been learned about the facilitation of memory retrieval by reminder treatments (see Gordon, 1981; Spear, 1978, 1981; Spear & Riccio, 1994). As I have described, contextual cues are especially effective in stimulating memory retrieval (Gordon & Klein, 1994; Hitchcock & Rovee-Collier, 1996; Zhou & Riccio, 1996). In addition, various other reminder procedures have been found to facilitate recall, including exposure to the *unconditioned stimulus* (Hunt, 1997; MacArdy & Riccio, 1995; Miller, Jagielo, & Spear, 1991; Quartermain, McEwen, & Azmitia, 1970), exposure to the *reinforced conditioned stimulus* (CS+) (Gisquet-Verrier & Alexinsky, 1990; Gordon & Mowrer, 1980), and exposure to a *nonreinforced conditioned stimulus* (CS−) that was present during training (Campbell & Randall, 1976; Miller, Jagielo, & Spear, 1990a, 1991, 1992).

Reminder treatments can be used to reverse many instances of memory loss. (For a review, see Miller, Kasprow, & Schachtman, 1986.) For example, reminder treatments have been used to facilitate memory retrieval from short-term memory (Feldman & Gordon, 1979; Kasprow, 1987). They can remind older animals (and babies) of forgotten early-life experiences (for example, Campbell & Randall, 1976; Fagen & Rovee-Collier, 1983; Haroutunian & Riccio, 1979; Galluccio & Rovee-Collier, 1999; Richardson, Riccio, & Jonke, 1983). Reminder treatments can counteract stimulus-generalization decrements that occur when learned behavior is tested in a new situation (Gordon, McCracken, Dess-Beech, & Mowrer, 1981; Mowrer & Gordon, 1983). They also have been observed to increase the low levels of conditioned responding that typically occur in latent inhibition, overshadowing, and blocking procedures (Kasprow, Cacheiro, Balaz, & Miller, 1982; Kasprow, Catterson, Schachtman, & Miller, 1984; Miller, Jagielo, & Spear, 1990b; Schachtman, Gee, Kasprow, & Miller, 1983; see also Gordon, McGinnis, & Weaver, 1985).

N. E. Spear

W. C. Gordon

BOX **11.2**

GENES AND LEARNING

The nervous system is composed of billions of neurons interconnected by chemical connections called synapses. In Box 11.1, I described how learning can alter behavior by producing a change in the way a synapse operates. In some cases, learning may bring about a lasting increase in synaptic strength, yielding a form of long-term potentiation (LTP). In other cases, experience will result in a downregulation known as long-term depression (LTD).

The mechanisms that mediate changes in synaptic strength operate in phases. Initially, local molecular mechanisms produce short-term and rapid changes in synaptic strength. Additional processes are then activated that result in lasting memories. Establishing a long-term memory depends on the activation of genes that manufacture new protein products that produce a lasting change in how a synapse works.

Using drugs that block protein synthesis, researchers demonstrated many years ago that the manufacture of new proteins contributes to the formation of long-term memories (Davis & Squire, 1984). More recently, it has been established that the same is true for the lasting forms of LTP and LTD (Mayford & Kandel, 1999). Even learning in the invertebrate *Aplysia* (see Box 2.3) depends on gene expression.

Modern molecular biology has given us a host of new techniques that allow researchers to uncover the genes involved in learning. These studies have revealed that a variety of learning mechanisms depend on the induction of common genetic codes, genes that encode some biological universals that have been well conserved through evolution. Just as the mechanisms that underlie the generation of a neural signal (the action potential) are well conserved across species, so too may be the mechanisms that underlie synaptic plasticity.

Modern genetics has also given us new tools for studying the role of gene expression in learning. We can read the genetic code, identify the locus of the relevant genes, and experimentally manipulate how those genes operate. If we believe that a particular protein plays an essential role in learning, we can test this by using mice in which the relevant gene has been knocked out. This provides a new and unique window into the molecular mechanisms that underlie learning.

Silva and his colleagues have been at the forefront of this new technology, creating genetically engineered mice that exhibit specific deficits in the way they learn and remember (see review by Silva & Giese, 1998). One of the earliest experiments focused on the role of a protein known as CaMKII. One way a synapse can be strengthened is by allowing calcium (Ca^{++}) into the cell. Ca^{++} is an electrically charged particle that normally has a higher concentration outside of the neuron than inside. When Ca^{++} is allowed into the neuron by the NMDA receptor (see Figure 11.15), it engages CaMKII, which enhances synaptic efficacy by activating the AMPA receptors that mediate the neural signal. Silva created mice that lacked the gene that underlies the production of CaMKII within the hippocampus. From other studies, Silva knew that the hippocampus plays a critical role in learning about spatial relations. He reasoned that if CaMKII is critical for learning, then knockout mice that lack this gene should have difficulty remembering where a hidden platform is in a Morris water maze. That is precisely what occurred, providing a link between learning and a particular protein product.

A difficulty with studies of knockout mice is that the mice may not develop normally. When a gene is missing, other biochemical mechanisms can be enlisted that help the organism compensate for its deficiency. This could yield a brain that differs in a variety of ways from a normal brain. The abnormal neural environment may make it difficult to interpret the consequences of the genetic manipulation. Neuroscientists are solving this problem by making mice in which the expression of a gene can be experimentally controlled. An interesting application of this technology involves the creation of a transgenic mouse. Instead of losing a gene (a knockout), the transgenic mouse has an extra gene that makes a new protein product.

In one example, mice were engineered that made a mutant version of CaMKII that did not work properly. These mice did not exhibit normal LTP and exhibited a learning deficit in the Morris water maze (Mayford, Bach, Huang,

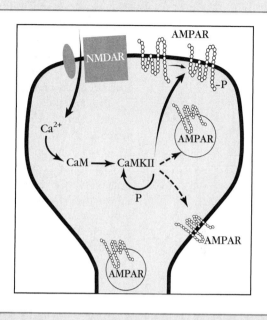

Figure 11.15 The molecular mechanisms that underlie long-term potentiation. The NMDA receptor allows CA^{++} to enter the cell, which engages the enzyme CaMKII. CaMKII plays a critical role in strengthening the synaptic response. It does so, in part, by awakening silent AMPA receptors. (Adapted from Malenka & Nicoll, 1999.)

Wang, Hawkins, & Kandel, 1996). The expression of the added gene in these mice was controlled by a molecular switch. This switch, which had been added by the researchers, was controlled by a novel chemical (doxycycline). To turn the switch off, and stop production of the mutant CaMKII, all the researchers had to do was add some doxycycline to the diet of the mice. When this was done, the mice once again exhibited normal LTP. They also recovered their ability to learn and remember spatial locations. As long as doxycycline was present, their brains worked normally. Only when this chemical was removed, and the mutant gene was expressed, was LTP and learning disrupted.

All of the genetic manipulations I described so far produced deficits in memory. Researchers are also exploring the possibility that modifying gene expression might improve memory. A good example is provided by a genetically engineered mouse named Doogie, after the ficticious TV boy genius, Doogie Howser. As I discussed in Box 11.1, the induction of LTP depends on the NMDA receptor. This receptor is formed from components (subunits), one of which changes with development. Early in development, animals have a subunit called NR2B that appears to promote the induction of LTP. In adults, this subunit is replaced by an alternative form (NR2A) that downregulates LTP. The change from the juvenile form (NR2B) to the adult form (NR2A) could make it more difficult for an adult animal to learn about new environmental relations. To explore this possibility, Tsien and his colleagues created mice that continued to make the juvenile form of the subunit (NR2B) into adulthood (Tang et al., 1999). As expected, these mice showed stronger LTP as adults. The mice also exhibited enhanced learning on an object recognition task and improved spatial memory in the Morris water maze. Across a range of tests, Doogie mice seemed smarter.

If the juvenile form of the NMDA receptor works better, why would nature replace it with one that undermines learning and memory? The answer is still being debated. Perhaps this change helps to protect some early memories that are crucial to survival. For example, once we have learned the words of our language, this information should not be readily unlearned. By enabling learning early in development, nature may open a critical window, only to close it later in life to help protect what was learned.

—J. W. Grau

FORGETTING

Forgetting is the flip side of memory. We are said to exhibit forgetting when memory fails and we don't respond in accordance with past experience or learning, but as Kraemer and Golding (1997) have argued, forgetting should not be viewed simply as the absence of remembering. Forgetting should instead be considered an important phenomenon in its own right (see also White, 2001). Forgetting can be adaptive because it increases behavioral variability. That behavioral variability is not a welcome experience when you cannot remember something on a test, but it can be useful when you move to a new job or a new city and have to learn new skills. Forgetting can also reduce the context specificity of learning and thereby permit learned behavior to occur in a broader range of situations (Riccio, Rabinowitz, & Axelrod, 1994).

The common experience is that failures of memory become more likely as time passes after a learning episode. However, it is not informative to view time as a "cause" of forgetting. As Piaget is reputed to have said, "Time is not a cause but a vehicle of causes." And there may be a variety of causes of forgetting. As I have described, memory mechanisms involve many different factors. Some of these concern coding and the acquisition of information. Others involve rehearsal and the retention of information. Still others involve processes of retrieval. Things can go wrong at any point along the way. Therefore, failures of memory, or forgetting, can occur for a variety of reasons.

Forgetting has been extensively investigated in the context of two types of phenomena—interference effects and retrograde amnesia. In the concluding sections of this chapter, I describe these phenomena in turn.

Proactive and Retroactive Interference

The most common sources of memory disruption arise from exposure to prominent stimuli either before or after the event that one is trying to remember. Consider meeting people at a party, for example. If the only new person you meet is Alice, chances are you will not have much trouble remembering her name. However, if you are introduced to a number of new people before and/or after meeting Alice, you may find it much harder to remember her name.

There are numerous well-documented and well-analyzed cases of **proactive interference**—situations in which memory for something is disrupted by earlier exposure to other information. In these cases, the interfering of information acts forward to disrupt the memory of a future target event. In cases of **retroactive interference,** memory for something is disrupted by subsequent exposure to other information. In these situations, the interfering stimulus acts backward to disrupt the memory of a preceding target event.

The mechanisms of proactive and retroactive interference have been extensively investigated in studies of human memory (Postman, 1971; Slamecka & Ceraso, 1960; Underwood, 1957). Proactive and retroactive interference have been also investigated in various animal memory paradigms. For examples of proactive interference, see Grant (1982, 2000), and Edhouse and White (1988a, 1988b). For examples of retroactive interference, see Harper and Garry (2000), Killeen (2001b), and Terry (1996).

Retrograde Amnesia

A sad and too frequent source of memory failure is severe head injury. For example, people who receive a concussion in a car accident often suffer memory loss. However, the amnesia is likely to be selective. They may forget how the injury occurred, where the accident took place, or who else was in the car at the time. But they will continue to remember their name and address, where they grew up, and what they prefer to eat for dessert. Thus, there is a gradient of memory loss, with forgetting limited to events that occurred close to the accident. This phenomenon is called **retrograde amnesia** (Russell & Nathan, 1946).

The clinical significance of retrograde amnesia resulting from closed-head injury received in traffic and sports accidents has encouraged investigators to develop techniques to study this phenomenon in laboratory animals. One experiment with laboratory rats, for example, examined the effects of closed-head injury on memory for a passive avoidance task (Zhou & Riccio, 1995). The rats received a single training trial in an experimental chamber that had two compartments, one white and the other black, separated by a sliding door. The rats were first confined in the white compartment for 15 seconds. The door was then opened allowing them to enter the black compartment. But as soon as the rats entered the black compartment, they encountered shock through the grid floor. The results of this single training trial were evaluated several days later, when the rats were again placed in the white compartment of the apparatus. This time when the door to the black compartment was opened, the rats were much slower to enter the black compartment. This hesitation was used as evidence of passive avoidance learning.

To evaluate the effects of closed-head injury, different groups of rats received a concussion at various times after the single conditioning trial. For one group, the concussion occurred 1 minute after the conditioning trial. For other groups, it occurred 6 hours, 1 day, 3 days, or 5 days later. Each of these groups was tested two days after the head injury. Two control groups did not receive a concussion and were tested at the same time as the 1-minute and 5-day experimental groups. The results of the experiment are summarized in Figure 11.16. The two control groups showed the maximum latencies (300 seconds) to enter the black compartment, indicating strong memory for the passive avoidance training trial. Strong learning was also evident in the subjects that received a concussion 5 days after the training trial. In contrast, a gradient of performance was evident in the other experimental

Courtesy of D. C. Riccio

D. C. Riccio

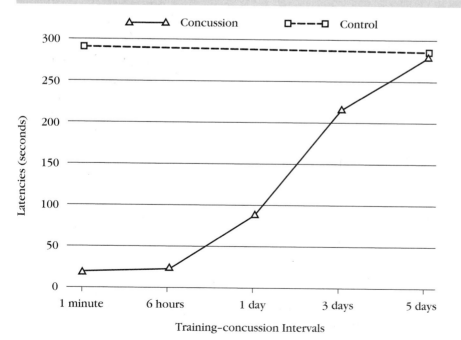

Figure 11.16 Median latencies to enter the black compartment after a passive avoidance conditioning trial. Control groups did not receive a concussion after the training trial. In contrast, each of the other groups received a concussion at intervals ranging from 1 minute to 5 days after conditioning. The concussion resulted in a retrograde amnesia for the passive avoidance task. (From Zhou & Riccio, 1995.)

groups. In general, less passive avoidance behavior occurred during the test session in groups that received shorter intervals between the training trial and the concussion. This illustrates the phenomenon on retrograde amnesia.

Many studies have provided convincing evidence of experimentally induced retrograde amnesia in a variety of learning tasks (for reviews, see McGaugh & Herz, 1972; Spear, 1978; Spear & Riccio, 1994). In addition, experiments have shown that retrograde amnesia can be produced by many different treatments that affect the nervous system, including anesthesia (McGaugh & Petrinovich, 1965); temporary cooling of the body, or hypothermia (Riccio, Hodges, & Randall, 1968); and injection of drugs that inhibit protein synthesis (Flexner, Flexner, & Stellar, 1963).

Why do various neural insults produce a graded loss of memory? The traditional explanation of retrograde amnesia involves the concept of **memory consolidation** (see McGaugh & Herz, 1972). According to the memory-consolidation hypothesis, when an event is first experienced, it enters a short-term, or temporary, memory store. While in short-term memory, the information is vulnerable and can be lost because of interfering stimuli or other disruptive events. However, if the proper conditions are met, the information gradually becomes consolidated into a relatively permanent form.

Memory consolidation is assumed to be a physiological process by which information is gradually transformed into a long-term or permanent state. Neurophysiological disturbances such as electroconvulsive shock, anesthesia, and body cooling are assumed to interfere with the consolidation process and thereby disrupt the transfer of information to long-term memory. Disruption of consolidation produces amnesia only for information stored in short-term memory. Once information has been transferred to long-term memory, it cannot be lost because of disruptions of consolidation. Amnesic agents presumably lead to loss of memory only for recently experienced events because only recent events are in short-term memory, and are thus susceptible to disruptions of consolidation.

Disruptions of performance caused by amnesic agents can also be explained in a very different way. According to this alternative account, amnesia results not from loss of the memory but from inability to retrieve or reactivate the memory (Lewis, 1979; Miller & Springer, 1973; Riccio & Richardson, 1984; Spear, 1973). This explanation is called the *retrieval-failure hypothesis*. The retrieval-failure hypothesis assumes that an amnesic agent alters the coding of new memories so as to make subsequent recovery of the information difficult. Thus, unlike the memory-consolidation view, the retrieval-failure hypothesis assumes that the information surrounding an amnesic episode is acquired and retained in memory, but in a form that makes it difficult to access.

What kinds of evidence would help decide between the memory-consolidation and retrieval-failure interpretations? If information is lost because of a failure of consolidation, it cannot ever be recovered. By contrast, the retrieval-failure view assumes that amnesia can be reversed if the proper procedure is found to reactivate the memory. To decide between the alternatives, researchers have to find techniques that can reverse the effects of amnesic agents. Several such procedures have been discovered.

Numerous experiments have shown that the memory deficits that characterize retrograde amnesia can be overcome by reminder treatments. Consider, for example, retrograde amnesia that was produced by a concussion. As I described earlier, rats that received a concussion within 3 days of their passive avoidance conditioning trial showed significant loss of memory for their conditioning experience (see Figure 11.16). In a follow-up experiment, Zhou and Riccio (1995, Experiment 3) examined whether the amnesia could be reversed by a reminder treatment.

The follow-up experiment included three groups of rats. Two of the groups received a single passive avoidance conditioning trial, as in the original study, and this was followed

1 minute later by a concussion. The third group was a "pseudo-training" group and received shock in another apparatus. All of the subjects were tested for their passive avoidance behavior 3 days later. However, shortly before this test, a brief shock was administered to one of the experimental groups in a novel environment to see if this US-alone reminder treatment would reverse the course of their amnesia. (The reminder treatment was also given to the pseudo-training group, but this was not expected to facilitate their recall since they did not learn the original task in the first place.)

The results of the experiment are summarized in Figure 11.17. The group that received a concussion after its training trial showed no evidence of learning. They stepped into the black compartment just as quickly during the test trial as they had during the training trial. This result confirms that the concussion produced amnesia. However, the amnesia was reversible. Subjects that received the concussion and were then given a US-alone reminder before the test showed strong passive avoidance performance. The results obtained with the pseudo-learning control group show that the strong passive avoidance performance of the second group was not due to new learning produced by the reminder treatment. The pseudo-learning group also received the reminder treatment but did not show evidence of passive avoidance behavior.

Results such as those in Figure 11.17 indicate that retrograde amnesia can be reversed by reminder treatments. Numerous similar studies have been conducted with similar results (see reviews by Gordon, 1981; Riccio & Richardson, 1984; Spear, 1978; Spear & Riccio, 1994). This body of evidence seriously calls into question the validity of consolidation failure as an explanation of retrograde amnesia. Rather, retrograde amnesia appears to be due to retrieval failure—the inability to retrieve information that was learned shortly before an amnesic treatment.

Interest in the consolidation hypothesis has been rekindled by recent findings that indicate that a recently activated memory is susceptible to the same kind of retrograde amnesia

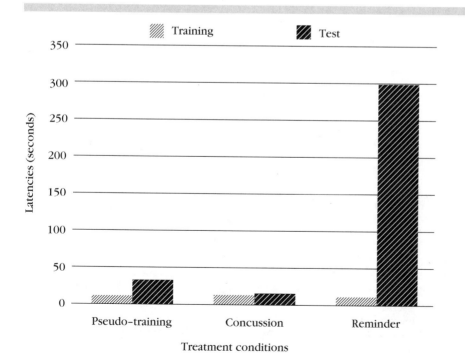

Figure 11.17 Effects of US-alone reminder treatment on recovery from amnesia for a passive avoidance training trial induced by a concussion. An increase in the response latency from training to testing is evidence of passive avoidance behavior. (Based on Zhou & Riccio, 1995.)

that can disrupt original learning (Nader, Schafe, & LeDoux, 2000). These data have been used to argue that memories have to be reconsolidated after each time that they are activated. As a number of commentators have pointed out, however, evidence contrary to the original consolidation hypothesis also presents problems for this reconsolidation hypothesis (for example, Miller & Matzel, 2000; Millin, Moody, & Riccio, 2001; Sara, 2000; see also Nader, Schafe, & LeDoux, 2000).

CONCLUDING COMMENTS

The study of memory processes is central to the understanding of animal cognition. Memory processes involve acquisition and coding of information, rehearsal and retention, and retrieval. Difficulties in any of these phases, or problems involving interactions among the phases, can result in failures of memory, or forgetting. Several ingenious techniques for the study of memory processes in animals have been developed in the past 30 years. These techniques have told us much about the coding of information, rehearsal processes, and retrieval processes. This information has, in turn, allowed us to better understand failures of memory that occur in interference paradigms and in retrograde amnesia.

SAMPLE QUESTIONS

1. Compare and contrast working memory and reference memory.
2. Describe the delayed-matching-to-sample procedure and alternative strategies that can be used to respond accurately in such a procedure. How can these response strategies be distinguished experimentally?
3. Describe the radial maze procedure and mechanisms that have been used to explain efficient performance in this situation.
4. Describe how retrospective coding and prospective coding may be differentiated experimentally?
5. Describe the complications involved in demonstrating directed forgetting in laboratory animals.
6. Describe the memory-consolidation and retrieval-failure explanations of retrograde amnesia and what evidence can be used to support one or the other hypothesis.

KEY TERMS

acquisition The original input of information in a learning or memory experiment.

amnesia Loss of memory due to concussion or other injury. (See also *retrograde amnesia*.)

animal cognition Theoretical constructs and models used to explain aspects of behavior that cannot be readily characterized in terms of simple S-R or reflex mechanisms. These mechanisms do not require consciousness, awareness, or intentionality.

cognitive ethology A branch of ethology that assumes that consciousness, awareness, and intentionality can be inferred from the complexity, flexibility, and cleverness of certain forms of behavior.

delayed matching to sample A procedure in which participants are reinforced for responding to a test stimulus that is the same as a sample stimulus that was presented some time earlier.

directed forgetting Forgetting that occurs because of a stimulus (a forget cue) that indicates that working memory will not be tested on that trial. Directed forgetting is an example of the stimulus control of memory.

memory A term used to characterize instances in which an organism's current behavior is determined by some aspect of its previous experience.

memory consolidation The establishment of a memory in relatively permanent form, or the transfer of information from short-term to long-term memory.

proactive interference Disruption of memory caused by exposure to stimuli before the event to be remembered.

procedural memory Memory that mediates the learning of behavioral and cognitive skills that are performed automatically, without conscious control, often reflecting knowledge about invariant relationships in the environment, such as CS-US contiguity (classical conditioning) or response-reinforcer contiguity (instrumental conditioning).

prospective memory Memory for an expected future event or response.

reference memory Long-term retention of background information necessary for successful use of incoming and recently acquired information. (Compare with *working memory*.)

rehearsal A theoretical process whereby information is maintained in an active state, available to influence behavior and/or the processing of other information.

retention interval The time between acquisition of information and a test of memory for that information.

retrieval The recovery of information from a memory store.

retrieval cues A stimulus related to an experience that facilitates the recall of other information related to that experience.

retrieval failure A deficit in recovering information from a memory store.

retroactive interference Disruption of memory caused by exposure to stimuli following the event to be remembered.

retrograde amnesia A gradient of memory loss going back in time from the occurrence of a major injury or physiological disturbance. Amnesia is greatest for events that took place closest to the time of injury.

retrospective memory Memory for a previously experienced event. Also called *retrospection*.

simultaneous matching to sample A procedure in which participants are reinforced for responding to a test stimulus that is the same as a sample stimulus. The sample and the test stimuli are presented at the same time. (Compare with *delayed matching to sample*.)

stimulus coding How a stimulus is represented in memory.

trace decay hypothesis The theoretical idea that exposure to a stimulus produces changes in the nervous system that gradually and automatically decrease after the stimulus has been terminated.

trials-unique procedure A matching-to-sample procedure in which different sample and comparison stimuli are used on each trial.

working memory Short-term retention of information that is needed for successful responding on the task at hand but not on subsequent (or previous) similar tasks. (Compare with *reference memory*.)

C hapter 12 explores a diversity of contemporary research areas in animal cognition involving the processing of various types of information. In each of these areas, it is important to consider basic conditioning mechanisms before accepting more complex cognitive interpretations of the behavior. This principle is nicely illustrated with transitive inference, the first area of research I discuss here. Transitive inference was initially thought to reflect complex cognitive processes, but recent research has provided a simpler associative account. Next, I describe a more specialized cognitive skill, memory (especially episodic memory) in food-storing birds. I then describe more widespread phenomena of animal cognition, including timing, serial pattern learning, and perceptual concept formation. In the last section of the chapter, I return to a more specialized form of cognition—namely, language—which is actually a collection of cognitive skills, some of which are clearly evident in a number of nonhuman species.

The various aspects of behavior discussed in Chapter 12 are not all reflections of a common underlying mechanism, nor are they all involved in the solution of a common behavioral problem or challenge to survival. However, they all involve major contemporary areas of research in animal cognition that have stimulated a great deal of interest. This interest has come in part because until recently the cognitive processes involved were considered to be characteristic primarily of human behavior. In addition, each of these areas of research has stimulated considerable controversy.

The controversies have centered on whether complex cognitive processes had to be postulated to explain the various behaviors that were observed. Opponents of cognitive interpretations have argued that the phenomena could be explained by traditional learning principles. By contrast, proponents of cognitive interpretations have argued that cognitive mechanisms provide simpler explanations for the phenomena and are more productive in stimulating new research. The work in this area has amply borne out this latter justification. Without a cognitive perspective, much of the research I describe in this chapter would never have been done, and many of the phenomena would never have been discovered. But, as the research on transitive inference has shown, not all cases of "intelligent" behavior require complex cognitive processes.

TRANSITIVE INFERENCE AND VALUE TRANSFER

Transitive inference refers to inferring that a set of stimuli is organized in a sequential order based on exposure to only two stimuli at a time. Consider, for example, the following puzzle. You have to figure out how to put five cards in order from "best" to "worst," but you are only given information about the cards in pairs. The five cards are labeled A, B, C, D, and E. During training trials, you are allowed to look at one pair of cards at a time. The training pairs are A-B, B-C, C-D, and D-E. Which stimulus is presented on the right or the left each time is varied randomly across trials, to prevent you from using position as a clue. With each stimulus pair, you are told that the card closer to the beginning of the alphabet is the better one. Thus, in a choice between A and B, you are told A is better than B (A+B–), but in a choice of B and C, you are told B is better than C (B+C–). In a choice between C and D, C is better than D (C+D–), and in a choice between D and E, D is better than E (D+E–). Could you figure out the order of the five cards from these paired trials, and what test would reveal your learning?

The critical test after training involves determining how a participant would respond during a test trial when she or he encountered the novel pair of stimuli, B versus D. Notice that during the training phase, cards B and D appeared equally often as "better" and "worse" cards. (The training pairs with these stimuli were A+B–, B+C–, C+D–, and D+E.) Based on how often cards B and D were "better" during training, there should be no basis for selecting between them. However, if during training you formed a mental representation of the sequence A through E, you should select B over D. This would be a transitive inferential choice.

Evidence of transitive inference was first obtained with chimpanzees (Gillan, 1981). Pairs of stimuli (AB, BC, CD, and DE) were presented at the same time to the chimpanzees. Which stimulus was "better" was indicated by providing food reinforcement for responding to that stimulus. Responding to the alternate ("worse") stimulus was not reinforced. Thus, just as in the card puzzle described above, the trials for the chimpanzees can be described as A+B–, B+C–, C+D–, and D+E–. After the subjects learned to perform with good accuracy on the stimulus pairs, they were tested in a choice between B and D.

They responded more to B than to D and this was considered evidence of "transitive inference," a form of complex cognition.

Since the chimpanzee experiment, transitive inference has also been demonstrated in pigeons. Furthermore, investigators have come to question the phenomenon as evidence of complex cognition. They have suggested that the phenomenon can be explained by the fairly elementary associative mechanism of *value transfer* (Couvillon & Bitterman, 1992; von Fersen, Wynne, Delius, & Staddon, 1991; Zentall & Sherburne, 1994). According to value transfer, a nonreinforced stimulus gains some "value" or excitatory strength through stimulus generalization if the stimulus is presented at the same time as another cue that is reinforced. Thus, when responding to A is reinforced in a choice between A and B, some generalized excitation also develops to B. That is, there is positive transfer from A+ to B− when these appear together. D will also gain some generalized excitation (or value transfer) on C+D− trials. However, C will have less value to transfer to D than A has to transfer to B. This is because C is reinforced only half the time it appears during training (B+C− and C+D−), whereas A is reinforced every time it appears (only in A+B−). Because B receives more value transfer than D during training, subjects will pick B over D during the test. (For additional studies of value transfer, see Clement & Zentall, 2000a; Dorrance, Kaiser, & Zentall, 1998; Lonon & Zentall, 1999; Zentall, Weaver, & Sherburne, 1996.)

The development of research on transitive inference is instructive because it illustrates that observers have to be careful in interpreting seemingly clever behavior as evidence of "complex" cognitive processes. On the face of it, transitive inference appears to require that subjects create a mental ordering of a series of stimuli based on their exposure to just pairs of stimuli. If that were in fact required to solve the task, it would represent fairly sophisticated cognitive activity. As the value transfer explanation indicates, however, a much simpler account of the behavior is available (and supported by experimental evidence). The concept of value transfer requires simply that the associative value of one stimulus generalize to a second stimulus that is present at the same time. Such generalization of associative value does not require sophisticated cognitive mechanisms.

MEMORY IN FOOD-STORING BIRDS

Memory in food-storing birds is another feat of cognition. A number of avian and mammalian species hoard food in various places during times of plenty and visit these caches later to recover the stored food items (for example, Barkley & Jacobs, 1998; Sherry, 1985, 1992; Shettleworth, 1995). One remarkable example of cache recovery is provided by the Clark's nutcracker (*Nucifraga columbiana*) (Balda & Turek, 1984; Kamil & Balda, 1990b). These birds live in alpine areas of the western United States and harvest seeds from pine cones in late summer and early autumn. They hide the seeds in underground caches and recover them months later in the winter and spring when other food sources are scarce. A Clark's nutcracker may store as many as 33,000 seeds in caches of 4 or 5 seeds each and recover several thousand of these during the next winter. Cache recovery also has been extensively investigated in the marsh tit (*Parus palustris*), a small, lively bird found in England, and in its North American relative, the chickadee (Shettleworth, 1983; Sherry, 1988). Marsh tits and chickadees store several hundred food items and recover them within a few days.

What mechanisms might food-storing birds use to recover food they previously placed in caches? One possibility is that they remember where they stored each food item and subsequently return to the remembered cache locations. However, before researchers can accept a memory interpretation, they have to rule out other possibilities. The possible alternatives to a memory interpretation are similar to those I discussed in the analysis of spatial memory in a radial maze. One possibility is that birds find caches by searching randomly among possible cache sites. Another possibility is that they store food only in particular types of locations and then go around to these favored places to recover the food items. They also may mark food-storage sites somehow and then look for these marks when it comes time to recover the food. Yet another possibility is that they are able to smell or see the stored food and identify caches in that way.

Ruling out nonmemory interpretations has required laboratory studies of the food-storing and retrieval behavior of the birds (for example, Kamil & Balda, 1990a, 1990b; Sherry, 1984; Sherry, Krebs, & Cowie, 1981; Shettleworth & Krebs, 1986). In one such laboratory study, for example, Kamil and Balda (1985) tested nutcrackers in a room that had a special floor with 180 recessed cups of sand (see left panel of Figure 12.1). After habituation to the experimental situation and while they were hungry, the birds were given three sessions during which they could store pinyon pine seeds in the sand cups. During each caching session, only 18 cups were available; the rest of the cups were covered with lids. This procedure forced the birds to store food in cups selected by the experimenter rather than in cups or locations the birds might have found especially attractive.

Starting 10 days after the seeds had been stored by the nutcrackers, four recovery sessions were conducted on successive days. During recovery sessions none of the 180 sand cups was covered with a lid, but seeds were located only in the cups where the birds had previously stored seeds. The results are summarized on the right side of Figure 12.1. Notice that on average the birds performed much better than chance in going to the sand cups where they had previously stored food. The correct locations could not be identified by disturbed sand because the experimenters raked the sand smooth at the start of each recovery session. Other tests showed that the correct locations were not identified by the smell of the

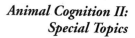

Figure 12.1   Left panel: Floor plan of the apparatus used by Kamil and Balda (1985) to test the spatial memory of Clark's nutcrackers. Filled circles represent sand cups. Other symbols represent rocks, logs, and a feeder in the middle. Right panel: Recovery accuracy, compared to chance, during four successive recovery sessions started 10 days after the birds stored pine seeds. (After Kamil & Balda, 1985.)

seeds buried in the sand because the birds visited places where they had previously stored food even if the food was removed before the test session. These control studies indicate that cache recovery reflects long-lasting spatial memory.

Having established that memory mechanisms are responsible for the cache-recovery behavior of food-storing birds, investigators turned their attention to identifying exactly what kinds of information are retained about a food-caching episode. It is clear that the birds remember *where* they previously stored food items, because without that information they could not return to the location of the stored items. How animals manage to return to locations where they previously stored or found food is the subject of studies of *spatial navigation*. Recent experiments have shown that Clark's nutcrackers use landmarks and the geometric relations between landmarks to guide their spatial navigation (Gibson & Kamil, 2001; Jones & Kamil, 2001; Kamil & Jones, 2000; for similar studies with rats, see Brown & Terrioni, 1996; Brown, DiGello, Milewski, Wilson, & Kozak, 2000; Greene & Cook, 1997).

In addition to remembering *where* they stored food, do the birds also remember *what* type of food they stored, and *when* they stored it? Clayton and Dickinson have been examining these questions in a series of experiments with scrub jays. If you store several different food items in a number of places, why should you care about which type of food is stored where? If you find all of the food items equally acceptable, then there is no reason to keep track of where specific food items are located. However, if you prefer one food over another, then knowing the location of each type of food will be useful. If you know where each type of food is located, you can retrieve the foods you like best before retrieving the less preferred items.

Why might it be useful to know *when* you stored a particular type of food? Information about the time of storage is useful if the food is likely to spoil or deteriorate the longer it is in storage. Without refrigeration, meat spoils much faster than nuts, for example. If you like meat better than nuts, which food you retrieve will depend on how long each has been stored. If both foods were stored less than an hour ago, the meat will be preferable over the nuts. However, if both foods were stored last week, the meat is probably spoiled by now and you might as well retrieve the nuts. Clayton and Dickinson (1999a, Experiment 1) used this type of situation to determine whether scrub jays remember what, when, and where they stored particular food items.

The birds were given practice trials in which they were allowed to store worms and peanuts in the compartments of an ice cube tray. A series of different trays was used, each made distinctive by placing different objects around it. A different tray was used for each type of food. To permit "hiding" the foods, the compartments of the ice trays were filled with sand. The training trials are depicted in Figure 12.2. Each trial consisted of a caching

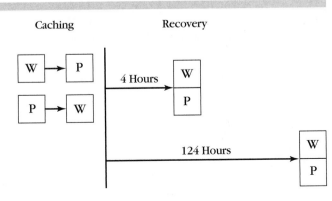

Figure 12.2 Procedure used to train scrub jays to remember what, where, and when they stored worms and peanuts. (Based on Clayton & Dickinson, 1999a.)

period, followed by a recovery period that occurred either 4 hours or 124 hours later. During the caching episodes one type of food was available at a time, and the order of the two foods was counterbalanced. During the recovery period, both foods were available simultaneously. On training trials with a 4-hour delay between caching and recovery, neither food deteriorated by the time the recovery or choice period occurred. In contrast, on training trials with the 124-hour delay between caching and recovery, the worms were in pretty bad shape by the time the recovery occurred.

As training progressed, the birds learned to select the worms during the recovery period if recovery was permitted after the 4-hour delay. If the recovery period was delayed 124 hours, the birds selected the peanuts instead. However, this behavior could have been cued by the smell of the peanut and worm caches during the recovery period. To prevent responding on the basis of olfactory cues, test trials were conducted at the end of the experiment during which fresh sand was put in the trays and all food was removed. The results of those test trials are summarized in Figure 12.3. Data for the scrub jays that learned that worms deteriorate if stored for 124 hours are presented in the left panel. (This was the "deteriorate" group.) As expected, these birds searched more in the worm tray than the peanut tray if the choice test occurred 4 hours after caching of the worms. In contrast, they searched more in the peanut tray than in the worm tray if the worms had been stored 124 hours earlier.

The right panel shows the results for a second group of scrub jays ("replenish") that received a different training history. For the "replenish" group, the fresh worms were always provided during the recovery or choice periods during training. Therefore, these birds did not get a chance to learn that worms deteriorate with time. Consistent with their training

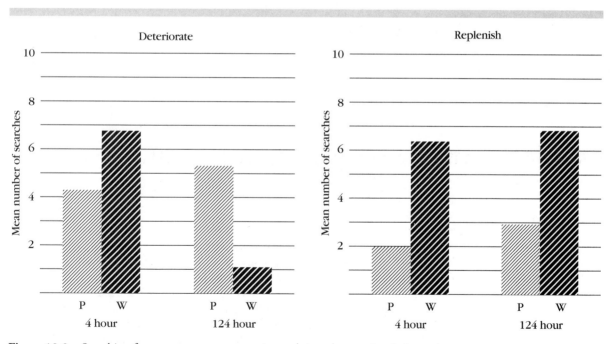

Figure 12.3 Searching for worms versus peanuts in scrub jays that previously learned that worms deteriorate with time ("deteriorate" group, top panel) and scrub jays for which worms were always replenished ("replenish" group, bottom panel). The choice tests were conducted 4 hours or 124 hours after the caching of worms. (Based on Clayton & Dickinson, 1999a.)

history, the "replenish" group showed a preference for worms whether caching had occurred 4 hours or 124 hours before the recovery or choice period.

The scrub jays in the Clayton and Dickinson study could not have returned to the compartments in which food had been stored if they had not remembered *where* they had stored the foods. The fact that the birds distinguished between the worm and peanut storage sites indicates that they remembered *what* type of food was stored in each site. The fact that the "deteriorate" group changed its choice depending on how long ago the worms had been stored indicates that they also remember *when* the food had been stored. These results indicate that scrub jays are able to remember not only *what* food items they stored, but *where* and *when* they stored them (see also Clayton & Dickinson, 1998, 1999b; Clayton, Yu, & Dickinson, 2001). Evidently scrub jays can remember many of the specifics of a particular caching episode. This is analogous to human episodic or declarative memory (Griffiths, Dickinson, & Clayton, 1999).

TIMING

Cache recovery is a highly specialized type of behavior, exhibited by a limited number of species. Timing, in contrast, is universally relevant. Everything occurs across time. All experience is embedded in a temporal context. Some events occur closely together; others are separated by longer intervals. In either case, the effects of stimuli are determined by their durations and distribution in time.

I have described numerous aspects of conditioning and learning that reflect the timing of events. Habituation, sensitization, and spontaneous recovery (Chapter 2) are all time-dependent effects. Pavlovian conditioning critically depends on the temporal relation between conditioned and unconditioned stimuli (Chapter 3), instrumental conditioning depends on the temporal relation between response and reinforcer (Chapter 5), and some schedules of reinforcement involve important temporal factors (Chapter 6). There are also important time-dependent effects in avoidance learning (Chapter 10) and memory (Chapter 11). These and related phenomena have been known for a long time. Only in the past 30 years, however, has substantial progress been made toward understanding the psychological processes that are responsible for the temporal control of behavior in human and nonhuman animals. (For reviews, see Bradshaw & Szabadi, 1997; Gibbon & Allan, 1984; Gibbon & Church, 1992; Killeen & Fetterman, 1988; Maier & Church, 1991; Richelle & Lejeune, 1980.)

Time intervals that are significant for biological systems vary greatly in scale. The 24-hour day/night cycle is one of the most important time cycles for biological systems. Other important time intervals operate on the order of fractions of a second (different components of the heartbeat, for example). Intervals in the range of seconds (and occasionally minutes) are important in conditioning procedures. Timing on this order, referred to as *interval timing*, has captivated the attention of investigators of learning.

A critical methodological requirement in studies of timing is to make sure that the passage of time is not correlated with an external stimulus, such as the noise of a clock ticking or the gradual increase in light that occurs as the sun comes up in the morning. Experimental situations have to be set up carefully to eliminate time-related external stimuli that might inadvertently "tip off" the organism and permit accurate responding without the use of an internal timing process. This methodological requirement is similar to that encountered in tests for memory. Like tests for memory, tests for timing have to make sure that the behavior is mediated by the internal cognitive process of interest rather than external cues or signals.

Techniques for the Measurement of Timing Behavior

Various powerful techniques have been developed to investigate timing in human and non-human animals (see review by Killeen, Fetterman, & Bizo, 1997). Some tasks involve **duration estimation.** A duration estimation task is basically a discrimination procedure in which the discriminative stimulus is the duration of an event. One study (Fetterman, 1995), for example, employed a modified matching-to-sample procedure. Pigeons were trained in an experimental chamber that had three pecking keys arranged in a row. The sample stimulus at the start of the trial was an amber light presented on the center key for either 2 seconds or 10 seconds. The sample was followed by illumination of one side key with a red light and the other side key with a green light. If the sample on that trial had been short (the 2-second stimulus), pecks on the red key were reinforced. If the sample had been long (the 10-second stimulus), pecks on the green key were reinforced. Pigeons and rats can learn to perform accurately in such tasks without too much difficulty (see also Church, Getty, & Lerner, 1976; Wasserman, DeLong, & Larew, 1984; for studies of duration estimation with people, see, for example, Wearden & Ferrara, 1996; Ferrara, Lejeune, & Wearden, 1997).

Other useful techniques for the study of timing have involved duration production instead of duration estimation. One popular technique, called the **peak procedure,** involves a discrete-trial variation of a fixed interval schedule. (Fixed interval schedules were described in Chapter 6.) Each trial begins with the presentation of a discriminative stimulus, a noise or a light. A specified duration after the start of the trial stimulus, a food pellet is set up, or made ready for delivery. Once the food pellet has been set up, the subject can obtain it by performing a specified instrumental response.

A study by Roberts (1981) nicely illustrates use of the peak procedure to investigate timing in laboratory rats. The subjects were tested in a standard lever-press chamber housed in a sound-attenuating enclosure to minimize extraneous stimuli. Some trials began with a light; others began with a noise. In the presence of the light, food was set up after 20 seconds; in the presence of the noise, food was set up after 40 seconds. Most of the trials ended when the rats responded and obtained the food pellet. However, some of the trials were designated as test trials and continued for 80 seconds or more and ended without food reward. These extralong trials were included to see how the participants would respond after the usual time of reinforcement had passed.

Figure 12.4 summarizes the results of the experiment in terms of rates of responding at various points during the test trials. The figure shows that during the 20-second signal, the highest rate of responding occurred around 20 seconds into the trial. By contrast, during the 40-second signal, the highest rate of responding occurred around 40 seconds into the

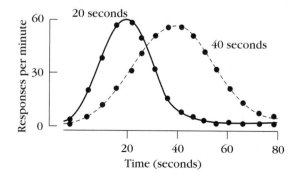

Figure 12.4   Rate of responding at various times during nonreinforced test trials. During training, food became available for delivery after 20 seconds in the presence of one stimulus (solid line) and after 40 seconds in the presence of another stimulus (dashed line). (From "Isolation of an Internal Clock," by S. Roberts, 1981, *Journal of Experimental Psychology: Animal Behavior Processes, 7,* pp. 242–268. Copyright © 1981 by the American Psychological Association. Reprinted by permission.)

trial. The results were remarkably orderly. The peak response rates occurred near the times that food became available during training, with lower response rates evident before and after that point. These features make the peak procedure especially useful in animal studies of timing. It should be noted, however, that results like those shown in Figure 12.4 emerge only after extensive training that includes numerous nonreinforced test trials that extend beyond the time when the reinforcer is usually set up (Kirkpatrick-Steger, Miller, Betti, & Wasserman, 1996; Papini & Hollingsworth, 1998; see also Cheng & Westwood, 1993; Cheng, Westwood, & Crystal, 1993; Church, Miller, Meck, & Gibbon, 1991; Church, Meck, & Gibbon, 1994).

The Concept of an Internal Clock

Results like those presented in Figure 12.4 also have been obtained with human participants (Rakitin, Gibbon, Penney, Malapani, Hinton, & Meck, 1998; Wearden & McShane, 1988) and clearly indicate that behavior can be exquisitely tuned to the passage of time. How might such findings be interpreted? An almost irresistible interpretation has been to assume that organisms use an internal clock and respond differentially based on the readings of this internal clock. Although the assumption of an internal clock may seem a bit fanciful at first glance, the suggestion is not that animals have a pocket watch that they can pull out and read now and then. Rather, the suggestion is that organisms have a timing mechanism localized somewhere in the nervous system that has clocklike properties.

Why should we entertain the possibility that organisms have an internal clock? The advantage of such a hypothesis is that it helps organize research. As Church (1978) pointed out, the concept of an internal clock may simplify explanation and discussion of instances of behavior controlled by time cues. The concept of a clock can also stimulate questions about animal timing that we would not be likely to ask otherwise, as I discuss shortly. Finally, an internal clock may be a physiological reality. We are more likely to find a biological clock if we first postulate its existence and investigate its properties at a behavioral level (for example, Hinton & Meck, 1997; Matell & Meck, 2000).

Characteristics of the Internal Clock

R. M. Church

If the concept of an internal clock is useful in explaining results of the peak procedure and other timing situations, we should be able to use the concept to generate interesting research questions. We may ask, for example, whether the clock can be stopped and restarted without loss of information about how much time has already elapsed. Roberts (1981) designed an experiment to answer this question (see also Roberts & Church, 1978). The experimental chamber used was ordinarily dark. Each trial started with the presentation of a light, and food was set up 40 seconds after the start of the trial. On special test trials without food reinforcement, the light was turned off for 10 seconds, beginning 10 seconds after the start of the trial. Roberts was interested in how the interruption influenced when the rats showed their peak responding.

Figure 12.5 shows the resulting distributions of response rates at various times during trials with and without the 10-second break. Introducing the 10-second break shifted the peak response rate to the right by a bit more than 10 seconds (13.3 seconds, to be exact). These results suggest that the internal clock of the rats stopped timing when the break was introduced. Some information about elapsed time was lost during the break, but when the stimulus resumed, the clock resumed timing without being reset (see also de Vaca, Brown, & Hemmes, 1994).

Other research on animal timing has shown that the internal clock of rats has many of the same properties as a stopwatch. For example, like a stopwatch, the internal clock mea-

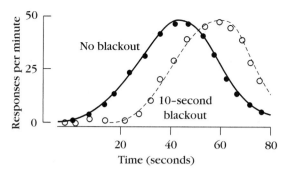

Figure 12.5 Rate of responding as a function of time during a signal in the presence of which food was set up after 40 seconds. On some trials, the signal was interrupted for a 10-second blackout period (dashed line). On other trials, no blackout occurred (solid line). (From "Isolation of an Internal Clock," by S. Roberts, 1981, *Journal of Experimental Psychology: Animal Behavior Processes, 7,* pp. 242–268. Copyright © 1981 by the American Psychological Association. Reprinted by permission.)

sures how much time has elapsed from the start of a stimulus (rather than how much time remains until the stimulus usually ends). Rats seem to use the same internal clock to measure the duration of stimuli from different sensory modalities (visual and auditory); they also use the same clock and clock speed to measure intervals of different durations (Meck & Church, 1982; Roberts, 1981, 1982; Roberts & Church, 1978). In contrast to rats, pigeons appear to use different clocks to measure the duration of visual and auditory stimuli (Brown, Hemmes, & de Vaca, 1992; Roberts, Cheng, & Cohen, 1989; Santi, Stanford, & Coyle, 1998).

Investigators have also started studying what determines the speed and accuracy of the internal clock. Increasing the rate of food reinforcement appears to increase the speed of the internal clock (Bizo & White, 1994, 1995a, 1995b; MacEwen & Killeen, 1991). The speed of the clock is also altered by diet (Meck & Church, 1987b), body temperature (Wearden & Penton-Voak, 1995), and psychoactive drugs. For example, methamphetamine has been observed to increase the speed of the internal clock, whereas other drugs, such as haloperidol, have been noted to decrease clock speed (see Maricq, Roberts, & Church, 1981; Meck, 1983; Meck & Church, 1987a).

Models of Timing

So far I have considered the notion of an internal clock somewhat loosely. What might be the details of a mechanism that permits organisms to respond on the basis of temporal information? This has been one of the thorniest theoretical questions in behavior theory. Time is not a physical reality. It is a human invention that helps us characterize certain aspects of our environment. We cannot see time; we can only see events that are distributed in time. Given that time itself is a conceptual abstraction, models of how organisms tell and use time are even more abstract.

Information Processing Model of Timing.   The first and most influential detailed account of timing is the information processing model proposed by Gibbon and Church (1984) (see also Gibbon, Church, & Meck, 1984; Church, Meck, & Gibbon, 1994). The model (also known as *scalar expectancy theory* or SET) is depicted in Figure 12.6. It assumes

Figure 12.6 Diagram of an information processing model of timing. (From "Sources of Variance in an Information Processing Theory of Timing," by J. Gibbon and R. M. Church. In H. L. Roitblat, T. G. Bever, and H. S. Terrace [Eds.], 1984, *Animal Cognition*. Copyright © 1984 Lawrence Erlbaum and Associates. Reprinted by permission.)

that interval timing is the product of three independent processes: a clock process, a memory process, and a decision process.

The clock process provides information about the duration of elapsed time. A key component of the clock process is a pacemaker that generates pulses at a certain rate (something like the beating of a metronome). The pacemaker pulses are fed to a switch, which is opened by the start of the interval to be timed. Opening the switch allows the pacemaker pulses to go to an accumulator that counts the number of pulses that come through. When the interval to be timed ends, the switch closes, thereby blocking any further accumulations of pacemaker pulses. Thus, the accumulator adds up the number of pulses that occurred during the timed interval. The greater the number of accumulated pulses, the longer the interval.

The number of accumulated pulses is then relayed to the memory process. The memory process thereby obtains information about the duration of the current stimulus. This information is stored in working memory. The memory process is also assumed to have information about the duration of similar stimuli in reference memory from past training. The contents of working and reference memory are then compared in the decision process, and this comparison provides the basis for the individual's response. For example, in the peak procedure, if the time information in working memory matches the information in reference memory concerning availability of reinforcement, the decision is to respond. If information in working and reference memory does not match closely enough, the decision is to not respond. This mechanism produces a peak response rate close to the time when reinforcement is set up.

A detailed hypothetical model of timing is necessary to guide analyses of fine-grained details of timing behavior (see Church, Meck, & Gibbon, 1994; Gibbon & Church, 1984). The model also helps explain different ways in which timing behavior can be altered. Evidence, for example, suggests that certain drugs alter timing behavior by changing the speed of the internal clock (altering the frequency of impulses generated by the pacemaker). By contrast, other drugs change timing behavior by altering the memory process, the remembered duration of past time intervals (Meck, 1983). These contrasting influences on timing behavior would be difficult to interpret without a model that distinguishes a clock process from a memory process.

The information processing model of timing has been useful in guiding our thinking about how timing might be accomplished and has been successfully applied to many experimental results. However, the theory has not been without its critics. The most vigorous challenge has come from Staddon and Higa (1999) who argued that key predictions of the model do not require a pacemaker and accumulator process (see also Staddon & Higa, 1996). The resultant discourse (for example, Donahoe & Burgos, 1999; Gallistel, 1999; Gibbon, 1999; Staddon, Higa, & Chelaru, 1999; Zeiler, 1999) has helped to identify critical theoretical issues and has also increased the range of explanatory models that are being considered in efforts to explain timing. It is unclear how these controversies will be resolved, but one can be sure that the debate will stimulate important new research and theoretical development.

P. R. Killeen

Behavioral Theory of Timing. A prominent alternative to the Gibbon-Church information processing model was offered by Killeen and Fetterman (1988, 1993; see also Killeen, 1991; Killeen, Fetterman, & Bizo, 1997; Machado, 1997) who characterized the timing process in more behavioral terms. This behavioral theory of timing (BeT) follows the Gibbon-Church model in postulating the existence of a pacemaker. However, the role of the pacemaker in BeT is quite different. BeT also characterizes the memory and decision processes differently (see especially Machado, 1997).

The behavioral theory of timing is based on the observation that situations in which the primary basis for the delivery of a reinforcer is the passage of time produce systematic time–related activities. These activities are akin to the pacing or finger tapping that people engage in during periods of forced waiting. In experimental situations these activities have been called **adjunctive behaviors** because they are not specifically required to pass the time but seem to emerge automatically when organisms are forced to wait for something important.

Clear examples of adjunctive behavior are evident in situations in which food is presented periodically at predictable intervals, say every 15 seconds. As I described in Chapter 5 (see discussion of "Skinner's superstition experiment" in Chapter 5), the feeding system (and its accompanying foraging responses) is activated in food-deprived animals that are periodically given small portions of food. Behavior under these circumstances reflects pre-organized species-typical foraging and feeding activities (Silva & Timberlake, 1998; Timberlake, 2001). Different behaviors occur depending on when food was last delivered and when food is going to occur again. Just after the delivery of food, the organism is assumed to display *postfood focal search* responses that involve activities near the food cup. In the middle of the interval between food deliveries (when the subjects are least likely to get food), *general search* responses are evident that take the subject away from the food cup. As time for the next food delivery approaches, subjects exhibit *prefood focal search* responses that bring the subject back to the food cup. (General search and prefood focal search responses have been also called **interim** and **terminal** responses [Staddon & Simmelhag, 1971].)

The behavioral theory of timing focuses on the successive behavioral states that are activated by periodic presentations of food. Because different responses emerge at different intervals in a forced waiting period, these contrasting responses can be used to tell time. The successive adjunctive responses are assumed to reflect a pacemaker or clock process. According to the behavioral theory of timing, participants in a timing experiment learn to use their adjunctive responses as discriminative stimuli for the experimentally required timing responses. Thus, instead of reading an internal clock, participants are assumed to "read" their adjunctive behavior to tell time.

If reading a clock basically consists of reading one's own adjunctive behavior, then we should be able to observe the timing mechanism by carefully observing an organism's adjunctive behaviors in a timing task. Thus, the behavior theory of timing should be easy to prove or disprove by direct observation. Based on this, one might argue that the behavioral theory of timing is preferable over the information processing model because more of its mechanisms are accessible to direct observation. Unfortunately, this apparent transparency is illusory. BeT is no easier to prove or disprove than the information processing theory. As Fetterman, Killeen, and Hall (1998) pointed out, if an investigator fails to find the adjunctive responses that are consistent with the theory, one can argue that the investigators did not look carefully enough. On the other hand, if the postulated adjunctive responses are found in a particular experiment, that does not prove that adjunctive responses are necessary for timing in other situations. Nevertheless, careful observations of the behavior of subjects in timing tasks have provided data supportive of BeT (for example, Lejeune, Cornet, Ferreira, & Wearden, 1998). In addition, in some cases adjunctive responses are better predictors of timing behavior than the actual passage of time (Fetterman et al., 1998).

SERIAL PATTERN LEARNING

Time is one ubiquitous characteristic of events in the environment. Another is serial order. Stimuli rarely occur randomly or independently of each other. Rather, many aspects of the environment involve orderly sequences of events. One thing leads to the next in a predictable fashion. Stimuli are arranged in orderly sequences as you walk from one end of a street to the other, as you work to open a package, or as you eat dinner, from the appetizer to the dessert. Stimulus order is also very important in language. "The hunters ate the bear" is very different from "The bear ate the hunters." Investigators of animal cognition have been interested in whether animals recognize order in a series of stimuli, whether they can form a representation of the serial order of stimuli, and what mechanisms they use to respond correctly to a series of stimuli.

Possible Bases of Serial Pattern Behavior

There are several possible ways in which to respond to a series of stimuli. By way of illustration, consider playing through a six-hole miniature golf course, a schematic of which is shown to the left in Figure 12.7. Each hole involves a unique set of stimuli and may be represented by letters of the alphabet: A, B, C, D, E, and F. Each hole also requires a unique response—a unique way in which the ball must be hit to get it into the hole. Let's label the responses R1, R2, . . . , R6. In playing the course, you have to go in order from the first to the last hole, A→F. In addition, you have to make the correct response on each hole: R1 on hole A, R2 on B, and so on.

How might you learn to play the course successfully? The simplest way would be to learn which response goes with which stimulus. This would involve learning a set of S-R associations: A-R1, B-R2, . . . , F-R6. In the presence of A, you would automatically make R1, which would get you to stimulus B; in the presence of B, you would automatically make R2, which would get you to C; in the presence of C, you would automatically make R3, which would get you to D, and so on. Such a mechanism is called a **response chain.** In a response chain, each response produces the stimulus for the next response in the sequence, and correct responses occur because the organism has learned a series of S-R associations.

Although a response chain can result in responding appropriately to a series of stimuli, it does not require learning the stimulus sequence or forming a mental representation of the order in which the stimuli or responses occur. Response chains do not require cognitive

Figure 12.7 Two possible layouts of a six-hole miniature golf course. A sequential arrangement is shown on the left, and a simultaneous arrangement is shown on the right.

mechanisms any more complex than S-R associations. A response-chain strategy works perfectly well on the usual miniature golf course, because the successive holes are laid out so that you are forced to go through them in the correct sequence, A→F.

Now, consider a course with a different layout. The rules are the same in that you have to play in order from A to F, but this course is laid out in such a way that you are not forced to go in that order. Imagine having the holes lined up next to each other in a random order on a playing field, as shown to the right in Figure 12.7. After having played hole A, for example, your movement would not be restricted to hole B. You could go to any other hole next. To earn points, however, you would still have to play B after having finished with A, and then go to C, then D, and so on. Learning a series of stimulus-response associations (A-R1, B-R2, and so on) would not be enough to succeed on such a course. Even if someone got you started at A, after playing hole A, you would not know where to go next because you would be confronted with the full array of possibilities, not just B.

What would you have to learn to respond in the correct sequence with a simultaneous stimulus array? This time, you would be forced to learn something about the order of the stimuli. You could get by with just knowing the order of successive pairs of stimuli. You could learn that A is followed by B, B is followed by C, and so forth. These would be a set of independent stimulus-stimulus associations (A-B, B-C, C-D, and so on). This type of mechanism is called **paired-associate learning.** Once you know the correct independent paired associates, having played hole A, you would know to go to B; having played B, you would know to go to C; and so on until you had completed the course.

Obviously, learning more than just the order of successive pairs of stimuli would also enable you to perform the task accurately. At the extreme, you might form a mental representation of the entire sequence: A-B-C-D-E-F. This alternative is called **serial representation learning.** A serial representation can be formed in different ways. One possibility is to string together a series of paired associates, such that A activates the representation of B, which in turn activates the representation of C, and so forth. Thus, a serial representation could consist of a chain of paired associates. Alternatively, you could learn the particular ordinal position of each stimulus. This would involve learning that stimulus A is in position 1, B is in position 2, and so forth.

How might we decide among possible mechanisms of serial pattern behavior? An especially powerful technique involves presenting carefully constructed test trials after training. Returning to the simultaneous layout of the miniature golf course (right side of Figure 12.7), consider being given a choice between holes C and E after having learned to respond to the entire sequence, A→F, in the correct order. In a choice between C and E, which hole would you play first? If you had learned a representation of the entire stimulus sequence, you could respond without difficulty because you would know that C occurs before E in the

365

sequence. Other possible mechanisms would create errors. For example, if you had learned a response chain in which one response leads to the next stimulus, you would be in trouble because the response preceding C is not available in a choice of only C and E. You would also be in trouble if you had learned just the order of successive pairs of stimuli because C and E do not form a successive pair.

Tests with Subsets after Training with a Simultaneous Stimulus Array

H. S. Terrace

Several different techniques have been developed to study the learning of serial representations in animals (for example, Hulse, 1978; Roitblat, Bever, Helweg, & Harley, 1991; Roitblat, Scopatz, Bever, 1987; Terrace, 1986a, 1986b). Straub and Terrace (1981) introduced the technique of training animals with a set of stimuli presented in a simultaneous array and then testing them with subsets of those stimuli (see also Terrace, 1987). This technique was then adopted by D'Amato and Colombo (1988) in a study with cebus monkeys (*Cebus apella*).

The monkeys were trained on a five-stimulus sequence, A→B→C→D→E. The stimuli were various visual patterns (dots, circles, and the like), which could be projected on any of five square panels. Which pattern appeared on which panel varied from one trial to the next, but all five stimuli were presented at the same time on each training trial. The task was to press the panels in the prescribed order, A→B→C→D→E. Training started with just stimulus A. After the monkeys learned to press A, B was added. After they learned the A→B sequence, C was added, and so forth. (For an alternative training strategy, see Swartz, Chen, & Terrace, 2000.)

Once the monkeys became proficient at responding to the simultaneous array with the correct sequence of responses, they were tested with subsets of the pattern that included just two or three of the stimuli. Two-element subsets could start with A, B, C, or D. Three-element subsets could start with A, B, or C. The monkeys performed with above-chance accuracy on all the subset test trials, including those that included only stimuli in the middle of the series (BC, CD, BD, and BCD). These results indicate that the monkeys learned the prescribed order of the five stimuli.

D'Amato and Colombo also measured the latencies of the correct responses during the tests with subsets of the five-element series. These results were particularly interesting and are shown in Figure 12.8. The left-hand graph shows the latency of responding to the first item of subsets of stimuli. Some of these subsets started with A (as in the subset AC, for example); some started with B (as in the subset BC or BD); some started with C (as in CD); and one started with D (DE).

When the first item of the subset was A, the monkeys responded rapidly. When the first item was B, responding was slower. Responding was slower still when the first item was C or D. Loosely speaking, these latencies suggest that at the start of a trial the monkeys started to walk through the sequence mentally. When they came to one of the stimuli presented on that trial, they responded to that stimulus. Since they encountered A first in this mental walk through the sequence, they responded to A quickest. Longer latencies occurred with items that came up later in their mental progression.

Additional evidence for mental scanning of the stimulus sequence was provided by how long it took for the subjects to respond to the second item in the subset tests. Some of the subsets involved adjacent items in the list, such as subset BC. Others involved one missing item, such as subset BD or CE. Still others involved two missing items (BE) or three missing items (AE). If the monkeys were walking through the list mentally as they performed

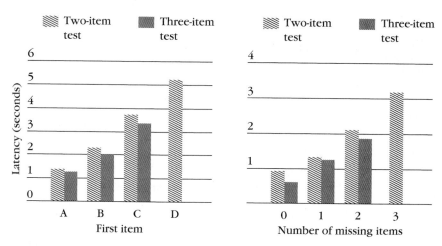

Figure 12.8 Latency of correct responses during tests of two- and three-item subsets of a five-item list with cebus monkeys. Left: Latency of responding to the first item of the subset as a function of the position of that item in the original sequence. Right: Latency of responding to the second item of the subset as a function of the number of items missing between the first and second items. (From "Representation of Serial Order in Monkeys (*Cebus apella*)," by M. R. D'Amato and M. Colombo, 1988, *Journal of Experimental Psychology: Animal Behavior Processes, 14,* pp. 131–139. Copyright © 1988 by the American Psychological Association. Reprinted by permission.)

the subset tests, how long they took to respond between the first and second items would depend on the number of missing items. With more missing items between stimuli in a subset, the monkeys should take longer to respond to the second item. This is exactly what occurred (see Figure 12.8, right). (For additional studies of the nature of that mental representation, see D'Amato and Colombo, 1989, 1990.)

Evidence of the Learning of Ordinal Position

The data presented in Figure 12.8 strongly indicates that the monkeys formed a mental representation of the prescribed order in which to respond to the stimuli presented in the simultaneous array. This mental representation no doubt included the knowledge that stimulus A was in position 1. However, the mental representation did not have to include knowing the specific ordinal position of each of the other stimuli. Once the monkeys started with stimulus A, they could have gotten through the sequence in the correct order if they just learned to associate stimulus A with B, B with C, C with D, and D with E. That is, a series of paired associates could have gotten them through the series correctly after they got started correctly with A.

More convincing evidence of the learning of ordinal positions was obtained in an experiment with two rhesus monkeys conducted by Chen, Swartz, and Terrace (1997). A simultaneous stimulus array was again used, but it included only four rather than five items. The items were color photographs of various objects and were presented in any of 9 positions on a stimulus display. As usual, the position of each stimulus was varied across trials. The subjects were first trained on one 4-item sequence, and then another, and another, until over the course of several years they became proficient on 15 different sequences.

TABLE 12.1

COMPOSITION OF STIMULUS ARRAYS IN A TEST OF ORDINAL POSITION LEARNING

ARRAY		COMPOSITION
Original 1	A1→B1→C1→D1	bird→flower→frog→shells
Original 2	A2→B2→C2→D2	tree→weasel→dragonfly→water
Original 3	A3→B3→C3→D3	elk→rocks→leaves→person
Original 4	A4→B4→C4→D4	mountain→fish→monkey→tomato
Derived: Order Preserved	A2→B4→C1→D3	tree→fish→frog→person
Derived: Order Preserved	A3→B1→C4→D2	elk→flower→monkey→water
Derived: Order Changed	B3→A1→D4→C2	rocks→bird→tomato→dragonfly
Derived: Order Changed	D1→C3→B2→A4	shells→leaves→weasel→mountain

Source: Based on Chen, Swartz, & Terrace, 1997.

Four of the original sequences the subjects learned are represented in Table 12.1. The letters A, B, C, and D represent the order of the stimuli in each array. (To obtain reinforcement, the subjects had to respond to stimulus A first, then B, then C, and finally D.) The number associated with each stimulus represents the array in which the item appeared. Thus, the first array involved stimuli A1→B1→C1→D1. The second array involved stimuli A2→B2→C2→D2, and so on.

The critical aspect of the experiment involved training subjects on new stimulus arrays that were constructed from earlier ones in special ways. In some of the new arrays, the correct ordinal positions of the stimuli were the same as in original training (order preserved), but stimuli from different arrays were selected. One such derived array was A2→B4→C1→D3. A2 was the first stimulus from array #2, B4 was the second stimulus from array #4, C1 was the third stimulus from array #1, and D3 was the fourth stimulus from array #3. In other derived arrays, the correct ordinal positions of the stimuli were changed compared with original training (order changed). B3→A1→D4→C2 is an example of such an array. Here the subjects had to respond first to the second item from list 3, then pick the first item in array 1, then the fourth item from array 3, and finally the third item from array 2.

How might the subjects perform on the derived stimulus arrays? If they learned a series of paired associates, they would treat the derived arrays as entirely new problems because none of the adjacent stimuli in the derived arrays had occurred after one another in the original problems. Thus, the subjects would treat A2→B4→C1→D3 as a new problem because they never had to pick B4 after A2 or C1 after B4 during original training. Prior paired associate learning would not help the subjects deal with the new A2→B4→C1→D3 array. In contrast, if the subjects previously learned the specific ordinal position of each stimulus, they would do very well on the new A2→B4→C1→D3 array. If the subjects previously learned the ordinal position of each stimulus, they would know that A2 was in the first position, B4 in the second position, C1 in the third, and D3 in the fourth, even though these particular stimuli were never presented in the same array before.

The results obtained by Chen, Swartz, and Terrace showed dramatically that the monkeys had learned the ordinal position of the stimuli during original training. They responded to the new A2→B4→C1→D3 array almost perfectly the first time even though they had never seen these stimuli together before. In contrast, they treated derived arrays in which the order of the stimuli was changed (B3→A1→D4→C2) as if these were entirely new problems.

It is important to keep in mind that the monkeys in this study were highly proficient in serial pattern learning. Their extensive training history was probably critical for their learning the ordinal position of the stimuli. Paired associate learning may characterize the serial pattern learning of novice subjects, with a shift toward ordinal position learning with the acquisition of expertise.

PERCEPTUAL CONCEPT LEARNING

Organisms experience a great variety of stimuli during their lifetime. However, as I have pointed out, they do not have to respond to stimuli as independent and isolated events. Serial pattern learning represents one type of cognitive organization of stimuli. An even more basic form of cognitive organization involves perceptual concept learning. Consider, for example, seeing a chair. You may note some of its specific features: its color, shape, height, and firmness. You would also immediately identify it as a "chair." We can all agree on which things are chairs and which things are not chairs even though chairs come in a variety of shapes, sizes, and colors. "Chair" is an example of a perceptual concept.

We rely on perceptual concepts in much of our interaction with the world. We have perceptual concepts of physical objects, such as chairs, houses, trees, water, cats, and cars. We also have perceptual concepts of events, such as rain and wind or day and night. Perceptual concepts are important because they help us organize or categorize the wide variety of stimuli that we encounter during the course of normal experience. Perceptual concepts are also important in language. Words are often labels for perceptual concepts.

In the rough and tumble of life, nothing occurs exactly the same way twice. Even the same tree viewed from the same vantage point appears slightly different each time you look at it. The sun may be shining on it from a different angle, clouds may be casting a different pattern of shadows, and a breeze may be moving the branches and leaves. Perceptual concepts help organisms navigate through the maze of ever-changing stimuli in the world.

Through perceptual concepts, certain variations among stimuli are ignored. For example, you recognize your cat as the same animal, even though, strictly speaking, the visual image the cat projects on your retina is different every time you see it. You also recognize various objects as chairs, even though they may differ in color, size, and firmness. By contrast, other differences are emphasized. You distinguish your cat from your neighbor's cat and from your parakeet. You also distinguish between things that are called chairs and things that are called tables. As these examples illustrate, perceptual concepts have two important and complementary characteristics, *generalization within a category* or set of stimuli and *discrimination between categories* or sets of stimuli.

The typical perceptual concept learning experiment involves instrumental discrimination training. Each trial begins with a stimulus. If the stimulus belongs to the category of interest (S+), responding is reinforced. If the stimulus does not belong to the target category (S−), responding is not reinforced. As training progresses, subjects come to respond more to the S+ stimuli than to the S− stimuli.

In one study with pigeons (Herrnstein, Loveland, & Cable, 1976), for example, color slides of various scenes were projected on one wall of the experimental chamber near a response key. If the scene included a tree or some part of a tree, the pigeons were reinforced with food for pecking the response key. If the picture did not include a tree or any part of one, pecking was not reinforced. Each experimental session consisted of 80 slide presentations, about 40 of which included a tree. During training, the stimuli for any given day were randomly selected from 500–700 pictures depicting various scenes from all four seasons of the year in New England. The same photographs were only occasionally used more than once. The reinforced stimuli included trees (or parts of trees) of all descriptions, but the trees were not necessarily the main point of interest in the pictures. Some slides showed a tree far in the distance, others showed trees that were partly obstructed so that only some of the branches were visible, for example.

The pigeons learned the requirements of the task without much difficulty. Soon they were pecking at a much higher rate in the presence of pictures that included a tree than in the presence of pictures without trees. What might have been responsible for the accuracy of their performance? One possibility is that the pigeons memorized what the reinforced and nonreinforced pictures looked like without paying particular attention to the presence or absence of trees. Although this may seem to be an unlikely possibility, it has to be seriously considered because pigeons are able to memorize several hundred pictures (Vaughan & Greene, 1984).

A common tactic for ruling out the role of memorization of the training exemplars is to test for transfer of performance to stimuli that did not appear during training. Herrnstein et al. (1976) did this by presenting a new set of photos that did and did not include trees. The pigeons performed nearly as accurately on the new pictures as on those used during prior training. Much higher rates of pecking occurred in the presence of new slides that included a tree (or part of one) than in the presence of new slides without trees. Such evidence of *generalization to novel exemplars* is critical for demonstrations of perceptual concept learning.

Much research has been done on the learning of perceptual concepts since this area of research was initiated by Herrnstein and Loveland (1964) nearly 40 years ago (for example, Commons, Herrnstein, Kosslyn, & Mumford, 1990; Herrnstein, 1984, 1990; Lea, 1984; Macintosh, 1995; Pearce, 1994a; Wasserman & Astley, 1994). In the tradition set by Herrnstein, much of the research has been done with pigeons responding to complex visual stimuli. Studies have demonstrated the learning of numerous different visual perceptual concepts. Pigeons have learned to respond to the presence or absence of water in various forms (lakes, oceans, puddles, and so on) and to the presence or absence of a particular person (in various types of clothing, in various situations, and engaged in various activities) (Herrnstein et al., 1976). In other studies, pigeons have been conditioned to respond to the presence or absence of fish in underwater photographs (Herrnstein & deVilliers, 1980), to the presence of the letter A as opposed to other letters of the alphabet in various fonts (Morgan, Fitch, Holman, & Lea, 1976), to various views of a particular location on campus (Honig & Stewart, 1988; Wilkie, Willson, & Kardal, 1989), and to video images of certain actions performed by other pigeons (Dittrich, Lea, Barrett, & Gurr, 1998; Jitsumori et al., 1999). As I noted in Chapter 8, pigeons have also been conditioned to distinguish samples of the music of Bach from that of Stravinsky (Porter & Neuringer, 1984) and to discriminate pictures of Monet from those of Picasso (Watanabe et al., 1995).

Studies have also demonstrated perceptual concept learning in other species, including monkeys, quail, rats, and dolphins (for example, D'Amato & Van Sant, 1988; Helweg, Roitblat, Nachtigall, & Hautus, 1996; Jitsumori, 1994; Kluender, Diehl, & Killeen, 1987; Martin-Malivel & Fagot, 2001; Roberts & Mazmanian, 1988; Schrier & Brady, 1987). In all of these cases, the participants learned to respond similarly to stimuli belonging to the category in question even though members of the category differed in numerous respects. As I noted in Chapter 8, perceptual concept learning is a form of stimulus equivalence learning. Because responding to various examples of the target category has the same (or

Courtesy of E. A. Wasserman

E. A. Wasserman

equivalent) reinforcing consequence, physically different stimuli come to be treated in the same (or equivalent) manner by the organism. Stimulus equivalence training produces generalization within a set of stimuli (Astley & Wasserman, 1998, 1999).

Discrimination between Perceptual Categories

In many of the studies of perceptual concept learning, the participants had to discriminate between stimuli that contained an exemplar of the concept from stimuli that did not—pictures of trees versus pictures without trees, for example. However, there was no common or unifying theme for the nonreinforced stimuli. The experiments demonstrated how one comes to discriminate stimuli that belong to a category from those that do not belong. However, the studies did not show how one comes to distinguish one category from another—how one learns to tell the difference between instances of oak trees from instances of pine trees, for example.

How one comes to discriminate between one concept and another depends not only on the reinforced category but also on the nonreinforced stimuli. Roberts and Mazmanian (1988), for example, found that both pigeons and monkeys had difficulty learning to discriminate pictures of birds from pictures of other types of animals. However, the participants had little trouble learning to distinguish pictures of birds from pictures not containing animals. Other aspects of their study demonstrated that the failure to discriminate birds from other animals was not due to a general inability to distinguish between two categories. Rather, the difficulty was related to the level of abstractness of the concepts. The pigeons and monkeys easily learned to discriminate various views of a particular bird, the common kingfisher, from pictures of other types of birds (see also Aitken, Bennett, McLaren, & Mackintosh, 1996; Macintosh, 1995; Wasserman, Kiedinger, & Bhatt, 1988).

Mechanisms of Perceptual Concept Learning

Perceptual concept learning is a well-established phenomenon. How animals do this, however, remains a lively topic of debate. The empirical analysis of perceptual categorization has turned out to be very difficult because of the complexity of the stimuli that are involved. Consider, for example, the learning of the concept "tree" by the pigeons that Herrnstein et al. (1976) tested. Photographs of natural scenes that do and do not include a tree (or part of a tree) are highly complex visual stimuli. Figuring out how the pigeons accomplish the categorization task requires closely examining not only their behavior but also the nature of the stimuli that control their behavior. What aspect(s) of the tree photographs led the pigeons to classify those photographs differently from the nontree photographs? Was it something about the color, shape, or texture of the photographs, and how were these (or some other) features used by the birds to make correct decisions?

Progress in categorization research was stymied by the stimulus problem for nearly a quarter century. However, this obstacle is finally being overcome by advances in computer image analysis and image production. Some investigators are examining perceptual categorization using computer-generated artificial images. The primary advantage of this approach is that the statistical properties of images can be perfectly specified. Unfortunately, however, researchers cannot be sure whether the mechanisms revealed in these experiments can be generalized to categorization involving complex natural stimuli. An alternative strategy has been to use computer image analysis (and complex statistical analyses of responses to these stimuli) to identify the features of complex natural stimuli that control categorization behavior. The tension between highly controlled studies with artificial stimuli and statistically more noisy studies of natural stimuli is not unique to categorization research. Ultimate progress will no doubt depend on both approaches.

Explanations of perceptual categorization have focused on three major alternatives: feature theory, exemplar theory, and prototype theory.

Feature Theory. The first and perhaps most obvious account of perceptual categorization is based on the concept of stimulus features. Feature theory assumes that members of a perceptual category have certain features in common—features to which the instrumental response becomes conditioned when the organism is reinforced. A chair, for example, is something that you can sit on. Therefore, it might be concluded that the property of supporting someone's sitting is a feature that defines a chair. Unfortunately, however, an individual feature such as this is rarely necessary or sufficient for membership in a category. The property of supporting someone's sitting, for example, is not sufficient to define a chair. You can also sit on the floor, but floors are not chairs. The property of being able to sit on the chair is also not a necessary feature. A chair suspended on the tip of a pole in the circus is still a chair, even though no one can sit on it.

Investigators of perceptual concept learning have argued against a simple feature-analysis explanation because a single feature common to all positive instances of natural perceptual concepts is often difficult (and sometimes impossible) to identify. Instead of focusing on a single critical feature, feature theorists have argued that category membership depends on an object having a number of features, no one of which is either necessary or sufficient for category membership. For example, features that are relevant to the concept of chair include having four legs, a back, a platform about 18 inches above the floor, a surface big enough to sit on, and a structure that will support the weight of a person. Exceptions to each of these features can be found, and no one of these features alone serves to identify a chair. However, if something has enough of these features, most of us would agree that it is a chair. This kind of reasoning involves a **polymorphic rule** (Herrnstein, 1984; Lea & Harrison, 1978; von Fersen & Lea, 1990).

According to a polymorphic rule, no one stimulus feature is necessary or sufficient for membership in a perceptual category. Rather, category membership is based on having a certain number of relevant features. For example, if something has three or four features that are relevant to chairs, one would conclude that it belongs in the chair category. Although polymorphic rules do not require a single critical feature, they still depend on stimulus features for perceptual categorization.

Research relevant to feature theory has been conducted using both artificial and natural stimuli. Huber and Lenz (1993), for example, used simple line drawings of faces, like those shown in Figure 12.9. Four features of the drawings were varied: the distance between the eyes, the height of the forehead, the length of the nose, and the size of the chin. Each of these features could take on one of three values, designated as -1, 0, and $+1$. Two categories were created from the resultant drawings by adding the values of the four features. One category (called "positive") was composed of drawings that had feature sums greater than zero; another category (called "negative") was made of drawings that had feature sums less than zero.

The drawing on the left in Figure 12.9 represents the face with the highest negative sum of the features, and the drawing on the right represents the face with the highest positive sum of the features. The pigeons were reinforced for pecking in the presence of faces with a positive feature sum and were not reinforced for pecking in the presence of faces with a negative feature sum. The birds learned the concept discrimination in about 20 sessions, and detailed analyses of their performance indicated that their behavior was controlled by the four features that were manipulated. Responding of each pigeon was highly correlated with the sum of the features that appeared in a test stimulus. Greater feature sums produced proportionately greater rates of responding. (For feature analysis of categorization of natural

Figure 12.9 Examples of drawings of faces used by Huber and Lenz (1993). The face on the left represents the highest negative sum of facial features. The face in the middle has a feature sum of zero, and the face on the right has the highest positive feature sum. (From "A Test of the Linear Feature Model of Polymorphous Concept Discrimination with Pigeons," by L. Huber and R. Lenz, 1993, *The Quarterly Journal of Experimental Psychology, 46B,* pp. 1–18. Copyright © 1993 by the Experimental Psychology Society. Reprinted by permission.)

face stimuli by pigeons and baboons, see Aust & Huber, 2001; Huber, Troje, Loidolt, Aust, & Grass, 2000; Jitsumori & Yoshihara, 1997; Martin-Malivel & Fagot, 2001.)

Exemplar Theory. The simplest, and in some ways the most successful, explanation of perceptual concept learning is the exemplar theory (Wasserman & Astley, 1994). This theory is based on conventional concepts of discrimination learning and stimulus generalization, such as those I described in Chapter 8. Reinforcement for responding in the presence of a stimulus is assumed to result in the conditioning of excitation to that stimulus. In contrast, nonreinforcement is assumed to result in the absence of excitation and perhaps the conditioning of inhibition to the stimulus. Both conditioned excitation and inhibition are assumed to generalize to other stimuli, with the degree of generalization determined by the degree of similarity between the new and old stimuli.

The basic ideas of exemplar theory are consistent with many aspects of perceptual concept learning. The theory explains generalization of a perceptual concept to new exemplars by assuming that the new test stimuli are in some ways similar to the stimuli that were used when the perceptual concept was originally trained. If the perceptual concept is that of a tree, for example, new pictures that include trees are treated as members of the category presumably because they resemble the pictures with trees that were reinforced during training. On the other hand, new pictures that do not include a tree are rejected because they have less in common with the reinforced stimuli that were used in training, and may even resemble some of the nonreinforced training stimuli.

Although exemplar theory is highly successful in explaining many aspects of perceptual concept learning, it should be pointed out that this theory may well operate in combination with the mechanisms of feature theory. In fact, exemplar theory is difficult to distinguish from feature theory in situations where organisms respond to examples of a perceptual concept in terms of the salient features that those examples have in common. The advantage of exemplar theory, however, is that it can predict various aspects of categorization behavior without first identifying which stimulus features are important to a perceptual category (for further details, see Wasserman & Astley, 1994).

Prototype Theory. Of the three theories of perceptual categorization, prototype theory relies most heavily on higher-order cognitive mechanisms. According to prototype theory, exposure to a number of exemplars of a perceptual category results in the abstraction of a **prototype** or "standard" representative of the concept. For the category "chair," for example, the prototype would be of an average or typical chair, one that has four legs and a back. Once the organism has abstracted or formed the prototype, it will respond to new instances of the category based on how similar these new instances are to the prototype.

In tests of this theory, the prototype has been assumed to be the arithmetic average of all of the examples of a category that are presented to a subject. Tests of prototype theory have typically involved artificial stimuli whose mean value can be computed relatively easily. Jitsumori (1996), for example, conducted a test of prototype theory with butterfly-like stimuli. The stimuli varied in the complexity of the pattern on the forewings, the shape of the hind wings, and the shading of the butterfly. Each of these features could take on one of six values.

To test prototype theory, Jitsumori (1996) created two sets of butterflies. The pigeons were reinforced for pecking in the presence of stimuli from one set (S+) and were not reinforced in the presence of stimuli from the contrasting set (S−). The S+ and S− stimuli were carefully selected so that they surrounded different average or prototype images. However, the actual average images were never presented during training. Thus, the pigeons were never explicitly reinforced for responding to the S+ prototype (and never received non-reward in the presence of the S− prototype). Despite never having seen the prototypes during training, the subjects responded most during a postconditioning test when the S+ prototype was presented. (For other evidence in support of prototype theory, see Huber & Lenz, 1996; Aydin & Pearce, 1994; Pearce, 1994a.)

Although evidence in support of prototype theory has been obtained, it has not been easy to differentiate predictions of this theory from predictions of other accounts, particularly exemplar theory. The differentiation between these two theories will require additional theoretical work.

LANGUAGE LEARNING IN NONHUMAN ANIMALS

Perhaps the most complex cognitive skill is linguistic competence. In fact, many have argued that linguistic skill is so complex and specialized that it is uniquely human. According to this view, the ability to use language depends on certain innate processes that have evolved only in our own species (for example, Chomsky, 1972; Lennenberg, 1967). By contrast, others have proposed that human beings are able to use language because they are especially intelligent and have experiences that permit language acquisition. This second view suggests that nonhuman organisms may also acquire language skills if they are sufficiently intelligent and encounter the requisite experiences. Encouraged by this possibility, investigators have tried to teach language skills to various species.

Early language training efforts attempted to determine whether nonhuman animals are capable of language. However, it has become evident that this is not an answerable question (Roitblat, Harley, & Helweg, 1993). Language is not a unitary entity that one either does or does not have; rather, it consists of component skills. A human infant's language abilities, for example, improve gradually as the infant acquires and integrates increasingly sophisticated language skills. In this developmental sequence, there is no one point at which the young child graduates from not having language to having it.

Some theoreticians remain interested in whether human-like language is possible in other species. Kako (1999), for example, recently proposed four elements of syntax that should be present to justify concluding that a particular species has human-like language.

However, investigators who have been on the front lines actually collecting the relevant data reject the value of trying to meet criteria that define human linguistic competence. Some have become impatient with this approach because the criteria keep changing. For example, E. Sue Savage-Rumbaugh, who has probably spent more effort studying language learning in apes than anyone else, recently commented (with two colleagues), "The history of comparative studies in animal learning and behavior has been marked by the constantly shifting demands made by those who want to preserve some species-specific attribute that will distinguish human behavior from all other primates" (Shanker, Savage-Rumbaugh, & Taylor, 1999).

If the goal is no longer to demonstrate human-like linguistic competence in nonhuman species, what is the goal of this type of research? There are several goals. One is to use language training as a vehicle to study the cognitive abilities of nonhuman species. This is the basic objective of the program of work directed by Irene Pepperberg (1999), who has been studying the cognitive abilities of a Grey parrot, Alex, since 1977. A related sentiment is expressed by Louis Herman, who directed language studies in dolphins: "The animal language work can help us to identify with more surety those processes in humans that may derive from general cognitive structures rather than from language-specific structures" (Herman & Uyeyama, 1999, p. 22). Research on language learning in nonhuman species can tell us a great deal about the cognitive prerequisites and components of language competence. Such research can also provide information about how best to teach linguistic skills. This information can then be put to good use in language instruction for persons with cognitive disabilities (Sevcik, Romski, & Wilkenson, 1991).

Early Attempts at Language Training

Most efforts to teach animals language have involved chimpanzees because chimpanzees have many characteristics in common with human beings. Despite these similarities, however, chimpanzees do not learn to speak when they are given the same types of experiences that children have as they learn to speak. Nadezhda Kohts, of the Darwinian Museum in Moscow, raised a chimpanzee in her home from 1913 to 1916 without once having it imitate the human voice or utter a word of Russian (see Premack, 1976). More detailed accounts of life with a chimpanzee are available from the experiences of Winthrop and Louise Kellogg, who raised a baby chimpanzee along with their baby boy (Kellogg, 1933). Their adopted charge also did not learn to speak like a person. Undaunted by this evidence, Cathy and Keith Hayes raised a chimpanzee named Viki with the explicit intent of teaching her to talk (Hayes & Hayes, 1951). Despite several years of training, Viki learned to say only three words: mama, papa, and cup.

The failure of the Hayeses to teach Viki to talk despite their great efforts discouraged others from trying again. However, people remained intrigued with the possibility that animals might acquire some language skills. The search for linguistic competence in chimpanzees got a big boost from the innovative work of Allen and Beatrice Gardner and their students (Gardner & Gardner, 1969, 1975, 1978). Instead of trying to teach their chimpanzee, Washoe, to talk using vocal speech, the Gardners taught her American Sign Language.

American Sign Language consists of manual gestures in place of words. Chimpanzees are much more adept at making hand movements and gestures than they are at making the vocal-laryngeal movements required for the production of speech sounds. Washoe was a good student. She learned to sign well over 100 words. Washoe's success suggested that earlier efforts to teach speech to chimpanzees may have failed not because of the inability of the chimpanzee to learn linguistic skills but because an inappropriate response medium (vocalization) was used. Washoe held out the promise that animals would acquire linguistic competence with the appropriate response medium.

The success of the Gardners with Washoe encouraged other language training efforts with chimpanzees as well as with other species. These included a gorilla (Patterson, 1978); dolphins (Herman, 1987); sea lions (Gisiner & Schusterman, 1992; Schusterman & Gisiner, 1988); and an African Grey parrot (Pepperberg, 1990). Some investigators followed the approach of the Gardners in using American Sign Language to train chimpanzees (see Gardner, Gardner, & Van Cantfort, 1989) and gorillas (Patterson, 1978). Others adopted alternative procedures.

Language Training Procedures

A variety of procedures have been employed to train language skills. For example, the program of research on African Grey parrots directed by Irene Pepperberg (for example, 1990, 1993, 1999) employed an observational learning procedure known as the **model-rival technique.** The first subject trained by Pepperberg was Alex. The model-rival technique involves two people interacting with the subject. One research assistant acts as a trainer and the other acts as a rival student who competes with Alex for the attention of the trainer. The trainer may present an object of interest to Alex and ask what color it is. The person acting as the student then responds, sometimes correctly and sometimes incorrectly. An incorrect response results in a reprimand from the trainer and temporary removal of the object. A correct response results in praise and a chance to manipulate the object. Alex observes these interactions and attempts to gain the attention of the trainer (and obtain the object) by responding correctly before the rival human "student" does so.

In the dolphin and sea lion language training projects, more conventional stimulus discrimination procedures have been used (for example, Herman, Pack, & Morrel-Samuels, 1993; Schusterman & Krieger, 1986). The instructional stimuli were provided by a person making a particular gesture (arms crossed against the chest, for example) at the edge of the pool. The correct response on the part of the marine mammal to the gesture was reinforced with food; incorrect responses were not reinforced. Thus, the training procedures used with the African Grey parrot and the marine mammals differ in numerous respects, including opportunities for observational learning and the reinforcers employed. These differences complicate comparisons between the species.

Starting with the pioneering work of the Gardners in training sign language to Washoe, language training has been conducted with more than a dozen chimpanzees. Sign language training was usually conducted within the context of an established social relationship between the trainers and the chimpanzees. The chimpanzees lived in a rich homelike environment and were cared for by a small number of people throughout the day, each of whom was adept in sign language. Every effort was made to engage the chimpanzees in active conversation (through signing) during their waking hours. New signs were learned during games, in the course of getting dressed, or in going from place to place. The intent was to teach language to the chimpanzees in the way that children presumably learn to talk during the normal course of interacting with parents and other children.

Although the naturalistic context for teaching sign language used by the Gardners seemed to facilitate learning, the informality of the approach made it difficult to document the course of language acquisition in detail. In an effort to gain greater control, other investigators developed artificial languages for use with chimpanzees. One artificial language, developed and used by David Premack and his associates, consists of various shapes made of plastic in place of words (Premack, 1971b, 1976). Another artificial language developed by Duane Rumbaugh and his colleagues at the Language Research Center associated with

I. M. Pepperberg, with Alex

Courtesy of I. M. Pepperberg

Figure 12.10 Examples of lexigrams used at the Language Research Center of Georgia State University.

Courtesy of Duane Rumbaugh, Language Research Center, Georgia State University

Georgia State University used simple designs of various shapes and colors to represent words (Rumbaugh, 1977; see also Savage-Rumbaugh, 1986). These symbols, called lexigrams, are presented on a board (see Figure 12.10). The chimpanzee can select a word by pointing to or pressing the corresponding lexigram on the board. Computer records of these lexigram responses provide detailed information about the linguistic performance of the research participant.

The first chimpanzee trained with lexigrams was Lana (Rumbaugh, 1977). The lexigrams appeared on a modified keyboard hooked up to a computer. Lana could "talk" to the computer and make various requests. The computer, in turn, was programmed to reply with lexigrams presented on a display console.

Lana's training emphasized the naming of objects and the learning of short sequences of symbols. After Lana, two other chimpanzees, Austin and Sherman, entered the research program at the Georgia State University Language Research Center (see Savage-Rumbaugh, 1986). In contrast to Lana, Austin and Sherman were reared with more extensive human contact, and, perhaps more important, they learned language within the context of interacting not only with humans but also with each other. However, they were trained with the same lexigram language system that had been used in training Lana rather than American Sign Language. Austin and Sherman interacted with caretakers and with each other by pointing to or pressing lexigrams on a stimulus board. Portable versions of the lexigram board were available to extend training to a variety of settings.

The most sophisticated demonstrations of language competence to date have been obtained with Kanzi, a bonobo great ape (*Pan paniscus*) (Savage-Rumbaugh, Murphy, Sevcik, Brakke, Williams, & Rumbaugh, 1993; Savage-Rumbaugh, Sevcik, Brakke, & Rumbaugh, 1990). Bonobos are more similar to human beings than are chimpanzees, but they are rare both in the wild and in captivity. Kanzi's experience was unusual in comparison to previous language-trained chimpanzees in that Kanzi did not receive formal language training. During the first 2.5 years of his life, he lived with his mother, Matata, who was born in the wild and started language training at the Language Research Center of Georgia State University when Kanzi was 6 months old.

Matata was trained with standard procedures in which she had to indicate the lexigram names of food objects to obtain those foods. She progressed slowly, however, and never

377

Figure 12.11 Kanzi working with a lexigram board.

Courtesy of E. Sue Savage-Rumbaugh, Great Ape Trust

attained the language competence of Austin and Sherman. For several years, Kanzi observed these training sessions but did not participate in them. Matata was then removed for a period for breeding purposes. During this separation Kanzi began to interact with the lexigram board spontaneously (see Figure 12.11). The investigators took advantage of this spontaneous use of the lexigram board and allowed Kanzi to continue to use it in addition to communicating with manual gestures. They also allowed Kanzi to continue to learn language skills by listening to spoken English and observing humans communicating with gestures and lexigrams.

Every effort was made to provide Kanzi with as rich and as natural an environment as possible. He was allowed to go on excursions in a 50-acre wooded area adjacent to the laboratory. The woods were provisioned with food stations at fixed locations. Excursions in the woods provided numerous opportunities for conversation concerning which food site to visit, what to take along, and so on. Kanzi was also allowed to visit various areas of the laboratory, including areas in which other apes were housed, and periodically he was taken on car rides.

Spoken and lexical language were incorporated into Kanzi's daily activities, such as diaper changes, food preparation, and various games. The hope was that Kanzi would acquire language incidentally during his normal daily activities, as children do. No explicit language training sessions were conducted, and Kanzi's use of language was not explicitly reinforced with food. However, the reinforcement contingencies inherent in social interactions were probably important in Kanzi's language learning (Sundberg, 1996).

Documenting Language Skills

Documenting acquired language skill requires special test procedures because language training typically involves extensive interactions with the participant under conditions in which hints or prompts might be provided, or conditions in which a trainer might give the animal "the benefit of the doubt" and credit the animal with more intelligent behavior than is warranted. Terrace and his colleagues (Terrace, 1979; Terrace, Petitto, Sanders, & Bever, 1979), for example, studied videotaped records of the sign language behavior of their chimpanzee, Nim, and found that Nim often imitated signs previously made by the trainer. Imitative signing was poor evidence of language skill.

Not only must test procedures preclude inadvertent prompts, they must also be constructed to allow for objective measurement of behavior. In a test of sign language vocabulary, for example, Gardner and Gardner (1984), presented pictures to Washoe for her to identify by signing. Two observers recorded the signs Washoe made. To minimize the possibility of prompting, neither observer could see the picture Washoe was trying to name. To ensure objective independent observations, the observers also could not see each other. With these elaborate procedures, Washoe could not be given hints about the correct sign by the observers. Since the observers did not know what the correct sign was on each trial, they also could not give her credit for incorrect responses. Despite these precautions, Washoe responded correctly about 80% of the time.

Washoe's vocabulary test was a test of word production. Another important aspect of vocabulary is comprehension of words presented or spoken by others. An interesting opportunity for testing comprehension arose in the work that Savage-Rumbaugh and her colleagues were doing with Kanzi. In addition to learning lexigrams spontaneously, Kanzi also seemed to have learned to recognize spoken English words. Kanzi, like other chimpanzees, could not produce the sounds of English words, but he appeared to know their meaning. Savage-Rumbaugh decided to evaluate this comprehension in several systematic tests. In one test (Savage-Rumbaugh, McDonald, Sevcik, Hopkins, & Rubert, 1986), English words were "spoken" by a speech synthesizer to make sure Kanzi was not responding to the intonation of human speech. After each word, Kanzi was asked to select the lexical symbol for that word from a selection of three lexigrams (see Figure 12.12). The experimenter did not see the possible choices, and thus could not inadvertently indicate which was correct. The

Courtesy of E. Sue Savage-Rumbaugh, Great Ape Trust

Figure 12.12 The bonobo chimpanzee Kanzi participating in a test of English comprehension. Words were presented to him through the earphones, and he had to respond by pressing lexigrams on the panel in the background.

choice alternatives were presented by a second experimenter who then did not observe Kanzi's choices, so that she also could not prompt the correct response. Each of 66 words was presented three times. Kanzi responded correctly each time 51 of the words was presented. In a similar test with spoken human speech, Kanzi erred on only on once of the 66 words. Thus, synthesized speech was more difficult for Kanzi to comprehend, as it is for human listeners sometimes.

Components of Linguistic Competence

As I noted earlier, research on language learning has come to focus on various components of linguistic competence rather than on whether nonhuman animals are capable of language. Let us consider those components of linguistic competence in greater detail.

Learning a Vocabulary. One of the undisputed results of language training programs is that animals can learn to associate arbitrary symbols (be they manual signs or lexigrams) with objects. They can learn to name correctly a large number of different objects. To what extent does this skill represent having learned what we call words in human language?

A word in human language is an abstract representation that can be used in a variety of ways. One can use the word as a label for its referent object (as in saying "tomato" when presented with an example of the vegetable). One can also identify the referent object in response to the word (as in picking out a tomato when asked, "Which is the tomato?"). One can also use the word in relation to other words (as in saying "tomato" when asked to name examples of "vegetables").

Strong evidence of multiple uses of words was obtained with the chimpanzees Austin and Sherman (Savage-Rumbaugh, Rumbaugh, Smith, & Lawson, 1980). In one study, for example, Austin and Sherman were trained to label lexigrams of various foods (beancake, orange, and bread) and tools (key, money, and stick) as "food" and "tool." They were then tested with a variety of symbols of new tools (magnet, sponge, lever, string, for example) and foods (M&M, banana, corn, for example). They had previously learned the lexigrams for each of these new tools and foods. However, they had not been explicitly trained to categorize or label these items in terms of their uses ("tool" and "food"). Nevertheless, Austin and Sherman performed with nearly perfect accuracy in categorizing these new lexigrams. Thus, they were able to use words to label and categorize other words.

Evidence of "Grammar" in Great Apes. Although it is agreed that great apes (and Grey parrots, dolphins, and sea lions) can learn a vocabulary, language is more than just a collection of words. Language also involves arrangement of words into sequences according to certain rules set forth by the grammar or syntax of the language. Hence, a major issue in language research has been whether the subjects display evidence of using grammatical rules. There has been considerable debate about this and the debate is ongoing (for example, Kako, 1999).

The smallest word sequence contains two words. However, the utterance of a pair of words does not prove that the participant is using grammar to create the sequence. An often-recounted incident involving a two-word sequence occurred when the chimpanzee Washoe saw a swan in the water. She had never seen a swan before. When asked "What is that?" she signed "Water bird." In this sequence, was Washoe using "water" as an adjective to specify the kind of bird she saw? Perhaps. However, an equally plausible interpretation is that she signed "water" because she saw the water and "bird" because she saw a bird. That is, she may have signed "water bird" as two independent words rather than as an utterance of two words related to each other as adjective and noun (Terrace et al., 1979).

Early detailed studies of language production in the chimpanzee failed to provide convincing evidence of responding on the basis of some kind of grammar or set of rules for word combinations (Terrace, 1979; Terrace et al., 1979). The chimpanzee Nim, who was taught sign language by Terrace and his associates, performed sequences of signs, but these appeared to be imitations of the trainer and included meaningless repetitions. For example, Nim's most common four-sign combination was "eat-drink-eat-drink."

Convincing evidence of the development of grammatical word sequences has been obtained in studies with the bonobo ape Kanzi (Greenfield & Savage-Rumbaugh, 1990; see also Savage-Rumbaugh et al., 1990). Data for the analysis of the possible existence of grammatical structure in Kanzi's language production were first obtained when Kanzi was 5.5 years old (Greenfield & Savage-Rumbaugh, 1990). Over a 5-month period of observations, Kanzi communicated 13,691 "words." Of these, about 10% contained more than one element or "word." The analysis of word sequences was limited to spontaneous communications. Thus, responses to directed questions were excluded from the analyses, as were responses that Kanzi performed to obtain something that was otherwise withheld, or responses that involved some degree of imitation. Unlike Nim, Kanzi rarely repeated himself or combined words that did not make sense together. Analyses of the multiple-word communications revealed a structure indicative of rules for word order.

Kanzi's word combinations could be categorized according to the types of words that were involved. By way of example, Table 12.2 summarizes data from three different types of two-word combinations. The first type involves a word for an action and a word for an agent. A total of 132 such action/agent combinations were observed. Of these, in 119 instances the word identifying the action preceded the word identifying the agent. In only 13 of the 132 cases did the word for the agent precede the word for the action. A similar bias in favor of a particular word order is evident with the other types of two-word combinations, action/object and goal/action. Notice that the "grammatical" rule is not a simple one. One of the words in all three of these types of two-word combinations involved an action. However, the action word did not come first predominantly in all three types of two-word combinations. When talking about an action and a goal, Kanzi tended to state the goal first.

TABLE 12.2	FREQUENCY OF VARIOUS TWO-ELEMENT COMMUNICATIONS BY KANZI*

WORD ORDER	FREQUENCY	EXAMPLE OF DOMINANT ORDER
Action→Agent	119	CARRY→gesture to Phil, who agrees to carry Kanzi
Agent→Action	13	
Action→Object	39	KEEP AWAY BALLOON→wanting to tease Bill with
Object→Action	15	a balloon and start a fight
Goal→Action	46	COKE CHASE→researcher chases Kanzi to place
Action→Goal	10	in woods where Coke is kept

*Lexigram responses are indicated by small capital letters.
Source: Adapted from Greenfield and Savage-Rumbaugh, 1990.

Some of the rules for word order that were manifest in Kanzi's word combinations were probably learned by observing his human caretakers. However, other grammatical rules appeared to be Kanzi's original inventions. Perhaps the most prominent of these concerned word combinations that Kanzi made involving a lexigram and a hand gesture. In such cases, Kanzi nearly always performed the lexigram response first, followed by the gesture. For example, in requesting to be carried, Kanzi would press the lexigram for CARRY, followed by a gesture pointing to the caretaker. Kanzi faithfully followed the rule of making the lexigram response before any manual gestures, but the caretakers usually performed such word sequences in the opposite order.

Language Comprehension versus Production.   Historically, studies of ape language have focused on whether apes can learn to produce orderly linguistic responses, be those words or word sequences. Starting with the findings obtained with Kanzi, the focus has shifted toward investigations of language comprehension. The initial observations of Kanzi's language competence were incidental and serendipitous. Recall that Kanzi was not in an organized language training program but was present while his mother received explicit language training. Savage-Rumbaugh and her colleagues noticed that Kanzi seemed to understand the words that were being used with his mother. This incidental observation led them to investigate language comprehension rather than production in a systematic fashion. The shift in emphasis has provided dramatic results (for example, Brakke & Savage-Rumbaugh, 1995; Savage-Rumbaugh et al., 1993).

Comprehension precedes the ability to speak a language in human language learning. Individuals learning a second language, for example, can often understand more of that language than they are able to speak. This raises the possibility that studies of language comprehension may reveal sophisticated aspects of linguistic competence that are not evident in language production.

A prominent feature of human language is its variety and flexibility. A limited set of words can be combined to form a great variety of different sentences, and you can understand a new sentence even if you have never seen that particular sequence of words before. It has been difficult to prove that animals can use language in as flexible a fashion as human beings (see, for example, Thompson & Church, 1980). Tests of comprehension conducted with Kanzi provided promising results.

Savage-Rumbaugh et al. (1993) conducted detailed evaluations of the language comprehension of Kanzi when he was 8 years old and compared his performance to that of a 2-year-old child, Alia. Alia's mother, Jeannine Murphy, was one of Kanzi's caretakers. She worked with Kanzi in the mornings and spent the afternoons with Alia in a double-wide mobile home at the Language Research Center that was set up like Kanzi's laboratory. Alia participated in games and other activities similar to those that were used with Kanzi and received similar exposure to lexigrams and spoken English.

The test sentences involved instructions to manipulate various objects that were familiar and available to Kanzi and Alia. Kanzi faced up to 12 objects, and Alia was given up to 8. In the critical test phase, the sentences were spoken by an experimenter hidden by a one-way mirror so that the experimenter could not make gestures that might prompt the correct response. All trials were recorded on videotape. Usually two or three other people were present in the room so that sentences involving interactions with these people could be included in the test. However, the additional individuals wore headphones that played loud music so that they could not hear the instructions given Kanzi or Alia. To further preclude inadvertent influences on the data, the results of tests with Kanzi were not known to the person conducting the tests with Alia, and vice versa.

Kanzi was tested with 415 sentences, and Alia was tested with 407. The sentences were distributed among seven different types. Some were fairly simple, such as "Put object X in object Y," "Give object X to person A," "Do action A on object X," and "Take object X to location Y." Others were more complicated, such as "Make pretend animate A do action A on recipient Y." (For example, "Make the [toy] doggie bite the [toy] snake.") Both Kanzi and Alia did remarkably well. Each responded correctly more than 50% of the time on all but one sentence type. Overall, Kanzi did a bit better than Alia. Kanzi responded correctly on 74% of the trials, and Alia responded correctly on 65% of the trials.

Both Kanzi and Alia responded correctly when tested with sentences involving the same words but in different orders. For example, they responded correctly to the sentences "Take the umbrella outdoors," and "Go outdoors and get the umbrella"; "Take the potato to the bedroom," and "Go to the bedroom and get the potato"; "Put some water on the carrot," and "Put the carrot in the water"; and "Kanzi/Alia is going to chase Liz/Nathaniel," and "Liz/Nathaniel is going to chase Kanzi/Alia." Kanzi was more accurate on sentence pairs involving the same words in different orders. Kanzi made the correct response on 66% of such pairs of sentences, whereas Alia was correct on 38% of them.

Kanzi and Alia also responded correctly to sentences involving unusual instructions that they had not previously encountered. For example, on one occasion the objects available to Kanzi included a tomato and a sponge ball. The ball was shaped in the form of a head, with eyes, a nose, and a mouth. One of Kanzi's test sentences was, "Feed your ball some tomato." Before this test item, the word "feed" had never been used with "ball." Nevertheless, in response to "Feed your ball some tomato," Kanzi took the tomato and put it into the mouth on the sponge ball (see Figure 12.13).

Both Kanzi and Alia also came up with some unusual solutions to the instructions they were given. Both had seen food washed in the kitchen sink. Therefore, in response to "Wash

Figure 12.13 Video sequence showing Kanzi's response to the instruction, "Feed your ball some tomato."

Courtesy of E. Sue Savage-Rumbaugh, Great Ape Trust

the hot dogs," the experimenters expected that they would take the hot dogs to the sink. But, neither did so. Rather, they responded in a way that did not require going to the sink. Kanzi washed the hot dogs with a hose that was in the room to clean the floor. Alia, in contrast, rubbed the hot dogs with a sponge that was close at hand.

Kanzi's performance provides the best evidence available so far that a nonhuman mammal can acquire sophisticated linguistic skills. Kanzi acquired a substantial vocabulary and also showed evidence of syntax in language production. In addition, he mastered some of the flexibility of language. He could understand differences in meaning created by different word orders and new messages created by combining familiar words in unfamiliar sentences. The language sophistication of Kanzi proves that many important linguistic skills are not uniquely human attributes. Thus, these findings vindicate Darwin's belief that seemingly unique human abilities and skills do not reflect a discontinuity in the animal kingdom. (For a discussion of the broader philosophical implications of this research, see Savage-Rumbaugh, Shanker, & Taylor, 1998.)

SAMPLE QUESTIONS

1. Describe the phenomenon of transitive inference, and explain how it could occur through simple associative mechanisms.
2. Describe how the behavior of food-storing birds can be used to provide evidence of episodic memory.
3. Describe the peak procedure and how results obtained with the peak procedure may be explained by an information processing model.
4. Compare and contrast the information processing model of timing and the behavioral theory of timing.
5. Explain why tests with subsets of items from a simultaneous array are useful in assessing the mechanisms of serial pattern learning.
6. Compare and contrast three different theories of perceptual concept learning.
7. Describe how responsiveness to word order may be evaluated in the language comprehension of chimpanzees and children.

KEY TERMS

adjunctive behaviors Systematic activities or responses that occur when reinforcers are delivered at fixed intervals.

duration estimation A discrimination procedure in which the discriminative stimulus is the duration of an event.

interim response A response that increases in frequency after the delivery of a periodic reinforcer and then declines as time for the the next reinforcer approaches.

model-rival technique An observational learning procedure in which the participant observes a trainer teaching a student and tries to compete with that student for the trainer's attention.

paired-associate learning Learning of associations between successive pairs of an ordered list of stimuli.

peak procedure A discrete-trial variation of a fixed interval schedule used to study timing in animals.

polymorphic rule A criterion for membership in a perceptual category, according to which categorization is determined by the exemplar having a certain number of stimulus features that are relevant to the category. However, no one feature alone (or in combination with other features) is assumed to be necessary or sufficient for category membership.

prototype An exemplar of a category that is the average, typical, or "standard" representation of that category.

response chain A consecutively ordered series of responses in which each response produces the cue for the next response in the sequence.

serial representation learning The learning of a mental representation of the order of an entire list or series of stimuli.

terminal response A response that is most likely to occur at the end of the interval between successive reinforcements that are presented at fixed intervals.

REFERENCES

Abramson, L. Y., Metalsky, G. I., & Alloy, L. B. (1989). Hopelessness depression: A theory-based subtype of depression. *Psychological Review, 96,* 358–372.

Acediano, F., Matute, H., Miller, R. R. (1997). Blocking of Pavlovian conditioning in humans. *Learning & Motivation, 28*(2), 188–199.

Aitken, M. R. F., Bennett, C. H., McLaren, I. P. L., & Mackintosh, N. J. (1996). Perceptual differentiation during categorization learning by pigeons. *Journal of Experimental Psychology: Animal Behavior Processes, 22,* 43–50.

Akins, C. K. (1998). Context excitation and modulation of conditioned sexual behavior. *Animal Learning & Behavior, 26,* 416–426.

Akins, C. K. (2000). Effects of species-specific cues and the CS-US interval on the topography of the sexually conditioned response. *Learning and Motivation, 31,* 211–235.

Akins, C. K., & Domjan, M. (1996). The topography of sexually conditioned behaviour: Effects of a trace interval. *Quarterly Journal of Experimental Psychology, 49B,* 346–356.

Akins, C. K., Domjan, M., & Gutiérrez, G. (1994). Topography of sexually conditioned behavior in male Japanese quail (*Coturnix japonica*) depends on the CS-US interval. *Journal of Experimental Psychology: Animal Behavior Processes, 20,* 199–209.

Albert, M., & Ayres, J. J. B. (1997). One-trial simultaneous and backward excitatory fear conditioning in rats: Lick suppression, freezing, and rearing to CS

compounds and their elements. *Animal Learning & Behavior, 25,* 210–220.

Allan, R. W., & Zeigler, H. P. (1994). Autoshaping the pigeon's gape response: Acquisition and topography as a function of reinforcer type and magnitude. *Journal of the Experimental Analysis of Behavior, 62,* 201–223.

Allison, J. (1983). *Behavioral economics.* New York: Praeger.

Allison, J. (1989). The nature of reinforcement. In S. B. Klein & R. R. Mowrer (Eds.), *Contemporary learning theories: Instrumental conditioning and the impact of biological constraints on learning* (pp. 13–39). Hillsdale, NJ: Erlbaum.

Allison, J. (1993). Response deprivation, reinforcement, and economics. *Journal of the Experimental Analysis of Behavior, 60,* 129–140.

Allison, J., Buxton, A., & Moore, K. E. (1987). Bliss points, stop lines, and performance under schedule constraint. *Journal of Experimental Psychology: Animal Behavior Processes, 13,* 331–340.

Amsel, A. (1958). The role of frustrative nonreward in noncontinuous reward situations. *Psychological Bulletin, 55,* 102–119.

Amsel, A. (1962). Frustrative nonreward in partial reinforcement and discrimination learning. *Psychological Review, 69,* 306–328.

Amsel, A. (1967). Partial reinforcement effects on vigor and persistence. In K. W. Spence & J. T. Spence (Eds.), *The psychology of learning and motivation* (Vol. 1, pp. 1–65). New York: Academic Press.

Amsel, A. (1989). *Behaviorism, neobehaviorism, and cognitivism in learning theory.* Hillsdale, NJ: Erlbaum.

Amsel, A. (1992). *Frustration theory.* Cambridge, England: Cambridge University Press.

Anderson, D. C., Crowell, C. R., Cunningham, C. L., & Lupo, J. V. (1979). Behavior during shock exposure as a determinant of subsequent interference with shuttle box escape-avoidance learning in the rat. *Journal of Experimental Psychology: Animal Behavior Processes, 5,* 243–257.

Anderson, M. C., & Shettleworth, S. J. (1977). Behavioral adaptation to fixed-interval and fixed-time food delivery in golden hamsters. *Journal of the Experimental Analysis of Behavior, 25,* 33–49.

Anger, D. (1963). The role of temporal discrimination in the reinforcement of Sidman avoidance behavior. *Journal of the Experimental Analysis of Behavior, 6,* 477–506.

Anisman, H., de Catanzaro, D., & Remington, G. (1978). Escape performance following exposure to inescapable shock: Deficits in motor response maintenance. *Journal of Experimental Psychology: Animal Behavior Processes, 4,* 197–218.

Anisman, H., Hamilton, M., & Zacharko, R. M. (1984). Cue and response-choice acquisition and reversal after exposure to uncontrollable shock: Induction of response perseveration. *Journal of Experimental Psychology: Animal Behavior Processes, 10,* 229–243.

Aparicio, C. F. (2001). Overmatching in rats: The barrier choice paradigm. *Journal of* the *Experimental Analysis of Behavior, 75,* 93–106.

Arcediano, F., Ortega, N., & Matute, H. (1996). A behavioural preparation for the study of human Pavlovian conditioning. *Quarterly Journal of Experimental Psychology, 49B,* 270–283.

Astley, S. L., & Wasserman, E. A. (1998). Novelty and functional equivalence in superordinate categorization by pigeons. *Animal Learning & Behavior, 26,* 125–138.

Astley, S. L., & Wasserman, E. A. (1999). Superordinate category formation in pigeons: Association with a common delay or probability of food reinforcement makes perceptually dissimilar stimuli functionally equivalent. *Journal of Experimental Psychology: Animal Behavior Processes, 25,* 415–432.

Aust, U., & Huber, L. (2001). The role of item- and category-specific information in the discrimination of people versus nonpeople images by pigeons. *Animal Learning & Behavior, 29,* 107–119.

Aydin, A., & Pearce, J. M. (1994). Prototype effects in categorization by pigeons. *Journal of Experimental Psychology: Animal Behavior Processes, 20,* 264–277.

Ayres, J. J. B. (1998). Fear conditioning and avoidance. In W. O'Donohue (Ed.), *Learning and behavior therapy* (pp. 122–145). Boston: Allyn and Bacon.

Ayres, J. J. B., Haddad, C., & Albert, M. (1987). One-trial excitatory backward conditioning as assessed by suppression of licking in rats: Concurrent observations of lick suppression and defensive behaviors. *Animal Learning & Behavior, 15,* 212–217.

Azorlosa, J. L., & Cicala, G. A. (1986). Blocking of conditioned suppression with 1 or 10 compound trials. *Animal Learning & Behavior, 14,* 163–167.

Azrin, N. H. (1956). Some effects of two intermittent schedules of immediate and non-immediate punishment. *Journal of Psychology, 42,* 3–21.

Azrin, N. H. (1958). Some effects of noise on human behavior. *Journal of the Experimental Analysis of Behavior, 1,* 183–200.

Azrin, N. H. (1959). Punishment and recovery during fixed ratio performance. *Journal of the Experimental Analysis of Behavior, 2,* 301–305.

Azrin, N. H. (1960). Effects of punishment intensity during variable-interval reinforcement. *Journal of the Experimental Analysis of Behavior, 3,* 123–142.

Azrin, N. H., & Holz, W. C. (1961). Punishment during fixed-interval reinforcement. *Journal of the Experimental Analysis of Behavior, 4,* 343–347.

Azrin, N. H., & Holz, W. C. (1966). Punishment. In W. K. Honig (Ed.), *Operant behavior: Areas of research and application* (pp. 380–447). New York: Appleton-Century-Crofts.

Azrin, N. H., Holz, W. C., & Hake, D. F. (1963). Fixed-ratio punishment. *Journal of the Experimental Analysis of Behavior, 6,* 141–148.

Azrin, N. H., Hutchinson, R. R., & Hake, D. F. (1966). Extinction-induced aggression. *Journal of the Experimental Analysis of Behavior, 9,* 191–204.

Babkin, B. P. (1949). *Pavlov: A biography.* Chicago: University of Chicago Press.

Baer, D. M., & Wolf, M. M. (1970). The entry into natural communities of reinforcement. In R. Ulrich, T. Stachnik, & J. Mabry (Eds.), *Control of human behavior* (Vol. 2, pp. 319–324). Glenview, IL: Scott, Foresman.

Baerends, G. P. (1988). Ethology. In R. C. Atkinson, R. J. Herrnstein, G. Lindzey, & R. D. Luce (Eds.), *Stevens' handbook of experimental psychology* (Vol. 1, pp. 765–830). New York: Wiley.

Baerends, G. P., & Drent, R. H. (Eds.). (1982). The herring gull and its egg. Part II. The responsiveness to egg features. *Behaviour, 82,* 1–417.

Baker, A. G., & Baker, P. A. (1985). Does inhibition differ from excitation? Proactive interference, contextual conditioning, and extinction. In R. R. Miller & N. E. Spear (Eds.), *Information processing in animals: Conditioned inhibition* (pp. 151–183). Hillsdale, NJ: Erlbaum.

Baker, T. B., & Tiffany, S. T. (1985). Morphine tolerance as habituation. *Psychological Review, 92,* 78–108.

Balaz, M. A., Kasprow, W. J., & Miller, R. R. (1982). Blocking with a single compound trial. *Animal Learning & Behavior, 10,* 271–276.

Balda, R. P., & Turek, R. J. (1984). The cache-recovery system as an example of memory capabilities in Clark's nutcracker. In H. L. Roitblat, T. G. Bever, & H. S. Terrace (Eds.), *Animal cognition* (pp. 513–532). Hillsdale, NJ: Erlbaum.

Balleine, B. W. (2001). Incentive processes in instrumental conditioning. In R. R. Mowrer and S. B. Klein (Eds.), *Handbook of contemporary learning theories* (pp. 307–366). Mahwah, NJ: Erlbaum.

Balsam, P. D. (1985). The functions of context in learning and performance. In P. D. Balsam & A. Tomie (Eds.), *Context and learning* (pp. 1–21). Hillsdale, NJ: Erlbaum.

Balsam, P. D. (1988). Selection, representation, and equivalence of controlling stimuli. In R. C. Atkinson, R. J. Herrnstein, G. Lindzey, & R. D. Luce (Eds.), *Stevens' handbook of experimental psychology: Vol. 2. Learning and cognition* (pp. 111–166). New York: Wiley.

Balsam, P. D., & Tomie, A. (Eds.). (1985). *Context and learning.* Hillsdale, NJ: Erlbaum.

Balsam, P. D., Deich, J. D., Ohyama, T., & Stokes, P. D. (1998). Origins of new behavior. In W. O'Donohue (Ed.), *Learning and behavior therapy* (pp. 403–420). Boston: Allyn and Bacon.

Banks, R. K. (1976). Resistance to punishment as a function of intensity and frequency of prior punishment experience. *Learning and Motivation, 7,* 551–558.

Bargh, J. A., & Chartrand, T. L. (1999). The unbearable automaticity of being. *American Psychologist, 54,* 462–479.

Barker, L. M., Best, M. R., & Domjan, M. (Eds.). (1977). *Learning mechanisms in food selection.* Waco, TX: Baylor University Press.

Barkley, C. L., & Jacobs, L. F. (1998). Visual environment and delay affect cache retrieval accuracy in a food-storing rodent. *Animal Learning & Behavior, 26,* 439–447.

Barnet, R. C., & Miller, R. R. (1996). Second-order excitation mediated by a backward conditioned inhibitor. *Journal of Experimental Psychology: Animal Behavior Processes, 22,* 279–296.

Barnet, R. C., Arnold, H. M., & Miller, R. R. (1991). Simultaneous conditioning demonstrated in second-order conditioning: Evidence for similar associative structure in forward and simultaneous conditioning. *Learning and Motivation, 22,* 253–268.

Barnet, R. C., Cole, R. P., & Miller, R. R. (1997). Temporal integration in second-order conditioning and sensory preconditioning. *Animal Learning & Behavior, 25,* 221–233.

Baron, A. (1965). Delayed punishment of a runway response. *Journal of Comparative and Physiological Psychology, 60,* 131–134.

Baron, A., & Herpolsheimer, L. R. (1999). Averaging effects in the study of fixed-ratio response patterns. *Journal of the Experimental Analysis of Behavior, 71,* 145–153.

Baron, A., & Leinenweber, A. (1994). Molecular and molar analyses of fixed-interval performance. *Journal of the Experimental Analysis of Behavior, 61,* 11–18.

Baron, A., & Menich, S. R. (1985). Reaction times of younger and older men: Effects of compound samples and a prechoice signal on delayed matching-to-sample performances. *Journal of the Experimental Analysis of Behavior, 44,* 1–14.

Barrett, J. E., & Hoffmann, S. M. (1991). Neurochemical changes correlated with behavior maintained under fixed-interval and fixed-ratio schedules of reinforcement. *Journal of the Experimental Analysis of Behavior, 56,* 395–405.

Barton, L. E., Brulle, A. R., & Repp, A. C. (1986). Maintenance of therapeutic change by momentary DRO. *Journal of Applied Behavior Analysis, 19,* 277–282.

Bashinski, H., Werner, J., & Rudy, J. (1985). Determinants of infant visual attention: Evidence for a two-process theory. *Journal of Experimental Child Psychology, 39* 580–598.

Batsell, W. R., Jr., & Batson, J. D. (1999). Augmentation of taste conditioning by a preconditioned odor. *Journal of Experimental Psychology: Animal Behavior Processes, 25,* 374–388.

Batsell, W. R., Jr., & Brown, A. S. (1998). Human flavor-aversion learning: A comparison of traditional aversions and cognitive aversions. *Learning and Motivation, 29,* 383–396.

Batsell, W. R., Jr., Paschall, G. Y., Gleason, D. I., & Batson, J. D. (2001). Taste preconditioning augments odor-aversion learning. *Journal of Experimental Psychology: Animal Behavior Processes, 27,* 30–47.

Batson, J. D., & Batsell, W. R., Jr. (2000). Augmentation, not blocking, in an A+/AX+ flavor-conditioning procedure. *Psychonomic Bulletin & Review, 7,* 466–471.

Baum, M. (1969). Extinction of avoidance response following response prevention: Some parametric investigations. *Canadian Journal of Psychology, 23,* 1–10.

Baum, M. (1970). Extinction of avoidance responding through response prevention (flooding). *Psychological Bulletin, 74,* 276–284.

Baum, W. M. (1974). On two types of deviation from the matching law: Bias and undermatching. *Journal of the Experimental Analysis of Behavior, 22,* 231–242.

Baum, W. M. (1975). Time allocation in human vigilance. *Journal of the Experimental Analysis of Behavior, 23,* 45–53.

Baum, W. M. (1979). Matching, undermatching, and overmatching in studies of choice. *Journal of the Experimental Analysis of Behavior, 32,* 269–281.

Baum, W. M. (1981). Optimization and the matching law as accounts of instrumental behavior. *Journal of the Experimental Analysis of Behavior, 36,* 387–403.

Baum, W. M. (1993). Performances on ratio and interval schedules of reinforcement: Data and theory. *Journal of the Experimental Analysis of Behavior, 59,* 245–264.

Baum, W. M., & Aparicio, C. F. (1999). Optimality and concurrent variable-interval variable-ratio schedules. *Journal of the Experimental Analysis of Behavior, 71,* 75–89.

Baum, W. M., & Kraft, J. R. (1998). Group choice: Competition, travel, and the ideal free distribution. *Journal of the Experimental Analysis of Behavior, 69,* 227–245.

Baxter, D. J., & Zamble, E. (1982). Reinforcer and response specificity in appetitive transfer of control. *Animal Learning & Behavior, 10,* 201–210.

Beatty, W. W., & Shavalia, D. A. (1980a). Rat spatial memory: Resistance to retroactive interference at long retention in-tervals. *Animal Learning & Behavior, 8,* 550–552.

Beatty, W. W., & Shavalia, D. A. (1980b). Spatial memory in rats: Time course of working memory and effects of anesthetics. *Behavioral and Neural Biology, 28,* 454–462.

Bechterev, V. M. (1913). *La psychologie objective.* Paris: Alcan.

Beck, C. D. O., & Rankin, C. H. (1997). Long-term habituation is produced by distributed training at long ISIs and not by massed training or short ISIs in *Caenorhabditis elegans. Animal Learning & Behavior, 25,* 446–457.

Bee, M. A. (2001). Habituation and sensitization of aggression in bullfrogs (*Rana catesbeiana*): Testing the dual-process theory of habituation. *Journal of Comparative Psychology, 115,* 307–316.

Belke, T. W. (1992). Stimulus preference and the transitivity of preference. *Animal Learning & Behavior, 20,* 401–406.

Belke, T. W. (1998). Qualitatively different reinforcers and parameters of Herrnstein's (1970) response-strength equation. *Animal Learning & Behavior, 26,* 235–242.

Belke, T. W., & Heyman, G. M. (1994a). A matching law analysis of the reinforcing efficacy of wheel running in rats. *Animal Learning & Behavior, 22,* 267–274.

Belke, T. W., & Heyman, G. M. (1994b). Increasing and signaling background reinforcement: Effect on the foreground response-reinforcer relation. *Journal of the Experimental Analysis of Behavior, 61,* 65–81.

Belke, T. W., & Spetch, M. (1994). Choice between reliable and unreliable reinforcement alternatives revisited: Preference for unreliable reinforcement. *Journal of the Experimental Analysis of Behavior, 62,* 353–366.

Bell, M. C. (1999). Pavlovian contingencies and resistance to change in a multiple schedule. *Journal of the Experimental Analysis of Behavior, 72,* 81–96.

Bernstein, I. L. (1978). Learned taste aversions in children receiving chemotherapy. *Science, 200,* 1302–1303.

Bernstein, I. L. (1991). Aversion conditioning in response to cancer and cancer treatment. *Clinical Psychology Review, 11,* 185–191.

Bernstein, I. L., & Borson, S. (1986). Learned food aversion: A component of anorexia syndromes. *Psychological Review, 93,* 462–472.

Bernstein, I. L., & Webster, M. M. (1980). Learned taste aversions in humans. *Physiology and Behavior, 25,* 363–366.

Berridge, K. C. (2001). Reward learning: Reinforcement, incentives, and expectations. In D. L. Medin (Ed.), *The psychology of learning and motivation* (Vol. 40, pp. 223–278). San Diego: Academic Press.

Berridge, K. C., & Schulkin, J. (1989). Palatability shift of a salt-associated incentive during sodium depletion. *Quarterly Journal of Experimental Psychology, 41B,* 121–138.

Best, M. R., Dunn, D. P., Batson, J. D., Meachum, C. L., & Nash, S. M. (1985). Extinguishing conditioned inhibition in flavour-aversion learning: Effects of repeated testing and extinction of the excitatory element. *Quarterly Journal of Experimental Psychology, 37B,* 359–378.

Bevins, R. A., & Ayres, J. J. B. (1994). Factors affecting rats' location during conditioned suppression training. *Animal Learning and Behavior, 22,* 302–308.

Bevins, R. A., Delzer, T. A., & Bardo, M. T. (1996). Second-order conditioning detects unexpressed morphine-induced salt aversion. *Animal Learning & Behavior, 24,* 221–229.

Bhatt, R. S., Rovee-Collier, C., & Shyi, G. C.-W. (1994). Global and local processing of incidental information and memory retrieval at 6 months. *Journal of Experimental Child Psychology, 52,* 141–162.

Bickel, W. K., DeGrandpre, R. J., Hughes, J. R., & Higgins, S. T. (1991). Behavioral economics of drug self-administration. II. A unit-price analysis of cigarette smoking. *Journal of the Experimental Analysis of Behavior, 55,* 145–154.

Bickel, W. K., Green, L., & Vuchinich, R. E. (1995). Behavioral economics. *Journal of the Experimental Analysis of Behavior, 64,* 257–262.

Bickel, W. K., Madden, G. J., & DeGrandpre, R. J. (1997). Modeling the effects of combined behavioral and pharmacological treatment on cigarette smoking: Behavioral-economic analyses. *Experimental and Clinical Psychopharmacology, 5,* 334–343.

Bickel, W. K., Odum, A. L., & Madden, G. J. (1999). Impulsivity and cigarette smoking: Delay discounting in current, never, and ex-smokers. *Psychopharmacology, 146,* 447–454.

Biegler, R. (2000). Possible uses of path integration in animal navigation. *Animal Learning & Behavior, 28,* 257–277.

Bitterman, M. E. (1964). Classical conditioning in the goldfish as a function of the CS-US interval. *Journal of Comparative and Physiological Psychology, 58,* 359–366.

Bitterman, M. E. (1988). Vertebrate-invertebrate comparisons. In H. J. Jerison & I. Jerison (Eds.), *Intelligence and evolutionary biology* (NATO ASI Series, Vol. G17, pp. 251–276). Berlin: Springer.

Bitterman, M. E. (1996). Comparative analysis of learning in honeybees. *Animal Learning & Behavior, 24,* 123–141.

Bizo, L. A., Bogdanov, S. V., & Killeen, P. R. (1998). Satiation causes within-session decreases in instrumental responding. *Journal of Experimental Psychology: Animal Behavior Processes, 24,* 439–452.

Bizo, L. A., Kettle, L. C., & Killeen, P. R. (2001). Rats don't always respond faster for more food: The paradoxical incentive effect. *Animal Learning & Behavior, 29,* 66–78.

Bizo, L. A., & Killeen, P. R. (1997). Models of ratio schedule performance. *Journal of Experimental Psychology: Animal Behavior Processes, 23,* 351–367.

Bizo, L. A., & White, K. G. (1994). Pacemaker rate in the behavioral theory of timing. *Journal of Experimental Psychology: Animal Behavior Processes, 20,* 308–321.

Bizo, L. A., & White, K. G. (1995a). Biasing the pacemaker in the behavioral theory of timing. *Journal of the Experimental Analysis of Behavior, 64,* 225–235.

Bizo, L. A., & White, K. G. (1995b). Reinforcement context and pacemaker rate in the behavioral theory of timing. *Animal Learning & Behavior, 23,* 376–382.

Bjork, R. A. (1972). The updating of human memory. In G. H. Bower (Ed.), *The psychology of learning and motivation* (Vol. 12, pp. 235–259). New York: Academic Press.

Black, A. H. (1971). Autonomic aversive conditioning in infrahuman subjects. In F. R. Brush (Ed.), *Aversive conditioning and learning* (pp. 3–104). New York: Academic Press.

Black, A. H. (1977). Comments on "Learned helplessness: Theory and evidence" by Maier and Seligman. *Journal of Experimental Psychology: General, 106,* 41–43.

Blackman, D. (1977). Conditioned suppression and the effects of classical conditioning on operant behavior. In W. K. Honig & J. E. R. Staddon (Eds.), *Handbook of operant behavior* (pp. 340–363). Englewood Cliffs, NJ: Prentice-Hall.

Blaisdell, A. P., Gunther, L. M., & Miller, R. R. (1999). Recovery from blocking achieved by extinguishing the blocking CS. *Animal Learning & Behavior, 27,* 63–76.

Blakely, E., & Schlinger, H. (1988). Determinants of pausing under variable-ratio schedules: Reinforcer magnitude, ratio size, and schedule configuration. *Journal of the Experimental Analysis of Behavior, 50,* 65–73.

Blakemore, C., & Cooper, G. F. (1970). Development of the brain depends on visual environment. *Science, 228,* 477–478.

Blanchard, D. C. (1997). Stimulus, environmental, and pharmacological control of defensive behaviors. In M. E. Bouton & M. S. Fanselow (Eds.), *Learning, motivation, and cognition* (pp. 283–303). Washington, DC: American Psychological Association.

Blass, E. M., Ganchrow, J. R., & Steiner, J. E. (1984). Classical conditioning in newborn humans 2–48 hours of age. *Infant Behavior and Development, 7,* 223–235.

Bliss, T. V. P., & Lomo, T. (1973). Long-lasting potentiation of synaptic transmission in the dentate area of the anesthetized rabbit following stimulation of the perforant path. *Journal of Physiology, 232,* 331–356.

Blough, D. S. (1959). Delayed matching in the pigeon. *Journal of the Experimental Analysis of Behavior, 2,* 151–160.

Blough, D. S. (1996). Error factors in pigeon discrimination and delayed matching. *Journal of Experimental Psychology: Animal Behavior Processes, 22,* 118–131.

Blumberg, M. S., & Wasserman, E. A. (1995). Animal mind and the argument from design. *American Psychologist, 50,* 133–144.

Boakes, R. A. (1984). *From Darwin to behaviourism.* Cambridge: Cambridge University Press.

Boakes, R. A., & Halliday, M. S. (Eds.). (1972). *Inhibition and learning.* London: Academic Press.

Boakes, R. A., Westbrook, R. F., Elliott, M., & Swinbourne, A. L. (1997). Context dependency of conditioned aversions to water and sweet tastes. *Journal of Experimental Psychology: Animal Behavior Processes, 25,* 324–333.

Boice, R. (1973). Domestication. *Psychological Bulletin, 80,* 215–230.

Boice, R. (1977). Burrows of wild and albino rats: Effects of domestication, outdoor raising, age, experience, and maternal state. *Journal of Comparative and Physiological Psychology, 91,* 649–661.

Boice, R. (1981). Behavioral comparability of wild and domesticated rats. *Behavior Genetics, 11,* 545–553.

Bolles, R. C. (1969). Avoidance and escape learning: Simultaneous acquisition of different responses. *Journal of Comparative and Physiological Psychology, 68,* 355–358.

Bolles, R. C. (1970). Species-specific defense reactions and avoidance learning. *Psychological Review, 71,* 32–48.

Bolles, R. C. (1971). Species-specific defense reaction. In F. R. Brush (Ed.), *Aversive conditioning and learning* (pp. 183–233). New York: Academic Press.

Bolles, R. C. (1972a). The avoidance learning problem. In G. H. Bower (Ed.), *The psychology of learning and motivation* (Vol. 6, pp. 97–145). New York: Academic Press.

Bolles, R. C. (1972b). Reinforcement, expectancy, and learning. *Psychological Review, 79,* 394–409.

Bolles, R. C., & Fanselow, M. S. (1980). A perceptual defensive-recuperative model of fear and pain. *Behavioral and Brain Sciences, 3,* 291–323.

Bolles, R. C., & Grossen, N. E. (1969). Effects of an informational stimulus on the acquisition of avoidance behavior in rats. *Journal of Comparative and Physiological Psychology, 68,* 90–99.

Bolles, R. C., Holtz, R., Dunn, T., & Hill, W. (1980). Comparisons of stimulus learning and response learning in a punishment situation. *Learning and Motivation, 11,* 78–96.

Bolles, R. C., & Riley, A. L. (1973). Freezing as an avoidance response: Another look at the operant-respondent distinction. *Learning and Motivation, 4,* 268–275.

Bolles, R. C., Stokes, L. W., & Younger, M. S. (1966). Does CS termination reinforce avoidance behavior? *Journal of Comparative and Physiological Psychology, 62,* 201–207.

Bonardi, C. (1996). Transfer of occasion setting: The role of generalization decrement. *Animal Learning & Behavior, 24,* 277–289.

Bonardi, C., Rey, V., Richmond, M., & Hall, G. (1993). Acquired equivalence of cues in pigeon autoshaping: Effects of training with common consequences and with common antecedents. *Animal Learning & Behavior, 21,* 369–376.

Borovsky, D., & Rovee-Collier, C. (1990). Contextual constraints on memory retrieval at six months. *Child Development, 61,* 1569–1583.

Borszcz, G. S., Cranney, J., & Leaton, R. N. (1989). Influence of long-term sensitization on long-term habituation of the acoustic startle response in rats: Central gray lesions, preexposure, and extinction. *Journal of Experimental Psychology: Animal Behavior Processes, 15,* 54–64.

Bouton, M. E. (1984). Differential control by context in the inflation and reinstatement paradigms. *Journal of Experimental Psychology: Animal Behavior Processes, 10,* 56–74.

Bouton, M. E. (1986). Slow reacquisition following the extinction of conditioned suppression. *Learning and Motivation, 17,* 1–15.

Bouton, M. E. (1988). Context and ambiguity in the extinction of emotional learning: Implications for exposure therapy. *Behaviour Research and Therapy, 26,* 137–149.

Bouton, M. E. (1991). Context and retrieval in extinction and in other examples of interference in simple associative learning. In L. Dachowski & C. F. Flaherty (Eds.), *Current topics in animal learning* (pp. 25–53). Hillsdale, NJ: Erlbaum.

Bouton, M. E. (1993). Context, time, and memory retrieval in the interference paradigms of Pavlovian learning. *Psychological Bulletin, 114,* 80–99.

Bouton, M. E. (1994). Conditioning, remembering, and forgetting. *Journal of Experimental Psychology: Animal Behavior Processes, 20,* 219–231.

Bouton, M. E. (2001). Classical conditioning and clinical psychology. In N. J. Smelser & P. B. Baltes (Eds.), *Encyclopedia of the social and behavioral sciences.* (Vol. 3, pp. 1942–1945). Oxford: Elsevier Science.

Bouton, M. E., & Bolles, R. C. (1980). Conditioned fear assessed by freezing and by the suppression of three different baselines. *Animal Learning & Behavior, 8,* 429–434.

Bouton, M. E., Kenney, F. A., & Rosengard, C. (1990). State-dependent fear extinction with two benzodiazepine tranquilizers. *Behavioral Neuroscience, 104,* 44–55.

Bouton, M. E., & King, D. A. (1983). Contextual control of the extinction of conditioned fear: Tests for the associative value of the context. *Journal of Experimental Psychology: Animal Behavior Processes, 9,* 248–265.

Bouton, M. E., Mineka, S., & Barlow, D. H. (2001). A modern learning theory perspective on the etiology of panic disorder. *Psychological Review, 108,* 4–32.

Bouton, M. E., & Nelson, J. B. (1998). The role of context in classical conditioning: Some implications for behavior therapy. In O'Donohue, W. (Ed.), *Learning and behavior therapy* (pp. 59–84). Boston: Allyn and Bacon.

Bouton, M. E., & Peck, C. A. (1989). Context effects on conditioning, extinction, and reinstatement in an appetitive conditioning preparation. *Animal Learning & Behavior, 17,* 188–198.

Bouton, M. E., & Ricker, S. T. (1994). Renewal of extinguished responding in a second context. *Animal Learning & Behavior, 22,* 317–324.

Bouton, M. E., & Swartzentruber, D. (1986). Analysis of the associative and occasion-setting properties of contexts participating in a Pavlovian discrimination. *Journal of Experimental Psychology: Animal Behavior Processes, 12,* 333–350.

Bouton, M. E., & Swartzentruber, D. (1989). Slow reacquisition following extinction: Context, encoding, and retrieval mechanisms. *Journal of Experimental Psychology: Animal Behavior Processes, 15,* 43–53.

Bowe, C. A., Miller, J. D., & Green, L. (1987). Qualities and locations of stimuli and responses affecting discrimination learning of chinchillas (*Chinchilla laniger*) and pigeons (*Columbia livia*). *Journal of Comparative Psychology, 101,* 132–138.

Bradshaw, C. M., & Szabadi, E. (Eds.). (1997). *Time and behaviour: Psychological and neurobiological analyses.* Oxford: Elsevier Science.

Brakke, K. E., & Savage-Rumbaugh, E. S. (1995). The development of language skills in bonobo and chimpanzee. I. Comprehension. *Language & Communication, 15,* 121–148.

Branch, M. N., & Hackenberg, T. D. (1998). Humans are animals, too: Connecting animal research to human behavior and cognition. In W. O'Donohue (Ed.), *Learning and behavior therapy* (pp. 15–35). Boston: Allyn and Bacon.

Braveman, N. S., & Bronstein, P. (Eds.). (1985). *Annals of the New York Academy of Sciences: Vol. 443. Experimental assessments and clinical applications of conditioned food aversions.* New York: New York Academy of Sciences.

Breland, K., & Breland, M. (1961). The misbehavior of organisms. *American Psychologist, 16,* 681–684.

Brener, J., & Mitchell, S. (1989). Changes in energy expenditure and work during response acquisition in rats. *Journal of Experimental Psychology: Animal Behavior Processes, 15,* 166–175.

Brogden, W. J., Lipman, E. A., & Culler, E. (1938). The role of incentive in conditioning and extinction. *American Journal of Psychology, 51,* 109–117.

Brooks, D. C. (2000). Recent and remote extinction cues reduce spontaneous recovery. *Quarterly Journal of Experimental Psychology, 53B,* 25–58.

Brooks, D. C., & Bouton, M. E. (1993). A retrieval cue for extinction attenuates spontaneous recovery. *Journal of Experimental Psychology: Animal Behavior Processes, 19,* 77–89.

Brooks, D. C., Palmatier, M. I., Garcia, E. O., & Johnson, J. L. (1999). An extinction cue reduces spontaneous recovery of a conditioned taste aversion. *Animal Learning & Behavior, 27,* 77–88.

Brown, B. L., Hemmes, N. S., & de Vaca, S. C. (1992). Effects of intratrial stimulus change on fixed-interval performance: The roles of clock and memory processes. *Animal Learning & Behavior, 20,* 83–93.

Brown, B. L., Hemmes, N. S., & de Vaca, S. C. (1997). Timing of the CS-US interval by pigeons in trace and delay autoshaping. *Quarterly Journal of Experimental Psychology, 50B,* 40–53.

Brown, J. S. (1969). Factors affecting self-punitive behavior. In B. Campbell & R. M. Church (Eds.), *Punishment and aversive behavior.* New York: Appleton-Century-Crofts.

Brown, J. S., & Cunningham, C. L. (1981). The paradox of persisting self-punitive behavior. *Neuroscience & Biobehavioral Reviews, 5,* 343–354.

Brown, J. S., & Jacobs, A. (1949). The role of fear in the motivation and acquisition of responses. *Journal of Experimental Psychology, 39,* 747–759.

Brown, M. F., & Bing, M. N. (1997). In the dark: Spatial choice when access to spatial cues is restricted. *Animal Learning & Behavior, 25,* 21–30.

Brown, M. F., DiGello, E., Milewski, M., Wilson, M., & Kozak, M. (2000). Spatial pattern learning in rats: Conditional control by two patterns. *Animal Learning & Behavior, 28,* 278–287.

Brown, M. F., & Moore, J. A. (1997). In the dark II: Spatial choice when access to extrinsic spatial cues is eliminated. *Animal Learning & Behavior, 25,* 335–346.

Brown, M. F., & Terrinoni, M. (1996). Control of choice by the spatial configuration of goals. *Journal of Experimental Psychology: Animal Behavior Processes, 22,* 438–446.

Brown, M. F., Wheeler, E. A., & Riley, D. A. (1989). Evidence for a shift in the choice criterion of rats in a 12–arm radial maze. *Animal Learning & Behavior, 17,* 12–20.

Brown, P. L., & Jenkins, H. M. (1968). Auto-shaping the pigeon's key peck. *Journal of the Experimental Analysis of Behavior, 11,* 1–8.

Bruner, D., Gibbon, J., & Fairhurst, S. (1994). Choice between fixed and variable delays with different reward amounts. *Journal of Experimental Psychology: Animal Behavior Processes, 20,* 331–346.

Budzynski, C. A., & Bingman, V. P. (1999). Time-of-day discriminative learning in homing pigeons, *Columba livia. Animal Learning & Behavior, 27,* 295–302.

Burkhard, B., Rachlin, H., & Schrader, S. (1978). Reinforcement and punishment in a closed system. *Learning and Motivation, 9,* 392–410.

Burns, M., & Domjan, M. (1996). Sign tracking versus goal tracking in the sexual conditioning of male Japanese quail (*Coturnix japonica*). *Journal of Experimental Psychology: Animal Behavior Processes, 22,* 297–306.

Burns, M., & Domjan, M. (2000). Sign tracking in domesticated quail with one trial a day: Generality across CS and US parameters. *Animal Learning & Behavior, 28,* 109–119.

Burns, M., & Domjan, M. (2001). Topography of spatially directed conditioned responding: Effects of context and trial duration. *Journal of Experimental Psychology: Animal Behavior Processes, 27,* 269–278.

Cadieu, N., El Ghadraoui, L., & Cadieu, J. C. (2000). Egg-laying preference for ethanol involving learning has adaptive significance in *Drosophila melanogaster. Animal Learning & Behavior, 28,* 187–194.

Cameron, J., & Pierce, W. D. (1994). Reinforcement, reward, and intrinsic motivation: A meta-analysis. *Review of Educational Research, 64,* 363–423.

Camhi, J. M. (1984). *Neuroethology.* Sunderland, MA: Sinauer.

Camp, D. S., Raymond, G. A., & Church, R. M. (1967). Temporal relationship between response and punishment. *Journal of Experimental Psychology, 74,* 114–123.

Campbell, B. A., & Church, R. M. (Eds.). (1969). *Punishment and aversive behavior.* New York: Appleton-Century-Crofts.

Campbell, B. A., & Randall, P. K. (1976). The effect of reinstatement stimulus conditions on the maintenance of long-term memory. *Developmental Psychobiology, 9,* 325–333.

Cándido, A., Maldonado, A., & Vila, J. (1991). Effects of duration of feedback on signaled avoidance. *Animal Learning & Behavior, 19,* 81–87.

Capaldi, E. D., Hunter, M. J., & Lyn, S. A. (1997). Conditioning with taste as the CS in conditioned flavor preference learning. *Animal Learning & Behavior, 25,* 427–436.

Capaldi, E. J. (1967). A sequential hypothesis of instrumental learning. In K. W. Spence & J. T. Spence (Eds.), *The psychology of learning and motivation* (Vol. 1, pp. 67–156). New York: Academic Press.

Capaldi, E. J. (1971). Memory and learning: A sequential viewpoint. In W. K. Honig & P. H. R. James (Eds.), *Animal memory* (pp. 115–154). New York: Academic Press.

Capaldi, E. J., Alptekin, S., & Birmingham, K. M. (1996). Instrumental performance and time between reinforcements: Intimate relation to learning or memory retrieval? *Animal Learning & Behavior, 24,* 211–220.

Capaldi, E. J., Alptekin, S., Miller, D. J., & Barry, K. (1992). The role of instrumental responses in memory retrieval in a T-maze. *Quarterly Journal of Experimental Psychology, 45B,* 65–76.

Carew, T. J., Hawkins, R. D., & Kandel, E. R. (1983). Differential classical conditioning of a defensive withdrawal reflex in *Aplysia californica. Science, 219,* 397–400.

Carlton, J. L., Mitchell, K. G., Schachtman, T. R. (1996). Conditioned inhibition produced by extinction of a conditioned stimulus. *Learning and Motivation, 27,* 335–361.

Carr, D., & Blackman, D. E. (2001). Relations among equivalence, naming, and conflicting baseline control. *Journal of the Experimental Analysis of Behavior, 75,* 55–76.

Carr, D., Wilkinson, K. M., Blackman, D., & McIlvane, W. J. (2000). Equivalence classes in individuals with minimal verbal repertoires. *Journal of the Experimental Analysis of Behavior, 74,* 101–114.

Carrell, L. E., Cannon, D. S., Best, M. R., & Stone, M. J. (1986). Nausea and radiation-induced taste aversions in cancer patients. *Appetite, 7,* 203–208.

Carroll, M. E., Carmona, G. G., & May, S. A. (1991). Modifying drug-reinforced behavior by altering the economic conditions of the drug and nondrug reinforcer. *Journal of the Experimental Analysis of Behavior, 56,* 361–376.

Carroll, M. E., & Overmier, J. B. (2001). *Animal research and human health.* Washington, DC: American Psychological Association.

Carter, M. M., Hollon, S. D., Carson, R., & Shelton, R. C. (1995). Effects of a safe person on induced distress following a biological challenge in panic disorder with agoraphobics. *Journal of Abnormal Psychology, 104,* 156–163.

Caspy, T., & Lubow, R. E. (1981). Generality of US preexposure effects: Transfer from food to shock or shock to food with and without the same response requirements. *Animal Learning & Behavior, 9,* 524–532.

Catania, A. C. (1999). Thorndike's legacy: Learning, selection, and the law of effect. *Journal of the Experimental Analysis of Behavior, 72,* 425–428.

Cerutti, D., & Catania, A. C. (1997). Pigeons' preference for free choice: Number of keys versus key area. *Journal of the Experimental Analysis of Behavior, 68,* 349–356.

Chance, P. (1999). Thorndike's puzzle boxes and the origins of the experimental analysis of behavior. *Journal of the Experimental Analysis of Behavior, 72,* 433–440.

Charlop, M. H., Kurtz, P. F., & Casey, F. G. (1990). Using aberrant behaviors as reinforcers for autistic children. *Journal of Applied Behavior Analysis, 23,* 163–181.

Chelonis, J. J., Calton, J. L., Hart, J. A., & Schachtman, T. R. (1999). Attenuation of the renewal effect by extinction in multiple contexts. *Learning and Motivation, 30,* 1–14.

Chen, J.-S., & Amsel, A. (1980). Learned persistence at 11–12 but not at 10–11 days in infant rats. *Developmental Psychobiology, 13,* 481–491.

Chen, S., Swartz, K. B., & Terrace, H. S. (1997). Knowledge of the ordinal position of list items in rhesus monkeys. *Psychological Science, 8,* 80–86.

Cheng, K. (2000). How honeybees find a place: Lessons from a simple mind. *Animal Learning & Behavior, 28,* 1–15.

Cheng, K., & Spetch, M. L. (1995). Stimulus control in the use of landmarks by pigeons in a touch-screen task. *Journal of the Experimental Analysis of Behavior, 63,* 187–201.

Cheng, K., Spetch, M. L., & Johnson, M. (1997). Spatial peak shift and generalization in pigeons. *Journal of Experimental Psychology: Animal Behavior Processes, 23,* 469–481.

Cheng, K., & Westwood, R. (1993). Analysis of single trials in pigeons' timing performance. *Journal of Experimental Psychology: Animal Behavior Processes, 19,* 56–67.

Cheng, K., Westwood, R., & Crystal, J. D. (1993). Memory variance in the peak procedure of timing in pigeons. *Journal of Experimental Psychology: Animal Behavior Processes, 19,* 68–76.

Cherot, C., Jones, A., & Neuringer, A. (1996). Reinforced variability decreases with approach to reinforcers. *Journal of Experimental Psychology: Animal Behavior Processes, 22,* 497–508.

Chomsky, N. (1972). *Language and mind.* New York: Harcourt Brace Jovanovich.

Church, R. M. (1963). The varied effects of punishment on behavior. *Psychological Review, 70,* 369–402.

Church, R. M. (1969). Response suppression. In B. A. Campbell & R. M. Church (Eds.), *Punishment and aversive behavior* (pp. 111–156). New York: Appleton-Century-Crofts.

Church, R. M. (1978). The internal clock. In S. H. Hulse, H. Fowler, & W. K. Honig (Eds.), *Cognitive processes in animal behavior* (pp. 277–310). Hillsdale, NJ: Erlbaum.

Church, R. M., Getty, D. J., & Lerner, N. D. (1976). Duration discrimination by rats. *Journal of Experimental Psychology: Animal Behavior Processes, 2,* 303–312.

Church, R. M., Meck, W. H., & Gibbon, J. (1994). Application of scalar timing theory to individual trials. *Journal of Experimental Psychology: Animal Behavior Processes, 20,* 135–155.

Church, R. M., Miller, K. D., Meck, W. H., & Gibbon, J. (1991). Symmetrical and asymmetrical sources of variance in temporal generalization. *Animal Learning & Behavior, 19,* 207–214.

Cicala, G. A., & Owen, J. W. (1976). Warning signal termination and a feedback signal may not serve the same function. *Learning and Motivation, 7,* 356–367.

Clark, R. E., & Squire, L. R. (1998). Classical conditioning and brain systems: The role of awareness. *Science, 280,* 77–81.

Clark, R. E., & Squire, L. R., (1999). Human eyeblink classical conditioning: Effects of manipulating awareness of the stimulus contingencies. *Psychological Science, 10,* 14–18.

Clayton, N. S., & Dickinson, A. (1998). Episodic-like memory during cache recovery by scrub jays. *Nature, 395,* 272–274.

Clayton, N. S., & Dickinson, A. (1999a). Scrub jays (*Aphelocoma coerulescens*) remember the relative time of caching as well as the location and content of their caches. *Journal of Comparative Psychology, 113,* 403–416.

Clayton, N. S., & Dickinson, A. (1999b). Memory for the content of caches by scrub jays (*Aphelocoma coerulescens*). *Journal of Experimental Psychology: Animal Behavior Processes, 25,* 82–91.

Clayton, N. S., Yu, K. S., & Dickinson, A. (2001). Scrub jays (*Aphelocoma coerulescens*) form integrated memories of the multiple features of caching episodes. *Journal of Experimental Psychology: Animal Behavior Processes, 27,* 17–29.

Cleaveland, J. M. (1999). Interresponse-time sensitivity during discrete-trial and free-operant concurrent variable-interval schedules. *Journal of the Experimental Analysis of Behavior, 72,* 317–330.

Cleland, G. G., & Davey, G. C. L. (1982). The effects of satiation and reinforcer devaluation on signal centered behavior in the rat. *Learning and Motivation, 13,* 343–360.

Cleland, G. G., & Davey, G. C. L. (1983). Autoshaping in the rat: The effects of localizable visual and auditory signals for food. *Journal of the Experimental Analysis of Behavior, 40,* 47–56.

Clement, T. S., & Zentall, T. R. (2000a). Determinants of value transfer and contrast in simultaneous discriminations by pigeons. *Animal Learning & Behavior, 28,* 195–200.

Clement, T. S., & Zentall, T. R. (2000b). Development of a single-code/default coding strategy in pigeons. *Psychological Science, 11,* 261–264.

Cohen, L. B. (1988). An information processing view of infant cognitive development. In L. Weiskrantz (Ed.), *Thought without language* (pp. 211–228). Oxford: Oxford University Press.

Cohen, S. L. (1998). Behavioral momentum: The effect of the temporal separation of rates of reinforcement. *Journal of the Experimental Analysis of Behavior, 69,* 29–47.

Cole, M. R. (1994). Response-rate differences in variable-interval and variable-ratio schedules: An old problem revisited. *Journal of the Experimental Analysis of Behavior, 61,* 441–451.

Cole, M. R. (1999). Molar and molecular control in variable-interval and variable-ratio schedules. *Journal of the Experimental Analysis of Behavior, 71,* 319–328.

Cole, R. P., Barnet, R. C., & Miller, R. R. (1995a). Effect of relative stimulus validity: Learning or performance deficit? *Journal of Experimental Psychology: Animal Behavior Processes, 21,* 293–303.

Cole, R. P., Barnet, R. C., & Miller, R. R. (1995b). Temporal encoding in trace conditioning. *Animal Learning & Behavior, 23,* 144–153.

Cole, R. P., Barnet, R. C., & Miller, R. R. (1997). An evaluation of conditioned inhibition as defined by Rescorla's two-test strategy. *Learning and Motivation, 28,* 323–341.

Cole, R. P., & Miller, R. R. (1999). Conditioned excitation and conditioned inhibition acquired through backward conditioning. *Learning and Motivation, 30,* 129–156.

Cole, R. P., Oberling, P., & Miller, R. R. (1999). Recovery from one-trial overshadowing. *Psychonomic Bulletin & Review, 6,* 424–431.

Collier, G., & Johnson, D. F. (1997). Who is in charge? Animal vs. experimenter control. *Appetite, 29,* 159–180.

Collier, G., & Johnson, D. F. (2000). Sucrose intake as a function of its cost and the cost of chow. *Physiology & Behavior, 70,* 477–487.

Collier, G., Johnson, D. F., & Morgan, C. (1992). The magnitude-of-reinforcement function in closed and open economies. *Journal of the Experimental Analysis of Behavior, 57,* 81–89.

Colwill, R. M. (1994). Associative representations of instrumental contingencies. *The psychology of learning and motivation* (Vol. 31, pp. 1–72). San Diego: Academic Press.

Colwill, R. M., & Delameter, B. A. (1995). An associative analysis of instrumental biconditional discrimination learning. *Animal Learning & Behavior, 23,* 218–233.

Colwill, R. M., Goodrum, K., & Martin, A. (1997). Pavlovian appetitive discriminative conditioning in *Aplysia californica*. *Animal Learning & Behavior, 25,* 268–276.

Colwill, R. M., & Motzkin, D. K. (1994). Encoding of the unconditioned stimulus in Pavlovian conditioning. *Animal Learning & Behavior, 22,* 384–394.

Colwill, R. M., & Rescorla, R. A. (1986). Associative structures in instrumental learning. In G. H. Bower (Ed.), *The psychology of learning and motivation* (Vol. 20, pp. 55–104). Orlando, FL: Academic Press.

Colwill, R. M., & Rescorla, R. A. (1990). Evidence for the hierarchical structure of instrumental learning. *Animal Learning & Behavior, 18,* 71–82.

Commons, M. L., Herrnstein, R. J., Kosslyn, S. M., & Mumford, D. B. (Eds.). (1990). *Quantitative analyses of behavior: Vol. 8. Behavioral approaches to pattern recognition and concept formation.* Hillsdale, NJ: Erlbaum.

Commons, M. L., Herrnstein, R. J., & Rachlin, H. (Eds.). (1982). *Quantitative analyses of behavior: Vol. 2. Matching and maximizing accounts*. Cambridge, MA: Ballinger.

Conger, R., & Killeen, P. (1974). Use of concurrent operants in small group research. *Pacific Sociological Review, 17,* 399–416.

Conn, P. M., & Parker, J. (1998). Animal rights: Reaching the public. *Science, 282,* 1417.

Cook, M., & Mineka, S. (1990). Selective associations in the observational conditioning of fear in rhesus monkeys. *Journal of Experimental Psychology: Animal Behavior Processes, 16,* 372–389.

Cook, M., Mineka, S., & Trumble, D. (1987). The role of response-produced and exteroceptive feedback in the attenuation of fear over the course of avoidance learning. *Journal of Experimental Psychology: Animal Behavior Processes, 13,* 239–249.

Cook, R. G., Brown, M. F., & Riley, D. A. (1985). Flexible memory processing by rats: Use of prospective and retrospective information in the radial maze. *Journal of Experimental Psychology: Animal Behavior Processes, 11,* 453–469.

Coulter, X., Riccio, D. C., & Page, H. A. (1969). Effects of blocking an instrumental avoidance response: Facilitated extinction but persistence of "fear." *Journal of Comparative and Physiological Psychology, 68,* 377–381.

Couvillon, P. A., & Bitterman, M. E. (1992). A conventional conditioning analysis of "transitive inference" in pigeons. *Journal of Experimental Psychology: Animal Behavior Processes, 18,* 308–310.

Craig, W. (1918). Appetites and aversions as constituents of instinct. *Biological Bulletin, 34,* 91–107.

Craske, M. G., Glover, D., & DeCola, J. (1995). Predicted versus unpredicted panic attacks: Acute versus general distress. *Journal of Abnormal Psychology, 104,* 214–223.

Crespi, L. P. (1942). Quantitative variation in incentive and performance in the white rat. *American Journal of Psychology, 55,* 467–517.

Critchfield, T. S., & Lattal, K. A. (1993). Acquisition of a spatially defined operant with delayed reinforcement. *Journal of the Experimental Analysis of Behavior, 59,* 373–387.

Cronin, P. B. (1980). Reinstatement of post response stimuli prior to reward in delayed-reward discrimination learning by pigeons. *Animal Learning & Behavior, 8,* 352–358.

Crossman, E. K., Bonem, E. J., & Phelps, B. J. (1987). A comparison of response patterns on fixed-, variable-, and random-ratio schedules. *Journal of the Experimental Analysis of Behavior, 48,* 395–406.

Crown, E. D., & Grau, J. W. (2001). Preserving and restoring behavioral potential within the spinal cord using an instrumental training paradigm. *Journal of Neurophysiology, 86,* 845–855.

Cumming, W. W. (1999). A review of Geraldine Jonçich's *The sane positivist: A biography of Edward L. Thorndike. Journal of the Experimental Analysis of Behavior, 72,* 429–432.

Cunningham, C. L. (1979). Alcohol as a cue for extinction: State dependency produced by conditioned inhibition. *Animal Learning & Behavior, 7,* 45–52.

Cunningham, C. L. (1998). Drug conditioning and drug-seeking behavior. In W. O'Donohue (Ed.) *Learning and behavior therapy.* (pp. 518–544). Boston: Allyn and Bacon.

Cusato, B., & Domjan, M. (1998). Special efficacy of sexual conditioned stimuli that include species typical cues: Tests with a conditioned stimulus preexposure design. *Learning and Motivation, 29,* 152–167.

Cusato, B., & Domjan, M. (2000). Facilitation of appetitive conditioning with naturalistic conditioned stimuli: CS and US factors. *Animal Learning & Behavior, 28,* 247–256.

Cusato, B., & Domjan, M. (2001). *CS-US similarity effects in sexual conditioning.* Paper presented at meetings of the Psychonomic Society, Orlando, FL, November, 2001.

Dallery, J., McDowell, J. J., & Lancaster, J. S. (2000). Falsification of matching theory's account of single-alternative responding: Herrnstein's K varies with sucrose concentration. *Journal of the Experimental Analysis of Behavior, 73,* 23–43.

D'Amato, M. R. (1973). Delayed matching and short-term memory in monkeys. In G. H. Bower (Ed.), *The psychology of learning and motivation* (Vol. 7, pp. 227–269). New York: Academic Press.

D'Amato, M. R., & Colombo, M. (1985). Auditory matching-to-sample in monkeys (*Cebus apella*). *Animal Learning & Behavior, 13,* 375–382.

D'Amato, M. R., & Colombo, M. (1988). Representation of serial order in monkeys (*Cebus apella*). *Journal of Experimental Psychology: Animal Behavior Processes, 14,* 131–139.

D'Amato, M. R., & Colombo, M. (1989). Serial learning with wild card items by monkeys (*Cebus apella*): Implications for knowledge of ordinal position. *Journal of Comparative Psychology, 103,* 252–261.

D'Amato, M. R., & Colombo, M. (1990). The symbolic distance effect in monkeys (*Cebus apella*). *Animal Learning & Behavior, 18,* 133–140.

D'Amato, M. R., Fazzaro, J., & Etkin, M. (1968). Anticipatory responding and avoidance discrimination as factors in avoidance conditioning. *Journal of Comparative and Physiological Psychology, 77,* 41–47.

D'Amato, M. R., & Salmon, D. P. (1982). Tune discrimination in monkeys (*Cebus apella*) and in rats. *Animal Learning & Behavior, 10,* 126–134.

D'Amato, M. R., & Van Sant, P. (1988). The person concept in monkeys (*Cebus apella*). *Journal of Experimental Psychology: Animal Behavior Processes, 14,* 43–55.

Dardano, J. F., & Sauerbrunn, D. (1964). An aversive stimulus as a correlated block counter in FR performance. *Journal of the Experimental Analysis of Behavior, 7,* 37–43.

Darwin, C. (1897). *The descent of man and selection in relation to sex.* New York: Appleton-Century-Crofts.

Davey, G. C. L. (1995). Preparedness and phobias: Specific evolved associations or a generalized expectancy bias? *Behavioral and Brain Sciences, 18,* 289–325.

Davey, G. C. L., & Cleland, G. G. (1982). Topography of signal-centered behavior in the rat: Effects of deprivation state and reinforcer type. *Journal of the Experimental Analysis of Behavior, 38,* 291–304.

Davey, G. C. L., Phillips, S., & Cleland, G. G. (1981). The topography of signal-centered behaviour in the rat: The effects of solid and liquid food reinforcers. *Behaviour Analysis Letters, 1,* 331–337.

Davidson, T. L., Aparicio, J., & Rescorla, R. A. (1988). Transfer between Pavlovian facilitators and instrumental discriminative stimuli. *Animal Learning & Behavior, 16,* 285–291.

Davidson, T. L., Flynn, F. W., & Jarrard, L. E. (1992). Potency of food deprivation intensity cues as discriminative stimuli. *Journal of Experimental Psychology: Animal Behavior Processes, 18,* 174–181.

Davis, D. G., Staddon, J. E., Machado, A., & Palmer, R. G. (1993). The process of recurrent choice. *Psychological Review, 100,* 320–341.

Davis, E. R., & Platt, J. R. (1983). Contiguity and contingency in the acquisition and maintenance of an operant. *Learning and Motivation, 14,* 487–512.

Davis, H. (1968). Conditioned suppression: A survey of the literature. *Psychonomic Monograph Supplements, 2* (14, Whole No. 30), 283–291.

Davis, H. P., & Squire, L. R. (1984). Protein synthesis and memory: A review. *Psychological Bulletin, 96,* 518–559.

Davis, M. (1974). Sensitization of the rat startle response by noise. *Journal of Comparative and Physiological Psychology, 87,* 571–581.

Davis, M. (1989). Sensitization of the acoustic startle reflex by footshock. *Behavioral Neuroscience, 103,* 495–503.

Davis, M., Hitchcock, J. M., & Rosen, J. B. (1987). Anxiety and the amygdala: Pharmacological and anatomical analysis of the fear-potentiated startle paradigm. In G. H. Bower (Ed.), *The psychology of learning and motivation* (Vol. 21, pp. 263–304). Orlando, FL: Academic Press.

Davis, R. L. (1996). Physiology and biochemistry of *Drosophila* learning mutants. *American Physiological Society, 76,* 299–317.

Davison, M. (1991). Choice, changeover, and travel: A quantitative model. *Journal of the Experimental Analysis of Behavior, 55,* 47–61.

Davison, M., & Jones, B. M. (1995). A quantitative analysis of extreme choice. *Journal of the Experimental Analysis of Behavior, 64,* 147–162.

Davison, M., & McCarthy, D. (1988). *The matching law: A research review.* Hillsdale, NJ: Erlbaum.

Davison, M., & Nevin, J. A. (1999). Stimuli, reinforcers, and behavior: An integration. *Journal of the Experimental Analysis of Behavior, 71,* 439–482.

Dawson, G. R., & Dickinson, A. (1990). Performance on ratio and interval schedules with matched reinforcement rates. *Quarterly Journal of Experimental Psychology, 42B,* 225–239.

Dean, S. J., & Pittman, C. M. (1991). Self-punitive behavior: A revised analysis. In M. R. Denny (Ed.), *Fear, avoidance and phobias* (pp. 259–284). Hillsdale, NJ: Erlbaum.

DeCarlo, L. T. (1985). Matching and maximizing with variable-time schedules. *Journal of the Experimental Analysis of Behavior, 43,* 75–81.

DeCola, J. P., & Rosellini, R. A. (1990). Unpredictable/uncontrollable stress proactively interferes with appetitive Pavlovian conditioning. *Learning and Motivation, 21,* 137–152.

DeCola, J. P., Rosellini, R. A., & Warren, D. A. (1988). A dissociation of the effects of control and prediction. *Learning and Motivation, 19,* 269–282.

DeGrandpre, R. J., Bickel, W. K., Rizvi, S. A. T., & Hughes, J. R. (1993). Effect of income on drug choice in humans. *Journal of the Experimental Analysis of Behavior, 59,* 483–500.

Deich, J. D., Allan, R. W., & Zeigler, H. P. (1988). Conjunctive differentiation of gape during food-reinforced key pecking in the pigeon. *Animal Learning & Behavior, 16,* 268–276.

DeKeyne, A., & Deweer, B. (1990). Interaction between conflicting memories in the rat: Contextual pretest cuing reverses control of behavior by testing context. *Animal Learning & Behavior, 18,* 1–12.

Delameter, A. R. (1996). Effects of several extinction treatments upon the integrity of Pavlovian stimulus-outcome associations. *Animal Learning & Behavior, 24,* 437–449.

Delprato, D. J. (1969). Extinction of one-way avoidance and delayed warning signal termination. *Journal of Experimental Psychology, 80,* 192–193.

DeMarse, T. B., & Urcuioli, P. J. (1993). Enhancement of matching acquisition by differential comparison-outcome associations. *Journal of Experimental Psychology: Animal Behavior Processes, 19,* 317–326.

Denniston, J. C., Blaisdell, A. P., & Miller, R. R. (1998). Temporal coding affects transfer of serial and simultaneous inhibitors. *Animal Learning & Behavior, 26,* 336–350.

Denniston, J. C., Cole, R. P., & Miller, R. R. (1998). The role of temporal relationships in the transfer of conditioned inhibition. *Journal of Experimental Psychology: Animal Behavior Processes, 24,* 200–214.

Denniston, J. C., Savastano, H. I., & Miller, R. R. (2001). The extended comparator hypothesis: Learning by contiguity, responding by relative strength. In R. R. Mowrer & S. B. Klein (Eds.), *Handbook of contemporary learning theories* (pp. 65–117). Mahwah, NJ: Erlbaum.

deVaca, S. C., Brown, B. L., & Hemmes, N. S. (1994). Internal clock and memory processes in animal timing. *Journal of Experimental Psychology: Animal Behavior Processes, 20,* 184–198.

Devenport, L. D. (1998). Spontaneous recovery without interference: Why remembering is adaptive. *Animal Learning & Behavior, 26,* 172–181.

deVilliers, P. A. (1974). The law of effect and avoidance: A quantitative relationship between response rate and shock-frequency reduction. *Journal of the Experimental Analysis of Behavior, 21,* 223–235.

DeVito, P. L., & Fowler, H. (1987). Enhancement of conditioned inhibition via an extinction treatment. *Animal Learning & Behavior, 15,* 448–454.

Dewsbury, D. A. (1998). Celebrating E. L. Thorndike a century after *Animal intelligence. American Psychologist, 53,* 1121–1124.

Dickinson, A. (2001). Causal learning: Association versus computation. *Current Directions in Psychological Science, 10,* 127–132.

Dickinson, A., & Balleine, B. (1994). Motivational control of goal-directed behavior. *Animal Learning & Behavior, 22,* 1–18.

Dickinson, A., & Dearing, M. F. (1979). Appetitive aversive interactions and inhibitory processes. In A. Dickinson & R. A. Boakes (Eds.), *Mechanisms of learning and motivation* (pp. 203–231). Hillsdale, NJ: Erlbaum.

Dickinson, A., Nicholas, D. J., & Macintosh, N. J. (1983). A re-examination of one-trial blocking in conditioned suppression. *Quarterly Journal of Experimental Psychology, 35,* 67–79.

Dickinson, A., Watt, A., & Griffiths, W. J. H. (1992). Free-operant acquisition with delayed reinforcement. *The Quarterly Journal of Experimental Psychology, 45B,* 241–258.

Dickinson, A., Watt, A., & Varga, Z. I. (1996). Context conditioning and free-operant acquisition under delayed reinforcement. *Quarterly Journal of Experimental Psychology, 49B,* 97–110.

Didden, R., Prinsen, H., & Sigafoos, J. (2000). The blocking effect of pictorial prompts on sight-word reading. *Journal of Applied Behavior Analysis, 33,* 317–320.

Dinsmoor, J. A. (1952). A discrimination based on punishment. *Quarterly Journal of Experimental Psychology, 4,* 27–45.

Dinsmoor, J. A. (1954). Punishment: I. The avoidance hypothesis. *Psychological Review, 61,* 34–46.

Dinsmoor, J. A. (1962). Variable-interval escape from stimuli accompanied by shocks. *Journal of the Experimental Analysis of Behavior, 5,* 41–48.

Dinsmoor, J. A. (1977). Escape, avoidance, punishment: Where do we stand? *Journal of the Experimental Analysis of Behavior, 28,* 83–95.

Dinsmoor, J. A. (1995). Stimulus control: Part I. *The Behavior Analyst, 18,* 51–68.

Dinsmoor, J. A. (1998). Punishment. In W. O'Donohue (Ed.), *Learning and behavior therapy* (pp. 188–204). Boston: Allyn and Bacon.

Dinsmoor, J. A. (2001a). Still no evidence for temporally extended shock-frequency reduction as a reinforcer. *Journal of the Experimental Analysis of Behavior, 75,* 367–378.

Dinsmoor, J. A. (2001b). Stimuli inevitably generated by behavior that avoids electric shock are inherently reinforcing. *Journal*

of the Experimental Analysis of Behavior, 75, 311–333.

Dinsmoor, J. A., & Sears, G. W. (1973). Control of avoidance by a response-produced stimulus. *Learning and Motivation, 4,* 284–293.

Dittrich, W. H., Lea, S. E. G., Barrett, J., & Gurr, P. R. (1998). Categorization of natural movement by pigeons: Visual concept discrimination and biological motion. *Journal of the Experimental Analysis of Behavior, 70,* 281–299.

Dobrzecka, C., Szwejkowska, G., & Konorski, J. (1966). Qualitative versus directional cues in two forms of differentiation. *Science, 153,* 87–89.

Dollard, J., & Miller, N. E. (1950). *Personality and psychotherapy.* New York: McGraw-Hill.

Dollard, J., Miller, N. E., Doob, L. W., Mowrer, O. H., & Sears, R. R. (1939). *Frustration and aggression.* New Haven, CT: Yale University Press.

Domjan, M. (1980). Ingestional aversion learning: Unique and general processes. In J. S. Rosenblatt, R. A. Hinde, C. Beer, & M. Busnel (Eds.), *Advances in the study of behavior* (Vol. 11, pp. 275–336). New York: Academic Press.

Domjan, M. (1983). Biological constraints on instrumental and classical conditioning: Implications for general process theory. In G. H. Bower (Ed.), *The psychology of learning and motivation* (Vol. 17, pp. 215–277). New York: Academic Press.

Domjan, M. (1987). Animal learning comes of age. *American Psychologist, 42,* 556–564.

Domjan, M. (1993). *The principles of learning and behavior* (3rd ed.). Pacific Grove, CA: Brooks/Cole.

Domjan, M. (1997). Behavior systems and the demise of equipotentiality: Historical antecedents and evidence from sexual conditioning. In M. E. Bouton & M. S. Fanselow (Eds.), *Learning, motivation, and cognition* (pp. 31–51). Washington, DC: American Psychological Association.

Domjan, M. (1998). Going wild in the laboratory: Learning about species typical cues. In D. L. Medin (Ed.), *The psychology of learning and motivation* (Vol. 38, pp. 155–186). San Diego: Academic Press.

Domjan, M. (2000). Learning: Overview. In A. E. Kazdin (Ed.), *Encyclopedia of psychology* (Vol. 5, pp. 1–3). New York: Oxford University Press.

Domjan, M., Blesbois, E., & Williams, J. (1998). The adaptive significance of sexual conditioning: Pavlovian control of sperm release. *Psychological Science, 9,* 411–415.

Domjan, M., & Burkhard, B. (1982). *The principles of learning and behavior.* Pacific Grove, CA: Brooks/Cole.

Domjan, M., & Burkhard, B. (1986). *The principles of learning and behavior* (2nd ed.). Pacific Grove, CA: Brooks/Cole.

Domjan, M., Cusato, B., & Villarreal, R. (2000). Pavlovian feed-forward mechanisms in the control of social behavior. *Behavioral and Brain Sciences, 23,* 235–249.

Domjan, M., & Hollis, K. L. (1988). Reproductive behavior: A potential model system for adaptive specializations in learning. In R. C. Bolles & M. D. Beecher (Eds.), *Evolution and learning* (pp. 213–237). Hillsdale, NJ: Erlbaum.

Domjan, M., & Holloway, K. S. (1998). Sexual learning. In G. Greenberg & M. M. Haraway (Eds.), *Comparative psychology: A handbook* (pp. 602–613). New York: Garland.

Domjan, M., & Mahometa, M. (2001). Learning and fertilization success in the domesticated quail. Paper presented at meetings of the Winter Conference on Learning and Behavior, Winter Park, CO, January, 2001.

Donahoe, J. W., & Burgos, J. E. (1999). Timing without a timer. *Journal of the Experimental Analysis of Behavior, 72,* 257–263.

Donahoe, J. W., & Burgos, J. E. (2000). Behavioral analysis and reevaluation. *Journal of the Experimental Analysis of Behavior, 74,* 331–346.

Donahoe, J. W., Palmer, D. C., & Burgos, J. E. (1997). The S-R issue: Its status in behavior analysis and in Donahoe and Palmer's *Learning and complex behavior. Journal of the Experimental Analysis of Behavior, 67,* 193–211.

Dorrance, B. R., Kaiser, D. H., & Zentall, T. R. (1998). Value transfer in a simultaneous discrimination by pigeons: The value of the S+ is not specific to the simultaneous discrimination context. *Animal Learning & Behavior, 26,* 257–263.

Dougherty, D. M., & Lewis, P. (1991). Stimulus generalization, discrimination learning, and peak shift in horses. *Journal of the Experimental Analysis of Behavior, 56,* 97–104.

Dragoi, V., & Staddon, J. E. R. (1999). The dynamics of operant conditioning. *Psychological Review, 106,* 20–61.

Dreyfus, L. R., DePorto-Callan, D., & Pesillo, S. A. (1993). Changeover contingencies and choice on concurrent schedules. *Animal Learning & Behavior, 21,* 203–213.

Dube, W. V., & McIlvane, W. J. (2001). Behavioral momentum in computer-presented discriminations in individuals with severe mental retardation. *Journal of the Experimental Analysis of Behavior, 75,* 15–23.

Ducharme, M. J., & Santi, A. (1993). Alterations in the memory code for temporal events induced by differential outcome expectancies in pigeons. *Animal Learning & Behavior, 21,* 73–81.

Dudai, Y. (1989). *The neurobiology of memory: Concepts, findings, trends.* Oxford: Oxford University Press.

Dudley, R. T., & Papini, M. R. (1995). Pavlovian performance of rats following unexpected reward omissions. *Learning and Motivation, 26,* 63–82.

Dudley, R. T., & Papini, M. R. (1997). Amsel's frustration effect: A Pavlovian replication with control for frequency and distribution of rewards. *Physiology & Behavior, 61,* 627–629.

Dugdale, N., & Lowe, C. F. (2000). Testing for symmetry in the conditional discriminations of language-trained chimanzees. *Journal of the Experimental Analysis of Behavior, 73,* 5–22.

Durkin, M., Prescott, L., Furchtgott, E., & Cantor, J. (1993). Concomitant eyeblink and heart rate classical conditioning in young, middle-aged, and elderly human subjects. *Psychology and Aging, 8,* 571–581.

Dweck, C. S., & Wagner, A. R. (1970). Situational cues and correlation between conditioned stimulus and unconditioned stimulus as determinants of the conditioned emotional response. *Psychonomic Science, 18,* 145–147.

Dworkin, B. R. (1993). *Learning and physiological regulation.* Chicago and London: University of Chicago Press.

Edgerton, V. R., Roy, R. R., & de Leon, R. D. (2001). Neural Darwinism in the mammalian spinal cord. In M. M. Patterson & J. W. Grau (Eds.), *Spinal cord plasticity: Alterations in reflex function* (pp. 185–206). Boston: Kluwer Academic Publishers.

Edhouse, W. V., & White, K. G. (1988a). Cumulative proactive interference in animal memory. *Animal Learning & Behavior, 16,* 461–467.

Edhouse, W. V., & White, K. G. (1988b). Sources of proactive interference in animal memory. *Journal of Experimental Psychology: Animal Behavior Processes, 14,* 56–70.

Ehrman, R. N., Robbins, S. J., Childress, A. R., & O'Brien, C. P. (1992). Conditioned responses to cocaine-related stimuli in cocaine abuse patients. *Psychopharmacology, 107,* 523–529.

Eisenberger, R., & Adornetto, M. (1986). Generalized self-control of delay and effort. *Journal of Personality and Social Psychology, 51,* 1020–1031.

Eisenberger, R., & Cameron, J. (1996). Detrimental effects of reward: Reality or myth? *American Psychologist, 51,* 1153–1166.

Eisenberger, R., Karpman, M., & Trattner, J. (1967). What is the necessary and sufficient condition for reinforcement in the contingency situation? *Journal of Experimental Psychology, 74,* 342–350.

Elliffe, D., & Alsop, B. (1996). Concurrent choice: Effects of overall reinforcer rate and the temporal distribution of reinforcers. *Journal of the Experimental Analysis of Behavior, 65,* 445–463.

Ellins, S. R., Cramer, R. E., & Martin, G. C. (1982). Discrimination reversal learning in newts. *Animal Learning & Behavior, 10,* 301–304.

Ellison, G. D. (1964). Differential salivary conditioning to traces. *Journal of Comparative and Physiological Psychology, 57,* 373–380.

Emmerton, J. (1998). Numerosity differences and effects of stimulus density on pigeon's discrimination performance. *Animal Learning & Behavior, 26,* 243–256.

English, J. A., Rowlett, J. K., & Woolverton, W. L. (1995). Unit-price analysis of opioid consumption by monkeys responding under a progressive-ratio schedule of drug injection. *Journal of the Experimental Analysis of Behavior, 64,* 361–371.

Epstein, L. H., Rodefer, J. S., Wisniewski, L., & Caggiula, A. R. (1992). *Physiology & Behavior, 51,* 945–950.

Escobar, M., Matute, H., & Miller, R. R. (2001). Cues trained apart compete for behavioral control in rats: Convergence with the associative interference literature. *Journal of Experimental Psychology: General, 130,* 97–115.

Estes, W. K. (1943). Discriminative conditioning: I. A discriminative property of conditioned anticipation. *Journal of Experimental Psychology, 32,* 150–155.

Estes, W. K. (1944). An experimental study of punishment. *Psychological Monographs, 57* (3, Whole No. 263).

Estes, W. K. (1948). Discriminative conditioning: II. Effects of a Pavlovian conditioned stimulus upon a subsequently established operant response. *Journal of Experimental Psychology, 38,* 173–177.

Estes, W. K. (1969). Outline of a theory of punishment. In B. A. Campbell & R. M. Church (Eds.), *Punishment and aversive behavior* (pp. 57–82). New York: Appleton-Century-Crofts.

Estes, W. K., & Skinner, B. F. (1941). Some quantitative properties of anxiety. *Journal of Experimental Psychology, 29,* 390–400.

Fagen, J. W., & Ohr, P. S. (2001). Learning and memory in infancy: Habituation, instrumental conditioning, and expectancy information. In L. T. Singer & P. S. Zeskind (Eds.), *Biobehavioral assessment of the infant* (pp. 233–273). New York: Guilford.

Fagen, J. W., & Rovee-Collier, C. (1983). Memory retrieval: A time-locked process in infancy. *Science, 222,* 1349–1351.

Falls, W. A. (1998). Extinction: A review of theory and the evidence suggesting that memories are not erased with nonreinforcement. In W. O'Donohue (Ed.),

Learning and behavior therapy (pp. 205–229). Boston: Allyn and Bacon.

Falls, W. A., & Davis, M. (1994). Fear-potentiated startle using three conditioned stimulus modalities. *Animal Learning & Behavior, 22,* 379–383.

Fanselow, M. S. (1989). The adaptive function of conditioned defensive behavior: An ecological approach to Pavlovian stimulus-substitution theory. In R. J. Blanchard, P. F. Brain, D. C. Blanchard, & S. Parmigiani (Eds.), *Ethoexperimental approaches to the study of behavior* (NATO ASI Series D, Vol. 48, pp. 151–166). Boston: Kluver Academic Publishers.

Fanselow, M. S. (1991). Analgesia as a response to aversive Pavlovian conditioned stimuli: Cognitive and emotional mediators. In M. R. Denny (Ed.), *Fear, avoidance and phobias* (pp. 61–86). Hillsdale, NJ: Erlbaum.

Fanselow, M. S. (1997). Species-specific defense reactions: Retrospect and prospect. In M. E. Bouton & M. S. Fanselow (Eds.), *Learning, motivation, and cognition.* (pp. 321–341). Washington, DC: American Psychological Association.

Fanselow, M. S. (1999). Learning theory and neuropsychology: Configuring their disparate elements in the hippocampus. *Journal of Experimental Psychology: Animal Behavior Processes, 25,* 275–283.

Fanselow, M. S., & Lester, L. S. (1988). A functional behavioristic approach to aversively motivated behavior: Predatory imminence as a determinant of the topography of defensive behavior. In R. C. Bolles & M. D. Beecher (Eds.), *Evolution and learning* (pp. 185–212). Hillsdale, NJ: Erlbaum.

Fanselow, M. S., Lester, L. S., & Helmstetter, F. J. (1988). Changes in feeding and foraging patterns as an antipredator defensive strategy: A laboratory simulation using aversive stimulation in a closed economy. *Journal of the Experimental Analysis of Behavior, 50,* 361–374.

Farley, J., & Alkon, D. L. (1980). Neural organization predicts stimulus specificity for a retained associative behavioral change. *Science, 210,* 1373–1375.

Fath, S. J., Fields, L., Malott, M. K., & Grossett, D. (1983). Response rate, latency, and resistance to change. *Journal*

of the Experimental Analysis of Behavior, 39, 267–274.

Feldman, D. T., & Gordon, W. C. (1979). The alleviation of short-term retention decrements with reactivation. *Learning and Motivation, 10,* 198–210.

Felton, M., & Lyon, D. O. (1966). The post-reinforcement pause. Journal of the *Experimental Analysis of Behavior, 9,* 131–134.

Fendt, M., & Fanselow, M. S. (1999). The neuroanatomical and neurochemical basis of conditioned fear. *Neuroscience and Biobehavioral Reviews, 23,* 743–760.

Ferguson, E., & Job, R. F. S. (1997). Uncontrollable water deliveries and subsequent finickiness. *Animal Learning & Behavior, 25,* 62–67.

Ferrara, A., Lejeune, H., & Wearden, J. H. (1997). Changing sensitivity to duration in human scalar timing: An experiment, a review, and some possible explanations. *Quarterly Journal of Experimental Psychology, 50B,* 227–237.

Ferster, C. B., & Skinner, B. F. (1957). *Schedules of reinforcement.* New York: Appleton-Century-Crofts.

Fetterman, J. G. (1995). The psychophysics of remembered duration. *Animal Learning & Behavior, 23,* 49–62.

Fetterman, J. G. (1996). Dimensions of stimulus complexity. *Journal of Experimental Psychology: Animal Behavior Processes, 22,* 3–18.

Fetterman, J. G., Killeen, P. R., & Hall, S. (1998). Watching the clock. *Behavioural Processes, 44,* 222–224.

Field, D. P., Tonneau, F., Ahearn, W., & Hineline, P. N. (1996). Preference between variable-ratio and fixed-ratio schedules: Local and extended relations. *Journal of the Experimental Analysis of Behavior, 66,* 283–295.

Fiori, L. M., Barnet, R. C., & Miller, R. R. (1994). Renewal of Pavlovian conditioned inhibition. *Animal Learning & Behavior, 22,* 47–52.

FitzGerald, R. E., Isler, R., Rosenberg, E., Oettinger, R., & Battig, K. (1985). Maze patrolling by rats with and without food reward. *Animal Learning & Behavior, 13,* 451–462.

Flaherty, C. F., Grigson, P. S., & Lind, S. (1990). Chlordiazepoxide and the moderation of the initial response to reward reduction. *Quarterly Journal of Experimental Psychology. B, Comparative & Physiological Psychology, 42,* (B-1) 87–105.

Flaherty, C. F. (1982). Incentive contrast: A review of behavioral changes following shifts in reward. *Animal Learning & Behavior, 10*(4), 409–440.

Flaherty, C. F. (1991). Incentive contrast and selected animal models of anxiety. In L. Dachowski & C. F. Flaherty (Eds.) *Current topics in animal learning: Brain, emotion, and cognition* (pp. 207–243). Hillsdale, NJ: Erlbaum.

Flaherty, C. F. (1996). *Incentive relativity.* New York: Cambridge University Press.

Flaherty, C. F., Greenwood, A., Martin, J., & Leszczuk, M. (1998). Relationship of negative contrast to animal models of fear and anxiety. *Animal Learning & Behavior, 26,* 397–407.

Flaten, M. A., & Blumenthal, T. D. (1999). Caffeine-associated stimuli elicit conditioned responses: An experimental model of the placebo effect. *Psychopharmacology, 145,* 105–112.

Flexner, J. B., Flexner, L. B., & Stellar, E. (1963). Memory in mice as affected by intracerebral puromycin. *Science, 141,* 57–59.

Foa, E. B., Zinbarg, R., & Rothbaum, B. O. (1992). Uncontrollability and unpredictability in post-traumatic stress disorder: An animal model. *Psychological Review, 112,* 218–238.

Foltin, R. W. (1991). An economic analysis of "demand" for food in baboons. *Journal of the Experimental Analysis of Behavior, 56,* 445–454.

Foltin, R. W. (1994). Does package size matter? A unit-price analysis of "demand" for food in baboons. *Journal of the Experimental Analysis of Behavior, 62,* 293–306.

Foltin, R. W. (1997). Food and amphetamine self-administration by baboons: Effects of alternatives. *Journal of the Experimental Analysis of Behavior, 68,* 47–66.

Foltin, R. W. (1999). Food and cocaine self-administration by baboons: Effects of alternatives. *Journal of the Experimental Analysis of Behavior, 72,* 215–234.

Foree, D. D., & LoLordo, V. M. (1973). Attention in the pigeon: The differential effects of food-getting vs. shock avoidance procedures. *Journal of Comparative and Physiological Psychology, 85,* 551–558.

Forestell, P. H., & Herman, L. M. (1988). Delayed matching of visual materials by a bottlenosed dolphin aided by auditory symbols. *Animal Learning & Behavior, 16,* 137–146.

Forzano, L. B., & Corry, R. J. (1998). Self-control and impusiveness in adult human females: Effects of visual food cues. *Learning and Motivation, 29,* 184–199.

Foster, T. M., Blackman, K. A., & Temple, W. (1997). Open versus closed economies: Performance of domestic hens under fixed-ratio schedules. *Journal of the Experimental Analysis of Behavior, 67,* 67–89.

Foster, T. M., Temple, W., Robertson, B., Nair, V., & Poling, A. (1996). Concurrent-schedule performance in dairy cows: Persistent undermatching. *Journal of the Experimental Analysis of Behavior, 65,* 57–80.

Fowler, H., Kleiman, M., & Lysle, D. (1985). Factors controlling the acquisition and extinction of conditioned inhibition suggest a "slave" process. In R. R. Miller & N. E. Spear (Eds.), *Information processing in animals: Conditioned inhibition* (pp. 113–150). Hillsdale, NJ: Erlbaum.

Fowler, H., Lysle, D. T., & DeVito, P. L. (1991). Conditioned excitation and conditioned inhibition of fear: Asymmetrical processes as evident in extinction. In M. R. Denny (Ed.), *Fear, avoidance and phobias* (pp. 317–362). Hillsdale, NJ: Erlbaum.

Foxx, R. M., & Azrin, N. H. (1973). The elimination of autistic self-stimulatory behavior by overcorrection. *Journal of Applied Behavioral Analysis, 6,* 1–14.

France, K. G., & Hudson, S. M. (1990). Behavior management of infant sleep disturbance. *Journal of Applied Behavior Analysis, 23,* 91–98.

Frankel, F. D. (1975). The role of response-punishment contingency in the suppression of a positively reinforced operant. *Learning and Motivation, 6,* 385–403.

Frankland, P. W., & Yeomans, J. S. (1995). Fear-potentiated startle and electrically evoked startle mediated by synapses in rostrolateral midbrain. *Behavioral Neuroscience, 109,* 669–680.

Friedman, B. X., Blaisdell, A. P., Escobar, M., & Miller, R. R. (1998). Comparator mechanisms and conditioned inhibition: Conditioned stimulus preexposure disrupts Pavlovian conditioned inhibition but not explicitly unpaired inhibition. *Journal of Experimental Psychology: Animal Behavior Processes, 24,* 453–466.

Gaffan, E. A., & Davies, J. (1981). The role of exploration in win-shift and win-stay performance on a radial maze. *Learning and Motivation, 12,* 282–299.

Galbicka, G. (1988). Differentiating the behavior of organisms. *Journal of the Experimental Analysis of Behavior, 50,* 343–354.

Gallistel, C. R. (1990). *The organization of behavior.* Cambridge, MA: MIT Press.

Gallistel, C. R. (1999). Can a decay process explain the timing of conditioned responses? *Journal of the Experimental Analysis of Behavior, 72,* 264–272.

Gallistel, C. R., & Gibbon, J. (2000). Time, rate, and conditioning. *Psychological Review, 107,* 289–344.

Gallistel, C. R., & Gibbon, J. (2001). Computational versus associative models of simple conditioning. *Current Directions in Psychological Science, 10,* 146–150.

Galluccio, L., & Rovee-Collier, C. (1999). Reinstatement effects on retention at 3 months of age. *Learning and Motivation, 30,* 296–316.

Gallup, G. G., Jr., & Suarez, S. D. (1985). Alternatives to the use of animals in psychological research. *American Psychologist, 40,* 1104–1111.

Gamzu, E. R., & Williams, D. R. (1971). Classical conditioning of a complex skeletal act. *Science, 171,* 923–925.

Gamzu, E. R., & Williams, D. R. (1973). Associative factors underlying the pigeon's key pecking in autoshaping procedures. *Journal of the Experimental Analysis of Behavior, 19,* 225–232.

Gantt, W. H. (1966). Conditional or conditioned, reflex or response? *Conditioned Reflex, 1,* 69–74.

Garb, J. J., & Stunkard, A. J. (1974). Taste aversions in man. *American Journal of Psychiatry, 131,* 1204–1207.

Garber, J., & Seligman, M. E. P. (Eds.). (1980). *Human helplessness: Theory and application.* New York: Academic Press.

Garcia, J., Ervin, F. R., & Koelling, R. A. (1966). Learning with prolonged delay of reinforcement. *Psychonomic Science, 5,* 121–122.

Garcia, J., & Koelling, R. A. (1966). Relation of cue to consequence in avoidance learning. *Psychonomic Science, 4,* 123–124.

Gardner, E. T., & Lewis, P. (1976). Negative reinforcement with shock-frequency increase. *Journal of the Experimental Analysis of Behavior, 25,* 3–14.

Gardner, R. A., & Gardner, B. T. (1969). Teaching sign language to a chimpanzee. *Science, 165,* 664–672.

Gardner, R. A., & Gardner, B. T. (1975). Early signs of language in child and chimpanzee. *Science, 187,* 752–753.

Gardner, R. A., & Gardner, B. T. (1978). Comparative psychology and language acquisition. *Annals of the New York Academy of Science, 309,* 37–76.

Gardner, R. A., & Gardner, B. T. (1984). A vocabulary test for chimpanzees (*Pan troglodytes*). *Journal of Comparative Psychology, 98,* 381–404.

Gardner, R. A., Gardner, B. T., & Van Cantfort, T. E. (Eds.). (1989). *Teaching sign language to chimpanzees.* Albany: State University of New York Press.

Gawley, D. J., Timberlake, W., & Lucas, G. A. (1987). System-specific differences in behavior regulation: Overrunning and underdrinking in molar nondepriving schedules. *Journal of Experimental Psychology: Animal Behavior Processes, 13,* 354–365.

Gemberling, G. A., & Domjan, M. (1982). Selective association in one-day-old rats: Taste-toxicosis and textureshock aversion learning. *Journal of Comparative and Physiological Psychology, 96,* 105–113.

George, J. T., & Hopkins, B. L. (1989). Multiple effects of performance-contingent pay for waitpersons. *Journal of Applied Behavior Analysis, 22,* 131–141.

Gershoff, E. T. (2002). Parental corporal punishment and associated child behaviors and experiences: A meta-analytic and theoretical review. *Psychological Bulletin,* in press.

Gewirtz, J. C., Brandon, S. E., & Wagner, A. R. (1998). Modulation of the acquisition of the rabbit eyeblink conditioned response by conditioned contextual stimuli. *Journal of Experimental Psychology: Animal Behavior Processes, 24,* 106–117.

Gharib, A., Derby, S., & Roberts, S. (2001). Timing and the control of variation. *Journal of Experimental Psychology: Animal Behavior Processes, 27,* 165–178.

Gibbon, J. (1999). Multiple time scales is well named. *Journal of the Experimental Analysis of Behavior, 72,* 272–275.

Gibbon, J., & Allan, L. (Eds.). (1984). Time and time perception. *Annals of the New York Academy of Sciences, 423.*

Gibbon, J., & Balsam, P. (1981). Spreading association in time. In C. M. Locurto, H. S. Terrace, & J. Gibbon (Eds.), *Autoshaping and conditioning theory* (pp. 219–253). New York: Academic Press.

Gibbon, J., & Church, R. M. (1984). Sources of variance in an information processing theory of timing. In H. L. Roitblat, T. G. Bever, & H. S. Terrace (Eds.), *Animal cognition.* Hillsdale, NJ: Erlbaum.

Gibbon, J., & Church, R. M. (1992). Comparison of variance and covariance patterns in parallel and serial theories of timing. *Journal of the Experimental Analysis of Behavior, 57,* 393–406.

Gibbon, J., Church, R. M., & Meck, W. H. (1984). Scalar timing in memory. *Annals of the New York Academy of Sciences, 423,* 52–77.

Gibbon, J., & Fairhurst, S. (1994). Ratio versus difference comparators in choice. *Journal of the Experimental Analysis of Behavior, 62,* 409–434.

Gibson, B. M., & Kamil, A. C. (2001). Search for a hidden goal by Clark's nutcrackers (*Nucifraga columbiana*) is more accurate inside than outside a landmark array. *Animal Learning & Behavior, 29,* 234–249.

Giftakis, J., & Tait, R. W. (1998). Blocking of the rabbit's classically conditioned nictitating membrane response: Effects of

modifications of context associative strength. *Learning and Motivation, 29,* 23–48.

Gillan, D. J. (1981). Reasoning in the chimpanzee: II. Transitive inference. *Journal of Experimental Psychology: Animal Behavior Processes, 7,* 150–164.

Gillan, D. J., & Domjan, M. (1977). Taste-aversion conditioning with expected versus unexpected drug treatment. *Journal of Experimental Psychology: Animal Behavior Processes, 3,* 297–309.

Gillette, K., Martin, G. M., & Bellingham, W. P. (1980). Differential use of food and water cues in the formation of conditioned aversions by domestic chicks (*Gallus gallus*). *Journal of Experimental Psychology: Animal Behavior Processes, 6,* 99–111.

Gisiner, R., & Schusterman, R. J. (1992). Sequence, syntax, and semantics: Responses of a language-trained sea lion (*Zalophus californianus*) to novel sign combinations. *Journal of Comparative Psychology, 106,* 78–91.

Gisquet-Verrier, P., & Alexinsky, T. (1990). Facilitative effect of a pretest exposure to the CS: Analysis and implications for the memory trace. *Animal Learning & Behavior, 18,* 323–331.

Goddard, M. J. (1996). Effect of US signal value on blocking of a CS-US association. *Journal of Experimental Psychology: Animal Behavior Processes, 22,* 258–264.

Goddard, M. J. (1999). Renewal to the signal value of an unconditioned stimulus. *Learning and Motivation, 30,* 15–34.

Goddard, M. J., & Holland, P. C. (1996). Type of feature affects transfer in operant serial feature-positive discriminations. *Animal Learning & Behavior, 24,* 266–276.

Goldshmidt, J. N., Lattal, K. M., & Fantino, E. (1998). Context effects on choice. *Journal of the Experimental Analysis of Behavior, 70,* 301–320.

Goodall, G. (1984). Learning due to the response-shock contingency in signalled punishment. *Quarterly Journal of Experimental Psychology, 36B,* 259–279.

Goodall, G., & Mackintosh, N. J. (1987). Analysis of the Pavlovian properties of signals for punishment. *Quarterly Journal of Experimental Psychology, 39B,* 1–21.

Gordon, W. C. (1981). Mechanisms for cue-induced retention enhancement. In N. E. Spear & R. R. Miller (Eds.), *Information processing in animals: Memory mechanisms.* Hillsdale, NJ: Erlbaum.

Gordon, W. C., & Klein, R. L. (1994). Animal memory: The effects of context change on retention performance. In N. J. Mackintosh (Ed.), *Animal learning and cognition* (pp. 255–279). San Diego: Academic Press.

Gordon, W. C., McCracken, K. M., Dess-Beech, N., & Mowrer, R. R. (1981). Mechanisms for the cueing phenomenon: The addition of the cueing context to the training memory. *Learning and Motivation, 12,* 196–211.

Gordon, W. C., McGinnis, C. M., & Weaver, M. S. (1985). The effect of cuing after backward conditioning trials. *Learning and Motivation, 16,* 444–463.

Gordon, W. C., & Mowrer, R. R. (1980). An extinction trial as a reminder treatment following electroconvulsive shock. *Animal Learning & Behavior, 8,* 363–367.

Gormezano, I. (1966). Classical conditioning. In J. B. Sidowski (Ed.), *Experimental methods and instrumentation in psychology.* New York: McGraw-Hill.

Gormezano, I., Kehoe, E. J., & Marshall, B. S. (1983). Twenty years of classical conditioning research with the rabbit. In J. M. Prague & A. N. Epstein (Eds.), *Progress in psychobiology and physiological psychology* (Vol. 10). New York: Academic Press.

Gosling, S. D. (2001). From mice to men: What can we learn about personality from animal research? *Psychological Bulletin, 127,* 45–86.

Gosling, S. D., John, O. P., Craik, K. H., & Robins, R. W. (1998). Do people know how they behave? Self-reported act frequencies compared with on-line codings by observers. *Journal of Personality and Social Psychology, 74,* 1337–1349.

Grace, R. C. (1994). A contextual model of concurrent-chains choice. *Journal of the Experimental Analysis of Behavior, 61,* 113–129.

Grace, R. C. (1995). Independence of reinforcement delay and magnitude in concurrent chains. *Journal of the Experimental Analysis of Behavior, 63,* 255–276.

Grace, R. C. (1999). The matching law and amount-dependent exponential discounting as accounts of self-control choice. *Journal of the Experimental Analysis of Behavior, 71,* 27–44.

Grace, R. C., & Nevin, J. A. (2000). Response strength and temporal control in fixed-interval schedules. *Animal Learning & Behavior, 28,* 313–331.

Graham, J. M., & Desjardins, C. (1980). Classical conditioning: Induction of luteinizing hormone and testosterone secretion in anticipation of sexual activity. *Science, 210,* 1039–1041.

Graham, N. J., Barnet, R. C., Gunther, L. M., & Miller, R. R. (1994). Latent inhibition as a performance deficit resulting from CS-context associations. *Animal Learning & Behavior, 22,* 395–408.

Grant, D. S. (1976). Effect of sample presentation time on long-delay matching in the pigeon. *Learning and Motivation, 7,* 580–590.

Grant, D. S. (1982). Intratrial proactive interference in pigeon short-term memory: Manipulation of stimulus dimension and dimensional similarity. *Learning and Motivation, 13,* 417–433.

Grant, D. S. (1991). Symmetrical and asymmetrical coding of food and no-food samples in delayed matching in pigeons. *Journal of Experimental Psychology: Animal Behavior Processes, 17,* 186–193.

Grant, D. S. (1993). Coding processes in pigeons. In T. R. Zentall (Ed.), *Animal cognition* (pp. 193–216). Hillsdale, NJ: Erlbaum.

Grant, D. S. (2000). Influence of intertrial interval duration on the intertrial agreement effect in delayed matching-to-sample with pigeons. *Animal Learning & Behavior, 28,* 288–297.

Grant, D. S., & Spetch, M. L. (1993). Analogical and nonanalogical coding of samples differing in duration in a choice-matching task in pigeons. *Journal of Experimental Psychology: Animal Behavior Processes, 19,* 15–25.

Grau, J. W., & Joynes, R. L. (2001). Spinal cord injury: From animal research to human therapy. In M. E. Carroll & J. B. Overmier (Eds.), *Animal research and*

human health: Advancing human welfare through behavioral science (pp. 209–226). Washington, DC: American Psychological Association.

Green, J. T., Ivry, R. B., & Woodruff-Pak, D. S. (1999). Timing in eyeblink classical conditioning and timed-interval tapping. *Psychological Science, 10,* 19–23.

Green, L., & Freed, D. E. (1993). The substitutability of reinforcers. *Journal of the Experimental Analysis of Behavior, 60,* 141–158.

Green, L., & Freed, D. E. (1998). Behavioral economics. In W. O'Donohue (Ed.), *Learning and behavior therapy* (pp. 274–300). Boston: Allyn and Bacon.

Greene, C. M., & Cook, R. G. (1997). Landmark geometry and identity controls spatial navigation in rats. *Animal Learning & Behavior, 25,* 312–323.

Greenfield, P. M., & Savage-Rumbaugh, E. S. (1990). Grammatical combination in *Pan paniscus:* Processes of learning and invention in the evolution and development of language. In S. T. Parker & K. R. Gibson (Eds.), *Language and intelligence in monkeys and apes* (pp. 540–578). Cambridge: Cambridge University Press.

Greenough, W. T., & Black, J. E. (2000). In A. E. Kazdin (Ed.), Learning: Molecular and Cellular Aspects. *Encyclopedia of psychology* (Vol. 5, pp. 3–5). New York: Oxford University Press.

Grice, G. R. (1948). The relation of secondary reinforcement to delayed reward in visual discrimination learning. *Journal of Experimental Psychology, 38,* 1–16.

Griffin, D. R. (1976). *The question of animal awareness.* New York: Rockefeller University Press.

Griffin, D. R. (1992). *Animal minds.* Chicago: University of Chicago Press.

Griffiths, D., Dickinson, A., & Clayton, N. (1999). Episodic memory: What can animals remember about their past? *Trends in Cognitive Sciences, 3,* 74–80.

Grossen, N. E., & Kelley, M. J. (1972). Species-specific behavior and acquisition of avoidance behavior in rats. *Journal of Comparative and Physiological Psychology, 81,* 307–310.

Groves, P. M., & Thompson, R. F. (1970). Habituation: A dual-process theory. *Psychological Review, 77,* 419–450.

Gunther, L. M., Denniston, J. C., & Miller, R. R. (1998). Conducting exposure treatment in multiple contexts can prevent relapse. *Behaviour Research and Therapy, 36,* 75–91.

Gunther, L. M., Miller, R. R., & Matute, H. (1997). CSs and USs: What's the difference? *Journal of Experimental Psychology: Animal Behavior Processes, 23,* 15–30.

Gunther, M. (1961). Infant behavior at the breast. In B. Foss (Ed.), *Determinants of infant behavior.* London: Wiley.

Gutiérrez, G., & Domjan, M. (1996). Learning and male-male sexual competition in Japanese quail (*Coturnix japonica*). *Journal of Comparative Psychology, 110,* 170–175.

Guttenberger, V. T., & Wasserman, E. A. (1985). Effects of sample duration, retention interval, and passage of time in the test on pigeons' matching-to-sample performance. *Animal Learning & Behavior, 13,* 121–128.

Guttman, N., & Kalish, H. I. (1956). Discriminability and stimulus generalization. *Journal of Experimental Psychology, 51,* 79–88.

Haggbloom, S. J., & Morris, K. M. (1994). Contextual cues and the retrieval of competing memories of goal events. *Animal Learning & Behavior, 22,* 165–172.

Haggbloom, S. J., Lovelace, L., Brewer, V. R., Levins, S. M., Owens, J. D. (1990). Replacement of event-generated memories of nonreinforcement with signal-generated memories of reinforcement during partial reinforcement training: Effects on resistance to extinction. *Animal Learning & Behavior, 18,* 315–322.

Hailman, J. P. (1967). The ontogeny of an instinct. *Behaviour Supplements, 15,* 1–159.

Hake, D. F., & Azrin, N. H. (1965). Conditioned punishment. *Journal of the Experimental Analysis of Behavior, 8,* 279–293.

Hall, G. (1991). *Perceptual and associative learning.* Oxford, England: Clarendon Press.

Hall, G. (1994). Pavlovian conditioning. In N. J. Mackintosh (Ed.), *Animal learning and cognition* (pp. 15–43). San Diego: Academic Press.

Hall, G., & Honey, R. C. (1989). Contextual effects in conditioning, latent inhibition, and habituation: Associative and retrieval functions of contextual cues. *Journal of Experimental Psychology: Animal Behavior Processes, 15,* 232–241.

Hall, G., Kaye, H., & Pearce, J. M. (1985). Attention and conditioned inhibition. In R. R. Miller & N. E. Spear (Eds.), *Information processing in animals: Conditioned inhibition* (pp. 185–207). Hillsdale, NJ: Erlbaum.

Hall, G., Ray, E., & Bonardi, C. (1993). Acquired equivalence between cues trained with a common antecedent. *Journal of Experimental Psychology: Animal Behavior Processes, 19,* 391–399.

Hall, R. V., Axelrod, S., Foundopoulos, M., Shellman, J., Campbell, R. A., & Cranston, S. S. (1971). The effective use of punishment to modify behavior in the classroom. *Educational Technology, 11*(4), 24–26.

Hall, S. M., Hall, R. G., & Ginsberg, D. (1990). Pharmacological and behavioral treatment for cigarette smoking. In M. Hersen, R. M. Eisler, & P. M. Miller (Eds.), *Progress in behavior modification* (Vol. 25, pp. 86–118). Newbury Park, CA: Sage.

Hallam, S. C., Grahame, N. J., Harris, K., & Miller, R. R. (1992). Associative structures underlying enhanced negative summation following operational extinction of a Pavlovian inhibitor. *Learning and Motivation, 23,* 43–62.

Hammond, L. J. (1968). Retardation of fear acquisition by a previously inhibitory CS. *Journal of Comparative and Physiological Psychology, 66,* 756–759.

Hanson, H. M. (1959). Effects of discrimination training on stimulus generalization. *Journal of Experimental Psychology, 58,* 321–333.

Hanson, J., & Green, L. (1986). Time and response matching with topographically different responses. *Animal Learning & Behavior, 14,* 435–442.

Hanson, S. J., & Timberlake, W. (1983). Regulation during challenge: A general model of learned performance under schedule constraint. *Psychological Review, 90,* 261–282.

Harlow, H. F. (1969). Age-mate or peer affectional system. In D. S. Lehrman, R. H. Hinde, & E. Shaw (Eds.), *Advances in the study of behavior* (Vol. 2). New York: Academic Press.

Haroutunian, V., & Riccio, D. C. (1979). Drug-induced "arousal" and the effectiveness of CS exposure in the reinstatement of memory. *Behavioral and Neural Biology, 26,* 115–120.

Harper, D. N., & Garry, M. (2000). Postevent cues bias recognition performance in pigeons. *Animal Learning & Behavior, 28,* 59–67.

Harper, D. N., & McLean, A. P. (1992). Resistance to change and the law of effect. *Journal of the Experimental Analysis of Behavior, 57,* 317–337.

Harris, J. A., Jones, M. L., Bailey, G. K., & Westbrook, R. F. (2000). Contextual control over conditioned responding in an extinction paradigm. *Journal of Experimental Psychology: Animal Behavior Processes, 9,* 248–265.

Hart, B. L. (1973). Reflexive behavior. In G. Bermant (Ed.), *Perspectives in animal behavior.* Glenview, IL: Scott, Foresman.

Hart, J. A., Bourne, M. J., & Schachtman, T. R. (1995). Slow reacquisition of a conditioned taste aversion. Animal Learning & Behavior, 23, *297–303.*

Hartl, J. A., Dougherty, D. H., & Wixted, J. T. (1996). Separating the effects of trial-specific and average sample-stimulus duration in delayed matching to sample in pigeons. *Journal of the Experimental Analysis of Behavior, 66,* 231–242.

Hartshorn, K., & Rovee-Collier, C. (1997). Infant learning and long-term memory at 6 months: A confirming analysis. *Developmental Psychobiology, 30,* 71–85.

Hastjarjo, T., & Silberberg, A. (1992). Effects of reinforcer delays on choice as a function of income level. *Journal of the Experimental Analysis of Behavior, 57, 119–125.*

Hastjarjo, T., Silberberg, A., & Hursh, S. R. (1990). Quinine pellets as an inferior good and a Giffen good in rats. *Journal of the Experimental Analysis of Behavior, 53,* 263–271.

Haug, M., & Whalen, R. E. (Eds.). (1999). *Animal models of human emotion and cognition.* Washington, DC: American Psychological Association.

Hayes, K. J., & Hayes, C. (1951). The intellectual development of a home-raised chimpanzee. *Proceedings of the American Philosophical Society, 95,* 105–109.

Healy, S. D., & Hurly, R. A. (1995). Spatial memory in rufous hummingbirds (*Selasphorus rufus*): A field test. *Animal Learning & Behavior, 23,* 63–68.

Hearst, E. (1968). Discrimination learning as the summation of excitation and inhibition. *Science, 162,* 1303–1306.

Hearst, E. (1969). Excitation, inhibition, and discrimination learning. In N. J. Mackintosh & W. K. Honig (Eds.), *Fundamental issues in associative learning.* Halifax: Dalhousie University Press.

Hearst, E. (1975). Pavlovian conditioning and directed movements. In G. Bower (Ed.), *The psychology of learning and motivation* (Vol. 9, pp. 215–262). New York: Academic Press.

Hearst, E. (1989). Backward associations: Differential learning about stimuli that follow the presence versus the absence of food in pigeons. *Animal Learning & Behavior, 17,* 280–290.

Hearst, E., & Franklin, S. R. (1977). Positive and negative relations between a signal and food: Approach withdrawal behavior to the signal. *Journal of Experimental Psychology: Animal Behavior Processes, 3,* 37–52.

Hearst, E., & Jenkins, H. M. (1974). *Sign-tracking: The stimulus-reinforcer relation and directed action.* Austin, TX: Psychonomic Society.

Hebb, D. O. (1949). *The organization of behavior.* New York: Wiley.

Hefner, H. E. (1999). The symbiotic nature of animal research. *Perspectives in Biology and Medicine, 43,* 128–139.

Heiligenberg, W. (1974). Processes governing behavioral states of readiness. In D. S. Lehrman, J. S. Rosenblatt, R. Hinde, & E. Shaw (Eds.), *Advances in the study of behavior* (Vol. 5, pp. 173–200). New York: Academic Press.

Helweg, D. A., Roitblat, H. L., Nachtigall, P. E., & Hautus, M. J. (1996). Recognition of aspect-dependent three-dimensional objects by an echolocating Atlantic bottlenose dolphin. *Journal of*

Experimental Psychology: Animal Behavior Processes, 22, 19–31.

Hendersen, R. W., Patterson, J. M., & Jackson, R. L. (1980). Acquisition and retention of control of instrumental behavior by a cue signaling airblast: How specific are conditioned anticipations? *Learning and Motivation, 11*, 407–426.

Hepper, P. G., & Shahidullah, S. (1992). Habituation in normal and Down's syndrome fetuses. *Quarterly Journal of Experimental Psychology, 44B*, 305–317.

Herman, L. M. (1987). Receptive competencies of language-trained animals. In J. S. Rosenblatt, C. Beer, M.-C. Busnel, & P. J. B. Slater (Eds.), *Advances in the study of behavior* (Vol. 17, pp. 1–60). Orlando, FL: Academic Press.

Herman, L. M., Pack, A. A., & Morrel-Samuels, P. (1993). Representational and conceptual skills of dolphins. In H. L. Roitblat, L. M. Herman, & P. E. Nachtigall (Eds.), *Language and communication: Comparative perspectives* (pp. 403–442). Hillsdale, NJ: Erlbaum.

Herman, L. M., & Uyeyama, R. K. (1999). The dolphin's grammatical competency: Comments on Kako. *Animal Learning & Behavior, 27*, 18–23.

Herman, R. L., & Azrin, N. H. (1964). Punishment by noise in an alternative response situation. *Journal of the Experimental Analysis of Behavior, 7*, 185–188.

Herrnstein, R. J. (1961). Relative and absolute strength of response as a function of frequency of reinforcement. *Journal of the Experimental Analysis of Behavior, 4*, 267–272.

Herrnstein, R. J. (1969). Method and theory in the study of avoidance. *Psychological Review, 76*, 49–69.

Herrnstein, R. J. (1970). On the law of effect. *Journal of the Experimental Analysis of Behavior, 13*, 243–266.

Herrnstein, R. J. (1984). Objects, categories, and discriminative stimuli. In H. L. Roitblat, T. G Bever, & H. S. Terrace (Eds.), *Animal cognition* (pp. 233–261). Hillsdale, NJ: Erlbaum.

Herrnstein, R. J. (1990). Levels of stimulus control: A functional approach. *Cognition, 37*, 133–166.

Herrnstein, R. J. (1997). *The matching law.* (H. Rachlin and D. I. Laibson, Eds.).

New York: Russell Sage; and Cambridge: Harvard University Press.

Herrnstein, R. J., & deVilliers, P. A. (1980). Fish as a natural category for people and pigeons. In G. H. Bower (Ed.), *The psychology of learning and motivation* (Vol. 14, pp. 60–97). New York: Academic Press.

Herrnstein, R. J., & Heyman, G. M. (1979). Is matching compatible with reinforcement maximization on concurrent variable interval, variable ratio? *Journal of the Experimental Analysis of Behavior, 31*, 209–223.

Herrnstein, R. J., & Hineline, P. N. (1966). Negative reinforcement as shock-frequency reduction. *Journal of the Experimental Analysis of Behavior, 9*, 421–430.

Herrnstein, R. J., & Loveland, D. H. (1964). Complex visual concept in the pigeon. *Science, 146*, 549–551.

Herrnstein, R. J., Loveland, D. H., & Cable, C. (1976). Natural concepts in pigeons. *Journal of Experimental Psychology: Animal Behavior Processes, 2*, 285–301.

Herrnstein, R. J., & Vaughan, W., Jr. (1980). Melioration and behavioral allocation. In J. E. R. Staddon (Ed.), *Limits to action.* New York: Academic Press.

Herzog, H. A., Jr. (1988). The moral status of mice. *American Psychologist, 43*, 473–474.

Heyman, G. M. (1983). Optimization theory: Close but no cigar. *Behaviour Analysis Letters, 3*, 17–26.

Heyman, G. M., & Herrnstein, R. J. (1986). More on concurrent interval-ratio schedules: A replication and review. *Journal of the Experimental Analysis of Behavior, 46*, 331–351.

Heyman, G. M., & Monaghan, M. M. (1994). Reinforcer magnitude (sucrose concentration) and the matching law theory of response strength. *Journal of the Experimental Analysis of Behavior, 61*, 505–516.

Hilgard, E. R., & Marquis, D. G. (1940). *Conditioning and learning.* New York: Appleton.

Hilliard, S. H., Domjan, M., Nguyen, M., & Cusato, B. (1998). Dissociation of conditioned appetitive and consummatory sexual behavior: Satiation and extinction tests. *Animal Learning & Behavior, 26*, 20–33.

Hineline, P. N. (1977). Negative reinforcement and avoidance. In W. K. Honig & J. E. R. Staddon (Eds.), *Handbook of operant behavior* (pp. 364–414). Englewood Cliffs, NJ: Prentice-Hall.

Hineline, P. N. (1981). The several roles of stimuli in negative reinforcement. In P. Harzem & M. D. Zeiler (Eds.), *Predictability, correlation, and contiguity* (pp. 203–246). Chichester, England: Wiley.

Hinson, J. M., & Cannon, C. B. (1999). Stimulus spacing, attention, and dimensional contrast. *Animal Learning & Behavior, 27*, 472–480.

Hinson, J. M., Cannon, C. B., & Tennison, L. R. (1999). Orthogonal stimulus variation and attention in dimensional contrast. *Animal Learning & Behavior, 27*, 181–189.

Hinson, J. M., & Staddon, J. E. R. (1983a). Hill-climbing by pigeons. *Journal of the Experimental Analysis of Behavior, 39*, 25–47.

Hinson, J. M., & Staddon, J. E. R. (1983b). Matching, maximizing, and hill-climbing. *Journal of the Experimental Analysis of Behavior, 40*, 321–331.

Hinton, S. H., & Meck, W. H. (1997). The "internal clocks" of circadian and interval timing. *Endeavour, 22*, 82–87.

Hintzman, D. L. (1991). Twenty-five years of learning and memory: Was the cognitive revolution a mistake? In D.E. Meyer & S. Kornblum (Eds.), *Attention and performance XIVP.* Hillsdale, NJ: Erlbaum.

Hitchcock, D. F. A., & Rovee-Collier, C. (1996). The effect of repeated reactivations on memory specificity in infancy. *Journal of Experimental Child Psychology, 62*, 378–400.

Ho, M.-Y., Wogar, M. A., Bradshaw, C. M., & Szabadi, E. (1997). Choice between delayed reinforcers: Interaction between delay and deprivation level. *Quarterly Journal of Experimental Psychology, 50B*, 193–202.

Hoffman, C. M., Timberlake, W., Leffel, J., & Gont, R. (1999). How is radial arm maze behavior in rats related to locomotor search tactics? *Animal Learning & Behavior, 27*, 426–444.

Hoffman, H. S., & Solomon, R. L. (1974). An opponent-process theory of motivation: III. Some affective dynamics in imprinting. *Learning and Motivation, 5,* 149–164.

Holland, P. C. (1977). Conditioned stimulus as a determinant of the form of the Pavlovian conditioned response. *Journal of Experimental Psychology: Animal Behavior Processes, 3,* 77–104.

Holland, P. C. (1980). Influence of visual conditioned stimulus characteristics on the form of Pavlovian appetitive conditioned responding in rats. *Journal of Experimental Psychology: Animal Behavior Processes, 6,* 81–97.

Holland, P. C. (1984). Origins of behavior in Pavlovian conditioning. In G. H. Bower (Ed.), *The psychology of learning and motivation* (Vol. 18, pp. 129–174). Orlando, FL: Academic Press.

Holland, P. C. (1985). The nature of conditioned inhibition in serial and simultaneous feature negative discriminations. In R. R. Miller & N. E. Spear (Eds.), *Information processing in animals: Conditioned inhibition* (pp. 267–297). Hillsdale, NJ: Erlbaum.

Holland, P. C. (1986). Temporal determinants of occasion setting in feature-positive discriminations. *Animal Learning and Behavior, 14,* 111–120.

Holland, P. C. (1989a). Feature extinction enhances transfer of occasion setting. *Animal Learning & Behavior, 17,* 269–279.

Holland, P. C. (1989b). Occasion setting with simultaneous compounds in rats. *Journal of Experimental Psychology: Animal Behavior Processes, 15,* 183–193.

Holland, P. C. (1989c). Transfer of negative occasion setting and conditioned inhibition across conditioned and unconditioned stimuli. *Journal of Experimental Psychology: Animal Behavior Processes, 15,* 311–328.

Holland, P. C. (1991). Acquisition and transfer of occasion setting in operant feature positive and feature negative discriminations. *Learning and Motivation, 22,* 366–387.

Holland, P. C. (1992). Occasion setting in Pavlovian conditioning. In D. L. Medin (Ed.), *The psychology of learning and motivation* (Vol. 28, pp. 69–125). San Diego, CA: Academic Press.

Holland, P. C. (2000). Trial and intertrial durations in appetitive conditioning in rats. *Animal Learning & Behavior, 28,* 121–135.

Holland, P. C., & Rescorla, R. A. (1975a). The effect of two ways of devaluing the unconditioned stimulus after first- and second-order appetitive conditioning. *Journal of Experimental Psychology: Animal Behavior Processes, 1,* 355–363.

Holland, P. C., & Rescorla, R. A. (1975b). Second-order conditioning with food unconditioned stimulus. *Journal of Comparative and Physiological Psychology, 88,* 459–467.

Holland, P. C., & Straub, J. J. (1979). Differential effect of two ways of devaluing the unconditioned stimulus after Pavlovian appetitive conditioning. *Journal of Experimental Psychology: Animal Behavior Processes, 5,* 65–78.

Holliday, M., & Hirsch, J. (1986). Excitatory conditioning of individual *Drosophila melanogaster. Journal of Experimental Psychology: Animal Behavior Processes, 12,* 131–142.

Hollis, K. L. (1997). Contemporary research on Pavlovian conditioning: A "new" functional analysis. *American Psychologist, 52,* 956–965.

Hollis, K. L., Cadieux, E. L., & Colbert, M. M. (1989). The biological function of Pavlovian conditioning: A mechanism for mating success in the blue gourami (Trichogaster trichopterus). *Journal of Comparative Psychology, 103,* 115–121.

Hollis, K. L., Pharr, V. L., Dumas, M. J., Britton, G. B., & Field, J. (1997). Classical conditioning provides paternity advantage for territorial male blue gouramis (*Trichogaster trichopterus*). *Journal of Comparative Psychology, 111,* 219–225.

Holloway, K. S., & Domjan, M. (1993). Sexual approach conditioning: Tests of unconditioned stimulus devaluation using hormone manipulations. *Journal of Experimental Psychology: Animal Behavior Processes, 19,* 47–55.

Holman, J. G., & Mackintosh, N. J. (1981). The control of appetitive instrumental responding does not depend on classical conditioning to the discriminative stimulus. *Quarterly Journal of Experimental Psychology, 33B,* 21–31.

Holz, W. C., & Azrin, N. H. (1961). Discriminative properties of punishment. *Journal of the Experimental Analysis of Behavior, 4,* 225–232.

Honey, R. C., Good, M., & Manser, K. L. (1998). Negative priming in associative learning: Evidence from a serial-habituation procedure. *Journal of Experimental Psychology: Animal Behavior Processes, 24,* 229–237.

Honey, R. C., & Hall, G. (1989). Acquired equivalence and distinctiveness of cues. *Journal of Experimental Psychology: Animal Behavior Processes, 15,* 338–346.

Honey, R. C., & Hall, G. (1991). Acquired equivalence and distinctiveness of cues using a sensory-preconditioning procedure. *Quarterly Journal of Experimental Psychology, 43B,* 121–135.

Honey, R. C., & Watt, A. (1998). Acquired relational equivalence: Implications for the nature of associative structures. *Journal of Experimental Psychology: Animal Behavior Processes, 24,* 325–334.

Honey, R. C., & Watt, A. (1999). Acquired relational equivalence between contexts and features. *Journal of Experimental Psychology: Animal Behavior Processes, 25,* 324–333.

Honey, R. C., Willis, A., & Hall, G. (1990). Context specificity in pigeon autoshaping. *Learning and Motivation, 21,* 125–136.

Honig, W. K. (1978). Studies of working memory in the pigeon. In S. H. Hulse, H. Fowler, & W. K. Honig (Eds.), *Cognitive processes in animal behavior* (pp. 211–248). Hillsdale, NJ: Erlbaum.

Honig, W. K., Boneau, C. A., Burstein, K. R., & Pennypacker, H. S. (1963). Positive and negative generalization gradients obtained under equivalent training conditions. *Journal of Comparative and Physiological Psychology, 56,* 111–116.

Honig, W. K., & Stewart, K. E. (1988). Pigeons can discriminate locations presented in pictures. *Journal of the Experimental Analysis of Behavior, 50,* 541–551.

Honig, W. K., & Thompson, R. K. R. (1982). Retrospective and prospective processing in animal working memory. In G. H. Bower (Ed.), *The psychology of learning and motivation* (Vol. 16, pp. 239–283). Orlando, FL: Academic Press.

Honig, W. K., & Urcuioli, P. J. (1981). The legacy of Guttman and Kalish (1956): 25 years of research on stimulus generalization. *Journal of the Experimental Analysis of Behavior, 36,* 405–445.

Horne, P. J., & Lowe, C. F. (1996). On the origins on naming and other symbolic behavior, *Journal of the Experimental Analysis of Behavior, 65,* 185–241.

Horne, P. J., & Lowe, C. F. (1997). Toward a theory of verbal behavior. *Journal of the Experimental Analysis of Behavior, 68,* 271–296.

Hoyert, M. S. (1992). Order and chaos in fixed-interval schedules of reinforcement. *Journal of the Experimental Analysis of Behavior, 57,* 339–363.

Huber, L., & Lenz, R. (1993). A test of the linear feature model of polymorphous concept discrimination with pigeons. *The Quarterly Journal of Experimental Psychology, 46B,* 1–18.

Huber, L., & Lenz, R. (1996). Categorization of prototypical stimulus classes by pigeons. *Quarterly Journal of Experimental Psychology, 49B,* 111–133.

Huber, L., Troje, N. F., Loidolt, M., Aust, U., & Grass, D. (2000). Natural categorization through multiple feature learning in pigeons. *Quarterly Journal of Experimental Psychology, 53B,* 341–357.

Hull, C. L. (1930). Knowledge and purpose as habit mechanisms. *Psychological Review, 30,* 511–525.

Hull, C. L. (1931). Goal attraction and directing ideas conceived as habit phenomena. *Psychological Review, 38,* 487–506.

Hulse, S. H. (1958). Amount and percentage of reinforcement and duration of goal confinement in conditioning and extinction. *Journal of Experimental Psychology, 56,* 48–57.

Hulse, S. H. (1978). Cognitive structure and serial pattern learning by animals. In S. H. Hulse, H. Fowler, & W. K. Honig (Eds.), *Cognitive processes in animal behavior* (pp. 311–340). Hillsdale, NJ: Erlbaum.

Hulse, S. H., Fowler, H., & Honig, W. K. (Eds.). (1978). *Cognitive processes in animal behavior.* Hillsdale, NJ: Erlbaum.

Hulse, S. H., Page, S. C., & Braaten, R. F. (1990). Frequency range size and the frequency range constraint in auditory perception by European starlings (*Sturnus vulgaris*). Animal Learning & Behavior, 18, 238–245.

Hunt, M., Parr, W. V., & Smith, P. (1999). Local and global sources of control in pigeon delayed matching-to-sample performance. Quarterly Journal of Experimental Psychology, 52B, 203–233.

Hunt, P. S. (1997). Retention of conditioned autonomic and behavioral responses in preweanling rats: Forgetting and reinstatement. *Animal Learning & Behavior, 25,* 301–311.

Hunter, W. S. (1913). The delayed reaction in animals and children. *Behavior Monographs, 2,* serial #6.

Hursh, S. R. (1984). Behavioral economics. *Journal of the Experimental Analysis of Behavior, 42,* 435–452.

Hursh, S. R. (1991). Behavioral economics of drug self-administration and drug abuse policy. *Journal of the Experimental Analysis of Behavior, 56,* 377–393.

Hursh, S. R., Raslear, T. G., Shurtleff, D., Bauman, R., & Simmons, L. (1988). A cost-benefit analysis of demand for food. *Journal of the Experimental Analysis of Behavior, 50,* 419–440.

Hutt, P. J. (1954). Rate of bar pressing as a function of quality and quantity of food reward. *Journal of Comparative and Physiological Psychology, 47,* 235–239.

Innis, N. K., Reberg, D., Mann, B., Jacobson, J., & Turton, D. (1983). Schedule-induced behavior for food and water: Effects of interval duration. *Behaviour Analysis Letters, 3,* 191–200.

Innis, N. K., Simmelhag-Grant, V. L., & Staddon, J. E. R. (1983). Behavior induced by periodic food delivery: The effects of interfood interval. *Journal of the Experimental Analysis of Behavior, 39,* 309–322.

Irwin, J., Suissa, A., & Anisman, H. (1980). Differential effects of inescapable shock on escape performance and discrimination learning in a water escape task. *Journal of Experimental Psychology: Animal Behavior Processes, 6,* 21–40.

Ishida, M., & Papini, M. R. (1997). Massed-trial overtraining effects on extinction

and reversal performance in turtles (*Geoclemys reevesii*). *Quarterly Journal of Experimental Psychology, 50B,* 1–16.

Israel, A. C., Devine, V. T., O'Dea, M. A., & Hamdi, M. E. (1974). Effect of delayed conditioned stimulus termination on extinction of an avoidance response following differential termination conditions during acquisition. *Journal of Experimental Psychology, 103,* 360–362.

Ito, M., & Nakamura, K. (1998). Human's choice in a self-control choice situation: sensitivity to reinforcer amount, reinforcer delay, and overall reinforcement density. *Journal of the Experimental Analysis of Behavior, 69,* 87–102.

Iversen, I. H. (1993a). Acquisition of matching-to-sample performance in rats using visual stimuli on nose keys. *Journal of the Experimental Analysis of Behavior, 59,* 471–482.

Iversen, I. H. (1993b). Techniques for establishing schedules with wheel running as reinforcement in rats. *Journal of the Experimental Analysis of Behavior, 60,* 219–238.

Ivkovich, D., Collins, K. L., Eckerman, C. O., Krasnegor, N. A., & Stanton, M. E. (1999). Classical delay eyeblink conditioning in 4– and 5–month-old human infants. *Psychological Science, 10,* 4–8.

Jackson, R. L., & Minor, T. R. (1988). Effects of signaling inescapable shock on subsequent escape learning: Implications for theories of coping and "learned helplessness." *Journal of Experimental Psychology: Animal Behavior Processes, 14,* 390–400.

Jackson, R. L., Alexander, J. H., & Maier, S. F. (1980). Learned helplessness, inactivity, and associative deficits: Effects of inescapable shock on response choice escape learning. *Journal of Experimental Psychology: Animal Behavior Processes, 6,* 1–20.

Janssen, M., Farley, J., & Hearst, E. (1995). Temporal location of unsignaled food deliveries: Effects on conditioned withdrawal (inhibition) in pigeon signtracking. *Journal of Experimental Psychology: Animal Behavior Processes, 21,* 116–128.

Jarrard, L. E., & Moise, S. L. (1971). Short-term memory in the monkey. In L. E. Jarrard (Ed.), *Cognitive processes of non-*

human primates. New York: Academic Press.

Jenkins, H. M. (1962). Resistance to extinction when partial reinforcement is followed by regular reinforcement. *Journal of Experimental Psychology, 64,* 441–450.

Jenkins, H. M. (1977). Sensitivity of different response systems to stimulus-reinforcer and response-reinforcer relations. In H. Davis & H. M. B. Hurwitz (Eds.), *Operant-Pavlovian interactions* (pp. 47–62). Hillsdale, NJ: Erlbaum.

Jenkins, H. M., Barnes, R. A., & Barrera, F. J. (1981). Why autoshaping depends on trial spacing. In C. M. Locurto, H. S. Terrace, & J. Gibbon (Eds.), *Autoshaping and conditioning theory* (pp. 255–284). New York: Academic Press.

Jenkins, H. M., & Harrison, R. H. (1960). Effects of discrimination training on auditory generalization. *Journal of Experimental Psychology, 59,* 246–253.

Jenkins, H. M., & Harrison, R. H. (1962). Generalization gradients of inhibition following auditory discrimination learning. *Journal of the Experimental Analysis of Behavior, 5,* 435–441.

Jenkins, H. M., & Moore, B. R. (1973). The form of the autoshaped response with food or water reinforcers. *Journal of the Experimental Analysis of Behavior, 20,* 163–181.

Jennings, H. S. (1976). *Behavior of the lower organisms.* Bloomington: Indiana University Press. (Original work published 1904)

Jitsumori, M. (1994). Discrimination of artificial polymorphous categories by rhesus monkeys (*Macaca mulatta*). *The Quarterly Journal of Experimental Psychology, 47B,* 371–386.

Jitsumori, M. (1996). A prototype effect and categorization of artificial polymorphous stimuli in pigeons. *Journal of Experimental Psychology: Animal Behavior Processes, 22,* 405–419.

Jitsumori, M., Natori, M., & Okuyama, K. (1999). Recognition of moving video images of conspecifics by pigeons: Effects of individuals, static and dynamic motion cues, and movement. *Animal Learning & Behavior, 27,* 303–315.

Jitsumori, M., & Yoshihara, M. (1997). Categorical discrimination of human fa-

cial expressions by pigeons: A test of the linear feature model. *Quarterly Journal of Experimental Psychology, 50B,* 253–268.

Job, R. F. S. (1987). Learned helplessness in an appetitive discrete-trial T-maze discrimination test. *Animal Learning & Behavior, 15,* 342–346.

Job, R. F. S. (1989). A test of proposed mechanisms underlying the interference effect produced by noncontingent food presentations. *Learning and Motivation, 20,* 153–177.

Johnson, H. M. (1994). Processes of successful intentional forgetting. *Psychological Bulletin, 116,* 274–292.

Jordan, W. P., Strasser, H. C., & McHale, L. (2000). Contextual control of long-term habituation in rats. *Journal of Experimental Psychology: Animal Behavior Processes, 26,* 323–339.

Kaiser, D. H., Sherburne, L. M., & Zentall, T. R. (1997). Directed forgetting in pigeons resulting from reallocation of memory-maintaining processes on forget-cue trials. *Psychonomic Bulletin & Review, 4,* 559–565.

Kaiser, L., & De Jong, R. (1995). Induction of odor preference in a specialist insect parasitoid. *Animal Learning & Behavior, 23,* 17–21.

Kako, E. (1999). Elements of syntax in the systems of three language-trained animals. *Animal Learning & Behavior, 27,* 1–14.

Kamil, A. C. (1978). Systematic foraging by a nectarfeeding bird, the amakihi (*Loxops virens*). *Journal of Comparative and Physiological Psychology, 92,* 388–396.

Kamil, A. C., & Balda, R. P. (1985). Cache recovery and spatial memory in Clark's nutcrackers (Nucifraga columbiana). *Journal of Experimental Psychology: Animal Behavior Processes, 11,* 95–111.

Kamil, A. C., & Balda, R. P. (1990a). Differential memory for different cache sites by Clark's nutcrackers (*Nucifraga columbiana*). *Journal of Experimental Psychology: Animal Behavior Processes, 16,* 162–168.

Kamil, A. C., & Balda, R. P. (1990b). Spatial memory in seed-caching corvids. In G. H. Bower (Ed.), *The psychology of learning and motivation* (Vol. 26, pp. 1–25). San Diego: Academic Press.

Kamil, A. C., & Jones, J. E. (2000). Geometric rule learning by Clark's nutcrackers (*Nucifraga columbiana*). *Journal of Experimental Psychology: Animal Behavior Processes, 26,* 439–453.

Kamin, L. J. (1956). The effects of termination of the CS and avoidance of the US on avoidance learning. *Journal of Comparative and Physiological Psychology, 49,* 420–424.

Kamin, L. J. (1965). Temporal and intensity characteristics of the conditioned stimulus. In W. F. Prokasy (Ed.), *Classical conditioning* (pp. 118–147). New York: Appleton-Century-Crofts.

Kamin, L. J. (1968). "Attention-like" processes in classical conditioning. In M. R. Jones (Ed.), *Miami Symposium on the Prediction of Behavior: Aversive stimulation* (pp. 9–31). Miami: University of Miami Press.

Kamin, L. J. (1969). Predictability, surprise, attention, and conditioning. In B. A. Campbell & R. M. Church (Eds.), *Punishment and aversive behavior* (pp. 279–296). New York: Appleton-Century-Crofts.

Kamin, L. J., & Brimer, C. J. (1963). The effects of intensity of conditioned and unconditioned stimuli on a conditioned emotional response. *Canadian Journal of Psychology, 17,* 194–198.

Kamin, L. J., Brimer, C. J., & Black, A. H. (1963). Conditioned suppression as a monitor of fear of the CS in the course of avoidance training. *Journal of Comparative and Physiological Psychology, 56,* 497–501.

Kamin, L. J., & Schaub, R. E. (1963). Effects of conditioned stimulus intensity on the conditioned emotional response. *Journal of Comparative and Physiological Psychology, 56,* 502–507.

Kandel, E. R. (1976). *Cellular basis of behavior.* San Francisco: Freeman.

Kandel, E. R., & Schwartz, J. H. (1982). Molecular biology of learning: Modulation of transmitter release. *Science, 218,* 433–443.

Kandel, E. R., Schwartz, J. H., & Jessell, T. M. (Eds.). (1991). *Principles of neural science.* New York: Elsevier.

Kandel, E. R., Schwartz, J. H., & Jessell, T. M. (Eds.). (2000). *Principles of neural science.* New York: McGraw-Hill.

Kaplan, P. S., Goldstein, M. H., Huckeby, E. R., & Cooper, R. P. (1995). Habituation, sensitization, and infants' responses to motherese speech. *Developmental Psychobiology, 28,* 45–57.

Kaplan, P. S., & Hearst, E. (1982). Bridging temporal gaps between CS and US in autoshaping: Insertion of other stimuli before, during, and after the CS. *Journal of Experimental Psychology: Animal Behavior Processes, 8,* 187–203.

Kaplan, P. S., Werner, J. S., & Rudy, J. W. (1990). Habituation, sensitization, and infant visual attention. In C. Rovee-Collier & L. P. Lipsitt (Eds.), *Advances in infancy research* (Vol. 6, pp. 61–109). Norwood, NJ: Ablex.

Karpicke, J. (1978). Directed approach responses and positive conditioned suppression in the rat. *Animal Learning & Behavior, 6,* 216–224.

Kasprow, W. J. (1987). Enhancement of short-term retention by appetitive-reinforcer reminder treatment. *Animal Learning & Behavior, 15,* 412–416.

Kasprow, W. J., Cacheiro, H., Balaz, M. A., & Miller, R. R. (1982). Reminder-induced recovery of associations to an overshadowed stimulus. *Learning and Motivation, 13,* 155–166.

Kasprow, W. J., Catterson, D., Schachtman, T. R., & Miller, R. R. (1984). Attenuation of latent inhibition by post-acquisition reminder. *Quarterly Journal of Experimental Psychology, 36B,* 53–63.

Kasprow, W. J., Schachtman, T. R., & Miller, R. R. (1987). The comparator hypothesis of conditioned response generation: Manifest conditioned excitation and inhibition as a function of relative excitatory strengths of CS and conditioning context at the time of testing. *Journal of Experimental Psychology: Animal Behavior Processes, 13,* 395–406.

Kastak, D., & Schusterman, R. J. (1994). Transfer of visual identity matching-to-sample in two California sea lions (*Zalophus californianus*). *Animal Learning & Behavior, 22,* 427–435.

Kastak, D., & Schusterman, R. J. (1998). Low-frequency amphibious hearing in pinnipeds: Methods, measurement, noise, and ecology. *Journal of the Acoustical Society of America, 103,* 2216–2228.

Kastak, D., Schusterman, R. J., Southall, B. L., & Reichmuth, C. J. (1999). Underwater temporary threshold shift induced by octave-band noise in three species of pinniped. *Journal of the Acoustical Society of America, 106,* 1142–1148.

Katzev, R. D. (1967). Extinguishing avoidance responses as a function of delayed warning signal termination. *Journal of Experimental Psychology, 75,* 339–344.

Katzev, R. D. (1972). What is both necessary and sufficient to maintain avoidance responding in the shuttle box? *Quarterly Journal of Experimental Psychology, 24,* 310–317.

Katzev, R. D., & Berman, J. S. (1974). Effect of exposure to conditioned stimulus and control of its termination in the extinction of avoidance behavior. *Journal of Comparative and Physiological Psychology, 87,* 347–353.

Kaufman, L. W., & Collier, G. (1983). Cost and meal pattern in wild-caught rats. *Physiology and Behavior, 30,* 445–449.

Keehn, J. D., & Nakkash, S. (1959). Effect of a signal contingent upon an avoidance response. *Nature, 184,* 566–568.

Keen, R., & Machado, A. (1999). How pigeons discriminate the relative frequency of events. *Journal of the Experimental Analysis of Behavior, 72,* 151–175.

Kehoe, E. J., Cool, V., & Gormezano, I. (1991). Trace conditioning of the rabbit's nictitating membrane response as a function of CS-US interstimulus interval and trials per session. *Learning and Motivation, 22,* 269–290.

Kelly, M. J. (1986). Selective attention and stimulus reinforcer interactions in the pigeon. *Quarterly Journal of Experimental Psychology, 38B,* 97–110.

Kellogg, W. N. (1933). *The ape and the child.* New York: McGraw-Hill.

Kesner, R. P., & DeSpain, M. J. (1988). Correspondence between rats and humans in the utilization of retrospective and prospective codes. *Animal Learning & Behavior, 16,* 299–302.

Kessler, R. C., McGonagle, K. A., Zhao, S., Nelson, C. B., Hughes, M., Eshleman, S., Wittchen, H.-U., & Kendler, K. S. (1994). Lifetime and 12-month prevalence of DSM-III-R psychiatric disorders in the United States: Results from the National Comorbidity Survey. *Archives of General Psychiatry, 51,* 8–19.

Khallad, Y., & Moore, J. (1996). Blocking, unblocking, and overexpectation in autoshaping with pigeons. *Journal of the Experimental Analysis of Behavior, 65,* 575–591.

Killeen, P. R. (1991). Behavior's time. In G. H. Bower (Ed.), *The psychology of learning and motivation* (Vol. 27, pp. 295–334). San Diego: Academic Press.

Killeen, P. R. (1995). Economics, ecologics, and mechanics: The dynamics of responding under conditions of varying motivation. *Journal of the Experimental Analysis of Behavior, 64,* 405–431.

Killeen, P. R. (2001a). The four causes of behavior. *Current Directions in Psychological Science, 10,* 136–140.

Killeen, P. R. (2001b). Writing and overwriting short-term memory. *Psychonomic Bulletin & Review, 8,* 18–43.

Killeen, P. R., & Fetterman, J. G. (1988). A behavioral theory of timing. *Psychological Review, 95,* 274–295.

Killeen, P. R., & Fetterman, J. G. (1993). The behavioral theory of timing: Transition analyses. *Journal of the Experimental Analysis of Behavior, 59,* 411–422.

Killeen, P. R., Fetterman, J. G., & Bizo, L. A. (1997). Time's causes. In C. M. Bradshaw & E. Szabadi (Eds.), *Time and behaviour: Psychological and neurobiological analyses* (pp. 79–139). Amsterdam: Elsevier Science.

Killeen, P. R., & Hall, S. S. (2001). The principal components of response strength. *Journal of the Experimental Analysis of Behavior, 75,* 111–134.

Kim, J. J., D. J. Krupa, et al. (1998). Inhibitory cerebello-olivary projections and blocking effect in classical conditioning. *Science, 279,* 570–573.

Kim, S. D., Rivers, S., Bevins, R. A., & Ayres, J. J. B. (1996). Conditioned stimulus determinants of conditioned response form in Pavlovian fear conditioning. *Journal of Experimental Psychology: Animal Behavior Processes, 22,* 87–104.

Kimble, G. A. (1961). *Hilgard and Marquis' conditioning and learning* (2nd ed.). New York: Appleton.

Kirby, K. N., Petry, N. M., & Bickel, W. K. (1999). Heroin addicts have higher discount rates for delayed rewards than non-drug-using controls. *Journal of Experimental Psychology: General, 128,* 78–87.

Kirkpatrick, K., & Church, R. M. (2000). Independent effects of stimulus and cycle duration in conditioning: The role of timing processes. *Animal Learning & Behavior, 28,* 373–388.

Kirkpatrick-Steger, K., Miller S. S., Betti, C. A., & Wasserman, E. A. (1996). Cyclic responding by pigeons on the peak timing procedure. *Journal of Experimental Psychology: Animal Behavior Processes, 22,* 447–460.

Klein, B. G., LaMon, B., & Zeigler, H. P. (1983). Drinking in the pigeon (*Columba livia*): Topography and spatiotemporal organization. *Journal of Comparative Psychology, 97,* 178–181.

Klein, M., & Rilling, M. (1974). Generalization of free operant avoidance behavior in pigeons. *Journal of the Experimental Analysis of Behavior, 21,* 75–88.

Kluender, K. R., Diehl, R. L., & Killeen, P. R. (1987). Japanese quail can learn phonetic categories. *Science, 237,* 1195–1197.

Köhler, W. (1939). Simple structural functions in the chimpanzee and in the chicken. In W. D. Ellis (Ed.), *A source book of Gestalt psychology* (pp. 217–227). New York: Harcourt Brace Jovanovich.

Koob, G. F., Caine, S. B., Parsons, L., Markou, A., & Weiss, F. (1997). Opponent-process model and psychostimulant addiction. *Pharmacology Biochemistry and Behavior, 57,* 531–521.

Kraemer, P. J., & Golding, J. M. (1997). Adaptive forgetting in animals. *Psychonomic Bulletin & Review, 4,* 480–491.

Kraemer, P. J., Hoffmann, H., Randall, C. K., & Spear, N. E. (1992). Devaluation of Pavlovian conditioning in the 10-day-old rat. *Animal Learning & Behavior, 20,* 219–222.

Kraemer, P. J., & Roberts, W. A. (1985). Short-term memory for simultaneously presented visual and auditory signals in the pigeon. *Journal of Experimental Psy-*

chology: *Animal Behavior Processes, 11,* 13–39.

Kremer, E. F. (1978). The Rescorla-Wagner model: Losses in associative strength in compound conditioned stimuli. *Journal of Experimental Psychology: Animal Behavior Processes, 4,* 22–36.

Kriekhaus, E. E., & Wolf, G. (1968). Acquisition of sodium by rats: Interaction of innate and latent learning. *Journal of Comparative and Physiological Psychology, 65,* 197–201.

Kruse, J. M., Overmier, J. B., Konz, W. A., & Rokke, E. (1983). Pavlovian conditioned stimulus effects upon instrumental choice behavior are reinforcer specific. *Learning and Motivation, 14,* 165–181.

Lansdell, H. (1988). Laboratory animals need only humane treatment: Animal "rights" may debase human rights. *International Journal of Neuroscience, 42,* 169–178.

Lashley, K. S., & Wade, M. (1946). The Pavlovian theory of generalization. *Psychological Review, 53,* 72–87.

Lattal, K. A. (1998). A century of effect: Legacies of E. L. Thorndike's *Animal intelligence* monograph. *Journal of the Experimental Analysis of Behavior, 70,* 325–336.

Lattal, K. A., & Abreu-Rodrigues, J. (1997). Response independent events in the behavior stream. *Journal of the Experimental Analysis of Behavior, 68,* 375–398.

Lattal, K. A., & Gleeson, S. (1990). Response acquisition with delayed reinforcement. *Journal of Experimental Psychology: Animal Behavior Processes, 16,* 27–39.

Lattal, K. A., & Metzger, B. (1994). Response acquisition by Siamese fighting fish (*Betta spendens*) with delayed visual reinforcement. *Journal of the Experimental Analysis of Behavior, 61,* 35–44.

Lattal, K. A., & Neef, N. A. (1996). Recent reinforcement-schedule research and applied behavior analysis. *Journal of Applied Behavior Analysis, 29,* 213–230.

Lattal, K. A. Reilly, M. P., & Kohn, J. P. (1998). Response persistence under ratio and interval reinforcement schedules. *Journal of the Experimental Analysis of Behavior, 70,* 165–183.

Lattal, K. M. (1999). Trial and intertrial durations in Pavlovian conditioning: Issues of learning and performance. *Journal of Experimental Psychology: Animal Behavior Processes, 25,* 433–450.

Lattal, K. M., & Nakajima, S. (1998). Overexpectation in appetitive Pavlovian and instrumental conditioning. *Animal Learning & Behavior, 26,* 351–360.

Lavin, M. J. (1976). The establishment of flavor-flavor associations using a sensory preconditioning training procedure. *Learning and Motivation, 7,* 173–183.

Lawler, C. P., & Cohen, P. S. (1992). Temporal patterns of schedule-induced drinking and pawgrooming in rats exposed to periodic food. *Animal Learning & Behavior, 20,* 266–280.

Lea, S. E. G. (1978). The psychology and economics of demand. *Psychological Bulletin, 85,* 441–466.

Lea, S. E. G. (1984). In what sense do pigeons learn concepts? In H. L. Roitblat, T. G. Bever, & H. S. Terrace (Eds.), *Animal cognition* (pp. 263–276). Hillsdale, NJ: Erlbaum.

Lea, S. E. G., & Harrison, S. N. (1978). Discrimination of polymorphous stimulus sets by pigeons. *Quarterly Journal of Experimental Psychology, 30,* 521–537.

Leaton, R. N. (1976). Long-term retention of the habituation of lick suppression and startle response produced by a single auditory stimulus. *Journal of Experimental Psychology: Animal Behavior Processes, 2,* 248–259.

LeDoux, J. (1996). Emotional networks and motor control: A fearful view. *Progress in Brain Research, 107,* 437–446.

Lee, R. K. K., & Maier, S. F. (1988). Inescapable shock and attention to internal versus external cues in a water discrimination escape task. *Journal of Experimental Psychology: Animal Behavior Processes, 14,* 302–310.

Leinbach, M. D., & Fagot, B. I. (1993). Categorical habituation to male and female faces: Gender schematic processing in infancy. *Infant Behavior and Development, 16,* 317–332.

Lejeune, H., Cornet, S., & Ferreira, M. A., & Wearden, J. H. (1998). How do Mongolian gerbils (*Meriones unguiculatus*) pass the time? Adjunctive behavior during temporal differentiation in gerbils. *Journal of Experimental Psychology: Animal Behavior Processes, 24,* 352–368.

Lejeune, H., & Wearden, J. H. (1991). The comparative psychology of fixed-interval responding: Some quantitative analyses. *Learning and Motivation, 22,* 84–111.

Lejuez, C. W., O'Donnell, J., Wirth, O., Zvolensky, M. J., & Eifert, G. H. (1998). Avoidance of 20% carbon dioxide-enriched air with humans. *Journal of the Experimental Analysis of Behavior, 70,* 79–86.

Lennenberg, E. H. (1967). *Biological foundations of language.* New York: Wiley.

Lepper, M. R., Greene, D., & Nisbett, R. E. (1973). Undermining children's intrinsic interest with extrinsic reward: A test of the "overjustification" hypothesis. *Journal of Personality & Social Psychology, 28*(1), 129–137.

Lerman, D. C., Iwata, B. A., Shore, B. A., & DeLeon, I. G. (1997). Effects of intermittent punishment on self-injurious behavior: An evaluation of schedule thinning. *Journal of Applied Behavioral Analysis, 30,* 187–201.

Lerman, D. C., Iwata. B. A., & Wallace, M. D. (1999). Side effects of extinction: Prevalence of bursting and aggression during the treatment of self-injurious behavior. *Journal of Applied Behavior Analysis, 32,* 1–8.

Leslie, J. C., Boyle, C., & Shaw, D. (2000). Effects of reinforcement magnitude and ratio values on behaviour maintained by a cyclic ratio schedule of reinforcement. *Quarterly Journal of Experimental Psychology, 53B,* 289–308.

Levenson, D. H., & Schusterman, R. J. (1999). Dark adaptation and visual sensitivity in shallow and deep-diving pinnipeds. *Marine Mammal Science, 15,* 1303–1313.

Levis, D. J. (1976). Learned helplessness: A reply and alternative S-R interpretation. *Journal of Experimental Psychology: General, 105,* 47–65.

Levis, D. J. (1981). Extrapolation of two-factor learning theory of infrahuman avoidance behavior to psychopathology. *Neuroscience & Biobehavioral Reviews, 5,* 355–370.

Levis, D. J. (1989). The case for a return to a two-factor theory of avoidance: The failure of non-fear interpretations. In S. B. Klein & R. R. Mowrer (Eds.), *Contemporary learning theories: Pavlovian conditioning and the status of learning theory* (pp. 227–277). Hillsdale, NJ: Erlbaum.

Levis, D. J. (1991). A clinician's plea for a return to the development of nonhuman models of psychopathology: New clinical observations in need of laboratory study. In M. R. Denny (Ed.), *Fear, avoidance and phobias* (pp. 395–427). Hillsdale, NJ: Erlbaum.

Levis, D. J. (1995). Decoding traumatic memory: Implosive theory of psychopathology. In W. O'Donohue & L. Krasner (Eds.), *Theories of behavior therapy* (pp. 173–207). Washington, DC: American Psychological Association.

Levis, D. J., & Brewer, K. E. (2001). The neurotic paradox: Attempts by two-factor fear theory and alternative avoidance models to resolve the issues associated with sustained avoidance responding in extinction. In R. R. Mowrer & S. B. Klein (Eds.), *Handbook of contemporary learning theories* (pp. 561–597). Mahwah, NJ: Erlbaum.

Lewis, D. J. (1979). Psychobiology of active and inactive memory. *Psychological Bulletin, 86,* 1054–1083.

Lewis, M., Alessandri, S. M., & Sullivan, M. W. (1990). Violation of expectancy, loss of control, and anger expression in young infants. *Developmental Psychology, 26,* 745–751.

Lieberman, D. A., & Thomas, G. V. (1986). Marking, memory and superstition in the pigeon. *Quarterly Journal of Experimental Psychology, 38B,* 449–459.

Lieberman, D. A., Davidson, F. H., & Thomas, G. V. (1985). Marking in pigeons: The role of memory in delayed reinforcement. *Journal of Experimental Psychology: Animal Behavior Processes, 11,* 611–624.

Lieberman, D. A., McIntosh, D. C., & Thomas, G. V. (1979). Learning when reward is delayed: A marking hypothesis. *Journal of Experimental Psychology: Animal Behavior Processes, 5,* 224–242.

Lieberman, D. A., Sunnucks, W. L., & Kirk, J. D. J. (1998). Reinforcement without awareness: I. Voice level. *Quarterly Journal of Experimental Psychology, 51B,* 301–316.

Limebeer, C. L., & Parker, L. A. (1999). Delta-9-tetrahydrocannabinol interferes with the establishment and the expression of conditioned rejection reactions produced by cyclophosphamide: A rat model of nausea. *NeuroReport, 10,* 3769–3772.

Limebeer, C. L., & Parker, L. A. (2000). The antiemetic drug ondansetron interferes with lithium-induced conditioned rejection reactions, but not lithium-induced taste avoidance in rats. *Journal of Experimental Psychology: Animal Behavior Processes, 26,* 371–384.

Lindberg, J. S., Iwata, B. A., Kahng, S. W., & DeLeon, I. G. (1999). DRO contingencies: An analysis of variable-momentary schedules. *Journal of Applied Behavior Analysis, 32,* 123–136.

Linscheid, T. R., & Cunningham, C. E. (1977). A controlled demonstration of the effectiveness of electric shock in the elimination of chronic infant rumination. *Journal of Applied Behavior Analysis, 10,* 500.

Lipp, O. V., Sheridan, J., & Siddle, D. A. T. (1994). Human blink startle during aversive and nonaversive Pavlovian conditioning. *Journal of Experimental Psychology: Animal Behavior Processes, 20,* 380–389.

Lockard, R. B. (1968). The albino rat: A defensible choice or a bad habit? *American Psychologist, 23,* 734–742.

Locurto, C. M., Terrace, H. S., & Gibbon, J. (Eds.). (1981). *Autoshaping and conditioning theory.* New York: Academic Press.

Loeb, J. (1900). *Comparative physiology of the brain and comparative psychology.* New York: G. P. Putman.

Logue, A. W. (1985). Conditioned food aversion learning in humans. *Annals of the New York Academy of Sciences, 433,* 316–329.

Logue, A. W. (1988a). A comparison of taste aversion learning in humans and other vertebrates: Evolutionary pressures in common. In R. C. Bolles & M. D. Beecher (Eds.), *Evolution and learning* (pp. 97–116). Hillsdale, NJ: Erlbaum.

Logue, A. W. (1988b). Research on self-control: An integrating framework. *Behavioral and Brain Sciences, 11,* 665–709.

Logue, A. W. (1995). *Self-control: Waiting until tomorrow for what you want today.* Englewood Cliffs, NJ: Prentice-Hall.

Logue, A. W. (1998a). Laboratory research on self-control: Applications to administration. *Review of General Psychology, 2,* 221–238.

Logue, A. W. (1998b). Self-control. In W. O'Donohue (Ed.), *Learning and behavior therapy* (pp. 252–273). Boston: Allyn and Bacon.

Logue, A. W., Forzano, L. B., & Ackerman, K. T. (1996). Self-control in children: Age, preference for reinforcer amount and delay, and language ability. *Learning and Motivation, 27,* 260–277.

Logue, A. W., Ophir, I., & Strauss, K. E. (1981). The acquisition of taste aversions in humans. *Behaviour Research and Therapy, 19,* 319–333.

LoLordo, V. M. (1971). Facilitation of food-reinforced responding by a signal for response-independent food. *Journal of the Experimental Analysis of Behavior, 15* 49–55.

LoLordo, V. M. (1979). Selective associations. In A. Dickinson & R. A. Boakes (Eds.), *Mechanisms of learning and motivation* (pp. 367–398). Hillsdale, NJ: Erlbaum.

LoLordo, V. M., & Fairless, J. L. (1985). Pavlovian conditioned inhibition: The literature since 1969. In R. R. Miller & N. E. Spear (Eds.), *Information processing in animals: Conditioned inhibition* (pp. 1–49). Hillsdale, NJ: Erlbaum.

LoLordo, V. M., Jacobs, W. J., & Foree, D. D. (1982). Failure to block control by a relevant stimulus. *Animal Learning & Behavior, 10,* 183–193.

LoLordo, V. M., McMillan, J. C., & Riley, A. L. (1974). The effects upon food-reinforced pecking and treadle-pressing of auditory and visual signals for response-independent food. *Learning and Motivation, 5,* 24–41.

LoLordo, V. M., & Taylor, T. L. (2001). Effects of uncontrollable aversive events: Some unsolved puzzles. In R. R. Mowrer & S. B. Klein (Eds.), *Handbook of contemporary learning theories* (pp. 469–504). Mahwah, NJ: Erlbaum

Lonon, A. M., & Zentall, T. R. (1999). Transfer of value from S+ to S− in simultaneous discriminations in humans. *American Journal of Psychology, 112,* 21–39.

Losey, G. S., & Sevenster, P. (1995). Can three-spined sticklebacks learn when to display? Rewarded displays. *Animal Behaviour, 49,* 137–150.

Lovibond, P. F. (1983). Facilitation of instrumental behavior by a Pavlovian appetitive conditioned stimulus. *Journal of Experimental Psychology: Animal Behavior Processes, 9,* 225–247.

Lubow, R. E. (1989). *Latent inhibition and conditioned attention theory.* Cambridge, England: Cambridge University Press.

Lubow, R. E., & Gewirtz, J. C. (1995). Latent inhibition in humans: Data, theory, and implications for schizophrenia. *Psychological Bulletin, 117,* 87–103.

Lubow, R. E., Weiner, I., & Schnur, P. (1981). Conditioned attention theory. In G. H. Bower (Ed.), *The psychology of learning and motivation* (Vol. 15, pp. 1–49). Orlando, FL: Academic Press.

Lucas, G. A., Timberlake, W., & Gawley, D. J. (1988). Adjunctive behavior of the rat under periodic food delivery in a 24–hour environment. *Animal Learning & Behavior, 16,* 19–30.

Lyon, D. O. (1968). Conditioned suppression: Operant variables and aversive control. *Psychological Record, 18,* 317–338.

Lysle, D. T., & Fowler, H. (1985). Inhibition as a "slave" process: Deactivation of conditioned inhibition through extinction of conditioned excitation. *Journal of Experimental Psychology: Animal Behavior Processes, 11,* 71–94.

MacArdy, E. A., & Riccio, D. C. (1995). Time-dependent changes in the effectiveness of a noncontingent footshock reminder. *Learning and Motivation, 26,* 29–42.

MacDonald, S. E. (1993). Delayed matching-to-successive-samples in pigeons: Short-term memory for item and order information. *Animal Learning & Behavior, 21,* 59–67.

MacDonall, J. S. (1998). Run length, visit duration, and reinforcers per visit in concurrent performance. *Journal of the Experimental Analysis of Behavior, 69,* 275–293.

MacDonall, J. S. (1999). A local model of concurrent performance. *Journal of the Experimental Analysis of Behavior, 71,* 57–74.

MacDonall, J. S. (2000). Synthesizing concurrent interval performances. *Journal of the Experimental Analysis of Behavior, 74,* 189–206.

Mace, F. C., Lalli, J. S., Shea, M. C., Lalli, E. P., West, B. J., Roberts, M., & Nevin, J. A. (1990). The momentum of human behavior in a natural setting. *Journal of the Experimental Analysis of Behavior, 54,* 163–172.

MacEwen, D., & Killeen, P. (1991). The effects of rate and amount of reinforcement on the speed of the pacemaker in pigeons' timing behavior. *Animal Learning & Behavior, 19,* 164–170.

Machado, A. (1989). Operant conditioning of behavioral variability using a percentile reinforcement schedule. *Journal of the Experimental Analysis of Behavior, 52,* 155–166.

Machado, A. (1992). Behavioral variability and frequency-dependent selection. *Journal of the Experimental Analysis of Behavior, 58,* 241–263.

Machado, A. (1994). Polymorphic response patterns under frequency-dependent selection. *Animal Learning & Behavior, 22,* 53–71.

Machado, A. (1997). Learning the temporal dynamics of behavior. *Psychological Review, 104,* 241–265.

Machado, A., & Cevik, M. (1997). The discrimination of relative frequency by pigeons. *Journal of the Experimental Analysis of Behavior, 67,* 11–41

Machado, A., & Cevik, M. (1998). Acquisition and extinction under periodic reinforcement. *Behavioural Processes, 44,* 237–262.

Machado, A., & Keen, R. (1999). The learning of response patterns in choice situation. *Animal Learning & Behavior, 27,* 251–271.

Mackintosh, N. J. (1974). *The psychology of animal learning.* New York: Academic Press.

Mackintosh, N. J. (1975). A theory of attention: Variations in the associability of stimuli with reinforcement. *Psychological Review, 82,* 276–298.

Mackintosh, N. J. (1995). Categorization by people and pigeons: The twenty-second Bartlett memorial lecture. *The Quarterly Journal of Experimental Psychology, 48B,* 193–214.

Mackintosh, N. J., Bygrave, D. J., & Picton, B. M. B. (1977). Locus of the effect of a surprising reinforcer in the attenuation of blocking. *Quarterly Journal of Experimental Psychology, 29,* 327–336.

Mackintosh, N. J., & Dickinson, A. (1979). Instrumental (Type II) conditioning. In A. Dickinson & R. A. Boakes (Eds.), *Mechanisms of learning and motivation* (pp. 143–169). Hillsdale, NJ: Erlbaum.

Madden, G. J., & Bickel, W. K. (1999). Abstinence and price effects on demand for cigarettes: A behavioral-economic analysis. *Addiction, 94,* 577–588.

Madden, G. J., Bickel, W. K., & Jacobs, E. A. (1999). Discounting of delayed rewards in opioid-dependent outpatients: Exponential or hyperbolic discounting functions? *Experimental and Clinical Psychopharmacology, 7,* 284–293.

Madden, G. J., Bickel, W. K., & Jacobs, E. A. (2000). Three predictions of the economic concept of unit price in a choice context. *Journal of the Experimental Analysis of Behavior, 73,* 45–64.

Madden, G. J., Petry, N. M., Badger, G. J., & Bickel, W. K. (1997). Impulsive and self-control choices in opioid-dependent patients and non-drug-using control participants: Drug and monetary rewards. *Experimental and Clinical Psychopharmacology, 5,* 256–262.

Maier, S. F. (1990). Role of fear in mediating shuttle escape learning deficit produced by inescapable shock. *Journal of Experimental Psychology: Animal Behavior Processes, 16,* 137–149.

Maier, S. F., & Church, R. M. (Eds.). (1991). Special issue on animal timing. *Learning and Motivation, 22,* 1–252.

Maier, S. F., & Jackson, R. L. (1979). Learned helplessness: All of us were right (and wrong): Inescapable shock has multiple effects. In G. H. Bower (Ed.), *The psychology of learning and motivation* (Vol.

13, pp. 155–218). New York: Academic Press.

Maier, S. F., Jackson, R. L., & Tomie, A. (1987). Potentiation, overshadowing, and prior exposure to inescapable shock. *Journal of Experimental Psychology: Animal Behavior Processes, 13,* 260–270.

Maier, S. F., Rapaport, P., & Wheatley, K. L. (1976). Conditioned inhibition and the UCS-CS interval. *Animal Learning and Behavior, 4,* 217–220.

Maier, S. F., & Seligman, M. E. P. (1976). Learned helplessness: Theory and evidence. *Journal of Experimental Psychology: General, 105,* 3–46.

Maier, S. F., Seligman, M. E. P., & Solomon, R. L. (1969). Pavlovian fear conditioning and learned helplessness. In B. A. Campbell & R. M. Church (Eds.), *Punishment and aversive behavior* (pp. 299–342). New York: Appleton-Century-Crofts.

Maier, S. F., & Warren, D. A. (1988). Controllability and safety signals exert dissimilar proactive effects on nociception and escape performance. *Journal of Experimental Psychology: Animal Behavior Processes, 14,* 18–25.

Maki, W. S. (1987). On the nonassociative nature of working memory. *Learning and Motivation, 18,* 99–117.

Maki, W. S., Beatty, W. W., Hoffman, N., Bierley, R. A., & Clouse, B. A. (1984). Spatial memory over long retention intervals: Nonmemorial factors are not necessary for accurate performance on the radial arm maze by rats. *Behavioral and Neural Biology, 41,* 1–6.

Maki, W. S., Moe, J. C., & Bierley, C. M. (1977). Short-term memory for stimuli, responses, and reinforcers. *Journal of Experimental Psychology: Animal Behavior Processes, 3,* 156–177.

Malenka, R. C., & Nicoll, R. A. (1999). Long-term potentiation—A decade of progress? *Science, 285,* 1870–1874.

March, J., Chamizo, V. D., & Mackintosh, N. J. (1992). Reciprocal overshadowing between intra-maze and extra-maze cues. *Quarterly Journal of Experimental Psychology, 45,* 49–63.

Marchand, A. R., & Kamper, E. (2000). Time course of cardiac conditioned responses in restrained rats as a function of the trace CS-US interval. *Journal of Ex-

perimental Psychology: Animal Behavior Processes, 26,* 385–398.

Marchant, H. G., III, Mis, F. W., & Moore, J. W. (1972). Conditioned inhibition of the rabbit's nictitating membrane response. *Journal of Experimental Psychology, 95,* 408–411.

Maricq, A. V., Roberts, S., & Church, R. M. (1981). Methamphetamine and time estimation. *Journal of Experimental Psychology: Animal Behavior Processes, 7,* 18–30.

Marsh, G. (1972). Prediction of the peak shift in pigeons from gradients of excitation and inhibition. *Journal of Comparative and Physiological Psychology, 81,* 262–266.

Martens, B. K., Lochner, D. G., & Kelly, S. Q. (1992). The effects of variable-interval reinforcement on academic engagement: A demonstration of matching theory. *Journal of Applied Behavior Analysis, 25,* 143–151.

Martin, S. J., Grimwood, P. D., & Morris, R. G. M. (2000). Synaptic plasticity and memory: An evaluation of the hypothesis. *Annual Review of Neuroscience, 23,* 649–711.

Martin-Malivel, J., & Fagot, J. (2001). Perception of pictorial human faces by baboons: Effects of stimulus orientation on discrimination performance. *Animal Learning & Behavior, 29,* 10–20.

Masserman, J. H. (1946). *Principles of dynamic psychiatry.* Philadelphia: Saunders.

Mast, M., Blanchard, R. J., & Blanchard, D. C. (1982). The relationship of freezing and response suppression in a CER situation. *Psychological Record, 32,* 151–167.

Matell, M. S., & Meck, W. H. (2000). Neuropsychological mechanisms of interval timing behaviour. *BioEssays, 22,* 94–203.

Matthews, T. J., Bordi, F., & Depollo, D. (1990). Schedule induced kinesic and taxic behavioral stereotypy in the pigeon. *Journal of Experimental Psychology: Animal Behavior Processes, 16,* 335–344.

Matzel, L. D., Gladstein, L., & Miller, R. R. (1988). Conditioned excitation and conditioned inhibition are not mutually exclusive. *Learning and Motivation, 19,* 99–121.

Mayford, M., Bach, M. E., Huang, Y.-Y., Wang, L., Hawkins, R. D., & Kandel, E. R. (1996). Control of memory formation through regulated expression of a CaMKII transgene. *Science, 274,* 1678–1683.

Mayford, M., & Kandel, E. R. (1999). Genetic approaches to memory storage. *Trends in Genetics, 15,* 463–470.

Mazur, J. E. (1987). An adjusting procedure for studying delayed reinforcement. In M. L. Commons, J. E. Mazur, J. A. Nevin, & H. Rachlin (Eds.), *Quantitative analyses of behavior: Vol. 5. The effect of delay and intervening events on reinforcement value* (pp. 55–73). Hillsdale, NJ: Erlbaum.

Mazur, J. E. (1991). Choice with probabilistic reinforcement: Effects of delay and conditioned reinforcers. *Journal of the Experimental Analysis of Behavior, 55,* 63–77.

Mazur, J. E. (1998). Choice with delayed and probabilistic reinforcers: Effects of prereinforcer and postreinforcer stimuli. *Journal of the Experimental Analysis of Behavior, 70,* 253–265.

Mazur, J. E. (2000). Two- versus three-alternative concurrent-chain schedules: A test of three models. *Journal of Experimental Psychology: Animal Behavior Processes, 26,* 286–293.

Mazur, J. E. (2001). Hyperbolic value addition and general models of animal choice. *Psychological Review, 108,* 96–112.

Mazur, J. E., & Romano, A. (1992). Choice with delayed and probabilistic reinforcers: Effects of variability, time between trials, and conditioned reinforcers. *Journal of the Experimental Analysis of Behavior, 58,* 513–525.

McAdie, T. M., Foster, T. M., & Temple, W. (1996). Concurrent schedules: Quantifying the aversiveness of noise. *Journal of the Experimental Analysis of Behavior, 65,* 37–55.

McAllister, D. E., & McAllister, W. R. (1991). Fear theory and aversively motivated behavior: Some controversial issues. In M. R. Denny (Ed.), *Fear, avoidance and phobias* (pp. 135–163). Hillsdale, NJ: Erlbaum.

McAllister, W. R., & McAllister, D. E. (1971). Behavioral measurement of fear. In F. R. Brush (Ed.), *Aversive conditioning and learning* (pp. 105–179). New York: Academic Press.

McAllister, W. R., & McAllister, D. E. (1992). Fear determines the effectiveness of a feedback stimulus in aversively motivated instrumental learning. *Learning and Motivation, 23,* 99–115.

McAllister, W. R., & McAllister, D. E. (1995). Two-factor fear theory: Implications for understanding anxiety-based clinical phenomena. In W. O'Donohue & L. Krasner (Eds.), *Theories of behavior therapy* (pp. 145–171). Washington, DC: American Psychological Association.

McDevitt, M. A., & Williams, B. A. (2001). Effects of signaled versus unsignaled delay of reinforcement on choice. *Journal of the Experimental Analysis of Behavior, 75,* 165–182.

McDowell, J. J. (1982). The importance of Herrnstein's mathematical statement of the law of effect for behavior therapy. *American Psychologist, 37,* 771–779.

McDowell, J. J., & Dallery, J. (1999). Falsification of matching theory: Changes in the asymptote of Herrnstein's hyperbola as a function of water deprivation. *Journal of the Experimental Analysis of Behavior, 72,* 251–268.

McDowell, J. J., & Wixted, J. T. (1988). The linear system theory's account of behavior maintained by variable ratio schedules. *Journal of the Experimental Analysis of Behavior, 49,* 143–169.

McFarland, D., & Bösser, T. (1993). *Intelligent behavior in animals and robots.* Cambridge, MA: MIT Press.

McGaugh, J. L., & Herz, M. J. (1972). *Memory consolidation.* San Francisco: Albion.

McGaugh, J. L., & Petrinovich, L. F. (1965). Effects of drugs on learning and memory. *International Review of Neurobiology, 8,* 139–196.

McGee, G. G., Krantz, P. J., & McClannahan, L. E. (1986). An extension of incidental teaching procedures to reading instruction for autistic children. *Journal of Applied Behavior Analysis, 19,* 147–157.

McLaren, I. P. L., & Mackintosh, N. J. (2000). An elemental model of associative learning: I. Latent inhibition and perceptual learning. *Animal Learning & Behavior, 28,* 211–246.

McLean, A. P., & Blampied, N. M. (2001). Sensitivity to relative reinforcer rate in concurrent schedules: Independence from relative and absolute reinforcer duration. *Journal of the Experimental Analysis of Behavior, 75,* 25–42.

McLean, A. P., Campbell-Tie, P., & Nevin, J. A. (1996). Resistance to change as a function of stimulus-reinforcer and location-reinforcer contingencies. *Journal of the Experimental Analysis of Behavior, 66,* 169–191.

McMillan, D. E., & Li, M. (1999). Drug discrimination under a concurrent fixed-ratio fixed-ratio schedule. *Journal of the Experimental Analysis of Behavior, 72,* 187–204.

McMillan, D. E., & Li, M. (2000). Drug discrimination under two concurrent fixed-interval fixed-interval schedules. *Journal of the Experimental Analysis of Behavior, 74,* 55–77.

McMillan, D. E., Li, M., & Hardwick, W. C. (1997). Drug discrimination under a concurrent fixed-interval fixed-interval schedule. *Journal of the Experimental Analysis of Behavior, 68,* 193–217.

McNish, K. A., Betts, S. L., Brandon, S. E., & Wagner, A. R. (1997). Divergence of conditioned eyeblink and conditioned fear in backward Pavlovian training. *Animal Learning & Behavior, 25,* 43–52.

McPhee, J. E., Rauhut, A. S., & Ayres, J. J. B. (2001). Evidence for learning-deficit versus performance-deficit theories of latent inhibition in Pavlovian fear conditioning. *Learning & Motivation, 32*(3), 274–305.

McSweeney, F. K., Hinson, J. M., & Cannon, C. B. (1996). Sensitization-habituation may occur during operant conditioning. *Psychological Bulletin, 120,* 256–271.

McSweeney, F. K., & Melville, C. L. (1993). Behavioral contrast for key pecking as a function of component duration when only one component varies. *Journal of the Experimental Analysis of Behavior, 60,* 311–343.

McSweeney, F. K., Melville, C. L., Buck, M. A., & Whipple, J. E. (1983). Local rates of responding and reinforcement during concurrent schedules. *Journal of the Experimental Analysis of Behavior, 40,* 79–98.

McSweeney, F. K., & Roll, J. M. (1998). Do animals satiate or habituate to repeatedly presented reinforcers? *Psychonomic Bulletin & Review, 5,* 428–442.

McSweeney, F. K., & Swindell, S. (1999). General-process theories of motivation revisited: The role of habituation. *Psychological Bulletin, 125,* 437–457.

Meck, W. H. (1983). Selective adjustment of the speed of internal clock and memory processes. *Journal of Experimental Psychology: Animal Behavior Processes, 9,* 171–201.

Meck, W. H., & Church, R. M. (1982). Abstraction of temporal attributes. *Journal of Experimental Psychology: Animal Behavior Processes, 8,* 226–243.

Meck, W. H., & Church, R. M. (1987a). Cholinergic modulation of the content of temporal memory. *Behavioral Neuroscience, 101,* 457–464.

Meck, W. H., & Church, R. M. (1987b). Nutrients that modify the speed of internal clock and memory storage processes. *Behavioral Neuroscience, 101,* 465–475.

Meisch, R. A., & Spiga, R. (1998). Matching under nonindependent variable-ratio schedules of drug reinforcement. *Journal of the Experimental Analysis of Behavior, 70,* 23–34.

Mellgren, R. L. (1972). Positive and negative contrast effects using delayed reinforcement. *Learning and Motivation, 3,* 185–193.

Melvin, K. B. (1971). Vicious circle behavior. In H. D. Kimmel (Ed.), *Experimental psychopathology.* New York: Academic Press.

Melvin, K. B., & Ervey, D. H. (1973). Facilitative and suppressive effects of punishment of species-typical aggressive display in *Betta splendens. Journal of Comparative and Physiological Psychology, 83,* 451–457.

Mercado, E., III, Murray, S. O., Uyeyama, R. K., Pack, A. A., & Herman, L. M. (1998). Memory for recent actions in the bottlenosed dolphin (*Tursiops truncates*): Repetition of arbitrary behaviors using

an abstract rule. *Animal Learning & Behavior, 26,* 210–218.

Meyer, J.-A., & Wilson, S. W. (Eds.). (1991). *From animals to animats: Proceedings of the first international conference on simulation of adaptive behavior.* Cambridge, MA: MIT Press.

Meyer, J.-A., Berthoz, A., Floreano, D., Roitblat, H., & Wilson, S. W. (Eds.). (2000). *From animals to animats 6.* Cambridge, MA: MIT Press.

Midgley, M., Lea, S. E. G., & Kirby, R. M. (1989). Algorithmic shaping and misbehavior in the acquisition of token deposit by rats. *Journal of the Experimental Analysis of Behavior, 52,* 27–40.

Mikulincer, M. (1994). *Human learned helplessness.* New York: Plenum.

Miller, H. L. (1976). Matching-based hedonic scaling in the pigeon. *Journal of the Experimental Analysis of Behavior, 26,* 335–347.

Miller, J. S., Jagielo, J. A., & Spear, N. E. (1990a). Alleviation of short-term forgetting: Effects of the CS– and other conditioning elements in prior cueing or as context during test. *Learning and Motivation, 21,* 96–109.

Miller, J. S., Jagielo, J. A., & Spear, N. E. (1990b). Changes in the retrievability of associations to elements of the compound CS determine the expression of overshadowing. *Animal Learning & Behavior, 18,* 157–161.

Miller, J. S., Jagielo, J. A., & Spear, N. E. (1991). Differential effectiveness of various prior-cuing treatments in the reactivation and maintenance of memory. *Journal of Experimental Psychology: Animal Behavior Processes, 17,* 249–258.

Miller, J. S., Jagielo, J. A., & Spear, N. E. (1992). The influence of the information value provided by prior-cuing treatment on the reactivation of memory in preweanling rats. *Animal Learning & Behavior, 20,* 233–239.

Miller, N. E. (1951). Learnable drives and rewards. In S. S. Stevens (Ed.), *Handbook of experimental psychology.* New York: Wiley.

Miller, N. E. (1960). Learning resistance to pain and fear: Effects of overlearning, exposure, and rewarded exposure in con-

text. *Journal of Experimental Psychology, 60,* 137–145.

Miller, N. E., & Dollard, J. (1941). *Social learning and imitation.* New Haven, CT: Yale University Press.

Miller, R. R., Barnet, R. C., & Grahame, N. J. (1992). Responding to a conditioned stimulus depends on the current associative status of other cues present during training of that specific stimulus. *Journal of Experimental Psychology: Animal Behavior Processes, 18, 251–264.*

Miller, R. R., Barnet, R. C., & Grahame, N. J. (1995). Assessment of the Rescorla–Wagner model. *Psychological Bulletin, 117,* 363–386.

Miller, R. R., & Escobar, M. (2001). Contrasting acquisition-focused and performance-focused models of acquired behavior. *Current Directions in Psychological Science, 10,* 141–145.

Miller, R. R., Hallam, S. C., & Grahame, N. J. (1990). Inflation of comparator stimuli following CS training. *Animal Learning & Behavior, 18,* 434–443.

Miller, R. R., Kasprow, W. J., & Schachtman, T. R. (1986). Retrieval variability: Sources and consequences. *American Journal of Psychology, 99,* 145–218.

Miller, R. R., & Matute, H. (1996). Animal analogues of causal judgment. In G. H. Bower (Ed.), *The psychology of learning and motivation* (Vol. 34, pp. 133–166). San Diego, CA: Academic Press.

Miller, R. R., & Matzel, L. D. (1988). The comparator hypothesis: A response rule for the expression of associations. In G. H. Bower (Ed.), *The psychology of learning and motivation* (Vol. 22, pp. 51–92). Orlando, FL: Academic Press.

Miller, R. R., & Matzel, L. D. (1989). Contingency and relative associative strength. In S. B. Klein & R. R. Mowrer (Eds.), *Contemporary learning theories: Pavlovian conditioning and the status of learning theory* (pp. 61–84). Hillsdale, NJ: Erlbaum.

Miller, R. R., & Matzel, L. D. (2000). Memory involves far more than consolidation. *Nature Reviews Neuroscience, 1,* 214–216.

Miller, R. R., & Spear, N. E. (Eds.). (1985). *Information processing in animals: Conditioned inhibition.* Hillsdale, NJ: Erlbaum.

Miller, R. R., & Springer, A. D. (1973). Amnesia, consolidation, and retrieval. *Psychological Review, 80,* 69–79.

Miller, V., & Domjan, M. (1981). Selective sensitization induced by lithium malaise and footshock in rats. *Behavioral and Neural Biology, 31,* 42–55.

Millin, P. M., Moody, E. W., & Riccio, D. C. (2001). Interpretations of retrograde amnesia: Old problems redux. *Nature Reviews Neuroscience, 2,* 68–70.

Mineka, S. (1979). The role of fear in theories of avoidance learning, flooding, and extinction. *Psychological Bulletin, 86,* 985–1010.

Mineka, S., & Cook, M. (1988). Social learning and the acquisition of snake fear in monkeys. In T. Zentall & B. G. Galef, Jr. (Eds.), *Social learning* (pp. 51–73). Hillsdale, NJ: Erlbaum.

Mineka, S., & Gino, A. (1979). Dissociative effects of different types and amounts of nonreinforced CS exposure on avoidance extinction and the CER. *Learning and Motivation, 10,* 141–160.

Mineka, S., & Gino, A. (1980). Dissociation between conditioned emotional response and extended avoidance performance. *Learning and Motivation, 11,* 476–502.

Mineka, S., & Henderson, R. (1985). Controllability and predictability in acquired motivation. *Annual Review of Psychology, 36,* 495–530.

Mineka, S., Miller, S., Gino, A., & Giencke, L. (1981). Dissociative effects of flooding on a multivariate assessment of fear reduction and on jump-up avoidance extinction. *Learning and Motivation, 12,* 435–461.

Mineka, S., Suomi, S. J., & DeLizio, R. (1981). Multiple separations in adolescent monkeys: An opponent-process interpretation. *Journal of Experimental Psychology: General, 110,* 56–85.

Minor, T. R., Dess, N. K., & Overmier, J. B. (1991). Inverting the traditional view of "learned helplessness." In M. R. Denny (Ed.), *Fear, avoidance and phobias* (pp. 87–133). Hillsdale, NJ: Erlbaum.

Minor, T. R., Trauner, M. A., Lee, C.-Y., & Dess, N. K. (1990). Modeling signal features of escape response: Effects of cessation conditioning in "learned helplessness" paradigm. *Journal of Experimental Psychology: Animal Behavior Processes, 16,* 123–136.

Mitchell, S. H., & Brener, J. (1991). Energetic and motor responses to increasing food requirements. *Journal of Experimental Psychology: Animal Behavior Processes, 17,* 174–185.

Morgan, C. L. (1903). *Introduction to comparative psychology* (rev. ed.). New York: Scribner.

Morgan, L., & Neuringer, A. (1990). Behavioral variability as a function of response topography and reinforcement contingency. *Animal Learning & Behavior, 18,* 257–263.

Morgan, M. J., Fitch, M. D., Holman, J. G., & Lea, S. E. G. (1976). Pigeons learn the concept of an "A." *Perception, 5,* 57–66.

Morris, C. J. (1987). The operant conditioning of response variability: Free-operant versus discrete-response procedures. *Journal of the Experimental Analysis of Behavior, 47,* 273–277.

Morris, R. G. M. (1974). Pavlovian conditioned inhibition of fear during shuttle-box avoidance behavior. *Learning and Motivation, 5,* 424–447.

Morris, R. G. M. (1975). Preconditioning of reinforcing properties to an exteroceptive feedback stimulus. *Learning and Motivation, 6,* 289–298.

Morris, R. G. M. (1981). Spatial localization does not require the presence of local cues. *Learning and Motivation, 12,* 239–260.

Morris, R. G. M., Anderson, E., Lynch, G. S., & Baudry, M. (1986). Selective impairment of learning and blockade of long-term potentiation by an N-methyl-D-aspartate receptor antagonist, AP5. *Nature, 319,* 774–776.

Mowrer, O. H. (1947). On the dual nature of learning: A reinterpretation of "conditioning" and "problem-solving." *Harvard Educational Review, 17,* 102–150.

Mowrer, O. H. (1960). *Learning theory and behavior.* New York: Wiley.

Mowrer, O. H., & Lamoreaux, R. R. (1942). Avoidance conditioning and signal duration: A study of secondary motivation and reward. *Psychological Monographs, 54* (Whole No. 247).

Mowrer, R. R., & Gordon, W. C. (1983). Effects of cuing in an "irrelevant" context. *Animal Learning & Behavior, 11,* 401–406.

Mowrer, R. R., & Klein, S. B. (Eds.). (2001). *Handbook of contemporary learning theories.* Mahwah, NJ: Erlbaum.

Moye, T. B., & Thomas, D. R. (1982). Effects of memory reactivation treatments on postdiscrimination generalization performance in pigeons. *Animal Learning & Behavior, 10,* 159–166.

Murkerjee, M. (1997, February). Trends in animal research. *Scientific American,* 86–93.

Myers, H. H., & Siegel, P. S. (1985). The motivation to breastfeed: A fit to the opponent-process theory? *Journal of Personality and Social Psychology, 49,* 188–193.

Myers, K. M., Vogel, E. H., Shin, J., & Wagner, A. R. (2001). A comparison of the Rescorla–Wagner and Pearce models in a negative patterning and summation problem. *Animal Learning & Behavior, 29,* 36–45.

Nader, K., Schafe, G., & LeDoux, J. E. (2000). Reconsolidation: The labile nature of consolidation theory. *Nature Reviews Neuroscience, 1,* 216–219.

Nakajima, S. (1997a). Failure of inhibition by B over C after A+, AB−, and ABC+ training. *Journal of Experimental Psychology: Animal Behavior Processes, 23,* 482–490.

Nakajima, S. (1997b). Transfer testing after serial feature-ambiguous discrimination in Pavlovian keypeck conditioning. *Animal Learning & Behavior, 25,* 413–426.

Nakajima, S. (1998). Further investigation of responding elicited by BC and C after A+, AB−, and ABC+ training. *Quarterly Journal of Experimental Psychology, 51B,* 289–300.

Nakajima, S., Tanaka, S., Urushihara, K., & Imada, H. (2000). Renewal of extinguished lever-press responses upon return to the training context. *Learning and Motivation, 31,* 416–431.

Nakajima, S., & Urushihara, K. (1999). Inhibition and facilitation by B over C after A+, AB−, and ABC+ training with multimodality stimulus combinations. *Journal of Experimental Psychology: Animal Behavior Processes, 25,* 68–81.

Nation, J. R., & Cooney, J. B. (1982). The time course of extinction-induced aggressive behavior in humans: Evidence for a stage model of extinction. *Learning and Motivation, 13,* 95–112.

Neill, J. C., & Harrison, J. M. (1987). Auditory discrimination: The Konorski quality-location effect. *Journal of the Experimental Analysis of Behavior, 48,* 81–95.

Neuenschwander, N., Fabrigoule, C., & Mackintosh, N. J. (1987). Fear of the warning signal during overtraining of avoidance. *Quarterly Journal of Experimental Psychology, 39B,* 23–33.

Neuringer, A. (1991). Operant variability and repetition as functions of interresponse time. *Journal of Experimental Psychology: Animal Behavior Processes, 17,* 3–12.

Neuringer, A. (1992). Choosing to vary and repeat. *Psychological Science, 3,* 246–250.

Neuringer, A. (1993). Reinforced variation and selection. *Animal Learning & Behavior, 21,* 83–91.

Neuringer, A., Deiss, C., & Olson, G. (2000). Reinforced variability and operant learning. *Journal of Experimental Psychology: Animal Behavior Processes, 26,* 98–111.

Neuringer, A., Kornell, N., & Olufs, M. (2001). Stability and variability in extinction. *Journal of Experimental Psychology: Animal Behavior Processes, 27,* 79–94.

Nevin, J. A. (1969). Interval reinforcement of choice behavior in discrete trials. *Journal of the Experimental Analysis of Behavior, 12,* 875–885.

Nevin, J. A. (1979). Overall matching versus momentary maximizing: Nevin (1969) revisited. *Journal of Experimental Psychology: Animal Behavior Processes, 5,* 300–306.

Nevin, J. A. (1988). Behavioral momentum and the partial reinforcement extinction effect. *Psychological Bulletin, 103,* 44–56.

Nevin, J. A. (1992). An integrative model for the study of behavioral momentum. *Journal of the Experimental Analysis of Behavior, 57,* 301–316.

Nevin, J. A. (1998). Choice and momentum. In W. O'Donohue (Ed.), *Learning and behavior therapy* (pp. 230–251). Boston: Allyn and Bacon.

Nevin, J. A., & Grace, R. C. (1999). Does the context of reinforcement affect resistance to change? *Journal of Experimental Psychology: Animal Behavior Processes, 25,* 256–268.

Nevin, J. A., & Grace, R. C. (2000). Behavioral momentum and the law of effect. *Behavioral and Brain Sciences, 23,* 73–130.

Nevin, J. A., Mandell, G., & Atak, J. R. (1983). The analysis of behavioral momentum. *Journal of the Experimental Analysis of Behavior, 39,* 49–59.

Noll, J. P. (1995). The matching law as a theory of choice in behavior therapy. In W. O'Donohue & L. Krasner (Eds.), *Theories of behavior therapy* (pp. 129–144). Washington, DC: American Psychological Association.

O'Donnell, J., Crosbie, J., Williams, D. C., & Saunders, K. J. (2000). Stimulus control and generalization of point-loss punishment with humans. *Journal of the Experimental Analysis of Behavior, 73,* 261–274.

O'Donohue, W. (1998). Conditioning and third-generation behavior therapy. In W. O'Donohue (Ed.), *Learning and behavior therapy* (pp. 1–14). Boston: Allyn and Bacon.

Oades, R. D., Roepcke, B., & Schepker, R. (1996). A test of conditioned blocking and its development in childhood and adolescence: Relationship to personality and monoamine metabolism. *Developmental Neuropsychology, 12,* 207–230.

Oberling, P., Gosselin, O., & Miller, R. R. (1997). Latent inhibition in animals as a model of acute schizophrenia: A reanalysis. In M. Haug & R. E. Whalen (Eds.), *Animal models of human emotion and cognition* (pp. 97–102). Washington, DC: American Psychological Association.

Oden, D. L., Thompson, R. K. R., & Premack, D. (1988). Spontaneous transfer of matching by infant chimpanzees (*Pan troglodytes*). *Journal of Experimental Psychology: Animal Behavior Processes, 14,* 140–145.

Odum, A. L., Madden, G. J., Badger, G. J., & Bickel, W. K. (2000). Needle sharing in opioid-dependent outpatients: Psychological process underlying risk. *Drug and Alcohol Dependence, 60,* 259–266.

Öhman, A., Dimberg, U., & Öst, L. G. (1985). Animal and social phobias: Biological constraints on learned fear responses. In S. Reiss & R. R. Bootzin (Eds.), *Theoretical issues in behavior therapy.* Orlando, FL: Academic Press.

Ohyama, T., Gibbon, J., Deich, J. D., & Balsam, P. (1999). Temporal control during maintenance and extinction of conditioned keypecking in ring doves. *Animal Learning & Behavior, 27,* 89–98.

Olton, D. S. (1978). Characteristics of spatial memory. In S. H. Hulse, H. Fowler, & W. K. Honig (Eds.), *Cognitive processes in animal behavior* (pp. 341–374). Hillsdale, NJ: Erlbaum.

Olton, D. S. (1979). Mazes, maps, and memory. *American Psychologist, 34,* 583–596.

Olton, D. S., Collison, C., & Werz, M. A. (1977). Spatial memory and radial arm maze performance of rats. *Learning and Motivation, 8,* 289–314.

Olton, D. S., & Samuelson, R. J. (1976). Remembrance of places passed: Spatial memory in rats. *Journal of Experimental Psychology: Animal Behavior Processes, 2,* 97–116.

Ost, J. W. P., & Lauer, D. W. (1965). Some investigations of salivary conditioning in the dog. In W. F. Prokasy (Ed.), *Classical conditioning* (pp. 192–207). New York: Appleton-Century-Crofts.

Overmier, J. B. (1999). On the nature of animal models of human behavioral dysfunction. In M. Haug & R. E. Whalen (Eds.), *Animal models of human emotion and cognition* (pp. 15–24). Washington, DC: American Psychological Association.

Overmier, J. B., & Lawry, J. A. (1979). Pavlovian conditioning and the mediation of behavior. In G. H. Bower (Ed.), *The psychology of learning and motivation* (Vol. 13, pp. 1–55). New York: Academic Press.

Overmier, J. B., & LoLordo, V. M. (1998). Learned helplessness. In W. O'Donohue (Ed.), *Learning and behavior therapy* (pp. 352–373). Boston: Allyn and Bacon.

Overmier, J. B., & Seligman, M. E. P. (1967). Effects of inescapable shock upon subsequent escape and avoidance learning. *Journal of Comparative and Physiological Psychology, 63*, 23–33.

Owen, J. W., Cicala, G. A., & Herdegen, R. T. (1978). Fear inhibition and species specific defense reaction termination may contribute independently to avoidance learning. *Learning and Motivation, 9*, 297–313.

Page, S., & Neuringer, A. (1985). Variability as an operant. *Journal of Experimental Psychology: Animal Behavior Processes, 11*, 429–452.

Palya, W. L. (1993). Bipolar control in fixed interfood intervals. *Journal of the Experimental Analysis of Behavior, 60*, 345–359.

Papadouka, V., & Matthews, T. J. (1995). Motivational mechanisms and schedule-induced behavioral stereotypy. *Animal Learning & Behavior, 23*, 461–469.

Papini, M. R. (2002). Pattern and process in the evolution of learning. *Psychological Review, 109*, 186–201.

Papini, M. R., & Bitterman, M. E. (1990). The role of contingency in classical conditioning. *Psychological Review, 97*, 396–403.

Papini, M. R., & Bitterman, M. E. (1993). The two-test strategy in the study of inhibitory conditioning. *Journal of Experimental Psychology: Animal Behavior Processes, 19*, 342–352.

Papini, M. R., & Dudley, R. T. (1997). Consequences of surprising reward omissions. *Review of General Psychology, 1*, 175–197.

Papini, M. R., & Hollingsworth, P. R. (1998). Role of nonreinforcement in the fixed-interval performance of pigeons. *Psychonomic Bulletin & Review, 5*, 84–90.

Parker, B. K., Serdikoff, S. L., Kaminski, B. J., & Critchfield, T. S. (1991). Stimulus control of Pavlovian facilitation. *Journal of the Experimental Analysis of Behavior, 55*, 275–286.

Patterson, F. G. (1978). The gestures of a gorilla: Language acquisition in another pongid. *Brain and Language, 5*, 56–71.

Patterson, M. M., & Grau, J. W. (2001). *Spinal cord plasticity: Alterations in reflex function*. Boston: Kluwer Academic Publishers.

Pavlov, I. P. (1927). *Conditioned reflexes* (G. V. Anrep, trans.). London: Oxford University Press.

Pear, J. J., & Legris, J. A. (1987). Shaping by automated tracking of an arbitrary operant response. *Journal of the Experimental Analysis of Behavior, 47*, 241–247.

Pearce, J. M. (1987). A model for stimulus generalization in Pavlovian conditioning. *Psychological Review, 94*, 61–73.

Pearce, J. M. (1994a). Discrimination and categorization. In N. J. Mackintosh (Ed.), *Animal learning and cognition* (pp. 109–134). San Diego: Academic Press.

Pearce, J. M. (1994b). Similarity and discrimination: A selective review and a connectionistic model. *Psychological Review, 101*, 587–607.

Pearce, J. M., Aydin, A., & Redhead, E. S. (1997). Configural analysis of summation in autoshaping. *Journal of Experimental Psychology: Animal Behavior Processes, 23*, 84–94.

Pearce, J. M., & Bouton, M. E. (2001). Theories of associate learning in animals. *Annual Review of Psychology, 52*, 111–139.

Pearce, J. M., & Dickinson, A. (1975). Pavlovian counterconditioning: Changing the suppressive properties of shock by association with food. *Journal of Experimental Psychology: Animal Behavior Processes, 1*, 170–177.

Pearce, J. M., & Hall, G. (1980). A model for Pavlovian learning: Variations in the effectiveness of conditioned but not of unconditioned stimuli. *Psychological Review, 87*, 532–552.

Pearce, J. M., Redhead, E. S., & Aydin, A. (1997). Partial reinforcement in appetitive Pavlovian conditioning in rats. *Quarterly Journal of Experimental Psychology, 50B*, 273–294.

Pecoraro, N. C., Timberlake, W. D., & Tinsley, M. (1999). Incentive downshifts evoke search repertoires in rats. *Journal of Experimental Psychology: Animal Behavior Processes, 25*, 153–167.

Pedreira, M. E., Romano, A., Tomsic, D., Lozada, M., & Maldonado, H. (1998). Massed and spaced training build up different components of long-term habituation in the crab *Chasmagnathus*. *Animal Learning & Behavior, 26*, 34–45.

Pelchat, M. L., & Rozin, P. (1982). The special role of nausea in the acquisition of food dislikes by humans. *Appetite, 3*, 341–351.

Pepperberg, I. M. (1990). Some cognitive capacities of an African grey parrot (Psittacus erithacus). In P. J. B. Slater, J. S. Rosenblatt, & C. Beer (Eds.), *Advances in the study of behavior* (Vol. 19, pp. 357–409). San Diego: Academic Press.

Pepperberg, I. M. (1993). Cognition and communication in an African Grey parrot (*Psittacus erithacus*): Studies on a nonhuman, nonprimate, nonmammalian subject. In H. L. Roitblat, L. M. Herman, & P. E. Nachtigall (Eds.), *Language and communication: Comparative perspectives* (pp. 221– 248). Hillsdale, NJ: Erlbaum.

Pepperberg, I. M. (1999). *The Alex studies: Cognitive and communicative abilities of Grey Parrots*. Cambridge, MA: Harvard University Press.

Pérez, C., Fanizza, L. J., & Sclafani, A. (1999). Flavor preferences conditioned by intragastric nutrient infusions in rats fed chow or a cafeteria diet. *Appetite, 32*, 155–170.

Perry, D. G., & Parke, R. D. (1975). Punishment and alternative response training as determinants of response inhibition in children. *Genetic Psychology Monographs, 91*, 257–279.

Peterson, C., Maier, S. F., & Seligman, M. E. P. (1993). *Learned helplessness: A theory for the age of personal control*. New York: Oxford University Press.

Peterson, C., & Seligman, M. E. P. (1984). Causal explanations as a risk factor for depression: Theory and evidence. *Psychological Review, 91*, 347–374.

Peterson, G. B., Ackil, J. E., Frommer, G. P., & Hearst, E. S. (1972). Conditioned approach and contact behavior toward signals for food and brain-stimulation reinforcement. *Science, 177*, 1009–1011.

Peterson, G. B., & Trapold, M. A. (1980). Effects of altering outcome expectancies on pigeons' delayed conditional discrimination performance. *Learning and Motivation, 11*, 267–288.

Petry, N. M., & Bickel, W. K. (1998). Polydrug abuse in heroin addicts: A behavioral economic analysis. *Addiction, 93*, 321–335.

Petry, N. M., & Heyman, G. M. (1994). Effects of qualitatively different reinforcers on the parameters of the response-strength equation. *Journal of the Experimental Analysis of Behavior, 61*, 97–106.

References

417

Petry, N. M., & Heyman, G. M. (1995). Behavioral economics of concurrent ethanol-sucrose and sucrose reinforcement in the rat: Effects of altering variable-ratio requirements. *Journal of the Experimental Analysis of Behavior, 64,* 331–359.

Pilz, P. K., & Schnitzler, H.-U. (1996). Habituation and sensitization of the acoustic startle response in rats: Amplitude, threshold, and latency measures. *Neurobiology of Learning and Memory, 66,* 67–79.

Pisacreta, R. (1982). Some factors that influence the acquisition of complex, stereotyped, response sequences in pigeons. *Journal of the Experimental Analysis of Behavior, 37,* 359–369.

Platt, J. R. (1973). Percentile reinforcement: Paradigms for experimental analysis of response shaping. In G. H. Bower (Ed.), *The psychology of learning and motivation* (Vol. 7, pp. 271–296). Orlando, FL: Academic Press.

Ploog, B. O. (2001). Net amount of food affects autoshaped response rate, response latency, and gape amplitude in pigeons. *Learning and Motivation, 32,* 383–400.

Ploog, B. O., & Zeigler, H. P. (1996). Effects of food-pellet size on rate, latency, and topography of autoshaped key pecks and gapes in pigeons. *Journal of the Experimental Analysis of Behavior, 65,* 21–35.

Plous, S. (1991). An attitude survey of animal rights activists. *Psychological Science, 2,* 194–196.

Plous, S. (1998). Signs of change within the animal rights movement: Results from a follow-up survey of activists. *Journal of Comparative Psychology, 112,* 48–54.

Poling, A., Nickel, M., & Alling, K. (1990). Free birds aren't fat: Weight gain in captured wild pigeons maintained under laboratory conditions. *Journal of the Experimental Analysis of Behavior, 53,* 423–424.

Porter, D., & Neuringer, A. (1984). Music discrimination by pigeons. *Journal of Experimental Psychology: Animal Behavior Processes, 10,* 138–148.

Postman, L. (1971). Transfer, interference, and forgetting. In J. W. Kling & L. A. Riggs (Eds.), *Woodworth and Schlosberg's experimental psychology* (3rd ed.). New York: Holt, Rinehart and Winston.

Poulos, C. X., & Cappell, H. (1991). Homeostatic theory of drug tolerance: A general model of physiological adaptation. *Psychological Review, 98,* 390–408.

Premack, D. (1962). Reversibility of the reinforcement relation. *Science, 136,* 255–257.

Premack, D. (1965). Reinforcement theory. In D. Levine (Ed.), *Nebraska symposium on motivation* (Vol. 13, pp. 123–180). Lincoln: University of Nebraska Press.

Premack, D. (1971a). Catching up with common sense, or two sides of a generalization: Reinforcement and punishment. In R. Glaser (Ed.), *The nature of reinforcement.* New York: Academic Press.

Premack, D. (1971b). Language in chimpanzee? *Science, 172,* 808–822.

Premack, D. (1976). *Intelligence in ape and man.* Hillsdale, NJ: Erlbaum.

Puente, G. P., Cannon, D. S., Best, M. R., & Carrell, L. E. (1988). Occasion setting of fluid ingestion by contextual cues. *Learning and Motivation, 19,* 239–253.

Quartermain, D., McEwen, B. S., & Azmitia, E. C., Jr. (1970). Amnesia produced by electroconvulsive shock or cycloheximide: Conditions for recovery. *Science, 169,* 683–686.

Rachlin, H. (1989). *Judgement, decision, and choice.* New York: Freeman.

Rachlin, H. (1995). Behavioral economics without anomalies. *Journal of the Experimental Analysis of Behavior, 64,* 397–404.

Rachlin, H. C., Battalio, R., Kagel, J., & Green, L. (1981). Maximization theory in behavioral psychology. *Behavioral and Brain Sciences, 4,* 371–417.

Rachlin, H. C., & Green, L. (1972). Commitment, choice, and self-control. *Journal of the Experimental Analysis of Behavior, 17,* 15–22.

Rachlin, H. C., Green, L., Kagel, J. H., & Battalio, R. C. (1976). Economic demand theory and studies of choice. In G. H. Bower (Ed.), *The psychology of learning and motivation* (Vol. 10, pp. 129–154). New York: Academic Press.

Rachlin, H. C., & Herrnstein, R. L. (1969). Hedonism revisited: On the negative law of effect. In B. A. Campbell & R. M. Church (Eds.), *Punishment and aversive behavior* (pp. 83–109). New York: Appleton-Century-Crofts.

Raia, C. P., Shillingford, S. W., Miller, H. L., Jr., & Baier, P. S. (2000). Interaction of procedural factors in human performance on yoked schedules. *Journal of the Experimental Analysis of Behavior, 74,* 265–281.

Rakitin, B. C., Gibbon, J., Penney, T. B., Malapani, C., Hinton, S. C., & Meck, W. H. (1998). Scalar expectancy theory and peak-interval timing in humans. *Journal of Experimental Psychology: Animal Behavior Processes, 24,* 25–33.

Ramirez, I. (1997). Carbohydrate-induced stimulation of saccharin intake: Yoked controls. *Animal Learning & Behavior, 25,* 347–356.

Ramsey, D. S., & Woods, S. C. (1997). Biological consequences of drug administration: Implications for acute and chronic tolerance. *Psychological Review, 104,* 170–193.

Randell, T., & Remington, B. (1999). Equivalence relations between visual stimuli: The functional role of naming. *Journal of the Experimental Analysis of Behavior, 71,* 395–415.

Randich, A. (1981). The US preexposure phenomenon in the conditioned suppression paradigm: A role for conditioned situational stimuli. *Learning and Motivation, 12,* 321–341.

Randich, A., & LoLordo, V. M. (1979). Associative and non-associative theories of the UCS preexposure phenomenon: Implications for Pavlovian conditioning. *Psychological Bulletin, 86,* 523–548.

Rashotte, M. E., Griffin, R. W., & Sisk, C. L. (1977). Second-order conditioning of the pigeon's keypeck. *Animal Learning & Behavior, 5,* 25–38.

Rauhut, A. S., Thomas, B. L., & Ayres, J. J. B. (2001). Treatments that weaken Pavlovian conditioned fear and thwart its renewal in rats: Implications for treating human phobias. *Journal of Experimental Psychology: Animal Behavior Processes, 27,* 99–114.

Raymond, J. L., Lisberger, S. G., & Mauk, M. D. (1996). The cerebellum: A neuronal learning machine? *Science, 272,* 1126–1131.

Reberg, D., Innis, N. K., Mann, B., & Eizenga, C. (1978). "Superstitious" behavior resulting from periodic response-independent presentations of food or water. *Animal Behaviour, 26,* 506–519.

Reed, P. (1991). Multiple determinants of the effects of reinforcement magnitude on free-operant response rates. *Journal of the Experimental Analysis of Behavior, 55,* 109–123.

Reed, P. (1999). Role of stimulus filling an action-outcome delay in human judgements of causal effectiveness. *Journal of Experimental Psychology: Animal Behavior Processes, 25,* 92–102.

Reed, P., Soh, M., Hildebrandt, T., DeJongh, J., & Shek, W. Y. (2000). Free-operant performance on variable interval schedules with a linear feedback loop: No evidence for molar sensitivities in rats. *Journal of Experimental Psychology: Animal Behavior Processes, 26,* 416–427.

Reed, P., & Wright, J. E. (1989). Effects of magnitude of food reinforcement on free-operant response rates. *Journal of the Experimental Analysis of Behavior, 49,* 75–85.

Reid, A. K., Chadwick, C. Z., Dunham, M., & Miller, A. (2001). The development of functional response units: The role of demarcating stimuli. *Journal of the Experimental Analysis of Behavior, 72,* 81–96.

Repp, A. C., & Singh, N. N. (Eds.). (1990). *Perspectives on the use of nonaversive and aversive interventions for persons with developmental disabilities.* Sycamore, IL: Sycamore.

Rescorla, R. A. (1967a). Inhibition of delay in Pavlovian fear conditioning. *Journal of Comparative and Physiological Psychology, 64,* 114–120.

Rescorla, R. A. (1967b). Pavlovian conditioning and its proper control procedures. *Psychological Review, 74,* 71–80.

Rescorla, R. A. (1968a). Pavlovian conditioned fear in Sidman avoidance learning. *Journal of Comparative and Physiological Psychology, 65,* 55–60.

Rescorla, R. A. (1968b). Probability of shock in the presence and absence of CS in fear conditioning. *Journal of Comparative and Physiological Psychology, 66,* 1–5.

Rescorla, R. A. (1969a). Conditioned inhibition of fear resulting from negative CS-US contingencies. *Journal of Comparative and Physiological Psychology, 67,* 504–509.

Rescorla, R. A. (1969b). Pavlovian conditioned inhibition. *Psychological Bulletin, 72,* 77–94.

Rescorla, R. A. (1973). Effect of US habituation following conditioning. *Journal of Comparative and Physiological Psychology, 82,* 137–143.

Rescorla, R. A. (1980a). *Pavlovian second-order conditioning.* Hillsdale, NJ: Erlbaum.

Rescorla, R. A. (1980b). Simultaneous and successive associations in sensory preconditioning. *Journal of Experimental Psychology: Animal Behavior Processes, 6,* 207–216.

Rescorla, R. A. (1982a). Effect of a stimulus intervening between CS and US in autoshaping. *Journal of Experimental Psychology: Animal Behavior Processes, 8,* 131–141.

Rescorla, R. A. (1982b). Some consequences of associations between the excitor and the inhibitor in a conditioned inhibition paradigm. *Journal of Experimental Psychology: Animal Behavior Processes, 8,* 288–298.

Rescorla, R. A. (1985). Conditioned inhibition and facilitation. In R. R. Miller & N. E. Spear (Eds.), *Information processing in animals: Conditioned inhibition* (pp. 299–326). Hillsdale, NJ: Erlbaum.

Rescorla, R. A. (1986). Extinction of facilitation. *Journal of Experimental Psychology: Animal Behavior Processes, 12,* 16–24.

Rescorla, R. A. (1987). Facilitation and inhibition. *Journal of Experimental Psychology: Animal Behavior Processes, 13,* 250–259.

Rescorla, R. A. (1988a). Facilitation based on inhibition. *Animal Learning & Behavior, 16,* 169–176.

Rescorla, R. A. (1988b). Pavlovian conditioning: It's not what you think it is. *American Psychologist, 43,* 151–160.

Rescorla, R. A. (1990a). Evidence for an association between the discriminative stimulus and the response-outcome association in instrumental learning. *Journal of Experimental Psychology: Animal Behavior Processes, 16,* 326–334

Rescorla, R. A. (1990b). The role of information about the response-outcome relation in instrumental discrimination learning. *Journal of Experimental Psychology: Animal Behavior Processes, 16,* 262–270.

Rescorla, R. A. (1991). Associative relations in instrumental learning: The eighteenth Bartlett memorial lecture. *Quarterly Journal of Experimental Psychology, 43B,* 1–23.

Rescorla, R. A. (1992). Association between an instrumental discriminative stimulus and multiple outcomes. *Journal of Experimental Psychology: Animal Behavior Processes, 18,* 95–104.

Rescorla, R. A. (1993a). Preservation of response–outcome associations through extinction. *Animal Learning & Behavior, 21,* 238–245.

Rescorla, R. A. (1993b). Inhibitory associations between S and R in extinction. *Animal Learning & Behavior, 21,* 327–336.

Rescorla, R. A. (1996a). Preservation of Pavlovian associations through extinction. *Quarterly Journal of Experimental Psychology, 49B,* 245–258.

Rescorla, R. A. (1996b). Response-outcome associations remain functional through interference treatments. *Animal Learning & Behavior, 24,* 450–458.

Rescorla, R. A. (1996c). Spontaneous recovery after training with multiple outcomes. *Animal Learning & Behavior, 24,* 11–18.

Rescorla, R. A. (1997a). Response-inhibition in extinction. *Quarterly Journal of Experimental Psychology, 50B,* 238–252.

Rescorla, R. A. (1997b). Spontaneous recovery after Pavlovian conditioning with multiple outcomes. *Animal Learning & Behavior, 25,* 99–107.

Rescorla, R. A. (1997c). Spontaneous recovery of instrumental discriminative responding. *Animal Learning & Behavior, 25,* 485–497.

Rescorla, R. A. (1997d). Spontaneous recovery of instrumental discriminative responding. *Animal Learning & Behavior, 27,* 485–497. (b)

Rescorla, R. A. (1997e). Summation: Assessment of a configural theory. *Animal Learning Behavior, 25,* 200–209.

Rescorla, R. A. (1999a). Associative changes in elements and compounds when the other is reinforced. *Journal of Experimental Psychology: Animal Behavior Processes, 25,* 247–255.

Rescorla, R. A. (1999b). Summation and overexpectation with qualitatively different outcomes. *Animal Learning & Behavior, 27,* 50–62.

Rescorla, R. A. (1999c). Within-subject partial reinforcement extinction effect in autoshaping. *Quarterly Journal of Experimental Psychology, 52B,* 75–87.

Rescorla, R. A. (2000a). Associative changes with a random CS-US relationship. *Quarterly Journal of Experimental Psychology, 53B,* 325–340.

Rescorla, R. A. (2000b). Extinction can be enhanced by a concurrent excitor. *Journal of Experimental Psychology: Animal Behavior Processes, 26,* 251–260.

Rescorla, R. A. (2001a). Experimental extinction. In R. R. Mowrer & S. B. Klein (Eds.), *Contemporary learning theories* (pp. 119–154). Mahwah, NJ: Erlbaum.

Rescorla, R. A. (2001b). Retraining of extinguished Pavlovian stimuli. *Journal of Experimental Psychology: Animal Behavior Processes, 27,* 115–124.

Rescorla, R. A., & Durlach, P. J. (1981). Within-event learning in Pavlovian conditioning. In N. E. Spear & R. R. Miller (Eds.), *Information processing in animals: Memory mechanisms* (pp. 81–112). Hillsdale, NJ: Erlbaum.

Rescorla, R. A., Durlach, P. J., & Grau, J. W. (1985). Contextual learning in Pavlovian conditioning. In P. Balsam & A. Tomie (Eds.), *Context and learning* (pp. 23–56). Hillsdale, NJ: Erlbaum.

Rescorla, R. A., & Furrow, D. R. (1977). Stimulus similarity as a determinant of Pavlovian conditioning. *Journal of Experimental Psychology: Animal Behavior Processes, 3,* 203–215.

Rescorla, R. A., & Heth, C. D. (1975). Reinstatement of fear to an extinguished conditioned stimulus. *Journal of Experimental Psychology: Animal Behavior Processes, 104,* 88–96.

Rescorla, R. A., & Solomon, R. L. (1967). Two-process learning theory: Relationships between Pavlovian conditioning and instrumental learning. *Psychological Review, 74,* 151–182.

Rescorla, R. A., & Wagner, A. R. (1972). A theory of Pavlovian conditioning: Variations in the effectiveness of reinforcement and nonreinforcement. In A. H. Black & W. F. Prokasy (Eds.), *Classical conditioning II: Current research and theory* (pp. 64–99). New York: Appleton-Century-Crofts.

Revusky, S. H., & Garcia, J. (1970). Learned associations over long delays. In G. H. Bower & J. T. Spence (Eds.), *The psychology of learning and motivation* (Vol. 4, pp. 1–84). New York: Academic Press.

Reynolds, G. S. (1961). Attention in the pigeon. *Journal of the Experimental Analysis of Behavior, 4,* 203–208.

Reynolds, G. S. (1975). *A primer of operant conditioning.* Glenview, IL: Scott, Foresman.

Riccio, D. C., Hodges, L. A., & Randall, P. R. (1968). Retrograde amnesia produced by hypothermia in rats. *Journal of Comparative and Physiological Psychology, 3,* 618–622.

Riccio, D. C., MacArdy, E. A., & Kissinger, S. C. (1991). Associative processes in adaptation to repeated cold exposure in rats. *Behavioral Neuroscience, 105,* 599–602.

Riccio, D. C., Rabinowitz, V. C., & Axelrod, S. (1994). Memory: When less is more. *American Psychologist, 49,* 917–926.

Riccio, D. C., & Richardson, R. (1984). The status of memory following experimentally induced amnesias: Gone, but not forgotten. *Physiological Psychology, 12,* 59–72.

Richardson, R., Duffield, T. Q., Bailey, G. K., & Westbrook, R. F. (1999). Reinstatement of fear to an extinguished conditioned context. *Animal Learning & Behavior, 27,* 399–415.

Richardson, R., Riccio, D. C., & Jonke, T. (1983). Alleviation of infantile amnesia in rats by means of a pharmacological contextual state. *Developmental Psychobiology, 16,* 511–518.

Richelle, M., & Lejeune, H. (1980). *Time in animal behavior.* New York: Pergamon.

Ricker, S. T., & Bouton, M. E. (1996). Reacquisition following extinction in appetitive conditioning. *Animal Learning & Behavior, 24,* 423–436.

Riley, A. L., & Simpson, G. R. (2001). The attenuating effects of drug preexposure on taste aversion conditioning: Generality, experimental parameters, underlying mechanisms, and implications for drug use and abuse. In R. R. Mowrer & S. B. Klein (Eds.), *Handbook of contemporary learning theories* (pp. 505–559). Mahwah, NJ: Erlbaum.

Riley, A. L., & Tuck, D. L. (1985). Conditioned food aversions: A bibliography. *Annals of the New York Academy of Sciences, 433,* 381–437.

Rilling, M., Kendrick, D. F., & Stonebraker, T. B. (1984). Directed forgetting in context. In G. H. Bower (Ed.), *The psychology of learning and motivation* (Vol. 18). New York: Academic Press.

Ristau, C. A. (Ed.). (1991). *Cognitive ethology.* Hillsdale, NJ: Erlbaum.

Robbins, S. J. (1988). Role of context in performance on a random schedule of autoshaping. *Journal of Experimental Psychology: Animal Behavior Processes, 14,* 413–424.

Robbins, S. J. (1990). Mechanisms underlying spontaneous recovery in autoshaping. *Journal of Experimental Psychology: Animal Behavior Processes, 16,* 235–249.

Roberts, A. D. L., & Pearce, J. M. (1999). Blocking in the Morris swimming pool. *Journal of Experimental Psychology: Animal Behavior Processes, 25,* 225–235.

Roberts, S. (1981). Isolation of an internal clock. *Journal of Experimental Psychology: Animal Behavior Processes, 7,* 242–268.

Roberts, S. (1982). Cross-modal use of an internal clock. *Journal of Experimental Psychology: Animal Behavior Processes, 8,* 2–22.

Roberts, S., & Church, R. M. (1978). Control of an internal clock. *Journal of Experimental Psychology: Animal Behavior Processes, 4,* 318–337.

Roberts, W. A. (1979). Spatial memory in the rat on a hierarchical maze. *Learning and Motivation, 10,* 117–140.

Roberts, W. A. (1984). Some issues in animal spatial memory. In H. L. Roitblat, T. G. Bever, & H. S. Terrace (Eds.), *Animal cognition* (pp. 425–443). Hillsdale, NJ: Erlbaum.

Roberts, W. A. (1998). *Animal cognition.* Boston: McGraw-Hill.

Roberts, W. A., Cheng, K., & Cohen, J. S. (1989). Timing light and tone signals in pigeons. *Journal of Experimental Psychology: Animal Behavior Processes, 15,* 23–35.

Roberts, W. A., & Grant, D. S. (1976). Studies of short-term memory in the pigeon using the delayed matching to sample procedure. In D. L. Medin, W. A. Roberts, & R. T. Davis (Eds.), *Processes of animal memory.* Hillsdale, NJ: Erlbaum.

Roberts, W. A., & Mazmanian, D. S. (1988). Concept learning at different levels of abstraction by pigeons, monkeys, and people. *Journal of Experimental Psychology: Animal Behavior Processes, 14,* 247–260.

Rodd, Z. A., Rosellini, R. A., Stock, H. S., & Gallup, G. G., Jr. (1997). Learned helplessness in chickens (*Gallus gallus*): Evidence for attentional bias. *Learning and Motivation, 28,* 43–55.

Rogers, R. F., Schiller, K. M., & Matzel, L. D. (1996). Chemosensory-based contextual conditioning in *Hermissenda crassicornis. Animal Learning & Behavior, 24,* 28–37.

Roitblat, H. L., Bever, T. G., & Terrace, H. S. (Eds.). (1984). *Animal cognition.* Hillsdale, NJ: Erlbaum.

Roitblat, H. L., Bever, T. G., Helweg, D. A., & Harley, H. E. (1991). On-line choice and the representation of serially structured stimuli. *Journal of Experimental Psychology: Animal Behavior Processes, 17,* 55–67.

Roitblat, H. L., Harley, H. E., & Helweg, D. A. (1993). Cognitive processing in artificial language research. In H. L. Roitblat, L. M. Herman, & P. E. Nachtigall (Eds.), *Language and communication: Comparative perspectives* (pp. 1–23). Hillsdale, NJ: Erlbaum.

Roitblat, H. L., & Meyer, J.-A. (Eds.). (1995). *Comparative approaches to cognitive science.* Cambridge, MA: MIT Press.

Roitblat, H. L., Penner, R. H., & Nachtigall, P. E. (1990). Matching-to-sample by an echo locating dolphin (*Tursiops truncatus*) *Journal of Experimental Psychology: Animal Behavior Processes, 16,* 85–95.

Roitblat, H. L., Scopatz, R. A., & Bever, T. G. (1987). The hierarchical representation of three-item sequences. *Animal Learning & Behavior, 15,* 179–192.

Romanes, G. J. (1882). *Animal intelligence.* New York: Appleton.

Romaniuk, C. B., & Williams, D. A. (2000). Conditioning across the duration of a backward conditioned stimulus. *Journal of Experimental Psychology: Animal Behavior Processes, 26,* 454–461.

Roper, K. L., Kaiser, D. H., & Zentall, T. R. (1995). True directed forgetting in pigeons may occur only when alternative working memory is required on forget-cue trials. *Animal Learning & Behavior, 23,* 280–285.

Roper, K. L., & Zentall, T. R. (1993). Directed forgetting in animals. *Psychological Bulletin, 113,* 513–532.

Rosas, J. M., & Bouton, M. E. (1996). Spontaneous recovery after extinction of a conditioned taste aversion. *Animal Learning & Behavior, 24,* 341–348.

Rosas, J. M., & Bouton, M. E. (1997). Additivity of the effects of retention interval and context change on latent inhibition: Toward resolution of the context forgetting paradox. *Journal of Experimental Psychology: Animal Behavior Processes, 23,* 283–294.

Rosas, J. M., & Bouton, M. E. (1997). Renewal of a conditioned taste aversion upon return to the conditioning context after extinction in another one. *Learning and Motivation, 28,* 216–229.

Rose, S. A., & Orlian, E. K. (2001). Visual information processing. In L. T. Singer and P. S. Zeskind (Eds.), *Biobehavioral assessment of the infant* (pp. 274–292). New York: Guilford.

Rosellini, R. A., & DeCola, J. P. (1981). Inescapable shock interferes with the acquisition of a low-activity response in an appetitive context. *Animal Learning & Behavior, 9,* 487–490.

Rosellini, R. A., DeCola, J. P., & Shapiro, N. R. (1982). Cross-motivational effects of inescapable shock are associative in nature. *Journal of Experimental Psychology: Animal Behavior Processes, 8,* 376–388.

Rosellini, R. A., DeCola, J. P., Plonsky, M., Warren, D. A., & Stilman, A. J. (1984). Uncontrollable shock proactively increases sensitivity to response-reinforcer independence in rats. *Journal of Experimental Psychology: Animal Behavior Processes, 10,* 346–359.

Rosellini, R. A., Warren, D. A., & DeCola, J. P. (1987). Predictability and controllability: Differential effects upon contextual fear. *Learning and Motivation, 18,* 392–420.

Ross, R. T. (1983). Relationships between the determinants of performance in serial feature-positive discriminations. *Journal of Experimental Psychology: Animal Behavior Processes, 9,* 349–373.

Ross, R. T., & Holland, P. C. (1981). Conditioning of simultaneous and serial feature-positive discriminations. *Animal Learning & Behavior, 9,* 293–303.

Rovee-Collier, C., & Bhatt, R. S. (1993). Evidence of long-term memory in infancy. In R. Vasta (Ed.), *Annals of child development* (Vol. 9, pp. 1–45). London: Jessica Kingsley.

Rozin, P., & Zellner, D. (1985). The role of Pavlovian conditioning in the acquisition of food likes and dislikes. *Annals of the New York Academy of Sciences, 443,* 189–202.

Rumbaugh, D. M. (Ed.). (1977). *Language learning by a chimpanzee: The Lana project.* New York: Academic Press .

Russell, M. S., & Burch, R. L. (1959). *The principles of humane experimental technique.* London: Methuen.

Russell, W. R., & Nathan, P. W. (1946). Traumatic amnesia. *Brain, 69,* 280–300.

Sahley, C., Rudy, J. W., & Gelperin, A. (1981). An analysis of associative learning in a terrestrial mollusc: I. Higher-order conditioning, blocking, and a transient US-pre-exposure effect. *Journal of Comparative Physiology-A, 144,* 1–8.

Sajwaj, T., Libet, J., & Agras, S. (1974). Lemon-juice therapy: The control of life-threatening rumination in a six-month-old infant. *Journal of Applied Behavior Analysis, 7,* 557–563.

Saladin, M. E., ten Have, W. N., Saper, Z. L., Labinsky, J. S., & Tait, R. W. (1989). Retardation of rabbit nictitating membrane conditioning following US preexposures depends on the distribution and numbers of US presentations. *Animal Learning & Behavior, 17,* 179–187.

Santi, A., Musgrave, S., & Bradford, S. A. (1988). Utilization of cues signaling different test stimulus dimensions in delayed matching to sample by pigeons. *Learning and Motivation, 19,* 87–98.

Santi, A., Stanford, L., & Coyle, J. (1998). Pigeons' memory for event duration: Differences between visual and auditory signals. *Animal Learning & Behavior, 26,* 163–171.

Sara, S. J. (2000). Reconsolidation: Strengthening the shaky trace through retrieval. *Nature Reviews Neuroscience, 1,* 212–213.

Sargisson, R. J., & White, K. G. (2001). Generalization of delayed matching to sample following training at different delays. *Journal of the Experimental Analysis of Behavior, 75,* 1–14.

Saunders, R. R., & Green, G. (1999). A discrimination analysis of training structure effects on stimulus equivalence outcomes. *Journal of the Experimental Analysis of Behavior, 74,* 117–137.

Savage-Rumbaugh, E. S. (1986). *Ape language.* New York: Columbia University Press.

Savage-Rumbaugh, E. S., McDonald, K., Sevcik, R. A., Hopkins, W. D., & Rubert, E. (1986). Spontaneous symbol acquisition and communicative use by pigmy chimpanzees (*Pan paniscus*). *Journal of Experimental Psychology: General, 115,* 211–235.

Savage-Rumbaugh, E. S., Murphy, J., Sevcik, R. A., Brakke, K. E., Williams, S. L., & Rumbaugh, D. M. (1993). Language comprehension in ape and child. *Monographs of the Society for Research in Child Development,* Vol. 58 (Nos. 3–4), Serial No. 233.

Savage-Rumbaugh, E. S., Rumbaugh, D. M., Smith, S. T., & Lawson, J. (1980). Reference: The linguistic essential. *Science, 210,* 922–925.

Savage-Rumbaugh, E. S., Sevcik, R. A., Brakke, K. E., & Rumbaugh, D. M. (1990). Symbols: Their communicative use, comprehension, and combination by bonobos (*Pan paniscus*). In C. Rovee-Collier & L. P. Lipsitt (Eds.), *Advances in infancy research* (Vol. 6, pp. 221–278). Norwood, NJ: Ablex.

Savage-Rumbaugh, S., Shanker, S. G., & Taylor, T. J. (1998). *Apes, language, and the human mind.* New York: Oxford University Press.

Savastano, H. I., Cole, R. P., Barnet, R. C., & Miller, R. R. (1999). Reconsidering conditioned inhibition. *Learning and Motivation, 30,* 101–127.

Savastano, H., & Fantino, E. (1994). Human choice in concurrent ratio-interval schedules of reinforcement. *Journal of the Experimental Analysis of Behavior, 61,* 453–463.

Savastano, H. I., & Fantino, E. (1996). Differences in delay, not ratios, control choice in concurrent chains. *Journal of the Experimental Analysis of Behavior, 66,* 97–116.

Savastano, H. I., & Miller, R. R. (1998). Time as content in Pavlovian conditioning. *Behavioural Processes, 44,* 147–162.

Sawa, K., Nakajima, S., & Imada, H. (1999). Facilitation of sodium aversion learning in sodium-deprived rats. *Learning and Motivation, 30,* 281–295.

Scavio, M. J., Jr., & Gormezano, I. (1974). CS intensity effects on rabbit nictitating membrane conditioning, extinction and generalization. *Pavlovian Journal of Biological Science, 9,* 25–34.

Schaal, D. W., McDonald, M. P., Miller, M. A., & Reilly, M. P. (1996). Discrimination of methadone and cocaine by pigeons without explicit discrimination training. *Journal of the Experimental Analysis of Behavior, 66,* 193–203.

Schaal, D. W., Shahan, T. A., Kovera, C. A., & Reilly, M. P. (1998). Mechanisms underlying the effects of unsignaled delayed reinforcement on key pecking of pigeons under variable interval schedules. *Journal of the Experimental Analysis of Behavior, 69,* 103–122.

Schachter, D. L., & Tulving, E. (1994). What are the memory systems of 1994? In D. L. Schachter & E. Tulving (Eds.), *Memory systems* (pp. 1–38). Cambridge, MA: MIT Press.

Schachtman, T. R., Brown, A. M., Gordon, E. L., Catterson, D. A., & Miller, R. R. (1987). Mechanisms underlying retarded emergence of conditioned responding following inhibitory training: Evidence for the comparator hypothesis. *Journal of Experimental Psychology: Animal Behavior Processes, 13,* 310–322.

Schachtman, T. R., Brown, A. M., & Miller, R. R. (1985). Reinstatement-induced recovery of a taste-LiCl association following extinction. *Animal Learning & Behavior, 13,* 223–227.

Schachtman, T. R., Gee, J.-L., Kasprow, W. J., & Miller, R. R. (1983). Reminder-induced recovery from blocking as a function of the number of compound trials. *Learning and Motivation, 14,* 154–164.

Schachtman, T. R., Kasprow, W. J., Meyer, R. C., Bourne, M. J., & Hart, J. A. (1992). Extinction of the overshadowing CS after overshadowing in conditioned taste aversion. *Animal Learning & Behavior, 20,* 207–218.

Schachtman, T. R., Threlkeld, R., & Meyer, K. (2000). Retention of conditioned inhibition produced by extinction. *Learning and Motivation, 31,* 283–300.

Schiff, R., Smith, N., & Prochaska, J. (1972). Extinction of avoidance in rats as a function of duration and number of blocked trials. *Journal of Comparative and Physiological Psychology, 81,* 356–359.

Schindler, C. W., & Weiss, S. J. (1982). The influence of positive and negative reinforcement on selective attention in the rat. *Learning and Motivation, 13,* 304–323.

Schlinger, H., Blakely, E., & Kaczor, T. (1990). Pausing under variable-ratio schedules: Interaction of reinforcer magnitude, variable-ratio size, and lowest ratio. *Journal of the Experimental Analysis of Behavior, 53,* 133–139.

Schlosberg, H. (1934). Conditioned responses in the white rat. *Journal of Genetic Psychology, 45,* 303–335.

Schlosberg, H. (1936). Conditioned responses in the white rat: II. Conditioned responses based upon shock to the foreleg. *Journal of Genetic Psychology, 49,* 107–138.

Schmajuk, N. A., & Holland, P. C. (Eds.). (1998). *Occasion setting: Associative learning and cognition in animals.* Washington, DC: American Psychological Association.

Schneider, A. M., Tyler, J., & Jinich, D. (1974). Recovery from retrograde amnesia: A learning process. *Science, 184,* 87–88.

Schneiderman, N., & Gormezano, I. (1964). Conditioning of the nictitating membrane of the rabbit as a function of CS-US interval. *Journal of Comparative and Physiological Psychology, 57,* 188–195.

Schreibman, L., Koegel, R. L., Charlop, M. H., & Egel, A. L. (1990). Infantile autism. In A. S. Bellack, M. Hersen, & A. E. Kazdin (Eds.), *International handbook of behavior modification and therapy* (pp. 763–789). New York: Plenum.

Schreurs, B. G. (1998). Long-term memory and extinction of rabbit nictitating membrane trace conditioning. *Learning and Motivation, 29,* 68–82.

Schrier, A. M., & Brady, P. M. (1987). Categorization of natural stimuli by monkeys (*Macaca mulatta*): Effects of stimulus set size and modification of exemplars. *Journal of Experimental Psychology: Animal Behavior Processes, 13,* 136–143.

Schultz, L. A., Collier, G., & Johnson, D. F. (1999). Behavioral strategies in the cold: Effects of feeding and nesting costs. *Physiology & Behavior, 67,* 107–115.

Schuster, R. H., & Rachlin, H. (1968). Indifference between punishment and free shock: Evidence for the negative law of effect. *Journal of the Experimental Analysis of Behavior, 11,* 777–786.

Schusterman, R. J., & Gisiner, R. (1988). Artificial language comprehension in dolphins and sea lions: The essential cognitive skills. *Psychological Record, 38,* 311–348.

Schusterman, R. J., & Kreiger, K. (1986). Artificial language comprehension and size transposition by a California sea lion (*Zalophus californianus*). *Journal of Comparative Psychology, 100,* 348–355.

Schwartz, B. (1976). Positive and negative conditioned suppression in the pigeon: Effects of the locus and modality of the CS. *Learning and Motivation, 7,* 86–100.

Schwartz, B. (1980). Development of complex, stereotyped behavior in pigeons. *Journal of the Experimental Analysis of Behavior, 33,* 153–166.

Schwartz, B. (1981). Reinforcement creates behavioral units. *Behavioural Analysis Letters, 1,* 33–41.

Schwartz, B. (1985). On the organization of stereotyped response sequences. *Animal Learning & Behavior, 13,* 261–268.

Schwartz, B. (1988). The experimental synthesis of behavior: Reinforcement, behavioral stereotypy, and problem solving. In G. H. Bower (Ed.), *The psychology of learning and motivation* (Vol. 22, pp. 93–138). Orlando, FL: Academic Press.

Schweitzer, J. B., & Sulzer-Azaroff, B. (1988). Self-control: Teaching tolerance for delay in impulsive children. *Journal of the Experimental Analysis of Behavior, 50,* 173–186.

Sclafani, A. (1997). Learned controls of ingestive behaviour. *Appetite, 29,* 153–158.

Seligman, M. E. P. (1971). Phobias and preparedness. *Behavior Therapy, 2,* 307–320.

Seligman, M. E. P. (1975). *Helplessness: On depression, development and death.* San Francisco: W. H. Freeman.

Seligman, M. E. P., & Maier, S. F. (1967). Failure to escape traumatic shock. *Journal of Experimental Psychology, 74,* 1–9.

Senkowski, P. C. (1978). Variables affecting the overtraining extinction effect in discrete-trial lever pressing. *Journal of Experimental Psychology: Animal Behavior Processes, 4,* 131–143.

Sevcik, R. A., Romski, M. A., & Wilkenson, K. (1991). Roles of graphic symbols in the language acquisition process for persons with severe cognitive disabilities. *Journal of Augmentative and Alternative Communication, 7,* 161–170.

Sevenster, P. (1973). Incompatibility of response and reward. In R. A. Hinde & J. Stevenson-Hinde (Eds.), *Constraints on learning* (pp. 265–283). London: Academic Press.

Shah, K., Bradshaw, C. M., & Szabadi, E. (1991). Relative and absolute reinforcement frequency as determinants of choice in concurrent variable interval schedules. *Quarterly Journal of Experimental Psychology, 43,* 25–38.

Shanker, S. G., Savage-Rumbaugh, E. S., & Taylor, T. J. (1999). Kanzi: A new beginning. *Animal Learning & Behavior, 27,* 24–25.

Shanks, D. R., & Dickinson, A. (1987). Associative accounts of causality judgment. In G. H. Bower (Ed.), *The psychology of learning and motivation* (Vol. 21, pp. 229–261). San Diego, CA: Academic Press.

Shapiro, K. L., & LoLordo, V. M. (1982). Constraints on Pavlovian conditioning of the pigeon: Relative conditioned reinforcing effects of red-light and tone CSs paired with food. *Learning and Motivation, 13,* 68–80.

Shapiro, K. L., Jacobs, W. J., & LoLordo, V. M. (1980). Stimulus-reinforcer interactions in Pavlovian conditioning of pigeons: Implications for selective associations. *Animal Learning & Behavior, 8,* 586–594.

Sheffield, F. D. (1948). Avoidance training and the contiguity principle. *Journal of Comparative and Physiological Psychology, 41,* 165–177.

Sheffield, F. D., Roby, T. B., & Campbell, B. A. (1954). Drive reduction versus consummatory behavior as determinants of reinforcement. *Journal of Comparative and Physiological Psychology, 47,* 349–354.

Sherburne, L. M., & Zentall, T. R. (1998). The differential outcomes effect in pigeons is not reduced by eliminating response-outcome associations: Support for a two-process account. *Animal Learning & Behavior, 26,* 378–387.

Sherry, D. F. (1984). Food storage by black-capped chickadees: Memory for the location and contents of caches. *Animal Behaviour, 32,* 451–464.

Sherry, D. F. (1985). Food storage by birds and mammals. *Advances in the Study of Behavior, 15,* 153–188.

Sherry, D. F. (1988). Learning and adaptation in food-storing birds. In R. C. Bolles & M. D. Beecher (Eds.), *Evolution and learning* (pp. 79–95). Hillsdale, NJ: Erlbaum .

Sherry, D. F. (1992). Memory, the hippocampus, and natural selection: Studies of food-storing birds. In L. R. Squire & N. Butters (Eds.), *Neuropsychology of memory* (2nd ed., pp. 521–532). New York: Gilford.

Sherry, D. F., Krebs, J. R., & Cowie, R. J. (1981). Memory for the location of stored food in marsh tits. *Animal Behaviour, 29,* 1260–1266.

Shettleworth, S. J. (1975). Reinforcement and the organization of behavior in golden hamsters: Hunger, environment, and food reinforcement. *Journal of Experimental Psychology: Animal Behavior Processes, 1,* 56–87.

Shettleworth, S. J. (1983). Memory in food-hoarding birds. *Scientific American, 248,* 102–110.

Shettleworth, S. J. (1995). Comparative studies of memory in food storing birds. In E. Alleva, A. Fasolo, H. Lipp, L. Nadel, & L. Ricceri (Eds.), *Behavioral brain research in natural and semi-natural settings: Possibilities and perspectives* (pp. 159–192). Dordrecht: Kluwer.

Shettleworth, S. J. (1998). *Cognition, evolution, and behavior.* New York: Oxford University Press.

Shettleworth, S. J., & Krebs, J. R. (1986). Stored and encountered seeds: A comparison of two spatial memory tasks in marsh tits and chickadees. *Journal of Experimental Psychology: Animal Behavior Processes, 12,* 248–257.

Shi, C., & Davis, M. (1999). Pain pathways involved in fear conditioning measured with fear-potentiated startle: Lesion studies. *Journal of Neuroscience, 19,* 420–430.

Shimp, C. P. (1966). Probabilistically reinforced choice behavior in pigeons. *Journal of the Experimental Analysis of Behavior, 9,* 443–455.

Shimp, C. P. (1969). Optimum behavior in free-operant experiments. *Psychological Review, 76,* 97–112.

Shurtleff, D., & Ayres, J. J. B. (1981). One-trial backward excitatory fear conditioning in rats: Acquisition, retention, extinction, and spontaneous recovery. *Animal Learning & Behavior, 9,* 65–74.

Sidman, M. (1953a). Avoidance conditioning with brief shock and no exteroceptive warning signal. *Science, 118,* 157–158.

Sidman, M. (1953b). Two temporal parameters of the maintenance of avoidance behavior by the white rat. *Journal of Comparative and Physiological Psychology, 46,* 253–261.

Sidman, M. (1962). Reduction of shock frequency as reinforcement for avoidance behavior. *Journal of the Experimental Analysis of Behavior, 5,* 247–257.

Sidman, M. (1966). Avoidance behavior. In W. K. Honig (Ed.), *Operant behavior* (pp. 448–498). New York: Appleton-Century-Crofts.

Sidman, M. (1990). Equivalence relations: Where do they come from? In D. E. Blackman & H. Lejeune (Eds.), *Behavioral analysis in theory and practice: Contributions and controversies* (pp. 93–114). Hillsdale, NJ: Erlbaum.

Sidman, M. (1994). *Equivalence relations and behavior: A research story.* Boston: Authors Cooperative.

Sidman, M. (2000). Equivalence relations and the reinforcement contingency. *Journal of the Experimental Analysis of Behavior, 74,* 127–146.

Sidman, M., & Tailby, W. (1982). Conditional discrimination vs. matching to sample: An expansion of the testing paradigm. *Journal of the Experimental Analysis of Behavior, 37,* 5–22.

Siegel, S. (1983). Classical conditioning, drug tolerance, and drug dependence. In Y. Israel, F. B. Glaser, H. Kalant, R. E. Popham, W. Schmidt, & R. G. Smart (Eds.), *Research advances in alcohol and drug problems* (Vol. 7). New York: Plenum.

Siegel, S. (1989). Pharmacological conditioning and drug effects. In A. J. Goudie & M. W. Emmett-Oglesby (Eds.), *Psychoactive drugs: Tolerance and sensitization* (pp. 115–180). Clifton, NJ: Humana Press.

Siegel, S. (1999). Drug anticipation and drug addiction. The 1998 H. David Archibald lecture. *Addiction, 94,* 1113–1124.

Siegel, S., & Allan, L. G. (1996). The widespread influence of the Rescorla–Wagner model. *Psychonomic Bulletin & Review, 3,* 314–321.

Siegel, S., & Allan, L. G. (1998). Learning and homeostasis: Drug addiction and the McCollough effect. *Psychological Bulletin, 124,* 230–239.

Siegel, S., Baptista, M. A. S., Kim, J. A., McDonald, R. V., & Weise-Kelly, L. (2000). Pavlovian psychopharmacology: The associative basis of tolerance. *Experimental and Clinical Psychopharmacology, 8,* 276–293.

Siegel, S., & Domjan, M. (1971). Backward conditioning as an inhibitory procedure. *Learning and Motivation, 2,* 1–11.

Sigmundi, R. A. (1997). Performance rules for problem-specific defense reactions. In M. E. Bouton & M. S. Fanselow (Eds.), *Learning, motivation, and cognition* (pp. 305–319). Washington, DC: American Psychological Association.

Sigmundi, R. A., & Bolles, R. C. (1983). CS modality, context conditioning, and conditioned freezing. *Animal Learning & Behavior, 11,* 205–212.

Silberberg, A., Warren-Bouton, F. R., & Asano, T. (1987). Inferior-good and Giffen-good effects in monkey choice behavior. *Journal of Experimental Psychology: Animal Behavior Processes, 13,* 292–301.

Silva, A. J., & Giese, K. P. (1998). Gene targeting: A novel window into the biology of learning and memory. In J. L. Martinez & R. P. Kesner (Eds.), *Neurobiology of learning and memory* (pp. 89–142). San Diego: Academic Press.

Silva, F. J., & Timberlake, W. (2000). A clarification of the nature of backward excitatory conditioning. *Learning and Motivation, 31,* 67–80.

Silva, F. J., Timberlake, W., & Cevik, M. O. (1998). A behavior systems approach to the expression of backward associations. *Learning and Motivation, 29,* 1–22.

Silva, K. M., & Timberlake, W. (1997). A behavior systems view of conditioned states during long and short CS-US intervals. *Learning and Motivation, 28,* 465–490.

Silva, K. M., & Timberlake, W. (1998). The organization and temporal properties of appetitive behavior in rats. *Animal Learning & Behavior, 26,* 182–195.

Simons, R. C. (1996). *Boo! Culture, experience, and the startle reflex.* New York: Oxford University Press.

Singh, N. N., & Solman, R. T. (1990). A stimulus control analysis of the picture-word problem in children who are mentally retarded: The blocking effect. *Journal of Applied Behavior Analysis, 23,* 525–532.

Skinner, B. F. (1938). *The behavior of organisms.* New York: Appleton-Century-Crofts.

Skinner, B. F. (1948). "Superstition" in the pigeon. *Journal of Experimental Psychology, 38,* 168–172.

Skinner, B. F. (1953). *Science and human behavior.* New York: Macmillan.

Skinner, D. M. (2000). Modulation of taste aversions by a pentobarbital drug state: An assessment of its transfer properties. *Learning and Motivation, 31,* 381–401.

Slamecka, N. J., & Ceraso, J. (1960). Retroactive and proactive inhibition of verbal learning. *Psychological Bulletin, 57,* 449–475.

Small, W. S. (1899). An experimental study of the mental processes of the rat: I. *American Journal of Psychology, 11,* 133–164.

Small, W. S. (1900). An experimental study of the mental processes of the rat: II. *American Journal of Psychology, 12,* 206–239.

Smith, J. C., & Roll, D. L. (1967). Trace conditioning with X-rays as an aversive stimulus. *Psychonomic Science, 9,* 11–12.

Smith, M. C., Coleman, S. R., & Gormezano, I. (1969). Classical conditioning of the rabbit's nictitating membrane response at backward, simultaneous, and forward CS-US intervals. *Journal of Comparative and Physiological Psychology, 69,* 226–231.

Smith, S. M., & Vela, E. (2001). Environmental context-dependent memory: A review and meta-analysis. *Psychonomic Bulletin & Review, 8,* 203–220.

Smotherman, W. P., & Robinson, S. R. (1992). Habituation in the rat fetus. *Quarterly Journal of Experimental Psychology, 44B,* 215–230.

Snodgrass, S. H., & McMillan, D. E. (1996). Drug discrimination under a concurrent schedule. *Journal of the Experimental Analysis of Behavior, 65,* 495–512.

Solomon, R. L. (1964). Punishment. *American Psychologist, 19,* 239–253.

Solomon, R. L. (1977). An opponent-process theory of acquired motivation: The affective dynamics of addiction. In J. D. Maser & M. E. P. Seligman (Eds.), *Psychopathology: Experimental models* (pp. 66–103). San Francisco: W. H. Freeman.

Solomon, R. L., & Corbit, J. D. (1973). An opponent-process theory of motivation: II. Cigarette addiction. *Journal of Abnormal Psychology, 81,* 158–171.

Solomon, R. L., & Corbit, J. D. (1974). An opponent-process theory of motivation: I. The temporal dynamics of affect. *Psychological Review, 81,* 119–145.

Solomon, R. L., Kamin, L. J., & Wynne, L. C. (1953). Traumatic avoidance learning: The outcomes of several extinction procedures with dogs. *Journal of Abnormal and Social Psychology, 48,* 291–302.

Solomon, R. L., & Wynne, L. C. (1953). Traumatic avoidance learning: Acquisition in normal dogs. *Psychological Monographs, 67* (Whole No. 354).

Soltysik, S. S., Wolfe, G. E., Nicholas, T., Wilson, W. J., & Garcia-Sanchez, L. (1983). Blocking of inhibitory conditioning within a serial conditioned stimulus conditioned inhibitor compound: Maintenance of acquired behavior without an unconditioned stimulus. *Learning and Motivation, 14,* 1–29.

Spear, N. E. (1973). Retrieval of memory in animals. *Psychological Review, 80,* 163–194.

Spear, N. E. (1978). *The processing of memories: Forgetting and retention.* Hillsdale, NJ: Erlbaum.

Spear, N. E. (1981). Extending the domain of memory retrieval. In N. E. Spear & R. R. Miller (Eds.), *Information processing in animals: Memory mechanisms* (pp. 341–378). Hillsdale, NJ: Erlbaum.

Spear, N. E., & Riccio, D. C. (1994). *Memory: Phenomena and principles.* Boston: Allyn and Bacon.

Spence, K. W. (1936). The nature of discrimination learning in animals. *Psychological Review, 43,* 427–449.

Spence, K. W. (1937). The differential response in animals to stimuli varying within a single dimension. *Psychological Review, 44,* 430–444.

Spence, K. W. (1956). *Behavior theory and conditioning.* New Haven, CT: Yale University Press.

Spetch, M. L. (1987). Systematic errors in pigeons' memory for event duration: Interaction between training and test delays. *Animal Learning & Behavior, 15,* 1–5.

Spetch, M. L. (1990). Further studies of pigeons' spatial working memory in the open-field task. *Animal Learning & Behavior, 18,* 332–340.

Spetch, M. L. (1995). Overshadowing in landmark learning: Touch-screen studies with pigeons and humans. *Journal of Experimental Psychology: Animal Behavior Processes, 21,* 166–181.

Spetch, M. L., Mondloch, M. V., Belke, T. W., & Dunn, R. (1994). Determinants of pigeons' choice between certain and probabilistic outcomes. *Animal Learning & Behavior, 22,* 239–251.

Spetch, M. L., Wilkie, D. M., & Pinel, J. P. J. (1981). Backward conditioning: A reevaluation of the empirical evidence. *Psychological Bulletin, 89,* 163–175.

Spetch, M. L., Wilkie, D. M., & Skelton, R. W. (1981). Control of pigeons' key-pecking topography by a schedule of alternating food and water reward. *Animal Learning & Behavior, 9,* 223–229.

Staddon, J. E. R. (1979). Operant behavior as adaptation to constraint. *Journal of Experimental Psychology: General, 108,* 48–67.

Staddon, J. E. R. (1983). *Adaptive behavior and learning.* Cambridge: Cambridge University Press.

Staddon, J. E. R., & Higa, J. (1996). Multiple time scales in simple habituation. *Psychological Review, 203,* 720–733.

Staddon, J. E. R., & Higa, J. J. (1999). Time and memory: Towards a pacemaker-free theory of interval timing. *Journal of the Experimental Analysis of Behavior, 72,* 225–252.

Staddon, J. E. R., Higa, J. J., & Chelaru, I. M. (1999). Time, trace, memory. *Journal of the Experimental Analysis of Behavior, 72,* 293–302.

Staddon, J. E. R., & Simmelhag, V. L. (1971). The "superstition" experiment: A reexamination of its implications for the principles of adaptive behavior. *Psychological Review, 78,* 3–43.

Staddon, J. E. R., Wynne, C. D. L., & Higa, J. J. (1991). The role of timing in reinforcement schedule performance. *Learning and Motivation, 22,* 200–225.

Stafford, D., & Branch, M. N. (1998). Effects of step size and break point criterion on progressive-ratio performance. *Journal of the Experimental Analysis of Behavior, 70,* 123–138.

Stanhope, K. J. (1992). The representation of the reinforcer and the force of the pigeon's keypeck in first- and second-order conditioning. *The Quarterly Journal of Experimental Psychology, 44B,* 137–158.

Starr, M. D. (1978). An opponent-process theory of motivation: Vl. Time and intensity variables in the development of separation-induced distress calling in ducklings. *Journal of Experimental Psychology: Animal Behavior Processes, 4,* 338–355.

Starr, M. D., & Mineka, S. (1977). Determinants of fear over the course of avoidance learning. *Learning and Motivation, 8,* 332–350.

Steinert, P., Fallon, D., & Wallace, J. (1976). Matching to sample in goldfish (*Carassuis auratus*). *Bulletin of the Psychonomic Society, 8,* 265.

Steinmetz, J. E. (1999). A renewed interest in human classical eyeblink conditioning. *Psychological Science, 10,* 24–25.

Steinmetz, J. E., Gluck, M. A., & Solomon, P. R. (2001). *Model systems and the neurobiology of associative learning: A festschrift in honor of Richard F. Thompson.* Hillsdale, NJ: Erlbaum.

Stephenson, D., & Siddle, D. (1983). Theories of habituation. In D. Siddle (Ed.), *Orienting and habituation: Perspectives in human research* (pp. 183–236). Chichester, England: Wiley.

Stevens, S. S. (1951). Mathematics, measurement and psychophysics. In S. S. Stevens (Ed.), *Handbook of experimental psychology* (pp. 1–49). New York: Wiley.

Stewart, J., & Eikelboom, R. (1987). Conditioned drug effects. In L. L. Iversen, S. D. Iversen, & S. H. Snyder (Eds.), *Handbook of psychopharmacology* (Vol. 19, pp. 1–57). New York: Plenum.

Stokes, P. D. (2001). Variability, constraints, and creativity: Shedding light on Claude Monet. *American Psychologist, 56,* 355–359.

Stokes, P. D., & Balsam, P. D. (1991). Effects of reinforcing preselected approximations on the topography of the rat's bar press. *Journal of the Experimental Analysis of Behavior, 55,* 213–231.

Stokes, P. D., Mechner, F., & Balsam, P. D. (1999). Effects of different acquisition procedures on response variability. *Animal Learning & Behavior, 27,* 28–41.

Stokes, T. F., & Baer, D. M. (1977). An implicit technology of generalization. *Journal of Applied Behavior Analysis, 10,* 349–367.

Straub, R. O., & Terrace, H. S. (1981). Generalization of serial learning in the pigeon. *Animal Learning & Behavior, 9,* 454–468.

Strijkstra, A. M., & Bolhuis, J. J. (1987). Memory persistence of rats in a radial maze varies with training procedure. *Behavioral and Neural Biology, 47,* 158–166.

Suarez, S. D., & Gallup, G. G. (1981). An ethological analysis of open-field behavior in rats and mice. *Learning and Motivation, 12,* 342–363.

Sumpter, C. E., Temple, W., & Foster, T. M. (1998). Response form, force, and number: Effects on concurrent-schedule performance. *Journal of the Experimental Analysis of Behavior, 70,* 45–68.

Sumpter, C. E., Temple, W., & Foster, T. M. (1999). The effects of differing response types and price manipulations on demand measures. *Journal of the Experimental Analysis of Behavior, 71,* 329–354.

Sundberg, M. L. (1996). Toward granting linguistic competence to apes: A review of Savage-Rumbaugh et al.'s *Language comprehension in ape and child. Journal of the Experimental Analysis of Behavior, 65,* 477–492.

Suomi, S. J., Mineka, S., & Harlow, H. F. (1983). Social separation in monkeys as viewed from several motivational perspectives. In E. Satinoff & P. Teitelbaum (Eds.), *Handbook of neurobiology: Vol. 6. Motivation.* New York: Plenum.

Susswein, A. J., & Schwarz, M. (1983). A learned change of response to inedible food in Aplysia. *Behavioral and Neural Biology, 39,* 1–6.

Sutphin, G., Byrne, T., & Poling, A. (1998). Response acquisition with delayed reinforcement: A comparison of two-lever procedures. *Journal of the Experimental Analysis of Behavior, 69,* 17–28.

Suzuki, S., Augerinos, G., & Black, A. H. (1980). Stimulus control of spatial behavior on the eight-arm maze in rats. *Learning and Motivation, 11,* 1–18.

Svartdal, F. (2000). Persistence during extinction: Conventional and reversed PREE under multiple schedules. *Learning and Motivation, 31,* 21–40.

Swartz, K. B., Chen, S., & Terrace, H. S. (2000). Serial learning by rhesus monkeys: II. Learning four-item lists by trial and error. *Journal of Experimental Psychology: Animal Behavior Processes, 26,* 274–285.

Swartzentruber, D. (1993). Transfer of contextual control across similarly trained conditioned stimuli. *Animal Learning & Behavior, 21,* 14–22.

Swartzentruber, D. (1995). Modulatory mechanisms in Pavlovian conditioning. *Animal Learning & Behavior, 23,* 123–143.

Swartzentruber, D. (1997). Modulation by the stimulus properties of excitation. *Journal of Experimental Psychology: Animal Behavior Processes, 23,* 434–440.

Symonds, M., & Hall, G. (1997). Contextual conditioning with lithium-induced nausea as the US: Evidence from a blocking procedure. *Learning and Motivation, 28,* 200–215.

Tait, R. W., & Saladin, M. E. (1986). Concurrent development of excitatory and inhibitory associations during backward conditioning. *Animal Learning & Behavior, 14,* 133–137.

Tang, Y.-P., Shimizu, E., Dube, G. R., Rampon, C., Kerchner, G. A., Zhuo, M., Liu, G., & Tsien, J. Z. (1999). Genetic enhancement of learning and memory in mice. *Nature, 401,* 63–69.

Terrace, H. S. (1979). *Nim.* New York: Knopf.

Terrace, H. S. (1984). Animal cognition. In H. L. Roitblat, T. G. Bever, & H. S. Terrace (Eds.), *Animal cognition* (pp. 7–28). Hillsdale, NJ: Erlbaum.

Terrace, H. S. (1986a). A nonverbal organism's knowledge of ordinal position in a serial learning task. *Journal of Experimental Psychology: Animal Behavior Processes, 12,* 203–214.

Terrace, H. S. (1986b). Positive transfer from sequence production to sequence discrimination in a nonverbal organism. *Journal of Experimental Psychology: Animal Behavior Processes, 12,* 215–234.

Terrace, H. S. (1987). Chunking by a pigeon in a serial learning task. *Nature, 325,* 149–151.

Terrace, H. S., Petitto, L. A., Sanders, R. J., & Bever, T. G. (1979). Can an ape create a sentence? *Science, 206,* 891–1201.

Terry, W. S. (1996). Retroactive interference effects of surprising reward omission on serial spatial memory. *Journal of Experimental Psychology: Animal Behavior Processes, 22,* 472–479.

Theios, J. (1962). The partial reinforcement effect sustained through blocks of continuous reinforcement. *Journal of Experimental Psychology, 64,* 1–6.

Theios, J., & Brelsford, J. (1964). Overlearning-extinction effect as an incentive phenomena. *Journal of Experimental Psychology, 67,* 463–467.

Thomas, B. L., & Papini, M. R. (2001). Adrenalectomy eliminates the extinction spike inn autoshaping with rats. *Physiology & Behavior, 72,* 543–547.

Thomas, D. R. (1993). A model for adaptation-level effects on stimulus generalization. *Psychological Review, 100,* 658–673.

Thomas, D. R., Cook, S. C., & Terrones, J. P. (1990). Conditional discrimination learning by pigeons: The role of simultaneous versus successive stimulus presentations. *Journal of Experimental Psychology: Animal Behavior Processes, 16,* 390–401.

Thomas, D. R., Curran, P. J., & Russell, R. J. (1988). Factors affecting conditional discrimination learning by pigeons: II. Physical and temporal characteristics of stimuli. *Animal Learning & Behavior, 16,* 468–476.

Thomas, D. R., & Empedocles, S. (1992). Novelty vs. retrieval cue value in the study of long-term memory in pigeons. *Journal of Experimental Psychology: Animal Behavior Processes, 18,* 22–23.

Thomas, D. R., McKelvie, A. R., & Mah, W. L. (1985). Context as a conditional cue in operant discrimination reversal learning. *Journal of Experimental Psychology: Animal Behavior Processes, 11,* 317–330.

Thomas, G. V., & Lieberman, D. A. (1990). Commentary: Determinants of success and failure in experiments on marking. *Learning and Motivation, 21,* 110–124.

Thomas, J. R. (1968). Fixed ratio punishment by timeout of concurrent variable-interval behavior. *Journal of the Experimental Analysis of Behavior, 11,* 609–616.

Thompson, C. R., & Church, R. M. (1980). An explanation of the language of a chimpanzee. *Science, 208,* 313–314.

Thompson, R. F. (1986). The neurobiology of learning and memory. *Science, 233,* 941–947.

Thompson, R. F. (1993). *The brain: A neuroscience primer.* New York: W. H. Freeman.

Thompson, R. F., Groves, P. M., Teyler, T. J., & Roemer, R. A. (1973). A dual-process theory of habituation: Theory and behavior. In H. V. S. Peeke & M. J. Herz (Eds.), *Habituation.* New York: Academic Press.

Thompson, R. H., Iwata, B. A., Conners, J., & Roscoe, E. M. (1999). Effects of reinforcement for alternative behavior during punishment of self-injury. *Journal of Applied Behavior Analysis, 32,* 317–328.

Thompson, R. F., & Spencer, W. A. (1966). Habituation: A model phenomenon for the study of neuronal substrates of behavior. *Psychological Review, 73,* 16–43.

Thorndike, E. L. (1898). Animal intelligence: An experimental study of the association processes in animals. *Psychological Review Monograph, 2* (Whole No. 8).

Thorndike, E. L. (1911). *Animal intelligence: Experimental studies.* New York: Macmillan.

Thorndike, E. L. (1932). *The fundamentals of learning.* New York: Teachers College, Columbia University.

Tierney, K. J. (1995). Molar regulatory theory and behavior therapy. In W. O'Donohue & L. Krasnerr (Eds.), *Theories of behavior therapy* (pp. 97–128). Washington, DC: American Psychological Association.

Tierney, K. J., & Bracken, M. (1998). Stimulus equivalence and behavior therapy. In W. O'Donohue (Ed.), *Learning and behavior therapy* (pp. 392–402). Boston: Allyn and Bacon.

Tierney, K. J., Smith, H. V., & Gannon, K. N. (1987). Some tests of molar models of instrumental performance. *Journal of Experimental Psychology: Animal Behavior Processes, 13,* 341–353.

Timberlake, W. (1980). A molar equilibrium theory of learned performance. In G. H. Bower (Ed.), *The psychology of learning and motivation* (Vol. 14, pp. 1–58). New York: Academic Press.

Timberlake, W. (1983a). The functional organization of appetitive behavior: Behavior systems and learning. In M. D. Zeiler & P. Harzem (Eds.), *Advances in analysis of behavior: Vol. 3. Biological factors in learning* (pp. 177–221). Chichester, England: Wiley.

Timberlake, W. (1983b). Rats' responses to a moving object related to food or water: A behavior-systems analysis. *Animal Learning & Behavior, 11,* 309–320.

Timberlake, W. (1984). Behavior regulation and learned performance: Some misapprehensions and disagreements. *Journal of the Experimental Analysis of Behavior, 41,* 355–375.

Timberlake, W. (1990). Natural learning in laboratory paradigms. In D. A. Dewsbury (Ed.), *Contemporary issues in comparative psychology* (pp. 31–54). Sunderland, MA: Sinauer.

Timberlake, W. (1994). Behavior systems, associationism, and Pavlovian conditioning. *Psychonomic Bulletin & Review, 1*(4), 405–420.

Timberlake, W. (1995). Reconceptualizing reinforcement: A causal-system approach to reinforcement and behavior change. In W. O'Donohue & L. Krasnerr (Eds.), *Theories of behavior therapy* (pp. 59–96). Washington, DC: American Psychological Association.

Timberlake, W. (2001). Motivational modes in behavior systems. In R. R. Mowrer & S. B. Klein (Eds.), *Handbook of contemporary learning theories* (pp. 155–209). Mahwah, NJ: Erlbaum.

Timberlake, W., & Allison, J. (1974). Response deprivation: An empirical approach to instrumental performance. *Psychological Review, 81,* 146–164.

Timberlake, W., & Farmer-Dougan, V. A. (1991). Reinforcement in applied settings: Figuring out ahead of time what will work. *Psychological Bulletin, 110,* 379–391.

Timberlake, W., & Grant, D. S. (1975). Auto-shaping in rats to the presentation of another rat predicting food. *Science, 190,* 690–692.

Timberlake, W., Leffel, J., & Hoffman, C. M. (1999). Stimulus control and function of arm and wall travel by rats on a radial arm floor maze. *Animal Learning & Behavior, 27,* 445–460.

Timberlake, W., & Lucas, G. A. (1985). The basis of superstitious behavior: Chance contingency, stimulus substitution, or appetitive behavior? *Journal of the Experimental Analysis of Behavior, 44,* 279–299.

Timberlake, W., & Lucas, G. A. (1989). Behavior systems and learning: From misbehavior to general principles. In S. B. Klein & R. R. Mowrer (Eds.), *Contemporary learning theories: Instrumental conditioning and the impact of biological constraints on learning* (pp. 237–275). Hillsdale, NJ: Erlbaum.

Timberlake, W., & Lucas, G. A. (1991). Period water, interwater interval, and adjunctive behavior in a 24–hour multiresponse environment. *Animal Learning & Behavior, 19,* 369–380.

Timberlake, W., Wahl, G., & King, D. (1982). Stimulus and response contingencies in the misbehavior of rats. *Journal of Experimental Psychology: Animal Behavior Processes, 8,* 62–85.

Timberlake, W., & Washburne, D. L. (1989). Feeding ecology and laboratory predatory behavior toward live and artificial moving prey in seven rodent species. *Animal Learning & Behavior, 17,* 2–11.

Timberlake, W., & White, W. (1990). Winning isn't everything: Rats need only food deprivation and not food reward to efficiently traverse a radial arm maze. *Learning and Motivation, 21,* 153–163.

Tinbergen, N. (1951). *The study of instinct.* Oxford: Clarendon Press.

Tinbergen, N., & Perdeck, A. C. (1950). On the stimulus situation releasing the begging response in the newly hatched herring gull chick (*Larus argentatus argentatus Pont.*). *Behaviour, 3,* 1–39.

Todes, D. P. (1997). From the machine to the ghost within: Pavlov's transition from digestive physiology to conditioned reflexes. *American Psychologist, 52,* 947–955.

Tomie, A., Brooks, W., & Zito, B. (1989). Sign-tracking: The search for reward. In S. B. Klein & R. R. Mowrer (Eds.), *Contemporary learning theories: Pavlovian conditioning and the status of learning theory* (pp. 191–223). Hillsdale, NJ: Erlbaum.

Tomie, A., Carelli, R., & Wagner, G. C. (1993). Negative correlation between tone (S–) and water increases target biting during S– in rats. *Animal Learning & Behavior, 21,* 355–359.

Tomsic, D., Pedreira, M. E., Romano, A., Hermitte, G., & Maldonado, H. (1998). Context-US association as a determinant of long-term habituation in the crab *Chasmagnathus*. *Animal Learning & Behavior, 26,* 196–209.

Tracy, J. A., Ghose, S. S., Stecher, T., McFall, R. M. & Steinmetz, J. E. (1999). Classical conditioning in a nonclinical obsessive-compulsive population. *Psychological Science, 10,* 9–13.

Trenholme, I. A., & Baron, A. (1975). Immediate and delayed punishment of human behavior by loss of reinforcement. *Learning and Motivation, 6,* 62–79.

Turkkan, J. S. (1989). Classical conditioning: The new hegemony. *The Behavioral and Brain Sciences, 12,* 121–179.

Twitmyer, E. B. (1974). A study of the knee jerk. *Journal of Experimental Psychology, 103,* 1047–1066.

Tzeng, O. C. S., & Gomez, M. (1992). Physiological paradigm of love. In O. C. S. Thzeng (Ed.), *Theories of love development, maintenance, and dissolution: Octagonal cycle and differential perspectives* (pp. 102–116). New York: Praeger.

Underwood, B. J. (1957). Interference and forgetting. *Psychological Review, 64,* 49–60.

Ungless, M. A. (1998). A Pavlovian analysis of food-attraction conditioning in the snail *Helix aspersa*. *Animal Learning & Behavior, 26,* 15–19.

United States Department of Agriculture, National Agricultural Statistics Service, 2001.

United States Department of Health and Human Services. (1996). *Smoking cessation: Clinical practice guideline.* AHCPR Publication No. 96–0692.

Urcuioli, P. J., & DeMarse, T. (1996). Associative processes in differential outcome discriminations. *Journal of Experimental Psychology: Animal Behavior Processes, 22,* 192–204.

Urcuioli, P. J., DeMarse, T. B., & Lionello, K. M. (1999). Sample duration effects on pigeons' delayed matching as a function of predictability of durations. *Journal of the Experimental Analysis of Behavior, 72,* 279–297.

Urcuioli, P. J., & Kasprow, W. J. (1988). Long-delay learning in the T-maze: Effects of marking and delay-interval location. *Learning and Motivation, 19,* 66–86.

Vaughan, W., Jr. (1981). Melioration, matching, and maximizing. *Journal of the Experimental Analysis of Behavior, 36,* 141–149.

Vaughan, W., Jr. (1985). Choice: A local analysis. *Journal of the Experimental Analysis of Behavior, 43,* 383–405.

Vaughan, W., Jr., & Greene, S. L. (1984). Pigeon visual memory capacity. *Journal of Experimental Psychology: Animal Behavior Processes, 10,* 256–271.

Viken, R. J., & McFall, R. M. (1994). Paradox lost: Implications of contemporary reinforcement theory for behavior therapy. *Current Directions in Psychological Science, 4,* 121–125.

Vollmer, T. R., & Bourret, J. (2000). An application of the matching law to evaluate the allocation of two- and three-point shots by college basketball players. *Journal of Applied Behavior Analysis, 33,* 137–150.

von Fersen, L., & Lea, S. E. G. (1990). Category discrimination by pigeons using five polymorphous features. *Journal of the Experimental Analysis of Behavior, 54,* 69–84.

von Fersen, L., Wynne, C. D. L., Delius, J. D., & Staddon, J. E. R. (1991). Transitive inference in pigeons. *Journal of Experimental Psychology: Animal Behavior Processes, 17,* 334–341.

Vyse, S. A., & Belke, T. W. (1992). Maximizing versus matching on concurrent variable-interval schedules. *Journal of the Experimental Analysis of Behavior, 58,* 325–334.

Wagner, A. R. (1961). Effects of amount and percentage of reinforcement and number of acquisition trials on conditioning and extinction. *Journal of Experimental Psychology, 62*, 234–242.

Wagner, A. R. (1976). Priming in STM: An information processing mechanism for self-generated or retrieval generated depression in performance. In T. J. Tighe & R. N. Leaton (Eds.), *Habituation: Perspectives from child development, animal behavior, and neurophysiology* (pp. 95–128). Hillsdale, NJ: Erlbaum.

Wagner, A. R. (1981). SOP: A model of automatic memory processing in animal behavior. In N. E. Spear & R. R. Miller (Eds.), *Information processing in animals: Memory mechanisms* (pp. 5–47). Hillsdale, NJ: Erlbaum.

Wagner, A. R., & Brandon, S. E. (2001). A componential theory of Pavlovian conditioning. In R. R. Mowrer & S. B. Klein (Eds.), *Handbook of contemporary learning theories* (pp. 23–64). Mahwah, NJ: Erlbaum.

Wagner, A. R., Logan, F. A., Haberlandt, K., & Price, T. (1968). Stimulus selection in animal discrimination learning. *Journal of Experimental Psychology, 76*, 171–180.

Wagner, A. R., & Rescorla, R. A. (1972). Inhibition in Pavlovian conditioning: Application of a theory. In R. A. Boakes & M. S. Halliday (Eds.), *Inhibition and learning*. London: Academic Press.

Wagner, A. R., Rudy, J. W., & Whitlow, J. W. (1973). Rehearsal in animal conditioning. *Journal of Experimental Psychology, 97*, 407–426.

Walters, E. T. (1994). Injury related behavior and neuronal plasticity: An evolutionary perspective on sensitization, hyperalgesia, and analgesia. *International Review of Neurobiology, 36*, 325–427.

Walters, G. C., & Glazer, R. D. (1971). Punishment of instinctive behavior in the Mongolian gerbil. *Journal of Comparative and Physiological Psychology, 75*, 331–340.

Walters, G. C., & Grusec, J. F. (1977). *Punishment*. San Francisco: W. H. Freeman.

Ward-Robinson, J., & Hall, G. (1996). Backward sensory preconditioning. *Journal of Experimental Psychology: Animal Behavior Processes, 22*, 395–404.

Ward-Robinson, J., & Hall, G. (1998). Backward sensory preconditioning when reinforcement is delayed. *Quarterly Journal of Experimental Psychology, 51*, 349–362.

Ward-Robinson, J., & Hall, G. (1999). The role of mediated conditioning in acquired equivalence. *Quarterly Journal of Experimental Psychology, 52B*, 335–350.

Wasserman, E. A. (1986). Prospection and retrospection as processes of animal short-term memory. In D. F. Kendrick, M. E. Rilling, & M. R. Denny (Eds.), *Theories of animal memory* (pp. 53–75). Hillsdale, NJ: Erlbaum.

Wasserman, E. A. (1990). Detecting response-outcome relations: Toward an understanding of the causal texture of the environment. In G. H. Bower (Ed.), *The psychology of learning and motivation* (Vol. 26, pp. 27–82). San Diego, CA: Academic Press.

Wasserman, E. A. (1993). Comparative cognition: Beginning the second century of the study of animal intelligence. *Psychological Bulletin, 113*, 211–228.

Wasserman, E. A., & Astley, S. L. (1994). A behavioral analysis of concepts: Its application to pigeons and children. In D. L. Medin (Ed.), *The psychology of learning and motivation* (Vol. 31, pp. 73–132). San Diego: Academic Press.

Wasserman, E. A., DeLong, R. E., & Larew, M. B. (1984). Temporal order and duration: Their discrimination and retention by pigeons. *Annals of the New York Academy of Sciences, 423*, 103–115.

Wasserman, E. A., Franklin, S. R., & Hearst, E. (1974). Pavlovian appetitive contingencies and approach versus withdrawal to conditioned stimuli in pigeons. *Journal of Comparative and Physiological Psychology, 86*, 616–627.

Wasserman, E. A., Kiedinger, R. E., & Bhatt, R. S. (1988). Conceptual behavior in pigeons: Categories, subcategories, and pseudocategories. *Journal of Experimental Psychology: Animal Behavior Processes, 14*, 235–246.

Wasserman, E. A., & Miller, R. R. (1997). What's elementary about associative learning? *Annual Review of Psychology, 48*, 573–607.

Watanabe, S., Sakamoto, J., & Wakita, M. (1995). Pigeons' discrimination of paintings by Monet and Picasso. *Journal of the Experimental Analysis of Behavior, 63*, 165–174.

Watson, J. B., & Rayner, R. (1920). Conditioned emotional reactions. *Journal of Experimental Psychology, 3*, 1–14. Reprinted in *American Psychologist, 55*, 313–317.

Wearden, J. H., & Burgess, I. S. (1982). Matching since Baum (1979). *Journal of the Experimental Analysis of Behavior, 38*, 339–348.

Wearden, J. H., & Clark, R. B. (1988). Interresponse-time reinforcement and behavior under aperiodic reinforcement schedules: A case study using computer modeling. *Journal of Experimental Psychology: Animal Behavior Processes, 14*, 200–211.

Wearden, J. H., & Ferrara, A. (1996). Stimulus range effects in temporal bisection by humans. *Quarterly Journal of Experimental Psychology, 49B*, 24–44.

Wearden, J. H., & McShane, B. (1988). Interval production as an analogue of the peak procedure: Evidence for similarity of human and animal timing processes. *Quarterly Journal of Experimental Psychology, 40B*, 363–375.

Wearden, J. H., & Penton-Voak, I. S. (1995). Feeling the heat: Body temperature and the rate of subjective time, revisited. *The Quarterly Journal of Experimental Psychology, 48B*, 129–141.

Weavers, R., Foster, T. M., & Temple, W. (1998). Reinforcer efficacy in a delayed matching-to-sample task. *Journal of the Experimental Analysis of Behavior, 69*, 77–85.

Wegner, D. M., & Wheatley, T. (1999). Apparent mental causation: Sources of the experience of will. *American Psychologist, 54*, 480–492.

Weinberger, N. (1965). Effect of detainment on extinction of avoidance responses. *Journal of Comparative and Physiological Psychology, 60*, 135–138.

Weisman, R. G., & Litner, J. S. (1972). The role of Pavlovian events in avoidance training. In R. A. Boakes & M. S. Halliday (Eds.), *Inhibition and learning*. London: Academic Press.

Weisman, R. G., & Premack, D. (1966). *Reinforcement and punishment produced by the same response depending upon the probability relation between the instrumental and contingent responses.* Paper presented at the meeting of the Psychonomic Society, St. Louis.

Weiss, S. J., Kearns, D. N., Cohn, S. I., Schindler, C. W., & Panlilio, L. V. (in press). Stimulus control of cocaine self-administration. *Journal of the Experimental Analysis of Behavior.*

Weiss, S. J., & Panlilio, L. V. (1999). Blocking a selective association in pigeons. *Journal of the Experimental Analysis of Behavior, 71,* 13–24.

Weiss, S. J., Panlilio, L. V., & Schindler, C. W. (1993a). Selective associations produced solely with appetitive contingencies: The stimulus-reinforcer interaction revisited. *Journal of the Experimental Analysis of Behavior, 59,* 309–322.

Weiss, S. J., Panlilio, L. V., & Schindler, C. W. (1993b). Single-incentive selective associations produced solely as a function of compound-stimulus conditioning context. *Journal of Experimental Psychology: Animal Behavior Processes, 19,* 284–294.

Weiss, S. J., & Schindler, C. W. (1981). Generalization peak shift in rats under conditions of positive reinforcement and avoidance. *Journal of the Experimental Analysis of Behavior, 35,* 175–185.

Weiss, S. J., & Weissman, R. D. (1992). Generalization peak shift for autoshaped and operant key pecks. *Journal of the Experimental Analysis of Behavior, 57,* 27–143.

Wernig, A., Muller, S., Nanassy, A., & Cagol, E. (1995). Laufband therapy based on "rules of spinal locomotion" is effective in spinal cord injured persons. *European Journal of Neuroscience, 7,* 823–829.

Westbrook, R. F., Jones, M. L., Bailey, G. K., & Harris, J. A. (2000). Contextual control over conditioned responding in a latent inhibition paradigm. *Journal of Experimental Psychology: Animal Behavior Processes, 26,* 157–173.

White, K. G. (2001). Forgetting functions. *Animal Learning and Behavior, 29,* 193–207.

White, K. G., & Wixted, J. T. (1999). Psychophysics of remembering. *Journal of the Experimental Analysis of Behavior, 71,* 91–113.

Whitlow, J. W., Jr., & Wagner, A. R. (1984). Memory and habituation. In H. V. S. Peeke & L. Petrinovich (Eds.), *Habituation, sensitization, and behavior.* New York: Academic Press.

Wilkie, D. M., & Slobin, P. (1983). Gerbils in space: Performance on the 17–arm radial maze. *Journal of the Experimental Analysis of Behavior, 40,* 301–312.

Wilkie, D. M., & Summers, R. J. (1982). Pigeons' spatial memory: Factors affecting delayed matching of key location. *Journal of the Experimental Analysis of Behavior, 37,* 45–56.

Wilkie, D. M., Willson, R. J., & Kardal, S. (1989). Pigeons discriminate pictures of a geographic location. *Animal Learning & Behavior, 17,* 163–171.

Williams, A. M., & Lattal, K. A. (1999). The role of the response-reinforcer relation in delay-of-reinforcement effects. *Journal of the Experimental Analysis of Behavior, 71,* 187–194.

Williams, B. A. (1983). Another look at contrast in multiple schedules. *Journal of the Experimental Analysis of Behavior, 39,* 345–384.

Williams, B. A. (1988). Reinforcement, choice, and response strength. In R. C. Atkinson, R. J. Herrnstein, G. Lindzey, & R. D. Luce (Eds.), *Stevens' handbook of experimental psychology: Vol. 2. Learning and cognition* (pp. 167–244) New York: Wiley.

Williams, B. A. (1990). Pavlovian contingencies and anticipatory contrast. *Animal Learning & Behavior, 18,* 44–50.

Williams, B. A. (1991). Marking and bridging versus conditioned reinforcement. *Animal Learning & Behavior, 19,* 264–269.

Williams, B. A. (1992a). Dissociation of theories of choice via temporal spacing of choice opportunities. *Journal of Experimental Psychology: Animal Behavior Processes, 18,* 287–297.

Williams, B. A. (1992b). Inverse relations between preference and contrast. *Journal of the Experimental Analysis of Behavior, 58,* 303–312.

Williams, B. A. (1993). Molar versus local reinforcement probability as determinants of stimulus value. *Journal of the Experimental Analysis of Behavior, 59,* 163–172.

Williams, B. A. (1994a). Conditioned reinforcement: Neglected or outmoded explanatory construct? *Psychonomic Bulletin & Review, 1,* 457–475.

Williams, B. A. (1994b). Reinforcement and choice. In N. J. Mackintosh (Ed.), *Animal learning and cognition* (pp. 81–108). San Diego: Academic Press.

Williams, B. A. (1997a). Conditioned reinforcement dynamics in three-link chained schedules. *Journal of the Experimental Analysis of Behavior, 67,* 145–159.

Williams, B. A. (1997b). Varieties of contrast: A review of *Incentive relativity* by Charles F. Flaherty. *Journal of the Experimental Analysis of Behavior, 68,* 133–141.

Williams, D. A., Butler, M. M., & Overmier, J. B. (1990). Expectancies of reinforcer location and quality as cues for a conditional discrimination in pigeons. *Journal of Experimental Psychology: Animal Behavior Processes, 16,* 3–13.

Williams, D. A., & Hurlburt, J. L. (2000). Mechanisms of second-order conditioning with a backward conditioned stimulus. *Journal of Experimental Psychology: Animal Behavior Processes, 26,* 340–351.

Williams, D. A., & Overmier, J. B. (1988a). Backward inhibitory conditioning with signaled and unsignaled unconditioned stimuli: Distribution of trials across days and intertrial interval. *Journal of Experimental Psychology: Animal Behavior Processes, 14,* 26–35.

Williams, D. A., & Overmier, J. B. (1988b). Some types of conditioned inhibitors carry collateral excitatory associations. *Learning and Motivation, 19,* 345–368.

Williams, D. A., Overmier, J. B., & LoLordo, V. M. (1992). A reevaluation of Rescorla's early dictums about Pavlovian conditioned inhibition. *Psychological Bulletin, 111,* 275–290.

Williams, D. A., & Sly, C. A. (1999). Recovery of conditioned suppression after backward pairings. *Animal Learning & Behavior, 27,* 152–167.

Willis, W. D. (2001). Mechanisms of central sensitization of nociceptive dorsal horn neurons. In M. M. Patterson & J. W. Grau (Eds.), *Spinal cord plasticity: Alterations in reflex function* (pp. 127–161). Boston: Kluwer Academic Publishers.

Wills, S., & Mackintosh, N. J. (1998). Peak shift on an artificial dimension. *Quarterly Journal of Experimental Psychology, 51B,* 1–31.

Willson, R. J., & Wilkie, D. M. (1991). Discrimination training facilitates pigeons' performance on one-trial-per-day delayed matching of key location. *Journal of the Experimental Analysis of Behavior, 55,* 201–212.

Wilson, S. W. (1991). The animal path to AI. In J. A. Meyer & S. W. Wilson (Eds.), *From animals to animats: Proceedings of the first international conference on simulation of adaptive behavior.* Cambridge, MA: MIT Press.

Winter, J., & Perkins, C. C. (1982). Immediate reinforcement in delayed reward learning in pigeons *Journal of the Experimental Analysis of Behavior, 38,* 169–179.

Witcher, E. S., & Ayres, J. J. B. (1984). A test of two methods for extinguishing Pavlovian conditioned inhibition. *Animal Learning & Behavior, 12,* 149–156.

Wolpe, J. (1990). *The practice of behavior therapy* (4th ed.). New York: Pergamon.

Woodworth, R. S., & Schlosberg, H. (1954). *Experimental psychology.* New York: Holt, Rinehart and Winston.

Wright, A. A. (1990). Markov choice processes in simultaneous matching-to-sample at different levels of discriminability. *Animal Learning & Behavior, 18,* 277–286.

Wright, A. A. (1992). Learning mechanisms in matching to sample. *Journal of Experimental Psychology: Animal Behavior Processes, 18,* 67–79.

Wright, A. A. (1997). Concept learning and learning strategies. *Psychological Science, 8,* 119–123.

Wright, A. A., Cook, R. G., Rivera, J. J., Sands, S. F., & Delius, J. D. (1988). Concept learning by pigeons: Matching-to-sample with trial-unique video picture

stimuli. *Animal Learning & Behavior, 16,* 436–444.

Wright, A. A., & Delius, J. D. (1994). Scratch and match: Pigeons learn matching and oddity with gravel stimuli. *Journal of Experimental Psychology: Animal Behavior Processes, 20,* 108–112.

Wright, A. A., Shyan, M. R., & Jitsumori, M. (1990). Auditory same/different concept learning by monkeys. *Animal Learning & Behavior, 18,* 287–294.

Wright, A. A., & Sands, S. F. (1981). A model of detection and decision processes during matching to sample by pigeons: Performance with 88 different wavelengths in delayed and simultaneous matching tasks. *Journal of Experimental Psychology: Aminal Behavior Process, 7,* 191–216.

Wynne, C. D. L., Staddon, J. E. R., & Delius, J. D. (1996). Dynamics of waiting in pigeons. *Journal of the Experimental Analysis of Behavior, 65,* 603–618.

Yerkes, R. M., & Morgulis, S. (1909). The method of Pavlov in animal psychology. *Psychological Bulletin, 6,* 257–273.

Yin, H., Barnet, R. C., & Miller, R. R. (1994). Second-order conditioning and Pavlovian conditioned inhibition: Operational similarities and differences. *Journal of Experimental Psychology: Animal Behavior Processes, 20,* 419–428.

Zamble, E., Hadad, G. M., Mitchell, J. B., & Cutmore, T. R. H. (1985). Pavlovian conditioning of sexual arousal: First- and second-order effects. *Journal of Experimental Psychology: Animal Behavior Processes, 11,* 598–610.

Zarcone, T. J., & Ator, N. A. (2000). Drug discrimination: stimulus control during repeated testing in extinction. *Journal of the Experimental Analysis of Behavior, 74,* 283–294.

Zarcone, T. J., Branch, M. N., Hughes, C. E., & Pennypacker, H. S. (1997). Key pecking during extinction after intermittent or continuous reinforcement as a function of the number of reinforcers delivered during training. *Journal of the Experimental Analysis of Behavior, 67,* 91–108.

Zeiler, M. D. (1984). The sleeping giant: Reinforcement schedules. *Journal of the Ex-*

perimental Analysis of Behavior, 42, 485–493.

Zeiler, M. D. (1999). Time without clocks. *Journal of the Experimental Analysis of Behavior, 72,* 288–292.

Zentall, T. R. (Ed.). (1993). *Animal cognition.* Hillsdale, NJ: Erlbaum.

Zentall, T. R. (1998). Symbolic representation in animals: Emergent stimulus relations in conditional discrimination learning. *Animal Learning & Behavior, 26,* 363–377.

Zentall, T. R. (2001). The case for a cognitive approach to animal learning and behavior. *Behavioural Processes, 54,* 65–78.

Zentall, T. R., Edwards, C. A., Moore, B. S., & Hogan, D. E. (1981). Identity: The basis for both matching and oddity learning in pigeons. *Journal of Experimental Psychology: Animal Behavior Processes, 7,* 70–86.

Zentall, T. R., Jagielo, J. A., Jackson-Smith, P. & Urcuioli, P. J. (1987). Memory codes in pigeon short-term memory: Effects of varying the number of sample and comparison stimuli. *Learning and Motivation, 18,* 21–33.

Zentall, T. R., Roper, K. L., Kaiser, D. H., & Sherburne, L. M. (1997). A critical analysis of directed-forgetting research in animals. In J. M. Golding & C. MacLeod (Eds.), *Interdisciplinary approaches to intentional forgetting* (pp. 265–287). Hillsdale, NJ: Erlbaum.

Zentall, T. R., Roper, K. L., & Sherburne, L. M. (1995). Most directed forgetting in pigeons can be attributed to the absence of reinforcement of forget trials during training or to other procedural artifacts. *Journal of the Experimental Analysis of Behavior, 63,* 127–137.

Zentall, T. R., & Sherburne, L. M. (1994). Transfer of value from S+ to S− in a simultaneous discrimination. *Journal of Experimental Psychology: Animal Behavior Processes, 20,* 176–183.

Zentall, T. R., & Smeets, P. M. (Eds.). (1996). *Stimulus class formation in humans and animals. Advances in Psychology* Vol. 117. New York: North-Holland (Elsevier Science).

Zentall, T. R., Steirn, J. N., & Jackson-Smith, P. (1990). Memory strategies in pigeons' performance of a radial-arm-maze analog task. *Journal of Experimental Psychology: Animal Behavior Processes, 16,* 358–371.

Zentall, T. R., Urcuioli, P. J., Jagielo, J. A., & Jackson-Smith, P. (1989). Interaction of sample dimension and sample comparison mapping on pigeons' performance of delayed conditional discriminations. *Animal Learning & Behavior, 17,* 172–178.

Zentall, T. R., Weaver, J. E., & Sherburne, L. M. (1996). Value transfer in concurrent-schedule discriminations by pigeons.

Animal Learning & Behavior, 24, 401–409.

Zhou, Y., & Riccio, D. C. (1995). Concussion-induced retrograde amnesia in rats. *Physiology & Behavior, 57,* 1107–1115.

Zhou, Y., & Riccio, D. C. (1996). Manipulation of components of context: The context shift effect and forgetting of stimulus attributes. *Learning and Motivation, 27,* 400–407.

Zhuikov, A. Y., Couvillon, P. A., & Bitterman, M. E. (1994). Quantitative two-process analysis of avoidance condition-

ing in goldfish. *Journal of Experimental Psychology: Animal Behavior Processes, 20,* 32–43.

Zimmer-Hart, C. L., & Rescorla, R. A. (1974). Extinction of Pavlovian conditioned inhibition. *Journal of Comparative and Physiological Psychology, 86,* 837–845.

Zoladek, L., & Roberts, W. A. (1978). The sensory basis of spatial memory in the rat. *Animal Learning & Behavior, 6,* 77–81.

NAME INDEX

Quartermain, D., 343

Rabinowitz, V. C., 346
Rachlin, H. C., 178, 180, 184, 186, 209, 215, 310, 311
Raia, C. P., 170
Rakitin, B. C., 360
Ramsey, D. S., 102, 104
Randall, C. K., 109
Randall, P. K., 343, 348
Randell, T., 242
Randich, A., 93
Rankin, C. H., 39, 47
Rapaport, P., 78
Rashotte, M., 109
Raslear, T. G., 212
Rauhut, A. S., 93, 260
Ray, E., 241
Raymond, G. A., 304, 305
Rayner, R., 63, 64
Reberg, D., 151
Redhead, E. S., 229
Reed, P., 131, 143, 147, 171
Reichmuth, C. J., 235
Reid, A. K., 131
Reilly, M. P., 148, 171, 235
Remington, B., 242
Remington, G., 153
Repp, A. C., 136, 313
Rescorla, R. A., 6, 71, 77, 78, 80, 82, 85, 86, 97, 98, 100, 108, 109, 110, 112–116, 194, 196, 197, 198, 229, 245, 246, 247, 248, 255, 256, 257, 261, 263, 264, 265, 266, 267, 268, 269, 296, 297
Revusky, S. H., 73
Rey, V., 241
Reynolds, G. S., 169, 170, 218, 219, 220, 222
Riccio, D. C., 102, 292, 316, 317, 343, 346, 347, 348, 349, 350
Richardson, R., 263, 343, 348, 349
Richelle, M., 358
Richmond, M., 241
Ricker, S. T., 259, 269
Riley, A. L., 72, 93, 195, 299
Riley, D. A., 336, 337
Rilling, M., 339
Ristau, C. A., 316
Rivera, J. J., 326
Rivers, S., 106
Rizvi, S. A. T., 213
Robbins, S. J., 102, 103, 116, 121, 256
Roberts, A. D. L., 110
Roberts, M., 274
Roberts, S., 254, 359, 360, 361
Roberts, W. A., 225, 322, 323, 328, 329, 334, 361, 370

Robertson, B., 176
Robins, R. W., 3
Robinson, S. R., 44
Roby, T. B., 199
Rodd, Z. A., 155
Rodefer, J. S., 38
Roepcke, B., 110
Rogers, R. F., 20
Roitblat, H. L., 11, 14, 316, 325, 362, 366, 370, 374
Rokke, E., 196
Roll, D. L., 73
Roll, J. M., 39, 56
Romanes, G., 10, 11, 14
Romaniuk, C. B., 79
Romano, A., 47, 183
Romski, M. A., 375
Roper, K. L., 339, 340, 341
Rosas, J. M., 93, 256, 259
Roscoe, E. M., 307
Rose, S. A., 44
Rosellini, R. A., 152, 153, 155, 156
Rosen, J. B., 45
Rosenberg, E., 327
Rosengard, C., 259
Ross, R. T., 246, 248, 249
Rothbaum, B. O., 154
Rovee-Collier, C., 48, 341, 342, 343
Rowlett, J. K., 213
Roy, R. R., 159
Rozin, P., 72, 96
Rubert, E., 379
Rudy, J. W., 20, 36, 37, 48, 338
Rumbaugh, D. M., 377, 380
Russell, M. S., 24
Russell, R. J., 249
Russell, W. R., 347

Sahley, C., 20
Sajwaj, T., 302
Sakamoto, J., 234
Saladin, M. E., 93, 116
Salmon, D. P., 233
Samuelson, R. J., 326, 328
Sanders, R. J., 379, 380
Sands, S. F., 325, 326
Santi, A., 336, 361
Saper, Z. L., 93
Sara, S. J., 350
Sargisson, R. J., 323, 324
Sauerbrunn, D., 305
Saunders, K. J., 303
Saunders, R. J., 241
Savage-Rumbaugh, E. S., 375, 377, 379, 380, 381, 382, 384
Savastano, H. I., 9, 79, 81, 83, 86, 118, 119, 180, 184

Sawa, K., 93
Scavio, M. R., Jr., 93
Schaal, D. W., 148, 235
Schachter, D. L., 319
Schachtman, T. R., 120, 225, 260, 261, 269, 343
Schafe, G. E., 349
Schepker, R., 110
Schiff, R., 291
Schiller, K. M., 20
Schindler, C. W., 225, 226, 232, 239
Schlinger, H., 167
Schlosberg, H., 173, 281
Schmajuk, N. A., 9, 245
Schneiderman, N., 77
Schnitzler, H.-U., 45
Schnur, P., 93
Schrader, S., 311
Schreibman, L., 223
Schreurs, B. G., 79
Schrier, A. M., 370
Schulkin, J., 100
Schultz, L. A., 211
Schuster, R. H., 310
Schusterman, R. J., 235, 322, 376
Schwartz, B., 49, 50, 131, 137, 195, 254
Schwartz, J. H., 11, 331
Schwarz, M., 20
Schweitzer, J. B., 188
Sclafani, A., 72
Scopatz, R. A., 366
Sears, R. R., 12
Sears, G. W., 296
Sechenov, I. M., 7, 8
Seligman, M. E. P., 96, 152, 153, 154, 155, 157
Senkowski, P. C., 269
Serdikoff, S. L., 246
Sevcik, R. A., 375, 377, 379
Sevenster, P., 125, 140
Shah, K., 177
Shahan, T. A., 148
Shahidullah, S., 44
Shanker, S. G., 375, 384
Shanks, D. R., 87
Shapiro, K. J., 96
Shapiro, K. L., 225
Shapiro, N. R., 152
Shavalia, D. A., 328, 329
Shaw, D., 143
Shea, N. C., 274
Sheffield, F. D., 199, 290
Shek, W. Y., 171
Shellman, J., 302
Shelton, R. C., 84
Sherburne, L. M., 196, 339, 340, 341, 354
Sheridan, J., 45

SUBJECT INDEX

PHOTO CREDITS

Chapter 1: 4, Bettmann / CORBIS **8,** Sovfoto **10,** Bettmann / CORBIS **20,** Robert W. Allan, Lafayette College **Chapter 2: 31,** Courtesy of Allen Zak **33,** Courtesy of G. P. Baerends **51,** Courtesy of Donald A. Dewsbury **Chapter 3: 62,** Bettmann Archive **65,** Courtesy of the author **67,** Courtesy of I. Gormezano **73,** Courtesy of Donald A. Dewsbury **82,** Courtesy of Donald A. Dewsbury **87,** Courtesy of Donald A. Dewsbury **88,** Courtesy of Donald A. Dewsbury **Chapter 4: 102,** Courtesy of Donald A. Dewsbury **107,** Courtesy of C. K. Akins **110,** Courtesy of L. J. Kamin **112,** Courtesy of Donald A. Dewsbury **117,** Courtesy of Donald A. Dewsbury **118,** Courtesy of J. Gibbon **119,** top, Courtesy of M. Burns; bottom, Courtesy of Donald A. Dewsbury **120,** Courtesy of R. R. Miller **Chapter 5: 130,** Bettmann Archive **131,** Omikron / Photo Researchers, Inc. **138,** Courtesy of A. Neuringer **140,** Courtesy of Donald A. Dewsbury **141,** top, Animal Behavior Enterprises; bottom, Courtesy of Courtesy of Donald A. Dewsbury **144,** Courtesy of Donald A. Dewsbury **145,** Courtesy of Donald A. Dewsbury **147,** Courtesy of D. A. Lieberman **150,** Courtesy of Donald A. Dewsbury **153,** top, Courtesy of Donald A. Dewsbury; bottom, Courtesy of M. E. P. Seligman **155,** Courtesy of N. K. Dess **156,** Courtesy of UCLA Department of Psychology **Chapter 6: 174,** Courtesy of Donald A. Dewsbury **176,** Courtesy of W. M. Baum **179,** Courtesy of B. A. Williams **184,** top, Courtesy of Donald A. Dewsbury; bottom, Courtesy of L. Green **185,** Courtesy of A.W. Logue **Chapter 7: 204,** top, Courtesy of W. Timberlake; bottom, Courtesy of J. Allison **Chapter 8: 224,** Courtesy of the author **225,** Courtesy of Donald A. Dewsbury **229,** Courtesy of Donald A. Dewsbury **240,** Courtesy of Donald A. Dewsbury **Chapter 9: 272,** Courtesy of A. Amsel **273:** Courtesy of E. J. Capaldi **Chapter 10: 283,** Courtesy of Donald A. Dewsbury **288,** Courtesy of Donald A. Dewsbury **295,** Courtesy of Donald A. Dewsbury **298,** Courtesy of Donald A. Dewsbury **300,** Courtesy of UCLA Department of Psychology **302,** Courtesy of N. H. Azrin **Chapter 11: 322,** Courtesy of D. S. Grant **324,** Courtesy of M. Spetch **325,** Courtesy of Donald A. Dewsbury **327,** Courtesy of Catherine Green, from Patricia Sharp Lab, Department of Psychology, Yale University **334,** Courtesy of Dr. D. M. Wilkie **336,** Courtesy of P. Urcuioli **338,** Courtesy of T. Zentall **342,** Courtesy of C. Rovee-Collier **343,** top, Courtesy of N.E. Spear; bottom, Courtesy of W. C. Gordon **347,** Courtesy of D. C. Riccio **Chapter 12: 360,** Courtesy of R. M. Church **363,** Arizona State University photo **366,** Courtesy of Donald A. Dewsbury **370,** Courtesy of E. A. Wasserman **376,** Courtesy of I. M. Pepperberg **378,** Courtesy of E. Sue Savage-Rumbaugh, Great Ape Trust **379,** Courtesy of E. Sue Savage-Rumbaugh, Great Ape Trust **383,** Courtesy of E. Sue Savage-Rumbaugh, Great Ape Trust

Workbook Designed for Michael Domjan's
The Principles of Learning and Behavior, 5th edition

Mark A. Krause
University of Portland

Table of Contents

Preface

Your course on learning will be full of terminology, concepts, and theories that have developed over the long history of this discipline. Organizing and making sense of the material is challenging. But you will reap the rewards that go with understanding the complex process of learning. This workbook is designed to help you enhance and solidify your knowledge of the psychology of learning.

Students who are working to grasp the basic foundations of the field find it challenging to organize the vast amount of information that is standard for most courses in learning. The learning course you are taking probably involves lectures from your professor, discussions and demonstrations done in class, assignments using Sniffy the virtual rat, and, for some, an actual laboratory opportunity. This workbook will provide you with another active, hands-on approach to studying learning.

As you encounter the terminology and concepts of learning it is important that you are actively engaged with the material. This workbook facilitates hands-on, active learning and has a chapter that coincides with the material from each chapter of your text, The Principles of Learning and Behavior (5th edition) by Michael Domjan. The workbook is not a condensed alternative to the text. I do not recommend that you attempt to work through any of the exercises *before* reading the corresponding text chapter. I recommend that you first carefully read each textbook chapter before attempting the corresponding workbook exercises. I do not devote much time and space to reiterating background information from the text. However, once you have read the text the terminology and concepts in the exercises will be familiar. I frequently refer you to textbook pages to refresh your memory of specific topics we cover. For this workbook it was not possible to cover *all* terms and concepts in your textbook. This does not imply that some of the material in your textbook is not important.

The problems in the chapters that follow take a variety of forms. Many are designed to reflect how learning is studied. For example, research on learning involves frequent experimentation on human and nonhuman subjects. Thus, many of the exercises ask you to design experiments. You will also work with some small data sets from actual and hypothetical experiments. I frequently ask you to use graphs to illustrate and summarize results from experiments. This allows you to more clearly picture the concepts you are learning about, and encourages you to think carefully about the material.

Some of the exercises in this workbook ask you to apply concepts to your own experiences. For example, the terminology from classical conditioning is often confusing to students so I have provided exercises that will allow you to apply these terms to new situations. Many of the problems in the workbook involve exercises. In addition, I have included something called "concept questions". These questions typically ask you to elaborate and apply ideas and theories presented in your text.

Your professor may have required you to use Sniffy the Virtual Rat (Pro version 2.0). Throughout the workbook I include an icon

SNIFFY APPLICATION

that refers to exercises and corresponding page numbers from your Sniffy manual. The purpose of this is to coordinate the Sniffy exercises with your textbook and workbook.

Studying the psychology of learning is a highly rewarding undertaking. Theories of learning are foundational to the field of psychology and apply to its many sub-disciplines. There are numerous practical applications of learning as well, from educational to therapeutic settings. One thing we know, as both psychologists and students, is that learning involves *doing*. Sometimes this means going beyond your textbook to get information. Thus, it is my hope that you find the exercises in this workbook helpful and that they facilitate your learning about learning.

Finally, I would like to thank your textbook author, Michael Domjan, for inviting me to write this and for helping to develop many of the exercises. I would also like to acknowledge the reviewers who helped improve the project: Shawn Charlton, San Diego Mesa College; Heide Island, The University of Montana; and Martin Shapiro, Cal Sate Fresno. In addition, much credit is due to Marianne Taflinger for her guidance and support in initiating, developing, and completing the project.

Mark A. Krause
University of Portland

1 Introduction

The first chapter of your text serves to orient you toward the basic questions that psychologists ask about learning, and the theoretical perspectives that contemporary researchers in learning adopt. We will start this workbook with several exercises based on **chapter 1** of your text. First, we ask you some concept questions about topics such as reflexes, nativism, empiricism, and functional neurology (**section 1-1**). Following this series of questions are exercises that serve to clarify our definition of learning (**section 1-2**). Our knowledge of learning is almost exclusively derived from carefully designed experiments. Familiarity with terminology and concepts associated with experimental methodology is essential to understanding the text material. **Sections 1-3** and **1-4** serve to help you brush up on your knowledge of common experimental concepts and with graphing and interpreting results.

After completing these exercises you should be able to:
- Understand the nature of reflexes and their importance to the psychology of learning,
- Distinguish between the positions of nativism and empiricism and relate these perspectives to the study of learning,
- Understand the role of functional neurology in the study of learning,
- Distinguish between changes in behavior due to learning and other processes such as fatigue, maturation, and motivation,
- Identify and apply basic terminology associated with the experimental method,
- Read and create clear, interpretable graphs.

1-1 Historical Viewpoints

1-1.1 Concept Questions

1) Draw a reflex arc as Descartes would have drawn it, labeling the sources of input and output.

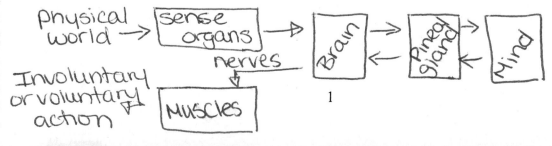

1

2) Draw a reflex arc that is based on the subsequent work of Charles Bell and Francois Magendie. How is this different from the Cartesian reflex circuit? Why is it different?

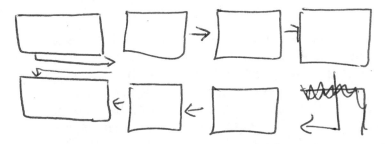

3) Provide an example of an association between two stimuli from your daily experience. Which is the triggering stimulus? What memory is activated by the stimulus? Is this association based on learning?

4) What were Aristotle's laws of association? Provide an example of each from your personal experience.

5) What is functional neurology? Why are studies of learning relevant to it?

6) What are the critical features of a model system that is designed to represent other species or situations?

1-2 Defining Learning

One of the defining features of learning is that behavior changes as a result of experience. However, this feature alone does not distinguish learned behaviors from changes resulting from other processes such as fatigue, maturation, or motivational and physiological states. It may be helpful to review **pages 14-16** of your text before completing this exercise. First, we should reiterate the definition of learning from your text:

....*an enduring change in the mechanisms of behavior involving specific stimuli and/or responses that results from prior experience with those or similar stimuli and responses* (**p. 14**)

1-2.1 Concept Questions
---

1) How does the definition of learning quoted above distinguish between learning and fatigue or motivational changes?

2) How does the definition distinguish between learning and maturation?

3) What is performance? How does the definition of learning distinguish between learning and performance?

4) What aspect of the definition makes learning a causal mechanism?

1-2.2   Applying the definition. Below are descriptions of ten different behaviors that involve change. Your task will be to identify the situations in which learning, as opposed to some other process, has occurred. Circle the option you choose. If you answer 'no' or 'maybe' attempt to identify what other process may account for the change in behavior. Some alternative processes could include maturation and physical growth, motivational influences, genetic change, or insightful problem solving.

1) A rat is placed in a t-maze. The left arm of the maze is lighted and the right arm of the maze is dark. The dark portion of the maze has food at the end of it. On the first 20 trials the rat enters the dark portion on 10 of the trials. On the next set of 20 trials the rat enters the dark portion on all 20 trials. Is the change in behavior between the first 20 trials and the second 20 trials due to learning?

(a. Yes)   b. No   c. Maybe

If b. or c., why did you choose this answer?

Do rats prefer dark ?
is the change enduring

---

2) Infants rely on the rooting reflex to initiate breast feeding. When infants are weaned and stop rooting, is the loss of the reflex due to learning?

a. Yes   b. No   (c. Maybe)

If b. or c., why did you choose this answer?

---

3) One set of cats observed their mothers killing mice from an early age and subsequently killed mice when given the chance. Other cats did not observe their mothers killing mice and were much less likely to become mouse killers. Do cats *learn* the "killing instinct"?

a. Yes   b. No   c. Maybe

If b. or c., why did you choose this answer?

4) An infant makes the transition between crawling and walking. Is the transition due to learning?

            a. Yes   b. No   c. Maybe

If b. or c., why did you choose this answer?

5) You compete against a computer at a video game. During an initial 20 games the computer responds to your moves in a random fashion. During the final 20 games the computer responds to your moves using information based on the first 20 games. Did the computer learn?

            a. Yes   b. No   c. Maybe

If b. or c., why did you choose this answer?

6) Jeb sits in his cubicle typing reports at an average of 20 words per minute. As the day progresses his productivity increases to 45 words per minute until he completes his assigned work. Is the increase in productivity due to learning?

            a. Yes   b. No   c. Maybe

If b. or c., why did you choose this answer?

7) A plant orients the surfaces of its leaves toward sunlight to facilitate photosynthesis. Did the plant learn?

a. Yes   b. No   c. Maybe

If b. or c., why did you choose this answer?

8) A chimpanzee sits in its enclosure with a long stick and a wooden crate. A banana is placed out of the chimpanzee's reach. After an hour of staring at the banana, the crate, and the stick, it places the crate beneath the banana, stands on it, and knocks the banana into the enclosure with the pole. Assuming the chimpanzee has not used a long stick or crate of this sort before, is this an example of learning?

a. Yes   b. No   c. Maybe

If b. or c., why did you choose this answer?

9) George works overtime the night before taking the Graduate Record Examination. His combined verbal-quantitative score is 950 out of 1600. George retakes the GRE the following week after a full night of sleep and scores 1190. Is the rise in his score due to learning?

a. Yes   b. No   c. Maybe

If b. or c., why did you choose this answer?

10) The sound of a toilet flushing signaled a major change in shower water temperature in an old apartment building where John was living. The result was that John would jump at the sound of the toilet flushing after only a few times that he took a shower in that apartment. A plumber fixed the problem and the jumping response declined over the course of two weeks. Was the jumping response learned?

a. Yes   b. No   c. Maybe

If b. or c., why did you choose this answer?

1-2.3 Concept Questions

1) Why does the study of learning require conducting true experiments?

2) Describe an instance of learning from your personal experience? How can you be sure that it is an example of learning and not some other process?

1-3 Experimental Terminology

Throughout you textbook you will read about the details of key experiments that relate to the theories and concepts of conditioning and learning. The purpose of this section is to refresh your memory of some of the terminology and concepts associated with experiments. Box 1-3 lists some of these terms.

Box 1-3. Key terms in experimental methods.

Independent variable (IV): The variable(s) controlled and manipulated by the experimenter.

Dependent variable (DV): The response measured by an experimenter to determine whether the independent variable was effective.

Extraneous or confounding variable: Uncontrolled variable that causes systematic changes in the dependent variable.

Experimental group: The group exposed to the independent variable.

Control group: The group compared with the experimental group that is not exposed to the independent variable.

1-3.1 In each example below, identify the IV and DV in the study described. Identify some possible extraneous variables that may need to be controlled. (Note: a study can have more than one IV and more than one DV).

---

1) A psychologist examined how different amounts of food reward affected the frequency of bar pressing by rats.

IV:

DV:

Possible extraneous variables to control?

2) A behavioral neuroscientist examined the effects of a drug on maze running performance in 10 female rats that came from a strain of animals bred for efficient spatial learning and memory.

IV:

DV:

Possible extraneous variables to control?

3) An applied psychologist tested whether different computer screen displays influenced productivity in office workers.

IV:

DV:

Possible extraneous variables to control?

1-4   How to Read and Create Graphs

Throughout your text you will find numerous figures that consist of graphs reporting key experimental results. Experiments in learning often involve dependent variables that yield numerical values such as time or frequency. Graphing is an effective way of revealing the effects of an independent variable(s) on a dependent variable(s). Many of the exercises in this workbook ask that you graph and interpret data. The purpose of this section is to provide you with some practice with reading, interpreting, and creating graphs.

1-4.1 Reading graphs. Consider a straightforward example from some early research in learning done by Tolman and Honzik (1930). Two groups of rats ran through a maze in order to receive food. The dependent variable was the number of times the rats made errors, such as entering wrong alleys of the maze. The independent variable was food deprivation. One group of rats was food deprived at the onset of the experiment and another was fed prior to the experiment and therefore was not hungry. Below are hypothetical data generated by the two groups of rats. The numbers in the cells represent the number of errors made while traveling through the maze.

Trial	Fed group	Food deprived group
1	200	205
2	194	200
3	188	185
4	180	165
5	179	156
6	175	130
7	170	100
8	160	75
9	161	60
10	165	45
Total averages	177.2	132.1

The averages for the two groups suggest that the food deprived group made fewer errors in this experiment. However, often in research on learning we are interested in examining the *pattern* of the results in addition to overall effects. Thus, we should plot the results using a line graph:

12

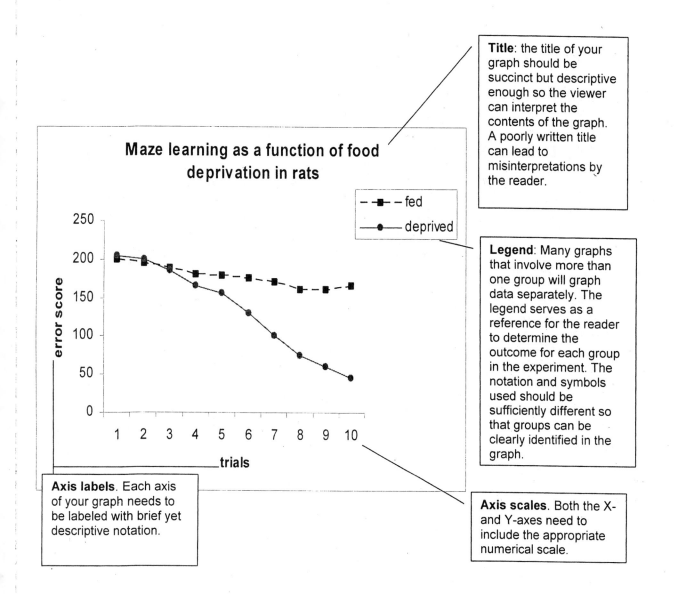

Title: the title of your graph should be succinct but descriptive enough so the viewer can interpret the contents of the graph. A poorly written title can lead to misinterpretations by the reader.

Legend: Many graphs that involve more than one group will graph data separately. The legend serves as a reference for the reader to determine the outcome for each group in the experiment. The notation and symbols used should be sufficiently different so that groups can be clearly identified in the graph.

Axis labels. Each axis of your graph needs to be labeled with brief yet descriptive notation.

Axis scales. Both the X- and Y-axes need to include the appropriate numerical scale.

There are many other ways of graphing data, including bar graphs, which will be used in subsequent chapters. The same general guidelines mentioned in the graph above still apply. Graphs are an important feature of a research report. Additionally, your interpretation of the graph is important. Your interpretation is written out in the body of the text and should include statements about how the independent variable affected the dependent variable. For example,

Food deprivation influenced the rate at which maze learning occurred. Rats that were deprived of food made fewer maze running errors over the course of 10 trials than did rats that were fed.

1-4.2 Creating graphs. Here we will practice creating a graph with the elements listed above. Imagine that two chimpanzees were taught to use American Sign Language using different methods. One chimpanzee was encouraged to imitate a human who formed the signs in her presence (Imitate). A second chimpanzee learned signs with the assistance of a human who molded the chimp's hands into the correct shape and moved them in the appropriate fashion (Molding). Below are data summarizing the cumulative number of signs learned by each chimp over the course of 8 weeks.

Week	Imitate	Molding
1	2	3
2	5	6
3	6	8
4	8	11
5	12	19
6	14	23
7	15	27
8	19	31

1) Plot these data on the axes below.
2) Be sure to scale and label the axes and include a title at the top.
3) Write out an interpretation below your graph.

Title:

Interpretation:

2 Elicited Behavior, Habituation, and Sensitization

This chapter introduces you to some basic categories of behavior, including reflexes and simple processes for changing behavior called habituation and sensitization. **Section 2-1** elaborates on the concept of a modal action pattern (MAP) described on **page 31** of your text. Following this are exercises that are designed to help you identify some factors that influence rates of habituation and sensitization (**section 2-2**). We conclude with a practice exercise in which you will apply the opponent process theory of emotion and motivation to your own experiences (**section 2-3**).

After completing these exercises you should be able to:

- Identify examples of modal action patterns,
- Apply concepts of ethology to various examples of behavior,
- Recognize several factors that influence the extent to which responses habituate and sensitize,
- Visualize how dual-process theory works,
- Apply the opponent-process theory of motivation and emotion to everyday examples.

2-1 Modal Action Patterns

Your text discusses the concept of a modal action pattern (MAP). On **pages 31-34** several examples of MAPs in animal behavior are described. For example, herring gulls use their bills to return eggs that have gone astray from their nests using a relatively stereotyped series of movements. This response has adaptive value. Clearly, *not* engaging in this behavior compromises the reproductive fitness of the birds. The concept of a MAP comes from the discipline of ethology, which focuses on the biological and evolutionary significance of behavior. One of ethology's major proponents, Niko Tinbergen (1963), identified four fundamental issues that ethologists try to address when studying behavior. The four issues are:

- Adaptation (survival value): focuses on how behavior influences survival and reproductive success. Research in this area typically searches for a direct link between a behavior and how it impacts survival of individuals and their offspring.

- Causation: focuses on the neurological and physiological processes that underlie and control behavior.
- Development (ontogeny): focuses on behavioral changes due to processes such as maturation, early experience, and learning.
- Evolution: examines similarities and differences in behavior between species.

2-1.1 Using the descriptions of the four ethological issues above, identify which of the four is being applied to each of the following examples based on published research:

---

1) Peter Marler studied how young birds acquire their songs by listening to members of their own species. **Answer:**_____

2) Konrad Lorenz studied the different cues that hatchling geese respond to as they imprint upon their mothers (or upon Lorenz himself, as he discovered during his work with these birds).
   Answer:_____

3) Esther Cullen compared nesting and social behavior of kittiwakes (*Rissa tridactyla*) that nest on cliffs with other sea dwelling gulls (*Larus argentatus*) that nest on open beaches. **Answer:**_____

4) Martha McClintock demonstrated that co-habitation by women in college dormitories results in menstrual synchrony, probably mediated by an olfactory cue. **Answer:**_____

5) Karl von Frisch described and experimented on the "language" that bees use to direct other bees in the hive toward food sources. Von Frisch examined the different movements the bees made that indicated the direction, distance, and quality of the food source so that hive-mates watching these movements could locate the food.
Answer:_____

6) Howard Evans compared various prey carrying strategies in different species of wasps. **Answer:**_____

7) Harry Harlow examined the effects of maternal deprivation on infant attachment and social behavior. **Answer:**_____

8) Erich von Holst examined how different regions of the brain control peripheral organs. **Answer:**_____

9) Robert Provine studied the specific facial features that elicit contagious yawning, a modal action pattern. **Answer:**_____

10) Niko Tinbergen demonstrated that gulls remove opened eggshells, which are highly visible to predators, from their nests, increasing survival rates in their young. **Answer:**_____

2-2 Habituation and Sensitization

Exposure to a stimulus can cause habituation, which is a decrease in responding, or sensitization, an increase in responding. The basic processes of habituation and sensitization are described on **pages 39-48** of your text. It would be helpful to review these pages before working on the exercises below. In these exercises we will explore some factors that influence whether habituation or sensitization occur. Below is a figure that depicts a decrease in startle responses across 10 trials.

2-2.1 Factor #1: The inter-stimulus interval. One factor influencing the degree to which habituation occurs is the amount of time that passes between one presentation of the stimulus and the next. As a general rule, a longer interval between stimulus presentations results in slower rates of habituation. For example, if you listen to a new song five times in succession in one day, habituation will be more pronounced than if you listen to the song once daily for five days. With this in mind, view the habituation curves below. Imagine that a habituation experiment was conducted with three groups:

Group 1: Exposed to novel stimulus for 5 seconds, once per minute
Group 2: Exposed to novel stimulus for 5 seconds, once per hour
Group 3: Exposed to novel stimulus for 5 seconds, once per day

The graph below shows hypothetical data for the three groups across the ten trial period. Specify in the graph below which curve represents the likely result for each of the three groups.

2-2.2   Factor #2: Stimulus duration. Another factor influencing levels of habituation and sensitization is the duration of the stimulus. For example, habituation to a 10 second stimulus will be slower than habituation to a 30 second stimulus. Now imagine a study with three groups treated as follows:

Group 1: Exposed to a novel stimulus for 1 minute each time for 10 trials
Group 2: Exposed to a novel stimulus for 2 minutes each time for 10 trials
Group 3: Exposed to a novel stimulus for 10 minutes each time for 10 trials

In the graph below, draw your own curves representing habituation in these three groups. Be sure to label the lines representing each group and give your graph a title.

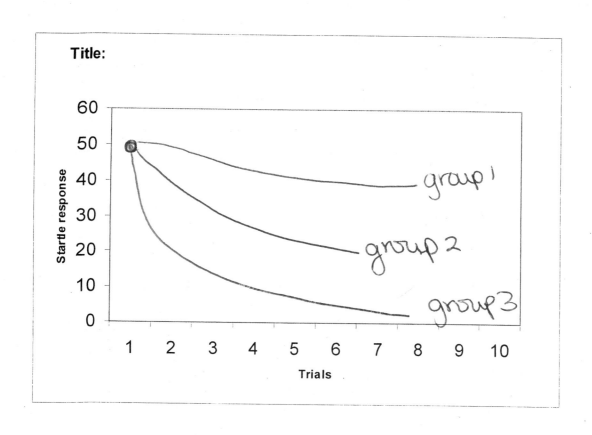

Title:

(y-axis) Startle response — 0, 10, 20, 30, 40, 50, 60

(x-axis) Trials — 1, 2, 3, 4, 5, 6, 7, 8, 9, 10

group 1

group 2

group 3

2-2.3 Factor #3: Stimulus specificity. Habituation tends to be stimulus specific, meaning that responding rebounds if the stimulus is changed. For example, imagine you have an ice cream cone with two scoops of differing flavors. As you work your way through the first scoop you may habituate to its flavor. Assuming you are sufficiently hungry, when you reach the second scoop you are likely to find that you are no longer habituated to the ice cream. Your interest in the ice cream will be renewed by the switch to the second flavor.

An example of stimulus specificity of habituation can be found in the alarm calls of vervet monkeys. These monkeys have three distinct sounding calls they emit when they spot a leopard, an eagle, or a snake. When they emit these calls other group members stop and scan either the sky or the ground for the predator. Curious researchers, including Cheney and Seyfarth (1990), have played pre-recorded vocalizations back to monkeys to examine their responses. For example, a leopard call could be played back repeatedly from a recording of a single monkey. Habituation, to the leopard call coming from *this* monkey should occur, as evidenced by group members ignoring it. However, playing a leopard call from a different monkey results in strong responses from group members.

In the blank graph below:
1) Draw a curve that indicates habituation to the test stimulus (a leopard call) after repeated presentations from Monkey A.
2) Indicate with a single data point how responding would occur to a single playback of Monkey B's leopard vocalization following habituation to Monkey A.

number of times call is played back

Remember that these monkeys are able to use three different types of alarm call. Now imagine that you have played Monkey A's leopard calls repeatedly, but this time you complete your experiment by presenting Monkey A's eagle and snake alarm calls. Given what you know about stimulus specificity and habituation, in the graph below draw a habituation curve for the leopard call and then add two data points indicating responses to the eagle and snake calls.

A

number of monkeys responding

number of times call is played back

X eagle X
snake

2-2.4 Dual-Process Theory. **Page 42** of your text introduces the dual-process theory of habituation and sensitization. This theory suggests that the net response to a stimulus reflects the simultaneous occurrence of habituation and sensitization. The exercises below provide you with practice visualizing how this theory works.

In the graph below draw curves that reflect a net response increase of 15 by the 10th trial. There should be 3 curves in total. One curve indicating habituation over 10 trials, one indicating sensitization, and a hypothetical curve representing net responding across the 10 trials. Reviewing **figure 2.12** on **page 42** will help you get started with this exercise. Be sure to label each of your three curves.

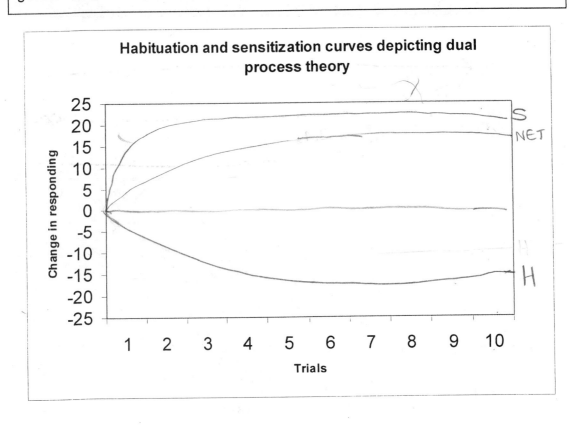

Habituation and sensitization curves depicting dual process theory

Next, in the graph below draw habituation, sensitization, and net responding curves that reflect a net response decrease of -10 by trial 10. Be sure to label each of your three curves.

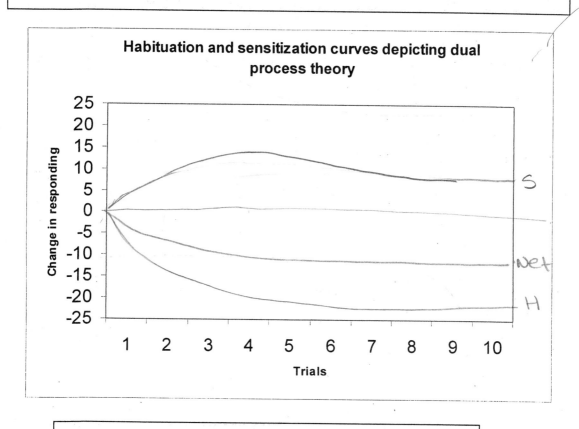

Habituation and sensitization curves depicting dual process theory

---

Concept Question

---

1) With regard to habituation and sensitization, what is an *S-R system* and what is a *state system*?

S-R System — habituation process, actuated by each stimuli presentation, some build up of H, reflex arc.

State system — sensitization process, actuated by arousing events, a general readiness to respond.

25.

2-3 Opponent Process Theory of Motivation

The opponent-process theory of motivation (**pp. 52-56** of your text) also involves two processes. However, the two processes are the primary and opponent processes. In addition, the opponent process theory is typically applied to complex emotional responses, such as happiness or sadness, rather than reflex responses. The exercise below asks you to apply opponent-process theory to your own experiences.

Try to recall an event that first elicited a strong emotional reaction, followed by a decreased reaction after repeated exposure. Describe the event, the emotions it elicited, and how your reaction changed over time.

mom + dad leave child at sitter, causing extreme seperation anxiety. After a while child could be left w/out a problem

What was the primary, or *a* process? anxiety

What was the secondary, or *b* process? Calm

In the blank graphs below plot hypothetical curves that depict an application of the opponent-process theory to the emotional event you described above. The top graph represents the manifest affective response, and the bottom graph represents the underlying opponent processes. Indicate both the *a* and *b* responses on the bottom graph. (hint: **pp. 54-55** of your text shows an example of how this might be done.)

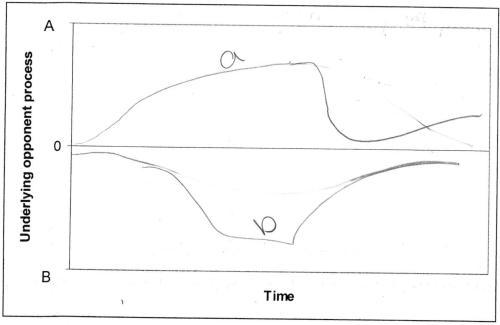

3   Classical Conditioning: Foundations

This chapter will familiarize you with the terminology, concepts, and theories of classical conditioning. We will continue to build upon some of the material from **chapter 2**, including graphing and interpreting data, and using the terminology of experiments. In **section 3-1** we will cover some terminology and applications of classical conditioning, and how to use suppression ratios. Following this are exercises that focus on the procedures of excitatory conditioning (**section 3-2**). **Section 3-3** focuses on inhibitory conditioning and the notation and procedures that are involved in designing experiments in classical conditioning.

After completing these exercises you should be able to:
- Apply the terminology of classical conditioning,
- Calculate and interpret suppression ratios,
- Compare and contrast the different excitatory conditioning procedures,
- Describe the relative effectiveness of the different excitatory procedures,
- Become familiar with notation and procedures for diagramming experiments in classical conditioning,
- Apply some different methods for studying conditioned inhibition.

3-1 Terminology and the Classical Conditioning Paradigm

Terminology is often a challenge for students learning about classical conditioning. Confusion over what is conditioned, what is unconditioned, what is a stimulus and what constitutes a response is common. The best way to meet this challenge is to practice. Before starting with the exercises I recommend that you review some of the key terms listed below. You may also refer to your text for definitions of these terms.

Key terms in classical conditioning

Unconditional stimulus (US): A stimulus that elicits a response without the necessity of prior training.

Unconditional response (UR): A response that occurs to a stimulus without prior training.

Conditional stimulus (CS): A stimulus that does not elicit a particular response initially, but comes to do so as a result of becoming associated with an unconditioned stimulus.

Conditional response (CR): The response that comes to be made to the conditioned stimulus as a result of classical conditioning.

Test trial: A trial in which a CR is measured in response to a CS (usually without the US present) to determine the strength of conditional responding.

Acquisition: The learning of a CR as a result of pairing the CS and US.

Your textbook described some of the early history of classical conditioning, including Ivan Pavlov's familiar examination of the conditioned salivary reflexes in dogs. The salivary reflex (the UR) occurs naturally in response to food cues such as taste and smell. We do not learn to salivate in response to food; we do so without conditioning (as do dogs). However, if a stimulus such as a tone (a CS) occurs in conjunction with food (the US), the tone can then also elicit salivation (a CR). The conditional eye blink response in rabbits, described in **chapter 3** of your text (**pp. 66-70**) involves the same type of learning. To review some key terms in classical conditioning, let's look at this example a little more closely in the schematic below.

Schematic of conditional eye blink responding

CS (tone) → US (puff of air to eye)

A puff of air directed at the eye (US) elicits a reflexive blink response (UR).

CR (eyeblink)

UR (eyeblink)

After repeated presentations of the tone (CS) paired with the airpuff, the tone alone will come to elicit conditional eyeblink responding (CR).

SNIFFY APPLICATION

Watch Sniffy acquire a conditioned response in exercise #1 (see Sniffy Pro 2.0 manual p. 37)

CS ———→ US

CR

UR

3-1.1 Applying terms and concepts. Now let's practice applying the terms and concepts reviewed above. Following are some examples of classical conditioning. Think about what is happening in each and identify the US, CS, UR, and CR in the spaces provided.

1) A nursing mother responds to the crying of her infant by putting the infant to her breast, which stimulates the delivery of milk. After this has occurred several times the sound of the baby crying stimulates the milk-letdown reflex.

   baby to breast *milk*

   US ~~baby to breast~~, UR ~~baby to~~ *breast*, CS ~~baby~~ *cry*,

   CR *milk let down*

2) A child has a routine of having his teddy bear with him when his parents comfortably tuck him in. When his parents are away the teddy bear comforts him.

   US *parents*, UR *comfort*, CS *teddy bear*

   CR *comfort*

3) A song continues to evoke arousal and nervousness in a person who heard the song during her first kiss with a person to whom she was wildly attracted. *(person)*

   US *Kiss (person)*, UR *Arousal*, CS *Song*,

   CR *Arousal*

30

4) A stuntman has a terrible accident causing immense pain while performing a stunt on a motorcycle. Thereafter motorcycles elicit fear.
US _pain/acc._, UR _pain pain_, CS _a motorcycle_
CR _fear_   _fear fear_

5) A cyclist was attacked by a dog while riding down "country road 5". On subsequent trips down that road the cyclist's heart pumps extra fast and he experiences heightened anxiety.
US _vicious bite_, UR _anxiety_, CS _road_,
CR _anxiety_

3-1.2 Conditioned suppression and suppression ratios. Suppression ratios are often used as indicators of conditioned fear or anxiety (see **p. 64** of text). What is suppressed is normal, ongoing behavior such as eating or drinking. Think of when you are extremely stressed. At such times, you are not likely to eat or drink. We can use this decrease as an index of your stress level.

The suppression ratio is calculated as follows:

$$\text{Suppression ratio} = \frac{CS_{\text{responding}}}{CS_{\text{responding}} + \text{pre-}CS_{\text{responding}}}$$

Where $CS_{\text{responding}}$ is the measure of conditioned responding during the test trial (e.g., amount of time spent moving), and pre-$CS_{\text{responding}}$ is a measure of the conditioned response *before* the CS is presented (also referred to as a "baseline" measure). So imagine that the day before an exam you spend 60 minutes at the breakfast table enjoying a large, leisurely breakfast. The following day you are stressed and food is therefore less appetizing so you spend only 15 minutes at the table. Your suppression ratio would be:

$$\frac{15}{15+60} = 0.20$$

31

Now imagine your roommate is also taking the exam, but is completely relaxed about it. If your roommate spends an hour eating on both days, what is his/her suppression ratio?

We will use rats as a way of further examining suppression ratios. Imagine the CS in this study is a 60 second presentation of white noise at a standard (dB) level. The US is a brief (1 second) shock presented immediately afterward. The conditional response is suppression of drinking activity. We measure drinking activity one minute prior to the onset of the CS (the pre-CS responding phase) and during a one minute CS presentation (the CS responding phase). Two groups of subjects were used. The experimental group experienced the CS and US together, while the control group experienced the CS and US one minute apart.

Below are sample data (in seconds) after five conditioning trials for six subjects (Ss), three in each group. These data come from the final test trial of the experiment.

- Calculate suppression ratios for each subject of the study, and then the average suppression ratio for each group.
- Graph the average suppression ratios for both groups with a bar graph below and write an interpretation:

		Pre-CS period	CS period	Pre-CS + CS period	Suppression ratio
Experimental group	Ss				
	1	20	1	21	.048
	2	17	2	19	.105
	3	19	5	24	.208
	Average suppression ratio =				.120
Control group	Ss				
	4	22	20	42	.476
	5	20	11	31	.355
	6	23	24	47	.511
	Average suppression ratio =				.447

Title:

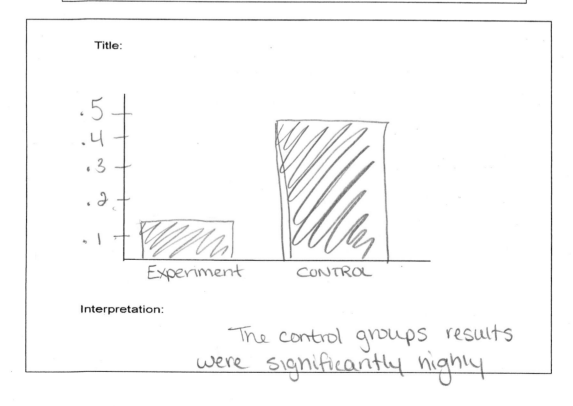

Interpretation:

The control groups results were significantly highly

3-2 Excitatory Conditioning Procedures

As you have learned from your textbook, classical conditioning is not always a simple matter of pairing a CS with a US. There are many other factors at work here. Numerous variables influence whether classical conditioning occurs. These include the arrangement in time between the CS and US, the number of CS-US pairings, the amount of experience one has had with the CS, and more. In this section we will focus on how various factors influence excitatory conditioning.

3-2.1 Excitatory conditioning procedures. The timing, or *temporal relationship*, between the CS and the US influences the extent to which a response is conditioned (**pp. 74-75**). There are four general ways to characterize the temporal characteristics of conditioning procedures: trace, delay, simultaneous, and backward conditioning (see **figure 3-7** reprinted from **p. 75** of your text below).

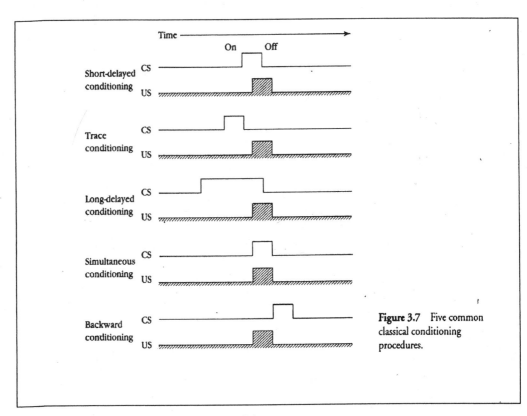

Figure 3.7 Five common classical conditioning procedures.

To visualize how the relationship between the CS and US affects conditioning, plot the following data in line graph format on the axes below and write out an interpretation of the patterns. The numbers below each type of conditioning (e.g., trace: 1, 5, 10, ...) represent the magnitude of the CR over the course of four conditioning trials. (You should have four separate lines, one for each type of conditioning, and four points per line representing each trial.)

Trials	Trace	Delay	Backward	Simultaneous
1	1	0	1	0
2	5	8	3	2
3	10	15	4	3
4	15	19	5	4

Title:

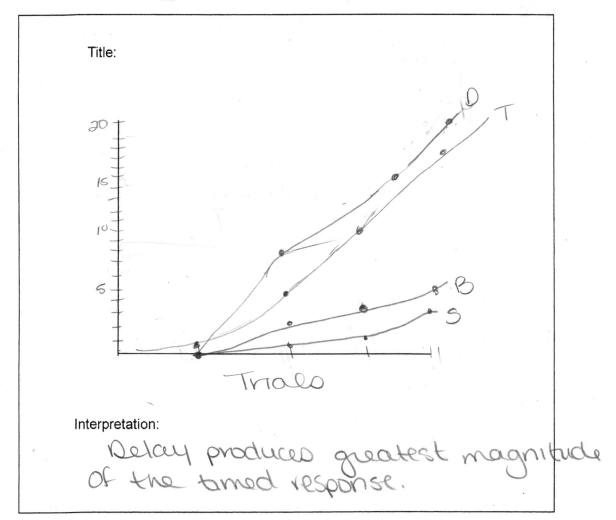

Trials

Interpretation:

Delay produces greatest magnitude of the timed response.

35

1) How does the temporal coding hypothesis relate to exercise 3-2.1?

3-2.2 Measuring excitatory responses. Conditioned responding can be measured in a variety of ways. Some common types of measure include.
  1) *Magnitude*
  2) *Probability*
  3) *Latency* time

The application of these measures is described on **page 76** of your text. Below are some examples of conditioned responding. Indicate (using numbers 1-3 above) which of the measures applies to each example.

1) Number of drops of saliva to the CS. Magnitude

2) Time taken to approach a light. Latency

3) Percentage of trials in which eyeblinking occurs. Probability

4) Level of anxiety as measured by galvanic skin responding. Magnitude

5) Supression of drinking as a measure of a conditioned taste aversion.

Magnitude

6) Time taken to reach ½ of maximum heart rate on a particular trial?

Latency

7) Percentage of times in which a leg withdrawal reflex occurs to a

CS. Probability

8) Amount of testosterone secreted in response to a CS. Magnitude

3-3 Diagramming and Designing Experiments in Classical Conditioning: Applications to the Measurement of Conditioned Inhibition

Our understanding of the mechanisms of classical conditioning is largely derived from carefully controlled laboratory experiments. One useful skill we recommend you develop is the ability to identify and use some of the symbols and strategies for diagramming experiments. Your professor may use some abbreviations and shorthand for diagramming experiments in class. Below are some recommended abbreviations, but keep in mind that people vary in how they communicate this information so you will probably encounter some minor differences.

- **Paired CS and US**: To indicate that two events are paired in time use an arrow: $\rightarrow$, as in CS $\rightarrow$US. This notation is also used to indicate that a stimulus is eliciting a response, as in US$\rightarrow$UR.

- **Unpaired CS and US**: To indicate that two events are unpaired or represent a negative contingency between the CS and US, use a forward slash: "/", as in CS/US. (note: Be aware, the "/" may also be used to indicate that two CSs occur together, such as CS+/CS-.)

- **Phase** of an experiment. Some experiments, such as those involving retardation of acquisition as a measure of conditioned inhibition, involve more than one phase (e.g., Phase 1 = inhibitory training, Phase 2 = excitatory conditioning).

- **Positive (+) and negative (-) signs**. In classical conditioning these typically mean that a CS signals a US (CS+) or that a CS signals the absence of a US (CS-).

For example, if you are designing an experiment on conditioned inhibition you might see something like this:

> Phase 1 establishes a CR after CS-US pairings

Phase 1:
  Group 1: CS+→US
  Group 2: CS+→US

Phase 2:
  Group 1 (control): CS+→US, [CS+ and CS-] → US (indicates alternating trials of both types)
  Group 2 (experimental): CS+→US, [CS+ and CS-] / US

Test: Group 1: CS-
  Group 2: CS-

> Phase 2 conditions the inhibitory response to the CS-. For Group 1 (control) the CS+ and CS- are always paired with a US. For Group 2 (experimental) the CS+ is paired with a US on some trials but the CS- is never paired with the US.

> A test procedure is conducted after phase 2 to determine whether the CS- is a conditioned inhibitor.

Concept Questions

1) Why was phase 1 necessary?

It's the cr when just CS is given

2) What was the purpose of treating Group 2 differently from Group 1 during Phase 2?

3) Which group should show stronger inhibition to the CS-?

Group 1

3-3.2 Inhibition procedures. Your text describes some common procedures for studies of conditioned inhibition (**pp. 82-86**). One involves bidirectional response systems, another involves doing a compound-stimulus, or summation, test, and the third involves the retardation-of-acquisition test. Before completing this exercise you should carefully review these pages.

Concept Question

1) What is a bidirectional response system and what is one limitation of using this type of system for a conditioned inhibition study?

Diagram a conditioned inhibition experiment that uses the retardation-of-acquisition procedure. Be sure to identify the different phases of the experiment and include control groups. In addition, be sure to indicate which groups receive paired and unpaired stimulus presentations in the different phases.

The figure below is a reprinted version of **figure 3.12** in your text (**p. 85**). The figure summarizes results from an experiment on conditioned inhibition that used a compound-stimulus test procedure. Review the details of this experiment and **figure 3.12** below and answer the concept questions that follow.

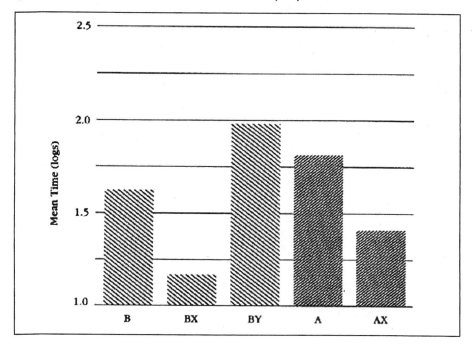

Concept Questions

1) What was the purpose of conditioning to both CSA and CSB?

2) Why were the mean times to complete 5 seconds of interrupted drinking comparatively short for the BX and AX tests?

3) What was the purpose of testing BY?

SNIFFY APPLICATION

Experiment with inhibitory
conditioning procedures in exercises
#10 & 11 (p. 78, 83)

4 Classical Conditioning: Mechanisms

Chapter 4 brings together many important concepts of classical conditioning. After reading this chapter you can probably appreciate that classical conditioning is not a simple matter of a CS being paired with a US. Conditioning depends on a variety of factors such as the novelty of the CS and US, their intensity, and their relevance to each other. **Section 4-1** provides exercises that allow you to examine how each of these affects the strength of conditioning. In addition, the *form* of a conditioned response is determined by several factors, such as the CS, the US, and the CS-US interval. How this occurs is examined by several thought questions that are posed in **section 4-2**. In **section 4-3** we consider some of the mechanisms that underlie CS-US relationships.

After completing these exercises you should be able to:
- Evaluate different ways that the CS affects conditioning,
- Evaluate different ways that the US affects conditioning,
- Describe how conditioning can occur with multiple CSs,
- Apply conditioning to examples such as fear and phobias,
- Describe how different aspects of the CS determines whether conditioning occurs,
- Explain different mechanisms that underlie classical conditioning.

4-1 Effectiveness of the CS and US

Conditioning is not always a simple matter of pairing a CS with a US and looking for a CR. Numerous variables influence whether conditioning occurs and to what degree. Here we explore several of these factors.

<u>**4-1.1 CS and US factors**</u>. The development of a CR depends on a variety of factors. Some factors include the type of CS, the type of US, and the degree to which the CS and US are related. **Pages 92-96** of your text describe several properties of CSs and USs that determine their effectiveness. You will need to review these pages prior to completing the exercises below.

Below are graphs showing final results from four experiments that examined some variables that influenced classical conditioning. Study each graph carefully and determine which variable was examined. Be sure to pay close attention to the variables studied, the values of the axes, and how the groups were affected by the treatments. Possible answers include:

1) Initial responses to the stimuli
2) Novelty of the CS or US
3) CS and US intensity/salience
4) CS-US relevance

1) **Variable examined**: CS and US intensity/salience

2) Variable examined:_____

3) Variable examined: CS and US intensity + salience

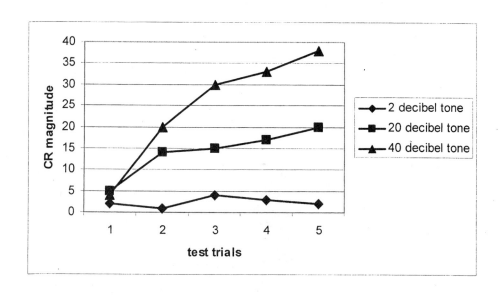

4) Variable examined: *CS-US relevance*

5) Which of the determinants listed above applies to the results in the figure reprinted from your text below? Explain your answer by referring to the results found for each group reported in the figure.

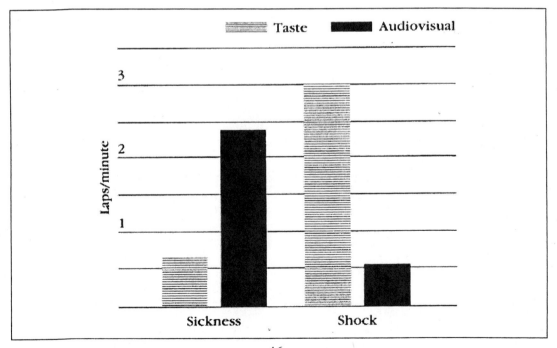

46

Answer: CS-US Relevance -
only when paired w/the appropriate
response ~~neither~~ does learning
take place

SNIFFY APPLICATION

Test the effects of CS and US strength/intensity on
conditioning Sniffy in exercises #4 & 5 (p. 45, 53)

4-1.2 Biological strength: Conditioning with multiple CSs. Students
frequently have trouble differentiating higher-order conditioning and sensory
preconditioning. The two are very similar in that both involve the pairing of at
least two CSs at some point in the process, but they are in fact quite different
phenomena (see **pp. 96-100** of your text). It may be helpful to review your text
before completing this exercise.

In the space below diagram an example of higher-order conditioning and
sensory preconditioning. Be sure to include actual examples of CSs and USs
in your diagrams and make them plausible situations. Avoid using examples
you already have seen in your text. After completing your diagrams answer
the question that follows.

Higher-order conditioning:

Sensory preconditioning:

1) Describe the key procedural difference between higher-order conditioning and sensory preconditioning.

SNIFFY APPLICATION

Experiment with sensory-preconditioning and higher-order conditioning in exercises #12 and 13 (p. 88, 94)

4-1.3 Application of fear conditioning. Applications of conditioned fear responding are described in your text (**pp. 98-99**). Out of concern for your well-being, we won't ask you to attempt to condition yourself to fear something of which you currently are not afraid. But perhaps you can apply the concept of a conditioned emotional fear reaction to your past experiences.

In the space below diagram and describe how you acquired a fear response via classical conditioning. Indicate the CS and US and indicate how many trials it took. You may have since overcome this fear, but describe it anyway. If higher-order conditioning was involved incorporate this aspect of your experience into the diagram.

Diagram:

Explanation:

If you have since overcome this fear, did you do so via counterconditioning? If so, explain. If you have not overcome the fear, describe how counterconditioning could be used to help you lose the fear.

4-1.4 Latent inhibition. Your text describes an interesting phenomenon called latent inhibition (**p. 92**), which refers to the inhibition of conditioning if a CS is experienced repeatedly prior to being paired with a US. For example, if a tone is heard several hundred times before being paired with a puff of air to the eye, conditioning may take longer than if the tone is not heard so frequently.

Let's consider an experiment conducted by Westbrook and colleagues (2000). In this experiment, conducted on rats, a 30 second clicking noise was used as the CS and the US was a mild shock to the feet. The researchers wanted to determine whether repeated exposure to the clicking noise without any shock would subsequently slow down the acquisition of conditioned fear responses. Rats are known to freeze when frightened, and CSs that predict the onset of foot shock elicit freezing behavior. Thus, the dependent variable was freezing behavior. Before continuing, think about how you would design this experiment. What would your independent variable be and how would you manipulate it?

The experiment can be summarized as follows:

Groups			
Pre-exposed		Not pre-exposed	
Paired	Unpaired	Paired	Unpaired

The independent variables involve exposure to the CS (pre-exposed or not pre-exposed) and pairings of the CS with the US (paired vs. unpaired). The experimenters decided to use four groups, summarized above, and note that there are two unpaired control groups, one for each level of the preexposure variable.

> **Question**

Before proceeding, state a hypothesis about what you predict for each of the four groups. (Which group(s) will show a high percentage of freezing behavior?)

Below are sample data based on the experiment. The numbers represent the mean percentage of freezing to the CS. Please graph and interpret the data below.

	Pre-exposed (paired)	Pre-exposed (unpaired)	Not pre-exposed (paired)	Not pre-exposed (unpaired)
Mean % freezing	23	25	97	39

52

Title:

Interpretation:

SNIFFY APPLICATION

Test the effects of CS and US pre-exposure in Sniffy in exercises #19, 20, & 21 (p. 123, 127, 129)

4-2 Determinants of the Conditioned Response

On **pages 100-109** of your text some factors that determine the form of the conditioned response are described. After reading these sections answer the following concept questions.

4-2.1 Concept Questions

1) Does the stimulus substitution model apply to salivary conditioning? Why or why not?

2) What are conditioned homeostatic responses and how are they relevant to drug tolerance?

3) What was the CS in Timberlake and Grant's (1975) study? What type of CR did this CS elicit? Why was this of theoretical interest?

4) What are general and focal searching behaviors? Give an example of each. What is a consummatory response? Provide an example.

5) How is the form of the CR determined by the CS-US interval?

4-2.2   S-R and S-S learning

Pages 108-109 of your text describe the important distinction between S-R and S-S learning. Review these pages carefully and answer the questions that follow.

1) Describe the distinction between S-S and S-R learning. It may be helpful to use an example of classical conditioning in your answer.

2) How can one change the value of the US after training?

3) How would this affect the CR if the behavior is mediated by S-R mechanisms and how it should affect the CR with S-S mechanisms?

4) Provide an actual example involving classical conditioning and describe how changing US value would address the questions above.

SNIFFY APPLICATION

Test S-R and S-S theories with Sniffy in the exercises from Chapter 7 of your Sniffy Pro manual

4-3 Mechanisms of Associating CSs and USs

4-3.1 Rescorla-Wagner. The Rescorla-Wagner model is one of the most influential models of learning that has been proposed in recent times. Its basic assumption is that the increment in learning that is produced by a conditioning trial depends on how surprising the outcome of the trial is. Furthermore, how surprising something is depends on all of the cues present during a conditioning trial.

> One stimulus that is always present in an experiment is the chamber in which the conditioning trials are conducted. In the following examples, explain how the conditioning context might influence learning about a discrete tone that is paired with food. Use the Rescorla-Wagner model as the basis for your predictions.

1) Subjects are first habituated to an experimental chamber. Then, a series of conditioning trials is conducted in which a tone is paired with food.

2) Subjects first receive several sessions in which food is presented periodically without warning in the experimental chamber. Then, a series of conditioning trials is conducted in which a tone is paired with food.

3) Subjects first receive several sessions in which food is presented periodically without warning in the experimental chamber. In the next phase of the experiment, the subjects are placed in the experimental chamber repeatedly for a week without getting food or any other US there. Then, a series of conditioning trials is conducted in which a tone is paired with food.

4) Subjects receive the tone paired with food 10 times during each experimental session. In addition, food is presented at random times between trials 10 times per day.

5) Subjects receive food presented 10 times at random intervals during each experimental session. A tone is also presented periodically, but any food presentations that might have occurred during a 2-min period after each tone are cancelled.

The basic Rescorla-Wagner equation is $\Delta V = k(\lambda - V)$. In this equation, V is the associative value of all of the cues present on a conditioning trial; λ is the asymptote of learning possible with the stimulus outcome (US or no US) that ends each trial; V is the change in associative value, or what is learned, as a result of a conditioning trial; and the parameter k represents a constant related to the salience of the CS and the US. The following questions provide practice in interpreting how various manipulations are represented in the equation.

1) At the beginning of training, what is the value of V?

2) In a typical learning experiment, subjects show large improvements early in training. However, as training progresses, the improvement that results from each conditioning trial gets smaller and smaller. Which term in the equation represents the size of the improvement that occurs with each trial? How does this term change as training progresses? What term on the right side of the equation causes this change?

3) Assume that after three sessions of training a CS has been conditioned to asymptote, and that is the only cue in the situation. What will be the value of V at the end of the three sessions?

4) Assuming the scenario described in the preceding question, what will be the value of ΔV if conditioning is continued past the asymptote of learning?

5) In extinction, each presentation of the CS ends without a US. Which term of the equation represents this stimulus outcome? What is the value of this term in extinction?

6) Assume that one group of subjects is conditioned with a US that consists of one pellet of food and another is conditioned with a US that consists of 4 pellets of food? Which term of the equation represents these differences in the magnitude of the US? How does the value of this term change with the increase from 1 to 4 food pellets?

SNIFFY APPLICATION

Experiment with the blocking effect in Exercise #7 (p. 64)

5 Instrumental Conditioning: Foundations

Chapter 5 of your text opens with some descriptions and examples of procedures used to study instrumental conditioning. For example, Edward Thorndike's research on trial and error learning with cats escaping from puzzle boxes was described. Since Thorndike's early experiments, we have learned a lot about the details of what is called *instrumental conditioning*, or, *operant learning*. The exercises below serve to familiarize you with the foundational terms and concepts that comprise instrumental conditioning. We start with an exercise designed to help you make the distinction between instrumental and classical conditioning (**section 5-1**). The differences between two general procedures for studying learning, discrete-trial and free-operant procedures, are explored in **section 5-2**. Exercises designed to help you apply the procedures of shaping and chaining are in **section 5-3**. Students first encountering the concepts of positive and negative reinforcement and punishment often find it challenging to apply these terms to new situations, and **section 5-4** has exercises to help you develop skills in doing this. **Section 5.5** focuses on how contingency and contiguity affect instrumental conditioning.

After completing these exercises you should be able to:

- Distinguish instrumental and classical conditioning,
- Identify situations that used discrete-trial and free-operant procedures,
- Identify target behaviors and devise methods for shaping them,
- Appreciate the importance of behavioral variability in shaping target behaviors,
- Successfully apply the concepts of positive and negative reinforcement, punishment, and omission training,
- Distinguish the effects of contingency and contiguity on instrumental conditioning.

5-1 Instrumental and Classical Conditioning Compared

These exercises are designed to help you distinguish between instrumental and classical conditioning. The two are often confused, so it is important to recognize some of the differences. The most important distinguishing characteristic is that with instrumental learning, there is a contingency between a response and a stimulus, and in classical conditioning there is a contingency between two stimuli (the CS and US), and no response is required for a stimulus to be presented.

Below are descriptions that summarize published experiments on either classical or instrumental conditioning. Based on the distinctions between the two types of learning that are described above and in your text to this point, review the following examples of conditioning, indicate which type of learning (instrumental or classical) has occurred, and explain your choice.

1) Rats learned that they can escape through a hole when a particular visual stimulus is presented. The rats were placed in an arena that had an escape hole leading to their home cages on one side. The home cage contained a drop of condensed milk, a rat favorite (Rossier et al., 2000).

Instrumental or Classical (circle one)

Explanation

2) Rats were transported from their home cages to a test box and were then shocked. The researchers then examined freezing behavior in response to both the test box and the procedures used to transport the rats to it. (Bevins, et al. 2000).

Instrumental or Classical (circle one)

Explanation

3) Rats were given intracranial stimulation to a reward center in the brain whenever they pressed a bar. The authors examined the relationship between the amount of pressing and the amount of brain stimulation provided. (Leon & Gallistel, 1998).

Instrumental or Classical (circle one)

Explanation

4) Rats were given food when (and only when) they directed an appropriate amount of force upon a bar. (Slifkin & Brener, 1998).

Instrumental or Classical (circle one)

Explanation

5) In a bar pressing task, rats were given food for making the discrimination between a drug (pentobarbital) and a control substance (saline). (McMillan & Hardwick, 2000).

Instrumental or Classical (circle one)

Explanation

6) Wallabies, a small marsupial species, were exposed to a model of a fox (a predator species) in conjunction with a human who acted as though he/she was going to capture the wallabies (a threatening event). Wallabies were then tested for their avoidance responses toward the model fox alone. (Griffin et al., 2001).

Instrumental or Classical (circle one)

Explanation

5-2 Discrete Trial and Free Operant Procedures.

Pages 127-130 of your text describe the differences between discrete-trial and free operant procedures and it may be helpful to review these pages before proceeding.

Remember that:

- In discrete trial procedures the behavior of the subject terminates the trial and the timing of successive trials (or repetitions of the response) is determined by the experimenter.

- In free operant procedures, the behavior of interest may be repeated any number of times. Thus, the timing of successive repetitions of the response is determined by the subject.

> Read the following examples and indicate whether each one involves a discrete trial or a free operant procedure (circle the correct option) and explain your choice.

---

1) A rat presses a lever that turns off a shock delivered to its feet.

discrete trials or free operant

Why?

---

2) A rat presses a lever 10 times and turns off a shock delivered to its feet.

discrete trials or free operant

Why?

---

3) Children are given as many crayons and sheets of paper as they want and are rewarded with praise for each drawing they complete.

discrete trials or free operant

Why?

---

4) A kitten is rewarded with treats each time it successfully uses a litter box.

discrete trials or free operant

Why?

---

5) A pigeon is placed in an operant chamber for two hours and receives reinforcement for every ten times it pecks a key.

discrete trials or free operant

Why?

---

6) An assembly line worker is paid $1 for every 5 widgets assembled during an 8 hour shift.

discrete trials or free operant

Why?

7) An assembly line worker is paid $100 for each 8 hour shift completed.

discrete trials or free operant

Why?

8) A caller frequently dials a number that is busy 90% of the time.

discrete trials or free operant

Why?

9) A runner's progress in completing a marathon in under five hours is monitored.

discrete trials or free operant

Why?

10) A child is rewarded with a story for inhibiting bedtime tantrums.

discrete trials or free operant

Why?

5-3 Shaping

In instrumental conditioning a subject either makes an appropriate response or avoids making an inappropriate response in order to receive reinforcement. A rat may need to press a lever to receive reinforcement. A child needs to try speaking in order to benefit from speech therapy. Without a response there is nothing to reinforce. As you know from reading **pages 130-133** shaping procedures can be used to bring about the target response. The following exercises are designed to familiarize you with some procedures and details involved in shaping.

5-3.1 Basic procedures

Identify a target behavior. Be creative. Choose a behavior that might not occur spontaneously but could be shaped. After identifying the target behavior list the successive approximations to that behavior below.

Target Behavior:_____

Successive approximations (note: there is no set number of successive approximations you need to come up with. Try to break down the response into several individual units):

Pages 130-133 of your text describe some variables that influence successful shaping. Prior to completing the exercise below you should review these pages. As you will see, effective shaping requires you to create a good balance between reinforcement and extinction. Consider the target behavior you selected above and answer the follow up questions below.

1) How could providing too much reinforcement for one of the approximations hinder reaching the final target response?

2) How could providing too much extinction have a hindering effect?

SNIFFY APPLICATION

Practice with magazine training and shaping Sniffy by completing exercises #22 and 23 (p. 147-148). The exercises will also familiarize you with cumulative recordings. More detail on cumulative recordings will be encountered in chapter 6 of your text. Also, you may want to try some of the more advanced shaping exercises in chapter 14 of your Sniffy Pro manual.

5-3.2 Response variability and shaping. Imagine that you have shaped four pigeons to reliably peck a disc. However, now you want the pigeons to peck the disc with their beaks open. This example is based on a study conducted by Deich, Allan, and Zeigler (1988), featured on **page 132** of your text. Below are frequency distributions representing data from your pigeons. The graphs show the number of times each pigeon opened its beak at various widths while pecking during a 1 hour baseline session (0 millimeters = beak closed, 25 millimeters = beak wide open). For example, pigeon 1 opened its beak 15mm 25% of the time. The pattern of results varies from pigeon to pigeon, which represents a challenge to you in your task.

Study each graph below and answer the questions that follow.

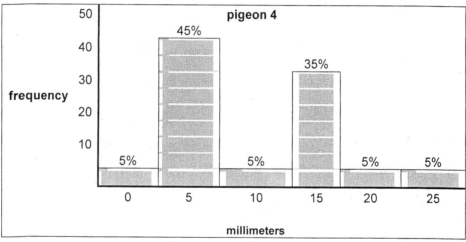

Questions

a) Which pigeon showed the greatest variability in responding during the baseline phase? Why did you conclude this?

b) Which showed the least variability? Why did you conclude this?

Remember that these data represent baseline levels of responding. With these same four pigeons you now want to attempt to shape the actual topography of their pecking behavior.

c) Which pigeon could you shape to peck with a 25mm gap most quickly? Why?

d) Which pigeon could you shape to peck with a 10mm gap most quickly? Why?

e) Which pigeon could you shape to peck with a 0mm gap most quickly? Why?

5-4 Procedures of Instrumental Conditioning

The terminology that describes the different procedures of instrumental learning is relatively straightforward. Terms such as positive reinforcement and punishment are easy enough to define. However, it can be challenging to apply these terms to various scenarios in which instrumental learning occurs. **Table 5.1**, reprinted from your text, lists the procedures of instrumental conditioning, the response-outcome contingency, and the results this has on responding. Take a few moments to review the contents of **table 5.1**.

TABLE 5.1	TYPES OF INSTRUMENTAL CONDITIONING PROCEDURES	
NAME OF PROCEDURE	**RESPONSE-OUTCOME CONTINGENCY**	**RESULT**
Positive reinforcement	*Positive:* Response produces an appetitive stimulus	*Reinforcement* or increase in response rate
Punishment (positive punishment)	*Positive:* Response produces an aversive stimulus	*Supression* or decrease in response rate
Negative reinforcement (escape or avoidance)	*Negative:* Response eliminates or prevents the occurrence of an aversive stimulus	*Reinforcement* or increase in response rate
Omission training (DRO)	*Negative:* Response eliminates or prevents the occurrence of an appetitive stimulus	*Supression* or decrease in response rate

It is helpful to practice applying these four outcomes to actual situations. Below are brief descriptions of common behaviors that can change as a result of instrumental conditioning. Read through each one and think about the behavior described, the consequence, and the likely effect of the consequence on behavior. For each example, **1)** identify the behavior, **2)** the response-outcome contingency (positive or negative), and **3)** the name of the procedure listed on the left-hand column of **table 5.1** (positive reinforcement, punishment, etc.)

1) Amy drove 70mph every day in a posted 45mph zone until she received a speeding ticket and fine for $500.

Behavior:_____

Response-outcome contingency:_____

Procedure:_____

2) Rachel's English 101 professor compliments her on her writing ability and she subsequently takes several composition classes.

Behavior:_____

Response-outcome contingency:_____

Procedure:_____

3) Geoff is expelled from school for cheating. (Assume in this example he wants to return to school)

Behavior:_____

Response-outcome contingency:_____

Procedure:_____

4) Cory works out at the health club and pushes himself so hard he becomes ill.

Behavior:_____

Response-outcome contingency:_____

Procedure:_____

5) Stephanie buys Eric a candy bar so that he will discontinue his public temper tantrum (answer from Stephanie's perspective, what is she learning?).

Behavior:_____

Response-outcome contingency:_____

Procedure:_____

6) A person with a heroin addiction begins feeling withdrawal symptoms and injects another dose to get rid of the unpleasant feelings.

Behavior:_____

Response-outcome contingency:_____

Procedure:_____

7) Laura complains to her fellow students about a professor she has. Her fellow students get tired of hearing it and no longer provide sympathy.

Behavior:_____

Response-outcome contingency:_____

Procedure:_____

8) Marty notices an improvement in his cardiovascular fitness when his building's elevator breaks down and he has to climb 6 flights of stairs several times per day. After the elevator is fixed Marty continues taking the stairs.

Behavior:_____

Response-outcome contingency:_____

Procedure:_____

5-5 Response and Reinforcer Relations

On **pages 145-159** of your text there is a detailed discussion on how responses and reinforcers are related. For example, contiguity and contingency between the response and reinforcer are important determinants of instrumental learning. The exercises below will help you to better see how contiguity and contingency have different roles in conditioning. In addition there are exercises that focus on marking procedures and learned-helplessness.

5-5.1 Contiguity and contingency.

For each of the following indicate whether there is contiguity between response and outcome, contingency between response and outcome, both, or neither. Examples of contiguity should indicate that the timing between responding and a reinforcer is a critical factor in learning. Examples of contingency should indicate that the consequences of responding were critical in influencing behavior.

1) John makes a left turn as he walks to the store and just then it starts raining.

Answer:

2) Mary buys a scratch-off lottery ticket and wins $20.

Answer:

3) Peter, a budding poet, tries to get his poems published and continues to submit them to magazines even though none has been accepted yet.

Answer:

4) Toby wakes up depressed. In an effort to feel better, he goes jogging. This gradually gets him out of his funk.

Answer:

5) Joe enjoys bowling and always wears a special shirt for important games.

Answer:

5-5.2   Learned helplessness.

Describe a situation in which you have no control over an aversive stimulus. How could you reduce the detrimental effects of this experience?

6

Schedules of Reinforcement and Choice Behavior

Chapter 6 covers a very important topic of operant learning. Schedules of reinforcement and their impact on rates of responding is a critical area of interest to psychologists. There are numerous types of schedules that are described in your text. The exercises below are designed to give you practice with identifying the schedules and to help you understand how each schedule influences responding. We will also examine some applications of research on schedules of reinforcement, such as choice behavior. Exercises in **section 6-1** provide an overview of some general features of cumulative recordings. **Section 6-2** serves to familiarize you with the differences between intermittent schedules of reinforcement. Namely, how intermittent schedules influence rates of responding. **Section 6-3** has exercises that will help you see how choice behavior is modeled using the matching law. **Section 6-4** covers the topics of self-control and value discounting.

After completing these exercises you should be able to:

- Differentiate between cumulative responding and response rates,
- Interpret cumulative recordings generated by different schedules of reinforcement,
- Describe, compare, and contrast the different types of intermittent schedules of reinforcement,
- Apply the different schedules of reinforcement to real-world scenarios,
- Describe and apply the matching law,
- Apply the concepts of self-control and value discounting.

6-1 Cumulative Response Recordings

Cumulative recordings were introduced on **page 164** of your text. Here we will be dealing with cumulative recordings in much more detail so first we will practice using and interpreting them.

6-1.1 Plotting data: Response rates vs. cumulative responding. Below are data on free operant responding over a 60-minute period for two subjects.

minute	subject a	cumulative responses for *a*	subject b	cumulative responses for *b*
0	0		1	
10	2		4	
20	3		6	
30	6		11	
40	14		14	
50	18		23	
60	20		30	

SNIFFY APPLICATION

Cumulative recordings in the Sniffy program were introduced earlier in chapter 5. Exercise #24 allows you to visualize Sniffy's cumulative responses.

In the blank graph below plot the number of responses for each 10 minute period for both subjects. Be sure to clearly label the two lines separately on your graph.

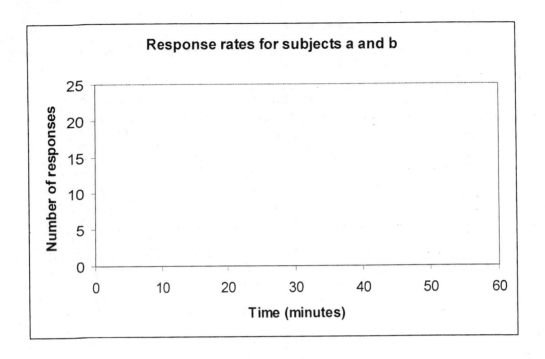

Response rates for subjects a and b

To the right of each subject's data above are blank cells for entering cumulative responses over time. Fill in these cells. Using these data plot the cumulative responses of subjects a and b in the blank graph below.

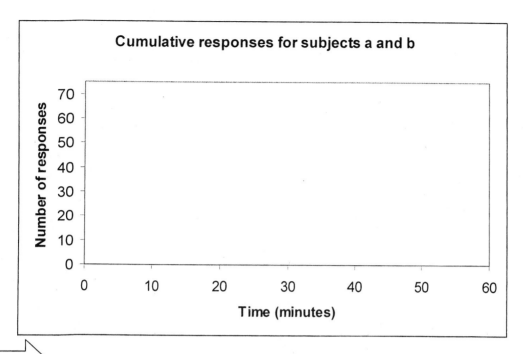

Cumulative responses for subjects a and b

Number of responses (y-axis): 0, 10, 20, 30, 40, 50, 60, 70

Time (minutes) (x-axis): 0, 10, 20, 30, 40, 50, 60

a) What was the average rate of responding for:

Subject A _____

Subject B _____

b) View your cumulative record graph above. Assuming both subjects were on the same schedule of reinforcement, which subject may have been given a higher quality reinforcer? Why did you choose this answer?

6-2 Simple Schedules of Intermittent Reinforcement

Simple schedules of reinforcement include continuous reinforcement (CRF), fixed ratio (FR) and variable ratio (VR) schedules, and fixed interval (FI) and variable interval (VI) schedules. In this exercise we will focus on the intermittent schedules of reinforcement; the FR, VR, FI, and VI schedules. **Figure 6-2** from your text is reprinted below because we will be referring to it several times in the coming exercises. Please review this figure and read the caption before proceeding.

Figure 6.2   Sample cumulative records of different pigeons pecking a response key on four simple schedules of food reinforcement: fixed ratio 120, variable ratio 360, fixed interval 4 minute, and variable interval 2 minute. (From *Schedules of Reinforcement*, by C. B. Ferster and B. F. Skinner, 1957, Appleton-Century-Crofts.)

6-2.1 Fixed ratio (FR) and variable ratio (VR) schedules.

a) How does increasing the ratio requirement (e.g., from an FR20 to an FR 50) affect responding on FR schedules? (hint. See **pp. 165-166** of your text)

b) Review the FR cumulative response curve from **figure 6-2** above. In the blank figure below fill in a likely cumulative response curve for a subject on a FR20 schedule and subject on a FR40 schedule. Be sure to include post reinforcement pauses and ticks where reinforcement has occurred.

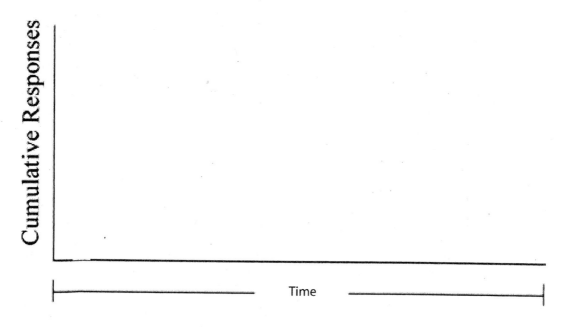

c) Why do VR schedules tend to maintain steady rates of responding?

d) Imagine you have two subjects that were reinforced on two different VR schedules. Subject 1 was reinforced after making the following number of responses: 4, 6, 4, 7, 2, 1, 4. Subject 2 was reinforced after 10, 10, 15, 20, 15, 12, 16 responses. What type of VR schedules were these two subjects on?

Subject 1 _____

Subject 2 _____

e) What is meant by "stretching the ratio" and "ratio strain", and describe how you would stretch a ratio from a CRF schedule to an FR50.

6-2.2   Fixed interval (FI) and variable interval (VI) schedules

Question a) Study the FI and VI cumulative recordings on **figure 6-2** above. Explain why the cumulative record of the subject with the FI schedule differs from that of the subject on the VI schedule.

b) Imagine you are taking two classes in which each of your professors plans to give 10 quizzes over the course the semester. One professor gives pop quizzes and the other professor gives scheduled quizzes. In the blank graphs below plot two plausible cumulative response curves representing your study efforts for both classes.

Cumulative Responses

Time

6-2.3 Applications of schedules of reinforcement. Students generally find the definitions of each schedule of reinforcement to be straightforward. However, actually applying these schedules can be a bit more challenging. In this exercise you can gain practice with applying schedules of reinforcement.

Scenario	Answer
1) How many reinforcers can be earned in an hour for a subject on an FR 5 schedule?	
2) What is the maximum number of reinforcers available per hour on a VI 2 min schedule?	
3) What is the maximum number of reinforcers per hour on a VR 2 schedule?	
4) Why do #2 and #3 above differ?	
5) A subject receives 20 reinforcers on a VI 3 min schedule (in an hour). How many reinforcers will it get if it doubles its response rate?	

Below is a list of examples in which reinforcement is being delivered on a type of schedule that was described in **pages 164-170** of your text. Identify the reinforcement schedule illustrated in these examples using the following abbreviations (Fixed ratio = **FR**, Variable ratio = **VR**, Fixed interval = **FI**, Variable interval = **VI**).

Remember,

- "Ratio" refers to schedules in which reinforcement is delivered based on how many times a subject responds.
- "Interval" refers to the amount of time that must pass before reinforcement is available following the last reinforcer.
- (Keep in mind these schedules are based on laboratory experimental procedures. They apply to real world situations but sometimes you have to be a bit flexible in how you apply them.)

1) A young child is allowed to go outside alone to play with friends, under the condition that she checks in with her mother every 30 minutes. Reinforcement in the form of praise is given each time she checks in at the agreed upon time. **Answer:** ~~VI~~ FI

2) Pop quizzes are a common motivator professors use to encourage studying material on a regular basis and for attending class. Which of the four schedules are being used by professors who give their students pop quizzes? **Answer:** VR

Could be VI if it was every 3 hrs of lecture. ✓

3) Playing slot machines at gambling casinos provide payoffs on occasion, as long as a person is performing the operant response of putting money in the machine and pulling the lever. **Answer:** VR

4) Checking your online bank account to see if checks you wrote to 10 different people have been cashed. **Answer:** FR

5) A factory worker paid on piecework (e.g., having to assemble a certain number of units to receive money). **Answer:** F.R

6) In contrast to normal fishing from the comfort of your boat, fly fishing involves frequent casting and reeling back before catching fish. Which type of schedule is a fly fisher on (hint: the more you cast the better your chances). **Answer:** VR

7) What type of schedule does a salesperson paid solely on commission experience? **Answer:** VR

8) Calling a friend and getting a busy signal because he or she is frequently on the phone. **Answer:** VI

9) Hitchhiking. **Answer:** VR

10) An executive's contract specifies salary increases to be negotiated every 6 months. **Answer:** FI

11) A custodian takes a break after each floor cleaned. **Answer:** _____

12) A person checks the front porch for the newspaper that is delivered between 6:00 and 7:00 am. **Answer:** _____

SNIFFY APPLICATION

Practice conditioning under various schedules of reinforcement with exercises #31-35 (pp. 181-185)

6-3 Schedules, Choice, and the Matching Law

Thus far our examples of schedules of reinforcement are comprised of situations in which a subject was responding to one schedule. However, after reading about choice behavior in your text (**pp. 172-189**) you have hopefully come to appreciate that we often encounter many different schedules at once. Furthermore, we can make choices about how we respond to different schedules and the degree to which we respond is proportional to the degree to which we find reinforcement. The matching law (**p. 174**) summarizes the relationship between effort and reinforcement using a simple equation (see **p. 175** of text) that is repeated here:

$$R_A/R_B = r_A/r_B$$

Where R_A and R_B are responses and r_A and r_B
are corresponding rates of reinforcement.

Remember that the matching law states that the relative rate of each behavior is equal to the relative rate of reinforcement that is provided for that behavior. Therefore, if we know the relative rates of reinforcement, then we should be able to predict relative rates of responding on those schedules. The following exercises will give you some practice with using the matching law.

6-3.1 Using the matching law equations. Imagine playing a video game in which you can press buttons to make things happen on the screen. There are two buttons (Left, R_A, and Right, R_B) that can be pressed and the consequences on the screen (reinforcers) are programmed on two different types of schedule. Based on this:

a) Fill in the missing value to satisfy the matching law in both
    scenarios below.

Responses to left (RA)	Responses to right (RB)
25	20
Reinforcers to left (rA)	Reinforcers to right (rB)
100	

Responses to left (R$_A$)	Responses to right (R$_B$) 80
Reinforcers to left (r$_A$) 12	Reinforcers to right (r$_B$) 96

Questions

Now let's assume that responding is reinforced on an FI5" schedule on side A and on an FI20" schedule on side B. Based on the matching law, what percentage of the total amount of time should be devoted to A and B?

FI5":____%

FI20":____%

b) Let's say we have two concurrent schedules and reinforcers are distributed as r$_B$ = 65%, and r$_A$ = 35%. Given this, what value(s) would we have for R$_A$ and R$_B$? (hint: there is more than one answer to this question, you must first decide on a total number of responses).

R$_A$ =

R$_B$ =

c) In the table below the number of reinforcers delivered under r$_A$ and r$_B$ are given. Also given is the total number of responses recorded during each one-hour session. Given this information, fill in the missing values of the table for R$_A$ and R$_B$. In other words, how many responses should occur when rates of reinforcement are distributed as indicated under r$_A$ and r$_B$?

R$_A$	R$_B$	r$_A$	r$_B$	Total responses recorded
		75	50	250
		1000	45	1253
		50	50	271

		12	26	50

d) Let's make some predictions about response rates based on the types of concurrent schedules we are using.

Estimate the proportion of responding you would expect a subject to devote to concurrent VI 20" and VI 30" schedules.

Questions →

VI 20"_____

VI 30" _____

Assume a total of 1200 responses were made during the course of this experiment. Write out the matching equation for a concurrent VI 20" and VI 30" schedule, assuming the subject obtained all of the reinforcers that were available.

6-4 Self-control and Value Discounting

   One application of instrumental conditioning is in self-control. We often face situations in which we must choose to be rewarded immediately, or to delay a reward. Drinking a high-calorie sweetened beverage brings immediate rewards. Drinking a glass of water has long term rewards because it is a healthier choice. As you learned from **pages 182-188** of your text we frequently face choices about the quantity of reinforcement. Furthermore, organisms are sensitive to the delay that intervenes between making a choice and receiving reinforcement. Reinforcers tend to lose their value when a delay is imposed. A $1000 reward right this moment is generally perceived of as more valuable than the same amount paid in five years. Value discounting describes this phenomenon. In the exercises below you can gain some practice with the concepts of self-control and value discounting.

6-4.1 Self-control. Describe a situation in which someone might have difficulty showing self control.

What are the two reinforcers in this situation?

Which one occurs with a shorter delay?

What tactics might help to encourage self-control in this situation?

6-4.2 Value discounting.

Value discounting refers to the fact that the perceived value of a reinforcer is less the longer you have to wait for it. Reinforcer value is discounted or reduced by waiting time or delay to the delivery of the reinforcer (see **pp. 185-188** for review).

Consider the perceived value of getting $100 today. To illustrate this in concrete terms, in the table below indicate how valuable $100 would be for you if you got the money today, tomorrow, 30 days from now, 150 days from now, or 300 days from now. Remember, we are asking for your *perceived* value of $100.

Delay to Delivery in Days	Perceived Value of $100
0	$100
1	
30	
150	
300	

Next, plot the values that you listed in the above table on the axes provided below. Draw a line connecting your points in the format similar to what you see on **figure 6.9** on **p. 187** of your text. Note that in this graphic representation, delay to delivery of the reinforcer is plotted from right to left.

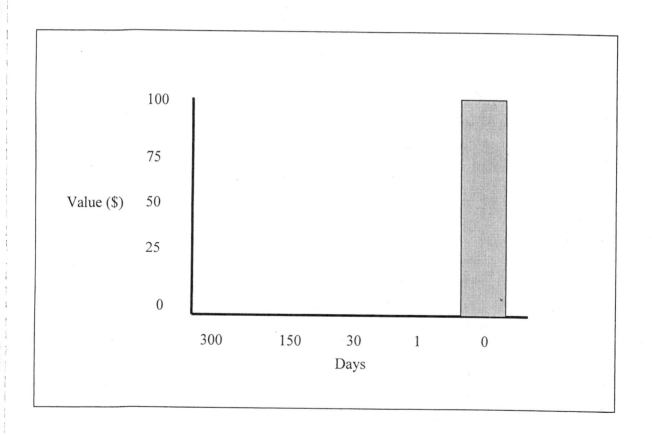

Let's assume that the value discounting function you drew is for a normally functioning individual. For certain types of individuals (heroin addicts, for example), reward value drops much faster the longer they have to wait to obtain the reward. On the graph below, indicate what a discounting function might look like for someone who is less able to appreciate the value of a delayed reinforcer.

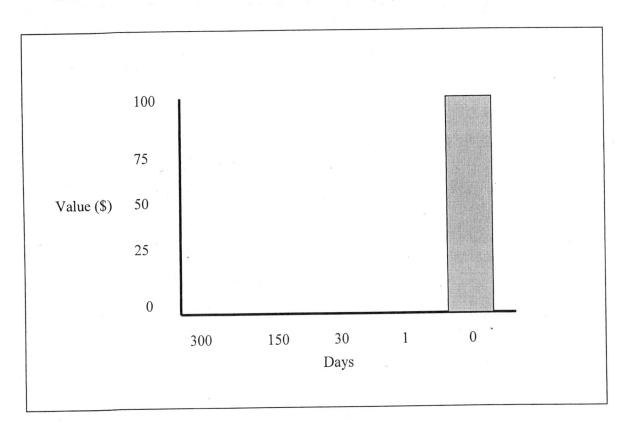

7 Instrumental Conditioning: Motivational Mechanisms

In **Chapters 5** and **6** you learned about many of the different concepts and phenomena of instrumental conditioning. Here we turn to examining the underlying mechanisms. **Chapter 7** of your text tackles two general approaches to the study of the motivational mechanisms of instrumental conditioning: *associative structure* and *behavioral regulation*. First we will explore the associative structure of instrumental conditioning. Classical conditioning can occur during the course of instrumental conditioning and helps to motivate the instrumental response. Thus, the two types of conditioning interact. In **Section 7-1** you will apply several different approaches to examining the nature of these interactions. In contrast to associative theories, theories of behavioral regulation examine instrumental learning in the context of goal-directedness and the constraints that operate on our ongoing behavioral activities. **Section 7-2** includes exercises that will help you to apply the different approaches to behavioral regulation.

After completing these exercises you should be able to:

- Compare and contrast the associative structure and behavioral regulation approaches to instrumental conditioning,
- Identify the differences between S-R, S-O, R-O, and S-(R-O) associations in instrumental conditioning,
- Apply each of these four types of associations to new examples,
- Understand and apply the Premack Principle to new examples,
- Apply the concept of behavioral bliss point to your own experiences.

7-1 The Associative Structure of Instrumental Learning

The exercises in this section are designed to help you identify and understand several different ways in which psychologists explain how associations underlie instrumentally learned responses. As you may recall in reading the first two pages of the chapter (**pp. 191-192**), psychologists examine the motivational mechanisms of instrumental learning from two approaches; associate structure and behavioral regulation.

7-1.1 Differentiating associative structure and behavioral regulation. Most of the chapter is devoted to these two approaches so we will start by contrasting them. For this exercise you should pay close attention to the introductory paragraphs on **page 192** of your text.

For each of the following, indicate whether it applies best to the *associative structure* approach or to the *behavioral regulation* approach to the analysis of instrumental conditioning, and briefly explain why.

1) It takes a more molar rather than molecular approach.

Circle one: associative structure   *behavioral regulation*

Why?

2) It considers reinforcers to be stimuli rather than responses.

Circle one: associative structure   *behavioral regulation*

Why?

3) It focuses only on the instrumental response that is involved in a particular instrumental conditioning procedure.

Circle one: associative structure   *behavioral regulation*

Why?

4) It ignores the concept of optimality.

Circle one: associative structure   *behavioral regulation*

Why?

5) It ignores the concept of reward expectancy.

Circle one: *associative structure*   *behavioral regulation*

Why?

6) It ignores changes in the reinforcer response.

Circle one: *associative structure*   *behavioral regulation*

Why?

7) It ignores the effect of other available reinforcers.

Circle one: *associative structure*   *behavioral regulation*

Why?

8) It can be tested with the use of transfer of control experiments.

Circle one: *associative structure*   *behavioral regulation*

Why?

7-1.2 Associative structure and the three-term contingency. On **pages 192-198** of your text there is detailed discussion on the associative structure of instrumental conditioning. One of the main issues addressed here concerns how the parts of the three-term contingency (stimulus-response-outcome; S, R, O) are related. In other words, which of these three terms are associated? and how? For example:

S-O: Stimulus-outcome. When a response is followed by a certain outcome (O) in the presence of a stimulus context (S), S can become associated with O. Once this occurs, S tells the organism that O will occur.

S-R: Stimulus-response. The association is between the stimulus context and the response it elicits. The outcome only creates the association, but is not itself associated with either the antecedent stimulus or the response.

R-O: Response-outcome. An association is formed between a response and its outcome.

S-(R-O): Stimulus-(response-outcome). The Stimulus context activates the response and outcome association. This is an association in hierarchical form.

The Law of Effect maintains that associations are of the S-R variety. However, as you saw in **pages 192-198** of your text and in the list above, there are numerous other ways to conceptualize the associative nature of instrumental learning. The purpose of this exercise is to allow you to apply these different associative structures to a common example. Below are **figures 5-1** and **5-2** reprinted from your text. Recall that Edward Thorndike examined trial and error learning in cats that were attempting to escape from the boxes shown below. The learning curve below is an example of Thorndike's data. Although the experiment appears rather simple, you may want to refer back to **pages 125-127** to refresh your memory of how it worked.

Box I

Figure 5.2 Latencies to escape from Box A during successive trials. The longest latency was 160 seconds; the shortest was 6 seconds. (Notice that the axes are not labeled, as in Thorndike's original report.)

In reference to Thorndike's procedures that used box 1 of **figure 5.1** above, what was the:

> Question

Stimulus?

Response?

Outcome?

> For this exercise you need to consider how each scenario of associative learning applies to the puzzle box learning example. In the spaces below, describe how S-O, S-R, R-O, and S-(R-O) learning applies to cats escaping from Thorndike's puzzle boxes. Be sure to identify what exactly is being associated and how that association develops.

S-O:

S-R:

R-O:

S-(R-O):

7-1.3 Concept Questions

1) What is a reason for doing a reinforcer devaluation procedure? Which type of association is this procedure most relevant to?

2) What is "reward expectancy" and why is it relevant to S-O associations?

3) According to two-process theory, how does a CS modify the rate of an instrumental response? Describe an example of how this happens.

4) How can an S-(R-O) association be involved in lever pressing for food in a Skinner box? What are the S, the R, and the O in this case?

5) Assume a rat reinforced with food for pressing a response lever only learns an R-O association. Could an R-O association alone explain lever press responding? Why or why not?

7-2 Behavioral Regulation

The behavioral regulation perspective on instrumental conditioning is quite distinct from that of the associative structure perspective you practiced above. You may recall from **page 199** of your text that one primary distinction is that behavioral regulation theories focus on the ways in which contingencies limit the ongoing behaviors of organisms. One such theory, called consummatory response theory, holds that the act of engaging in responses such as eating, drinking, and sex is inherently reinforcing. So in this case responses, not stimuli, are reinforcing. Theories that expanded on this perspective, such as the Premack Principle and the behavioral bliss point, comprise more modern approaches to behavioral regulation. The exercises below are designed to better acquaint you with these theories of behavioral regulation.

7-2.1 Premack Principle. A milestone on the road to the behavioral regulation perspective on instrumental conditioning is the differential probability, or Premack principle (**pp. 199-202**). The Premack principle maintains that response probabilities are critical features of instrumental conditioning. Recall that Premack dismissed the idea that there is a fundamental distinction between reinforcers and instrumental responses. A response itself can serve as a reinforcer. More specifically, a highly probable response can be used to reinforce a less probable response. For example, eating dessert is a more probable response than eating vegetables for many kids (and adults). Making the response of eating dessert contingent upon eating vegetables is an effective way of increasing the lower probability, vegetable eating response.

On **page 201** of your text an experiment conducted on rats by Premack was described. The responses involved wheel running and drinking and Premack designed an experiment to test the differential probability principle with these two responses. Before proceeding with the exercise below please review this study and, especially, **figure 7.4** which summarizes the results.

Figure 7.3 of your text, reprinted below, diagrams another experiment Premack (1965) conducted with children. Below this figure is a set of blank graphs. For this exercise, first review the Premack (1965) study described on **pages 200-201** of your text and think about his results. Next, fill in the blank graphs with probable results of the study. (hint: use **figure 7.4** as a guide). Be sure to label the axes of the graphs.

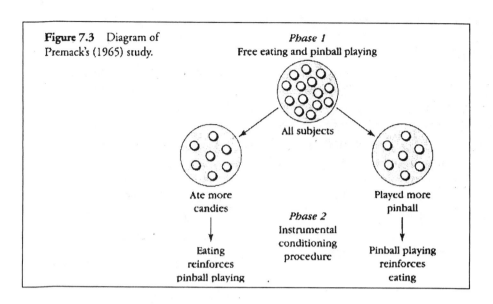

Figure 7.3 Diagram of Premack's (1965) study.

Phase 1
Free eating and pinball playing

All subjects

Ate more candies

Played more pinball

Phase 2
Instrumental conditioning procedure

Eating reinforces pinball playing

Pinball playing reinforces eating

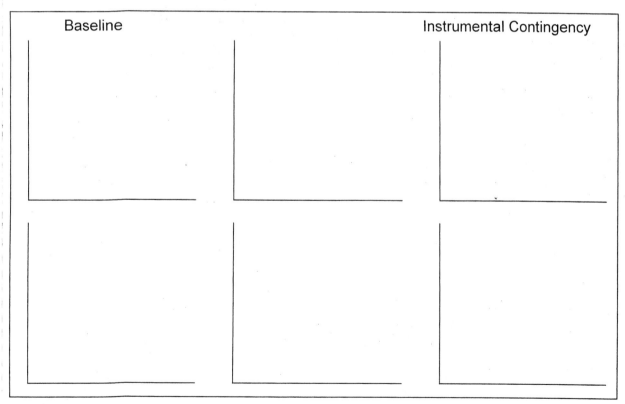

Baseline

Instrumental Contingency

7-2.2 The behavioral bliss point. A fundamental assumption of behavioral regulation is the concept of the *behavioral bliss point*. **Pages 204-208** discuss the concept of the bliss point and it will be helpful to review these pages before doing the exercises below. You probably notice some similarities between the behavioral bliss point and the Premack principle. Behavioral regulation theories assume that there is an optimal distribution of activities under free conditions. When there are no constraints on the activities we may perform we distribute our activities at our own individually-based optimum levels. However, sometimes we have to engage in less-preferred activities more than we would hope. This is because there are instrumental contingencies that cause deviations from the optimal distribution of activity. Before completing the exercises below first review **figure 7.6** reprinted below.

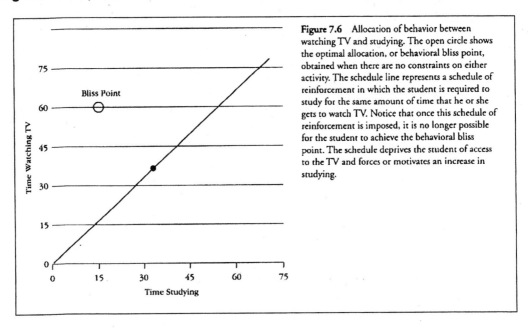

Figure 7.6 Allocation of behavior between watching TV and studying. The open circle shows the optimal allocation, or behavioral bliss point, obtained when there are no constraints on either activity. The schedule line represents a schedule of reinforcement in which the student is required to study for the same amount of time that he or she gets to watch TV. Notice that once this schedule of reinforcement is imposed, it is no longer possible for the student to achieve the behavioral bliss point. The schedule deprives the student of access to the TV and forces or motivates an increase in studying.

The figure below plots the baseline bliss point (open circle) of a child who was given the opportunity to play pinball and eat candy under unconstrained conditions. As you can see, at the bliss point, the child spent 20 minutes eating candy and 10 minutes playing pinball. Thus, at the baseline or bliss point the ratio of eating to playing pinball was 2:1. The line in the graph is a contingency line that represents the ratio when an instrumental conditioning procedure is introduced that constrains the child's choices. The instrumental contingency represented by the line requires that the child change from its baseline or "bliss" level of responding to one in which she spends 10 minutes eating candy for every 40 minutes she spends playing pinball. Thus, the ratio of times spent on the two responses required by the instrumental procedure is 1:4. Draw a point on the contingency line that shows how the child will redistribute her behavior under the 1:4 contingency.

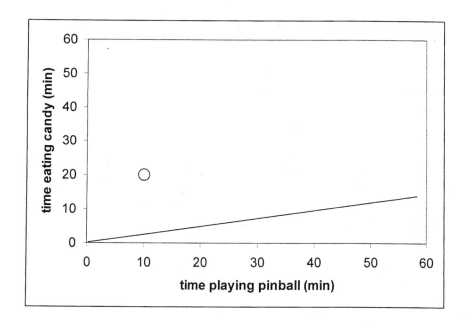

1) If the child were to insist on spending as much time eating when the instrumental procedure is in effect as during the bliss point, how much time will she have to devote to playing the pinball machine?

2) If she insists on playing the pinball machine as long as she did during the bliss point, how much time will she have to devote to eating?

3) In the above example, the bliss point involves 20 minutes of eating and 10 minutes of playing pinball. According to the Premack Principle, could playing pinball reinforce eating as the instrumental response? Why or why not? Could eating reinforce playing pinball as the instrumental response? Why of why not?

4) Given the schedule line, can she return to the bliss point? If not, how will the child have to redistribute her behavior under these conditions?

According to the response deprivation hypothesis, an activity will serve as a reinforcer if access to it is restricted to less time than what the subject is likely to perform under baseline or unrestricted conditions. Given the bliss point identified in the above figure, answer the following questions using the response deprivation hypothesis.

5) How could playing pinball reinforce eating as the instrumental response?

6) How could eating reinforce playing pinball as the instrumental response?

7-2.3 Personal application. The following exercise asks you to apply the behavioral bliss point approach to your own activities. First, think about how much time you devote to different activities during a normal weekday. How much time, in minutes, do you spend in class, with friends, eating, at work, etc.? Surely the numbers vary by day of the week, timing of the semester, etc. It may be helpful to just pick one particular day of the week in which you engage in most of the activities you list. The numbers you come up with probably differ from what you would have under less constrained conditions. Perhaps the way you allocate your time during winter or spring breaks better reflects your baseline level of responding for various activities such as watching television, spending time with friends, exercising, etc. The exercise below allows you to compare your time allocation under unconstrained and constrained conditions.

In the left hand column below list five common activities you engage in during a 24-hour period. Under the *Actual* column indicate the estimated amount of time (in minutes) you spend on these activities during a normal weekday that includes classes, studying, working, sleeping, etc. The time you spend on *actual* activities should reflect the constraints you experience with your busy school schedule. Under the *Ideal* column estimate the amount of time (in minutes) you would spend on each activity under ideal or unconstrained conditions. List the activities under each column from most frequent to least frequent. (Note: presumably you are going to list schoolwork as an activity. If so, treat this as a general category that includes attending class, doing assignments, studying, etc.)

	Activity	Actual amount of time spent (min)	Ideal amount of time spent (min)
1			
2			
3			
4			
5			

Of the five activities you listed above, pick two from under **Ideal** conditions. In the graph below plot the bliss point between the two activities. Be sure to label the axes of the graph and write out a title. Next plot the **Actual** point on the graph for the same two activities. Connect this point with the origin of the x- and y-axis.

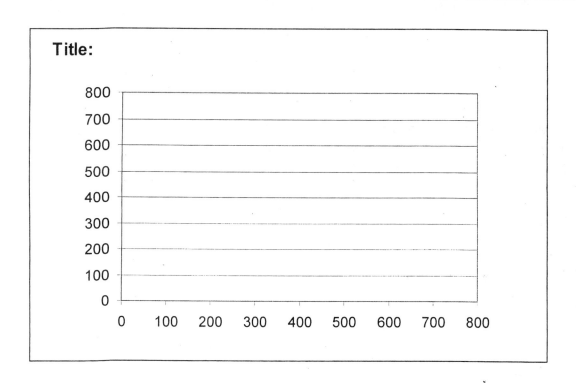

Title:

What is the ratio of time spent engaged in the two activities under ideal conditions?

1) What is the ratio of time spent in the two activities you chose under actual conditions?

2) What is the ratio of time spent under ideal conditions (the "bliss point)?

3) Which activity is further from the bliss point under actual conditions?

4) Could you conceive of a substitute for one of the activities? What instrumental requirements are needed to gain access to this substitute? What would be the impact of having access to this substitute?

8   Stimulus Control of Behavior

Chapter 8 covers some common processes that are found in both instrumental and classical conditioning. These processes are generalization, discrimination and stimulus control, and they reflect the dynamic interactions that occur between organisms and the stimuli they experience. At this point you can probably appreciate the importance of both flexibility and selectivity when it comes to learning. The exercises below are designed to enhance your understanding of the details of how these processes are studied and how they work. First we will examine some basics of how stimulus control is measured by focusing on the processes of discrimination and generalization (**section 8-1**). Next, you will consider some of the factors that influence stimulus control, and you will be asked to apply these factors to your own experiences (**section 8-2**). The exercises in **section 8-3** are designed to familiarize you with the details of how stimulus control is studied. Most studies that you will be reading about deal with stimuli that are *discrete*, that is, they usually appear for only a brief period of time. However, many of our responses are also under the stimulus control of more general, contextual features of our environment.

After completing these exercises you should be able to:
- Differentiate the processes of generalization and discrimination.
- Differentiate between stimulus control in instrumental and classically conditioned responding.
- Identify the ways in which stimulus control is established.
- Identify various factors that predispose organisms to stimulus control.
- Describe how experience with stimuli results in stimulus control.

8-1 Measuring stimulus control

Organisms must be able to determine which stimuli predict that a US or reinforcement is available. Sometimes a CS+ or S+ may be very similar to stimuli that do NOT signal a US (the CS-) or reinforcement (the S-). For example, long, long ago cell phones sounded very much alike when a call arrived. The difference between the S+ and S- was not so great. This was before a many different personalized ringing options became available. Because the S+ and S- were often very similar (if not identical), it was common to see several people in a crowd reflexively fumbling for their phone when they heard someone else's phone ring. In situations such as this, we notice that over time people may develop a heightened ability to discriminate one stimulus (their ring) from another very similar stimulus (someone else's ring).

Question

Describe two examples in which you have had to discriminate between stimuli in order for a response to be reinforced?

Generalization occurs when an organism responds in a similar fashion to two or more stimuli. Some examples of how generalization is studied are described in **pages 220-222** of your text. Based on our definition of generalization, it appears that a standard experiment on generalization requires at least two phases, a training phase and a testing phase. It is important to appreciate the importance of this. Therefore, before proceeding, answer the following question.

Question

Generally speaking, what happens during each phase of a generalization study and why?

Let's review how generalization is depicted graphically. **Figure 8.2** is reprinted below. Notice that this particular graph refers to an instrumental response that has generalized to different colored stimuli.

Figure 8.2 Stimulus generalization gradient for pigeons that were trained to peck in the presence of a colored light of 580-nm wavelength and were then tested in the presence of other colors. (From "Discriminability and Stimulus Generalization," by N. Guttman and H. I. Kalish, 1956, *Journal of Experimental Psychology, 51*, pp. 79–88.)

In the graph below plot generalization gradients for three people who have a fear of heights, ranging from light, moderate, to severe. Your y-axis refers to anxiety level (rated on a scale of 1-10) and the x-axis includes a measure of height. (Note: The style of this graph will be different from the one above because there is a zero point on the x-axis.)

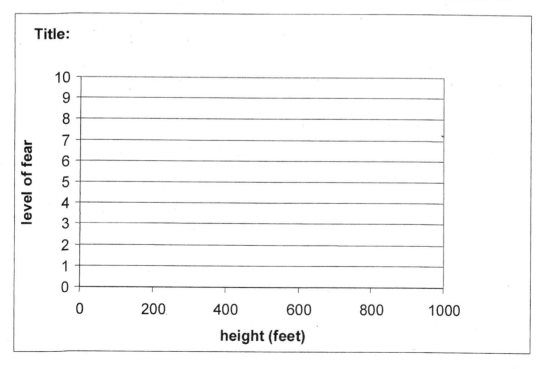

Title:

1) Which shows the most stimulus generalization? Which shows the least?

2) Which shows the strongest stimulus control by the stimulus dimension of "height"? Keep in mind that the strength of stimulus control is determined by the slope of the generalization gradient. The steeper the slope, the stronger is the behavior under the control of that stimulus dimension.

SNIFFY APPLICATION

Examine the processes of generalization, discrimination, and stimulus control in exercises #37-42 (pp. 203-209)

8-2 Stimulus and Response Factors

There are several factors that determine whether responding comes under stimulus control. Individual subjects may attend to different features of complex stimuli, and these are the features that may determine whether responding occurs (recall the experiment by Reynolds, 1961). In addition, the sensory capacities and biological predispositions of an individual or species may also determine whether stimulus control occurs. Several stimulus and response factors that influence stimulus control are discussed on **pages 222-230** of your text. For example:

- Sensory capacity and orientation
- Relative ease of conditioning various stimuli
- Type of reinforcement
- Type of instrumental response

From this list, choose two factors and describe an example of each as it applies to your own experiences. In your answer you need to identify the response that was learned, the stimulus or stimuli that controlled the response, and how that stimulus control developed.

1) Factor:_____

2) Factor:_____

8-3 Learning Factors in Stimulus Control

Discrimination training brings behavior under stimulus control. But how does that happen? Suppose we are studying color vision and want to train nonhuman primate subjects to discriminate a specific color— or light of a specific wavelength. For instance, how would we train monkeys to press a button when a color with a wavelength of 550 nm was presented? To demonstrate that pressing a button in response to a 550 nm stimulus is under stimulus control we could run an experiment with the appropriate control groups.

Imagine that during discrimination training monkeys are exposed to a screen that presents a colored stimulus measuring 550 nm. If a monkey presses a button while the stimulus is on, it receives food each time. The S+ is the 550 nm stimulus. The S- varies though. One group cannot receive food reinforcement while the screen is grey (group 1), and a second group learns that it cannot receive food when a slightly different color, a 540 nm stimulus, is presented (group 2). A third control group is not trained to discriminate. It is reinforced for all button presses, regardless of the color on the screen. The experimental design can be summarized as follows:

	Group 1	Group 2	Group 3 (control)
S+	550 nm	550 nm	No discrimination
S-	grey	540 nm	Training

After conducting several hundred trials with these different procedures, you run test trials in which you expose the monkeys to colors ranging from 500 to 600 nm. How do you think monkeys in each group will respond to colors ranging from 500-600 nm?

> In the graph below fill in three generalization gradients you would predict for the three groups and write a title and interpretation for your graph.

Title:

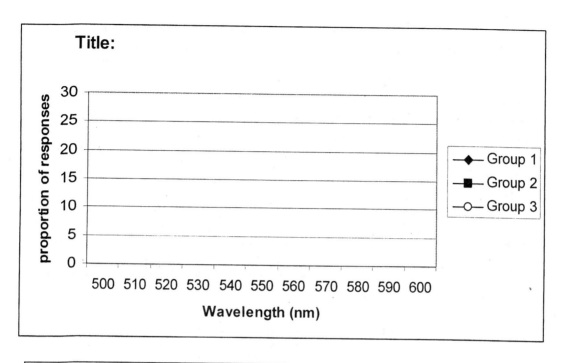

proportion of responses

30
25
20
15
10
5
0

500 510 520 530 540 550 560 570 580 590 600

Wavelength (nm)

◆ Group 1
■ Group 2
○ Group 3

Interpretation:

> Question

1) Why was group 3, the control group, needed when the S- for group 1 was a grey screen (with no color)?

2) State how stimulus control applies to this experiment. Which group showed the most stimulus control? Which showed the least? Why?

117

The discrimination learning theory of Spence has generated much research in the area of stimulus control. His theory focuses on both the excitatory and inhibitory components of learning. So far we have focused on excitatory conditioning. Discrimination training results in increased responding to the target stimulus, and less responding to stimuli that differ from the target stimulus. However, it is important to remember that during the CS- or S- phases of discrimination training an organism must inhibit responding, since the US or the reinforcer is not forthcoming. So excitatory and inhibitory conditioning interact during learning; Spence's theory tells us this. Let's now examine how the interaction between the two would look.

Imagine that you trained a pigeon to peck at a key following presentation of a 600 Hz tone. The S+ during training was the 600 Hz tone and the S- was a 400 Hertz tone. During testing, the pigeon was presented with tones ranging from 200 – 1000 Hz. Below are hypothetical data that show the level of both conditioned excitation and conditioned inhibition to each frequency during the test phase of the experiment.

Hertz	conditioned excitation	Conditioned inhibition
200	0	-.50
400	.50	-.75
600	1.0	-.50
800	.50	-.25
1000	.25	0

In the graph below plot these data, using separate lines for excitatory and inhibitory responding using the symbols (● or ■) provided in the legend of the graph and write an interpretation.

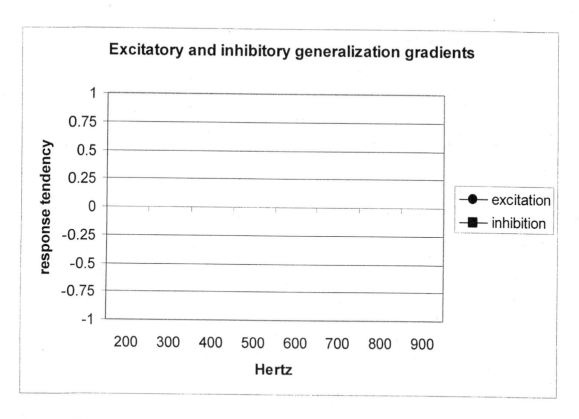

Excitatory and inhibitory generalization gradients

response tendency

1
0.75
0.5
0.25
0
-0.25
-0.5
-0.75
-1

200   300   400   500   600   700   800   900

Hertz

—●— excitation
—■— inhibition

Interpretation:

One phenomenon that is important to Spence's theory is "peak shift" (**p. 238** of your text). This is a very common occurrence in studies of stimulus control. If you indicated that peak shift occurred in the color discrimination study with monkeys described above, well done! If you did not indicate peak shift, take a moment to redraw the lines with peak shift included in the figure below.

Title:

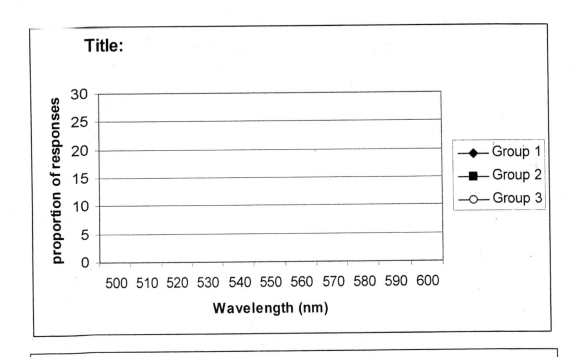

a) Compare and contrast Spence's explanation of peak shift with alternative accounts (**pp. 239-240**).

b) How might peak shift be maladaptive in some cases?

9 Extinction of Conditioned Behavior

Chapter 9 focuses on the process of extinction. Extinction is a very important phenomenon that has received a lot of attention in basic and applied research. It is also a process that is found in both instrumental and classical conditioning. Thus, an entire chapter devoted to the process of extinction is justified. First, in **section 9-1** you will have a chance to visualize some basic processes involved in extinction, and to practice working with the important role of context in learning and extinction. In **section 9-2** we will see how prior learning history affects extinction.

After completing these exercises you should be able to:

- Understand the processes of extinction and spontaneous recovery of conditioned responding,
- Describe the relevance of extinction to treating conditioned fear responses,
- Describe the importance of context in extinction,
- Distinguish between the renewal effect, reinstatement, and spontaneous recovery,
- Apply different characteristics of extinction to real-world examples.
- Describe paradoxical reward effects,
- Compare and contrast theories of the partial reinforcement extinction effect.

9-1 Extinction and Original Learning

9-1.1 Extinction and spontaneous recovery of conditioned responding.

Two processes of classical conditioning that have generated a lot of laboratory and applied research are extinction and spontaneous recovery (**pp. 255-257**). In this section you can gain some familiarity with these processes. First, in the graph below indicate in each panel how the data would look if an excitatory conditioned response was acquired, extinguished, and showed spontaneous recovery.

SNIFFY APPLICATION

Practice with the concepts of extinction and spontaneous recovery in exercises #2 & #3 (p. 41, 44) for classical conditioning and #s 25-27 (pp. 156-163) for instrumental conditioning.

Next let's examine an actual research application to extinction of conditioned responding.

9-1.2 Phobias: Treatments, relapse prevention, and the renewal effect.

Phobias are frequently treated with behavioral therapies, but there are some limitations to the therapy if sessions are only conducted in one setting. This exercise provides you with the opportunity to practice working with some sample data based on an actual experiment[1], conducted on rats, with implications for treating phobias in humans. On **page 260** of your text the applied, clinical significance of a phenomenon called the *renewal effect* is discussed. It will be helpful to review the text before completing this exercise. In this exercise we will consider a possible method for extinguishing conditioned phobic responses. The study examined acquisition and extinction in several different physical settings, or contexts.

One problem with phobias is that people who suffer from them frequently experience relapses when they encounter the phobic object in a context that differs from where they received treatment. Gunther et al. (1998) reasoned that exposure to phobia therapy in multiple contexts, accomplished by using extinction in each one, can provide a more robust treatment of phobias.

The experimenters conditioned a fear response in groups of rats placed in one of three test chambers that differed in physical characteristics, representing the different contexts. The CS used in this study was a brief presentation of white noise, and this was followed by foot shock delivered via the floor grid of the experimental chambers. Recall that freezing behavior is a common response found in rats when an aversive event is pending, and that a standard dependent variable in studies such as this is drinking behavior. Thus, we can predict that thirsty rats would spend less time drinking if they are in a context that elicits fear. We would expect drinking to *decrease* during conditioning, and return to normal levels during extinction. Three groups of rats were needed to test whether extinction in multiple contexts generalizes to a novel context that the rats never experienced:

1) a control group that received no extinction ("Group NE")
2) a group that received extinction in one context ("Group E1")
3) a group that received extinction in three different contexts ("Group E3")

Let's briefly return to the question of how this experiment applies to the treatment of phobias. Can you think of a real-world example that humans experience that is analogous to the rat study?

Think of how this might play out in people who want to overcome social anxieties. Imagine that several people are being treated for social phobia. You have three groups and you want to see which group, after extinction treatments, will show the least amount of anxiety while attending a large party. One group

---

[1] This example is adopted from Gunther, Denniston, & Miller (1998).

receives no extinction and is tested for anxiety at a large party. A second group receives extinction treatment at a small dinner party prior to testing. And a third group receives extinction treatment at the small dinner party, in a large classroom, and in a crowded restaurant. Which group of people should show the least amount of anxiety at the large party?

Question

Before proceeding, what do you predict for each of the three groups of rats in the Gunther et al. experiment? (In other words, how much conditioned responding do you expect to see in each group of rats when tested in the novel context at the end of extinction?).

NE:

E1:

E3:

The critical measure in this experiment is the amount of time it took the rats in each group to complete five cumulative seconds of drinking in the presence of the CS while placed in an experimental chamber or context they had never encountered before (the novel context). Below are hypothetical data that reflect the results of this study:

| | Group | | |
	NE	E1	E3
Time to complete 5 seconds of drinking	30	20	5

Graph these data on the axes below and write an interpretation.

Title:

Interpretation:

Questions

The renewal effect and spontaneous recovery seem like very similar effects. Students often confuse the two. How does the renewal effect differ from spontaneous recovery?

How are the renewal effect and reinstatement similar? How do the two phenomena differ?

9-2 What Is Learned in Extinction?

It makes intuitive sense that extinction involves "unlearning" something because the conditioned response is diminished. However, several research findings indicate that extinction is not a matter of unlearning something, but rather learning something new. In this section there are two sets of exercises that focus on some special properties of extinction. We will explore how prior learning histories affect extinction rates.

9-2.1 Paradoxical reward effects. There are three rather peculiar phenomena of extinction described on **pages 269-270** of your text:
- The overtraining extinction effect
- The magnitude reinforcement extinction effect
- The partial reinforcement extinction effect

First review these effects and then complete the exercise below.

> Following are some scenarios involving extinction of learned responses. Read these carefully and identify which of the three effects noted above apply. Answer the questions that follow.

> 1) Veronica answers phones for a company and is paid $2.50 per call for her work. Somehow, Derek does the same job at the same company for $1.50 per call. Following a recession **both** employees are not paid for several days. Which person would you predict will be less inclined to answer the phone when it rings during this period? Which effect explains your answer?

2) Dr. Burns has two students, Jacquie and Kelcy, who repeatedly smile when she attempts to humor the class during lectures. As a result, Dr. Burns makes eye contact with these students more often than with other students. Jacquie smiles at all of Dr. Burns' jokes. Kelcy smiles at some of her jokes. Unfortunately, both students earned Fs on their first exams and subsequently stop smiling at Dr. Burns' jokes. Following the exam, which of the two students do you think Dr. Burns will try looking to more frequently after she tells a joke? Which effect explains your answer?

3) In 1985 Coca-Cola Co. switched to "New Coke", which tasted quite different from traditional Coke. This created quite a stir among beverage drinkers, mostly because the New Coke product simply was not as good as the "Classic" Coke it replaced. Based on the theme of these exercises, do you think older, more experienced Classic Coke drinkers would extinguish drinking New Coke more or less rapidly than younger drinkers? Which effect explains your answer?

4) A rat was trained to press two levers for food on two CRF schedules. A red light indicated that the lever on the right could be pressed for one food pellet. A green light indicated that the lever on the left could be pressed for two food pellets. The lights came on, one after the other, at regular intervals. After responding on the two schedules was established the rat was placed on extinction. The red and green lights were switched on at regular intervals but no food was made available. Which lever will be pressed more frequently during extinction? Which effect explains your answer?

5) Mr. Simpson owns a lawnmower that has a starter cord that has to be pulled several times before it starts. His neighbor, Mr. Flanders, owns a mower that starts at a single pull of the cord. Neighborhood vandals stole spark plugs from both mowers one night. The next time the two go to start their mowers, which one will pull the cord more often before giving up? Which effect explains your answer?

9-2.2 Partial reinforcement extinction effect (PREE).

This particular effect of extinction is of considerable interest to many researchers of learning. There are a few competing theories explaining the mechanisms of the PREE, and **pages 270-273** of your text provide some background and explanations of it. Below we will explore some additional details of this effect.

In the graph below draw 3 hypothetical cumulative response recordings for subjects that were placed on CRF, VR5, and VR10 schedules of reinforcement until each schedule produced the same total number of lever press responses, and then indicate how the curves would look if extinction followed. Be sure your graph clearly shows how the three groups were differentially affected by the extinction procedure. Write an interpretation of your results below your graph.

Interpretation:

 Questions

The discrimination hypothesis. Based on the discrimination hypothesis, which of the following schedules would produce the greatest PREE and why? FR1, FR10, VR10

Frustration theory. Which of the following would produce the greatest level of frustration when extinction is introduced and why? FR1, FR10, VR10.

The sequential hypothesis. Assume that "R" indicates reward and "N" indicates no reward. Imagine there are three groups of subjects on intermittent reinforcement schedules that are reinforced as follows:

Subject 1: N R R N N R R N R R
Subject 2: R R R N R R N R R N
Subject 3: N N N R N R N R N R

Based on the sequential hypothesis, which subject is most likely to show the strongest evidence for PREE? Explain your answer.

SNIFFY APPLICATION

Examine reinforcement schedule
effects on PREE with exercise #36
(p. 187)

10 Aversive Control: Avoidance and Punishment

Our approach to studying learning changes a bit with this chapter. Here we will examine how aversive stimulation results in conditioned avoidance responding. Also we will explore the ways that punishment results in decreased instrumental responding. In our analysis of avoidance, we will approach the topic from procedural, theoretical, and applied perspectives (**section 10-1**). According to two-process theory, classical and instrumental conditioning interact during avoidance learning and we will explore how this occurs in **section 10-1**. In **section 10-2** we will turn our discussion to punishment. The exercises will cover some of the applied aspects of punishment.

After completing these exercises you should be able to:
- Distinguish the processes of avoidance and escape,
- Describe how two-process theory explains aversive conditioning,
- Apply two-process theory to real-world examples,
- Identify various procedures for measuring avoidance learning,
- Describe some alternatives to two-process theory,
- Identify different factors that influence the effectiveness of punishment.

10-1 Avoidance Behavior

First we will explore in detail the procedures and theories behind conditioned avoidance. The distinction between avoidance and escape will be made, followed by an exercise that tests two-process theory. Also, we will explore various experimental approaches to studying avoidance responding.

10-1.1 Avoidance, escape and two-process theory. Below are some examples of behaviors that reduce an aversive event. As you read on **page 282** we can either use avoidance or escape to remove something aversive. Avoidance and escape differ and it will be helpful to review the distinction between the two phenomena before proceeding.

The examples below involve different situations in which an aversive stimulus is present and a response is made to remove that stimulus. Indicate below which examples are instances of avoidance and which are instances of escape.

1. Opening an umbrella during a downpour of rain

Circle one: **Avoidance   Escape**

2. A rat runs to the opposite side of a shuttle box in response to a tone

Circle one: **Avoidance   Escape**

3. Switching off your alarm clock just before it goes off

Circle one: **Avoidance   Escape**

4. Turning off a noisy car alarm

Circle one: **Avoidance   Escape**

5. Taking calcium tablets before eating a large, spicy dinner

Circle one: **Avoidance   Escape**

10-1.2   Experimental analysis of avoidance. The exercises below provide you with some practice in differentiating different ways of analyzing avoidance behavior.

1) *Acquired drive experiments* (**pp. 284-288**)

Figure 10.4 from your text (**p. 283**) is reprinted on the next page. This is a standard apparatus used in experiments on avoidance conditioning.

Figure 10.4 A shuttle box. The box has a metal grid floor and is separated into two compartments by an archway. The instrumental response consists of crossing back and forth (shuttling) from one side of the box to the other.

I. In the space below describe how this apparatus might be modified for use in an acquired-drive experiment. Be sure to differentiate between classical and instrumental conditioning procedures.

II. How does this procedure demonstrate an "acquired drive"?

2) *Independent measurement of fear during acquisition and avoidance behavior* **(pp. 288-290)**

Figure 10.7 from your text (see next page) summarizes results from a study testing whether conditioned fear and avoidance are highly correlated. Before answering the questions below review the figure and your text.

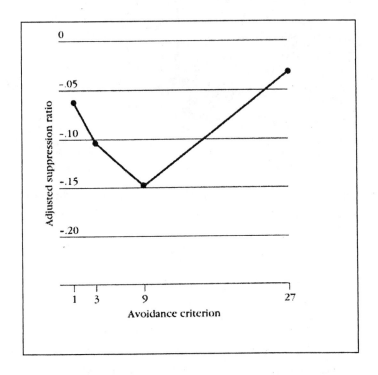

I. What happens to fearfulness following relatively extensive avoidance training? Why do you think this happens?

II. How might the data in **figure 10.7** above contradict two-process theory?

3) *Asymptotic avoidance performance* (**p. 290**)

    I. Describe how the process of extinction affects well-established avoidance responding.

    II. Describe how the mechanism of conservation of fear maintains avoidance behavior.

4) *Extinction of avoidance behavior through response-blocking and CS-alone exposure* (**pp. 290-292**)

    I. Imagine the following scenario.

When Emily was young she was attacked and bitten by a feisty house cat. She immediately acquired a strong fear of cats. Cats became a CS predicting pain (the US). Describe how response-blocking and CS-alone exposure could be used to help her overcome her fear of cats.

10-1.3 Alternative theories of avoidance. Two-process theory explains many phenomena of avoidance learning. However, there are alternatives to two-process theory and they are described on **pages 295-301** of your text. You may want to review these pages before answering the questions below. The alternatives/phenomena include:

1. positive reinforcement through conditioned inhibition
2. reinforcement of avoidance through reduction of shock frequency
3. avoidance and species-specific defense reactions
4. predatory imminence

Following are statements about avoidance learning. The statements are based on observations that suggest some alternatives to two-process theory. Read each statement carefully and identify (using numbers 1-4 above) which alternative to two-process theory applies (there may be more than one answer to each).

---

1. Avoidance behavior increases in frequency in response to stimuli that signal the onset of an aversive stimulus. _____

2. External and proprioceptive stimuli that are involved in making responses that reduce the number of shocks received become conditioned inhibitors of fear. _____

3. The avoidance responses that develop during the initial learning trials are of critical importance and reflect innate defensive responses.

   _____

4. The avoidance response that is elicited by a threat is directly related to the different levels of danger present in a given situation. _____

5. The most effective avoidance response is selected by the process of punishment. _____

6. Avoidance responses occur because they reduce the frequency of shock, irrespective of signals for shock or safety._____

SNIFFY APPLICATION

Examine how different types of punishment influence instrumental responding in exercises #28-30 (pp. 167-170)

10-2 Punishment

The next set of exercises deal with punishment. As you learned from your text this is a controversial topic and much of the research has been focused on identifying the effectiveness of various procedures, although some theoretical issues have been also addressed (**pp. 308-311**). Here we will explore various factors that influence the degree to which punishment is effective.

10-2.1 Punishment and instrumental responding. The intensity of a punisher can determine the extent to which operant responding decreases. We will explore this rule in more detail. But first we need to review a method used for studying punishment.

Recall that researchers use suppression ratios to measure the effects of an aversive stimulus on responding. In Pavlovian conditioning an aversive CS suppresses ongoing activity or produces a freezing response. In instrumental conditioning an aversive stimulus also suppresses an operant response. For example, free operant bar pressing will be suppressed if responding is followed by punishers such as loud noise or shock to the feet. The exercise below is designed to illustrate how suppression ratios are used in a study on the effects of punisher intensity on operant responding.

Smoking reduction. Imagine you are conducting a study with four people who are very heavy smokers (2-5 packs per day). The four people are motivated to quit smoking but find the addiction too strong to rely on self-control (so cold turkey is not an option). At the outset you collect four $500 checks from each participant. The checks are made out to each participant's least favorite person or organization. If they fail to reduce their smoking behavior at the end of each week a check is mailed to the payee. So each participant could lose up to $2000. Each person has a spouse or close friend who monitors the free operant responding of cigarette smoking during the study. The table below shows the number of packs each participant normally smoked (baseline) and the number of packs smoked at the end of each week of the four week study. What is the formula for the suppression ratio? I could not figure it out.

Participant	Baseline (packs/week)	Week 1	S.R. 1	Week 2	S.R. 2	Week 3	S.R. 3	Week 4	S.R. 4
1	35	35	0.5	35		34		8	
2	14	10	0.42	8		7		7	
3	21	14		10		6		3	
4	28	25		10		5		25	

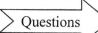

Questions

a) Calculate the suppression ratios (S.R. 1 – 4) for each subject at the end of each week. Write your answers in the shaded boxes to the right of the data for each week.

b) What would the suppression ratio be if each participant reduced the total number of packs smoked per week by one-half?

c) Imagine that this value is the criterion you adopted for all four weeks. Any suppression ratio **greater** than this value resulted in having the check sent for that week.

   a. How much money did subject 1 lose?_____

   b. How much money did subject 2 lose?_____

   c. How much money did subject 3 lose?_____

   d. How much money did subject 4 lose?_____

d) Do you think that altering your criterion could have had a positive effect (e.g., fewer cigarettes smoked) on your results? How so?

10-2.2   Introductory level of punishment. The effectiveness of punishment procedures depends in part on the introductory strength of the punishment. Generally, starting with a weak introductory level of punishment is less effective than starting with strong punishment.

   Imagine you are conducting a study to test this hypothesis using rats as subjects and foot shock as punishment. After training your rats to bar press for food you conduct five punishment sessions in which bar pressing results in the delivery of shock. Your design might look as follows.

Group	Introductory punishment level (volts)	Session 1 suppression ratio	Session 2 – 5 punishment level (volts)	Session 5 suppression ratio
Control	0		0	
Exp 1	50		150	
Exp 2	100		150	
Exp 3	150		150	

   Assume that the food delivered is not especially tasty to the rats, and is still delivered during the punishment sessions to rats in all four groups. Your control group is not shocked throughout the duration of the study. Your three experimental groups (Exp 1-3) receive varying introductory levels of punishment. In the table above you will notice empty cells for the suppression ratios for each group.

   Fill in the empty cells in the table above with likely suppression ratios for each group at session one and then at session five following a **standard** punishment level phase. Graph your results below with a separate line for each subject.

Title:

Interpretation:

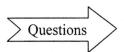
Questions

a) What do your results reveal about introductory levels of punishment?

b) Why was food delivered throughout the duration of the punishment sessions?

c) What might the effects on suppression ratios be if you were to use a highly preferred food?

10-2.3 Contingency and contiguity. In addition to punisher intensity, you read about several other factors that influence the effectiveness of punishment. Two such factors are response and stimulus contingency and contiguity.

Contingency: Design an experiment that demonstrates the importance of contingency in punishing a response. Be sure to include a control group. Use the graph below to write in hypothetical results demonstrating that your experiment worked and write an interpretation (see **pp. 304-305**) for ideas on how this might work.

Experimental design.

Title:

Interpretation:

Contiguity: Design an experiment that demonstrates the importance of temporal contiguity in punishing a response and graph and interpret the results below (see **p. 305**).

Experimental design.

Title:

Interpretation:

146

11 Animal Cognition I: Memory Mechanisms

The final two chapters of your text focus on the topic of animal cognition. This topic is different from others covered in your text in that it deals with some relatively complex forms of learning. In addition, a more focused discussion on the topic of memory is provided in **Chapter 11**. In the exercises below, you are first asked to consider a couple of concept questions that serve to help you distinguish animal cognition from other perspectives covered in the text (**section 11-1**). Next, we will turn our discussion to the various procedures used to study memory, namely delayed matching to sample (**section 11-2**). In **section 11-3** you will be asked to apply various mechanisms of memory to actual situations. The topic of forgetting is covered in **section 11-4** and you will be asked to differentiate between proactive and retroactive interference.

After completing these exercises you should be able to:

- Distinguish animal cognition from related fields,
- Describe the differences between procedural, working, and reference memories,
- Describe the delayed matching to sample procedure,
- Create your own examples of how the delayed matching to sample procedure works,
- Apply concepts behind different memory mechanisms to real-world examples,
- Differentiate between proactive and retroactive interference.

11-1 Animal Cognition Defined

The field of *animal cognition* is distinct from perspectives such as *animal learning* or *cognitive ethology*. The differences can be challenging to identify because there are many similarities between the perspectives. Here you are asked to consider a couple of questions that serve to help you conceptualize the field of animal cognition.

1) Describe a major difference between cognitive ethology and animal cognition. How are they similar?

2) Classical conditioning is traditionally presented as a relatively mechanical process that does not require any thinking on the part of the organism. This does not mean that a cognitive interpretation of classical conditioning cannot be offered. How might you apply a cognitive interpretation to conditioned salivary responding?

3) What aspects of the analysis of instrumental learning involve cognitive processes?

11-2 Memory Paradigms

Paradigms represent the ways in which we conceptualize information, and the methods we used to study phenomena. As you have seen, in the psychology of learning there are standard methods used to study things such as blocking, sensory preconditioning, schedules of reinforcement, and many other phenomena. The study of memory relies on standardized procedures as well, such as delayed matching to sample. In this section we will deal with some basic concepts of memory and the methods used to study them.

11-2.1 Procedural memory.   After reviewing **page 319** and the definition of procedural memory, list three activities you routinely engage in that utilize your procedural memory system.

1)

2)

3)

11-2.2 Working memory and reference memory.   In the examples below identify which task utilizes working memory and which task uses reference memory.

1) A server in a restaurant takes an order without writing it down. The information must be memorized until the order is placed with the cook.

Circle one: working   **reference**

2) A server memorizes the specials that she has to describe to each customer that evening.

Circle one: working   **reference**

3) John gets a job as a server in a new restaurant and has to familiarize himself with the standard items on the menu.

Circle one: working   reference

4) London cabbies have to pass a test demonstrating their knowledge of the streets of London before they are allowed to operate cabs.

Circle one: working   reference

5) A dentist doing a root canal runs into unexpected problems and decides she needs to consult a colleague before finishing the case. During the consultation, she is asked to describe what she has done so far and what she found.

Circle one: working   reference

6) A detective is trying to retrace the steps of a suspect and interviews a cab driver who picked up the suspect shortly before the crime. The detective is interested in the route the cab driver took.

Circle one: working   reference

7) To obtain a real-estate license, Mary has to pass a test on real estate laws and procedures in her state.

Circle one: working   reference

8) A pilot completing her pre-flight preparations has to keep in mind what aspects of the plane she has already looked at and what aspects she still has to check out.

Circle one: working   reference

11-2.3 Delayed matching to sample. The delayed matching to sample (DMTS) procedure was described on **pages 320-325** of your text. The figure below summarizes the basics of the DMTS procedure. As you go through the figure, imagine we are trying to do discrimination training with pigeons. The procedure consists of three phases:

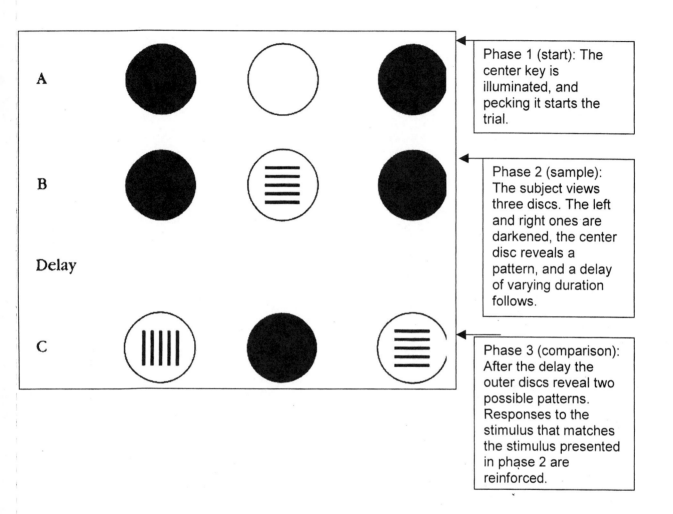

A

Phase 1 (start): The center key is illuminated, and pecking it starts the trial.

B

Phase 2 (sample): The subject views three discs. The left and right ones are darkened, the center disc reveals a pattern, and a delay of varying duration follows.

Delay

C

Phase 3 (comparison): After the delay the outer discs reveal two possible patterns. Responses to the stimulus that matches the stimulus presented in phase 2 are reinforced.

In the spaces below, diagram two different DMTS procedures using the same style as shown in the figure above. Your sample and comparison stimuli can vary across several dimensions, including shape, size, color, pattern, and combinations thereof. You can change the dimensions of the comparison stimuli relative to the sample so that they differ greatly, or hardly differ at all.

DMTS diagram #1

DMTS diagram #2

1) What are three procedural determinants of the DMTS task? (hint: refer to **page 322** of your text.)

2) Pick one of these procedural determinants of DMTS and design an experiment testing whether the determinant was effective. Be sure to state a hypothesis for the outcome you predict based on the determinant you chose.

3) Describe how *working memory* and *reference memory* systems are used during the DMTS procedure.

11-3 Memory Mechanisms

On **page 334** of your text three strategies used for navigation are described. These involve using,
- A Beacon
- A Landmark, or
- A Relation between landmarks

Read the following brief scenarios below and circle the strategy for navigation that applies to each example.

1) Finding a car that was parked behind a large S.U.V. in a parking lot.

Beacon   **Landmark**   **Relation between landmarks**

2) Locating a store in a shopping mall that is three doors down from the bookstore and directly across from the cell phone kiosk.

Beacon   **Landmark**   **Relation between landmarks**

3) Looking for the "Deli" sign in a grocery store to find a sandwich.

Beacon   **Landmark**   **Relation between landmarks**

4) Finding a home in the country that is one mile north of a large red barn.

Beacon   **Landmark**   **Relation between landmarks**

5) Paddling toward an island to find shelter.

Beacon   **Landmark**   **Relation between landmarks**

6) Approaching a light that has been associated with the delivery of food.

Beacon   **Landmark**   **Relation between landmarks**

7) Finding a campsite that is north of a stream and east of a particular waterfall.

Beacon   **Landmark**   **Relation between landmarks**

11-4 Forgetting

Page 346 of your text describes two different sources of forgetting. Review these and complete the exercise below.

Read the scenarios below and identify whether forgetting was due to proactive or retroactive interference (circle one).

1) Wade had two exams in a single day. His first exam was for a learning class at 8:00am. At 10:00am he then took an exam for his behavioral neuroscience class. During his neuroscience exam Wade forgot several details about the cerebellum because of what he memorized for his learning class.

   proactive   **retroactive**

2) Dan was a football player who transferred from the University of Kentucky to the University of North Carolina. Dan experienced difficulty memorizing the names for new plays he was learning at UNC, as many of them were similar to what he learned at Kentucky.

   proactive   **retroactive**

3) Each semester Dr. Matthews learns the names of her new students. Occasionally when she runs into students from previous semesters she has trouble recalling their names because of all of the new students she has met.

   proactive   **retroactive**

4) A cooking school student learns to identify the names of all the spices used in Asian cooking. She subsequently has difficultly remembering the names of some of them because of her learning about Indian cuisine.

   proactive   **retroactive**

5) Julie moved to a new city and frequently cites her previous area code when providing her new phone number.

   proactive   **retroactive**

12 Animal Cognition II: Special Topics

Here we will explore some additional aspects of animal cognition. In this chapter we consider some additional complex forms of cognition such as concept learning and language. In **section 12-1** we will focus on something called transitive inference, which requires the formation of a concept of how a series of stimuli are related based on experiences with just two of the stimuli at a time. Exercises in **section 12-2** deal with a specialized form of spatial memory found in birds. **Section 12-3** explores the ways in which animals process time. In our final set of exercises, we will further explore research that examines the language abilities of nonhuman species such as African grey parrots, chimpanzees, and bonobos (**section 12-4**).

After completing these exercises you should be able to:

- Apply the concept of transitive inference to real-world examples,
- Distinguish between transitive inference and value transfer,
- Evaluate several important variables that influence spatial memory in birds,
- Apply theories of timing to real-world examples,
- Compare and contrast two theories of timing,
- Evaluate different procedures used to test for language abilities in nonhuman primates.

12-1 Transitive Inference and Value Transfer

The complex cognitive ability of *transitive inference* is described on **pages 353-354** of your text. Transitive inference implies that an organism has conceptually placed a set of stimuli in a particular order and is then able to identify how a particular stimulus is related to the others in the series. The experiment with chimpanzees conducted by Gillan (1981) was described in your text. Recall that in this task the animals learned about relationships between stimuli A, B, C, D, and E. It may be helpful to review the details of the experiment in your text.

Understanding and appreciating the significance of transitive inference is aided by applying it to real-world situations. We can learn that A can be greater than B, that B is greater than C, and so on. However, the capacity for transitive inference can be used in social situations as well. For example, transitive inference may be the basis for social hierarchies– knowing who is the boss, who is second in command, and who is at the bottom of the hierarchy. Learning about social hierarchies is important for species that live in complex social groups.

This exercise is based on the work of Dasser (1987) done with monkeys. Most primate species are social and live in groups that form dominance hierarchies. Individuals must learn the status of different individuals in their group. Their survival and success within the group depends on their ability to recognize the order of the dominance hierarchy.

Imagine a monkey who joins a group that has five individuals that have a dominance hierarchy in order of most to least dominant: Otto, Moja, Boris, Flip, and Bunjie.

1) How would transitive inference aid the new monkey in determining the nature of the hierarchy between the five individuals in the group?

2) Assume the new monkey only saw two of the group members at a time. List all the possible pairs she might see.

3) How could the new monkey determine the dominance hierarchy or "pecking order" if she only saw two members of the group at a time? Which pairs would she have to see interacting to be able to decipher the entire hierarchy?

4) Once the newcomer has determined the pecking order on the basis of experience with a limited number of dyads or pairs of monkeys, she should be able to predict the dominance in all other pairs or dyads. Examine the pairs that you did not include in your previous answer and state which monkey in each of those pairs would be dominant over the other one.

5) How might value transfer explain the new monkey's "concept" of the dominance hierarchy?

6) Which explanation, value transfer or transitive inference, do you think Georges Romanes would be most likely to favor and why? (You may want to refer back to **chapter 1** of your text for a hint.)

12-2 Memory in Food-storing Birds

   The fascinating feats of memory found in food-storing birds such as Clark's nutcrackers are described on **pages 354-358** of your text. Carefully controlled experiments have shown that birds rely on memory for locating food stored in thousands of separate locations. In addition to remembering *where* food was stored, these birds appear to remember the type of food stored and when the food was stored. Clayton and Dickinson (1999) tested whether birds remember food quality and duration in which food has been stored. Below are results from their experiment, which is reprinted from **figure 12.3** of your text.

> Review the figure below and also the description of the study in your text and answer the questions that follow.

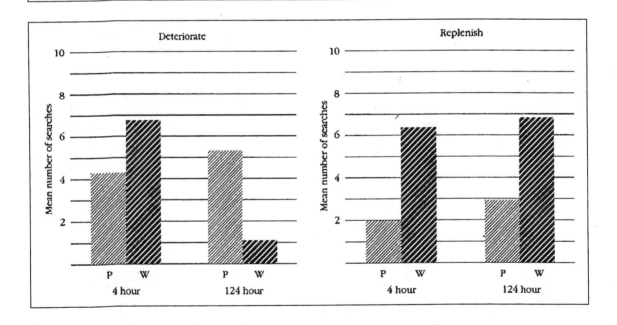

1) What do P and W represent in the figure?

160

2) What is the "Deteriorate" condition? How is this different from the "Replenish" condition?

3) What did the birds in the "deteriorate" condition experience?

4) What did the birds in the "replenish" condition experience?

5) What do the data of Clayton and Dickinson (1999) suggest about the variables of *what* and *when* in food storage?

12-3 Timing

Now we turn to how animals respond to the passage of time. The procedures used to study timing are important to understand. In the exercises below you are asked to consider some procedural issues in the study of timing, and also consider two alternative theories to timing behavior.

12-3.1 Concept questions

---

1) If you take a class in the basement of a building with no clocks or watches present, what cues might you use to estimate the amount of time that has passed since the beginning of the class period?

2) Subjects in timing experiments are often trained to respond on a Fixed Interval schedule. This leads to increased response rates as subjects get closer to the time that the reinforcer is made available. How is an FI schedule related to the "peak procedure" used to produce evidence of timing. Where does the "peak" occur in this procedure?

3) What would happen if a "blackout" period were introduced into the peak procedure? What does this demonstrate about timing?

12-3.2 Information processing model

> Study the *information processing model of timing* depicted in **figure 12.6** below (**p. 362 of your text**). At first it might seem a bit abstract. However, carefully thinking through each step will help you see how it applies to how you process time. Review the model and answer the following questions.

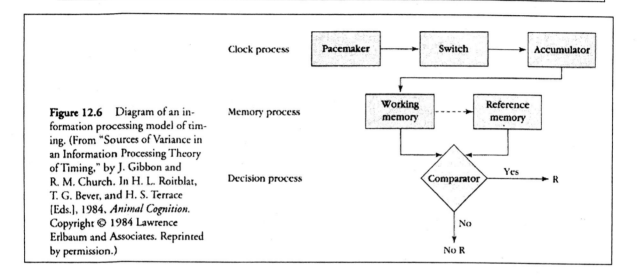

Figure 12.6 Diagram of an information processing model of timing. (From "Sources of Variance in an Information Processing Theory of Timing," by J. Gibbon and R. M. Church. In H. L. Roitblat, T. G. Bever, and H. S. Terrace [Eds.], 1984, *Animal Cognition.* Copyright © 1984 Lawrence Erlbaum and Associates. Reprinted by permission.)

1) What does the *accumulator* accumulate?

2) How are the *switch* and *accumulator* related?

3) How are *working memory* and *reference memory* systems processing the number of accumulated pulses?

4) What is the function of the *comparator*?

Imagine the coach of a football team calls a timeout that can last no more than two minutes to avoid incurring a penalty. During the timeout period the coach has to decide on a play and announce it to his team within 90 seconds of calling the timeout. Describe below how the information processing model of timing applies to this situation.

12-3.3   Information processing versus behavioral theory.

The *information processing theory* of timing contrasts with the *behavioral theory* of timing (**pp. 363-364**). The exercise below is designed to help you apply each theory, and to identify similarities and differences between the two.

> Read the following scenario and answer the questions that follow.

You have placed a takeout order at your favorite restaurant. The restaurant is as always very busy and there will be a wait before your food is ready. Based on past experience the wait could be 20 minutes or so. Assume that external cues such as a clock or watch are absent so your only cue is the passage of time that follows placing your order. Your decision to check the front counter of the restaurant to see if your food is ready is the instrumental response.

1) Based on this information, describe how the information processing model of timing applies to this example. Be sure to make reference to all components of the model (the pacemaker, switch, accumulator, working and reference memory, and comparator).

2) Describe how the behavioral theory of timing could be applied to this example. Be sure to refer to adjunctive behaviors, interim, and terminal responses.

3) How do the two theories differ? How are they similar?

12-4 Language

Sue Savage-Rumbaugh leads a productive group of researchers examining language abilities in primates. This work is featured on **pages 374-384** of your text. Dr. Savage-Rumbaugh initiated the work with the bonobo Kanzi while at the Language Research Center at Georgia State University. The work has continued for many years. Kanzi, as well as other language-trained apes, and Dr. Savage-Rumbaugh are currently located at the Great Ape Trust in Iowa. The work is featured at www.greatapetrust.org. Putting these web links in is terrific. Too bad we cannot do that with more topics.

As you learned in your text Kanzi communicates using an artificial language composed of lexigram symbols such as those pictured in **figure 12.10**, reprinted from your text below.

These symbols represent words of the Yerkish language. The work in animal language capacities is controversial. It is also somewhat difficult to evaluate if one only reads about it. To see some examples of Kanzi using lexigrams, visit the following site:

http://www.greatapetrust.org/media/avclips.cfm

Your text describes research on Kanzi's ability to recognize spoken English words. You can see Kanzi being tested for English word recognition at the website above. Click on the link to the media file called *"Kanzi understands spoken language"* and view the clip. Answer the questions about the clip that follow.

1) Why does Kanzi wear the headphones? And why does the experimenter sit behind Kanzi?

2) Based on your observations of this clip *alone*, do you think Kanzi understands the lexigrams as words?

3) Based on what you have learned about classical and instrumental conditioning, do you see how these forms of learning may apply to what Kanzi was doing in the clip you watched?

On **pages 382-383** of your text some experiments involving language comprehension are described. The experiments were designed to determine if Kanzi could understand language in a flexible way. For example, Kanzi was asked to do something unusual like "Make the (toy) doggie bite the (toy) snake". You can see sample trials of this experiment at the Great Ape Trust website.

View the media clip entitled "Kanzi and novel sentences" and answer the questions about the clip and the text that follow.

---

1) Why did the experimenter wear the face mask?

2) Why did the experimenter ask Kanzi to do things that seemed somewhat unusual?

3) Compared with the first video clip you watched, does this one demonstrate greater evidence of language ability in Kanzi? Why or why not?

References

Bevins, R., Rauhut, A. S., McPhee, J. E., & Ayers, J. J. B. (2000). One-trial context fear conditioning with immediate shock: The roles of transport and contextual cues. *Animal Learning and Behavior, 28*, 162-171.

Cheney, D. L., & Seyfarth, R. M. (1990). *How monkeys see the world.* Chicago: University of Chicago Press.

Clayton, N. S., & Dickinson, A. (1999). Scrub jays (Aphelocoma coerulescens) remember the relative time of caching as well as the location and content of their caches. *Journal of Comparative Psychology, 113*, 403-416.

Dasser, V. (1987). Slides of group members as representations of real animals (*Macaca fascicularis*). Ethology, 76, 65-73.

Deich, J. D., Allan, R. W., & Zeigler, H. P. (1988). Conjunctive differentiation of gape during food-reinforced key pecking in the pigeon. *Animal Learning and Behavior, 16*, 268-276.

Gillan, D. J. (1981). Reasoning in the chimpanzee: II. Transitive inference. *Journal of Experimental Psychology: Animal Behavior Processes, 7*, 150-164.

Griffin, A. S., Evans, C. S., & Blumstein, D. T. (2001). Learning specificity in acquired predator recognition. *Animal Behaviour, 62*, 577-589.

Gunther, L. M., Denniston, J. C., & Miller, R. R. (1998). Conducting exposure treatment in multiple contexts can prevent relapse. *Behaviour Research and Therapy, 36*, 75-91.

Leon, M. I. & Gallistel, C. R. (1998). Self-stimulating rats combine subjective reward magnitude and subjective reward rate multiplicatively. *Journal of Experimental Psychology: Animal Behavior Processes*, 24, 265-277.

McMillan, D. E., & Hardwick, W. C. (2000). Drug discrimination in rats under concurrent variable-interval variable-interval schedules. *Journal of the Experimental Analysis of Behavior, 73*, 103-120.

Reynolds, G. S. (1961). Attention in the pigeon. *Journal of the Experimental Analysis of Behavior, 4*, 203-208.

Rossier, J., Grobety, M-C., & Schenk, F. (2000). Spatial learning in rats across visually disconnected environments. *Animal Learning and Behavior, 28,* 16-27.

Slifkin, A. B., & Brener, J. (1998). Control of operant force production. *Journal of Experimental Psychology: Animal Behavior Processes, 24,* 1-8.

Timberlake, W., & Grant, D. S. (1975). Auto-shaping in rats to the presentation of another rat predicting food. *Science,* 190, 690-692.

Tinbergen, N. (1963). On aims and methods of ethology. *Zeitschrift für Tierpsychologie, 20,* 410-433.

Tolman, E. C., & Honzik, C. H. (1930). Degrees of hunger, reward and non-reward, and maze learning in rats. *University of California Publications in Psychology, 4,* 241-256.

Westbrook, R. F., Jones, M. L., Bailey, G. K., & Harris, J. A. (2000). Contextual control over conditioned responding in a latent inhibition paradigm. *Journal of Experimental Psychology: Animal Behavior Processes, 26,* 157-173.

Habituation

Banging on the pot startles the cat at first and disrupts its drinking.
After the startle response has become habituated, the cat resumes drinking.

Classical conditioning

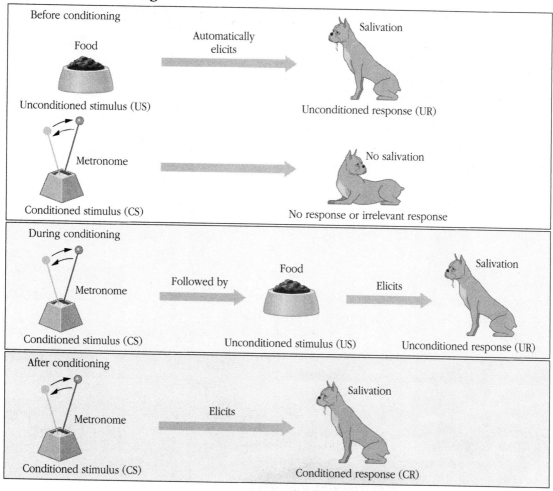

Before conditioning

Food — Automatically elicits → Salivation

Unconditioned stimulus (US) — Unconditioned response (UR)

Metronome → No salivation

Conditioned stimulus (CS) — No response or irrelevant response

During conditioning

Metronome — Followed by → Food — Elicits → Salivation

Conditioned stimulus (CS) — Unconditioned stimulus (US) — Unconditioned response (UR)

After conditioning

Metronome — Elicits → Salivation

Conditioned stimulus (CS) — Conditioned response (CR)

Second-order conditioning

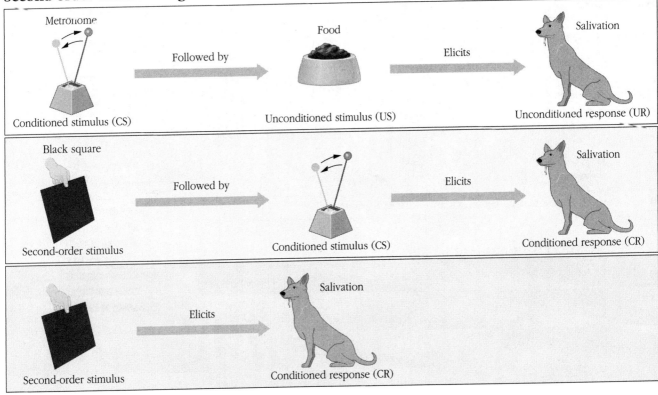

Classical and instrumental conditioning compared

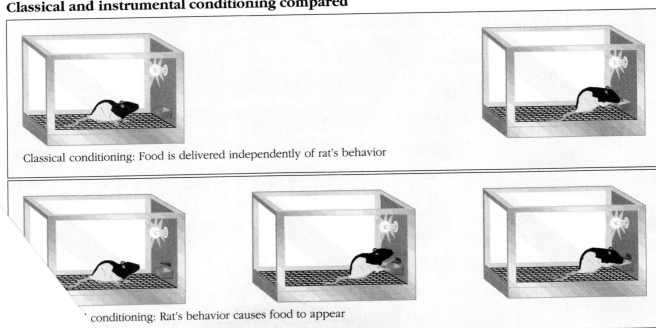

DO NOT STAPLE.   TAPE HERE   DO NOT STAPLE.   TAPE HERE

FOLD HERE

THOMSON ™

WADSWORTH

NO POSTAGE
NECESSARY
IF MAILED
IN THE
UNITED STATES

BUSINESS REPLY MAIL
FIRST-CLASS MAIL   PERMIT NO. 102   MONTEREY CA

POSTAGE WILL BE PAID BY ADDRESSEE

Attn: *Michael Domjan*

Wadsworth/Thomson Learning
60 Garden Ct Ste 205
Monterey CA 93940-9967

FOLD HERE

OPTIONAL:

Your name: Date:

May we quote you, either in promotion for *The Principles of Learning and Behavior: Active Learning Edition*, fifth edition, or in future publishing ventures?

Yes: _____ No: _____

Sincerely yours,

Michael Domjan

TO THE OWNER OF THIS BOOK:

I hope that you have found *The Principles of Learning and Behavior: Active Learning Edition,* fifth edition useful. So that this book can be improved in a future edition, would you take the time to complete this sheet and return it? Thank you.

School and address:_____

Department:_____

Instructor's name:_____

1. What I like most about this book is:_____

_____

_____

2. What I like least about this book is:

_____

_____

3. My general reaction to this book is:

_____

_____

4. The name of the course in which I used this book is:

_____

5. Were all of the chapters of the book assigned for you to read?_____

   If not, which ones weren't?_____

6. In the space below, or on a separate sheet of paper, please write specific suggestions for improving this book and anything else you'd care to share about your experience
   in using this book.

_____

_____

_____